RAILROADS OF THE ADIRONDACKS

A HISTORY

Also by Michael Kudish:

Where Did the Tracks Go:
Following Railroad Grades in the Adirondacks

Adirondack Upland Flora:
An Ecological Perspective

Paul Smith's Flora

Paul Smith's Flora II

RAILROADS OF THE ADIRONDACKS

A HISTORY

by Michael Kudish

Michael Kudish

PURPLE MOUNTAIN PRESS
Fleischmanns, New York

Railroads of the Adirondacks: A History

First Edition
1996

Published by
Purple Mountain Press, Ltd.
Main Street, P.O. Box E3
Fleischmanns, New York 12430-0378
914-254-4062
914-254-4476 (fax)

Copyright © 1996 by Michael Kudish

All rights reserved under International and Pan American Copyright Conventions. No part of this book may be reproduced or transmitted by any means without permission in writing from the publisher and copyright holder.

Library of Congress Cataloging-in-Publication Data

Kudish, Michael, 1943-
    Railroads of the Adirondacks : a history / by Michael Kudish. --
1st ed.
      p.   cm.
    Includes bibliographical references and index.
    ISBN 0-935796-75-4 (hardcover : alk. paper)
    1. Railroads--New York (State)--Adirondack Mountains Region--History. I. Title.
TF24.N7K83   1996
385'.09747'5--dc20
                                                                    96-16049
                                                                      CIP

Cover: Southbound D&H local beginning a late-winter run in the mid-1940s.
Fort Edward station is in the background.
Courtesy of the Chapman Historical Museum, Glens Falls.

Manufactured in the United States of America.
Printed on acid-free paper.

Table of Contents

Preface 7
Acknowledgements 9

Part One: By Discipline

Chapter 1: Geography and the Maps
(includes list of maps) 13
Chapter 2: Railroads and Passengers 26
Chapter 3: Railroads and Forests 30
Chapter 4: Railroads and Forest Fires 45
Chapter 5: Railroads and Agriculture 48
Chapter 6: Railroads and Mining 52
Chapter 7: Railroads and Miscellaneous Industries 59
Chapter 8: Unusual Railroads 70
Chapter 9: Abandonment 79
Chapter 10: Railroad Preservation 83

Part Two: By Geography

Section I: Into the Adirondacks from the Champlain Valley on the East

Chapter 11: Delaware & Hudson Mainline from Whitehall to Rouses Point 99
Chapter 12: Adirondac Company's Railroad to North Creek 131
Chapter 13: The Lake George Region 154
Chapter 14: Baldwin Branch 157
Chapter 15: Crown Point Iron Company's Railroad 159
Chapter 16: Lake Champlain & Moriah Railroad 166
Chapter 17: Elizabethtown Terminal Railroad and the NY&P Railroad at Willsboro 179
Chapter 18: Keeseville, Ausable Chasm and Lake Champlain Railroad 182
Chapter 19: Ausable Branch 185
Chapter 20: Chateaugay Railroad 200
Chapter 21: Mooers Branch 242
Chapter 22: Amtrak's *Adirondack* 246

Section II: Into the Adirondacks from the North

Chapter 23: New York & Ottawa Railroad 265
Chapter 24: Bombay & Moira Railroad 287

Chapter 25: Watson Page Lumber Company Railroad 289
Chapter 26: Brooklyn Cooperage Company Railroad 291
Chapter 27: Bay Pond Inc. Railroad 301
Chapter 28: Oval Wood Dish Corporation's Railroad at Kildare 304

Section III: Into the Adirondacks from the Saint Lawrence Valley on the Northwest and West

Chapter 29: Hannawa Railroad 325
Chapter 30: Clifton Iron Company's Railroad 328
Chapter 31: Carthage & Adirondack Railroad 331
Chapter 32: Six Short Railroads Connecting with the Carthage & Adirondack 355
Chapter 33: Three Peripheral Railroads: Adirondack & Saint Lawrence (DeKalb Junction to Hermon), Gouverneur & Oswegatchie, and the Lowville & Beaver River 360

Section IV: Into the Adirondacks from the Mohawk Valley on the South

Chapter 34: Jerseyfield Railroad 383
Chapter 35: Fonda, Johnstown, and Gloversville Railroad 387
Chapter 36: New York Central Adirondack Division 389
Chapter 37: Raquette Lake and Marion River Carry Railroads 429
Chapter 38: Mac-a-Mac and Whitney Industries Railroads at Brandreth 439
Chapter 39: Grasse River Railroad 443
Chapter 40: Paul Smith's Electric Railway 453
Chapter 41: Horse Shoe Forestry Company and Wake Robin Railroads 463
Chapter 42: Seven Short-Line Railroads along the New York Central Adirondack Division 466
Chapter 43: The Adirondack Railway, 1979-1980 472

Annotated Bibliography 477
Index 489

Preface

WHEN THIS WRITER arrived at Paul Smith's College in 1971, he had wished for a single, convenient reference which would provide a summary of railroad locations for the whole Adirondack region. None was available, although much had been written by many authors. This writer had to prepare such a reference for himself and hope that others would find it useful. *Where did the Tracks Go* (hereafter referred to as *Tracks*) was published by The Chauncy Press in 1985. *Tracks* went back to the printer several times but is now out of print. The present volume differs from it in three significant ways:

First, much additional detail on those lines and stations included in *Tracks* is presented in this book on the scale-four maps of mines, mining processing facilities, sawmills, and pulp mills. Examples are at Lyon Mountain, Standish, Port Henry, Mineville-Witherbee, Fisher Hill, Benson Mines, Hammondville-Ironville, Crown Point, Tahawus, North Creek, Conifer, Cranberry Lake, Saint Regis Falls, Santa Clara, Corinth-Palmer, Ticonderoga, Wanakena, and Newton Falls. Many additional logging spurs are shown for the Rich Lumber Company, Oval Wood Dish Company, and Brooklyn Cooperage Company.

Second, the geographic boundaries of *Tracks* have been expanded in this book. The eastern boundary is the Delaware & Hudson Mainline along Lake Champlain. The northern boundary is the Rutland Railroad, although this book provides detail on this line only where it crossed Adirondack regional lines at Rouses Point, Malone Junction, and Moira. The Saint Lawrence Division of the New York Central and the Rome, Watertown & Ogdensburg form the west boundary, but no detail is provided on these lines. The New York Central Mainline along the Mohawk River, not included, forms the south boundary.

Additional chapters on railroad lines not included in *Tracks* are Chapter 11 on the Delaware & Hudson Mainline, Chapter 13 on the Baldwin Branch, Chapter 17 on the Elizabethtown Terminal Railroad and the New York & Pennsylvania Company Railroad at Willsboro, Chapter 21 on the Mooers Branch, Chapter 29 on the Hannawa Railroad, Chapter 25 on the Watson Page Lumber Company Railroad, Chapter 30 on the Clifton Iron Company Railroad, and Chapter 33 on Three Peripheral Railroads from the Saint Lawrence and Black River Valleys. Chapter 13 on the Lake George Region, Chapter 34 on the Fonda Johnstown & Gloversville Railroad, and Chapter 35 on the Jerseyfield Railroad provide only brief sketches of these lines with abundant references for further reading. Chapters 22 and 43 are on the recent history of passenger service on Amtrak's *Adirondack* and the Adirondack Railway of 1979-1980, respectively.

The map of the Carthage & Adirondack Railroad (Chapter 31 here) terminated westward at Briggs in the 1985 edition. In this book the maps cover the line all the way to Carthage.

Third, *Tracks* treated the railroads only geographically. This book also provides ten introductory chapters arranged by industrial topics for those researchers who study history by topics—a land-use history overview. Chapters 3, 5, and 6 deal mainly with commodities exported from the Adirondacks, while Chapters 2 and 7 deal mainly with commodities (including tourists!) imported.

Objectives

The primary intent of this book is to assist the reader in the location of railroad grades in the field. For future historians, this book dates as best as possible the period of service of each line and major industry. Many references to further, more detailed reading on the lines are provided, especially on topics which cannot be included here: forestry, geology, finances, biographies of railroad builders, political and social aspects, etc..

This book does not consider railroads in isolation, but rather relates them to other industries which they tied together: forests, mining, agriculture, and hostelry. Railroads either led, followed, or arrived simultaneously with the migration and settlement into the Adirondack interior. Forest historians will know where not to look for old growth stands because logging railroads reached the scene before them. Chapters 11 and 22 may be used as an itinerary for passengers on Amtrak's *Adirondack*, while Chapters 36 and 43 may be used by potential future passengers on a resurrected Adirondack Railway from Remsen to Lake Placid.

Not Objectives

This book is not intended as a roster of locomotives, rolling stock, and other railroad equipment. Complete rosters are available in the references cited. Neither is it intended to be an analysis of timetable operations. Timetables for many of the lines are readily available in museums and libraries. Rosters and timetable analyses each could fill a whole volume the size of this book. There is no space for them here.

Unconfirmed Detail

Much detail has been obtained by this writer verbally from a number of people, some of them reliable railroad historians, over two decades. Most of this detail is probably correct, although some might be in error or in partial error. If this detail cannot be substantiated or confirmed by articles, books, maps, timetables, photographs or other documents from the historic period, then such detail is excluded from this book. The detail is being saved, however, because confirmation will allow inclusion in a future edition.

Text and Maps

This writer typed the text, constructed the maps himself, and is thus responsible for all errors. Pressing a typist and cartographer into service would have delayed publication of this book several years.

An important feature of the scale-four maps is that they are largely composite and, therefore, essentially timeless maps. They show trackage detail which accumulated over a period of decades and probably is incorrect for any given individual year. When this writer rides Amtrak's *Adirondack* from New York City northward, he is nearly overwhelmed by the changes made in a period as short as 25 years. Track diagrams must constantly be redrawn and updated, but the old ones are never discarded because of their historic value. Switches are pulled up, moved, replaced, added. Passing sidings disappear. Industries close. Industrial sidings disappear. Stubs remain intact but are disconnected from the main by removal of switches. Other industries open. Sidings appear. A section of double track is removed, creating single track. Whole branches are eliminated. For the whole Adirondack region, such changes have been going on constantly for a century and a half. Change is the rule, not the exception.

Private Lands

Many abandoned railroad grades cross land now privately-owned. It is wise to obtain permission from the owner before exploring the right-of-way, and not only out of respect for the owner's privacy. More importantly, the owner can often inform the historian about relicts and details which the historian would almost never locate on his/her own. Best of all is the land owner accompanying the historian in the field and the two sharing discoveries and discussion.

Acknowledgements

FOR AN ENORMOUS VOLUME of historic publications, photographs, timetables, maps, discussions, and field tours: Richard Wettereau.

For proofing, editing, and commenting upon the manuscript: Murray Heller, Madge Heller, Esther Kudish, Theodore Mack, and Kath Buffington.

For providing assistance in the printing of the map labels: Keith Tyo and Joseph Kepes.

For assisting in the use of aerial photographs: Russell C. McKittrick.

For loan of old fifteen-minute U.S.G.S. topographic quadrangles: Paul Smith's College Lands Department staff Stanley Ingison, Rolf Haugland, and Jane Mandeville.

For a mass of historic newspaper articles and a ride on the backyard railroad in Fine: Pauline Campbell and Kenneth Campbell.

For many reference checks: the staff of the Paul Smith's College Cubley Library and the Saranac Lake Free Library.

For miles of right-of-way field exploration: Fred Baker, Christopher Brescia, and Luke Wood.

For innumerable disruptions and interruptions by a multitude of eruptions: Hannah Keyes.

For their loan of photographs for the book: Chapman Historical Museum, Glens Falls; Feinberg Library, State University of New York Plattsburgh.

For their timely loan of photographs and research of captions: Tom Curran, Kip Grant, and Jeffrey Martin.

Chapter 11: William Rooke for a track schematic of the D&H Mainline, ca. 1928.

Map 12-14A of Palmer: International Paper Company staff Robert H. Mellon, Joe Hanley, and Jim Campopiano. Map 12-21 of North Creek: Field tour with Bill Bibby. Map 12-22 of Tahawus: Gordon Medema of Kronos Inc. (formerly National Lead Chemicals Company, MacIntyre Development) for field tour.

Maps 15-4 and 15-5 of Ironville and Hammondville, respectively: Dr. Elmer Eugene Barker's 1941 map of Hammondville and Stephen M. Barker's 1973 map of Ironville were major sources of detail. Both maps were done for The Penfield Foundation, Ironville, Crown Point, New York. Field tour by Leo Kudlacik.

Maps 16-1 through 16-8: Photographs in the Warren Dobson collection. Field tours by Leo Kudlacik and Brian Venne. An immense collection of detail by a historian who wishes to remain anonymous, but a good portion of his collection is most fortunately in the Sherman Library at Port Henry. Fisher Hill map from *Metallurgy* magazine.

Chapters 19 and 20 in Clinton County: Field tour and maps provided by James Bailey, City Historian. Map 19-5 of the Plattsburgh Traction Company: most of the detail comes from Borrup (1970-1971), especially the map by E. Bond, 1972.

Map 20-10. Morrisonville to Kent Falls: field tour by Leo Perry, Schuyler Falls Town Historian.

Map 21-2, Mooers Junction: Orville K. McKnight (1989, page 115).

Map 23-7, Moira: Nimke (1986 p. 21; 1989 pp. 148-151).

Maps 23-9 & 23-10, Saint Regis Falls and Santa Clara, respectively: Champion International Corp. staff Jane Gardner, Bud Delano, and John F. Flynn. Map 23-12, Brandon: field tour with Fred Joost. Maps 23-18 and 36-30 of Tupper Lake: valuation diagrams from Professor C. Creighton Fee.

Map 25-1 and 23-9, Watson Page Lumber Company Railroad: field tour by Russell Nelson.

Chapter 26: tour of Brooklyn Cooperage Plant and a published history: Andrew de Treville. Map 26-2, Everton area: field tour by Clayton Winters.

Maps 28-1 and 28-2 of Oval Wood Dish Company's Railroad from Bill Gove's collection.

Maps 30-1 and 30-2 of the Clifton Iron Company's Railroad: Information from John Thomas and Richard Palmer.

Map 31-15, Bacon, Kalurah and Jayville: field tour by Robert Burke. Map 31-16, Aldrich: field tour by Clint Shaw. Map 31-22, Newton Falls to Clifton Mines: field tour by Robert Burke and Keith Fuller. Maps 31-18 through 31-21, Carthage & Adirondack Railroad: valuation diagrams from Mark DeLawyer.

Map 36-15, Remsen: map in Hank Harter collection.

Map 37-5, Raquette Lake: track diagram from Jimmy Dillon. Maps 37-3 and 37-6, Raquette Lake and Marion River Carry Railroads: field tours by Warren Lipa and the Sagamore Institute.

Map 38-2, Brandreth: field tour by Dr. LeRoy Wardner and Donald B. Potter, plus historic videotape by F. Arthur Potter.

Map 39-7, Cranberry Lake: field tour by Dr. Ed Dreby.

Chapter 40, Paul Smith's Railway: electrical detail by Joseph Cunningham.

Map 42-33, Thendara: relief map on exhibit in 1992 in Thendara Station by Daryl Carman, Town of Webb Historical Society.

Part One

By Disipline

Chapter 1
Geography and the Maps

THIS BOOK is divided into two parts. The first part, Chapters 1 through 10, is arranged by discipline: passengers, forest products, forest fires, agriculture, mining, and miscellaneous industries. If the reader is interested in, for example, mining, information brought together from many different localities scattered throughout the Adirondacks along many different railroads can be found conveniently in Chapter 6. Following Chapters 1 through 7 is one on unusual, narrow gauge, wooden-railed, electric, inclined, and very short railroads, also railroads which did not connect with any other lines. Part one concludes with chapters on abandonment of railroads and attempts at preservation and restoration.

The second part, Chapters 11 through 43, is arranged geographically by railroad line and stations. If the reader is interested in, for example, the New York & Ottawa, all the information on that railroad has been brought together in Chapter 23. If the reader is interested in the area around Saint Regis Falls station, the diverse industries are in one convenient place in the text.

Railroads penetrated into the interior of the Adirondacks from all directions, always from the outside surrounding lowlands to the inside. Previously, penetrating the interior of the Adirondacks in much of the same way, were postglacial migration routes of plants and animals, and the settlement of people of European descent. Migration routes and railroads often follow the least steep grades and paths of least resistance, i.e. river valleys upstream.

Railroads were built into the Adirondacks primarily to tap the forest and mineral resources, and secondarily to provide easy access for passengers. The lowlands, because of their less rugged terrain, longer growing season and better soils, all conducive to agriculture, were settled first: mainly in the eighteenth and early nineteenth centuries. The Adirondacks, because of their rugged terrain, shorter growing season and poorer soils, were settled last: mainly after 1850.

Chapters 11 through 22 involve railroads which penetrated the Adirondacks from the east, Chapters 23 through 28 those from the north, Chapters 29 through 33 from the west and northwest, and Chapters 34 through 43 from the south.

Chapters 11 through 22 describe railroads which originated primarily from the Upper Hudson, Lake George, and Lake Champlain Lowlands. Because these Lowlands were settled early and were major barge trade routes on the waterways, the earliest railroad construction into the interior of the Adirondacks came from the east. Involved were the Delaware & Hudson Mainline, its branches, and several independent connecting railroads. Many of these were built to serve the iron industry: Chapters 15, 16, 19, and 20.

Chapter 11 deals with the D&H Mainline's Champlain Division from Whitehall at the south end of Lake Champlain to Rouses Point at the north end, a distance of about 113 miles.

Chapter 12 covers the Adirondac Company's Railroad, later the North Creek Branch of the D&H. This branch joins the mainline at Saratoga Springs in the Saratoga Division and thus south of the geographic limits of this book. The branch was later extended to Tahawus.

Chapter 13 introduces the reader to three railroads in the Lake George area, peripheral to the region covered in this book. Little detail is offered on these lines because of this and, also, because they are treated fully in other publications. The D&H

Caldwell Branch into Lake George diverged from the Saratoga Division at Fort Edward. The Prospect Mountain Inclined Railway ran only for several years. The Hudson Valley Electric Railway's line came up into Warrensburg from the Glens Falls-Lake George area.

Chapters 14 through 21 include branches off the D&H Champlain Division and several independent railroads which served as tributaries or feeders to the D&H main. The treatment in this book runs from south to north. Chapter 14 is on the Baldwin Branch which joined the mainline at Ticonderoga (Montcalm Landing). Chapter 15 concerns the Crown Point Iron Company's Railroad which ran as a narrow gauge from Crown Point to Hammondville. Chapter 16 is on the Lake Champlain and Moriah, another mining line and the steepest railroad in the Adirondacks. Chapter 17 involves the Elizabethtown Terminal Railroad, under construction in 1910 but never completed. Chapter 17 also involves the New York and Pennsylvania Company's Paper Mill Railroad and other industries at Willsboro. Chapter 18, on the Keeseville, Ausable Chasm and Lake Champlain Railroad, discusses a line that was electrified for a portion of its short existence. Chapter 19 includes the Ausable Branch, built originally as part of the D&H mainline, but then left only as a branch. Chapter 20 is on the Chateaugay and Lake Placid Branch, originally narrow gauge and built as the Chateaugay Railroad. Chapter 21 is on the Mooers Branch, originally not a branch at all but the mainline built from Mooers Junction to Plattsburgh; it was replaced by the current D&H mainline via Rouses Point and later abandoned. Chapter 22 provides a brief narrative of the recent resurrection of Amtrak passenger service on the D&H mainline from 1974 to the present after a three-year hiatus when only freight trains operated.

Chapters 23 through 28 include railroads which penetrated the Adirondacks from the north. The primary trunk line was the New York & Ottawa, a forest products railroad, which climbed out of the Saint Lawrence Valley from Moira (Chapter 23) with five connecting railroads. Chapter 24 is on the Bombay & Moira Railroad, a little-known ephemeral line which was more of a branch off the Ogdensburg & Lake Champlain than off the New York & Ottawa. Chapter 25 is on the Watson Page Lumber Company electric railroad from Saint Regis Falls to Lake Ozonia Outlet. Chapter 26 is on the Brooklyn Cooperage Company's branches from Saint Regis Falls over the old Everton Railroad, to Lake Ozonia, from Meno, from Tupper Lake Junction, and at Salisbury Center. Chapter 27 is on Bay Pond Inc.'s Railroad from McDonald Station. Chapter 28 is on the Oval Wood Dish Company's Railroad from Kildare and also with a spur off Bay Pond Inc.'s line.

Chapters 29 through 33 discuss railroads which penetrated the Adirondacks from the west, and to a lesser extent, from the northwest. These forest product and mining railroads were built into the interior from the Saint Lawrence and Black River Valleys, connecting with the major trunk lines which had been built at earlier date. The trunk lines were the New York Central's Saint Lawrence Division, completed from Watertown to Massena in 1857, and the Rome, Watertown & Ogdensburg, completed in the Black River Valley from Rome to Watertown in 1851. Chapter 29 is on the Hannawa Railroad which ran from Potsdam southward towards Hannawa Falls. Chapter 30 is on the Clifton Iron Company's Railroad which operated from East DeKalb to the Clifton Ore Bed on wooden rails. Chapter 31 concerns the Carthage & Adirondack Railroad, soon to become the Carthage & Adirondack Branch of the New York Central. This branch originated at Sackets Harbor and continued through Watertown and Carthage to Newton Falls with an extension to Newbridge and the Clifton Ore Beds. Chapter 32 includes five short line railroads, branches off the Carthage & Adirondack. Chapter 32 also deals with the Cranberry Lake Railroad which joined the Carthage & Adirondack at Benson Mines and headed southeast to Wanakena; in addition were many miles of logging spurs. Chapter 33 includes three short lines: (1) The Adirondack & Saint Lawrence from DeKalb Junction to Hermon, (2) The Gouverneur & Oswegatchie from Gouverneur to Edwards with a branch to Balmat, and (3) The Lowville & Beaver River railroad from Lowville to Croghan.

Chapters 34 through 40 involve penetration into the Adirondacks from the Mohawk Valley on the south. The New York Central's Adirondack Division (Chapter 36) and its connecting short line railroads and branches dominate. This Division was the only through-railroad which entered the Adirondacks at one end and emerged from the other; all other lines dead-ended in the Adirondack interior. Although the Adirondack Division entered the Adirondacks also from the north via Malone Junction and continued into the interior, most traffic was concentrated at the southern end of the line. Mileposts began at Herkimer, not Malone Junction. The Jerseyfield Railroad (Chapter 34) and the Fonda,

Johnstown, & Gloversville Railroad (Chapter 35), also penetrated the Adirondacks from the south, but were not connected to the New York Central's Adirondack Division.

The longer branches and connecting railroads, those which require several pages of text and/or cannot fit on a single-page map with a portion of the Adirondack Division, are placed in separate chapters: Chapter 37 is on the Raquette Lake and Marion River Carry Railroads. Chapter 38 is on the Mac-a-Mac and Whitney Railroads. Chapter 39 is on the Grasse River Railroad. Chapter 40 is on the Paul Smith's Electric Railway. Chapter 41 is on the Horseshoe Forestry Company and Wake Robin Railroads.

Chapter 42 includes seven short line railroads all but the first of which connected with the New York Central Adirondack Division. These are the Black River and Woodhull Railroad, the Moose River Lumber Company Railroad, the first Fulton Chain Railroad or "Peg Leg," the second Fulton Chain Railroad into Old Forge, the Champlain Realty Company Railroad at Woods Lake, the Partlow Lake Railway, and the Piercefield Spur.

Chapter 43 is an updating of Chapter 36: a brief narrative on the recent history of the Adirondack Railway, 1979-1980, and the Adirondack Railway Preservation Society's excursion line at Thendara which commenced operations in 1992.

The Brooklyn Cooperage Company, although it did connect with the Adirondack Division at Tupper Lake Junction, had the bulk of its operations off the Ottawa Division, and has been placed in Chapter 26 along those lines which penetrated from the north.

The D&H Chateaugay Branch, which entered the Adirondacks from the Plattsburgh area and connected with the Adirondack Division at Saranac Lake (later at Plumadore) is presented in Chapter 20 among those railroads which penetrated from the east.

The Four Scales of Maps

The main purpose of the maps is for the reader to locate railroad grades, facilities, and industries, especially abandoned ones, in the field.

Maps are divided in this book into four scales forming a geographic hierarchy. The scales, one through four, are described from the largest areas with least detail in scale-one to the smallest areas with most detail in scale-four. One may make an analogy here with a microscope: at low power, one sees a large field (or area) but little detail; this is like a scale-one map. When one switches to higher and higher power lenses, the field gets smaller and smaller and more and more detail appears; this is like going to scale-two and then scale-three maps. Finally, at highest power, one has the smallest field but the greatest detail; these are the scale-four maps.

Maps are identified by two numbers separated by a hyphen. The first number is the chapter number, and the second is the map sequence number within that chapter. For example, Map 16-6 is the 6th map in Chapter 16.

To reduce the already-overwhelming length of the mainline chapters (#11 D&H and #36 N.Y. Central Adirondack Division), detail on junctions with shorter railroads and branches is shifted into the short, or branch, line railroad chapter instead of into the main-line chapter. This shift does create an interruption in the main-line trend of thought. However, the advantage is that most of the branch lines had sidings and facilities at the junction point relating to those industries served by the branch. For example, Crown Point detail on the D&H Mainline is in Chapter 15 on the Crown Point Iron Company rather than in Chapter 11.

Track plans have been reconstructed from numerous sources, including explorations in the field, old photographs, and track schematics (track valuation diagrams) drawn by the railroad draftsmen or by other cartographers.

Scale-one Maps

Scale-one maps show the whole Adirondacks at 1:1,126,400 or 17.75 miles to the inch. The first scale-one map, Map 1-1, shows the geographic bounds of this book, the major junctions and the terminals. It identifies all the railroad lines, both extant and abandoned, all present together on a single page.

Legend to Map 1-1: Railroads of the Adirondacks

Railroad identification numbers 11 through 42 on Map 1-1 also serve as chapter numbers:

11. Delaware & Hudson Mainline (D&H).
12. D&H Adirondack Branch, formerly Durant's Adirondac Company's Railroad.
13C. Caldwell Branch of the D&H to Lake George.
13H. Hudson Valley Electric Railway to Warrensburg.
14. D&H Baldwin Branch.

15. Crown Point Iron Company's Railroad.
16. Lake Champlain & Moriah Railroad.
17. Elizabethtown Terminal Railroad (under construction but never completed).
17A. New York & Pennsylvania Company's Railroad.
18. Keeseville, Ausable Chasm & Lake Champlain Railroad.
19. D&H Ausable Branch.
20. D&H Chateaugay Branch.
20R. Roakdale Railroad.
21. D&H Mooers Branch.
(22 is a chapter on Amtrak's *Adirondack*, a train rather than a railroad).
23. Ottawa Division of the New York Central, formerly Hurd's Northern Adirondack Railroad, then New York & Ottawa.
24. Bombay & Moira Railroad.
25. Watson Page Lumber Company Railroad.
26. Brooklyn Cooperage Company Railroad.
26E. Everton Railroad.
27. Bay Pond Inc. Railroad.
28. Oval Wood Dish Company Railroad.
29. Hannawa Railroad.
30. Clifton Iron Company's Railroad.
31. Carthage & Adirondack Branch of the New York Central.
31M. Mecca Lumber Company Railroad.
31N. Newton Falls Paper Company Railroad.
31P. Post & Henderson Railroad.
31H. Higbie Lumber Company and Newton Falls & Northern Railroad; Hanna Ore Company Railroad.
32. Cranberry Lake and Rich Lumber Company Railroads.
33A. Adirondack & Saint Lawrence Railroad (2nd).
33G. Gouverneur & Oswegatchie Railroad.
33L. Lowville & Beaver River Railroad.
34. Jerseyfield Lumber Co. Railroad, an extension of the Little Falls & Dolgeville and the Dolgeville & Salisbury Railroads.
35. Fonda, Johnstown & Gloversville Railroad.
36. Adirondack Division of the New York Central, formerly Webb's Adirondack & Saint Lawrence (1st) or Mohawk & Malone.
36H. Hinckley Branch.
37R. Raquette Lake Railway.
37M. Marion River Carry Railroad.
38. Mac-a-Mac and Whitney Railroads.
39. Grasse River Railroad.
40. Paul Smith's Electric Railway.
41. Horseshoe Forestry and Wake Robin Railroads.

42B. Black River & Woodhull Railroad at Forestport.
42M. Moose River Lumber Company Railroad at McKeever.
42F. Fulton Chain (first), the "Peg Leg", Railroad at Minnehaha.
42C. Fulton Chain (second) Railroad or Old Forge Branch.
42W. Champlain Realty Company Railroad at Woods Lake.
42P. Partlow Lake Railway.
42I. Piercefield Spur of the International Paper Company.

There are no chapters in this book on the following peripheral railroads. These are shown on Map 1-1 for location purposes only.

101. New York Central Mainline.
102. Rome, Watertown & Ogdensburg.
103. Rutland Railroad, earlier the Northern New York, then Ogdensburg & Lake Champlain Railroads.
104. Saint Lawrence Division of The New York Central.
105. Norwood & Saint Lawrence Railroad, currently the Saint Lawrence Railroad.
106. Rutland Branch of the D&H.
107. Addison Branch of the Rutland Railroad.

Other scale-one maps are within Chapters 2 through 10, locating the industries individually, numbered 2-1 through 9-1. These are listed in the List of Maps at the end of this Chapter.

Scale-two Maps

Scale-two, or chapter-level, maps deal with those chapters on the longest railroads, those generally between 40 and 150 miles long, and requiring more than several scale-three maps. The purpose of the scale-two map is to show the whole line on a single page which allows for a broad overview of how the stations and any branch and/or connecting lines relate to one another. Scale-two maps also show how the several to many scale-three maps in the chapter link together. Scale-two maps include all passenger stations, all localities between the stations which had place-names (mostly industries or passing sidings), and junctions. Detail is available on the scale-four maps.

These scale-two maps are, in actuality, not at a single scale, but at several different similar scales. The longest three lines are at a scale of 1/830,951 or about

13.1 miles to the inch to fit onto a single page. They are:

Map 11-1, D&H Mainline, with 114 miles described in this book;

Map 12-1, D&H Adirondack Branch to North Creek & Tahawus, 86 miles long;

Map 36-1, New York Central Adirondack Division, 145 miles long.

Three more lines are at a scale of 1/356,958 or about 5.6 miles to the inch to fit onto a single page. They are:

Map 20-1, Chateaugay Railroad, 84 miles long;
Map 23-1, New York & Ottawa, 54 miles long;
Map 31-1, Carthage & Adirondack, 55 miles long.

The Grasse River Railroad, somewhere between 41 and 46 miles long and shown on Map 39-1, is at a scale of 1/250,000 or 3.9 miles to the inch. The Fonda, Johnstown & Gloversville Railroad is also shown at a scale of 1/250,000.

Note that the mileposts of these longer lines run in various directions, but with milepost zero always at the point of construction origin, and the highest-numbered milepost the most distant. The D&H Mainline and the N.Y. Central Adirondack Division mileposts both run from south to north, while the New York & Ottawa runs from north to south. The Carthage & Adirondack runs from west to east, while the Grasse River runs from east to west. The Chateaugay runs from zero at Plattsburgh and heads west, eventually turning south at Wolf Pond, and east at Saranac Lake.

Scale-three Maps

The purpose of the scale-three maps is to direct the reader in the field to the railroad grade, extant or abandoned. In order to further assist the reader to locate abandoned grades, often I have added new highways and relocations of older highways which were both non-existent when the older topographic 15-minute quadrangles were surveyed, 1892 to ca. 1930. Examples are the Northway (Interstate 87), Route 374 between Plattsburgh and Cadyville, and Route 3 between Wanakena and Cranberry Lake.

Scale-three maps are, unlike the scale-two maps, all at the same scale of 1/62,500, very close to the most convenient scale of one inch equals one mile (the exact ratio for one inch equals one mile is 1/63,360 where the denominator is the number of inches in a mile: 12 x 5280). The 1/62,500 scale, where one inch equals 0.9864 mile, was traditionally used by the United States Geological Survey for their 15-minute quadrangles from the 1890s through the 1950s. Most scale-three maps cover an area 9.5 miles long by 6.75 miles wide with the railroad running down the middle.

In *Where did the Tracks Go* (Kudish, 1985), these topographic quadrangles were used as the base maps upon which to superimpose the railroad lines. For the present edition, it was thought best to maintain the same scale, but to delete the clutter of contour lines, especially in steep places. Those natural and human features thought most useful in aiding the reader in how to get there have been maintained. The major streams, ponds, lakes, hills, mountain summits, roads, dams, tunnels, landmark buildings, and other locating features, as well as the railroads themselves, have been selected for tracing from the quadrangles. Some natural topographic features, especially those several miles from the railroad, have been omitted if they do not assist in locating the grade and do nothing but add to a confusing tangle of unnecessary detail.

In agricultural and village areas where the network of highways and streets, respectively, is dense, only those roads which closely parallel or cross the railroad grade are shown. To show all highways and streets within three or four miles of the railroad on the scale-three maps would create unnecessary and confusing clutter.

Errors in the topography on the older 15-minute quadrangles, Russell (1919) and Cranberry Lake (1916), have made it difficult to trace the North Tram of the Grasse River Railroad. Likewise, the Santa Clara (1921) Quadrangle has made it difficult to trace the Brooklyn Cooperage line east of Meno along the Onion River. The more recent 7.5-minute maps show the topography correctly, but are on a different, larger scale: 1:24,000. Hence, I have had to plot these railroad grades as best I could on the 1:24,000 maps, and then reduce them to the 1:62,500 standard of the scale-three maps. In these instances, the railroads will be observed to ascend and descend phenomenally steep grades which show on the older topographic quadrangles but which in reality are not there.

Station names are set in large type. Other features directly pertaining to the railroad are set in intermediate type. Features such as highways, lakes, rivers, and hills helping to locate the railroad but not directly pertaining to it are set in small type.

The symbol for a railroad on a scale-three map is the thickest, darkest line. On some occasions, earlier-abandoned trackage is shown by a broken thick dark line. Highways are shown as lines of intermediate thickness. County lines are shown typically as straight, thin lines. Rivers, brooks, lakes, and ponds are shown as wavy thin lines. Hilltops and mountain summits are denoted by triangles.

Large black dots along the railroad lines indicate stations, junctions, passing sidings, and other localities which the railroads had given place-names. Many of the passing sidings were long, up to a mile, so that the dot on a scale-three map always marks the center of the siding and not one of its ends. The only exceptions to this pattern are the long passing sidings on the D&H Mainline with cabins shown at both ends.

North arrows point most commonly to the top of the page, but in some maps, the north arrow points toward the right or left margin. In the latter case, the railroad line runs generally in an east-west direction. On a few maps, the north arrow points obliquely when the railroad line cuts obliquely, e.g. from northwest to southeast; a longer segment along the line can be shown obliquely thus and fewer maps are needed to cover the whole line.

Scale-three maps are arranged by increasing milepost numbers, not by any consistent north-to-south or east-to-west direction. (See the explanation on mileposts in the above section above on scale-two maps).

Sources for the names of highways, streets, brooks, hills and other non-railroad landmarks are largely the United States Geological Survey topographic quadrangles, old track schematics drawn by the railroads' real estate and valuation office, county highway maps, village street maps, and various other maps and books. Highway names and numbers often change over time so that one must carefully compare nineteenth century with contemporary maps to make certain that the same road is involved with a name change or that there are two different closely parallel roads. Saint Lawrence County seems to have the most frequent county highway number changes; in the last few years, for example, Conifer Highway 75 became 62, Wanakena Highway 58 became 61, Newton Falls highways 50 and 109 were joined together to make 60, Fine Highway 27 is now 27 or 122, and Pitcairn Highway 46 is now 23! Some highways have always had two names concurrently.

The northern segment of the New York Central Adirondack Division, from just south of Gabriels to just south of Malone Junction, has become a Niagara-Mohawk power line. The pole numbers along this power line are often useful in locating former railroad features, and are shown on Maps 36-11 through 36-14.

Old abandoned highways are shown only if they are useful in locating a railroad grade. The lines symbolizing highways are sometimes straightened on the scale-three maps for simplicity when in actuality the road is quite curvy. Railroad trackage on the maps is never straightened in this manner.

Highway symbol lines may be interrupted by place-name labels pertaining to railroad facilities or industries, but railroad track symbol lines are never interrupted. These interruptions in the highway symbol do not suggest that the highway is closed at that point.

If a former railroad grade, now a highway, ended, but the highway continues on further, the railroad terminus is shown as a black dot on the scale-three map. The portion of the highway formerly occupied by the railroad is shown as a thick, boldface line, while the continuing highway segment is shown as a finer line. An example is on Map 20-6 where Franklin County Highway 30 continues on east past the Roakdale Railroad terminus at Roakdale.

Where a railroad appears to run off the edge of one scale-three map and continues onto another scale-three map, an arrow is shown along with the number of the continuing map.

Scale-three maps also serve to locate which areas are shown in greatest detail on the scale-four maps: stations, sidings, yards, junctions, and industries.

Scale-four Maps

Scale-four maps cover in greatest detail the smallest areas such as a village, a yard, a junction, a mine, or a mill---each with great industrial density. Scale-four maps are the only ones in this book which are typically diagrammatic and thus not exactly to scale. The 9.5-inch length of a single page map often represents a distance of approximately one mile, so that the scale is very roughly 1/6,000 to 1/7,000, varying from map to map.

If a page has two or more scale-four maps on it, the lowest numbered map will determine the sequence that this page has among the other maps.

In a few instances, larger yard or mill areas require two or more maps. Each map will indicate, wherein trackage appears to run off the edge, the number of the adjacent map on which the trackage continues. Examples are Port Henry Maps 16-2 and 16-3; Plattsburgh Maps 19-3, 19-4, 19-5, and 19-9; Tupper Lake Maps 23-18 and 36-30; Saranac Lake Maps 20-23 and 20-24; and Benson Mines Maps 31-19 and 31-20.

Fonts on the scale-four maps range from large bold on the map title, large for names of depots and branch-line railroads, intermediate for names of industries and railroad facilities, and small for names of all other features not directly related to the railroad: highways, streets, streams, and hilltops.

North arrows may be approximate and point in various directions on the scale-four maps, depending on the orientation of the railroad. If the railroad is angling obliquely southwest-northeast, for example, north may be at the upper left corner so that the maximum trackage mileage can be included on the map. Examples are Maps 42-1, 42-2, 42-3, 42-4, and 40-1. If there are several maps combined on one page and only one north arrow is shown, then north is approximately in the same direction for all.

Changes in track plans over the years present one of the most difficult challenges in preparing this book. At some yards, depots, junctions, and mills there were frequent track relocations, removals, and additions. Such places should require several to many maps each, at intervals of perhaps a decade, to document all these changes. Instead, I have compiled the maximum trackage for each of these places on, in effect, a single composite timeless map. The reader must be constantly aware that not all of the spurs and sidings existed simultaneously. Thus few scale-four maps are accurate for any particular year. In only two instances I have made an exception: the Mineville-Witherbee area had experienced such drastic modifications over the 103-year history of the Lake Champlain & Moriah Railroad (because of the constant opening and closing of mine shafts and mills) that I have divided the area into Map 16-6 Nineteenth Century and Map 16-7 Twentieth Century. Benson Mines has been divided into a nineteenth century map, 31-18, and two twentieth century maps, 31-19 and 31-20.

Power poles can be helpful in locating former railroad features. On the New York Central Adirondack Division grade between a point south of Gabriels and a point south of Malone Junction, Niagara Mohawk Power Corporation has strung a power line. Power pole numbers are shown on Maps 36-33 through 36-44.

Mileposts can also be helpful in locating former or existing railroad features provided that, of course, the mileposts still stand. Mileposts are referred to in Chapter 11 on the D&H Mainline, in Chapter 12 on the D&H Adirondack Branch to North Creek, in Chapter 31 on the Carthage & Adirondack, and in Chapter 36 on the New York Central Adirondack Division. Because scale-four maps are typically not to scale, mileage is shown at highway crossings, depots, ends of sidings, bridges, etc., to help the reader determine distances more accurately.

On four scale-four maps with extremely dense trackage, it was thought better to use a thinner line to denote each track than the standard thickest line. The maps are 16-2 Port Henry South, 19-5 Plattsburgh Traction Company, 23-18 Tupper Lake, and 36-30 Tupper Lake Junction.

In Chapter 11 on the D&H Mainline, there are several junction points with complex trackage. Instead of showing scale-four maps of these junctions in the mainline chapter, the junction detail maps have been moved into the branch chapter scale-four maps as follows:

Ticonderoga is on Map 14-1 in the Baldwin Branch chapter;
Crown Point is on Map 15-3 in the Crown Point Iron Company's Railroad chapter;
Port Henry is on Maps 16-2 and 16-3 in the Lake Champlain & Moriah Railroad chapter;
Westport is on Map 17-1 in the Elizabethtown Terminal Railroad chapter;
Willsboro is on Map 17-3 in the New York & Pennsylvania Co. Railroad chapter;
Port Kent is on Map 18-2 on the Keeseville, Ausable Chasm & Lake Champlain Railroad chapter;
South Junction area (including Bluff Point and Cliff Haven) is on Map 19-6 of the Ausable Branch chapter;
Plattsburgh is on Maps 19-3, 19-4, 19-5, and 19-9 of the Ausable Branch chapter.

In Chapter 36 on the New York Central Adirondack Division, junction point scale-four maps have also been moved into branch line chapters as follows:

McKeever is on Map 42-1 on the Moose River Lumber Company Railroad;
Minnehaha is on Map 42-2 on the first Fulton Chain Railway;
Thendara is on Map 42-3 on the second Fulton Chain Railway;
Carter is on Map 37-4 of the Raquette Lake Railway chapter;

Brandreth is on Map 38-1 on the Mac-a-Mac and Whitney Railroads chapter;

Woods Lake is on Map 42-5 on the Champlain Realty Co.;

Partlow is on Map 42-6 on the Partlow Lake Railway;

Horseshoe is on Map 41-1 on the Horseshoe Forestry Co. RR chapter;

Childwold Station is on Map 39-6 on the Grasse River Railroad chapter;

Lake Clear Junction is on Map 40-1 on the Paul Smith's Electric Railway chapter;

Piercefield is on Map 42-7 on the Piercefield Spur.

This arrangement is used because most of the branch lines had sidings and facilities at these junction points relating to those industries served by the branch.

A legend to the symbols used on scale-four maps is shown on the last page of this chapter.

Sequence of Maps of Various Scales in Each Chapter: How the Maps Link Together

The sequence of maps in each chapter varies with the length and detail included in the chapter. The seven longest railroads, over 40 miles in length, begin with a scale-two map showing the whole line (see section on scale-two maps above). This is followed by a series of scale-three maps showing the location of the grade with respect to topography and highways. Any highly detailed scale-four maps will complete the chapter.

For the shorter lines, the maps begin with a series of scale-threes followed by, if needed, scale-fours. For the shortest lines, those serving a single industry such as the New York & Pennsylvania Company Railroad, one scale-four map should suffice.

List of Maps (all scales)

Map Scale Follows No.

No.			Page
1-1	1	Railroads of the Adirondacks	25
2-1	1	Railroads with Passenger Service	29
3-1	1	Railroads and Spurs Used Exclusively for Forest Products	37
3-2	1	Sawmills	38
3-3	1	Lumber Yards and Lumber Dealers	39
3-4	1	Pulp & Paper Mills, Pulp Rossing Plants & Pulpwood Loading Sidings	40
3-5	1	Charcoal	41
3-6	1	Stave & Heading Mills for Barrels	42
3-7	1	Other Forest Products	43
3-8	1	Jackworks	44
5-1	1	Creameries	50
5-2	1	Livestock	51
6-1	1	Railroads and Spurs Used Exclusively for Mining	55
6-2	1	Iron Mines	56
6-3	1	Mines Other Than Iron Mines	57
6-4	1	Sand & Gravel Pits; Ice & Spring Water	58
7-1	1	Coal for Locomotives	63
7-2	1	Coal for Heating	64
7-3	1	Fuel Oil & Bottled Gas	65
7-4	1	Miscellaneous Industries	66
7-5	1	Water for Locomotives	67
7-6	1	Engines Houses	68
7-7	1	Wyes, Reversing Loops & Turntables	69
8-1	1	Narrow Gauge Railroads	74
8-2	1	Electric Railroads	75
8-3	1	Wooden Rail Railroads	76
8-4	1	Disconnecting Inclined Railroads	77
8-5	1	Disconnecting Non-inclined Railroads	78
9-1	1	Recent Abandonments	82
11-1	2	Delaware & Hudson Mainline	114
11-2	3	Whitehall to Clemons	115
11-3	3	Dresden to Wrights	116
11-4	3	Montcalm Landing to Addison Junction	117
11-5	3	Crown Point to Port Henry	118
11-6	3	Cheever Ore Bed Company to Westport	119
11-7	3	Wadhams to Essex	120
11-8	3	Willsboro to Rockland Siding	121
11-9	3	Douglass to Valcour	122
11-10	3	South Junction to Plattsburgh	123
11-11	3	Beekmantown to Canada Junction	124
11-12	3	Chazy to Rouses Point	125
11-13	4	Whitehall	126
11-14	4	South Bay Siding	127
11-15	4	Clemons (Chubb's Dock)	127
11-16	4	Dresden	127
11-17	4	Putnam	127
11-18	4	Cummings Siding	127
11-19	4	I.P. (International Paper Co.) Mill	127
11-20	4	Porter's Spur	127
11-21	4	Burdick's Siding	127
11-22	4	HS Cabin	127
11-23	4	Howard's Siding	128
11-24	4	Allen's Siding	128
11-25	4	Wadhams	128
11-26	4	Merriam	128

11-27	4	Whallonsburg	128	16-2	4	Port Henry South	172
11-28	4	Essex	128	16-3	4	Port Henry North	173
11-29	4	Burnham's	128	16-4	4	Terio Wye	174
11-30	4	Douglass	128	16-5	4	Switchback	175
11-31	4	Beekmantown	129	16-6	4	Mineville, 19th Century	176
11-32	4	Spellmans	129	16-7	4	Mineville, 20th Century	177
11-33	4	West Chazy	129	16-8	4	Fisher Hill	178
11-34	4	Chazy	129				
11-35	4	Cooperville	129	17-1	3	Elizabethtown Terminal Railroad	180
11-36	4	Rouses Point	130	17-2	4	Westport	180
				17-3	4	Willsboro	181
12-1	2	Adirondac Company's Railroad to North Creek	138				
				18-1	4	Keeseville, Ausable Chasm & Lake Champlain Railroad at Port Kent	184
12-2	3	Saratoga Springs to South Corinth	139	18-2	4	K, AC & LC RR at Ausable Chasm & Keeseville	184
12-3	3	White's Sand to Hadley	140				
12-4	3	Wolf Creek to Stony Creek	141	19-1	3	Ausable Branch: Plattsburgh to Peru	191
12-5	3	Warrensburg Junction to The Glen	142	19-2	3	Ausable Branch: Harkness to Ausable Forks	192
12-6	3	Riverside to North Creek	143				
12-7	3	Ordway Siding to North River	144	19-3	4	Plattsburgh Yard	193
12-8	3	Stillwater	145	19-4	4	Plattsburgh	194
12-9	3	Tahawus	146	19-5	4	Plattsburgh Traction Company	195
12-10	4	Greenfield	147	19-6	4	South Junction Area	196
12-11	4	Kings	147	19-7	4	Peru, Harkness, and Arnold	197
12-12	4	South Corinth	147	19-8	4	Ausable Forks Area	198
12-13	4	White's Sand	147	19-9	4	Plattsburgh North	199
12-14	4	Corinth	148				
12-14A	4	Palmer	149	20-1	2	Chateaugay Railroad	219
12-15	4	Hadley	147	20-2	3	Plattsburgh to Woods Mills	220
12-16	4	Wolf Creek	147	20-3	3	Cadyville to Russia	221
12-17	4	Stony Creek	150	20-4	3	Chazy Lake Station to Twin Ponds Station	222
12-18	4	Warrensburg Junction and Thurman Station	151				
				20-5	3	Middle Kilns to Catamount	223
12-19	4	The Glen	150	20-5A	3	Kinsley Lumber Co. RR at Tekene	224
12-20	4	Riverside	150	20-6	3	Loon Lake to Vermontville Station	225
12-21	4	North Creek	152	20-7	3	Bloomingdale Station to Saranac Lake	226
12-22	4	Tahawus	153	20-8	3	Ames Mills to Lake Placid	227
				20-9	4	Freydenburg Falls Branch	228
13-1	3	Lake George Region	156	20-10	4	Morrisonville to Cadyville	229
				20-11	4	Dannemora	230
14-1	3	Baldwin Branch	158	20-12	4	Russia	230
				20-13	4	Chazy Lake	230
15-1	3	Crown Point Iron Company's Railroad (west end)	161	20-14	4	Lyon Mountain, standard gauge	231
				20-14A	4	Lyon Mountain, narrow gauge	232
15-2	3	Crown Point Iron Company's Railroad (east end)	162	20-15	4	Standish	233
				20-16	4	Twin Ponds	234
15-3	4	Crown Point	163	20-17	4	Middle Kilns	234
15-4	4	Ironville	164	20-18	4	Plumadore	234
15-5	4	Hammondville	165	20-19	4	Loon Lake	235
16-1	3	Lake Champlain & Moriah Railroad	171				

20-20	4	Onchiota 236
20-21	4	Bloomingdale Station. 237
20-22	4	Relocation North of Pecks Corners 237
20-23	4	Saranac Lake North 238
20-24	4	Saranac Lake South 239
20-25	4	Ray Brook 240
20-26	4	Lake Placid. 241
21-1	3	Mooers Branch. 243
21-2	4	Mooers Junction 244
21-3	4	Sciota 245
23-1	2	New York & Ottawa Railroad 275
23-2	3	Moira to Dickinson Center 276
23-3	3	Saint Regis Falls to Weidman. 277
23-4	3	Spring Cove to Brandon 278
23-5	3	McDonald to Willis Pond 279
23-6	3	Kildare to Tupper Lake 280
23-7	4	Moira 281
23-8	4	Dickinson Center 282
23-9	4	Saint Regis Falls 283
23-10	4	Santa Clara. 284
23-11	4	Spring Cove 282
23-12	4	Brandon and McDonald Station 285
23-13	4	Bay Pond 282
23-14	4	Black Rapids. 282
23-15	4	Derrick. 282
23-16	4	Willis Pond 282
23-17	4	Childwold 282
23-18	4	Tupper Lake 286
24-1	3	Bombay & Moira Railroad 288
25-1	3	Watson Page Lumber Company Railroad 290
26-1	2	Brooklyn Cooperage Company Railroad 295
26-2	3	Saint Regis Falls to Everton 296
26-3	3	Santa Clara to Lake Ozonia. 297
26-4	3	Meno 298
26-5	3	Meno West. 299
26-6	3	Tupper Lake Junction to Wawbeek. . . . 300
27-1	3	Bay Pond Inc. Railroad 303
28-1	3	Oval Wood Dish Co. RR (in Franklin County) 306
28-2	3	Oval Wood Dish Co. RR (in St. Lawrence Co.) 307
28-3	4	Kildare 308
29-1	3	Hannawa Railroad 327
29-2	4	Potsdam 327
30-1	3	Clifton Iron Company's RR (northwest end) 329
30-2	3	Clifton Iron Company's RR (southeast end) 330
31-1	2	Carthage & Adirondack Railroad and Cranberry Lake Railroad 338
31-2	3	Carthage to North Croghan. 339
31-3	3	Natural Bridge to Lake Bonaparte 340
31-4	3	Harrisville to Jayville 341
31-5	3	Briggs to Anderson 342
31-6	3	Benson Mines to Wanakena 343
31-7	3	Newton Falls to Clifton Mines 344
31-8	4	Carthage & Wilna 345
31-9	4	Natural Bridge 346
31-10	4	Rock 346
31-11	4	Diana 346
31-12	4	Harrisville. 347
31-13	4	Bacon, Kalurah, and Jayville. 348
31-14	4	Briggs 346
31-15	4	Collins 346
31-16	4	Aldrich to Oswegatchie 349
31-17	4	Anderson 346
31-18	4	Benson Mines, 19th Century 350
31-19	4	Benson Mines Southwest (20th Century) . 351
31-20	4	Benson Mines Northeast (20th Century) . 352
31-21	4	Newton Falls 353
31-22	4	Newbridge and Clifton Mines 354
32-1	4	Wanakena. 359
33-1	2	Three Peripheral Railroads. 362
33-2	3	Gouverneur & Oswegatchie Railroad . . . 363
33-3	4	Gouverneur & Oswegatchie Railroad (detail). 364
33-4	3	Lowville & Beaver River Railroad 365
33-5	4	Lowville & Beaver River Railroad (detail). 366
34-1	3	Jerseyfield Railroad (south end) 385
34-2	3	Jerseyfield Railroad (north end) 386
35-1	2	Fonda, Johnstown & Gloversville Railroad. 388
36-1	2	New York Central Adirondack Division. 406
36-2	3	Prospect Junction to Honnedaga 407
36-3	3	Kayuta to White Lake 408

36-4 3	White Lake Sand Pit to Onekio	409
36-5 3	Thendara to Carter Station	410
36-6 3	Big Moose to Little Rapids	411
36-7 3	Brandreth to Robinwood	412
36-8 3	Sabattis to Horseshoe	413
36-9 3	Mount Arab to Tupper Lake Junction	414
36-10 3	Floodwood to Saranac Inn	415
36-11 3	Lake Clear Junction to Gabriels	416
36-12 3	Rainbow Lake to Tekene Junction	417
36-13 3	Plumadore to Owls Head	418
36-14 3	Chasm Falls to Malone Junction	419
36-15 4	Remsen	420
36-16 4	Honnedaga	421
36-17 4	Forestport	421
36-18 4	Anos	421
36-19 4	Woodgate	421
36-20 4	Otter Lake	421
36-21 4	Nelson Lake	421
36-22 4	Big Moose	422
36-23 4	Beaver River	421
36-24 4	Keepawa	423
36-25 4	Nehasane	423
36-26 4	Robinwood	423
36-27 4	Sabattis	423
36-28 4	Mount Arab	423
36-29 4	Underwood	423
36-30 4	Tupper Lake Junction	424
36-31 4	Floodwood	423
36-32 4	Saranac Inn	423
36-33 4	Gabriels	425
36-34 4	Rainbow Lake	425
36-35 4	Stonywold	425
36-36 4	Tekene Junction	425
36-37 4	Little Bryants	426
36-38 4	Bryants Mill	426
36-39 4	Mountain View	426
36-40 4	Owls Head	426
36-41 4	Chasm Falls Station	427
36-42 4	Todds Pit	427
36-43 4	Whippleville Station	427
36-44 4	Duquettes Pit	427
36-45 4	Malone Junction	428
37-1 3	Raquette Lake Railway (west end)	432
37-2 3	Raquette Lake Railway (east end)	433
37-3 3	Marion River Carry Railroad	434
37-4 4	Carter Station	435
37-5 4	Raquette Lake	436
37-6 4	Marion River Carry	437
37-7 4	1913 Wreck Site	438
38-1 3	Mac-a-Mac and Whitney Railroads	441
38-2 4	Brandreth Station	442
39-1 2	Grasse River Railroad	446
39-2 3	Childwold Station to Shurtleffs	447
39-3 3	Brandy Brook Station to Pleasant Lake	448
39-4 3	Pleasant Lake to North Branch Grasse River	449
39-5 3	(end of North Tram)	450
39-6 4	Childwold Station and Conifer	451
39-7 4	Cranberry Lake	452
40-1 4	Lake Clear Junction	461
40-2 4	Paul Smiths	462
41-1 4	Horseshoe	465
42-1 4	McKeever	469
42-2 4	Minnehaha	469
42-3 4	Thendara	470
42-4 4	Old Forge	471
42-5 4	Woods Lake	471
42-6 4	Partlow	471
42-7 4	Piercefield	471

LEGEND TO SYMBOLS ON SCALE-FOUR MAPS

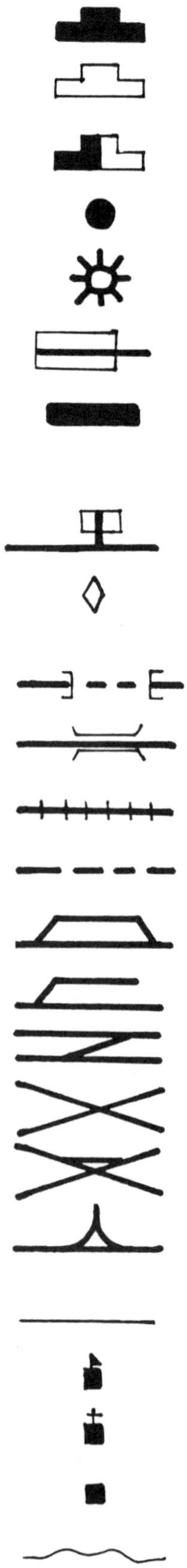

passenger station or depot

freight station

combination passenger and freight station

fuel oil tank

water tank

shop, enginehouse, or industrial building with internal track

other servicing or industrial buildings

round house with turntable

speeder shed

milepost

tunnel

bridge

track on trestle

earlier-abandoned trackage

passing or double-ended siding

stub or single-ended siding

crossover

crossing without connection

crossing with interchange connection

wye

highway

school

church

other buildings

brook

MAP 1-1 RAILROADS OF THE ADIRONDACKS

See legend on page 15

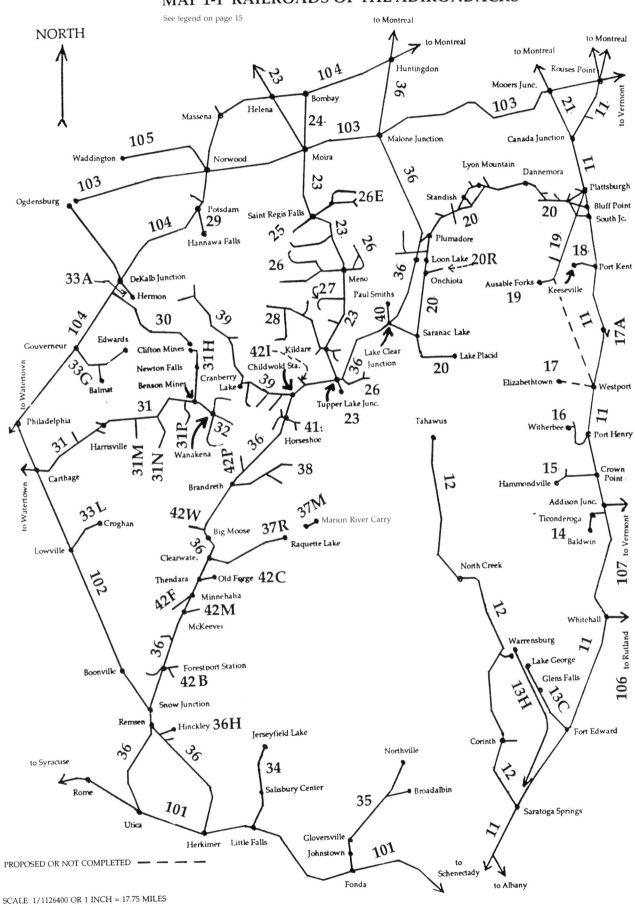

PROPOSED OR NOT COMPLETED − − − −

SCALE: 1/1126400 OR 1 INCH = 17.75 MILES

Chapter 2
Railroads and Passengers

ALTHOUGH most Adirondack regional railroads were originally built for transporting forest and/or mining products, some lines also carried a considerable number of passengers especially in summer.

Hotels

In the nineteenth and early twentieth centuries, most tourists who visited the Adirondacks came by rail and stayed at hotels. In the latter part of the twentieth century, this pattern changed: now most tourists travel by private automobile and stay in second homes, motels, or campgrounds.

The larger hotels had their own conveyances, originally horse-drawn, to meet the trains and transport the guests and their luggage to the hostelry. Some guests traveled by stagecoach lines not owned by the hotels. Distances to hotels from the depot ranged from a fraction of a mile to as many as fifty miles.

One line which carried tourists, but not necessarily to hotels, was the Keeseville, Ausable Chasm, and Lake Champlain Railroad. People were transported from Port Kent on the D&H mainline to Ausable Chasm, a natural tourist attraction, from 1890 to 1924.

Steamboats

Steamboats plied the waters of Lake Champlain with railroad connections scheduled to minimize travel time. These boats docked at landings at the following villages listed from north to south: North Hero (Vermont), Grand Isle (Vermont), Plattsburgh, Bluff Point, Valcour, Port Kent, Burlington (Vermont), Essex, Westport, Port Henry, Crown Point, and Ticonderoga. Detail is available in Shaughnessy (1967).

Steamboats also plied nearly the full length of Lake George from Caldwell (Lake George Village) to Baldwin.

Several lakes in the Adirondack interior had steamboat service. On Chazy Lake, a boat connected Chazy Lake Station on the D&H Chateaugay Branch with the Chazy Lake House in the 1896 era. The Tupper Lake Navigation Company operated the steamer "Altamont" in the 1896-1909 era; the boat, along with a stagecoach connection to Tupper Lake Junction depot, served several hotels on both Big and Little Tupper Lakes such as the Tupper Lake House and Moody's. Bog River Falls, a scenic stop without a hotel, was also made by the "Altamont." Steamboat service was also available on the Fulton Chain of Lakes out of Old Forge.

An exhibit at The Adirondack Museum superbly shows how the steamboats and railroads coordinated travel time into Blue Mountain Lake: passengers traveled by rail to Raquette Lake Station, crossed Raquette Lake by steamer, rode the Marion River Carry Railroad, and then boarded another steamer across Utowana, Eagle, and Blue Mountain Lakes. Other steamboats served other portions of Raquette Lake.

Several additional lakes with steamboat service, but without railroads directly reaching their shores, were Upper Saranac Lake, Schroon Lake, and Big Moose Lake.

Tuberculosis Sanatoria

After Dr. Edward Livingston Trudeau established his sanatorium at Saranac Lake in 1884, the tuberculosis curing "industry" grew rapidly. In addition, numerous smaller curing cottages were built in Saranac Lake.

Thousands of tuberculosis sufferers were brought by rail into the greater Saranac Lake area. The unfortunate left in coffins in baggage cars, while the fortunate either returned home by rail after curing or remained as residents of Saranac Lake. Most sanatoria closed in the 1950s as tuberculosis became much less prevalent a disease in the United States and the therapy did not include sanatorium rest.

Those sanatoria served by rail sidings for coal delivery were at Lake Kushaqua (Whitefathers), Gabriels (Sisters of Mercy), Ray Brook, and possibly Saranac Lake (Will Rogers). Other major sanatoria, without freight rail sidings but with railroads bringing in the majority of patients, were Sunmount in Tupper Lake and Rainbow Sanatorium in Rainbow Lake.

Local Residents

In addition to tourists, many local residents of the Adirondacks rode the trains, either between two communities in northern New York, or to and from cities outside the region. Most passenger service operated all year, although the number of trains daily was reduced to half or less in winter. The Marion River Carry Railroad operated only in summer mainly for tourists and owners of summer camps.

Specials

Special trains were occasionally run for specific purposes. Tyler (1968, pp. 35-37) describes special Sunday church trains run in the early 1890s by Hurd from Brandon to Santa Clara and Tupper Lake. Hyde (1970) and Dumas (1962) both mention the fact that blueberry pickers would come up from Malone Junction to Mountain View on the Sunday morning train and head back down in the evening; sometimes extra coaches were cut off at Mountain View during the day to accommodate the crowds. Kozma (1985) describes several special trains on the D&H mainline run for specific events such as the Essex County Fair at Westport in 1888, and excursions for the New York City Fresh Air Children to Willsboro in 1882. See Chapter 40 paragraphs on conductors' trip reports for special charters on the Paul Smith's Electric Railway.

Hotel Stagecoach Connections

The major hotels are listed under the individual railroad stations with their stagecoach and other conveyance connections:

Chapter 12: Hadley, Thurman, The Glen, Riverside, and North Creek.
Chapter 19: Plattsburgh, Bluff Point, and Ausable Forks.
Chapter 20: Chazy Lake, Lyon Mountain, Loon Lake, Bloomingdale Station, Saranac Lake, and Lake Placid.
Chapter 23: Moira, Saint Regis Falls, Santa Clara, Spring Cove, Brandon, Derrick, Childwold, and Tupper Lake.
Chapter 31: Oswegatchie and Newton Falls.
Chapter 32: Wanakena.
Chapter 36. Forestport, Otter Lake, Thendara, Beaver River, Sabattis, Childwold Station, Tupper Lake, Saranac Inn, Lake Clear Junction, Gabriels, Rainbow Lake, Loon Lake, and Mountain View.
Chapter 37: Uncas, Raquette Lake, and Marion River Carry.
Chapter 39: Conifer, Shurtleff's, Cranberry Lake.
Chapter 40: Paul Smith's.
Chapter 42: Thendara and Old Forge.

Legend to Map 2-1: Railroads with Passenger Service

The identifying numbers 11 through 42 also serve as chapter numbers for railroads:

11. D&H Mainline.
12. D&H Adirondack Branch to North Creek, formerly the Adirondac Company's Railroad.
13C. D&H Caldwell Branch to Lake George.
13H. Hudson Valley Electric Railway to Warrensburg.
14. D&H Baldwin Branch.
15. Crown Point Iron Company's Railroad.
16. Lake Champlain & Moriah Railroad, with passenger service for the miners from Port Henry to Mineville and Witherbee.
18. Keeseville, Ausable Chasm & Lake Champlain Railroad.
19. D&H Ausable Branch.
20. D&H Chateaugay Branch, formerly Chateaugay Railroad.
21. D&H Mooers Branch.

- 23. Ottawa Division of the New York Central, formerly New York & Ottawa Railroad.
- 31. Carthage & Adirondack Branch of New York Central Railroad.
- 32. Cranberry Lake Railroad.
- 33A. Adirondack & Saint Lawrence Railroad (2nd) from Dekalb Junction to Hermon.
- 33G. Gouverneur & Oswegatchie Railroad.
- 33L. Lowville & Beaver River Railroad.
- 34. Little Falls & Dolgeville Railroad and Dolgeville & Salisbury Railroad.
- 35. Fonda, Johnstown, & Gloversville Railroad.
- 36. New York Central Adirondack Division, formerly Webb's Mohawk & Malone Railroad or first Adirondack & Saint Lawrence RR.
- 36H. Hinckley Branch, New York Central Railroad.
- 37R. Raquette Lake Railway.
- 37M. Marion River Carry Railroad.
- 39. Grasse River Railroad.
- 40. Paul Smith's Electric Railway.
- 42F. first Fulton Chain Railway, or "Peg Leg."
- 42C. second Fulton Chain Railway, or Old Forge Branch.

The identifying numbers in the 100 series denote peripheral railroads which are not described in chapters in this book:

- 101. New York Central Railroad Mohawk Division (Mainline).
- 102. Rome, Watertown & Ogdensburg Railroad.
- 103. Rutland Railroad, formerly Ogdensburg & Lake Champlain.
- 104. New York Central Saint Lawrence Division.
- 106. Rutland Branch of the D&H.
- 107. Addison Branch of the Rutland Railroad.

The Paul Smith's Electric Railway carried passengers from 1906 to about 1930.
Author's collection.

MAP 2-1 RAILROADS WITH PASSENGER SERVICE
See legend on page 27

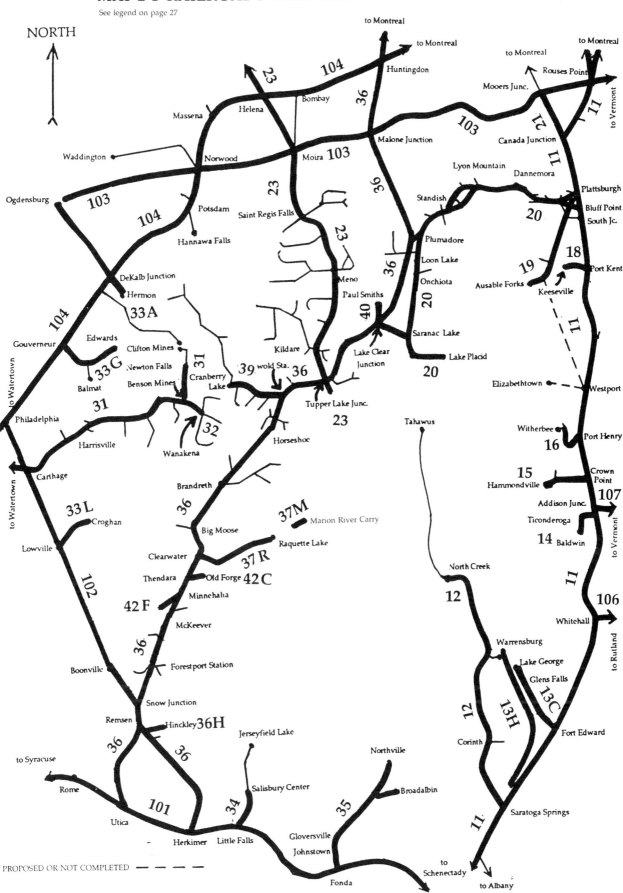

Chapter 3
Railroads and Forests

THE TWO PRIMARY INDUSTRIES for which railroads were built into the Adirondacks were forest products and mining. The sole purpose for the existence of at least eighteen railroads was to transport forest products out of the region.

**Legend to Map 3-1:
Railroads and Spurs Used Exclusively
for Forest Products (no passengers, no
mining, no other industries involved)**

The identifying numbers also serve as chapter numbers. The major mills and other industrial centers on these railroads and spurs are cross-referenced to Maps 3-2 through 3-8.

12. International Paper Co. mill spur into Palmer from Corinth: #406 on Map 3-4.
20I. International Paper Co. mill spurs in the Kents Falls-Woods Mills area: #416 on Map 3-4.
20C. Chateaugay Ore & Iron Co. charcoal spurs in the Lyon Mountain-Upper Kilns area: #444 on Map 3-5.
20R. Roakdale Railroad at Onchiota: #309 on Map 3-2.
23. Black Rapids spur to jackworks, probably of Ducey Lumber Co.: #917 on Map 3-8.
25. Watson Page Lumber Company Railroad at Saint Regis Falls: #313 on Map 3-2.
26E. Everton Railroad at Saint Regis Falls: #322 on Map 3-2.
26B. Brooklyn Cooperage Company Railroad at several locations including Saint Regis Falls, Tupper Lake Junction, and Salisbury Center: #451, #454, and #453, respectively, on Map 3-6.
27. Bay Pond, Inc. Railroad at McDonald: #901 and #902 on Map 3-8.
28. Oval Wood Dish Company Railroad at Kildare (mill was at Tupper Lake): #477 on Map 3-7.
31D. Two spurs at Harrisville leading to Diana and International Paper Co. paper mills: #423 and #424, respectively, on Map 3-4.
31M. Mecca Lumber Company Railroad at Kalurah: #323 on Map 3-2.
31N. Newton Falls Paper Company Railroad at Aldrich: #425 on Map 3-4.
31P. Post and Henderson Railroad at Benson Mines: #327 on Map 3-2.
31H. Higbie Lumber Company and the Newton Falls & Northern Railroad: #328 and #350 on Map 3-2.
32. Rich Lumber Company spurs out of Wanakena: #495 on Map 3-7 and #904 and #905 on Map 3-8.
34. Jerseyfield Railroad at Salisbury Center: #330 on Map 3-2.
36. Kinsley Brothers, later Baker Brothers, Railroad at Tekene: #436 on Map 3-4.
38. Mac-a-Mac and Whitney Industries Railroads at Brandreth: #341 on Map 3-2, #431 on Map 3-4, #908 to #911 on Map 3-8.
39. Grasse River Railroad's North Tram and other spurs between Conifer and Cranberry Lake: #342 and #343 on Map 3-2.
41. Horseshoe Forestry Company and Wake Robin Railroads at Horseshoe Lake: #345 on Map 3-2, #455 on Map 3-6, and #467 on Map 3-7.
42B. Black River & Woodhull Railroad at Forestport #331 and #332 on Map 3-2.
42M. Moose River Lumber Company Railroad at McKeever: #346 on Map 3-2.
42W. Woods Lake Spur of Champlain Realty Company Railroad: #433 on Map 3-4, #906 and #916 on Map 3-8.
42P. Partlow Lake Railway at Partlow.
42I. Piercefield Spur of the International Paper Company: #434 on Map 3-4.

107. Norwood & Saint Lawrence Railroad, owned by Saint Regis Paper Company (not included in this book).

Before the advent of the first railroads into the Adirondacks in the 1860s, almost all the timber cut was coniferous softwood and floatable down such rivers as the Hudson, Schroon, Bog, and Boquet to the mills. Mainly pine and spruce but also some fir and cedar were harvested. Railroads made it possible to transport timber which has greater specific gravity: hardwoods such as beech, maples, birches, cherry, and white ash which could not readily float.

The major concentration of logging railroads entered the Adirondacks from the north, northwest, and west, beginning in the mid-1880s. These include the New York & Ottawa and the Carthage & Adirondack trunk lines with all their branches. To this day, most logging in the Adirondacks still occurs in this north and northwest belt, but transportation is by truck rather than by rail.

Note that the northern and northwestern Adirondacks, once saturated with lumber railroads, has extensive nearly flat glacial outwash plains and low, rolling till hills, making construction easy for railroad grades. The occasional, medium-sized bedrock mountains, mainly 2000 to 2500 feet in elevation, presented only a minor obstacle to the railroads. The alternatives were to climb over them or tunnel through them, but the general pattern was to go around them. Swamps, marshes, and bogs had to be crossed creating larger obstacles, but glacial outwash and glacial till fill was almost always plentiful nearby.

Lumber companies in the northern and northwestern Adirondacks with their own railroad branches included the Watson Page Lumber Company (Chapter 25), the Brooklyn Cooperage Company (Chapter 26), Oval Wood Dish (Chapter 28), Bay Pond Inc. (Chapter 27), Rich Lumber Company (Chapter 32), Mecca Lumber Company (in Chapter 31A), Higbie Lumber Company (in Chapter 31A), Post & Henderson (in Chapter 31A), and Newton Falls Paper Company (in Chapter 31A).

The New York Central Adirondack Division was completed in 1892 on a diagonal across the Adirondacks from southwest to northeast (see Chapter 36). It opened the way for an additional number of branch logging and/or pulp railroads which soon followed. Another belt of intense forest product harvesting activity was thus created including more companies with their own branches: Moose River Lumber Company (Chapter 42); Champlain Realty Company, a division of International Paper (Chapter 42); Mac-a-Mac then Whitney industries at Brandreth (Chapter 38); Partlow Lake Railway, part of the Webb Estate (Chapter 42); Horseshoe Forestry Company (Chapter 41); and Baker Brothers, formerly Kinsley Lumber Company (Chapters 20 and 36). The Grasse River Railroad of the Emporium Forestry Company, although connected to the New York Central Adirondack Division at Childwold Station, was geographically positioned, however, in the northwest belt, between the Carthage & Adirondack branches on the west and the New York & Ottawa branches on the east. Chapter 39 is devoted to the Grasse River Railroad.

The Jerseyfield Railroad, a logging line, entered the region from the Mohawk Valley on the south as an extension of the Little Falls & Dolgeville and Dolgeville & Salisbury Railroads (see Chapter 34). The south-central Adirondacks including Long Lake, Indian Lake, Speculator, and Wells never had railroads built within ten miles of them. This is true as well for the Schroon River Valley above Warrensburg and the Ausable Valley above Ausable Forks.

Prior to the advent of mechanical skidders, trucks, and paved highways to transport logs to the mills, areas not served by railroads could not be easily and thoroughly logged. The timber in those areas served by railroads was far more accessible. However, some large tracts were never served by railroads for several reasons. The High Peaks south of Lake Placid, and other mountains exceeding 3000 feet in height to the southwest beyond Indian Lake, created a steep, rugged terrain difficult to construct railroads into. Once land became part of the State Forest Preserve, it was off-limits to the lumber companies. No main line, such as the D&H, New York Central Adirondack Division, Carthage & Adirondack, nor New York & Ottawa entered these areas from which lumber railroads could branch.

Many of the short spurs, typically one-half mile to one mile long, shown but not labeled on the old 15-minute United States Geological Survey topographic quadrangles dating to the turn-of-the-century, served pulp and/or paper mills. Examples are at Hadley, Kents Falls, two at Woods Mills, two at Harrisville, Corinth, Piercefield, Ausable Chasm, and Willsboro.

Legend to Map 3-2:
Sawmills

These are numbered, as best as possible, by increasing chapter numbers and by increasing mileage within each chapter. Specific locations for these mills are shown on the maps cross-referenced.

301. Northern Lumber Co. Sawmill, Riverside: Map 12-20.
302. Sawmill on pier at Port Henry, possibly Stimpson: Map 16-2, letter P.
303. Port Henry Iron Company Sawmill at Roe Pond, Witherbee: Map 16-6.
304. Baker Brothers Planing and Sawmill, Plattsburgh: Map 19-4, number 2.
305. A. Mason & Son Sawmill, Peru: Map 19-7.
306. Sawmill at Lyon Mountain (owner unknown but possibly the Chateaugay Ore & Iron Co.): Map 20-14.
307. Sawmill at Bradley Pond, probably owned by the Chateaugay Ore & Iron Company, and later moved to Onchiota possibly as #308: Map 20-14A.
308. Roak's Sawmill, Onchiota, possibly moved from Bradley Pond as #307: Map 20-20. Later Walker's, then Baker Brothers, and finally Plattsburgh Dock & Coal Company.
309. Roak's Sawmill, Roakdale: Map 20-20.
310. Shanley & Alfred Lumber Co. Sawmill, Shanleys: Map 23-3.
311. Leboeuf's Sawmill at LeBoeufs (site unknown): Map 23-4.
312. Ducey's Sawmill, Moira: Map 23-7.
313. Watson Page Sawmill, Saint Regis Falls: Map 23-9.
314. Hurd, Hotchkiss, & McFarlane Sawmill, Saint Regis Falls: Map 23-9.
315. Hurd's Sawmill, Santa Clara: Map 23-10.
316. Ducey's Sawmill, Brandon: Map 23-12.
317. Turner's Sawmill at Derrick: Map 23-15.
318. Hobson's Sawmill, Tupper Lake: Map 23-18.
319. Hurd's Big Mill, Tupper Lake: Map 23-18. Several owners followed, including Norwood; then Santa Clara Lumber Co.
322. Everton's Sawmill, Everton: Map 26-2.
323. Mecca Lumber Co. Sawmill, Kalurah: Map 31-13.
324. Post & Henderson Sawmill, Jayville (site unknown): Map 31-13.
325. Dean, Mitchell & Yousey Sawmill, Aldrich: Map 31-16.
326. Coffin's Sawmill at Coffins Mills (site unknown): Map 31-16.
327. Post & Henderson Sawmill, Benson Mines: Map 31-18.
328. Higbie Lumber Co. Sawmill, Newton Falls: Maps 31-21 and 31-22.
329. Ford Brothers Sawmill, Wanakena: Map 32-1.
330. Jerseyfield Railroad Sawmill, Salisbury Center: Map 34-1.
331. Black River & Woodhull Railroad Sawmill on Pine Creek near Forestport: Map 36-3.
332. Grant's Sawmill, Little Woodhull Creek: Map 36-3.
333. G. F. Hughes Sawmill, Remsen: Map 36-15.
334. Muncil's Sawmill, Gabriels: Map 36-33.
335. Morgans Mills, moved from Bryants as #337: Map 36-12.
336. Little Bryant's: Map 36-37.
337. Bryants Mill: Map 36-38.
338. Sawmill site at Mountain View (owner unknown): Map 36-39.
339. Boyce's Saw & Planing Mill, Owls Head: Map 36-40.
340. Bassett's Sawmill, Marion River Carry: Map 37-6.
341. Mac-a-Mac Sawmill, Brandreth: Map 38-1.
342. Emporium Forestry Co. Sawmill, Conifer: Map 39-6.
343. Emporium Forestry Co. Sawmill, Cranberry Lake: Map 39-7.
344. Paul Smith's Sawmill, Paul Smiths: off west edge of Map 40-2.
345. Horseshoe Forestry Co. Sawmill, Hitchins Pond: Map 41-1.
346. Moose River Lumber Co. Sawmill, McKeever: Map 42-1.
347. There were several mills at Thendara: Map 42-3----First Brown's Tract Lumber Company Mill, Second Brown's Tract Lumber Company Mill, and the Deis Mill (part of which is now Foley's Lumber & Hardware Company).
348. The Treadwells Mills Pulp and Paper Company had a sawmill at Treadwells Mills: Map 20-9.
349. Brooklyn Cooperage had a sawmill on Stony Brook west of Meno: Map 26-3.
350. Higbie Lumber Company at Newbridge: Map 31-22.

Legend to Map 3-3:
Lumber Yards and Lumber Dealers

(note: some of these lumber yards and lumber dealers may also have had a sawmill, but there is no evidence yet for such mills----specific locations for these lumber yards & dealers are shown on the maps cross-referenced)

371. Curtis Lumber Company & Building Materials, Warrensburg: Map 12-18.
372. A. C. Emerson Co., Lumber & Coal, Warrensburg: Map 12-18.
373. T. C. Murphy Lumber Co., Riverside: Map 12-20.
374. Finch Pruyn, North Creek: Map 12-21.

375. Great Eastern Lumber Co. Drykiln, North Creek: Map 12-21.
376. Stimpson Lumber & Coal, Port Henry: #302 on Map 3-2, letter N on Map 16-2.
377. Dock & Coal Co. Lumber Yard, Plattsburgh: Map 19-3.
378. W. Wilcox & Son Coal, Wood & Hay, woodshed at Plattsburgh: Map 19-9.
379. Branch & Callanan Lumber Yard, Saranac Lake: Map 20-23.
380. Lumber sheds at Oswegatchie: Map 31-16.
381. Lumber yard at Big Moose: Map 36-22.
382. Bowen Lumber Company, Malone Junction: Map 36-45.
383. Bissell's Lumber Yard, Wanakena: Map 32-1.

Legend to Map 3-4:
Pulp and Paper Mills, Pulp Rossing Plants, and Pulpwood Loading Sidings
(note: there are no detailed maps in this book on peripheral mills # 401, #402, #403, #404, and #415----specific locations of other mills are shown on the maps cross-referenced)

401. Finch Pruyn at Glens Falls.
402. Saint Regis, now Champion International, at Deferiet.
403. Domtar, Cornwall, Ontario.
404. Malone Paper, Malone.
405. International Paper Co. north of Ticonderoga: Map 11-19.
406. International Paper Co., Palmer (near Corinth): Map 12-14A.
407. Rockwell Falls Fiber Co., then Union Bag & Paper Co.; finally Nu-Era Paper Company, Hadley: Map 12-15.
408. Warrensburg Board & Paper Co., Warrensburg: Map 12-18.
409. International Paper Co. in Ticonderoga Village, 3 mills named A, B and C: Map 14-1.
410. New York & Pennsylvania Co., Willsboro: Map 17-3.
411. Georgia Pacific, Plattsburgh: Map 19-9.
412. J. & J. Rogers at Ausable Forks, 2 mills: Map 19-8.
413. Maine, Plattsburgh: Map 20-9.
414. Freydenburg Falls, Plattsburgh: Map 20-9.
415. Degrasse Paper Company Mill, Eddy.
416. International Paper Co., Mills A & B at Woods Mills and Mill C at Kents Falls: Map 20-10.
417. Saint Regis Paper Co., Saint Regis Falls: Map 23-9.
418. Johnston's, Saint Regis Falls: Map 23-9.
419. Santa Clara Lumber Company Pulp Rossing Plant at Tupper Lake Junction: Map 23-18.
420. Potsdam Red Sandstone Co., Hannawa Falls: Map 29-2.
421. James River, formerly Crown Zellerbach Corp., Carthage: Map 31-8.
422. Newton Falls Paper Company, Carthage (probably only a siding): Map 31-8.
423. Diana Paper Co., later Saint Regis Paper Co., Harrisville: Map 31-12.
424. International Paper Co., Harrisville: Map 31-12.
425. Newton Falls Paper Co., pulpwood loading siding at Aldrich. This company may have owned a pulp mill at Aldrich in 1920 next to sawmill #325: Maps 31-5 and 31-16.
426. Newton Falls Paper Co., Newton Falls: Map 31-21.
427. J. P. Lewis Paper Co., now Mountain Paper Co., Beaver Falls: Map 33-4.
428. Champlain Realty Co. pulpwood loading siding at Buck Pond: Map 36-22.
429. International Paper Co. Pulp Rossing Plant, Underwood: Map 36-29.
430. Whitney Industries pulpwood loading siding between Underwood and Tupper Lake Junction: Map 36-29.
431. Mac-a-Mac Co. at Brandreth (pulpwood shipped to the Saint Regis Paper Co. Mill at Deferiet): Map 38-1.
432. Moose River Lumber Co. pulp mill, McKeever later owned by the Gould Paper Co.: Map 42-1.
433. Champlain Realty Co., Woods Lake: Map 42-5.
434. International Paper Co., Piercefield: Map 42-7.
435. Pulpwood loading siding at Bryant's (owner unknown): Map 36-38.
436. Pulpwood loading siding at Tekene Junction on the New York Central, probably Kinsley Brothers': Map 36-36.
437. Saint Lawrence Pulp Mill Co. at Hailesboro: Map 33-3.
438. Aldrich Paper Co. at Emeryville: Map 33-3.
439. Gouverneur Wood & Pulp Co. at Emeryville (this company apparently shared a siding at Emeryville with #438 and the U.S. Talc Company #634, but did not have a plant here): Map 33-3.
440. Alice Falls Paper Mill, Ausable Chasm: Map 18-2.

Still operating are mills #401, #402, #403, #405, #406, #411, #421, #426, and #427. #421 is no longer served by rail.

Legend to Map 3-5:
Charcoal

In the mining areas with blast furnaces and/or forges, the forests were clearcut or nearly so that the wood could be made into charcoal fuel. Photos of these taken in the late nineteenth century reveal a landscape nearly as free of trees as an agricultural one, but the forests have since grown back. Localities 441 through 444, below, were part of the iron industry, while 445 through 447 were not.

441. Around the Hammondville-Irondale areas for the Crown Point Iron Company. Charcoal was made at Irondale. See, also, Map 15-4.
442. Around the Mineville-Witherbee-Port Henry area for the Witherbee Sherman and Port Henry Iron Companies. See Chapter 16.
443. The Ausable Forks area west and northwest to Black Brook, West Kilns, and Silver Lake had no blast furnace, but charcoal was also produced by the J.& J. Rogers Iron Works. See Chapter 19.
444. From Lyon Mountain to Plumadore, the Chateaugay Iron Company had numerous spurs and sidings for charcoal, including the Bradley Pond Switch, at Standish, the South Inlet Branch, the Upper Kilns Branch, and at Plumadore. In addition, but not along the railroad, were the Belmont Forges at the foot of the Chateaugay Lakes. See Chapter 20.
445. Charcoal was made at Spring Cove. See also Map 23-11.
446. Charcoal was made by Hurd at Tupper Lake adjacent to the Big Mill. See Map 23-18 for location of overhead tramway.
447. Charcoal was made by Brooklyn Cooperage Company in Tupper Lake, with Tupper Lake Chemical taking over production later. See also Map 36-30.

Legend to Map 3-6:
Stave and Heading Mills for Barrels
(specific locations of these mills are shown on the maps cross-referenced)

451. Brooklyn Cooperage Company, Saint Regis Falls: Map 23-9.
452. Venters & Buckley, Wanakena: Map 32-1.
453. Brooklyn Cooperage Company, Salisbury Center: Map 34-1.
454. Brooklyn Cooperage Company, Tupper Lake: Map 36-30.
455. Horseshoe Forestry Company, Hitchins Pond: Map 41-1.

Legend to Map 3-7:
Other Forest Products

In addition to the major forest products, lumber, pulp, charcoal and barrels, the Adirondacks provided many minor ones. Numerous factories and mills, many with railroad sidings, produced a variety of wooden products. These were located primarily in the northern third of the region where the bulk of the logging railroads were operating. Specific locations of these factories are shown on the maps cross-referenced.

461. Acetate of lime, Brooklyn Cooperage, Tupper Lake: Map 36-30.
462. Bobbin spools, U.S. Bobbin & Shuttle Co., Tupper Lake: Map 36-30.
463. Bobbin spools, Draper Corporation, Tupper Lake: Map 36-30.
464. Bowling pin blanks, Draper Corporation, Tupper Lake: Map 36-30.
465. Boxes, Hurd, Saint Regis Falls: Map 23-9.
466. Boxes, Hurd, Santa Clara: Map 23-10.
467. Boxes, Horseshoe Forestry, Hitchins Pond: Map 41-1.
468. Broomsticks, Hurd?, Saint Regis Falls: Map 23-9.
469. Broomsticks, Hurd, Santa Clara: Map 23-10.
470. Butter tubs, W.S. Coffin, Coffins Mills: Map 31-16.
471. Chairs & other furniture, Hurd, Santa Clara: Map 23-10.
472. Chairs & other furniture, O'Neil, later Cascade, Saint Regis Falls: Map 23-9.
473. Chairs & other furniture, Jamestown Adirondack, Tupper Lake: Map 36-30.
474. Chairs & other furniture, W. S. Coffin, Coffins Mills: Map 31-16.
475. Christmas trees, Asplin, Gabriels: Map 36-33.
476. Clapboards, manufacturer unknown, Saint Regis Falls: Map 23-9.
477. Dishes & other kitchen utensils, Oval Wood Dish, Tupper Lake: Map 23-18.
478. Firewood, Bryant, Bryants Mills: Map 36-38.
479. Hoe handles, manufacturer unknown, North Creek: Map 12-21.
480. Lath, Ryan & Shleder, Wanakena: Map 32-1.
481. Lath, manufacturer unknown, Saint Regis Falls: Map 23-9.
482. Lath, Hurd, Santa Clara: Map 23-10.
483. Mangle rolls for laundries, Elliott, Derrick: Map 23-15.
484. Mangle rolls for laundries, Elliott, Tupper Lake: Map 36-30.
485. Maple syrup, Horseshoe Forestry, Hitchins Pond: Map 41-1.

486. Pickets for fences, Hurd, Santa Clara: Map 23-10.
487. Shingles, Hurd, Santa Clara: Map 23-10.
488. Shoe lasts, Bates & Northrup, Wanakena: Map 32-1.
489. Shuttles for textiles, U.S.Bobbin & Shuttle, Tupper Lake: Map 36-30.
490. Veneer, Tupper Lake Veneer, Tupper Lake: Map 36-30.
491. Veneer, Setter Brothers, Wanakena: Map 32-1.
492. Whipbutts for buggies, Rich Lumber Co., Wanakena: Map 32-1.
493. Wood alcohol, Brooklyn Cooperage, Tupper Lake: Map 36-30.
494. Wood waste & chips, Hurd, Tupper Lake: Map 23-18.
495. Wood waste & chips, Rich Lumber Co., Wanakena: Map 32-1.
496. Piano sounding boards, Pullman Brothers, Thendara: Map 42-3.
497. Veneer mill, Moose River Lumber Company, McKeever.
793. A box factory was located southeast of Otis Junction, probably as a part of Carl B. Getman Concrete Building Supply Company: Maps 7-4 and 20-9; not Map 3-7.

Legend to Map 3-8: Jackworks

Jackworks were conveyor belts which hauled conifer logs out of, or occasionally into, bodies of water to railroad cars. Many of the saw and pulp mills had jackworks. Only those described in the literature and/or those with evidence found in the field are shown on the maps. Specific locations of these jackworks are shown on the maps cross-referenced.

901. Bay Pond Inc. at Augerhole Falls: Map 27-1.
902. Bay Pond Inc. at Wolf Pond: Map 27-1.
903. Newton Falls Paper Co. on the Middle Branch Oswegatchie River near Scanlon's Camp: Maps 31-5 and 31-16.
904. Rich Lumber Company, Oswegatchie River: Map 31-6.
905. Rich Lumber Company, Dead Creek: Map 31-6.
906. Champlain Realty Co. at Buck Pond: Map 36-22.
907. Whitney Industries at Raquette Pond: Map 36-29.
908. Mac-a-Mac Co. at North Pond Flowground: Map 38-1.
909. Mac-a-Mac Co. at Brandreth Lake: Map 38-1.
910. Mac-a-Mac Co. at West Pond: Map 38-1.
911. Mac-a-Mac Co. at Thayer Lake: Map 38-1.
912. Emporium Forestry Co. at Silver Lake: Map 39-7.
913. Paul Smith's Electric Railway at Lower Saint Regis Lake: Map 40-2.
914. Moose River Lumber Co. at McKeever: Map 42-1.
915. Second Brown Tract Mill, Thendara: Map 42-3.
916. Champlain Realty Co. at Twitchell Creek: Map 42-5.
917. Ducey's at Black Rapids: Map 23-14.

Reforestation

The area between Wolf Ponds and Middle Kilns along the Chateaugay Branch had been so denuded of forest to supply the Standish Blast Furnace with charcoal between 1885 and 1902 that the D&H itself established a reforestation program. In the Centennial History of the D&H, published in 1925, a photo of a red pine tree nursery at Bluff Point is included on page 456, and a Scots pine plantation at Wolf Pond on page 458. Linney (1934) includes two photos taken in 1915 of Scots pine plantations started in 1910: one at Wolf Ponds, page 133, and the other at Middle Kilns, page 134. Schwarz (1936, Jan. 1 & Feb. 1) wrote articles on "Forestry on the D&H."

The New York State Forest Commission had begun a reforestation program earlier with its first tree nursery at Axton in 1898. Some of the state lands planted with trees follow railroad grades, while many do not.

Old growth

Old growth, or first growth, can be defined as a forest which has not been cleared, logged, burned, nor otherwise severely disturbed during the last 300 years. There is still much old growth left in the Adirondacks, at least 200,000 acres, but it is widely scattered and most often in small parcels ranging in size from dozens of acres to several hundred. The largest area is the Five Ponds Wilderness Area between the Stillwater Reservoir and lands logged by the Rich Lumber Company south of Wanakena. The second largest area includes the High Peaks. There are many small old growth parcels in the Paul Smiths area from Jenkins Mountain southward to Saint Regis Mountain to Fish Pond, an area where railroads did not reach. Further north of Paul Smiths, logging railroads removed the old growth timber. Most old growth is now in the Forest Preserve. A map published by the New York State Forest Commission in 1891 shows those tracts in the Adirondacks still remaining in old growth in 1891; perhaps as much as a third of the Adirondacks had not been logged, burned, or cleared at that time. McMartin (1994) provides an updated history.

Forest historians searching for old growth in the Adirondacks need not visit localities served by railroads. This book instructs such historians where not to go.

Forest which had been logged by many lumber and paper companies, especially that in the northwestern Adirondacks, will not return to anything approaching its initial state for another 100 to 200 years. Abandoned agricultural fields and pastures will also require several centuries. Abandoned quarries, sand and gravel pits, and tailings piles may take longer.

Land-use history is chaotic: different people do different things to the land at different times without an overall, long-range region-wide perspective. Only recently have management plans for large parcels of land for many years into the future become common.

Brooklyn Cooperage railroad grade along the loop east of Meno, April 1986.
The line had been abandoned about 1920.
Author photo.

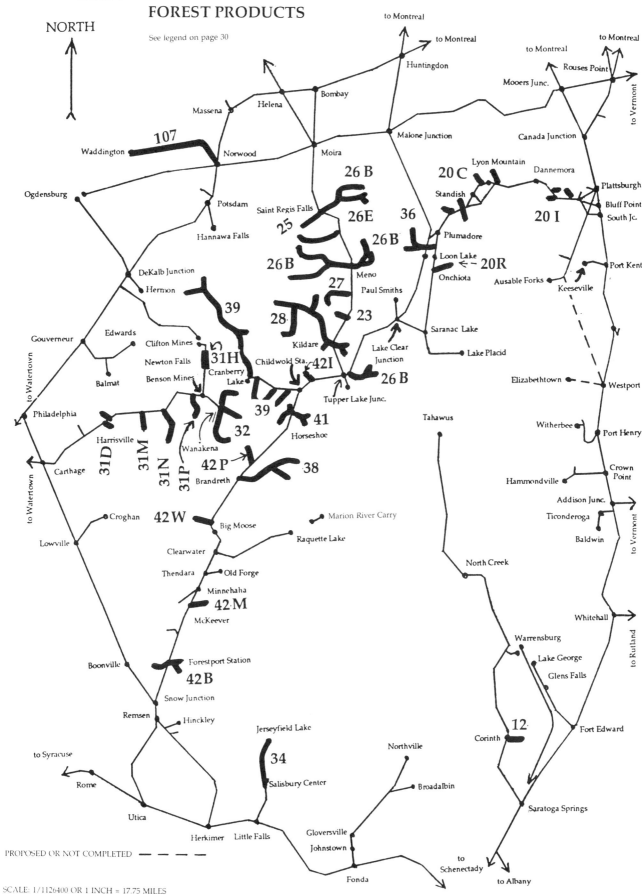

MAP 3-1 RAILROADS AND SPURS USED EXCLUSIVELY FOR FOREST PRODUCTS

MAP 3-2 SAWMILLS

See legend on page 32

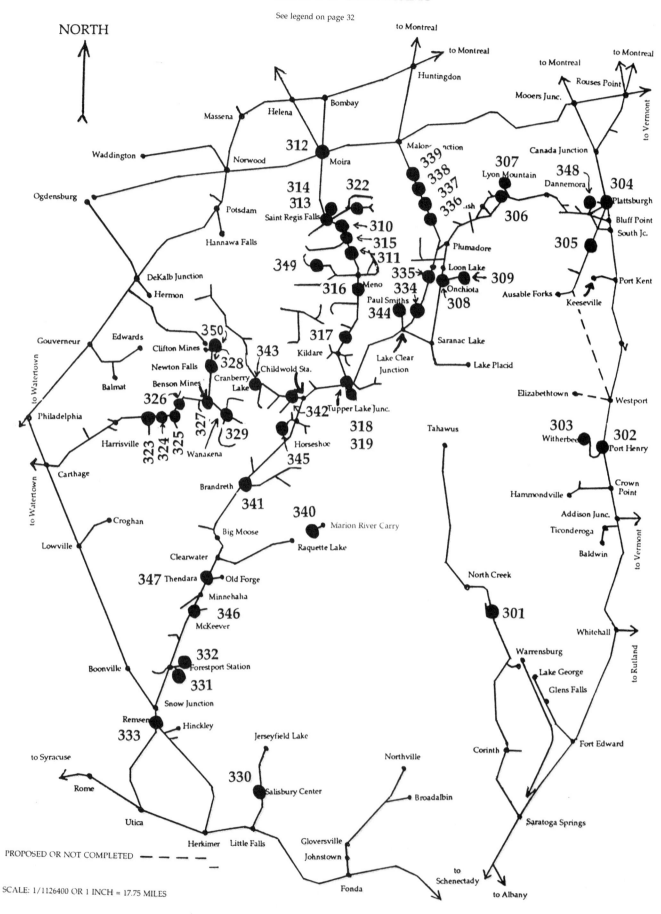

MAP 3-3 LUMBER YARDS AND LUMBER DEALERS

See legend on page 32

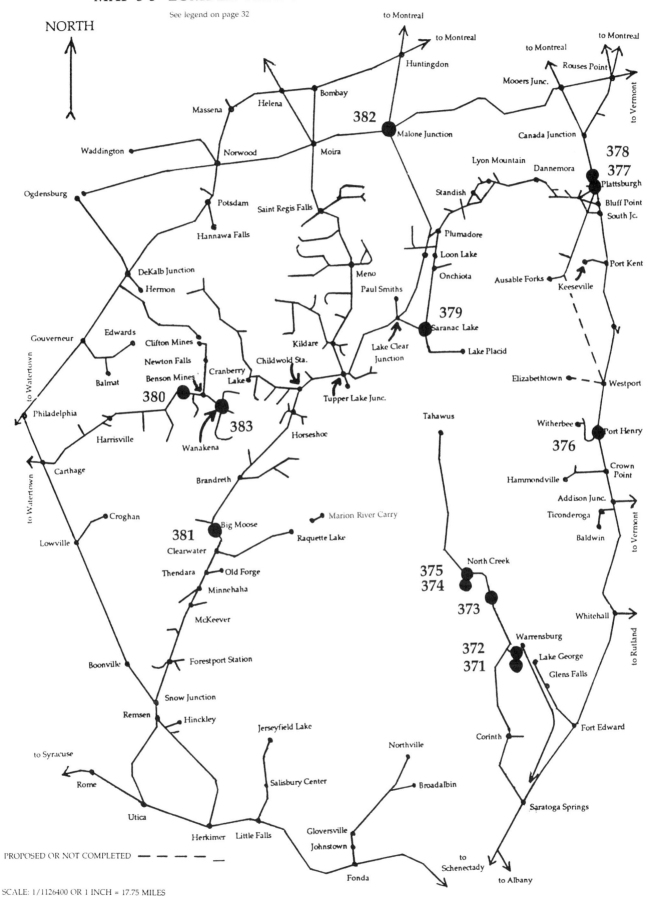

PROPOSED OR NOT COMPLETED – – – –

SCALE: 1/1126400 OR 1 INCH = 17.75 MILES

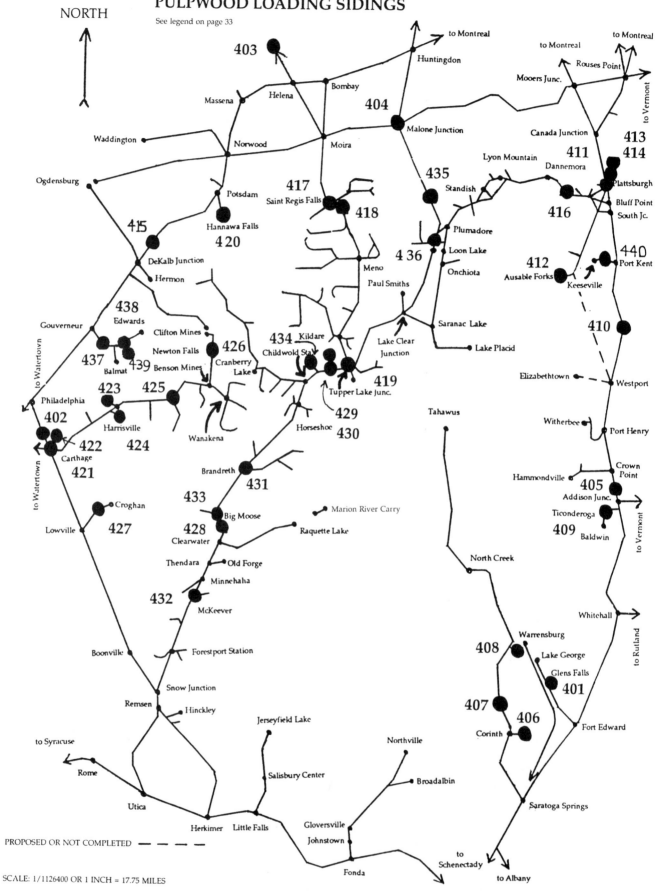

MAP 3-4 PULP & PAPER MILLS, PULP ROSSING PLANTS, & PULPWOOD LOADING SIDINGS

See legend on page 33

PROPOSED OR NOT COMPLETED -------

SCALE: 1/1126400 OR 1 INCH = 17.75 MILES

MAP 3-5 CHARCOAL

See legend on page 33

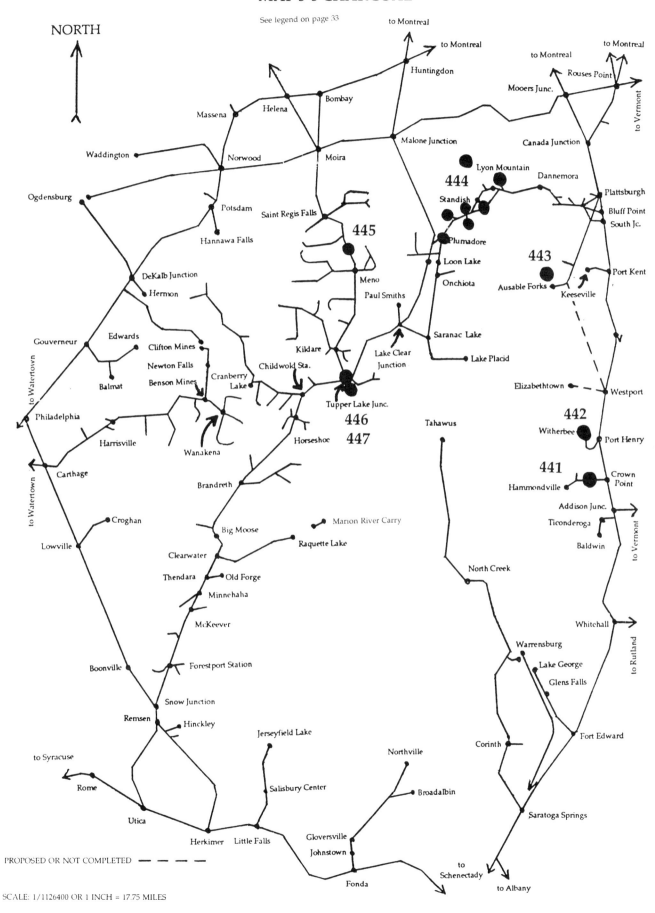

MAP 3-6 STAVE & HEADING MILLS FOR BARRELS
See legend on page 34

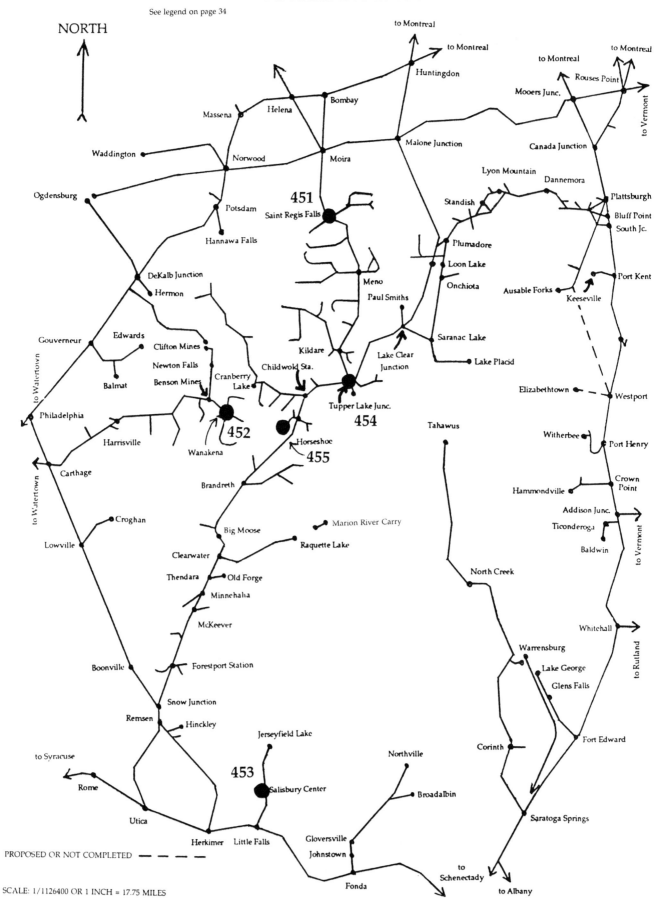

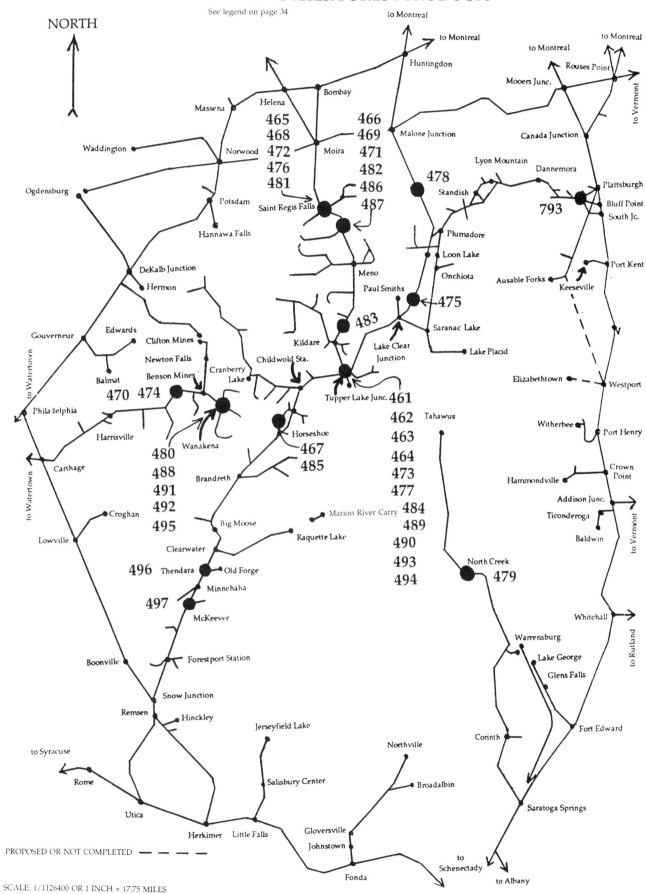
MAP 3-7 OTHER FOREST PRODUCTS
See legend on page 34

MAP 3-8 JACKWORKS

See legend on page 35

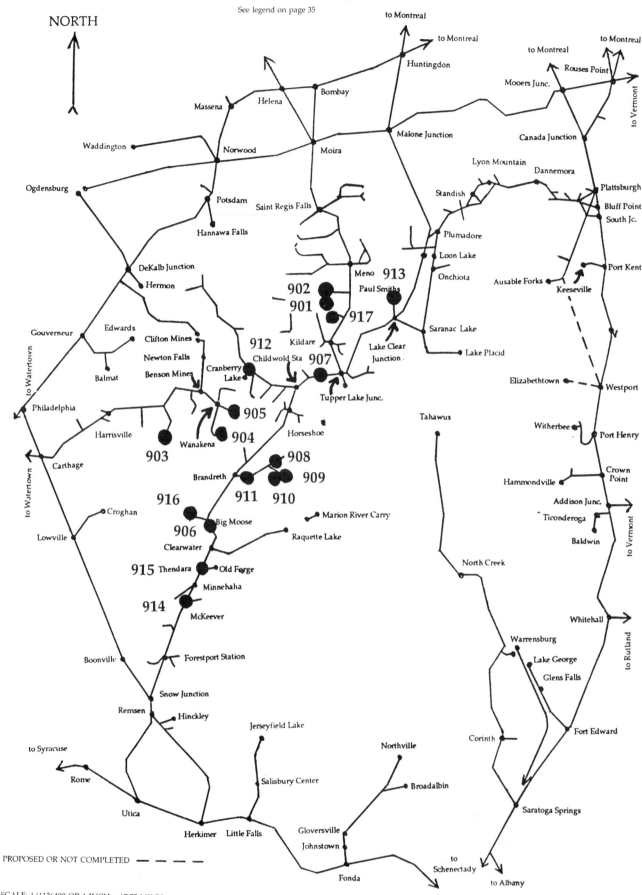

Chapter 4
Railroads and Forest Fires

COMMON CAUSES OF FIRES are the burning of brush, clearing of land, the covering of a trespass (illegal logging, often on State Forest Preserve lands), other forms of arson, campfires of hunters and fishermen, berry pickers, lightning, and railroads.

Statistics

A number of early publications offer much detail. The annual reports of the New York State Forest Commission (1884-1894), the Forest Fish and Game Commission (1895-1910), the Conservation Commission (1911-1926), and the Conservation Department (1927-1969), all predecessor organizations of the current Department of Environmental Conservation, included forest fire warden reports. In the early years, from 1885 through about 1910, some of these fire warden reports were highly detailed. Suter (1903) reported on forest fires of that year and provided a map of the Adirondacks showing the extent of the burns. Schmitt and the New York State Conservation Commission (1916) published a map of the Adirondacks showing forest history, including burns, from 1903 until 1916.

During the year 1903, the largest acreage burned. The total was estimated to be 464,000 for the whole of New York State, much of this occurring in the Adirondacks. During the year 1908, the second largest acreage burned, about 347,000 acres for the State as a whole and, again, much of this occurring in the Adirondacks. The annual reports of the New York State Forest Fish and Game Commission supply the data. By 1908, New York State had enough. Forest fire prevention and control programs burst forth on the scene in profusion. Fire towers grew atop dozens of summits in 1909 and 1910.

Some of the forest fires in the Adirondacks during the nineteenth century and first decade of the twentieth were caused by sparks from locomotives. The percentage of the number of forest fires caused by railroad locomotives can be obtained from the annual reports. The statistics are approximations because they vary from year to year. Some are for Fire Districts and others for Fire Towns, covering the whole of New York State and the Adirondack Park, respectively. These statistics still give us a general idea of just how large or small a role the railroads played in starting burns. The percentages in the following table refer to the number, not acreage, of fires.

First column: Period of years
Second column: Number of years data available for that period
Third-fifth columns: Percentage of fires caused by railroads in New York State as a whole

		minimum	maximum	mean
1893-1909	10	9%	32%	20.6%
1910-1919	7	11%	28%	18.6%
1920-1929	9	12%	25%	16.4%
1930-1939	10	5%	11%	6.7%
1940-1949	10	5%	17%	9.7%
1950-1959	10	2%	6%	3.5%
1960-1965	6	5%	8%	6.3%
All years	62	2%	32%	11.6%

Certain historic trends must be considered when examining the table, notably the decrease in the number and extent of forest fires after 1909. In 1909 began an intensive program of forest fire prevention and control, but not until the 1930s was the contribution of burns made by locomotives significantly reduced. Also, by the 1930s, there were fewer trains running to cause fires. By the late 1940s and early 1950s, dieselization and still fewer trains reduced the percentage further. For all 62 years for which data are available, locomotives caused only 11.6% of the fires on the average----not as many as one would be led to believe.

Railroads, Fires, and Soils

The relation between railroads and forest fires is a very complex one. Many fires were at least ten miles from the nearest railroad. Therefore, they could not have been started by flying sparks from locomotives. Other fires adjacent to railroads were sometimes set by locomotives, but we know that they were caused more often by human activities which were unrelated to railroad operations. A tract with a railroad through it generally had more such activity concentrated along it, e.g. in villages and industries, than a tract without a railroad. The greater the number of people in an area, the greater the probability of a burn.

Tracts in the Adirondacks which have not burned are located both with and without railroads passing through them.

A concentration of burned areas exists in the northern Adirondacks. These are glacial outwash plains with exceedingly sandy soils. Here, water retention is minimal so that in times of drought not only does the soil dry out, but so also does the vegetation upon it. Tree species which can tolerate such poor soils are predominantly coniferous: pines, spruces, fir, and hemlock, all very resinous and thus very flammable. When a burn occurs on an outwash plain, it is often severe. The plain remains in a semi-open, brushy state with scattered trees for decades. To this day, after nearly a century, the forest has not fully returned to many of these areas.

Forest fires were not limited to outwash plains. Some island bedrock hills and low mountains, projecting out of the sea of outwash and covered with glacial till soils, also burned. The soils were (and are) less sandy and retain water longer. The forests growing upon them are primarily northern hardwoods: beech, maples, birches, cherry, and white ash----less resinous and less flammable. Generally, a till slope burns less severely and reforests itself within several decades. Southwest- and south-facing till slopes are most prone to fires since they are the warmest and driest. Some fires on till slopes were caused by locomotives; others were not, not even if the slope were adjacent to a railroad.

Examples of Specific Burns

Examples of burned outwash plains with railroads once running through them include those in the New York Central Adirondack Division from Gabriels through Lake Clear Junction to Saranac Inn, others along the New York & Ottawa from south of Madawaska through Brandon southwest to Bay Pond, and still others along the Chateaugay Railroad from Loon Lake through Onchiota to Bloomingdale Station. Some portions of these plains were burned more than once. The railroads were not always the cause.

Marleau (1986, p. 246) and Bernard (1981) mention how a forest fire threatened Sabattis (Long Lake West) in 1908 and then burned the whole hamlet. Fire-fighting trains at first derailed due to the warping of the rails by excessive heat. Later trains made it in, but firefighters were too late to save it.

The forest fires at Wanakena and Horseshoe in 1908 so devastated the timber that the Rich Lumber Company and the Horseshoe Forestry Company, respectively, shut down operations within several years. See Gove (1973) and Keith (1972) on the former, and Clark (1974) and Hughes (1990) on the latter.

The logging exhibit at The Adirondack Museum includes a photo of Kildare in 1912 after a fire.

Harter (1979, pp. 121 to 131) devotes his whole Chapter XIV to railroads and forest fires. However, it is limited to the New York Central Adirondack Division and its branches.

A *D&H Bulletin* (1926) included an article: "Forest Fires Once a Handicap."

Bernard (1981) briefly describes a number of autumn 1908 fires, many of which began in the vicinity of railroads: between Stony Creek and Hadley, and another at Thurman on the D&H Adirondack Branch; between Plumadore and Owls Head on the New York Central Adirondack Division; along the New York & Ottawa (which Bernard oddly calls the Mohawk & Malone!) between Tupper Lake and Saint Regis Falls including Bay Pond; and the D&H Chateaugay Branch between Dannemora and Lake Placid.

Fire Prevention and Control

Locomotives had to burn fuel oil each year, by law, from April 1 to December 1 when fire danger was most severe, and could revert back to coal in winter when fires were unlikely due to snow cover. (Detail on limited operation of coal-burning locomotives in the Forest Preserve is available in the June 13, 1948 New York Central Adirondack Division's employees' timetable, page 2). In addition, spark arresters were required to be installed in locomotive smokestacks. Bernard (1981) states that not a single fire occurred along the Raquette Lake Railway which burned only fuel oil in 1908.

Fire prevention trains were established on the New York Central Adirondack and Ottawa Divisions (Seely, 1928): five flat cars bearing each a 7000-gallon water tank and pump with hose. Gove (1973) describes fire-fighting cars stationed at the Cranberry Lake Railroad engine house in Wanakena. Photos in Harter (1979, pages 124 and 125) show a Nehasane Park Fire Service Train and other fire service trains. Bernard (1981) has a fire service train photo and one is on exhibit at The Adirondack Museum's Logging Building.

Speeders followed trains to insure that sparks had not ignited vegetation (speeders, small gasoline-powered railroad cars which hold several persons and ride on four wheels, were originally powered by human muscle and were also called hand cars).

The area around Lake Clear Junction was burned probably more than once, the last time in 1903.
The ties of the Paul Smith's Railway are visible at left, ca. 1953.
Alan Thomas photo.

Chapter 5
Railroads and Agriculture

BECAUSE THE ADIRONDACK INTERIOR is not an agricultural region, few sidings here were used to ship farm products. Short growing seasons because of higher elevations plus frequently stony, sandy soils make agriculture difficult in the interior. There were some exceptions. For example, potatoes had been shipped from Gabriels.

Most agricultural products were shipped by rail out of areas peripheral to the Adirondacks: the Champlain, Saint Lawrence, and Black River Valleys. These lowlands have longer growing seasons and better limestone soils so that agriculture continues as a major industry. Dairy products still are shipped out, but most travel by truck today.

Dairy products were shipped by rail from the locations listed in the creameries legend below and are shown on Map 5-1. The Rutland Railroad in New York was a major dairy shipper. In fact, the first railroad refrigerator iced car was built by the Northern Railroad, a Rutland predecessor, in 1851 (Shaughnessy, 1964, page 58). Discussions of agricultural products transported by the Rutland Railroad are also found in Nimke (1986, 1989, and 1990); Berry (1948 through 1956); Shaw and Walsh (1982); and Doherty (1971). Two issues of the *D&H RR Bulletin* included articles on milk: 1933 and 1936 (Apr. 1).

Legend to Map 5-1:
Creameries
(These are numbered, as best as possible, by increasing chapter numbers and by increasing mileage within each chapter—specific locations of creameries are shown on the maps cross-referenced)

501. Dairymen's League Cooperative Association, Inc. Essex Plant, Essex: Map 11-28.
502. S. C. Millet, then Rutpro, finally Borden's Milk Station, Rouses Point: Map 11-36, letter Q.
503. Owner of milk plant unknown, Crown Point: Map 15-3.
504. Peru Butter and Cheese Company, Peru: Map 19-7.
505. Unidentified owner of creamery, Peru: Map 19-7.
506. Sheffield Farms Co., Inc., Harkness: Map 19-7.
507. Plattsburgh Creamery, Plattsburgh: Map 19-9.
508. Sheffield Farms Milk Plant, Morrisonville: Map 20-10.
509. Millett's, then Levy's, then Dairymen's League, Moira: Map 23-7.
510. Owner of milk plant unknown, Natural Bridge: Map 31-9.
511. Dairylea Creamery, Remsen: Map 36-15. Photo in Harter (1979, page 172).
512. Remsen Dairy Company, Remsen: Map 36-15.
513. B. K. Brown Cold Storage and Milk Plant, Remsen: Map 36-15.
514. Cheese factory, Honnedaga: Map 36-16.
515. Lowville Farmers' Coop. Inc., Lowville: Map 33-5.

There were many more creameries along the Rutland Railroad in northern New York. See Nimke (1986, 1989, and 1990).

Legend to Map 5-2:
Livestock
(feed, stock pens, and meat packing plants)

Dairy regions require a supply of feed and grain. Prior to the closing of Conrail's line into Malone Junction from Huntingdon, Quebec, on March 30, 1980, the author toured and photographed the Junction. The bulk of freight still entering Malone Junction in April 1976 was feed and grain for cattle and other domesticated animals (see #541 on Map 5-2). Specific locations of livestock facilities are shown on the maps cross-referenced.

531. Nutrena Feeds, West Chazy: Map 11-33.
532. Winterbottom Feeds, Chazy: Map 11-34.
533. Pasco Feed, Warrensburg: Map 12-18.
534. Waddell's Feed Store, Riverside: Map 12-20.
535. C. W. Sullivan Company (grain), North Creek: Map 12-21.
536. Stock pen, Port Kent: Map 18-1.
537. Agway, Plattsburgh: Map 19-9.
538. W. Wilcox & Son coal, wood and hay, Plattsburgh: Map 19-9 and #378 on Map 3-3.
539. G. L. F. Feed Store, Moira: Map 23-7.
540. General Mills, Inc., Moira: Map 23-7.
541. Various feed sidings along Rutland Railroad, Malone Junction: west of depot and off the west edge of Map 36-45.
542. County Livestock Exchange, Chazy: Map 11-34.
543. Swift Meats, Saranac Lake: Map 20-23.
544. D&H stock yard, Mooers Junction: Map 21-2.
545. Rutland stock yard, Mooers Junction: Map 21-2.
546. Cattle pen, Tupper Lake: Map 23-18.
547. Cattle chute, Oswegatchie: Map 31-16.
548. Armour Meat Co., Tupper Lake Junction: Map 36-30.
549. Cattle pen, Saranac Inn: Map 36-32.
550. Cattle ramp, Lake Clear Junction: Map 40-1.
551. Cattle chute, Beaver River: Map 36-23.
552. Central Vermont Railroad stock pen, Rouse Point: Map 11-36, letter U.

Miscellaneous Agricultural Industries:

Hop pole yard, Mooers Junction: Map 21-2.

Grist mill, Plattsburgh: Map 19-4, #19.

Northern Orchard Company (apples), Peru: Map 19-7 (Apples may have been shipped from Chazy also).

Grist mill, Benson Mines: Map 31-18.

Potatoes, Gabriels.

Berry pickers at Mountain View have been described in Chapter 2 on passengers in the section entitled Specials, but their harvesting was more for personal home use than for commerce.

Cranberries were harvested at Horseshoe Lake by Abbot Augustus Low.

Abandoned creamery building at Natural Bridge, July 1994.
Author photo.

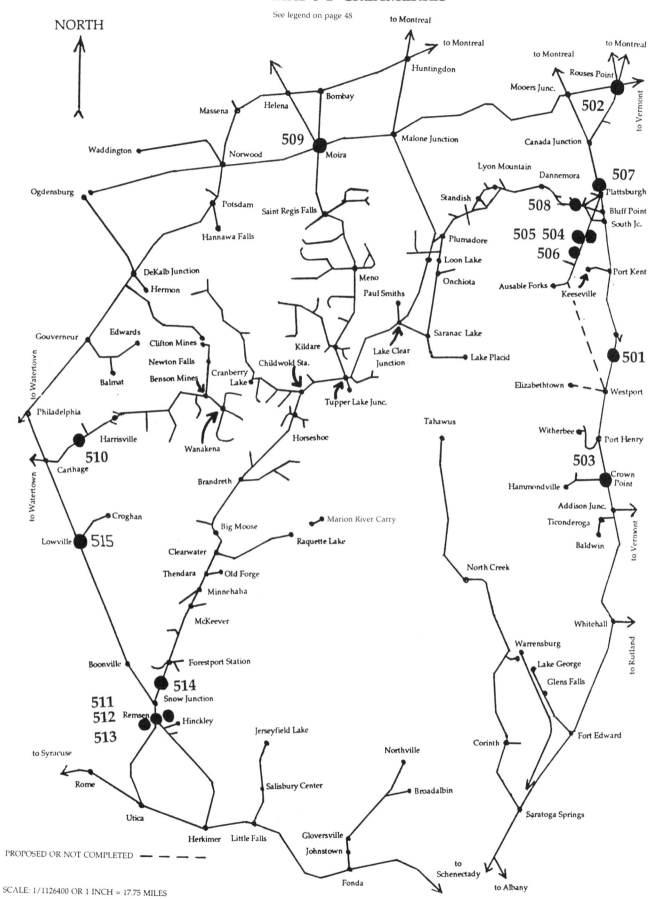

MAP 5-2 LIVESTOCK
See legend on page 48

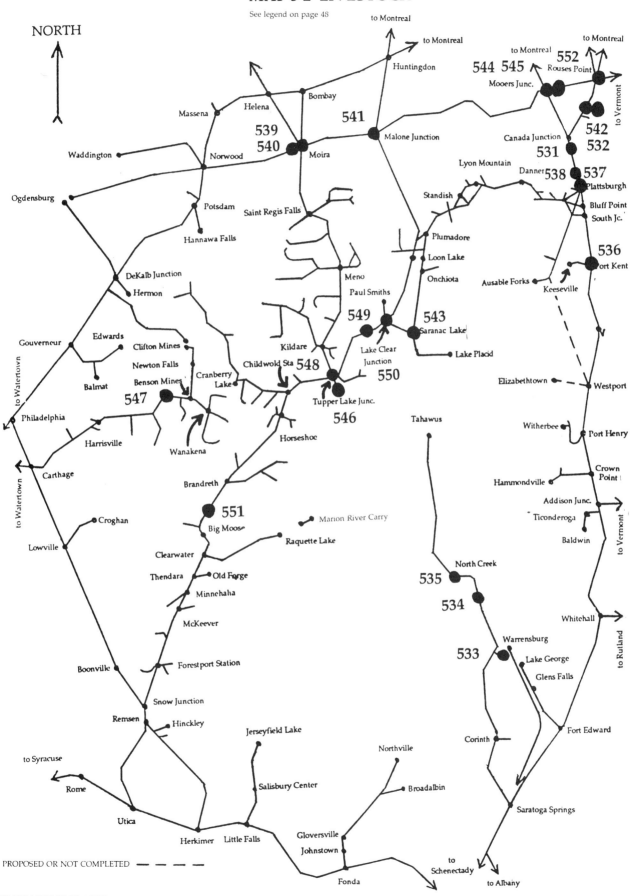

Chapter 6
Railroads and Mining

MINING AND FOREST PRODUCTS were the two most active industries in the Adirondacks for which railroads were built. Of the mineral products, iron was the primary, although several other minerals have been and still are shipped by rail. Only those mines served by railroads fall within the scope of this book. Several smaller mines had their own, mostly narrow gauge, railroads within the confines of their property and did not connect with any other railroads (see Chapter 8 Unusual Railroads).

Legend to Map 6-1: Railroads and Spurs Used Exclusively for Mining

The identification numbers on Map 6-1 also double as chapter numbers where detail can be found. Specific locations for these mines are shown on the maps cross-referenced.

11. International Lime & Stone Corporation, later Chazy Marble Lime Company Inc., spur: #621 on Map 6-3, Maps 11-11 and 11-12.
12. National Lead Company, now Kronos, Railroad from Ordway (near North Creek) to Tahawus: #622 on Map 6-3, Maps 12-7, 12-8, 12-9, 12-21, and 12-22.
15. Crown Point Iron Company's Railroad: #601 on Map 6-2.
16. Lake Champlain & Moriah Railroad: #602 on Map 6-2.
19. Peru Iron Company Railroad at Ferrona (Arnold): #603 on Map 6-2; Map 19-7.
30. Clifton Iron Company's Railroad: #605 on Map 6-2.
31. Spur into calcite quarry, owner unknown, from Burnett: #632 on Map 6-3; Map 31-3.
31H. Hanna Ore Company Railroad, built anew from Newbridge to Clifton Mines. Hanna had rebuilt the former Higbie Railroad from Newton Falls to Newbridge: #605 on Map 6-2; Maps 31-7 and 31-22.
33. Saint Joseph Lead Company zinc mine at Balmat: #635 on Map 6-3; Map 33-3.
36. White Lake Sand Pit spur: #654 on Map 3-4; Map 36-4.
36L. L&M Stone Company, later Eastern Rock Products, Inc., limestone quarry near Prospect Junction: #637 on Map 6-3; Map 36-2.

Legend to Map 6-2: Iron Mines (served by railroads)

These, as well as the mines on Map 6-3 and the industries on Map 6-4, are numbered, as best as possible, by increasing chapter numbers and by increasing mileage within each chapter. These iron mines have closed in the Adirondacks primarily because of competition with open pit operations in the Mesabi Range of Minnesota.

601. Crown Point Iron Company's Railroad from Crown Point to Irondale and Hammondville, 1874 to 1893. See Chapter 15 for detail. Several disconnecting inclined plane railroads operated at Hammondville, numbered 15 on Map 8-4.
602. Witherbee Sherman and Port Henry Iron Companies from Port Henry to Mineville, Witherbee, and Fisher Hill operated the Lake Champlain and Moriah Railroad, 1868-1937. From 1937 to 1971 it was operated by Republic Steel. See Chapter 16 for detail. A disconnecting railroad, #16 on Map 8-5, operated underground.
603. Peru Iron Company at Ferrona, later named Arnold, ca. 1868 to 1900? Inclined railroad numbered 19 on Map 8-4 served it and brought the ore down to

the Ausable Branch of the D&H. See Chapter 19 and Map 19-7 for detail.

604. Chateaugay Iron and Ore Company at Lyon Mountain on the D&H Chateaugay Branch, 1880 to 1938. Mines operated by Republic Steel from 1938 to 1967. See Chapter 20 and Map 20-14 for detail. A disconnecting railroad #20 on Map 8-5 operated underground. Chateaugay Iron and Ore Company also had an ore transfer facility at Plattsburgh (see Map 19-4) and a blast furnace at Standish (see Map 20-15).

605. Clifton Iron Company from East DeKalb to Clifton Mines in 1868 and 1869: #30 on Map 8-3. These mines reopened with the Hanna Ore Company in 1941 until 1952, but the access was from Newton Falls on the Carthage & Adirondack Railroad. See Chapter 30 and Map 31-22 for detail.

606. Thor and Magnetic Iron Company at Jayville, on the Carthage and Adirondack Railroad, 1887 to 1920. See Chapter 31 and Map 31-13 for detail.

607. Benson Mines, last owned by Jones and Laughlin Steel, from 1895 discontinuously to 1977. See Chapter 31 and Maps 31-18 through 31-20 for detail.

608. Dannemora: An iron mine and separator were located within the walls of the Clinton State Prison. See #20D on Map 8-5; also Map 20-11.

Legend to Map 6-3: Mines Other Than Iron Mines

There were mines and quarries in the Adirondack region which did not extract iron but which were still served by a railroad. In some cases, there was a railroad siding, only for shipping, and no additional trackage into the quarry or mine.

621. Chazy: Limestone was quarried with a spur into it from the D&H Mainline by the International Lime and Corporation, later the Chazy Lime & Marble Company. See Maps 11-11, 11-12, and 11-34.

622. Tahawus: Ilmenite was shipped from 1944 through 1989, although mining ceased about 1982. See Chapter 12 on the D&H North Creek Branch with the National Lead Company extension. See also Maps 12-9 and 12-22.

623. North Creek: While the National Lead Company Railroad was under construction between North Creek and Tahawus in the early 1940s, ilmenite ore was trucked over the highway from Tahawus. At North Creek, a facility existed during this period to load the ore from the trucks to railroad cars. See Map 12-21.

624. North Creek: Also at North Creek were garnet sheds for the loading of garnet ore from highway trucks to railroad cars. Because the mines at Gore Mountain were inaccessible by rail, the garnet ore had to be trucked over the highway to North Creek. See Map 12-21.

625. Crown Point: The Crown Point Feldspar Company had a siding south of here on the D&H Mainline. See Map 15-3.

626. Willsboro: Wollastonite is presently mined here by NYCO. The sidings into the processing plant opened in 1949. See Map 17A-1.

627. Bluff Point: The Vermont Marble Company had a siding here on the D&H Mainline. The bedrock here is limestone rather than marble. See Map 19-6.

628. Bluff Point: The Bluff Point Stone Company had a quarry (probably limestone) actually closer to South Junction than to Bluff Point. See Map 19-6.

629. Saint Regis Falls: There was a mica factory here. Whether or not there was a siding to serve it is uncertain. See Map 23-9.

630. Hannawa Falls: Sandstone was quarried from ca. 1899 to ca. 1917. See Chapter 29 on the Potsdam Red Sandstone Company.

631. Stellaville: Pyrite had been mined here on the second Adirondack and Saint Lawrence Railroad by the Saint Lawrence Pyrites Company. See Map 30-1.

632. Lewisburg: Calcite had been quarried near here at the end of a spur which diverged from the Carthage & Adirondack at Burnett, east of Natural Bridge. See Map 31-3.

633. Rock: A talc mine is still operating here, east of Natural Bridge, by Clark Minerals Inc.. Their Diana Plant mills and office are also on this site. See Map 31-10.

634. The area from Hailesboro to Talcville included several talc mines over the years. The major ones were the International Talc Company's Wight Mine along the Balmat Branch, Algalite Talc at Hailesboro, U.S. Talc Co. at Emeryville, and Gouverneur Talc Co. at Balmat. See Map 33-3.

635. Balmat: The Gouverneur & Oswegatchie Railroad still serves the Saint Joseph Lead Company zinc mines. See Map 33-3.

636. Norfolk: Dolostone is still quarried by Barrett Paving Materials but is no longer served by rail. The spur from the Norwood & Saint Lawrence Railroad was still in place in 1990.

637. Prospect Junction: The L & M Stone Company had a limestone quarry here with a spur into it active in the 1945 era, but now abandoned. See Map 36-2.

Legend to Map 6-4: Gravel and Sand Pits, Ice and Spring Water

Although sand and gravel are not obtained directly from bedrock, they are still mineral products, and should be included in this chapter. Along with sand and gravel pits were several ice-harvesting facilities and even one spring water bottling plant.

Gravel and sand pits were especially concentrated along the New York Central Adirondack Division. From south to north they were:

651. Pit Four sand pit, White Lake: Map 36-3.
652. Johnson Track (Johnson Siding), White Lake: Map 36-3.
653. Lo Fountain Siding, White Lake.
654. White Lake Sand Pit, White Lake: Map 36-4.
655. Beaver River: Map 36-23.
656. Floodwood: Map 36-31.
657. Owls Head: Map 36-13.
658. Todds Pit: Map 36-42.
659. Duquettes Pit: Map 36-44.

Several additional sand and gravel pits existed on other railroad lines:
661. The Paul Smith's Electric Railway also hauled sand, primarily for maintenance of the line: Chapter 40.
662. There was a sand and gravel pit in Saranac Lake with a track into it near the Payeville Road: Map 20-24.
663. White's Sand on the D&H North Creek Branch, between Corinth and South Corinth: Map 12-13.
664. The D&H had a sand tower for servicing locomotives, North Creek: Map 12-21.
665. Fran Smith's Sand Plant, Santa Clara (no detail available): Map 23-10.
666. The D&H had a sand tower at Rouses Point for servicing locomotives: Map 11-36.

Ice was cut at several locations and spring water bottled at one location:

671. Ice was cut from Lake Champlain, Port Henry.
672. Utica City Ice, White Lake: Map 36-4.
673. Ice was cut adjacent to the depot, Raquette Lake.
674. Spring water was bottled at Virgin Forest Springs by Abbot Augustus Low, Horse Shoe: Map 41-1.
675. Strong & Casey Coal & Ice, Rouses Point: Map 11-36.

A *D&H RR Bulletin* (1934, Mar. 1) included an article entitled "Harvesting the Ice for D&H Use."

The open-pit ilmenite quarry at Tahawus dwarfs the string of covered hoppers at the left, May 1983.
Author photo.

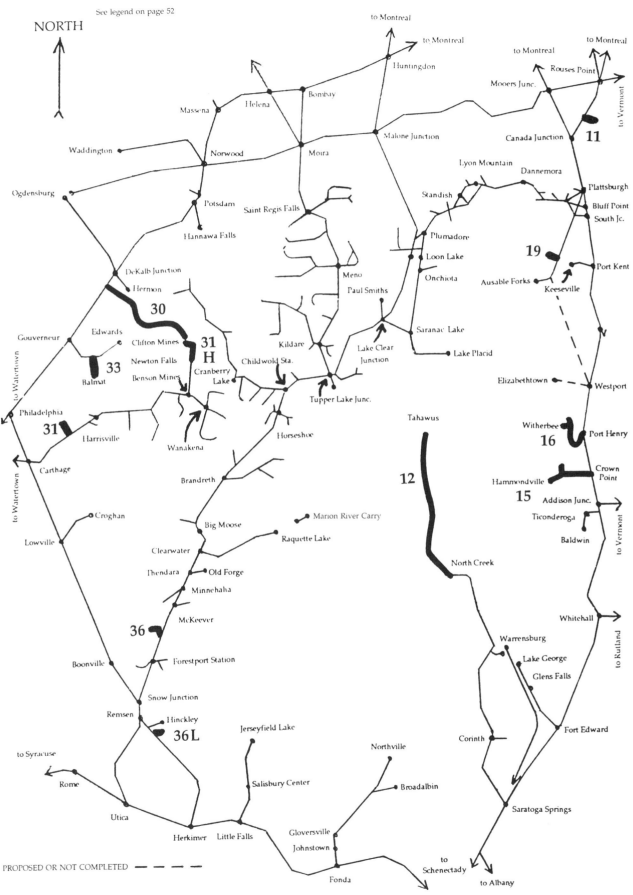
MAP 6-1 RAILROADS AND SPURS USED EXCLUSIVELY FOR MINING

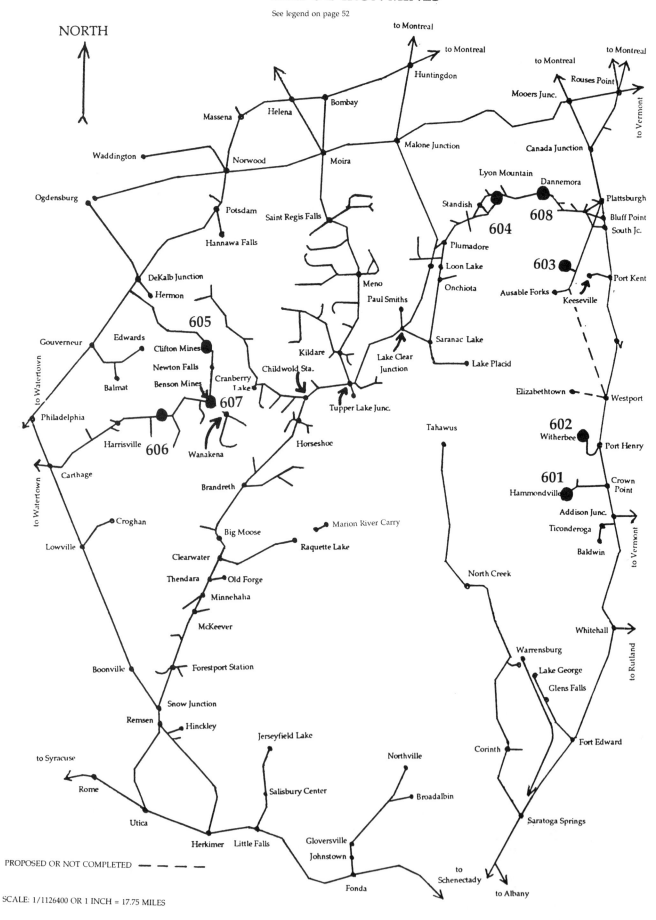

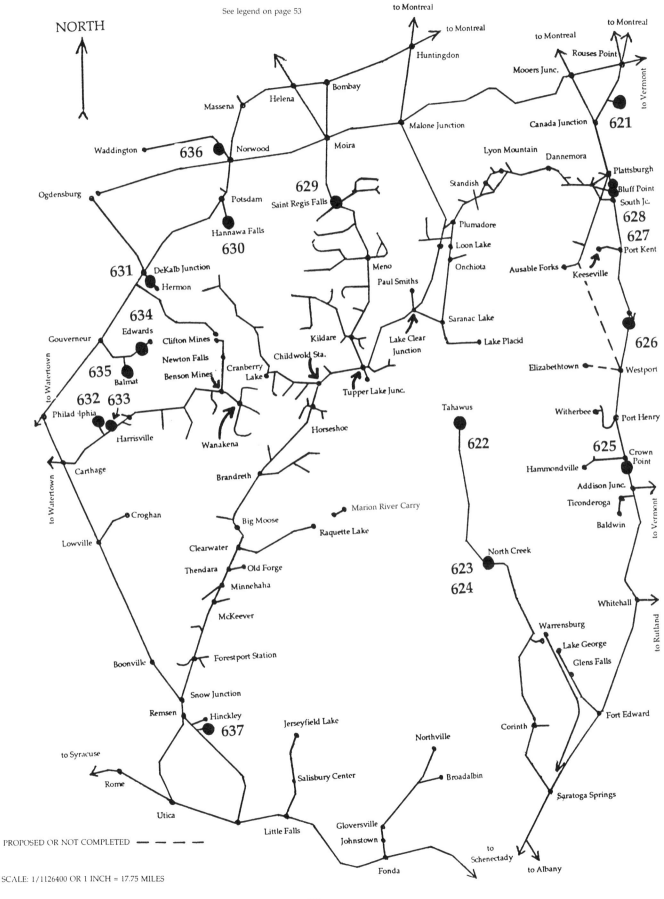

MAP 6-4 SAND & GRAVEL PITS; ICE & SPRING WATER

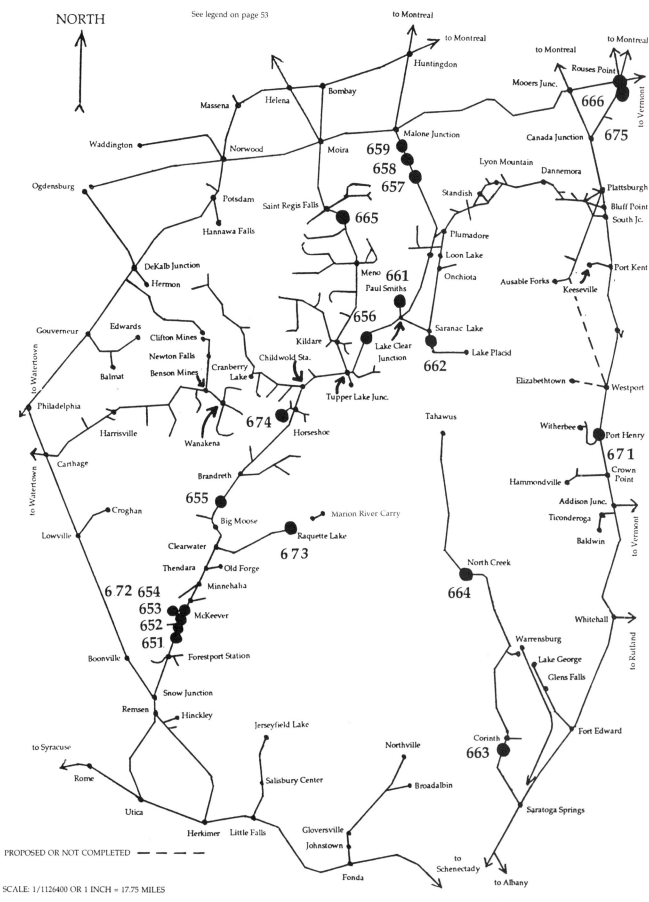

Chapter 7:
Railroads and Miscellaneous Industries

THERE WERE FREIGHT SIDINGS in the greater Adirondack region which did not serve any of the major industries: forest products, mining, and agriculture. Most of the freight involved here did not originate from northern New York as exports, but rather was brought into the region from the outside as imports. The major ones were fossil fuels such as coal, oil, and gas, and certain food items such as meat and bananas.

Legend to Maps 7-1 and 7-2:
Coal

One of the largest consumers of coal was the railroad itself (Map 7-1). There must have been many more small coaling facilities than those listed below. Coaling towers to fill locomotive tenders were located at:

701. South Junction on the D&H: Map 19-6.
702. Malone Junction on the N.Y. Central: Map 36-45.
703. Tupper Lake Junction on the N.Y. Central: Map 36-30.
704. Whitehall on the D&H: Map 11-13.

Coaling sheds to fill locomotive tenders were located at:

705. Lake Placid: Map 20-26.
706. Mooers Junction: See Map 21-2.
707. A coal shack for caboose stoves was located at North Creek: Map 12-21.
708. Lyon Mountain on the narrow gauge: Map 20-14A.
710. Marion River Carry, adjacent to engine house: Map 37-6.

Coaling trestles to fill locomotive tenders were located at:

709. Port Henry for the L.C.& M.R.R.: Map 16-4.
711. Moira coaling plant.

Coal, brought in mainly from Pennsylvania for heating, was delivered to tuberculosis sanatoria, prisons, sintering plants, powerhouses, and commercial coal dealers (Map 7-2). The following four institutions all had coal sidings:

721. Sisters of Mercy Sanatorium at Gabriels: Map 36-33.
722. Whitefathers Sanatorium at Lake Kushaqua: Map 36-35.
723. Ray Brook Sanatorium: Map 20-25.
724. Dannemora State Prison. One of the primary reasons for the construction of the Chateaugay Railroad to Dannemora was to deliver coal to the State Prison. The powerhouse was on the south side of the tracks: Map 20-11.

Coaling trestles to supply sintering plants and powerhouses generating electricity for the iron industry were located at:

731. Tahawus for the sinter plant: Map 12-22.
732. Crown Point for the blast furnace: See Map 15-3.
733. Witherbee: Central Power House for the New Bed mines such as Barton Hill: Map 16-7.
734. Mineville: Old Bed Powerhouse for Bonanza & Joker Shafts and Mills # 1 & #2: Map 16-7.
735. Switchback for Mill #7: Map 16-5.
736. Lyon Mountain Powerhouse, probably coal-fired but not certain: Map 20-14.
737. Port Henry Powerhouse near Mill Brook: Map 16-3.

Commercial coal dealers selling to the public had sidings to accommodate railroad hopper cars. Examples are:

741. Hurley Brothers, Lake Placid: Map 20-26.
742. Lake Placid Company Coal, Lake Placid: Map 20-26.
743. LaTour D&H Sterling Coal, Saranac Lake: Map 20-23.
744. Sterling Coal, Saranac Lake (a second dealer): Map 20-23.
745. Boyce & Roberson Blue Coal, Saranac Lake: Map 20-23.
746. Unknown coal dealer behind Bloomingdale Avenue, Saranac Lake: Map 20-23.
747. Texaco Oil-O-Matic & Coal, Tupper Lake: Map 36-30.
748. Pasco, Warrensburg: Map 12-18.
749. A. C. Emerson Lumber & Coal, Warrensburg: Map 12-18.
750. Stimpson Coal & Lumber, Port Henry: Map 16-2.
751. Dock & Coal Company, Plattsburgh: Map 19-3.
752. E. J. Griffith, Hadley: Map 12-15.
753. Strong & Casey Coal & Ice, Rouses Point: Map 11-36.
754. Unknown owner at Cadyville: Map 20-10.
755. W. Wilcox & Son, Plattsburgh: Map 19-9.
756. Marks & Wilcox and/or Old Forge Supply Corporation, Thendara: Map 42-3.
756A. Schleider Coal Company, Lowville: Map 33-5.

Legend to Map 7-3:
Fuel Oil and Bottled Gas

Except in winter, fuel oil instead of coal was consumed by the railroads after the disastrous fire years of 1903 and 1908. Fuel oil tanks were present at many locomotive servicing facilities such as at:

757. Saranac Lake: Map 20-23.
758. Malone Junction: Map 36-45.
759. Lake Placid: Map 20-26.
760. Bradley Pond, an oil house: Map 20-14A.

Fuel oil was also sold by commercial dealers to the public. Sidings were located at:

761. Raeoil, Lyons: Map 20-25.
762. Texaco, Tupper Lake: Map 36-30.
763. Standard Oil, later Mobil, Tupper Lake: Map 36-30.
764. Champlain Valley Oil, Saranac Lake: Map 20-23.
765. Standard Oil, later Hyde's, Saranac Lake: Map 20-23.
766. LaTour's, Saranac Lake: Map 20-23.
767. Dittmar Fuel, Hadley: Map 12-15.
768. Standard Oil, Mooers Junction: Map 21-2.
769. Chateaugay Oil Co. (on the Rutland Railroad), Rouses Point: Map 11-36.
770. Marks & Wilcox and/or Old Forge Supply Corporation, Thendara: Map 42-3.
770A. Suburban Atlantic States Gas Company (propane), Lowville: Map 33-5.

Sidings for bottled gas were located at:

771. Adirondack Bottled Gas, Saranac Lake: Map 20-24.
772. Pyrofax Gas, Saranac Lake: Map 20-23.
773. Adirondack Bottled Gas, Lyons: Map 20-25.
774. Pargas, Salmon River Junction: Map 19-6.

Legend to Map 7-4:
Other Miscellaneous Industries

781. Adirondack Hardware Company, Saranac Lake Map 20-23.
782. Cohen Hardware, Saranac Lake: Map 20-23.
783. Pabst Beverages, Plattsburgh: Map 19-3.
784. Hiland Beverages, Morrisonville: Map 20-10.
785. Imperial Wallpaper Mill, presently C&A Wallcoverings, is still served by the D&H (now Canadian Pacific), Plattsburgh: Map 20-9.
785A. Arpak Plastics, presently Mold Rite Plastics, is still served by the D&H (now Canadian Pacific), Plattsburgh: Map 20-9.
786. The Slack Chemical Company continues to have rail service in 1994, Carthage: Map 31-8.
787. Malone Concrete Products Co. had two plants, Malone Junction: Map 36-45.
788. Plattsburgh Heat and Power: hydroelectric plant, Plattsburgh: Map 19-4, #7.
789. Hydroelectric plant, Hannawa Falls: Map 29-1.
790. HHH Building Supply, Willsboro: Map 17A-1.
791. Carthage Machine Company, Carthage: Map 31-8.
792. Rudermann Machine Exchange ? (unclear lettering by New York Central draftsman on a valuation diagram), Carthage: Map 31-8.
793. Carl B. Getman Concrete Building Supply Company, two locations, one probably associated with the box factory, Otis Junction: Map 20-9.
794. Plattsburgh Ready Mix Concrete Company, Inc., Otis Junction: Map 20-9.
795. Northern Concrete Pipe Corporation, Dannemora: Maps 20-3 and 20-11.
796. Allied Chemical and Dye Corporation, Lyon Mountain: Map 20-14.
797. Aries Chemical Company, Beaver Falls: Map 33-5.

In the latter years of through freight service from Utica to Montreal via the New York Central Adirondack Division, especially in the late 1950s, many of the cars in the long consist were refrigerators filled with bananas for the Montreal area. The train was informally called the "Banana Train."

Maps 7-5, 7-6, and 7-7 do not deal exactly with industries, but rather with facilities for servicing trains. Chapter 7 is the most appropriate chapter for including these facilities because coal (Map 7-1) and fuel oil (Map 7-3) for locomotives are already presented here.

Legend to Map 7-5: Water for Locomotives

The following is a listing of locomotive watering facilities arranged by chapters and mileposts within each chapter:

Chapter 11: Whitehall, Fort Ticonderoga, Crown Point (could have been only for Crown Point Iron Company locomotives or shared with D&H), Port Henry, Westport, Willsboro, Port Kent, South Junction, and Rouses Point.

Chapter 12: Thurman and North Creek (the water tank at Palmer could have been industrial only?).

Chapter 15: Crown Point and Ironville.

Chapter 16: Port Henry.

Chapter 18: Port Kent (Did K.A.C.& L.C. R.R. share the water tank with the D&H?)

Chapter 19: Rome (industrial water tank only?) and Ausable Forks.

Chapter 20: Cadyville, Dannemora, Chazy Lake, Standish (two tanks, the first for narrow gauge and the second for standard), Loon Lake, Vermontville Station, and Lake Placid.

Chapter 21: Mooers Junction (shared with Rutland Railroad?).

Chapter 23: Moira, Saint Regis Falls, Meno, Kildare, and Tupper Lake Junction.

Chapter 27: McDonald Station.

Chapter 28: Kildare (apparently separate from N.Y. & Ottawa tank)

Chapter 30: Monterey

Chapter 31: Carthage (site unknown), Diana, Jayville (later moved to Kalurah), and Benson Mines.

Chapter 33: DeKalb Junction, Gouverneur, Edwards (later moved to Emeryville?), Lowville, and Croghan.

Chapter 36: Remsen, White Lake, Thendara, Clearwater, Beaver River, Horseshoe, Tupper Lake Junction, Lake Clear Junction, Lake Kushaqua, Owls Head, and Malone Junction.

Chapter 37: Clearwater (shared with Adirondack Division?), Raquette Lake, and Marion River Carry.

Chapter 39: Conifer.

Chapter 40: Lake Clear Junction (shared with Adirondack Division?).

Chapter 41: Horseshoe (shared with Adirondack Division?).

Chapter 42: about 1.75 miles northeast of McKeever on Moose River Lumber Company Railroad.

Certainly there were more locomotive watering facilities than those listed above, especially those of some of the smaller railroads, but no information has arrived to date to precisely locate these facilities on the maps.

Additional water facilities for those peripheral railroads not included in chapters in this book were as follows:

Rome, Watertown & Ogdensburg RR: Boonville, Lyons Falls, and Lowville.

Saint Lawrence Division: Philadelphia, Gouverneur, DeKalb Junction, Potsdam, Norwood, Massena Springs, and Ogdensburg.

Herkimer, Newport & Poland: Newport.

Legend to Map 7-6: Enginehouses

These facilities were used mainly for the overnight storage and often light repair and maintenance of steam and/or diesel locomotives. No turntable was involved so that these enginehouses were not roundhouses.

Chapter 11: Port Henry

Chapter 12: North Creek (with old refrigerator car inside), and Tahawus (with old plow inside).

Chapter 16: Mineville in 19th century, Port Henry in 20th.

Chapter 17A: Willsboro.

Chapter 23: Moira

Chapter 19: carbarn of Plattsburgh Traction Company.

Chapter 27: McDonald.

Chapter 31: Carthage (built between 1991 and 1994 by Mohawk, Adirondack & Northern Railroad), Benson Mines.

Chapter 32: Wanakena.

Chapter 36: Thendara (old freight house converted by Adirondack Railway 1979-1980, and Adirondack

Railway Preservation Society 1992), and Tupper Lake Junction.

Chapter 37: Raquette Lake and Marion River Carry.

Chapter 39: Conifer and Cranberry Lake.

Chapter 42: McKeever, 1.6 miles east of on Moose River Lumber Company Railroad.

Legend to Map 7-7: Wyes, Reversing Loops, and Turntables

These three devices were all used to turn locomotives. Wyes and reversing loops were also used to turn short trains. Some of the turntables were accompanied by roundhouses, but no roundhouse could exist without a turntable. Several one-stall roundhouses with turntables are listed as enginehouses on the maps because the railroads themselves called them enginehouses; examples are at Lake Placid (Map 20-26), and at Crown Point (Map 15-3).

Wyes

Chapter 11: Whitehall, and Addison Junction. The interchange at Rouses Point could have been used as a wye.

Chapter 12: Tahawus.

Chapter 16: Switchback in the 1940s and 1950s, and Mineville in the 19th century. (The Terio Wye was not a true wye at all, but a switchback).

Chapter 20: Bluff Point, Woods Mills at Mill C, Saranac Lake for the narrow gauge, Lake Placid in the 19th century.

Chapter 21: The interchange at Mooers Junction with the Rutland could have been used as a wye.

Chapter 23: Moira, Black Rapids Junction and the Draper Corporation near Tupper Lake Junction. The interchange at Tupper Lake Junction with the Adirondack Division could have been used as a wye.

Chapter 26: East of Tupper Lake Junction.

Chapter 31: Carthage north end, Benson Mines at the Post & Henderson Railroad, and at Newton Falls.

Chapter 32: Wanakena.

Chapter 33: DeKalb Junction, Balmat, Edwards, and Gouverneur Junction.

Chapter 36: Prospect Junction, Big Moose, possibly Beaver River at entrance to sand pit, Tupper Lake Junction, Lake Clear Junction, the Rutland interchange at Malone Junction could have been used as a wye, and Saranac Lake near Lake Colby.

Chapter 37: Clearwater.

Chapter 38: There was never a wye at Brandreth Station because the Mac-a-Mac and Whitney Railroad connections with the Adirondack Division were not operating simultaneously.

Chapter 39: Childwold Station, Conifer, and Dodge Brook Wye near Cranberry Lake.

Reversing Loops

Chapter 20: Loon Lake possibly had one temporarily for the narrow gauge when this station served as a terminus, 1886-1887.

Chapter 26: Brooklyn Cooperage line around Sugarloaf and Daniel Mountains east of Meno could have doubled as a reversing loop.

Chapter 37: Raquette Lake.

Chapter 41: Horseshoe Lake for Wake Robin Railroad.

Turntables
(R denotes accompanying roundhouse)

Chapter 11: Whitehall (R), Port Henry (R), Plattsburgh (R), and Rouses Point (R).

Chapter 12: Hadley and North Creek.

Chapter 15: Crown Point (R) and Hammondville.

Chapter 16: Port Henry (R).

Chapter 19: Ausable Forks.

Chapter 20: Plattsburgh (R) for the narrow gauge, Lyon Mountain (R) for both narrow gauge and standard gauge, Lake Placid (R).

Chapter 21: Mooers Junction.

Chapter 23: Brandon one, and Santa Clara (R) two.

Chapter 33: Croghan.

Chapter 36: Remsen, Thendara, and Malone Junction (R).

MAP 7-1 COAL FOR LOCOMOTIVES

See legend on page 59

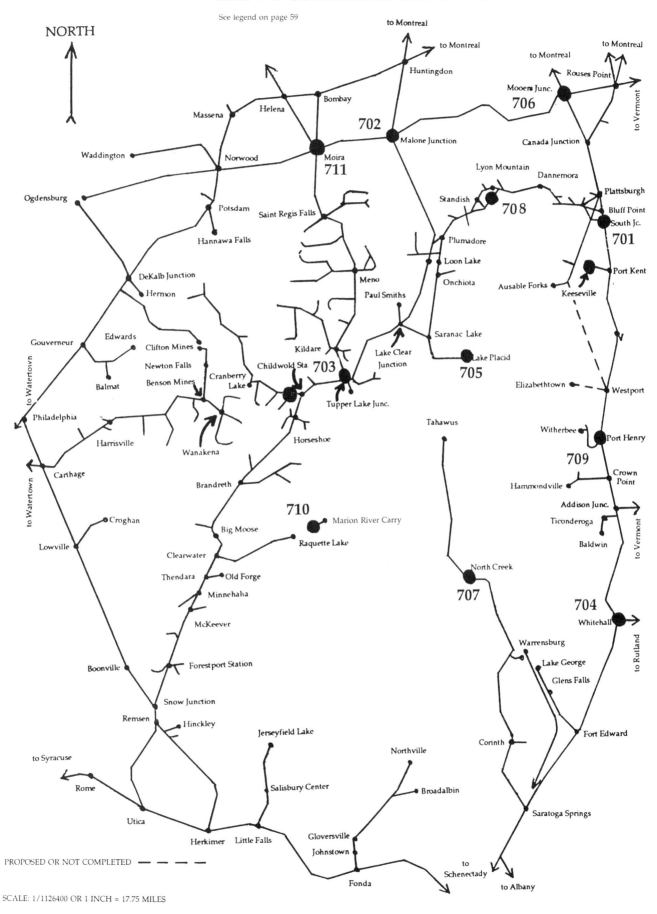

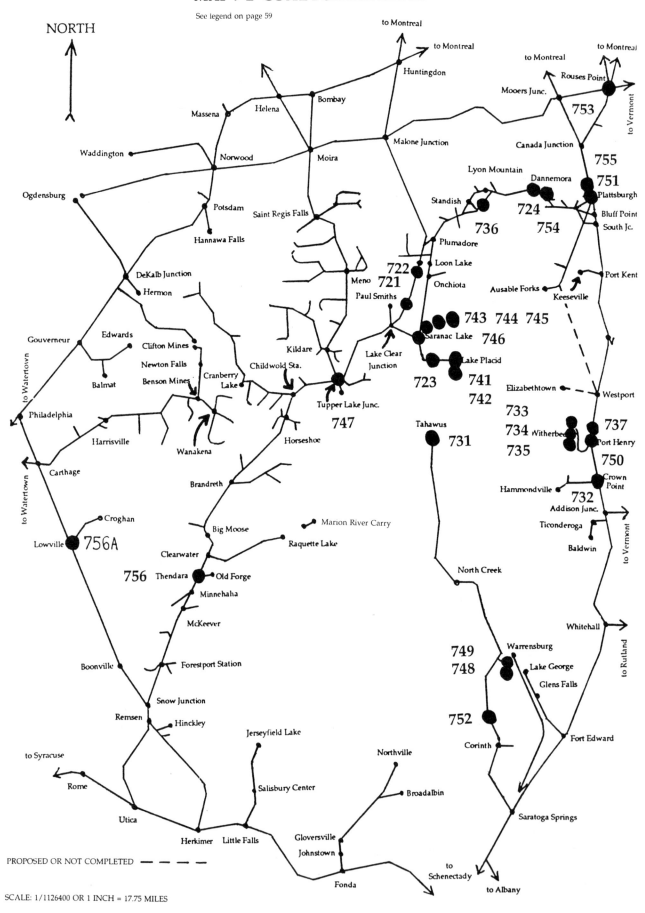

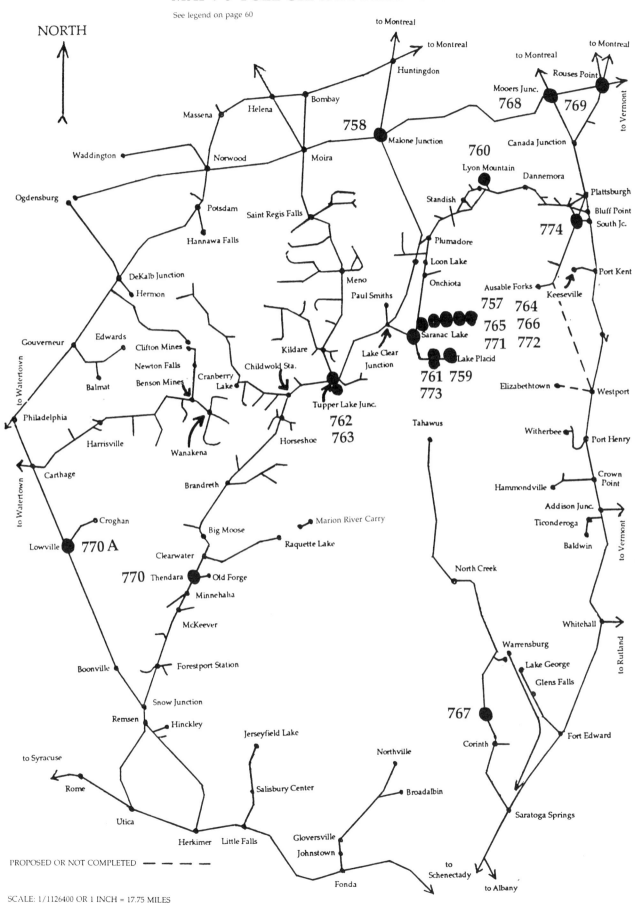

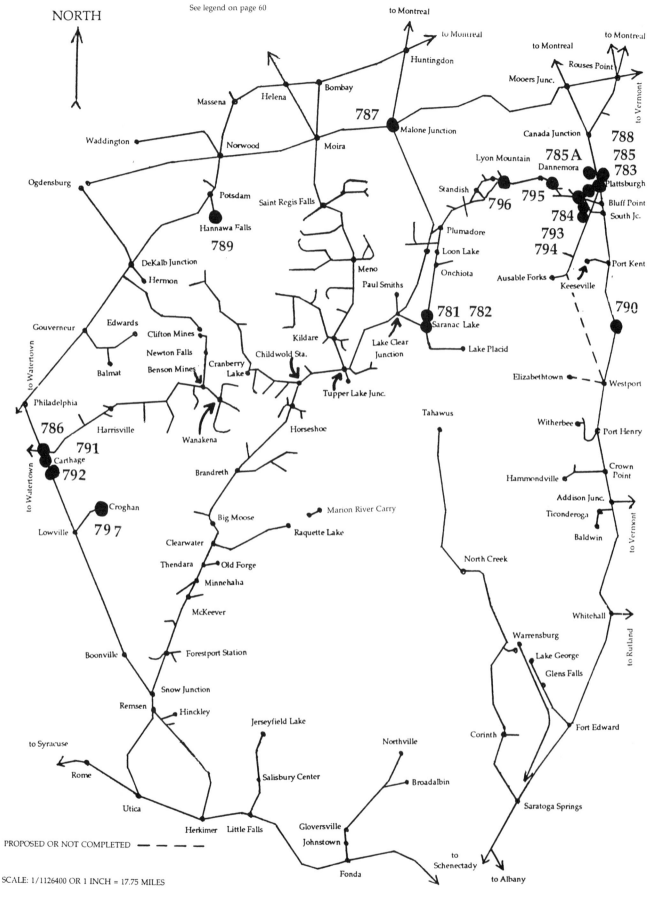

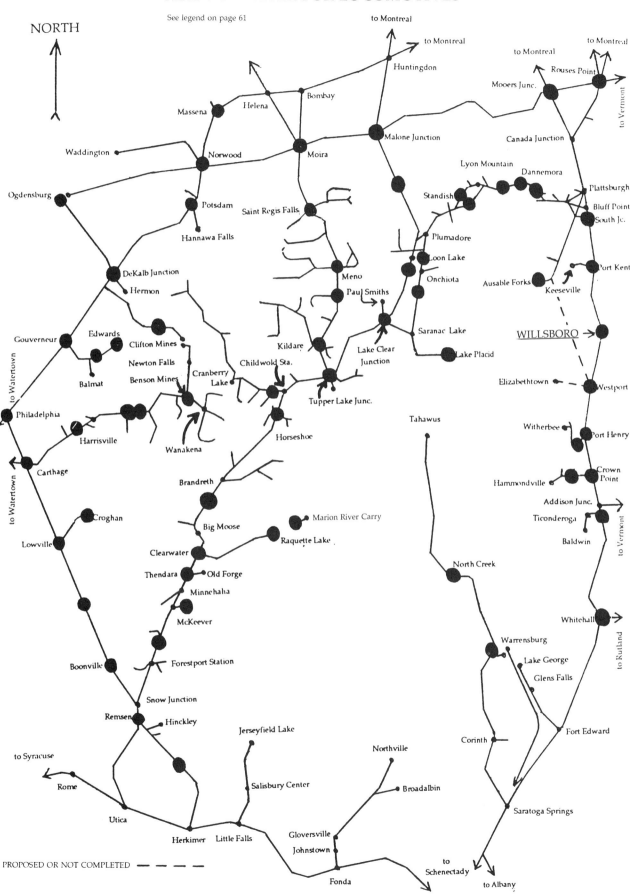

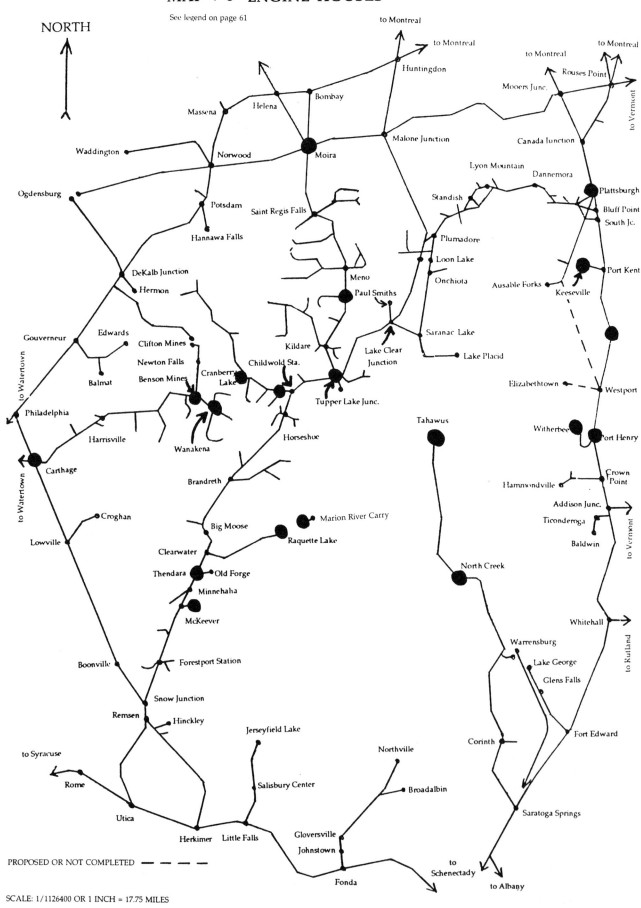

MAP 7-6 ENGINE HOUSES

See legend on page 61

PROPOSED OR NOT COMPLETED -----

SCALE: 1/1126400 OR 1 INCH = 17.75 MILES

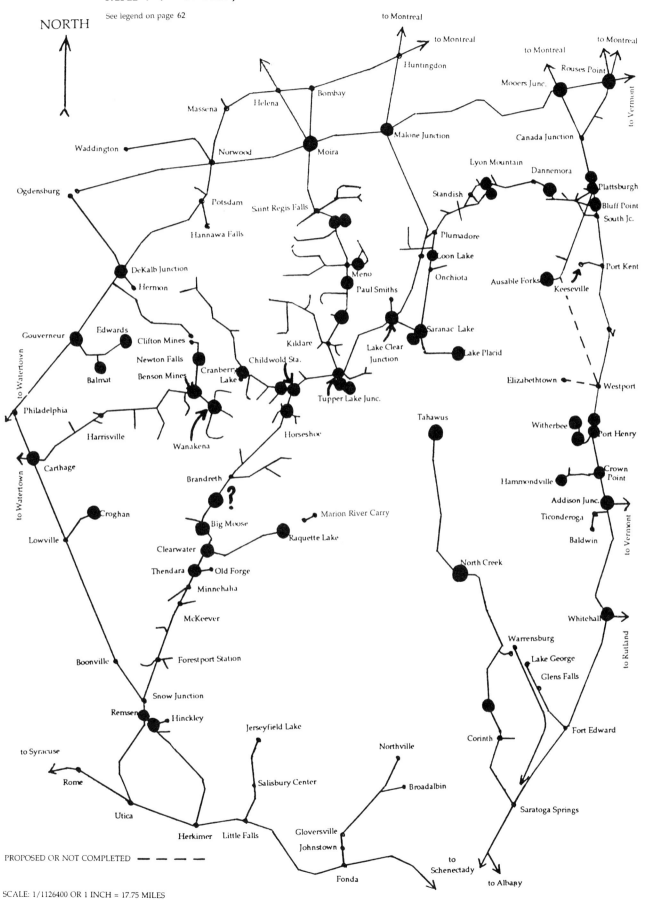

MAP 7-7 WYES, REVERSING LOOPS & TURNTABLES

See legend on page 62

PROPOSED OR NOT COMPLETED -----

SCALE: 1/1126400 OR 1 INCH = 17.75 MILES

Chapter 8:
Unusual Railroads

IN NORTHERN NEW YORK there were railroads which were atypical of most railroads in North America. These were either narrow gauge, short standard gauge, electric, wooden-railed, disconnecting and inclined, or disconnecting and non-inclined. Identifying numbers on Maps 8-1 through 8-5 double as chapter numbers whenever possible. Only those four railroads totally isolated from other lines: Roth's Forge, Whiteface Mountain, West Kilns, and Hague are numbered 801 through 804.

Legend to Map 8-1:
Narrow Gauge Railroads

Narrow gauge railroads are those in which the inner distance between the rails is less than the standard four-feet eight-and-one-half inches.

20. The Chateaugay Railroad until 1903.
20R. The Roakdale Railroad (See Maps 20-6 and 20-20 for detail; also #20R on Map 3-1 and #309 on Map 3-2).
15. The Crown Point Iron Company's Railroad.
36. The Herkimer, Newport & Poland Railroad.
25. Very likely the Watson Page Lumber Company Railroad.
41. The Horseshoe Forestry and Wake Robin Railroads (probably in their earlier years).
42F. The "Peg Leg" or first Fulton Chain Railway was also wooden-railed and appears on Map 8-3 as number 42F.

These were all of three-foot gauge except possibly Watson Page whose gauge is still yet undetermined. Many of the disconnecting railroads which were located entirely within one industry were narrow gauge railroads (see Map 8-5 and sections on disconnecting railroads below in this chapter).

Narrow gauge lines were built in North America primarily in the nineteenth century in hilly or mountainous areas. Narrow gauge meant narrow cuts and fills, and smaller radius curves for smaller trains—hence less expense and easier construction.

Dual gauge railroads were those which could accommodate both standard and narrow gauge trains. There were three rails, one of them being used by both gauges in common. Examples are the Saranac Lake and Lake Placid Railroad from 1893 to 1903, and the Chateaugay Railroad from Plattsburgh to possibly Morrisonville and Cadyville for a short while, 1902-1903, while standard-gauging was in progress. The Crown Point yard was also dual guage.

Short Standard Gauge Railroad

The Marion River Carry Railroad at 0.87 mile long was claimed to be the shortest standard-gauged railroad in the United States. It had to be standard-gauged to accommodate freight cars brought across Raquette Lake from the Raquette Lake Railway (see Chapter 37).

Legend to Map 8-2:
Electric Railroads

Electric railroads are still common around large cities, but they were few and far between in northern New York.
16. Republic Steel: Underground and battery-operated.
18. The Keeseville, Ausable Chasm & Lake Champlain Railroad.

20. Chateaugay Ore & Iron Company: underground and battery-operated.
40. The Paul Smith's Electric Railway.
25. The Watson Page Lumber Company Railroad.
19. The Plattsburgh Traction Company.
13H. The Hudson Valley Railway from Glens Falls to Warrensburg.
104. Ogdensburg Street Railway, i.e. trolley lines.
33. Wight Talc Mine near Balmat, underground and battery-operated.
35. Fonda, Johnstown, and Gloversville Railroad had an electrified division.

Railroads 16, 20, and 23 in the section on Disconnecting and Non-Inclined Railroads were also electric but underground. Watertown had an electric street railway, i.e., trolley lines, but it is beyond the border of Map 8-2. One reliable source informs me that there was an electric railway between Alexandria Bay and Redwood, operated by the International Electric Railroad, but I have not yet confirmed this; it, also, is beyond the border of Map 8-2.

Legend to Map 8-3:
Wooden Rail Railroads

Four railroads built in the 1860s had wooden rails instead of steel.

30. The Clifton Iron Company's Railroad.
42B. The Black River and Woodhull Railroad: #42B on Map 3-1.
42F. The first Fulton Chain Railway known informally as the "Peg Leg." This line was also narrow-gauged: #42F on Map 8-1.
16. The Lake Champlain & Moriah Railroad from 1868-1869, when it was built, for several years. By 1873, the rails were replaced by steel ones.

Legend to Maps 8-4 and 8-5:
Disconnecting Railroads

In and around large cities, small (in mileage only, not in importance), connecting railroads still facilitate the interchange of cars among the larger, long-distance railroads. In the Adirondacks there existed a number of small railroads which operated entirely within mines, sawmills, and charcoal kilns; these did not have track connections with the large carriers such as the New York Central and the Delaware & Hudson. I have termed these small lines as "disconnecting railroads" as opposed to the connecting ones.

The term "disconnected" is perhaps a more accurate description. There were at least twenty in the Adirondacks. Most of the disconnecting lines were also narrow gauge. Some were inclined, others were not.

Legend to Map 8-4:
Disconnecting and Inclined Railroads

Inclined railroads are those where freight and/or passenger cars are hauled up a steep plane by cable. A stationary steam or electric engine sits at the top of the grade and, often, two cars are present, serving as counterweights to each other. The operation is much like that of an elevator although not oriented vertically. Downstate, three notable inclines were the Otis Elevating Railway at Palenville, the Mount Beacon Railway which closed quite recently, and the Fenwick Lumber Company's Railroad at Hunter Mountain in the Catskills.

19. Peru Iron Company's Railroad from Ferrona to Arnold Hill. See Map 19-7 for detail, and #603 on Map 6-2.
13. Prospect Mountain Inclined Railway.
40. Marjorie Merriweather Post's Railway at Camp Topridge, three miles west-southwest of Paul Smiths, had two inclined cable railways running from her dock on Upper Saint Regis Lake to the buildings, an ascent of about sixty feet. The southerly incline was for passengers in a colorful red-and-white-canopied car. The northerly was for baggage and freight. Stationary electric engines and cable drums were housed at the summit of each incline in small buildings. (This author rode the passenger car in September 1985). Camp Topridge became part of the New York State Executive Department when Mrs. Post died in 1973. In 1986, the lands were transferred back to private ownership.
20. The Cone Family Camp Railroad is described briefly by R. Landon (1992): The largest camp on Lake Placid (lake, not village), owned by this North Carolina Family has an "inclined railroad (which) can lift a guest from the boathouse to the lodge."
16. The Cheever Ore Bed Company tramway north of Port Henry. See Map 16-1 for detail.
15. E. Barker (1942 and 1969, page 5) describes two small disconnecting railroads at Hammondville working the Crown Point Iron Company's mines. First, he describes the North Pit previous to 1876 and, second, one closer to the village after 1876. "The ore was hoisted on an inclined track with a two-horse whim. About that year a vertical shaft was put down from the top of the hill, tapping the ore body below. The ore was then hoisted with a

steam engine and carried on a gravity tramway down the south face of the hill to a spur on the new railroad." See #601 on Map 6-2 and Map 15-5 for detail.

Legend to Map 8-5: Disconnecting and Non-Inclined Railroads

20. Lewis (1880, pp. 307 and 311) described the early underground tramways which later used battery locomotives to haul five-ton cars. Photos of these trams appeared in D&H (1925, page 629), Linney (1934, p. 79), and *D&H RR Bulletin* (1935b). See #604 on Map 6-2 and #20 on Map 8-2.

801. At The Adirondack Museum in Blue Mountain Lake on exhibit is an ore car with a 24-inch gauge, ca. 1870, from Roth's Forge, near North Hudson.

12. Also at The Adirondack Museum on exhibit is a photo (#P30705) of the North River Garnet Company mine with its tracks on trestles at Ruby Mountain, near North River, about the year 1900. Krieger (1937, p. 105) includes a photo of a narrow-gauge railroad in the Barton Garnet Mine at Gore Mountain. Whether the Ruby Mountain and Gore Mountain railroads were one and the same, or two different railroads, I am not certain.

19. The J.&J. Rogers Company had a narrow gauge railway in their iron mine at Palmer Hill in the Town of Black Brook. An exhibit on mining at The Adirondack Museum in 1985 displayed a photo (# 73.93.28) of this narrow gauge railroad ca. 1885. This was an ore-car line and not connected to the Ausable Branch.

802. Atop Whiteface Mountain was a narrow gauge line which was not part of a mining operation, although it was used for moving rock. A newspaper article from Tupper Lake in 1937 (no specific name nor date of newspaper available), now housed in the Smallman Collection at the Paul Smith's College Cubley Library, describes an ephemeral railroad beneath the summit which had just ceased operating. It was used in the construction of the bore which connects the parking lot with the elevator shaft. Rock debris could then be brought easily out of the tunnel through which tourists walk today.

20D. Within the walls of the State Prison at Dannemora was a small railroad operating from an iron mine in 1869, a decade before the Chateaugay Railroad arrived. See Map 20-11, and #608 on Map 6-2. Detail is available in Beers' (1869) Clinton County Atlas.

11S. Kozma (1985, p. 20) describes the Sisco Furnace at Westport, built on Lake Champlain in 1846. "Railroads were laid to convey wood from the sheds to the kilns, and 1000 feet of railroad connected the kilns with the furnace." Detail on the Sisco (alternately spelled Siscoe) Furnace will be found in Poor (1849). The D&H at Westport did not open until 1875.

11. Kozma (1985, p.8) states: "The Lake Champlain Granite Company of Vergennes, Vermont, built a short piece of track from their granite quarry, terminating at Barn Rock Bay. . .grading the roadbed, including trestles and culverts. Work was completed in mid-October 1890." Barn Rock Bay is at the base of Split Rock Mountain, 4.5 miles east-northeast of the D&H Westport Depot.

16. Starbird (1967), included a photo on pp. 182-183 with the following caption: "Burrowing more than a mile into the earth, a shaft at Mineville, New York, four miles west of Lake Champlain, leads to one of the few underground iron mines still being worked in the United States. The train pulls its load along a horizontal passage to a storage area, where special lifts called skips hoist the ore to the surface." The locomotive shown in Starbird's article is a small industrial electrical engine owned by Republic Steel. Within four years of Starbird's article, the mines and railroad had shut down. This underground electric railway was already operating in 1910 in the Joker Mine. See #602 on Map 6-2.

16C. Granbery (1906, page 28) describes a narrow gauge track laid through the yard and into the casting house at the Cedar Point Blast Furnace. See #602 on Map 6-2.

26. A narrow-gauge railroad linked the Brooklyn Cooperage Company Stave Mill in Tupper Lake with its chemical plant from 1902 to ca. 1915. Clayton Elliott's Mangle Roller Plant, built in 1915, also had a small railroad. Whether he inherited the former Brooklyn Cooperage tramway or established a brand new one I am not certain.

37M. Bassett's Sawmill in the 1890s, before the opening of the Marion River Carry Railroad, had a set of tracks on high docks to move logs and lumber around. Timm (1989, page 240) has a photo.

803. Wilford LaHart, now living in what used to be the hamlet of West Kilns in the Clinton County Town of Black Brook, reports a fuel wood-hauling railroad which began at the very far west slopes of the Stephenson Range in the Town of Wilmington, Essex County. Hardwood logs were cut in this vicinity and loaded on a car which descended by gravity about 0.9 mile northward to the charcoal kilns at West Kilns. A horse hauled the empty car back up. The old railroad grade shows as a perfectly straight line on 1957 aerial photographs. A field check by the author revealed a narrow fill across the wetlands, hence narrow gauge, and tie impressions still extant at the county line in hair cap moss: definite railroad evidence. Mr. LaHart states that the line ran from ca. 1865 to ca. 1882

when the kilns closed; his father had observed the railroad operating as a boy.

804. Brown (1963, p. 183) has a photo of graphite mine at Hague with a horse-drawn railway.

33. An undated (but probably 1960s era) article in the *Watertown Daily Times* describes an undeground disconnecting railroad in the Wight Mine, owned by International Talc Company, between Emeryville and Balmat (see Map 33-3 for detail). This railroad was powered by battery-operated locomotive-sand, therefore, is also shown on Map 8-2 as an electric railroad.

12SR. A narrow gauge railroad was used in the construction of the Sacandaga Reservoir dam at Conklingville (Ashley Falls) beginning in 1927. Detail is available in the *D&H Bulletin* (1930, Dec. 1).

An unusual railroad: This disconnecting and inclined railroad served Marjorie Merriweather Post's Camp Topridge near Paul Smiths.
Author photo, September 1985.

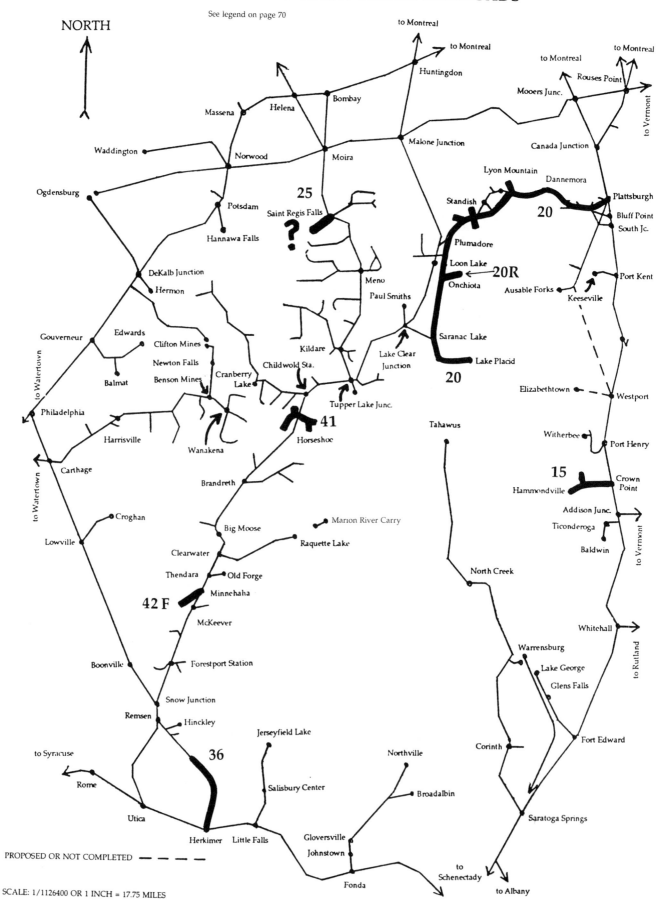

MAP 8-1 NARROW GAUGE RAILROADS

See legend on page 70

PROPOSED OR NOT COMPLETED - - - -

SCALE: 1/1126400 OR 1 INCH = 17.75 MILES

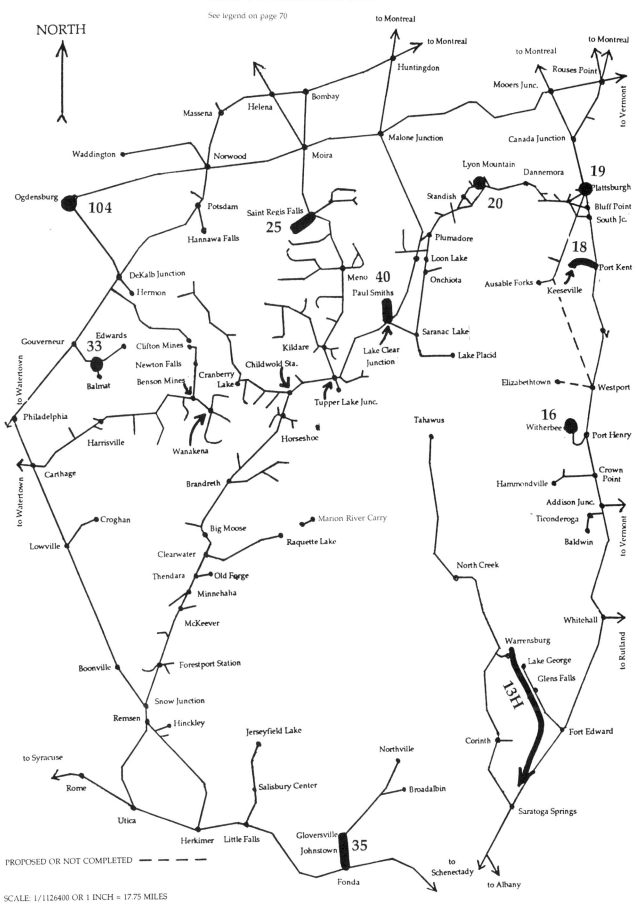

MAP 8-3 WOODEN-RAIL RAILROADS

See legend on page 71

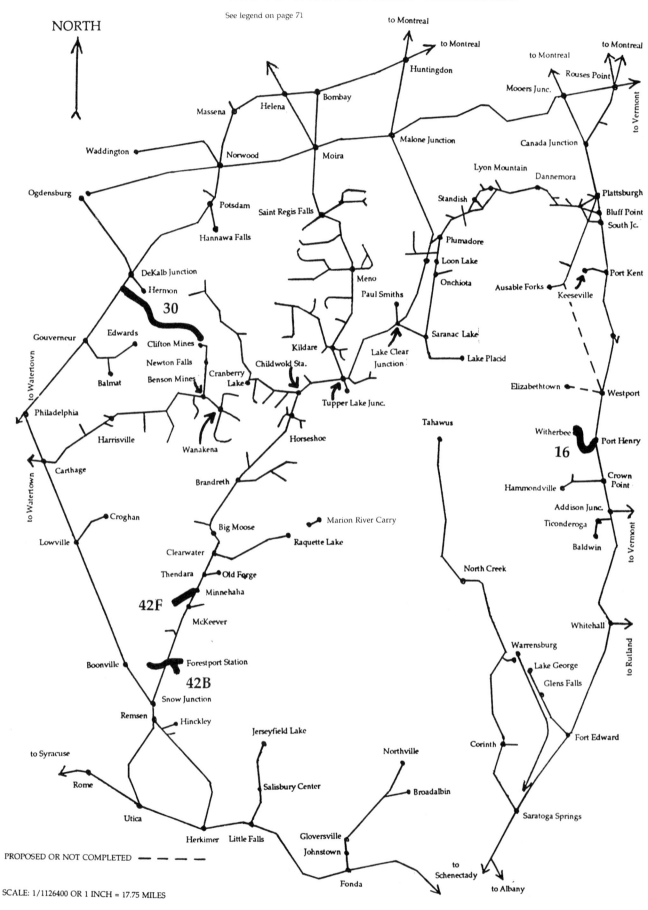

MAP 8-4 DISCONNECTING INCLINED RAILROADS

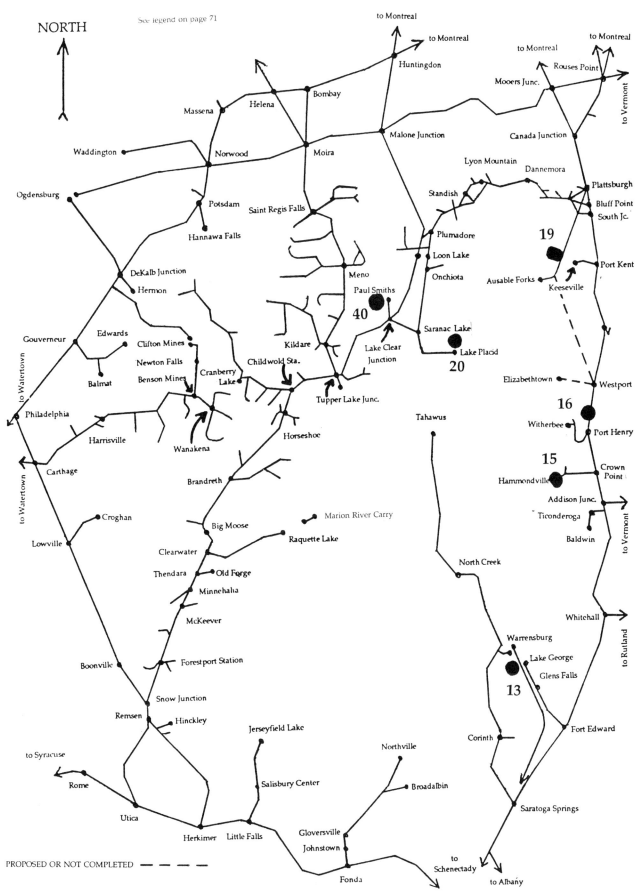

PROPOSED OR NOT COMPLETED — — —

SCALE: 1/1126400 OR 1 INCH = 17.75 MILES

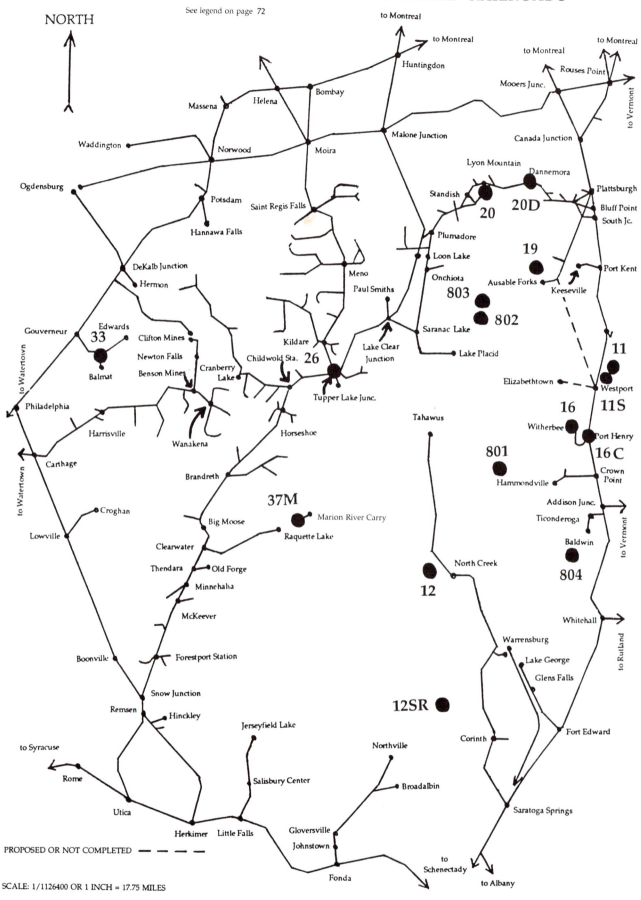

Chapter 9: Abandonment

RAILROADS ARE BUILT for mass passenger transportation, or, more often, to serve an industry or industries. If the industries close, or if other forms of transportation develop, then the railroad no longer has a reason for existence and it, too, closes. If the freight and/or passenger service expenses on the line exceed the income generated, the railroad might continue operations in the red until permission is granted by the Interstate Commerce Commission to abandon.

Recent Abandonments

During the twenty-four years in which I have lived in the Adirondacks, there has been a number of abandonments. Some take historians by surprise: unfortunately, the line closes before anyone can document its last days. Existing lines should be studied, mapped, and photographed before it is too late, and abandonment a fact.

Abandonments in the greater Adirondack region since 1971 have been:

11. D&H passenger service on the mainline abandoned between May 1971 and August 1974, but reinstated by Amtrak.
12. D&H North Creek Branch, Corinth to Tahawus, November 1989.
12W. Warrensburg Branch of the D&H, 1981.
14. D&H branch into Ticonderoga Village from Ticonderoga Station on the mainline, 1981.
19. D&H Ausable Branch, Salmon River Junction to Ausable Forks, 1981.
20. D&H Chateaugay Branch, Dannemora to Otis Junction, 1981.
35. Fonda, Johnstown and Gloversville Railroad, 1991.
36. New York Central Adirondack Division, from Remsen to Lake Placid, operated until the spring of 1972 by Penn Central. Resurrected temporarily by the Adirondack Railway in 1979 and 1980.
36M. Conrail line from Huntingdon, Quebec, to Malone Junction on March 30, 1980.
104. Conrail branch from DeKalb Junction to Ogdensburg in March 1987 (see the *Rip Van Winkle Flyer*, publication of the Ulster & Delaware Chapter of the National Railway Historical Society, #8, September 1987, page 3). This branch closed because its only customer, a paper mill, closed.

All these abandonments, except #11, were not due to the closing of a single major industry, but rather to the number of small industries and businesses which required so few carloads per year that the line became economically unprofitable. In addition, numbers 36 and 36M were abandoned because beaver flooding washouts had made the cost of repairs widen the gap further between expenditures and income. Abandonment number 11 was due to Amtrak's initial refusal in 1971 to operate international runs between the United States and Canada; this refusal was cancelled by August of 1974.

Disposition

Railroad grades can be disposed of in a multitude of ways and combinations so that each mile of a branch can have, and probably has had, a very different history. Each conceivable method of disposition which could possibly happen probably has happened. The primary controlling factor in the disposition of a grade is its ownership. The longer grades are often divided up and purchased by several owners, each treating his or her land segment differently.

Change in ownership of a single segment over time also creates different dispositions. Because most land transfers are not pre-planned with long-term overviews of how the land will be used, disposition of many railroad grades is chaotic, subject only to the whims of chance and human short-sightedness.

An exception to this nationwide chaos is the Rails to Trails Conservancy located in Washington, D.C., which purchases abandoned railroad grades and converts them into hiking and bicycling trails. To my knowledge, such purchases by Rails to Trails have not yet taken place in and around the Adirondacks.

Some railroads may continue to own the grade in the hopes that perhaps industries served will be resurrected and the trains will operate again, e.g. National Lead Company (now Kronos) and the ilmenite mines at Tahawus. The State of New York owns the line from Remsen to Lake Placid and had leased it to the Adirondack Railway Corporation in 1979 and 1980 to operate it during the Winter Olympics and after. It is possible that the line will run again, still owned by the State of New York, but this time leased to the Adirondack Railway Preservation Society. The tracks are still in place except for several beaver washouts and highway crossing pave-overs.

If the land upon which the grade is located is purchased by the State of New York and becomes part of the Forest Preserve, then it is likely that the land will revert back permanently to its natural condition, i.e. forest, which cannot be cleared, logged, developed, or reopened as a railroad in the future. Examples include the former Rich Lumber Company land south of Wanakena now part of the Five Ponds Wilderness Area, the former A. A. Low Horseshoe Forestry Company lands between Horseshoe and Hitchins Pond, and the Chateaugay Branch through much of the Bloomingdale Bog. Some railroad grades are privately owned; these have reverted back to their forested, natural state and are not currently being logged, cleared, or developed.

If a utility owns the grade, it can be used as a power line. An example is the former New York Central Adirondack Division from Malone Junction to a point about one mile south of Gabriels. The grade itself is a sand/gravel road, used by Niagara Mohawk Power Corporation to maintain the powerline and also by snowmobilers for recreation in winter.

Perhaps the most extensive mileage of abandoned grades in the Adirondacks is presently owned by the paper companies: Champion International (formerly Saint Regis), International Paper (which once included Champlain Realty Company), Finch Pruyn, Wagner Woodlands, and Domtar. Some of the grades are used currently by the owners to haul pulpwood and some logs out of the woods by truck. Most paper company lands are leased to fish and game clubs so that many additional miles of old grades are used for access to hunting camps and fishing holes.

Some railroad grades, because of their gentle ascents and broad curves, have been used as the subgrades for public highways. Examples are the Everton Railroad (later Brooklyn Cooperage Company) west of Everton, now Franklin County Highway 14; the D&H Chateaugay Branch north of Saranac Lake, now State Highway 86; Cranberry Lake Railroad between Benson Mines and Wanakena, now State Highway 3; and the D&H Chateaugay narrow gauge between Lyon Mountain and Standish, now Clinton County Route 1. Some public but unpaved highways occupying former railroad grades are maintained by the towns, and of these, some are not maintained in winter.

Other railroad grades are used as tourist lines. As already mentioned, the New York Central Adirondack Division was run by the Adirondack Railway from Remsen to Lake Placid in 1979 and 1980. The former Lowville and Beaver River, now operated by the Mohawk, Adirondack, & Northern Railroad, runs a summer tourist line from Lowville to Croghan. The Adirondack Railway Preservation Society began service between Thendara and Minnehaha in July of 1992 and continues through 1995.

Still other grades have been abandoned twice. There are three examples of this in the Adirondacks. The Everton Railroad, 1886 to ca. 1898, between Saint Regis Falls and Everton was rebuilt and extended by the Brooklyn Cooperage Company between 1904 and 1920; it was then abandoned again. Mac-a-Mac Corporation, 1912 to 1920, built a line from Brandreth Station to Brandreth Lake; Whitney Industries used much of the old line from 1936 to 1939, extended it to Rock Pond, and abandoned it for the second time. The Higbie Lumber Company, 1908 to 1919, built a line from Newton Falls to Newbridge as the Newton Falls and Northern Railroad; later, the grade was used by the Hanna Ore Company in 1941 and extended to Clifton Mines only to be reabandoned in 1952.

Some railroad grades are now under water. Beaver have dammed up the Onion River east of Meno and submerged a Brooklyn Cooperage Company junction. A branch of this line on the nearby divide between Mountain and Clear Brooks requires a detour unless one wants to swim to continue exploring the grade. In some cases, the railroad grade itself becomes a dam when the beavers plug a culvert and the stream rises and erodes the grade. There were at least three such washouts in 1992 along the Adirondack Railway: south of Floodwood near Rollins Pond, south of Nehasane, and just north of Thendara.

The D&H Chateaugay line south of Loon Lake Station has cabins built upon it. Nearby, the grade passes through a series of backyards.

An example of how a railroad line with a diverse disposition history can be abandoned is the Paul Smiths Electric Railway, only 6.5 miles long. All lands belong to Paul Smith's College except for a small tract at Lake Clear Junction and another where State Highway 30 crosses it. On the College Campus, the grade is now a lawn in front of the classroom buildings and, nearby, a parking lot. In two segments, it is used as a logging road. There are several beaver washouts where it is nearly impassable. There are ties still in place, however sporadically. The trolley catenary wire support poles have almost all rotted out. A logging spur is overgrown with trees nearly seventy years old.

A common practice in northern New York is that if a railroad is built and/or abandoned in segments rather than all at once, those segments of line last built into the interior of the Adirondacks are the first to be abandoned. A corollary follows that those segments of line first built at the periphery of the Adirondacks are last to be abandoned, indeed if they have been abandoned at all. Here are a few examples: (1) The Chateaugay Railroad was first built to Dannemora in 1879 and last abandoned to it in 1981. This line was last built to Lake Placid in 1893 and abandoned from it first in 1946. (2) The Little Falls & Dolgeville was built in 1892, then extended to Salisbury Center in 1908. The line was abandoned back to Dolgeville in 1945 and finally back to Little Falls in 1964. (3) The Adirondac Company's Railroad was built to North Creek in 1871 and extended to Tahawus in 1944. The line has recently, in 1989, been abandoned back through North Creek to Corinth, while the Saratoga Springs-Corinth section still runs. (4) The Grasse River Railroad, built to Conifer in 1913 was later extended as the North Tram between 1917 and 1920. It was abandoned back to Conifer in 1948 where it remained in service until 1957.

One must not confuse station closings with demolition of station buildings. Some buildings were demolished shortly after passenger service ceased, while others have persisted for decades afterward. Some are abandoned and dilapidated while others are extant with other functions. Still standing in 1994 on the D&H are: Ticonderoga Village, Merriam, West Chazy, Chazy, Dannemora, Lyon Mountain standard gauge, Saranac Lake, Ray Brook, Lake Placid, Willsboro, Crown Point, Corinth, Riverside, North Creek. Saratoga Springs, Port Henry, Westport, Plattsburgh, and Rouses Point still have Amtrak service. Still standing in 1994 on the N.Y. Central Adirondack Division are Forestport, Otter Lake, McKeever(?), Thendara, Big Moose, Lake Clear Junction, and Malone Junction. Carthage and Harrisville still stand on the C&A.

MAP 9-1 RECENT ABANDONMENTS

See legend on page 79

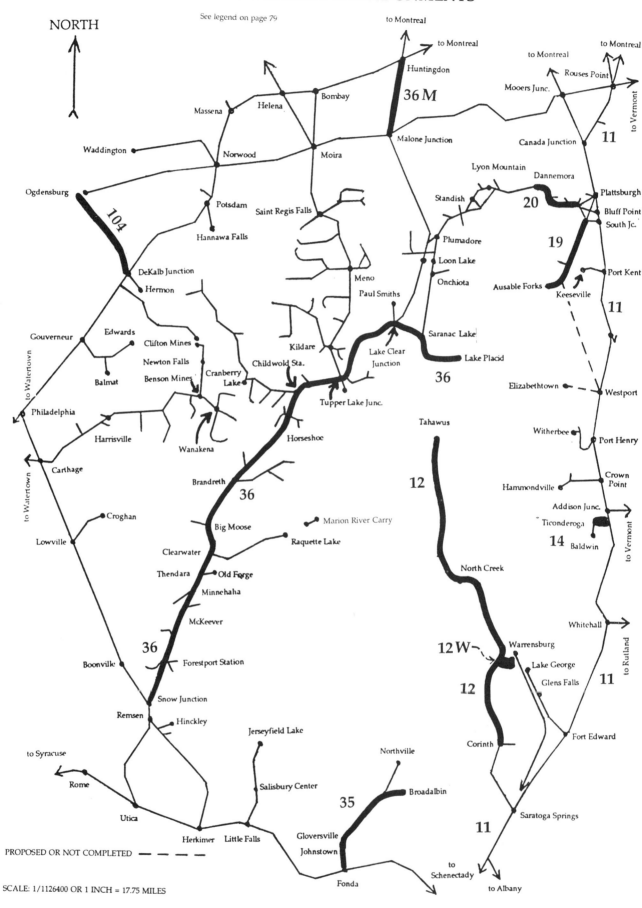

Chapter 10:
Railroad Preservation

RAILROADS IN THE ADIRONDACKS were built mostly in the nineteenth and very early twentieth centuries. Primarily because of tight-radius curves, they cannot compete with modern interstate highway speeds. Unlike highways, railroads, with the exception of slow-geared logging locomotive lines, cannot climb steep grades of more than several percent. They cannot go everywhere cars, trucks and buses can since the rail network is less dense than the highway network.

Yet reasons for preserving railroads are numerous. The practical transportation reasons include economic ones. Railroads are less expensive to build and maintain than highways because the right-of-way is narrower and less land is required. They are less expensive to operate in terms of salaries because one small crew on a freight train can replace dozens of truck drivers. We know that regularly-scheduled passenger and freight trains historically could not often turn a profit, but a railroad need not make a profit. It can be run by a not-for-profit corporation as a public service. Or it can even run at a deficit as a public service similar to those of many governmental agencies. Steam-powered trains attract large crowds from long distances and can be profitable. Chartered trains by special-interest organizations can be filled in advance; such trains do not run unless all seats are filled thus ensuring a profit.

Energy efficiency has become increasingly important in current decades. Railroads use less fuel than trucks, buses and automobiles to move the same cargo or number of people the same distance. One reason is less friction once a train accelerates. If the United States is the victim of another oil embargo, the railroads can most efficiently use what little oil we have. Fewer trucks on the highways means less exhaust pollution, less noise, less wear and tear on the roads, and fewer delays for passenger vehicles due to traffic congestion.

Safety has always been an important consideration. Railroad movements are planned. Unlike in highway travel, if the railroad is well-run and well-maintained, there are no by-chance meets where trains can collide.

Dependability is important, too. Because railroads are less affected by adverse weather than highway vehicles and not affected by highway traffic jams, trains can better maintain their schedules.

The educational advantages of railroads are almost unlimited. A benefit from studying the history of the railroads themselves results in the greater understanding of the history of the industries which they served: mining, forestry, hostelry, health (e.g. tuberculosis sanatoria), agriculture, and various forms of manufacturing.

In addition, railroads can aid in the study of the present, using tour guides in a coach via a public address system lecturing to a myriad of diverse special interest groups: geologists, soil scientists, botanists, wildlife biologists, photographers, governmental agencies, senior citizens, railroad buffs, climatologists, historians, painters, land-use planners, architects, civil engineers, astronomers, fall foliage watchers, scouts, museum buffs, and various other clubs and organizations. Trains can let some special interest groups off at various points along the line for field work, picking them up on a return trip or, if a charter, waiting for them.

Successful preserved railroads by the hundreds are all over North America operating as educational and entertainment organizations. Descriptions of most of these are published annually by the Empire

State Railway Museum in the *Steam Directory*. The National Association of Railroad Passengers also helps the cause.

Some people might enjoy studying the logistics of running a railroad----the movements of trains. Because trains are restricted to tracks, passing and switching must be planned in advance; this is one reason why railroads fascinate this writer. In contrast, highway vehicles and boats can more easily pass around each other, while aircraft and submarines can also pass above or below one another.

Social reasons for railroad preservation are numerous. There is more interaction among people in railroad coaches because they hold more people than automobiles, trucks, and vans. It is easier for people to move around in them than in a bus. People, especially young people, need to be retrained into thinking railroads not highways. Videos featuring them are readily available, as is a abundance of toys emulating them.

Because the Adirondacks provide such wonderful recreational areas, access can be made by trains dropping off and picking up passengers and their recreational equipment at predetermined points inaccessible by highway (Equipment includes skis, canoes, backpacks and camping gear, bicycles, motorbikes, and snowmobiles). The Adirondack Railway in 1979-1980 did just this. We have enough trails for recreation; let us not convert another railroad into one of these in the Adirondack region.

In addition to all the obvious advantages, there is another which is crucial to the human spirit: millions of people agree on the aesthetic effects of railroad sights, sounds, and smells. Railroads have inspired many paintings, photographs, songs, poetry, and prose. The sheer size of locomotives and cars, their weights, and train lengths are overwhelming. There is much drama in watching and riding on trains. Railroads are entertaining!

There are railroads in the greater Adirondack region which have been abandoned but which could be resurrected. If the mines reopen at Tahawus and/or Mineville, the North Creek line and Lake Champlain & Moriah, respectively, could reopen to serve them. The New York Central Adirondack Division (Remsen-Lake Placid line) should be resurrected for passenger tours, exported wood products, garbage and recycling, and imported goods such as coal and oil. The Tupper Lake to Lake Placid section via Lake Clear junction and Saranac Lake could reopen for local commuter traffic because of the higher population density in that area. The Fonda, Johnstown and Gloversville which closed just in 1991 could be reopened before it becomes more difficult and expensive to do so.

Those railroads which are still extant should all be preserved: the D&H mainline (now Canadian Pacific), the D&H Adirondack Branch to Corinth, Conrail and Canadian National to Massena, and the Mohawk Adirondack & Northern to Newton Falls, Croghan, and Lyons Falls.

Northbound Amtrak *Adirondack* at Westport, June 26, 1982. Amfleet and F40PH locomotive were new then.
Pages 105 & 246.
Author photo.

Southbound Amtrak *Adirondack* turboliner at Red Rocks, north of Willsboro, June 22, 1991.
Pages 107 & 246.
Author photo.

Red Rocks along Willsboro Bay, ca. 1914. Page 107.
Post card, author's collection.

Port Kent. The K.A.C.&L.C. Railroad came in behind the depot. Note the cattle pen at the right. Pages 108 & 182.
Post card, collection of Richard Wettereau.

D&H #1776, *Freedom*, specially painted for the Bicentennial, hauls a northbound freight from Corinth in 1976. **Page 132.**

Kip Grant photo.

The D&H's *Laurentian* southbound just south of Saratoga Springs. The train was discontinued on May 1, 1971 when Amtrak began operations but was reinstated on August 6, 1974 as the *Adirondack*. The Adirondac Company's railroad diverged not far from here. Page 132.

Thomas C. Curran photo.

The trestle over the Sacandaga River south of Hadley was made famous by a Seneca Ray Stoddard photo in the nineteenth century. Trains to Tahawus which crossed this trestle ceased operating on November 16, 1989. Looking south, July 1990. Page 133.

Author photo.

#1776 switching at the International Paper Company Mill at Palmer near Corinth. Page 133.
Kip Grant photo.

Leased Bangor & Aroostook GP-38 locomotive at North Creek on February 26, 1981. Page 135.
Jeffrey G. Martin photo.

D & H 4-4-0 at North Creek in 1901. Page 135.
Lawrence E. Corbett photo.

A nineteenth-century Adirondac Company combine, used in this century as a Northern Lumber Company office, is examined by Paul Smith's College head librarian, Ted Mack, on October 21, 1989. It is located about 0.7 mile south of Riverside. Page 135.
Author photo.

Old wooden snow plow at Tahawus, May 1983. Alco D&H RS-3 #4103 was built in 1952. Page 136.
Author photo.

D&H RS-3 #4115 switching in Glens Falls in November 1972. Page 154.
Kip Grant photo.

Part Two

By Geography

Section I:
Into the Adirondacks from the Champlain Valley and the East

Chapter 11:
Delaware & Hudson Mainline from Whitehall to Rouses Point

A MASS OF INFORMATION on the D&H Mainline has been accumulated since 1985 when *Where did the Tracks Go* was published. Enough material is available now to warrant a new chapter. The detail is presented in such a manner as to minimally duplicate that already available in D&H (1925), Shaughnessy (1967), Mohr (1974), Zimmermann (1978), Gardner (1990), Sweetland (1992) and Plant and Plant (1993). None of these works has detailed track schematics arranged geographically. The depot photographs in Gardner (1990) are reprints from the D&H Board of Directors *Inspection of Lines* (1928).

A great deal of detail is available on the Mainline for several reasons. It is a mainline with heavy traffic and many branches. It has been in service for many years: 144 into Whitehall and 117 through Westport, for example, as of this 1994 writing. Many changes have occurred during this long period. Many industries have risen, peaked, and declined. In addition, there has been a number of relocations creating a complex history: examples are the Port Henry tunnels, the Bulwagga Bay trestle, a shift from Mooers Junction to Rouses Point, and the junctions with both the Ausable and Chateaugay branches. Construction was complex, too: the line into the iron mines at Mineville did not initiate in Whitehall but in Leicester, Vermont. The Ausable line had been planned to be on the mainline but became only a branch. The first railroad into Plattsburgh came not from Albany but from Montreal.

The segment from Whitehall to Rouses Point was chosen for inclusion in this book for two reasons. First, the railroad itself is organized into operational divisions, one of these being the Champlain Division from Whitehall to Rouses Point. Built northward from Albany, the line terminated near Whitehall for 25 years before being extended northward to Plattsburgh and Montreal. Second, inclusion of detail south of Whitehall and in Quebec would have made this book unwieldy. This is a work on the

Adirondacks, and the bulk of the trackage should be in the Adirondacks. The segment on the mainline from Port Kent to Rouses Point is not geologically in the Adirondacks, but is so tied in with branches into the Adirondacks that it is included.

To avoid duplication of detail at the junction points of the mainline with its branches, such detail is shown only in the chapters on the branches. One reason is that the industries which the branches served often had yards and other facilities at the junction points: for example, the Crown Point Iron Company, the Lake Champlain & Moriah, and the Chateaugay Ore & Iron Company. The following table refers the reader to the proper chapter and page(s) for junction detail:

Junction, Branch or Railroad: Chapter Numbers

Junction	Branch or Railroad	See Chapter
Whitehall	Rutland Branch	not included
Ticonderoga	Baldwin Branch	14
Addison Junction	Rutland Railroad	14
Crown Point	Crown Point Iron Company's RR	15
Port Henry	Lake Champlain & Moriah RR	16
Westport	Elizabethtown Terminal RR	17
Willsboro	New York & Pennsylvania Company's RR	17
Port Kent	Keeseville, Ausable Chasm & Lake Champlain RR	18
South Junction to Plattsburgh	Ausable Branch and Chateaugay Branch	19/20
Canada Junction	Mooers Branch	21
Rouses Point	Rutland RR	23 (brief note)
	Canadian National RR	not included
	Napierville Junction RR	not included

The maps and text are arranged as if one were traveling from south to north along the Mainline from Whitehall to Rouses Point. Note the cabins. These are control points of the Centralized Train Control, C.T.C., system. The D&H began using the term cabin sometime between 1950 and 1962 and identified each of them with two capital letters: for example, SC, LC, TI, SR, CN.

The Champlain Transportation Company, a subsidiary of the D&H, operated from 1826 through 1933 so that steamboat service along Lake Champlain probably terminated by 1933.

Passengers aboard Amtrak's *Adirondack* may use this book as a guide to locate many of the historic remnants still extant along the line. The geology, flora and fauna of the Champlain Valley as seen from the train window are equally as fascinating as the history of the railroads themselves.

McNamara's D&H *Official Freight Shippers Directory* of 1914-1915 and other years lists its freight customers by (1) station, by (2) nature of freight involved and by (3) whether the customer was a receiver, shipper, dealer, manufacturer, or wholesaler. However, the *Directory* does not list which customers had their own sidings and which used only public team tracks. Those few customers who had their own sidings are included in this atlas. Because of the large number of freight customers who did not have their own sidings, these customers will not be listed in this book. This approach applies to all the D&H branch chapters as well: 12, 13, 14, 19, 20 and 21.

Mileages

Most of the mileages I have measured by scaling off from a D&H track schematic dating to about 1928. Other more detailed valuation diagrams were used where available, e.g. at Port Henry, Plattsburgh, and at Beekmantown. The *D&H Official List No. 57* (1941) of station mileages shows some discrepancies with the track schematic and valuation diagram mileages. The *Official List* mileages are consistently less than the mileages on the track schematic and valuation diagrams, but inconsistencies ranging from 0.10 to 0.20 mile occur in the SIZE of the discrepancy. Because the size of the discrepancies among the D&H documents themselves is so variable, a simple minor relocation of the mainline between 1928 and 1941 cannot be the cause; numerous minor relocations are more likely. One relocation might be because of the abandonment of the Port Henry tunnels.

Field checks using mileposts show that the track schematic and valuation diagrams are more accurate in tying in with the mileposts and original nineteenth century right-of-way. I have included both track schematic and *Official List* mileages for each station with a sizeable mileage discrepancy: Clemons, Putnam, Port Henry, Westport, Wadhams, Willsboro, Port Kent, Plattsburgh, Beekmantown, West Chazy, Chazy, Cooperville, and Rouses Point.

Station Descriptions

Whitehall. 77.39 miles from Albany. Elevation ca. 105 feet above sea level. Maps 11-2 and 11-13.

The Whitehall-Lake Station area was the terminus for the line for a period of 26 years from 1848 to 1874.

Passenger station: The line was opened to Whitehall from Albany in 1848, with the branch eastward into Rutland finished in 1850. Detail on the rebuilding and relocation of the passenger and freight stations will be found in the Legend to Map 11-13. This detail has been summarized from several sources: Gibbs (1931, May 1), MacMartin (1932, Jun. 1), *D&H RR Bulletin* (1934, Mar. 1), Morton (1977), Gardner (1990, Volume 3, front cover and page 66), and B. Martin (1995). Amtrak still stops at Whitehall, but the abandoned station was recently demolished by burning by the Whitehall Fire Department on April 28, 1987 (Norman, 1987). Amtrak had been using a small waiting shelter since the 1970s, but it has been replaced by a new one at 77.92 miles on November 14, 1994 according to B. Martin (1995, page 19).

Tunnel: At milepost 78 was a 682-foot-long tunnel within the village. Detail on this tunnel built in 1850 and its rebuilding in 1931-1934 is available in the 1931 (May 1), 1932 (Jun. 1), and 1934 (Mar. 1) publications listed above. In 1893 the Whitehall Quadrangle showed two spurs from the north end of the tunnel point down to the head of Lake Champlain; one spur still existed in 1977.

Photographs: Shaughnessy (1967) offers many photos of Whitehall: pp. 143, 240, 248, 399, 403, 404, 408, 412, 423, and 432. Zimmermann's (1978) photos are on pages 2, 8, 9, 10, 19, 23, 42, 44, 46, 48, 55, 68, 70, and 79. Sweetland (1992) has photos on pages 46-59, and Plant and Plant (1993) have photos on pages 32-35. Some of the references listed above in the paragraphs on the passenger station and tunnel also contain photographs.

Servicing facilities: The 1941 D&H *Official List No. 57* includes a coaling plant, a roundhouse with 25 stalls and an ice-storage area, a 75-foot electric turntable, a car repair shop, track scales for weighing cars, two stock pens, and two water tanks: one at the station and one at the roundhouse. B. Martin (1995) states that servicing facilities were closed during the 1979-1981 era.

Industrial sidings: In 1940 was the Champlain Coal Company track, and in 1950 and 1962 the Champlain Spinners, Inc. track; I cannot find precise locations for these from the Employees's Timetables. The location of the spur into Whitehall Harbor is known, however, and is shown on Map 11-13.

SC Cabin. 78.62 miles in 1969. Maps 11-2 and 11-13.

This was the north end of doubletrack through Whitehall. In 1940 it was called Elbow. The name SC Cabin was used later.

Lake Station. 79.30 miles. Elevation 101. Maps 11-2 and 11-13.

In 1851 the line was extended to here from Whitehall in order to meet the steamboats on Lake Champlain (Shaughnessy, 1967, page 144) until the railroad was extended further north to Port Henry in 1874 and to Plattsburgh in 1875. The mean elevation of Lake Champlain is 95 feet above sea level. The D&H here was six feet above the lake.

Here is the division point, i.e. the border between the Saratoga Division on the south and the Champlain Division on the north. Servicing facilities are common sights at division points, but in this instance these facilities were in Whitehall and not at Lake Station.

At about 79.6 miles, the 1893 Whitehall Quadrangle shows a stub on the east going down to the lake and an unknown industry. At 80.43 miles is the drawbridge over the outlet to South Bay.

South Bay Siding. 81.43 to 82.05 miles in 1928. Elevation 105. Maps 11-2 and 11-14.

This passing siding was in existence when the 1893 Whitehall Quadrangle was published. In 1942 it held 68 cars, but was gone by 1950.

Clemons (Chubb's Dock). 84.50 miles. Elevation 105. Maps 11-2 and 11-15.

Passenger station: The original name of this station was Chubb's Dock, but it was changed to Clemons sometime between the timetables of June 24, 1900 and June 24, 1906. Gardner (1990, Volume 4, page 37) tells us that the "original station was built for Lake Station in 1851. In 1873 it was moved to Clemons and set up about 250 feet south of the present station site on the lake side. 1903 it was removed to the present station site but was burned in 1909." (The second) combination passenger and freight station built in 1909. The station closed sometime between the timetables of June 26, 1932 and April 1, 1933. The *D&H Official list No. 57* (1941) places Clemons at 84.40 miles, south of a small bridge at 84.41 and of the siding.

Passing siding: A short passing siding was here in 1928 according to the D&H track schematic from milepost 84.47 to 84.65.

Dresden. 87.26 miles. Elevation 107. Maps 11-3 and 11-16.

Passenger station: This station was in existence in 1875 but closed between April 24, 1960 and July 23, 1960. Gardner (1990, Volume 4, page 37) informs us that the original waiting room, from 1875 to 1906, was in the general store. A new combination depot was built in 1906. A reliable source informed me in 1994 that the depot was a general store once again!
Passing siding: In 1928 the passing siding here began at milepost 87.10 and ended at 87.60. It must have been extended by 1942 when it held 120 cars. The siding had been removed by 1969.
Ferry connection: A ferry crossed Lake Champlain here into Vermont in 1893 (Whitehall Quadrangle).
Photographs: Zimmermann (1978) includes photos on pages 4 and 48.
Facilities: stock pen.

Putnam. 92.40 miles. Elevation 107. Maps 11-3 and 11-17.

Passenger station: This station existed from 1875 to 1888 as a waiting room inside a general store (Gardner, 1990, Volume 4, page 38). The combination passenger and freight station was built in 1888, but closed sometime between 1950 and 1955. The D&H *Official List* (1941) places Putnam at 92.30 miles.
Passing siding: A passing siding was present in 1928 from milepost 92.27 to 92.73, and held 41 cars in 1942. It was gone by 1969.
Ferry connection: Another ferry crossed Lake Champlain here according to the 1893 Whitehall Quadrangle.
Photograph: Shaughnessy (1967) has one on page 194.
Facilities: stock pen.

Cummings Siding. 95.65 to 96.25 miles in 1928. Elevation 143. Maps 11-3 and 11-18.

This siding held 66 cars in 1942 and 118 cars in 1962. By 1969 it was gone. Note the elevation above Lake Champlain: some 48 feet, the D&H Mainline descending in both directions.

Wrights (Patterson). 97.40 miles. Elevation ca. 120. Map 11-3.

Passenger station: Gardner (1990, Volume 4, page 38) states that the original station was part of a building in Comstock, and was moved to Patterson in 1875. It burned in 1885. Because it remained in service until sometime between September 10, 1931 and September 27, 1931, a second depot must have been built on the site. The name was changed from Patterson to Wrights sometime between a D&H map of 1890 and the timetable of April 15, 1892.
Siding: A dead-end stub siding was here in 1928 with the switch at milepost 97.29. At milepost 98.5 the track reached a lesser, compared to Cummings Siding, summit of 126 feet.
Ferry connection: The 1892 Ticonderoga Quadrangle shows a third ferry across Lake Champlain here, this one to Chipmans Point, Vermont.
Facilities: two stock pens.

Fort Ticonderoga (Montcalm Landing). 99.56 miles. Elevation 107. Maps 11-4 and 14-1.

Passenger station: When the New York & Canada opened in 1874, this station was not on shore but out in Lake Champlain on a long trestle with a steamboat dock. A photo in D&H (1925, page 261) taken in 1874 shows it. The 1892 Ticonderoga Quadrangle informs us that the trestle was about 0.3 mile long from milepost 99.4 to 99.7. Shaughnessy (1967, page 145) and Gardner (1990, Volume 4, page 39) also include a photo of the trestle, but the 1928 D&H track schematic no longer shows the structure.
Montcalm Landing: Sometime between the June 25, 1911 and February 11, 1912 D&H timetables, the name of the station was changed from Fort Ticonderoga to Montcalm Landing. A simultaneous station name change was made at milepost 101.47 from Addison Junction to Fort Ticonderoga. Then again, sometime between the April 1, 1933 and January 1934 timetables, the station name here at milepost 99.56 was changed back to Fort Ticonderoga from Montcalm Landing. This reversal occurred after the station at milepost 101.47 had closed. If these name changes are not confusing enough, yet a third station had the similar name "Ticonderoga," without the "Fort"! This depot was not on the D&H Mainline but on the Baldwin Branch in the Village of Ticonderoga. Amtrak trains still stopped at milepost 99.56 where the "station" had been reduced to a shed until about 1994. Now they stop at Addison Junction.

Passing siding: A passing siding existed from milepost 98.97 to milepost 100.05. In 1928 it was called Defiance Siding; Mount Defiance loomed over it. The name was changed to MD Siding by the April 28, 1940 employees' timetable; at that time it held 65 cars. In 1969 the south end of this siding was called LC Cabin and the north end TI Cabin.

Servicing facilities: The 1941 D&H *Official List No. 57* includes a watering facility for locomotives; the 1928 track schematic places it at milepost 99.35. There were two stock pens.

Baldwin Branch: At the north end of the passing siding, at milepost 100.03, the Baldwin Branch diverged. The June 22, 1890 timetable calls it Lake George Junction but it was not a station stop. The area around the junction was called Delano on the 1894 Ticonderoga Quadrangle. For details on the Baldwin Branch and track plans of the Fort Ticonderoga area from milepost 98.97 to 101.75, see Chapter 14.

Drawbridge and tunnel: At milepost 100.78 is a drawbridge, 94 feet long, over Ticonderoga Creek, the outlet to Lake George. At milepost 101.00 is the south end of a tunnel, some 439 feet long, located beneath the entrance road to the current Fort Ticonderoga museum.

Photographs: Additional photographs of Fort Ticonderoga occur in Shaughnessy (1967, page 428), Zimmermann (1978, pages 23, 46, and 48), Plant and Plant (1993, page 40).

Addison Junction. 101.47 miles. Elevation ca. 108. Maps 11-4 and 14-1.

Trestle to Vermont: Before there was a junction here, the first railroad built into this area was the Rutland's Addison Branch from Whiting Station, later Leicester Junction, Vermont. The line crossed Lake Champlain on a low trestle with a drawbridge in the middle (C. H. Miller, 1985), and headed northward to Port Henry and on into the Port Henry Iron Company mines at Mineville. This line from Vermont to Mineville was completed December 1, 1871 (D&H, 1925, page 246).

Passenger station: The Addison Railroad, which entered New York from Vermont across Lake Champlain, was the first to reach this point in 1868. Gardner (1990, Volume 4, page 42) shows photos of the 1868 station and freight house. The New York & Canada, later absorbed by the D&H, first opened from Whitehall to here November 30, 1874 (D&H, 1925, page 249). The first name of the D&H station was Addison Junction. Sometime between the timetables of June 25, 1911 and February 11, 1912 the name had been changed to Fort Ticonderoga. This was, to this writer, an unfortunate and confusing name change because the station at milepost 99.56 had its name altered simultaneously from Fort Ticonderoga to Montcalm Landing. Addison Junction station closed sometime between June 26, 1932 and April 1, 1933. I have been informed by a reliable source that Amtrak has recently (Spring of 1994?) moved its shelter and has been stopping its trains at Addison Junction rather than at milepost 99.56. The timetables do not reflect this change: 140 miles from Montreal on all timetables.

Trestle to Vermont abandoned: Addison Junction ceased to be a junction after February 27, 1921 when the Rutland Railroad timetable no longer showed Addison Branch trains crossing into New York State. They terminated instead at Larabee's Point, Vermont from 1927 through April 29, 1951. Currently, a ferry crosses Lake Champlain here. The access road to this ferry dock crosses the D&H Mainline at milepost 101.62.

Passing siding: The 1928 D&H track schematic shows a passing siding at Addison Junction from milepost 101.18 to milepost 101.70. The April 28, 1940 and November 1, 1942 D&H employees' timetables indicate a 67- then 64-car capacity and names it Pells. It was gone by 1950. For a detailed track plan of Addison Junction, see Chapter 14 on the Baldwin Branch.

International Paper Company Pulp Mill: At 103.5 miles, elevation 109, Map 11-19, is a pulp mill built about 1971. The mill is still served by the D&H today and includes a siding from 103.11 to 103.86 miles along the Mainline as well as a spur into the mill.

Crown Point. 109.10 miles. Elevation 121. Maps 11-5 and 15-3.

Passenger station: Originally this community was called Hammonds Corners, but by 1875 the D&H timetable already called it Crown Point. The photo caption in Gardner (1990, Volume 4, page 43) states that the station was built in 1868; this seems early because the Addison Railroad was not built to here until 1871. Additions and alterations were done on the building in 1912-1913. The station closed between April 24, 1960 and July 23, 1960.

Crown Point Iron Company's Railroad: From here, a narrow gauge railroad diverged and climbed to Ironville (Irondale) and Hammondville (see Chapter 15 for detailed maps) from 1873 through 1893.

Passing sidings: Several passing sidings were here in 1928 with a combined length beginning at 108.28 miles and ending at 109.33. One of them, Gunnisons, held 86 cars in 1940 and 78 in 1950; it was gone by 1962.

Industrial sidings: See Map 15-3. A stub had served a dairy just north of the station, but the building had been abandoned by 1977. At milepost 107.5 in 1928 was the Crown Point Feldspar Company stub track. See Chapter 15 on the Crown Point Iron Company's blast furnace.

Photographs: Photos of Crown Point appear in Shaughnessy (1967, pages 138, 141, 178, and 430) and in Allen (1973) as well as in publications on the Crown Point Iron Company (see Chapter 15).

Ferry: At milepost 109.28 was the crossing of a highway that led east to a steamboat and ferry dock. The ferry was later replaced by the Crown Point Bridge, about five miles to the North, which opened between 1924 and 1938.

Facility: stock pen.

Porter's Spur. 110.28 miles. Elevation 126. Function unknown in 1928.

Bulwagga Bay Trestle. Milepost 111.53 (elevation 145) to ca. 116.3 (elevation 106). Map 11-5.

Just south of Burdick's Crossing was a junction in the vicinity of milepost 111.53. The original line from Vermont to the mines at Mineville in 1871 diverged here in a north-northeast direction and was built out onto the Crown Point peninsula. Near the tip of this peninsula, not far from the west end of the present Crown Point Highway Bridge, the track curved west and crossed the head of Bulwagga Bay on a trestle, joining the mainland south of Port Henry at about milepost 116.3. On April 18, 1874 this trestle was destroyed by wind-driven ice floes (D&H, 1925, page 249). The railroad was then re-routed off the peninsula and along the west shore of Bulwagga Bay where it is today. Construction was completed and trains running again on November 30, 1874. The 1892 Port Henry Quadrangle indicates a pier jutting out into Lake Champlain with a track on it at about milepost 116.3. Could this be a remnant stub of the old Bulwagga Bay trestle? The 1871 Asher & Adams map shows the trestle.

Burdick's Crossing and Burdick's Siding. 111.87 miles. Elevation 148 at the south end. Maps 11-5 and 11-21.

This location on the 1892 Ticonderoga Quadrangle had a siding 0.55 mile long and stub-ended. By 1928, it was a multiple-track passing siding called Burdick's Siding, beginning at milepost 111.95 and ending at 112.55. It held 73 cars in 1940, 67 cars in 1950, and was gone by 1962. The highway crossing is at 111.87.

Currier's Crossing. 113.27 miles. Elevation 108. Map 11-5.

D&H RR Bulletin (1931, Oct. 15) describes the grade crossing elimination of the highway, now State Route 903, which leads to the Crown Point Bridge.

Port Henry. 116.72 miles. Elevation 103. Maps 11-5, 16-2 and 16-3.

As is stated earlier in this chapter, the first railroad to reach Port Henry in 1871 and continue on to the Port Henry Iron Company mines at Mineville did not come from Whitehall. The Addison Railroad came from Vermont and crossed Lake Champlain at Addison Junction. Construction from Whitehall came later and was to be completed here in the spring of 1874, but was delayed by the collapse of the Bulwagga Bay Trestle until November 30, 1874.

Passenger station: The station was already in existence in 1875, although the building which stands today was constructed in 1888 (Gardner, 1990, Volume 4, page 44). Amtrak trains still stop here. The D&H *Official List No. 57* (1941) places the depot at 116.58 miles, only 0.03 mile north of the 116.55 footbridge.

Freight house: Gardner's (1990, Volume 4, page 44) photo caption states "Portion of original combination station built in 1868, bought by D&H in 1874. It stood on No. 6 track. In 1888 one half was dismantled and the other half moved to north end of round house and used as oil and store room. It was torn down in 1927." Because the Addison Railroad did not reach Port Henry until 1871, Gardner does not state why the freight house was built three years in advance. A second freight house, also pictured in Gardner, was built in 1888 along with and directly southwest of the current depot.

Passing sidings: In 1928 a passing siding existed from milepost 115.80 to milepost 116.40 as shown on the 1928 track map blueprint. This siding in 1940 was named Sherman, and held 81, later 109, cars. In 1969 the south end at 115.43 was called SR cabin while the north end at 116.42 was called SN Cabin. The siding was removed sometime between 1983 and the summer of 1991. In 1942 another passing siding existed near the station, from milepost 116.40 to 116.91 and held 77 cars.

Servicing facilities: In addition to the servicing facilities of the Lake Champlain & Moriah Railroad described in Chapter 16, the D&H had its own facilities at Port Henry. Included over various years were a 65-foot turntable, an engine house which later became a roundhouse, track scales, and two water tanks. A storage building for maintenance of way equipment southwest of the depot was removed between the summer of 1991 and the summer of 1992.

Industrial sidings: In addition to the numerous sidings shown on Maps 16-2 and 16-3, the B.C. Manufacturing Company had a lumber shed on a siding along the D&H in 1876 at the south end of the Village. Kozma (1985, page 12) mentions that a side track existed in 1880 for Edgerly's ice harvesting (from Lake Champlain presumably) but does not locate it.

Lake Champlain and Moriah Railroad: From Port Henry this branchline diverged. See Chapter 16 for details.

Tunnels: Two tunnels, west of the present mainline track, were probably opened in 1875 when the D&H was completed to Plattsburgh. The mainline went inland for a short distance here because the Bay State Furnace was located on the lake shore. The tunnels were abandoned sometime between 1940 (low clearance listed in an employees' timetable) and 1945 (no longer shown on the Port Henry Quadrangle). The mainline was then relocated directly along the lake shore, but the tunnels still exist. The more southerly of the two tunnels, a covered cut in glacial till constructed of stonework, is at milepost 117.65 and the more northerly, blasted through bedrock, at 117.75. The residents of Port Henry are considering moving all the garbage which has accumulated in these tunnels and preparing the site for a historic landmark and, perhaps, a museum.

Photographs: See Shaughnessy (1967, pages 170 and 172), Zimmermann (1978, pages 11, 22, 38, 50, 54, and 68), Sweetland (1992, pages 62 and 63), and Plant and Plant (1993, pages 40-42).

Derailment: See R. Moore (1995) for an account of the major Canadian Pacific freight derailment of March 1, 1995 at milepost 119. Newspaper reports include Calkins (1995), LaMoureux (1995), McKinstry (1995), and Rosenquist (1995).

Cheever Iron Ore Company Railroad. 118.9 miles. Elevation 111.

See Chapter 16 for details on this line which pre-dated, and did not connect with, the D&H. At milepost 120, elevation 106, begins the long climb upward through Westport.

HS Cabin. 121.88 miles. Elevation ca. 160. Maps 11-6 and 11-22.

In 1969 this control point was listed in the D&H Employees' timetable of October 26. By 1977 no passing siding existed here, although a stub track serving a bottled gas plant, just south of the bridge over State Highway 22, remained. By 1992, the stub was gone.

Howard's Siding. 123.15 to 123.80 miles. Elevation 200 feet at the south end and 220 at the north. Maps 11-6 and 11-23.

This siding was in existence in 1928 and in 1942 and had a capacity of 68 cars. By 1962 it held 140 cars, but was abandoned by 1969.

Allen's Siding. 127.05 to 127.60 miles. Elevation 275 feet at the south end and 266 at the north. Maps 11-6 and 11-24.

This siding was in existence in 1928 and in 1942 and had a capacity of 55 cars. It was gone by 1950. Just south of Allen's Siding, at milepost 126.2, a summit is reached on the track at elevation 298 feet, the mainline descending in both directions. This is the second highest point on the Champlain Division; the highest is at milepost 129.26 at 320 feet.

Westport. 127.80 miles. Elevation 270. Maps 11-6, 17-1 and 17-2.

Passenger station: This combination passenger and freight station opened in 1875-1876 (Gardner, 1990, volume 4, photo caption on page 45). The building was remodeled and enlarged in 1891 with an extension built in 1908. The depot has been converted into an arts center, and Gates (1973) presents its history. Amtrak has constructed a small waiting shed between the depot and the Highway 9N overpass. The D&H *Official List No. 57* (1941) places Westport at 127.64 miles, some 0.19 mile south of the Highway 9N underpass at 127.83. In the field, the distance between the depot and the Highway 9N underpass seems closer to 0.02 or 0.03 mile and not anywhere near 0.19 mile.

Stagecoach connections: Kozma (1985, page 2) has some detail on Westport as well as on the three following stations. She lists stagecoach connections made at Westport especially for Elizabethtown and Lake Placid. The June 24, 1906 D&H timetable, page 10, announces Kellogg's Stages to Elizabethtown with a running time of 62 minutes.

Passing siding: From milepost 127.70 to 127.88 a short passing siding was in existence in 1928. By 1974 it had become a dead-end stub directly in front of the station. The switch had been removed before May 31, 1991.

Facilities: The 1928 track schematic and the 1941 D&H *Official List No. 57* include a water tank. There was a stock pen.

Elizabethtown Terminal Railroad: For details, see Chapter 17. This line, under construction from Westport in 1910, was never completed.

Highest point on the Champlain Division: The highest point is at milepost 129.26, 320 feet above sea level and 225 above Lake Champlain. State highway 22 crosses the track at this point and has been photographed in Zimmermann (1978, page 26).

Original proposed mainline inland route: The original proposed mainline route from Westport to Plattsburgh was not along the shore of Lake Champlain, but rather via an inland route. It was at first thought too difficult and expensive to construct the right-of-way as a shelf in a high bedrock ledge along the lake north of Willsboro at Red Rocks, but this engineering feat was accomplished in 1875. The proposed inland route was never built except for the Plattsburgh-Ausable River Station segment which became the Ausable Branch (see Chapter 19). An 1871 Asher & Adams map shows the proposed route. The inland route (see Map 11-1) would have diverged from the existing mainline at about the highest point at milepost 129.26. It would have passed to the west of the hamlet of Wadhams Mills instead of to the east where it is today. It would have passed east of the hamlets of Towers Forge (Stowersville) and Lewis, crossed what is now Highway 9 at Deerhead, and followed the North Branch Boquet River upstream.

Photographs: Photos of Westport occur in Shaughnessy (1967, pages 294 and 431), Gates (1973), Zimmermann (1978, pages 12 and 26), Sweetland (1992, pages 64-67) and Plant and Plant (1993, page 42).

Wadham's Mills. 130.81 miles. Elevation 295. Maps 11-7 and 11-25.

Passenger station: In 1875 this station was called Wadham's Mills, but the name was shortened to Wadham's sometime between the June 23, 1907 and June 21, 1908 timetables. Kozma (1985, page 6) states that the first station building was replaced by another in 1884. Gardner (1990, Volume 4, page 46) states that the combination passenger and freight station in her photo was built in 1902. Gray's 1876 *Atlas of Essex County*, page 45, locates it on the west side of the track north of the highway crossing. The D&H *Official List No. 57* (1941) places Wadham's at 130.59 miles, south of the crossing. The D&H timetable of February 15, 1928 documented the elimination of the Wadham's and Whallonsburg stops and the opening of Merriam station, roughly midway between, to replace them.

Passing siding: Two overlapping sidings already present in 1928 began at milepost 130.58 and, with combined length, ended at 131.47. One siding held 72 cars in 1942. In 1969, the south end of the siding was WD Cabin and the north end, DH Cabin. The northbound and southbound Amtrak trains are scheduled to meet here in 1994. The first of three crossings of the Boquet River occurs at 130.48 miles just south of WD Cabin.

Facilities: stock pen.

Merriam. 133.10 miles. Elevation 264. Maps 11-7 and 11-26.

Passenger station: This station resulted as a consolidation of the Wadham's and Whallonsburg stations. The change was documented by the D&H timetable of February 15, 1928. Gardner (1990, Volume 4, page 45) includes a photo of the Merriam depot; so does the *D&H RR Bulletin* (1928, Jul. 15). A short article on Merriam Station appears in the *D&H RR Bulletin* (1928, Sept. 15). Trains ceased stopping here between June 7, 1938 and June 25, 1939—a very ephemeral life for a station. The building still stood in 1992 and had until recently been used as a residence.

Pulpwood log boom: Kozma (1985, page 12) describes a boom in 1893 at Merriam to collect pulpwood cut upstream on the Boquet River. The pulpwood was then shipped by rail to the Champlain Pulp Mills built in 1882 in Willsboro.

Whallonsburg. 134.23 miles. Elevation 273. Maps 11-7 and 11-27.

Passenger station: According to Gardner (1990, Volume 4, pages 45 and 48), a combination passenger and freight station was built in 1875-1876. The building burned on December 1, 1887 and was replaced quickly by the moving of the station from Valcour. The *D&H RR Bulletin* of September 15, 1928 states that this second Valcour-Whallonsburg depot burned on November 10, 1925 and was eventually replaced by the Merriam depot on February 15, 1928. The Boquet River was crossed for a second time just south of the station at milepost 134.05.

Passing siding: It began at 134.10 and ended at 138.81 miles in 1928.

Facilities: The 1941 *D&H Official List No. 57* includes two stock pens; I do not know their location.

Essex. 137.25 miles. Elevation 272. Maps 11-7 and 11-28.

Passenger station: Gardner's (1990, Volume 4, page 46) caption states that this station opened in 1875 as a shelter built next to a general store. In 1886 a combination station was built by Essex townspeople and turned over to the D&H. This station burned in 1903 and apparently was replaced by a second combination station built in 1903 and shown in Gardner's photo. It closed between April 24, 1960 and September 23, 1960.

Siding: Essex Siding was unnamed but already present in 1928 from milepost 137.45 to 137.96. In 1942 it was named such and held 65 cars. It occasionally stores maintenance-of-way equipment today and is stub-ended.

Facilities: The 1941 *D&H Official List No. 57* includes a stock pen; I do not know its location.

Industries: The Dairymen's League Cooperative Association Inc. creamery was here.

Willsboro. 142.01 miles. Elevation 227. Maps 11-8 and 17A-1.

Passenger station: Gardner's (1990, Volume 4, page 46) photo caption states that it was built in 1875-1876. A name-change from Willsborough to Willsboro occurred between the timetables of June 29, 1919 and September 11, 1921. Amtrak trains stopped here all year through October 29, 1983, then summers only from 1984 through 1987. The station building is used by the D&H today for maintenance-of-way. Two section houses also stand across the main from the station with a stub siding. The D&H *Official List No. 57* (1941) places Willsboro at 141.87 miles, or well to the South of milepost 142. In the field, the depot is just north of milepost 142.

Passing siding: The siding was already in existence in 1928 from milepost 141.27 to 142.01; it held 74 cars in 1942.

Facilities: The 1941 D&H *Official List No. 57* indicates a water tank here but the 1928 track schematic does not reveal the location. A stock pen was here.

Industrial sidings: An exhibit at The Adirondack Museum's mining building in Blue Mountain Lake sets the opening of the wollastonite plant at milepost 141.0 as July 5, 1953 although other sources claim it was in 1949. Two stub-ended sidings serve the plant. See Chapter 17A on the New York and Pennsylvania Company's Railroad which connected with the D&H Mainline at Willsboro. A stub, south of the station, might have served the H.H.H. Building Supply whose building still stands; the lane leading to it is named "Dock and Coal Road," suggesting also a coal facility.

Boquet River Trestle: At 140.83 miles, the Boquet River is crossed for the third and last time. The span is 140 feet long.

Red Rocks. Approximately 144 to 148 miles. Elevations from 170 to 200 feet. Map 11-8.

This is the spectacularly scenic portion of the line which posed the great engineering challenge of the early 1870s. At milepost 144.5 is the sharpest curve on the Champlain Division, an 8-degree curve. The center of the 606-foot-long Willsboro Tunnel is at milepost 144.94 and at elevation 190 along Willsboro Bay. Leading to the tunnel on both sides, the track is blasted as a tortuous shelf into the bedrock wall 95 feet above the lake. At milepost 145.91 is the 158-foot-long high trestle 80 feet above Highby Brook made famous by Stoddard's nineteenth century photos. Photographs of the Red Rocks area abound in publications: D&H (1925, pages 250 and 254), Shaughnessy (1967, pp. 134, 146, 148, 149, 156, 198, 396, 413 and 418), Zimmermann (1978, pp. 47 and 52), and in Plant and Plant (1993, page 44). *D&H RR Bulletin* (1928, Jan. 1; 1928, Jan. 15; 1932, Nov. 1; and

1932, Dec. 1) feature photos and some text of Red Rocks and the Willsboro Tunnel.

Burnhams. 146.01 miles at the switch. Elevation 170. Maps 11-8 and 11-29.

Just a short distance north of the Highby Brook trestle was Burnhams, a dead-end stub track shown on a 1928 D&H track schematic. The function of this stub is unknown.

Douglass. 149.90 miles. Elevation 197. Maps 11-8, 11-9, and 11-30.

Passenger station: This station appeared sometime between the timetables of June 25, 1893 and October 2, 1898. The original name for this community on maps dating from 1874 or earlier through 1891 was Port Douglass, but when the D&H opened their station here, the "Port" was deleted from the name. The station closed between April 26, 1959 and April 24, 1960. Gardner (1990, Volume 4, page 47) notes that the shelter in the photo was built in 1911, but that it had replaced an original open shack located about one-half mile to the north.

Passing siding: In 1928 through at least 1962, the siding here was called Rockland. It held 71 cars in 1940 and 128 cars in 1950 and 1962. In 1928, it began at milepost 149.15 and ended at 149.83. In 1969, the extended south end at milepost 148.61 was called RW Cabin and the north end at milepost 149.83 RK cabin.

Fuel storage tanks: Several large tanks today mark the far north end of the Douglass area, but no railroad stub serves them.

Port Kent. 154.46 miles. Elevation 139. Maps 11-9 and 18-1.

Passenger station: Gardner's (1990, Volume 4, page 47) photo caption states that this combination passenger and freight station was built in 1875-1876. There was an alteration to the building in 1904 and the canopy extended in 1911. The building was removed probably between 1962 and 1969. Amtrak trains began stopping here all year from 1974 through October 29, 1983, then summers only from 1984 through the present primarily to meet the ferries to and from Burlington, Vermont. An open, but canopied, waiting shelter was constructed by Amtrak in May 1995. A photo of the station shows a sign at the north end of the building as 154.46 miles, yet the D&H *Official List No. 57* (1941) places Port Kent at 154.31.

Passing siding: A passing siding was here in 1928 from milepost 154.15 to 154.71. It held 57 cars in 1940 and 54 in 1950. It was gone by 1962, although a dead end stub track remained as late as 1977.

Facilities: A water tank stood south of the depot and a stock pen west of it along a spur track.

Keeseville, Ausable Chasm & Lake Champlain Railroad: This branch line, with detail presented in Chapter 18, diverged here.

Photographs: Shaughnessy (1967) presents some on pp. 260, 378, 381, 396, 400, and 418. Zimmermann (1978) includes some on pp. 39, 40, and 50.

North of Port Kent: At about milepost 155 are several hopper cars deliberately overturned and dumped to stabilize the steep bank along the lake from collapse; I first noticed them in 1977, and they are still visible down the embankment on the east. Just south of the Essex-Clinton County Line near milepost 156 is Wickham Marsh, west of the track and of botanical interest. At 157.21 and 157.35 miles are the twin spans across the Ausable River, built in 1909 and 1913; the D&H hops across an island here.

Valcour. 160.88 miles. Elevation 157. Maps 11-9 and 19-6.

Passenger station: Gardner's (1990, Volume 4, page 48) photo caption states that this combination freight and passenger station was built in 1875-1876. It was moved to Whallonsburg to replace the station which burned there on December 1, 1887. A second combination station was built at Valcour in 1888 and altered in 1910. It closed between the timetables of April 26, 1936 and June 7, 1938. I have been informed that this second building had been moved to the southeast corner of Laphams Mills Road and Rock Street and is now a private residence; I have not confirmed this.

Facilities: two stock pens.

Double track: At 160.60 miles began doubletrack which used to run clear to Plattsburgh in 1928, although by 1977 it began at South Junction and ran only to BU Cabin at milepost 165.21.

Model railroad: At about 159.8 miles is a private home on the east side with its backyard adjacent to the D&H. Until about 1990, this backyard accommodated a disconnected outdoor narrow gauge railroad which had been known by various names including the Kinney Junction, T.K.& P., and the Kinney & Palmer Railroad.

South Junction. 162.80 miles. Elevation 147. Maps 11-10 and 19-6.

Passenger station: A junction was built at milepost 162.77 in 1894 when the Ausable Branch (Chapter 19) was relocated (originally, the junction was at milepost 166.65). The South Junction station must have opened in 1894 and was certainly in service by 1898. Trains still stopped here according to the June 23, 1935 timetable. By September 29, 1935 and April 26, 1936, the station was still listed, but no longer did any trains stop here. By the June 7, 1938 timetable, the station was no longer listed.

Double trackage: In 1928, the mainline was doubletracked through here from Valcour to Plattsburgh. By 1977, SJ Cabin at milepost 162.35 marked the south end of a much shorter doubletracked segment.

Facilities: At 162.56 miles was the huge coaling plant built in 1922 and illustrated in Shaughnessy (1967, p. 422), in D&H (1925, p. 476), and in the *D&H Railroad Bulletin* (1927). The coaling tower stood until the end of steam, still present in 1950 but gone by 1962. A water tank was nearby to the southeast at 162.47.

Chateaugay Branch: Chateaugay Branch freight trains began to use South Junction in 1955, and still do, on their way up to Otis Junction and the Freydenburg Falls spur (see Chapter 20).

Bluff Point. 164.20 miles. elevation 144. Maps 11-10 and 19-6.

Passenger station: Gardner's (1990, Volume 4, page 63) photo caption states that the passenger station was built in 1890 and a canopy over the platform in 1899. The June 22, 1890 timetable does list it. Ausable Branch trains stopped here beginning in 1894 and Chateaugay Branch trains beginning in 1903. Apparently, Bluff Point was a summer stop only for D&H Mainline trains. The name listed on the timetables from 1898 through 1927 was "Bluff Point-Hotel Champlain." The April 2, 1928 timetable still lists the station but, because it was off-season, no longer indicates any trains stopping here. By July 2, 1928, the timetable no longer lists Bluff Point.

Facilities: The 1941 D&H *Official List No. 57* indicates track scales for weighing cars at Bluff Point but I cannot find the site.

Chateaugay Branch: The junction with the standard-gauge Chateaugay Branch from 1903 through 1955 was via a wye with the north switch on the mainline at milepost 164.18. See Chapter 20.

Hotel Champlain: Up the hill and east of the station on Bluff Point bluff was the Hotel Champlain which burned on May 25, 1910 (D&H, 1925, pp. 306 and 359 with photos). Shaughnessy (1967, p. 261) also offers a photo at Bluff Point. Today, the hotel site is marked by Clinton County Community College.

Industrial sidings: The former Chateaugay Branch wye still persists as a stub onto the Air Force Base after the Chateaugay Line was rerouted via South Junction in 1955. At 163.45 miles in 1928 was the Bluff Point Stone Company spur; in 1977 it served a bottled gas plant. At 163.95 miles in 1928 was the Vermont Marble Company spur.

Tree nursery: A photo of the tree nursery at Bluff Point appears on page 456 of D&H (1925). See Chapter 20, the segment on Middle Kilns and Wolf Ponds, for information on the plantations.

Plattsburgh Traction Company: Cars of this trolley line stopped near Bluff Point Station from 1895 to 1929 (Borrup, 1971). See Chapter 19.

Cliff Haven. 164.68 miles. Elevation 142. Maps 11-10 and 19-6.

Passenger station: Gardner's (1990, Volume 4, page 63) photo caption indicates that the station was built in 1902 and enlarged in 1908. The April 2, 1928 timetable lists it as "Cliff Haven, Summer Catholic School." After the very nearby Bluff Point station closed, the Cliff Haven station was listed in the July 2, 1928 timetable as "Cliff Haven (Bluff Point)," serving both localities. Cliff Haven station remained open only during the summers through 1944. By 1945, the summer timetable no longer lists it.

BU Cabin: At 165.21 miles in 1969 marked BU Cabin, the north end of double trackage. Double trackage as late as 1950 extended all the way to Plattsburgh.

Junction with original Ausable Branch and narrow gauge Chateaugay Railroad. 166.65 miles. Elevation 140. Maps 11-10 and 19-4.

See Chapters 19 and 20 for an explanation of this unnamed junction. Here the original Ausable Branch diverged from 1875 through 1894 and the narrow gauge Chateaugay Railroad from 1878 through 1903.

Plattsburgh. 167.51 miles. Elevation 112. Maps 11-10, 19-3, 19-4, 19-5, and 19-9.

Passenger station, facilities, yards, industries, and photographs: See Chapter 19 on the Ausable Branch for detail. The D&H *Official List No. 57* (1941) places Plattsburgh at 167.40 miles south of the Dock Street grade crossing. Careful measurements of more detailed valuation diagrams tying in with milepost 167 place the depot at 167.51 miles.

BT Cabin. 168.80 miles. Elevation 114. Maps 11-10 and 19-9.

The north end of industrial sidings in 1928 was here. At 168.9 miles in 1969 was BT Cabin, marking the north end of the industrial area at that time. At 170 miles, the track begins to climb again northward from elevation 104.

Beekmantown. 171.64 miles. Elevation 148. Maps 11-11 and 11-31.

Passenger station: Gardner's (1990, Volume 4, page 67) photo caption states that this station was built in 1852 and burned on July 20, 1912. An old passenger coach, removed from the track and propped up on a foundation, replaced it (on the same site) in 1912. The station closed sometime between the timetables of June 29, 1930 and June 28, 1931. The D&H *Official List No. 57* (1941) places Beekmantown at 171.48 miles or well south of the Burke Road grade crossing; this disagrees with a detailed 1914 valuation diagram which places the station north of the 171.63 grade crossing.

Passing siding: A short one was located here in 1928 from 171.55 to 171.69 miles. The two stubs were not yet present in 1914 but were in place by 1928. The passing siding and stubs were long gone by 1992.

Facilities: stock pen and coal shed of Ralston & Howes.

Spellmans. 173.42 miles. Elevation 200. Maps 11-11 and 11-32.

Passenger station: This station opened between the timetables of June 24, 1900 and June 24, 1906. It closed between the timetables of June 29, 1930 and June 28, 1931.

Passing siding: In 1928, a passing siding began at milepost 173.23 and ended at 173.80. It held 50 cars in 1942. It was gone by 1950.

West Chazy. 176.83 miles. Elevation 256. Maps 11-11 and 11-33.

Passenger station: Gardner's (1990, Volume 4, page 67) informs us that the combination station was built in 1852, moved in 1907 and then remodeled as a freight house. The original name was Chazy, but the name was changed to West Chazy in 1876 when the new line through Rouses Point and the Village of Chazy opened. A new passenger station was completed in 1907. The station closed between the timetables of April 24, 1960 and July 23, 1960. Today both passenger and freight stations still stand; this writer was most pleased and surprised in 1992 to see the following sign adjacent to the depot: "c. 1852 Plattsburgh-Montreal RR Sta. Built c. 1852 as Chazy. 1876 became West Chazy. 2nd station built 1905-1907. Chazy Friends of the Library." (All communities with extant stations should follow this example in preserving their depots!)

Passing siding: One was already here by 1928 from milepost 176.65 to 177.78. It held 119 cars in 1940 when it was named CY Siding. In 1950 and 1962 it held 105 cars. In 1969, the south end of it was named CY Cabin and the north end MB Cabin. It no longer exists in 1992.

Facilities: two stock pens.

Industrial siding: A dead-end stub track, probably a remnant of the former passing siding, still exists at West Chazy adjacent to the Nutrena Feeds-Beacon Feed Service-Cargill Hybrid Seed Sales building; personnel in the building told me that the railroad no longer served them in 1992.

Ketcham Bridge: At milepost 176.36 as recently as the late 1970s existed a narrow, old wooden bridge which carried Ketcham Bridge Road over the D&H main. A new grade crossing, first observed by this writer in 1992, replaced the old bridge sometime in the 1980s.

Subsummit: Here is another on the D&H, the mainline descending in both directions from West Chazy.

Canada Junction. Approximately 178 miles. Elevation 248. Maps 11-11 and 11-33.

A short distance north of what was MB Cabin in 1969 had been a junction from 1876 through 1925. The original line via Mooers Junction to Plattsburgh was built in 1852 (See Chapter 21), and the present line via Rouses Point not until 1876. Both lines operated until 1925 when the older Mooers Branch was abandoned. The Mooers Branch crossed Riley's (Slosson) Road about 0.2 mile west of the present D&H Mainline. At milepost 179, the existing Mainline begins the downgrade northbound from elevation 249 to Chazy and Cooperville.

Chazy. 183.16 miles. Elevation 159. Maps 11-12 and 11-34.

Passenger station: Gardner's (1990, Volume 4, page 68) states that a combination station was built in 1876, but moved in 1910 and remodeled as a freight house. A new Spanish-style stone depot was built in 1910 on the site of the combination station; the same photo of the 1910 depot appears in D&H (1925, page 460). It was in service until sometime between the timetables of April 24, 1960 and July 23, 1960. Both the depot and freight station still existed in 1994. The D&H *Official List No. 57* (1941) places Chazy at 183.01 miles well to the south of the 183.12 Route 9 underpass; however, the station is north of the underpass.

Passing siding: One existed here in 1928 from milepost 182.61 to 183.37. It held 88 cars in 1940, and 80 in 1942 and 1950, but it was removed by 1962.

Facilities: The 1941 D&H *Official List No. 57* indicates two stock pens.

Industrial sidings: Two dead-end stubs still exist in 1994, but are disconnected from the mainline. They had served the former freight house, now occupied by Winterbottom Feeds. At milepost 182.40, a spur once headed east, crossed U.S. Highway 9, and terminated nearly two miles from the mainline in a limestone quarry. In 1928 and 1950 the quarry was operated by the Chazy Marble Lime Company, but in 1962 and 1969 the operator had become the Chazy International Lime & Stone Corporation. A six-page untitled 1933 travel/freight pamphlet published by the D&H includes a photo of the 12-kiln lime plant with a yearly capacity of 36,000 tons. When the author visited the site in 1989, the spur, as well as the quarry it had served, had been abandoned for some time.

Cooperville. 186.90 miles. Elevation 115. Maps 11-12 and 11-35.

Passenger station: Gardner's (1990, Volume 4, page 69) photo caption tells us that the original combination station was built in 1876 but burned in 1924. The Sciota station, along the Mooers Branch which was abandoned that year, was moved to Cooperville and placed on the same site as the original depot. The station closed sometime between the timetables of January 6, 1929 and April 27, 1930. In 1940 and 1942 the locality was called Windsor. The D&H *Official List No. 57* (1941) places Cooperville at 186.75 miles, but a check in the field suggests that it was about 0.15 mile north of this.

CV Cabin: In 1950 and 1969, the south end of double trackage at milepost 186.73 was called CV Cabin. The double trackage was already present by 1928 and extended to Rouses Point.

NR Cabin: At milepost 189.39, elevation 150, was NR Cabin in 1950 and 1962, at a crossover between the two tracks of the D&H mainline and the south end of Rouses Point Yard.

Photographs: Zimmermann (1978) has two on pages 7 and 39.

Rouses Point. 190.95 miles. Elevation ca. 140. Maps 11-12 and 11-36.

Passenger station: Gardner's (1990, volume 4, page 70) photo caption indicates that the original combination station was built in 1877. In 1889 it was moved and converted into a freight house. Amtrak trains still stop at the present depot with the stone turret, built in 1889. The D&H *Official List No. 57* (1941) places Rouses Point at 190.78 miles, at the Chapman Street crossing two blocks south. Milepost 191 is immediately north of the customs building and could not be as far as 0.22 mile from the depot; in the field 0.05 mile seems more accurate.

Rutland Railroad: At milepost 191.09 was the crossing, with interchange tracks, of the Ogdensburg & Lake Champlain (later the Rutland Railroad). The latter opened in 1850 to Ogdensburg, the earliest railroad in northern New York (see Chapter 23 on the Rutland at Moira).

Napierville Junction and Canadian National Railways: North of the crossing, the D&H splits: the Napierville Junction Railway, built in 1906 and owned by the D&H, heads north-northwest, while the Canadian National Railway, built in 1876, heads north-northeast. At 192.05 miles is the Quebec border.

Photographs: There are many: Shaughnessy (1967, pp. 142, 171, 277, 304, 310, 383, 389, 398, 401, and 417), Zimmermann (1978, pp. 7, 13, 24, 39, 45, 50, and 68), Sweetland (1992, pages 68-73), and Plant and Plant (1993, page 46).

Servicing facilities: Rouses Point marked the north end of the Champlain Division. Facilities were elaborate over the years. In 1940 the roundhouse had seven stalls; it still stands in 1994, along with the adjacent sand tower, both abandoned in 1991. The

1941 D&H *Official List No. 57* indicates a 100-foot electric turntable, three stock pens, a coaling crane, a water tank, and ice storage within the roundhouse. Diesel servicing facilities came later.

Industrial sidings: Employees' timetables from 1940, 1950, and 1962 list the Inter-Provincial Lumber Company tracks.

Customs: *D&H RR Bulletin* (1930, Dec. 15; 1931, May 1; 1936, Aug. 1; 1936, Dec. 1) include articles about both Canadian and United States Customs.

Recent references: Manor (1991 and 1992) discusses the present status of the Rouses Point yard and the sale of the D&H to the Canadian Pacific Railway, respectively.

Equipment

Because the line from Whitehall to Rouses Point is part of the D&H mainline, almost any kind of locomotive (except the very largest articulateds on the tight curves at Red Rocks) and car could run along it. See any of the major references on the D&H for rosters and photos of equipment, e.g. Shaughnessy (1967), Zimmermann (1978), D&H (1925), Sweetland (1992), Plant and Plant (1993), and the Bridge Line Historical Society Bulletins (1991 to the present).

Timetable Operation

This can easily be reconstructed with a complete set of D&H, later Amtrak, timetables over the years. (An analysis here could fill a separate volume and would be beyond the realm of this treatment.)

Purchase by the Canadian Pacific

The first offer by the Canadian Pacific to purchase the financially-ailing D&H was on February 9, 1990. The actual purchase did not take place until January 1991 (see Manor, 1991 and 1992).

Legend to Map 11-13: Whitehall

Mileposts from south to north:

73.92 KG Cabin, south end of double trackage.
75.53 Crossover near weighing station.
76.68 Divergence of old and new mainlines at south end. Relocation construction began in late 1931 or early 1932 and was completed shortly after March 1934.
76.84 Crossover.
77.29 Crossover to south end of new (1934) wye.
77.39 Whitehall depot, built 1898.
77.48 New overpass of Highway 4 and north end of new wye. The old wye continued west and connected with the old mainline on Main Street. The 1898 depot sat in the middle of the old wye. The north leg of the new wye I have been informed was removed in the spring of 1994, but I have not yet been able to confirm this.
77.91 South portal of old 677- to 682-foot-long, single-track tunnel, and the divergence of old and new mainlines, north end, just south of Saunders Street.
77.92 South portal of new, 1934, 241-foot-long double-track tunnel under Saunders and Division Streets.
77.96 North portal of new tunnel.
78.04 North portal of old tunnel, between Clinton Avenue and Bellamy Street.
78.09 Junction with spur to Whitehall Harbor.
78.62 SC Cabin. North end of double trackage.
79.30 Lake Station. End of Saratoga Division and beginning of Champlain Division. Terminus of railroad from 1851 to 1875.

Buildings and Facilities from south to north:

A. Weighing station.
B. New 1934 freight yard west of Tub Mountain. 13 tracks. Yard area indicated by cross-hatching and not by precise trackage.
C. Yard office.
D. Coal tower.
E. Roundhouse and turntable.
F. Yards shown with cross-hatching because exact track plans are not available (Do not confuse cross-hatch lines with trackage). Diesel yard (about 5 tracks) with two fueling towers on west and caboose yard (about 6 tracks) on east.
G. Shop.
H. Old water tower. Still present in 1950.
I. Diesel fuel oil storage tank.
J. Section house?
K. Site of first, 1850 depot torn down in 1890-1893 era. Between the old (K) and new (M) depots was a yard of at least 13 tracks, removed during the relocation of the mainline in 1933-1934.
KK. Second freight house was built in 1890 probably just south-southwest of the first depot site.
L. Water plug, mainly for southbound trains.
M. Site of first, 1850 freight house, moved back to the east in 1892 and used as a store house by the main-

tenance-of-way department. Second depot built on this site in 1892-1893 and burned April 28, 1987 by Whitehall Fire Department.

N. New water tower. Already present in 1943, probably built after 1934 wye relocation (see R).
O. Foreman's office.
P. Passenger ramp leading down to main platform with canopy.
Q. Four passenger platforms without canopy, not all in service simultaneously.
R. The original pre-1934 wye, shown as a dashed line on Map 11-13, extended further west to join the original mainline.
S. Water plug, mainly for northbound trains.
T. Present Amtrak waiting shed.
U. Present bridges over barge canal on Rutland Branch built 1909.
V. D&H caboose in a park. The new 1934 mainline is just west of the caboose in an open cut. The original mainline, shown as a dashed line on Map 11-13, had run down the middle of Main Street and bisected the south end of Church Street.

Legend to Map 11-36: Rouses Point

D&H facilities:

A. Seven-stall roundhouse
B. Turntable
C. Shop?
D. Sand tower
E. Depot
F. U.S. Customs House
G. Diesel servicing area of yard
H. Grade crossing watchman's shanty

Rutland facilities:

I. Rouses Point Junction depot
J. Rouses Point depot (original)
K. Immigration Building (later depot)
L. Freight house
M. Water tank; site of early turntable and roundhouse in this vicinity
N. Section house
O. Strong & Casey coal & ice
P. Chateaugay Oil Company
Q. Milk station (creamery): S. C. Millet, then Rutpro Corp., finally Bordens----with coal shed & ice house
R. Trestle across Lake Champlain to Vermont: Rutland Railroad with Central Vermont Railroad gauntlet track

Central Vermont facilities:

S. Freight house (joint with Canadian National)
T. Open freight platform
U. Stock pen

Interchange points:

V. Central Vermont----Canadian National
W. Rutland----Canadian National
X. Rutland----Napierville Junction
Y. Delaware & Hudson----Canadian National
Z. Delaware & Hudson----Napierville Junction (a subsidiary of the D&H).

Napierville Junction Railway facility:

AA. Roundhouse and turntable at an early date

MAP 11-1 DELAWARE & HUDSON MAINLINE

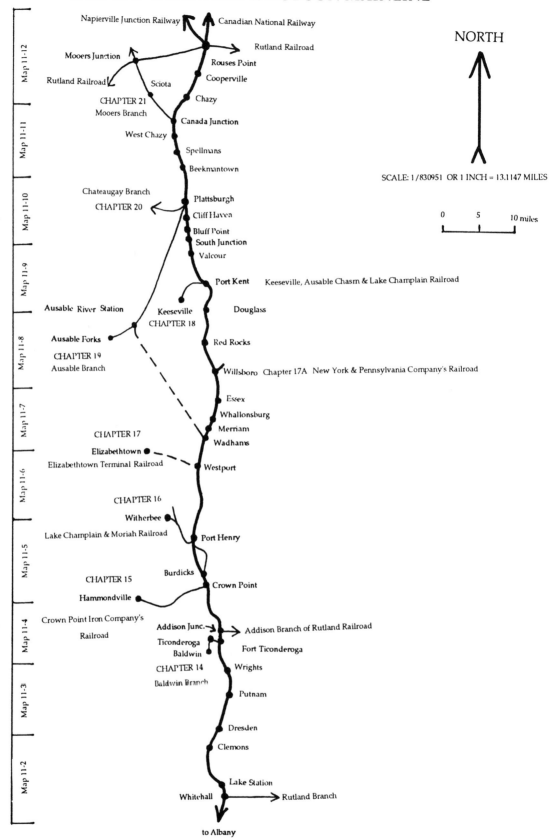

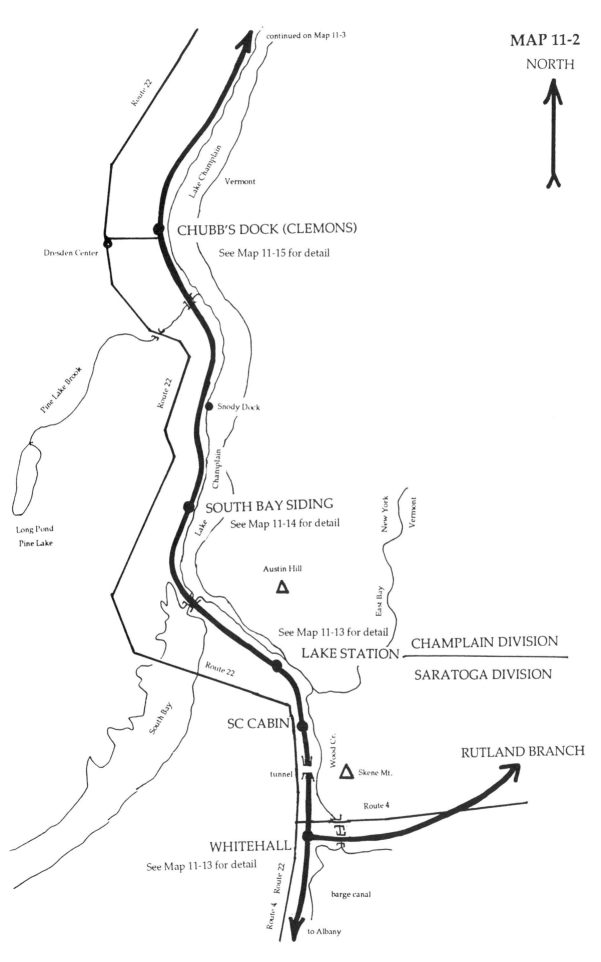

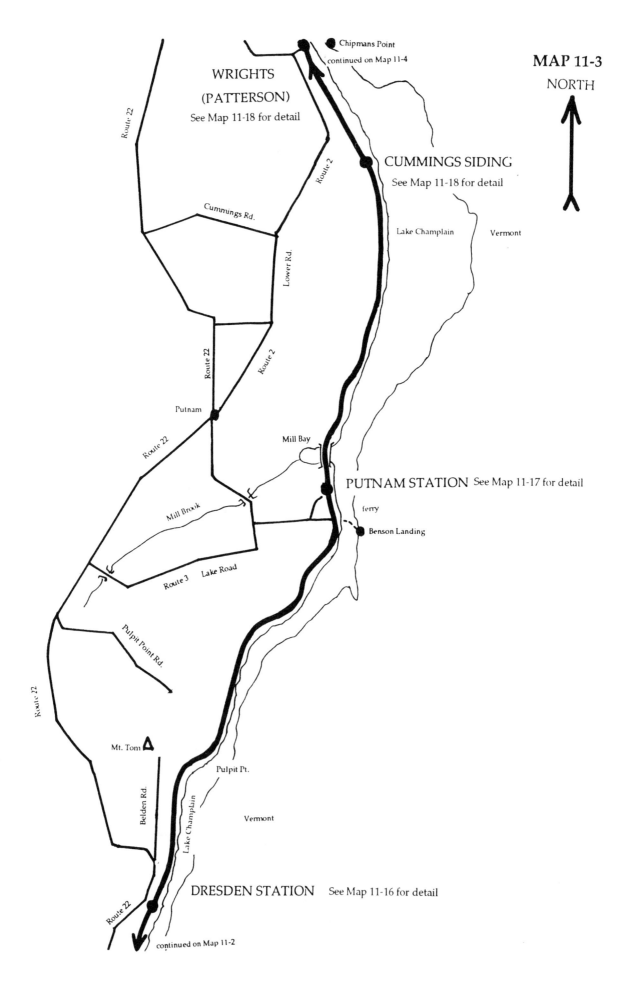

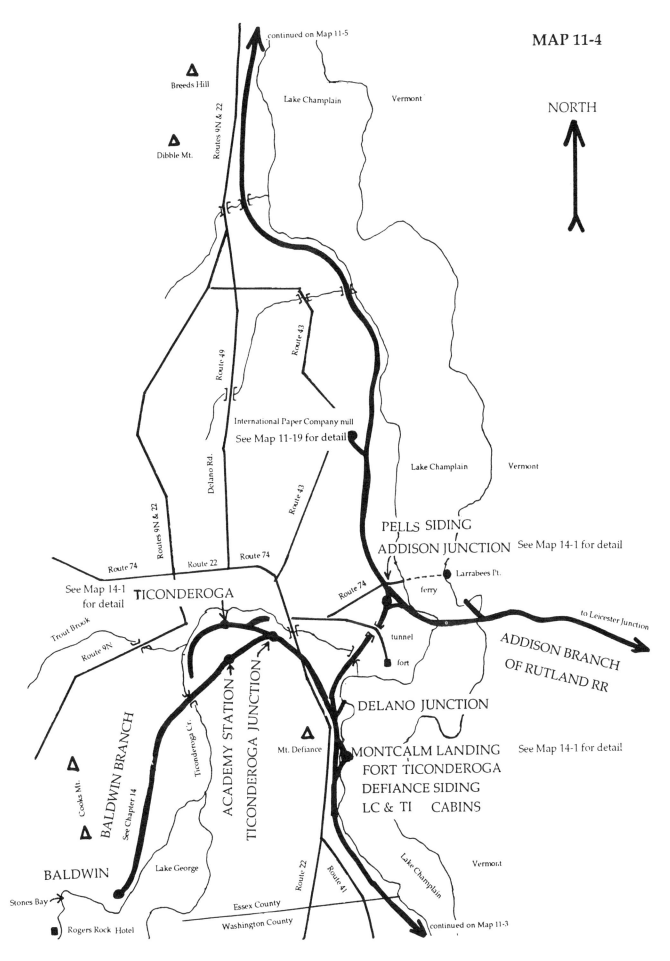

MAP 11-4

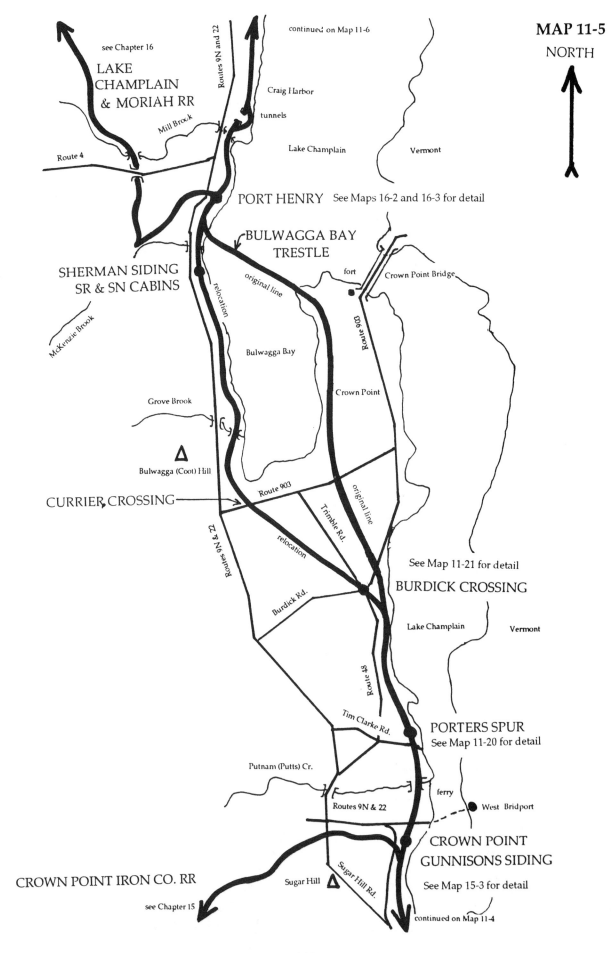

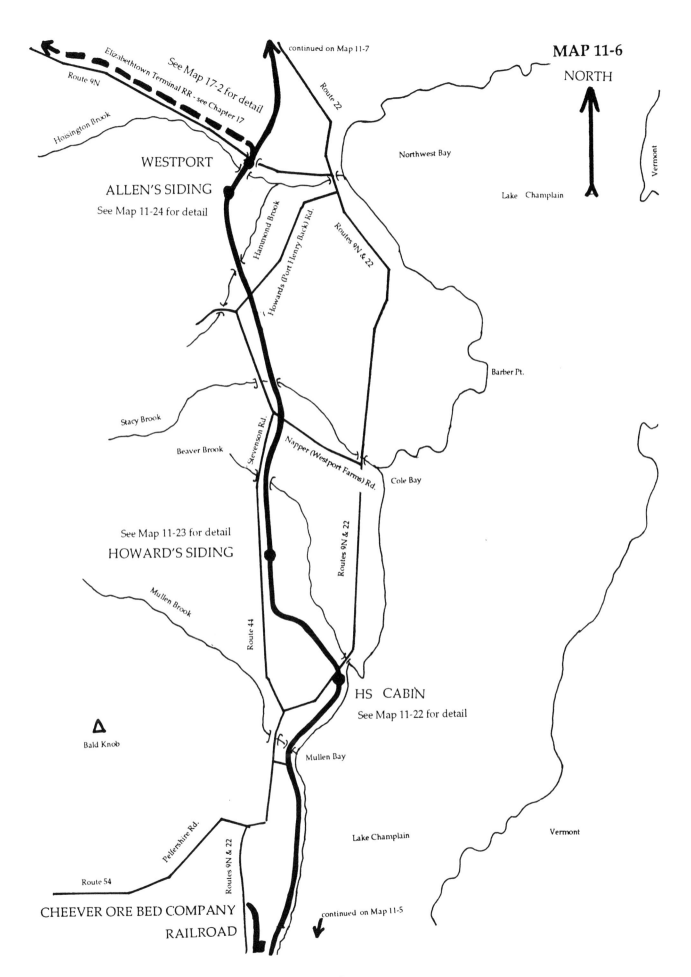

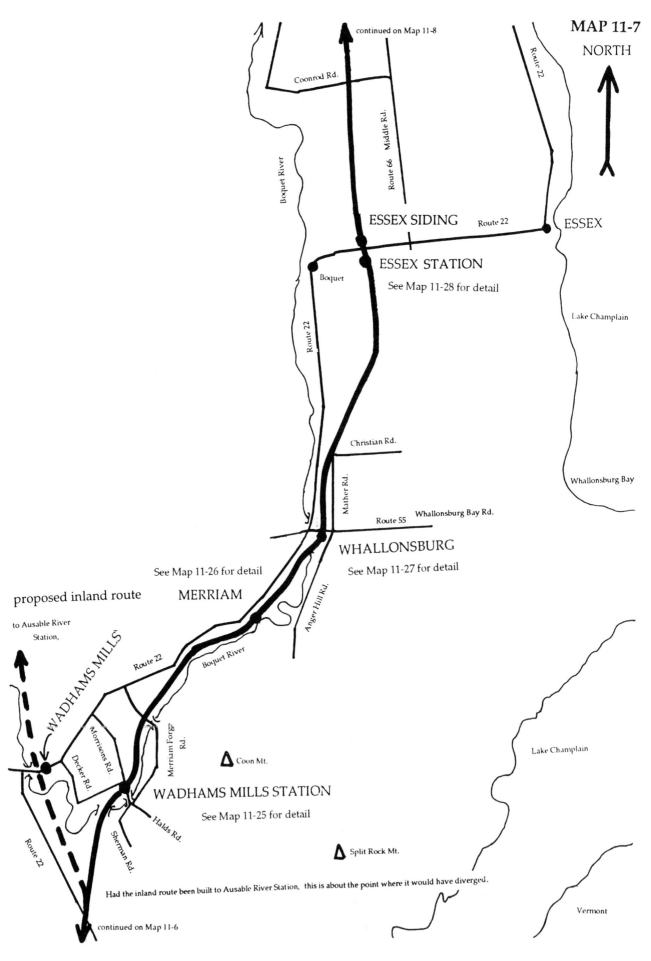

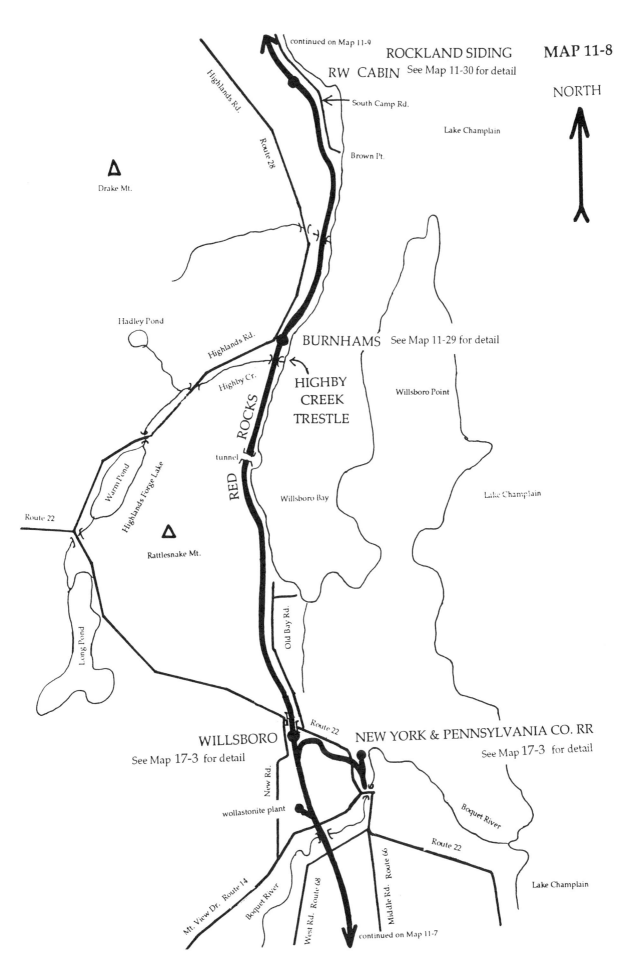

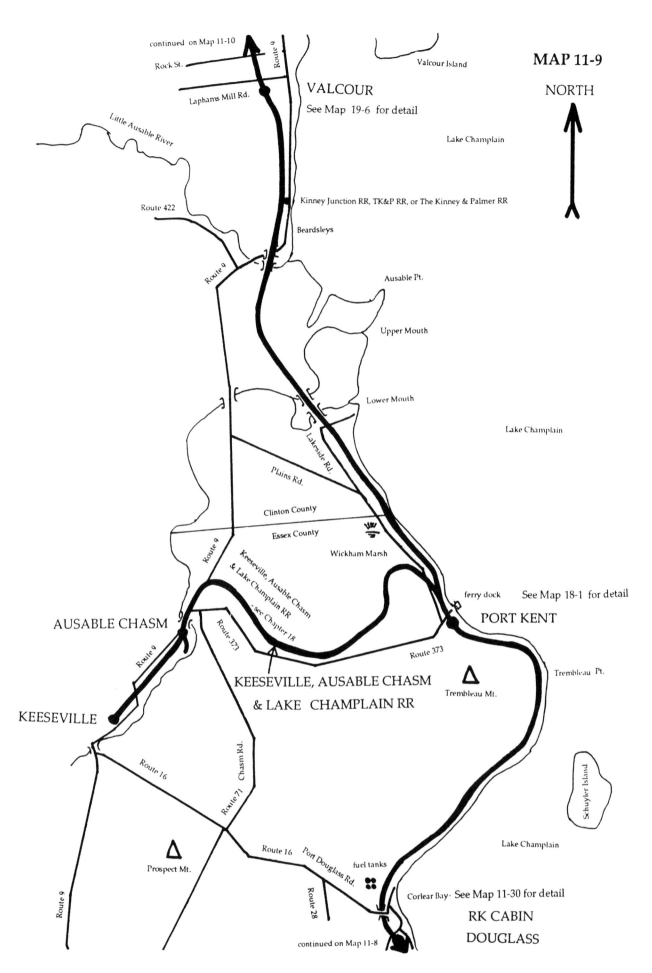

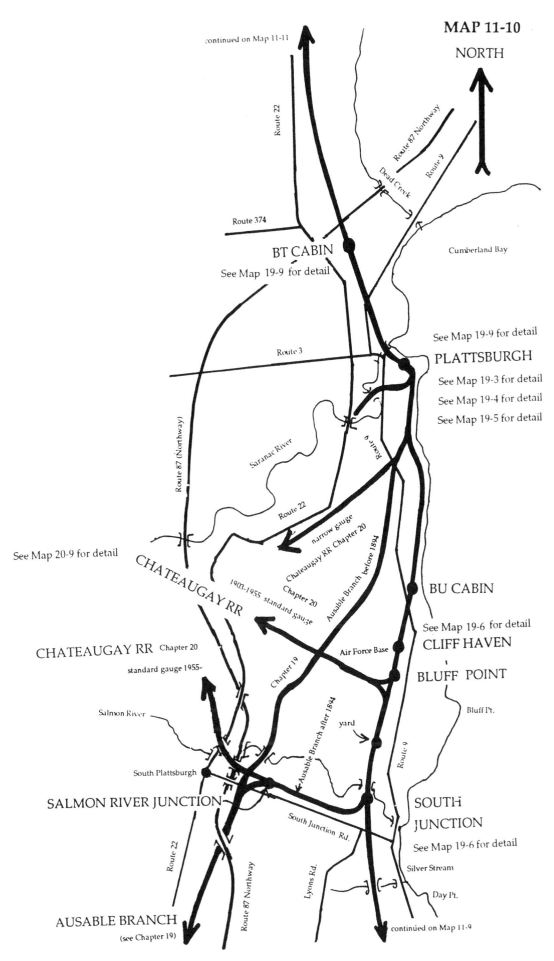

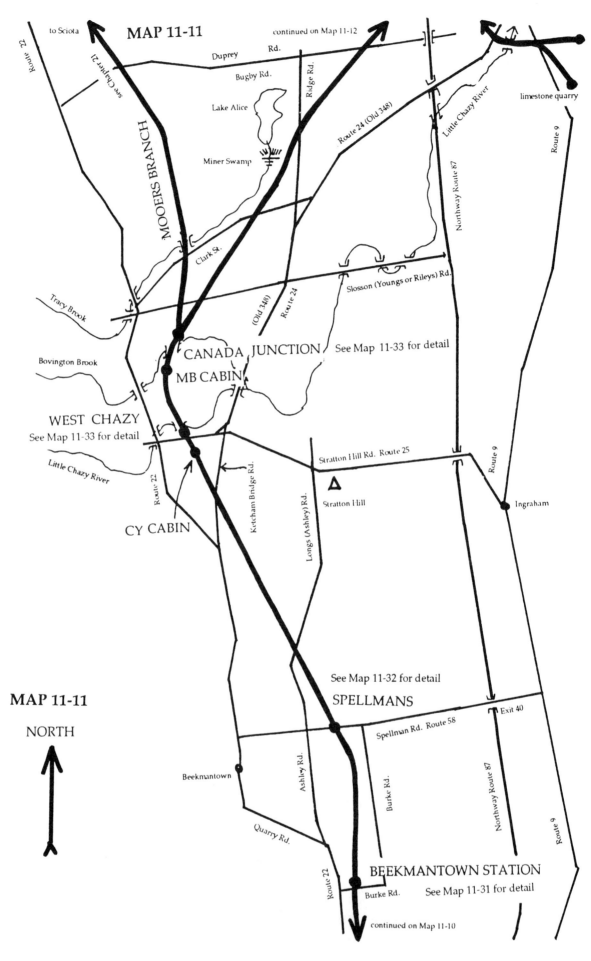

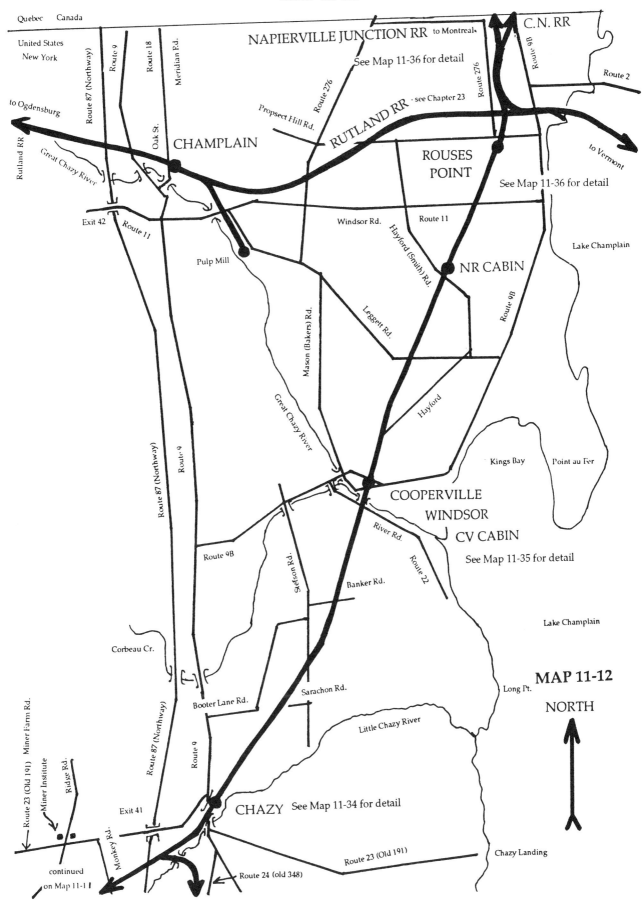

MAP 11-12

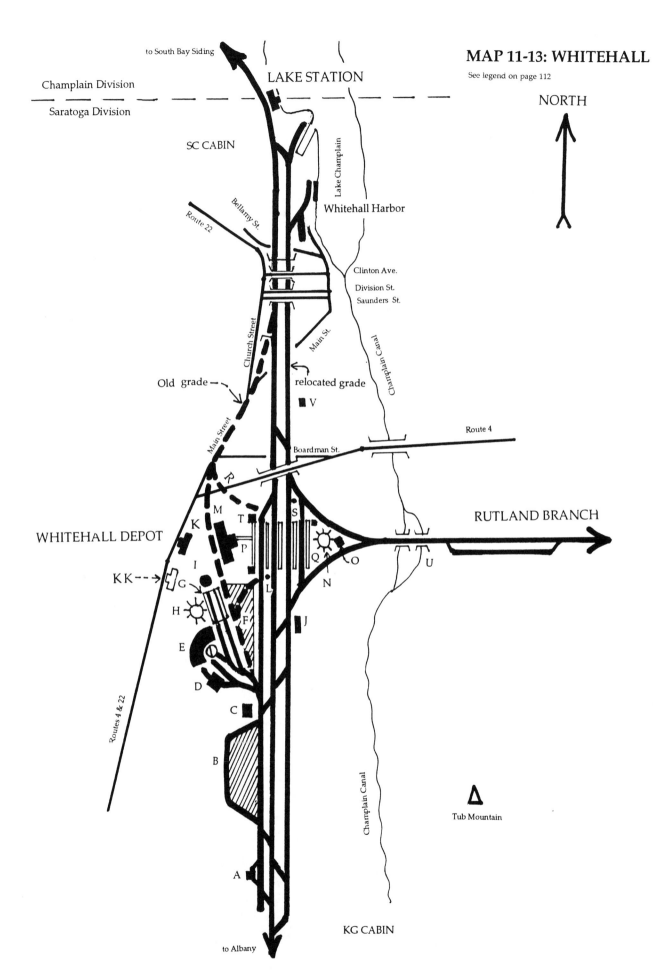

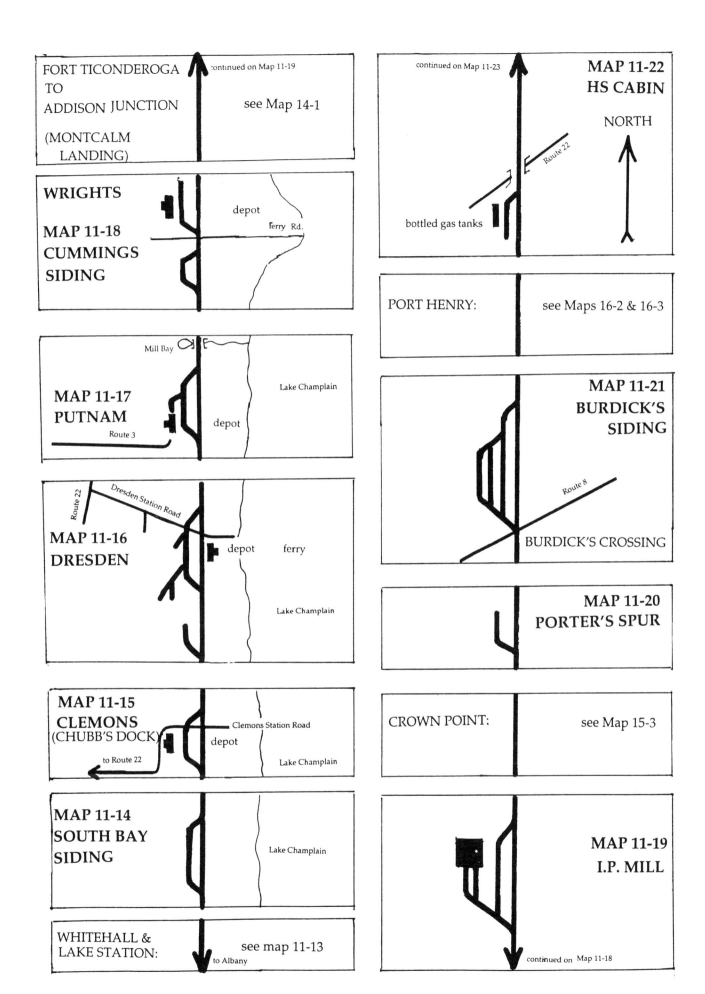

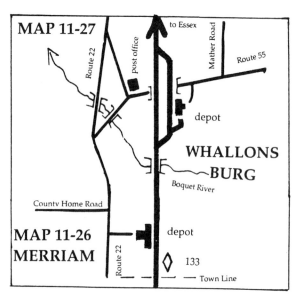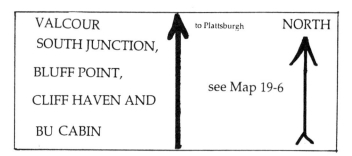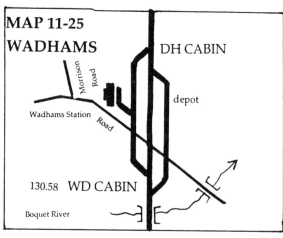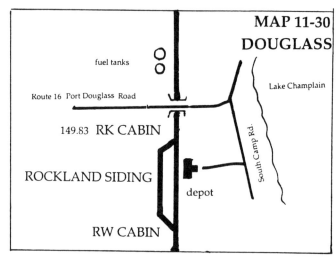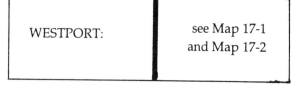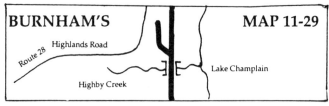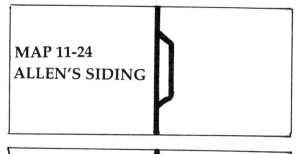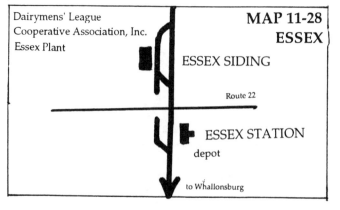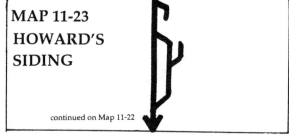

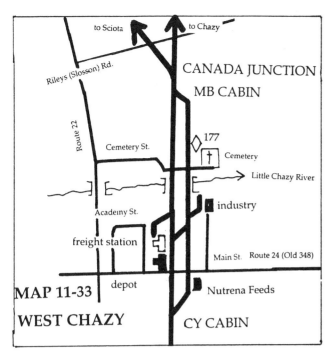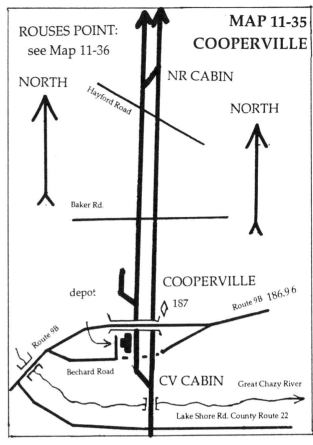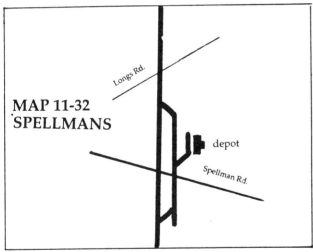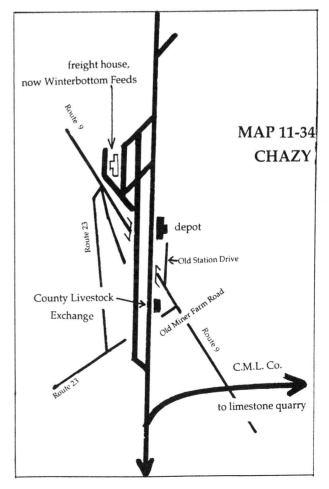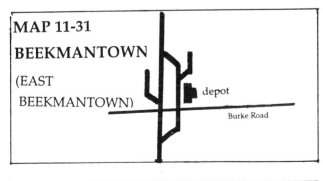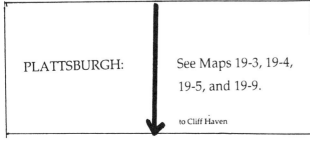

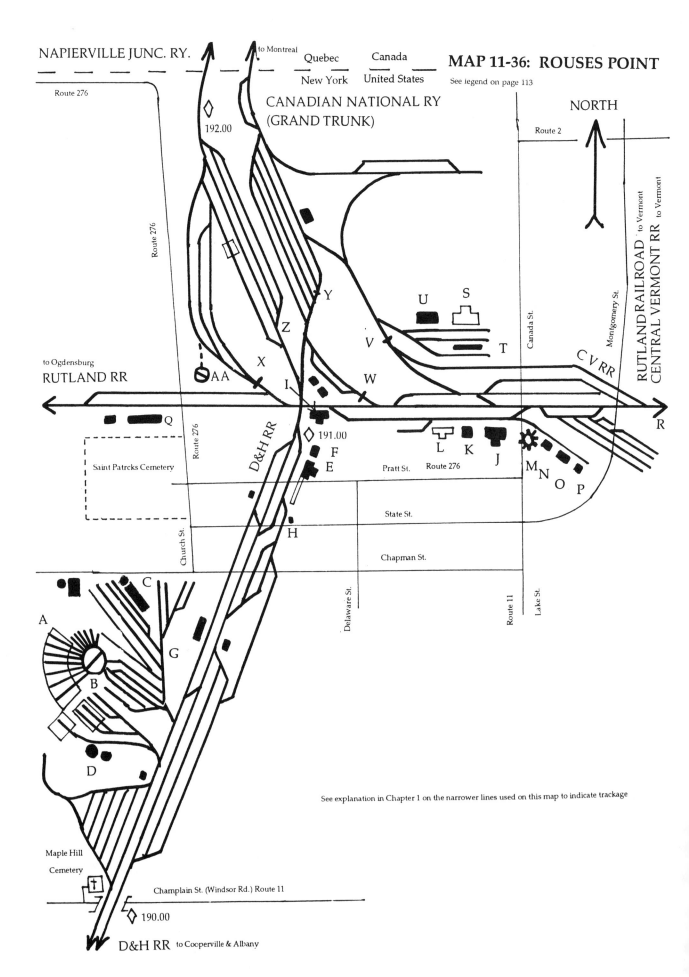

Chapter 12:
Adirondac Company's Railroad to North Creek

MUCH DETAIL on the Adirondac Company's railroad is presented in Hochschild (1961), and Shaughnessy (1967, Chapter 6, pp. 114-133). This line was the first to penetrate the interior of the Adirondack Mountains.

Construction

Construction began in 1865. One aim was to serve the iron mines at Sanford Lake (first realized in 1944!), and another to cross the Adirondacks to connect with the Great Lakes shipping at Ogdensburg (the latter aim never realized). Poor (1891) stated that the Adirondack Extension Railroad was incorporated May 1, 1891 to build a railroad from North Creek to Malone. This extension was never built to Malone, but slightly over a half-century later another extension plan did become realized to Tahawus.

By December 1, 1865 (Hochschild, 1961), trains terminated at Wolf Creek, Thurman in 1869, and Riverside in 1870. It was not until early 1871 that the first trains arrived in North Creek (Shaughnessy, pp. 121 and 296). One part of the Adirondac (the k was omitted from of their name) Company's contract was for completion of sixty miles of track from the original Saratoga Springs depot of the Rensselaer and Saratoga Railroad. North Creek was at 57.14 miles so that a 2.86-mile-long extension was built past North Creek Station and not used until 1944! The leading figure in the construction of this line was Dr. Thomas C. Durant; he was to the North Creek Line what Hurd was to the Northern Adirondack, and Webb to the Mohawk & Malone.

In 1889 the Adirondac Company's Railroad was sold to the D&H (Hochschild, 1961, p. 12). In 1959 the D&H Railroad mainline was rerouted from downtown Saratoga Springs to the west edge of the City, thus shortening the North Creek Branch by about 0.7 mile.

Mileage

There is much confusion in the method used to determine mileages along the North Creek line. The cause of this confusion before 1959 lies in where one starts measuring: whether it is Albany, at the junction of the North Creek Line with the D&H Main Line 0.45 mile south of the original Rensselaer & Saratoga Railroad depot, or at the depot itself. More confusion occurs after 1959 because of the relocation of the D&H Mainline from downtown Saratoga Springs to the west edge of the City. This relocation created a new junction, called AD Cabin (Is AD short for "Adirondack"?) about 1.4 miles north of the original junction, shortening the North Creek branch by this distance. Still more confusion after 1959 lies in where one starts measuring: from the new Saratoga Springs depot (currently used by Amtrak) or from AD Cabin, about 1.4 miles north of the depot.

I have decided to use the mileage shown on a D&H blueprint-atlas, drawn in 1891 by a civil engineer-draftsman who supplied us only with his initials, W.E.A. This valuation diagram is entitled "Adirondack Railway from Saratoga to North Creek." Those mileposts remaining in the ground today along the North Creek line agree with this blueprint-atlas and not with the mileages indicated in many of the more recent D&H timetables.

Station Descriptions

Saratoga Springs. 38.30 miles from Albany. Elevation 300 feet. Map 12-2.

The Adirondac Company's Railroad shared the depot with the Rensselaer & Saratoga Railroad (later part of the D&H mainline). The station, mainline and junction with the North Creek branch were all relocated in 1959. Photos occur in Shaughnessy (1967, pages 114, 119, 361, 399, and 408); in Sweetland (1992, pages 38-41); in Plant and Plant (1993, pages 26 and 27); and in Gardner (1990, Volume 3, pages 42 and 43).

Abundant detail on Saratoga Springs is readily available in publications on the D&H Mainline, but it is not within the realm of this book to present it. However, permit me to add this note for those historians interested in Saratoga Springs. The old Hudson Valley Railway trolley terminal still stands in 1996 as the Visitor Center, at the southwest corner of Broadway and Congress Street. A photo appeared in D&H (1925, page 493).

Junction with D&H Mainline. 37.85 miles from Albany. Elev. 300 ft. Map 12-2.

This junction was 0.45 mile south of the original Rensselaer & Saratoga depot on the D&H Mainline in downtown Saratoga Springs.

AD Cabin. 39.45 miles. Elevation 360. Map 12-2.

When the D&H Mainline was relocated to the west edge of Saratoga Springs in 1959, the new junction with the North Creek line was named AD Cabin.

Greenfield. 43.68 miles. Elevation 600. Maps 12-2 and 12-10.

This was a station from 1875 or earlier. It closed sometime between the September 10, 1931 and the June 26, 1932 timetables.
The photo caption in Gardner (1990, Volume 3, page 43) indicates that the shelter was built in 1911. The passing siding began at 43.57 miles and ended at 43.73.

Kings. 47.22 miles. Elevation 600. Maps 12-2 and 12-11.

This was a station from 1875 or earlier. It closed sometime between the June 26, 1932 and April 1, 1933 timetables. The photo caption in Gardner (1990, Volume 3, page 43) indicates that the combination passenger and freight station was built in 1887. The passing siding began at 47.15 miles and ended at 47.26. DeMarco (1992), Town of Greenfield Historian, reports that the Kings Station has been completely restored for Delaware & Hudson Railway Day festivities on September 22, 1992.

South Corinth. 50.53 miles. Elevation 620. Maps 12-2 and 12-12.

This was a station from 1875 or earlier. It closed sometime between the April 1, 1933 and January 1934 D&H timetables. The photo caption in Gardner (1990, Volume 3, page 45) indicates that the waiting room was built in 1880; formerly it was a combination station. The passing siding began at 50.47 miles and ended at 50.65.

White's Sand. 52.46 miles. Elevation 635. Maps 12-3 and 12-13.

A facility at this point was located in 1969 for loading sand into locomotives. In 1990, an old concrete loading dock remained with a stub track, both visible from State Highway 9N just north of the grade crossing.

Corinth (Jessup's Landing). 54.46 miles. Elevation 641. Maps 12-3, 12-14 and 12-14A.

Passenger station: This was a station from 1875 or earlier through June 25, 1955 and probably to 1956. It was originally called Jessup's Landing through October 5, 1890, but by October 2, 1892 had become Corinth. The photo caption in Gardner (Volume 3, 1990, page 45) indicates that a combination passenger and freight station was built in 1865 and remodeled into a freight house in 1891. This station stood west of the tracks and had been removed well before 1990. The present passenger station, still standing in 1990 and east of the tracks, was built in 1910-1911. The caption does not state which building was used for a passenger station during the interval between 1891 and 1911.
Passing siding: There was a siding here in 1871 (Shaughnessy, 1967, p. 122) and a photo appears in the same reference on page 397. It began at 54.39

miles and ended at 54.59. In 1990 it still exists and is called "East Track."

Industrial sidings: There were several, including a station track, freight house track, coal storage pocket track, Hanfield Straight Track and Hanfield Back Track. The station track and Hanfield Straight Track were still used for switching cars headed to and from Palmer in 1990.

Palmer Branch: From Corinth at milepost 54.30 leads a branch to the International Paper Company Mill at Palmer, about 2.5 miles. This mill is an old one; it is already present on the Saratoga 1899 15-minute Quadrangle. A photo of it, with trackage, can be found in New York State Fisheries Game and Forest Commission (1896, page 505). It has been rebuilt, however, and still runs in 1996. Trains operate to here at present, the line north of Corinth having been abandoned in November 1989.

Hadley (Lake Luzerne). 59.43 miles. Elevation 640. Maps 12-3 and 12-15.

Passenger station: This was a station from 1875 or earlier through probably 1956. The photo caption in Gardner (1990, Volume 3, page 47) indicates that the combination passenger and freight house was built in 1870.

Stagecoach connections: In 1875, there were connections for Conklingville and the Sacandaga Valley, and omnibuses for the hotels at Luzerne. In 1912, there was an auto stage for Conklingville, Day, West Day, Edinburgh, and Batchellerville.

Passing siding: The siding at the station, shown in Shaughnessy (p. 131), began at 59.30 miles and ended at 59.51. A stub-ended remnant of it remained in 1990.

Sacandaga Switch: A turntable was located at milepost 58.99 with a siding in the early years.

Trestle: Photos in Shaughnessy (1967, pp. 128, 130, and 354) are of the high truss bridge over the Sacandaga River from milepost 59.02 to 59.13. This impressive 750-foot-long trestle was first made famous by Stoddard's photographs in the 19th century. Plant and Plant (1993, page 29) include a more recent photo.

Industrial siding: Thomas (1979, p.54) states: "Toward the end of the century and into the 1900s a large woodenware factory was operated in Hadley close to the railroad station. Novelty items such as pill boxes, toothpicks, and match sticks were manufactured here." (Did this factory use the passing siding directly or was there a separate stub track into the industry?)

Branch: The 15-minute Luzerne Quadrangle, surveyed in 1900-1903, indicates a two-track spur at Hadley heading down from a point south of the station (milepost 59.28) toward a dam on the Hudson River just above its confluence with the Sacandaga River. Thomas (1979, p. 58) tells us what industry the spur served, but fails to offer the exact year of the spur's construction and removal. The Rockwell Falls Fiber Company built a mill at the dam in 1878. Between 1887 and 1900 the mill was enlarged and then sold to the Union Bag and Paper Company. By 1900, the spur was already in place as shown on the Quadrangle, but its date of construction is unknown. In 1915 the mill was sold again, this time to the Nu-Era Paper Company for "several years." The final owner, New York Power and Light Company, razed most of the buildings in 1936. The railroad spur probably existed through the Nu-Era Paper Company's era to ca. 1930, but whether the tracks continued to serve the Power and Light Company is undocumented.

Sacandaga Reservoir: *D&H RR Bulletin* (1930, Dec. 1) described the construction of the Conklingville Dam and included a photo. A caption stated: "From two narrow gauge railroad tracks, dump cars bringing material loaded by steamshovels. . . ." No mention of any connection with the North Creek standard gauge line at Hadley, five miles away, is made.

Wolf Creek (Quarry Switch). 62.28 miles. Elevation 630. Maps 12-4 and 12-16.

Passenger station: This station did not yet exist by June 24, 1900, but was already present by June 24, 1906. It closed between June 26, 1932 and April 1, 1933. The station was probably located at the highway crossing at milepost 62.28, and not at the bridge over Wolf Creek, a tributary of the Hudson, at milepost 62.65.

Quarry Switch: An 1875 timetable lists Quarry Switch at 25 miles from Saratoga Springs (about milepost 63 from Albany), but it is not certain that this site or a nearby one became Wolf Creek Station.

Passing siding: Trains met here in 1888 requiring a passing siding.

Water tank: About 1891, one was on the west side of the track at milepost 62.22.

Stony Creek. 67.01 miles. Elevation 604. Maps 12-4 and 12-17.

Passenger Station: This was a station from 1875 or earlier through 1955 or 1956. The photo caption in Gardner (1990, Volume 3, page 47) indicates that the combination passenger and freight house was built in 1870. Shaughnessy (1967, page 128) includes a photo of the station.

Passing siding: This siding began at milepost 66.97 and ended at 67.16. A 400-foot-long spur diverged from the main at 67.35 and headed northwest almost to the highway.

Bridge: A photo in Shaughnessy, page 131, shows the bridge over Stony Creek at milepost 66.62.

Thurman. 72.72 miles. Elevation 618. Maps 12-5 and 12-18.

Passenger station: This was a station from 1875 or earlier through 1955 or 1956. The photo caption in Gardner (1990, Volume 3, page 51) indicates that the combination passenger and freight house was built in 1870. Shaughnessy (1967, page 132) includes the same photo but with far better clarity.

Stage connections: In 1875, stages departed for Warrensburg and coaches for Lake George. In 1912, a stage met trains for Warrensburg, and another for Athol.

Passing siding: The siding began at milepost 72.60 and ended at milepost 72.79. It was later lengthened southward to 72.54 and was still extant on October 12, 1985.

College Boys at Student Camp: Adey (1928, Aug. 15) described how eight old coaches were set off on an additional siding east of the main to house, feed, and train engineering students during the summer of 1928. They were surveying for a relocation of a portion of the line between Hadley and Thurman.

Servicing facilities: The 1941 D&H *Official List 57* includes a water tank at Thurman. It was at milepost 73.34.

Warrensburg Branch: This 3.39-mile-long branch diverged from milepost 72.54 and headed east for Warrensburg. Shaughnessy (1967, p. 226) says that it was built in 1905. This is confirmed by the double span truss bridge over the Hudson River which has the date, 1905, on it. Midway along the branch was a spur into the Warrensburg Board and Paper Company plant along the Schroon River. In the Village of Warrensburg were the following industries as I have gathered from remnants extant on August 2, 1992: A. C. Emerson Company selling D&H anthracite coal and lumber; Design Concepts: More than a Furniture Store (presently); Curtis Lumber & Building Materials; and possibly Pasco Feed and Coal. Gardner (1990, Volume 3, page 49) includes two photographs in Warrensburg. The caption of the first photo indicates that a waiting room resulted when old coach #43 was placed there in 1907. This puzzles me because I have not yet seen a timetable indicating passenger service into Warrensburg from the North Creek Branch; the Hudson Valley Electric Railway had been providing such a service since 1902. The second photo shows a converted box car with the caption "freight room."

Abandonment of the Warrensburg Branch must have taken place in 1980 or 1981 when the D&H abandoned several lines, including the Chateaugay Branch to Dannemora, the Ausable Branch, and the branch into Ticonderoga.

The Glen (Friends Lake). 81.18 miles. Elevation 749. Maps 12-5 and 12-19.

Passenger station: This was a station from 1875 or earlier through 1955 or 1956. The photo caption in Gardner (1990, Volume 3, page 51) indicates that the combination passenger and freight house was built in 1870. Shaughnessy (1967, pp. 126, 132, and 133) offered photos of the area and Plant and Plant (1993, page 5) include a recent photo near The Glen.

Stage connections: In 1912 carriages left The Glen for Friends Lake.

Passing siding: It began at milepost 81.09 and ended at 81.25. The bridge over Glen Creek was at 81.27.

Miscellany: Washburn's Eddy, between The Glen and Riverside, was never a station, but appeared on a map in Hochschild (1961, page 7) dated to 1882.

Riverside (Riparius Station). 87.06 miles. Elevation 885. Maps 12-6 and 12-20.

Passenger station: This was a station from 1875 or earlier through 1955 or 1956. The photo captions in Gardner (1990, Volume 3, page 53) indicate that a combination passenger and freight station was built in 1875, then moved (to a site unknown to me, possibly what is now the remains of Waddell's Feed Store) and rebuilt into a freight station in 1914. The present passenger station, extant in 1989, was built in 1913-1914, but I am puzzled. The present building has an open breezeway between the north waiting room portion and the south baggage portion. Yet the photo in Gardner does not show it. Was the breezeway added later?

Shaughnessy (1967, p. 126) has a photo of the original combination station.

Stage connections: In 1875 coaches met the trains for Chestertown, Pottersville, and the steamboats on Schroon Lake; stages met the trains for Wevertown and Johnsburgh. In 1888 Tally-Ho coaches departed for Schroon Lake and Pottersville. In 1908, stages met trains for Schroon Lake. In 1912, one stage headed for Pottersville and Schroon Lake, while a second headed for Chestertown, Horicon, and Brant Lake, and a third for Johnsburgh.

Passing siding: The siding begins at milepost 86.95 and ends at 87.11. It was still present in 1989.

Industrial sidings: Waddell's Feed Store and T. C. Murphy Lumber Company receiving dock (lumber trucked to Wevertown for sale) were just south of the station. About 0.7 mile south of the station, approximately at milepost 86.4, was the Northern Lumber Company sawmill; a nineteenth century combine of The Adirondac Company's Railroad had been used as an office and still stood deteriorating in the woods in 1992!

North Creek. 94.65 miles. Elevation 1028. Maps 12-6 and 12-21.

Passenger station: This was a station from early 1871 until cessation of passenger service in 1956. The existing station was not the original according to Bill Bibby, a local D&H employee and historian. The smaller original building sat in 1989 a short distance south of the existing station, but on the east side of the tracks; if this fact is confirmed, then this temporary depot existed only for one year: 1871-1872. The photo captions in Gardner (1990, Volume 3, page 55) indicate that the passenger station was built in 1872 and the freight house in 1903. Additional photos of North Creek abound: R. B. Miller (1956), Hochschild (1961, p. 10), Shaughnessy (1967, pp. 121, 133, 196, 312, 314, and 418), Sweetland (1992, page 60), and Plant and Plant (1993, page 28). Hotaling (1993) described the restoration of this historic depot. (Let us all breathe a big sigh of relief that some people are preserving it!) Murray (1995) updates us on the restoration.

Theodore Roosevelt: At North Creek, Theodore Roosevelt was sworn in as the 26th President of the United States on September 14, 1901. The *D&H RR Bulletin* (1929) included an article on engineer Frank A. Myers who pulled Roosevelt's Special train. Shaughnessy (1967) offers detail on this event on pages 196 and 199. An exhibit of this event exists as a scale model at The Adirondack Museum in Blue Mountain Lake.

Ski trains: *D&H RR Bulletin* (1935, Apr. 1 and 1938, Mar. 1) described these special ski trains. Pages 312 and 314 in Shaughnessy (1967) also contain photos of these ski trains, begun in March of 1934 when the New York State ski center at Gore Mountain opened. Kaplan (1991) wrote a more recent article on *The North Creek Ski Train* and provides detail on this service from 1934 through about 1941.

Stagecoach connections: Connections here were numerous. In 1875, stages departed for Minerva, North River, Indian River (Jackson's), and Cedar River Falls (Wakely's). Conveyances operated from Indian Lake to Blue Mountain Lake, and from Minerva to Newcomb, Long Lake, and Tahawus. In 1888 Tally-Ho coaches ran to Blue Mountain Lake with additional stage and boat connections there. In 1908 stages ran to Blue Mountain Lake. In 1912, stages departed for North River, Indian Lake, Blue Mountain Lake, and Long Lake. Stages also ran to Olmsteadville, Minerva, Alden Lair, and Newcomb.

Passing sidings: The long one had two crossovers in the middle and ranged from milepost 94.36 to 94.75.

Servicing facilities: At North Creek were a water tank, an ice house for passenger cars, a locomotive shop (rebuilt about 1944 or 1945 for diesels), a sand tower, a coal shack for caboose stoves, an oil tank for fueling steam locomotives, a 60-foot turntable, and a section house (see Map 12-21). An old wooden D&H milk refrigerator car, rebuilt ca. 1962 as tool maintenance car #30643, still sat in the locomotive shop in 1989! Cupp (1994), in the *Bridge Line Historical Society Bulletin* reports this car as # 30043 and offers detail on its trucks.

Industrial sidings: See Map 12-21. Included were Barton Mines garnet sheds, Finch Pruyn lumber, C. W. Sullivan Company Blue Seal Grain storage (currently a woodworking plant in part), W. R. Waddell Stores (Purina Chows, building supplies, and coal), a hoe handle factory (used later for garnet), and Great Eastern Lumber Company dry kiln dismantled by Torrington Concrete in 1989. The ore tipple at milepost 94.36 was for ilmenite, not garnet. It was a temporary facility in operation while the railroad was being extended to Tahawus during World War II, 1941-1944. The ilmenite was trucked by highway to North Creek where it was loaded into railroad cars. The back cover of Bourcier (1985) presents a portion of Beer's *1876 County Atlas of Warren, New York*, and includes some freight sidings south of the depot. Dr. Thomas C. Durant had two sawmills here in 1876 on the west side of the tracks and a lumber yard on the east.

National Lead Company Trackage. Milepost 0.0 (94.85 miles D&H). Elevation ca. 1030. Map 12-21.

From 1944 to 1989, here, 0.2 mile north of North Creek Station, were the end of Delaware & Hudson trackage and the beginning of the extension by National Lead Company to Tahawus. From this point north, mileages indicated are National Lead's, not D&H.

Ordway Siding. 0.9 to 1.43 miles. Elevation ca. 1030. Maps 12-7 and 12-21.

When National Lead Company opened the mines at Tahawus in 1944, an interchange track was required between the D&H and National Lead Company trains. Ordways Siding was used for that purpose until the very end of service in November 1989. It held about 50 ore hopper cars. Ordway Crossing with State Highway 28 was at 2.1 miles.

Milepost 60. 2.66 miles. Elevation 1037. Map 12-7.

Here in 1871, the Adirondac Company's Railroad track terminated, in the "middle of nowhere" near Ordway Pond! When the line was built from Saratoga Springs in the late 1860s, the contract specified a line precisely sixty miles long from Saratoga Springs (and thus 98.30 miles from Albany).

From here, the National Lead Company track continued on through the hamlet of North River and up the Boreas River Gorge. A photo of the gorge appears in Shaughnessy (1967, p. 354).

Stillwater Siding. 13 miles. Elevation 1500. Map 12-8.

When the National Lead Company extended the railroad from North Creek to Tahawus in 1941-1944, their civil engineers found that the grade northward along the Boreas River was quite steep for a railroad. The river and the railroad climbed from elevation 1140 to elevation 1500 feet in 3.5 miles, an average grade of 1.95%. At the summit of this grade, a siding was built about 0.7 mile long with a capacity of from 63 to 80 cars (depending on the length of the cars) at the same time as the main track. The siding was named "Stillwater." Whether the name was taken from Stillwater Brook, about four miles upstream to the north, I am not sure. (This siding should not be confused with the large reservoir of the same name which the New York Central's Adirondack Division crossed north of Beaver River; see Map 36-6).

The purpose of Stillwater Siding was for doubling the hill. This procedure involved the temporary storage of a section of cars while the locomotives returned alone to North Creek for another section. The train would be reassembled at Stillwater and continue on its way to Tahawus. The siding was also used to set off "cripples," i.e. freight cars in need of repairs. Bill Bibby, a D&H employee who has provided me with much of the history of Stillwater and North Creek, says that the siding had been used through 1989 for these two functions.

Tahawus (Sanford Lake). 29 miles at the wye. Elevation 1740. Maps 12-9 and 12-22.

The Defense Plant Corporation, a federal agency, acquired lands from Milepost 60 to Tahawus and leased these lands to the National Lead Company. National Lead began to mine ilmenite, titanium ore, at Tahawus and, along with the Federal Government, commenced construction of an extension of the railroad from Milepost 60 to the mine in 1941-1942. The Delaware & Hudson Railway was employed to haul the tonnage over the new line. The first train reached Tahawus on June 19, 1944 (Shaughnessy, 1967, pp. 296, 353-355 with photos) pulled by a diesel.

In 1962, the then twenty-year old village of Tahawus was moved from its original site southwest of Sanford Hill to Newcomb. Once the buildings were shipped, the present quarry pit was excavated and reached a depth of about 300 feet by 1983.

References on the geology and operation of these mines include Hochschild (1962, "The MacIntyre Mine---"), Hyde (1974, pp. 173-176, 193-196), and C. H. Miller (1983). More recently, in the *Bridge Line Historical Society Bulletin*, Wright (1991) and Phelan (1994) have written on the subject.

Railroad Operation, Timetable Operation and Equipment

Enough detail has accumulated in my files on these subjects to warrant a virtual doubling of the length of this chapter. Much of the detail is available from the references cited throughout the chapter and from D&H timetables over the years. Some of the information has been shared with me, verbally, by reliable people but it still would need confirmation before inclusion in this book. (Operations and equipment really should fill a separate volume).

Controversy and Closure

The last winter for regularly-scheduled passenger service to North Creek was in 1949-1950, and the last train in 1950 was on September 30. Passenger trains ran summers only from 1951 through 1956, the last train being on September 9, 1956 (Shaughnessy, 1967, page 418).

An article by Bird (1971) described the proposed sale of the federally-owned line to its lessee, National Lead Industries. At that time, 1971, the ilmenite mines and railroad were very active and environmentalists were concerned that New York State Forest Preserve lands along the line would be commercially exploited. The *New York State Conservationist* in 1972 reported that the New York State Department of Environmental Conservation protested the sale of the line from Milepost 60 to Sanford Lake. The sale never took place. Miller's 1985 article reviewed the history of the proposed controversial sale and stated that all operations were to cease in the mines in the near future. Indeed, this has been the case. On Thursday, November 16, 1989 the last train left Tahawus at 7 AM in two sections of about 30 cars each. The cars were brought to Ordways Siding. The next day the D&H hauled the cars to Saratoga Springs. At the time of this writing, the D&H operates the North Creek Line as far as the International Paper Mill at Palmer, outside Corinth. North of here, it is abandoned.

Legend to Map 12-14A: Palmer and the Hudson River Mill 3 of the International Paper Company

1. Track number 1
2. Track number 2
3. Track number 3
4. Track number 4
5. Track number 5
6. Track number 6
A. Tool house
B. Track scales
C. Track for wing conveyor to stacker
D. Track for stacker (storage conveyor)
E. Wood room
F. Office
G. Crossyard conveyor
H. Substation
I. Sulphite wood room
J. Ground wood and barker building
K. Ground wood mill digester house
L. Sulphite track
M. Clay shed
N. Bindarene coating & color preparation
O. steep 4.3% grade down
P. Lower trestle
Q. Engine house for industrial switcher
R. Switchback (two of them)
S. Waste treatment plant
T. Riffler room, core plant, bleach kraft, and storage & repulping
U. Paper mill
V. Boiler house
W. Lower boiler house coal track
X. Palmer Falls hydro station
Y. Hudson River
Z. Dam
AA. Curtis Dam
BB. Curtis Mill & hydro plant
CC. Water tower
DD. Machine building (?)

MAP 12-1   ADIRONDAC COMPANY'S RAILROAD TO NORTH CREEK

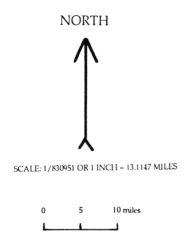
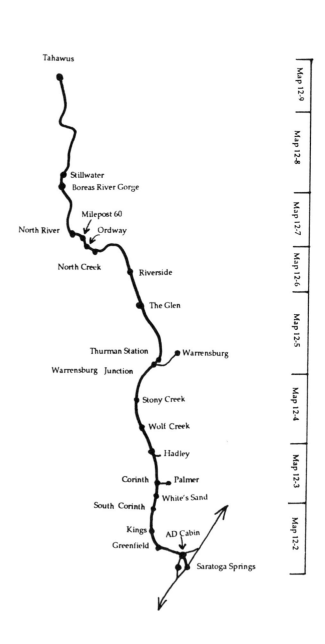

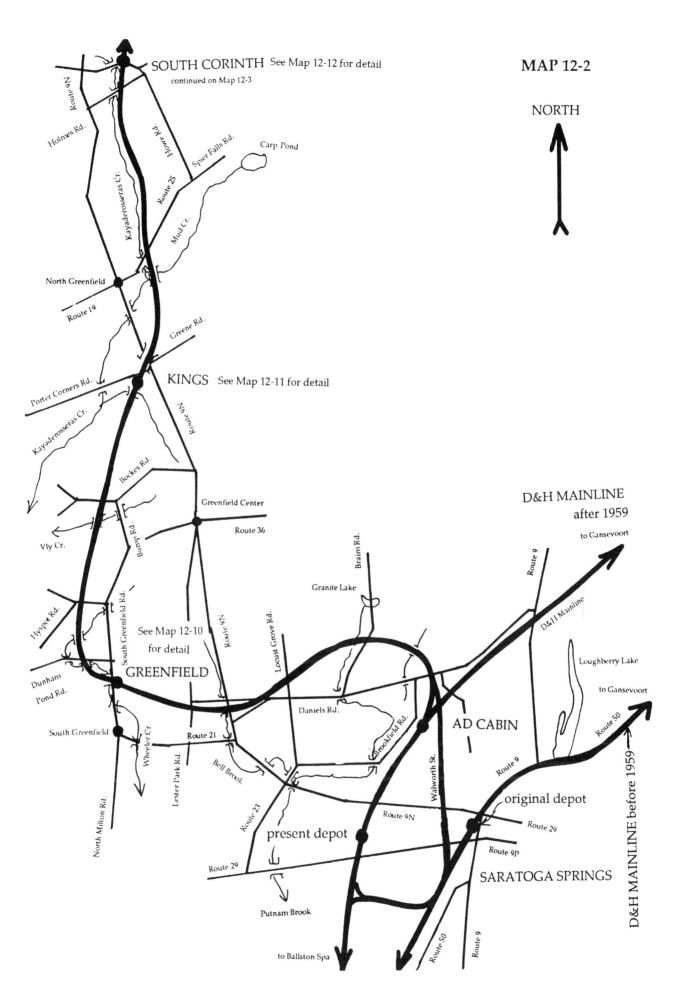

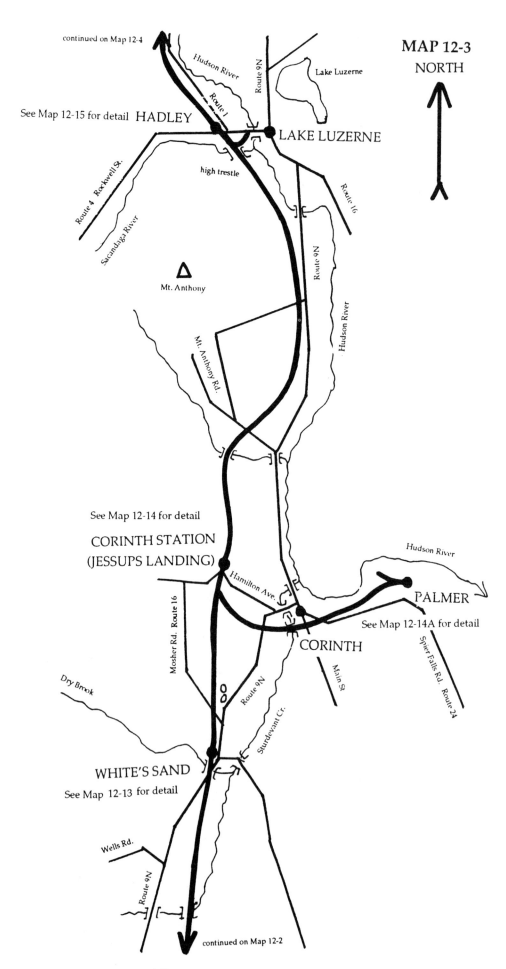

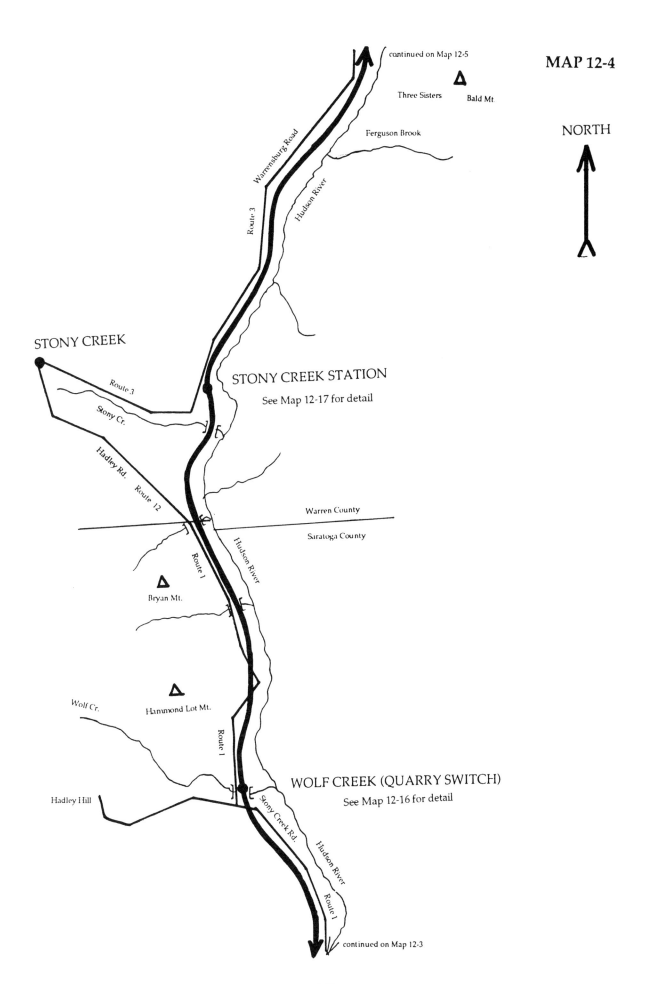

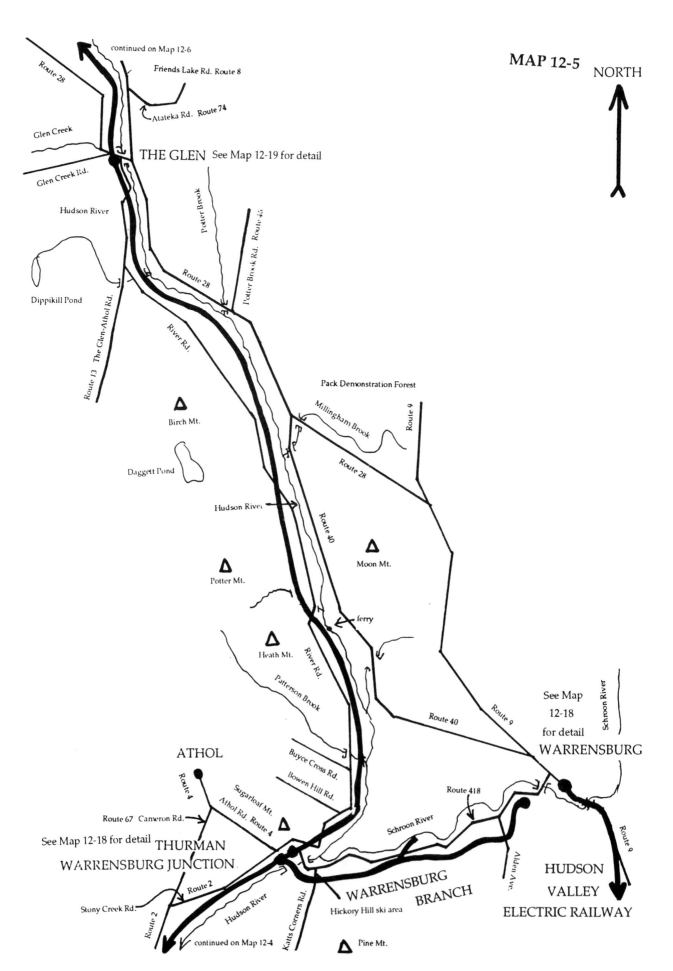

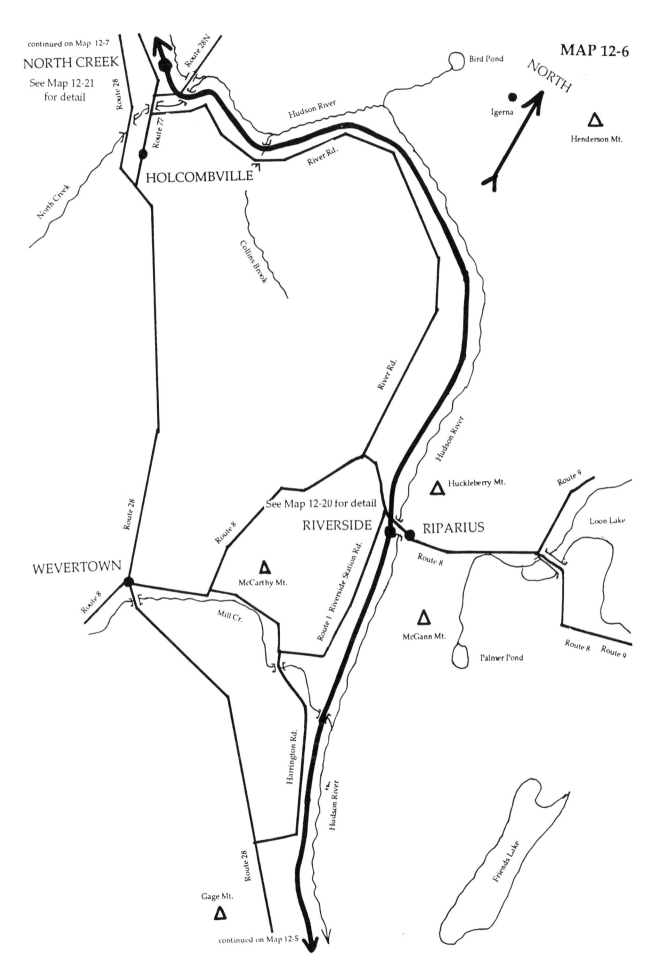

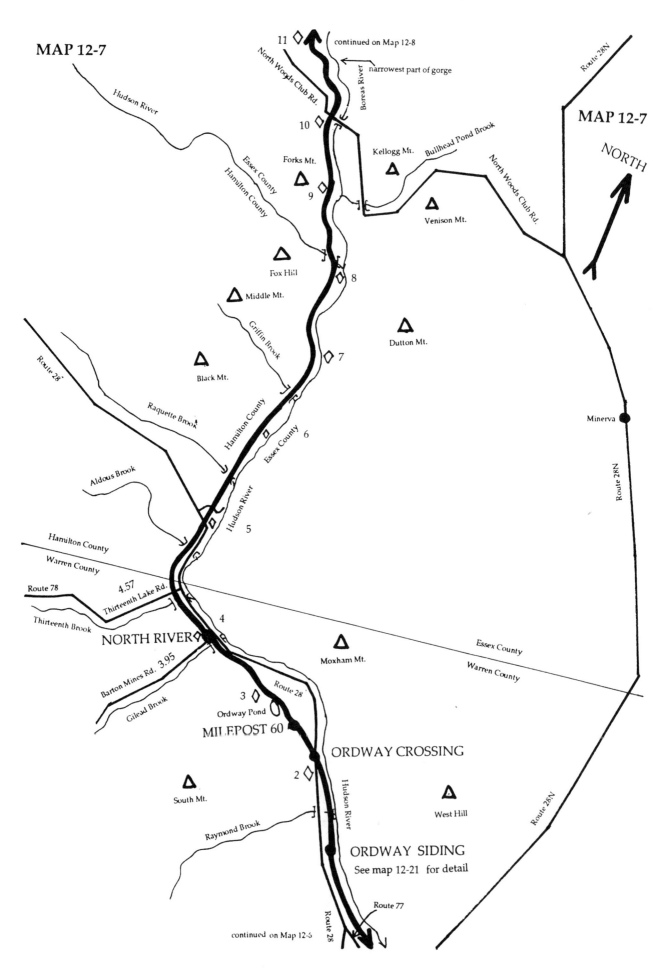

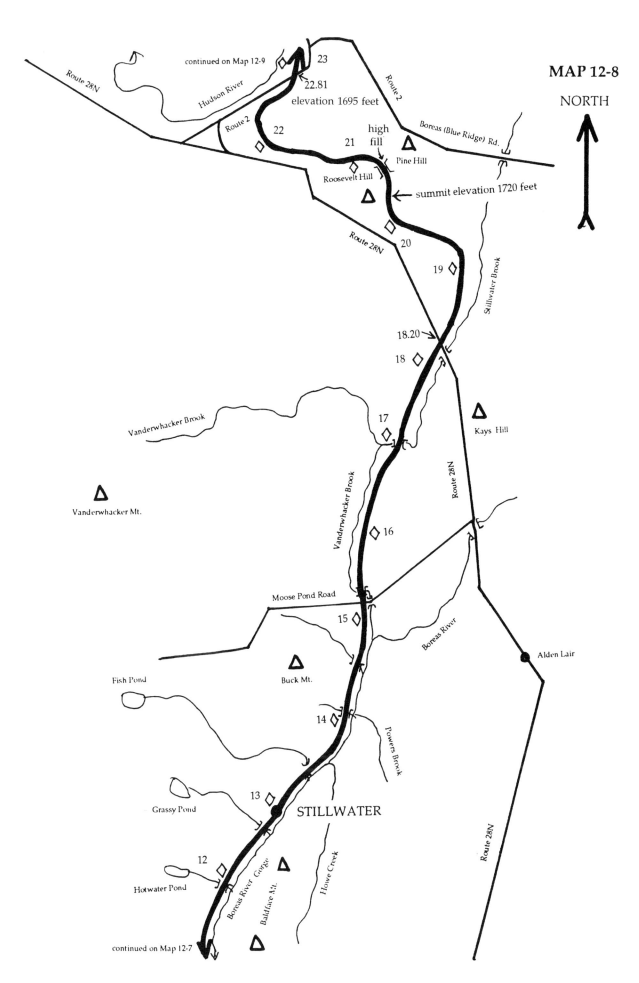

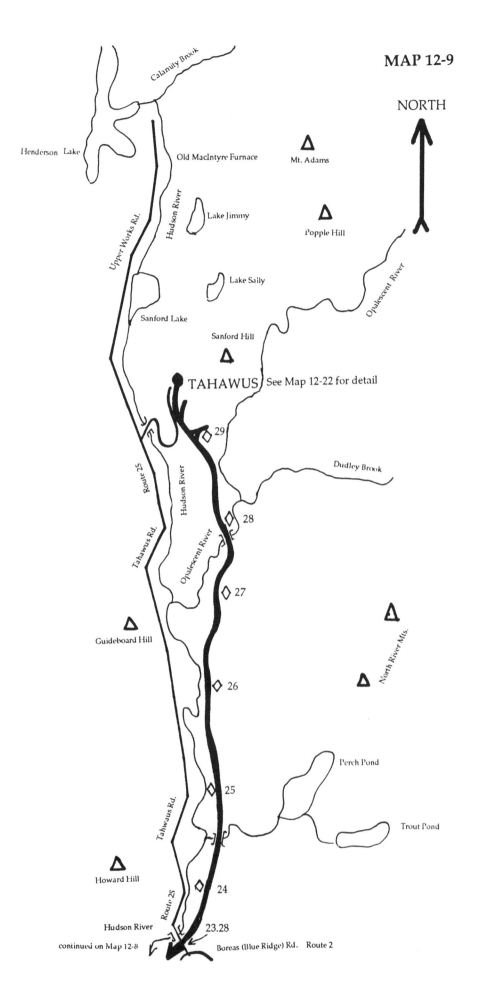

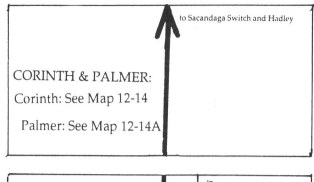

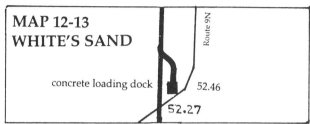

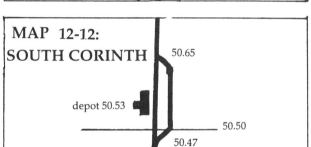

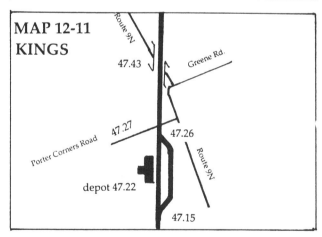

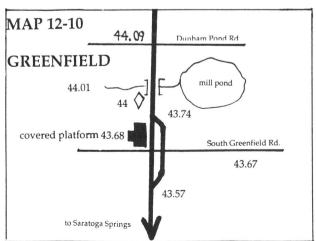

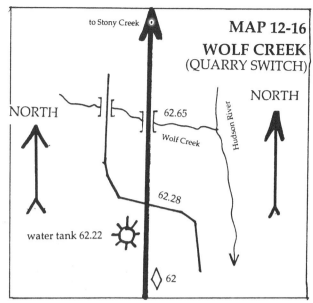

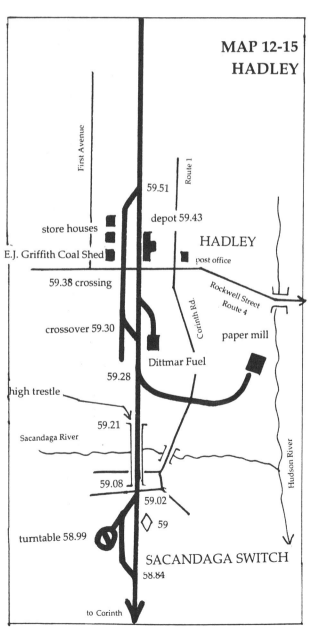

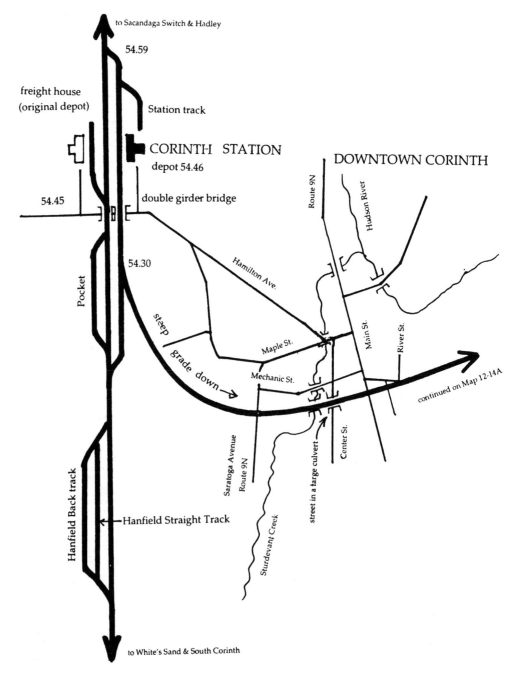

MAP 12-14 CORINTH

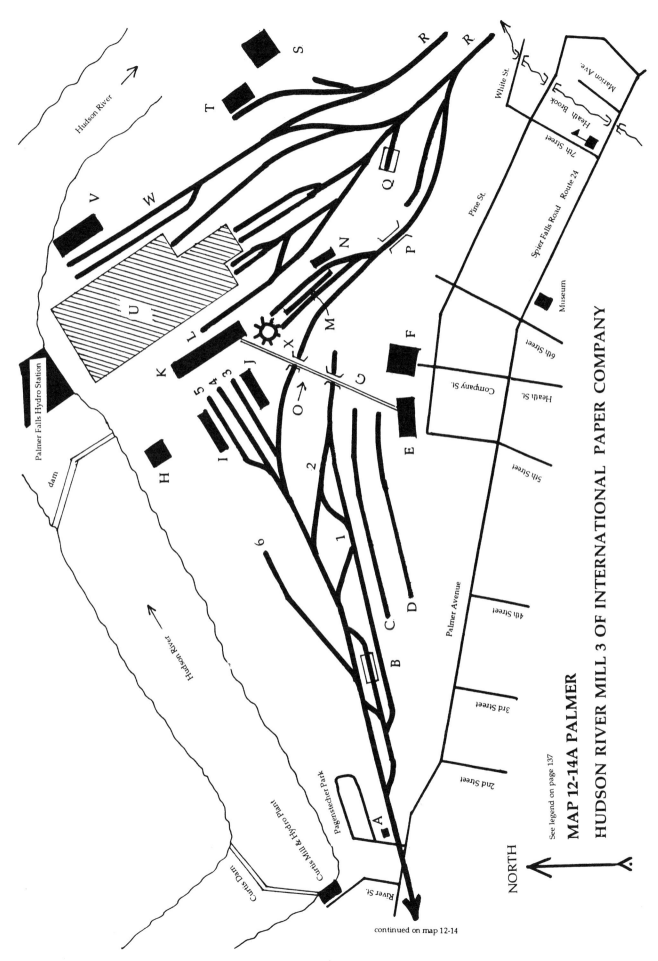

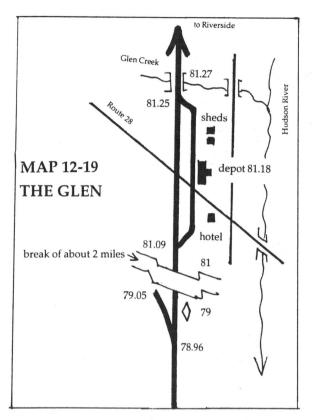
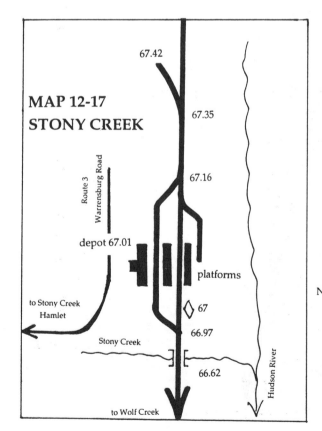
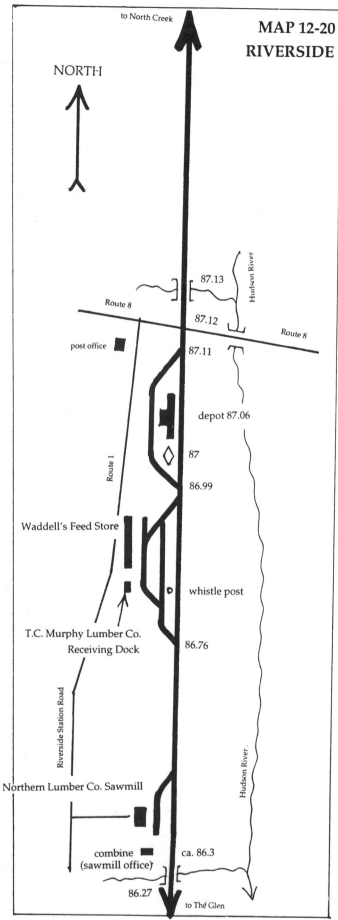

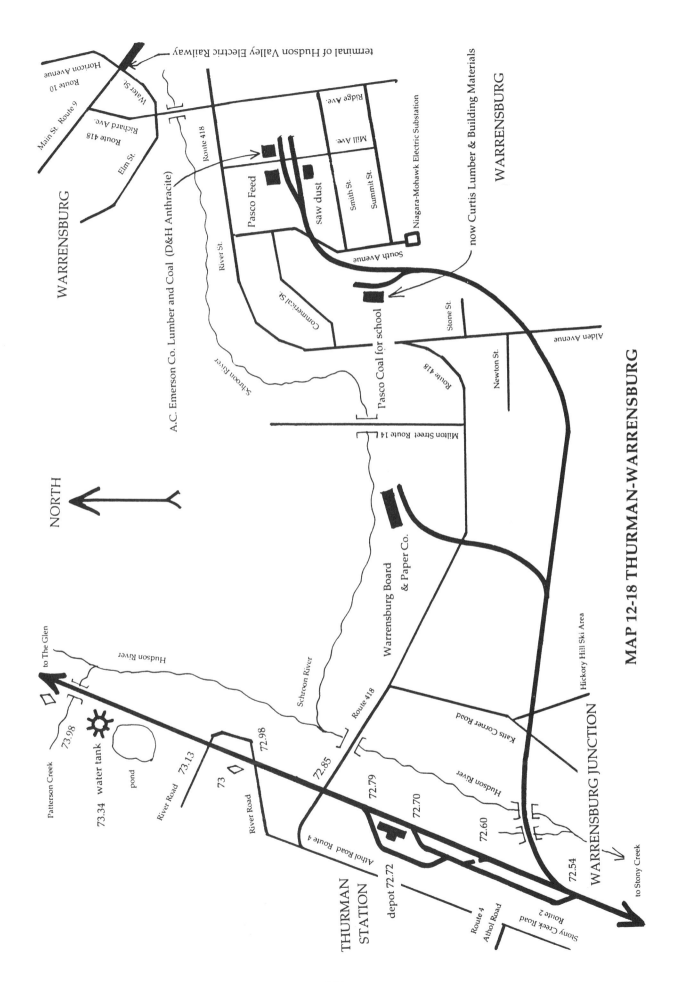

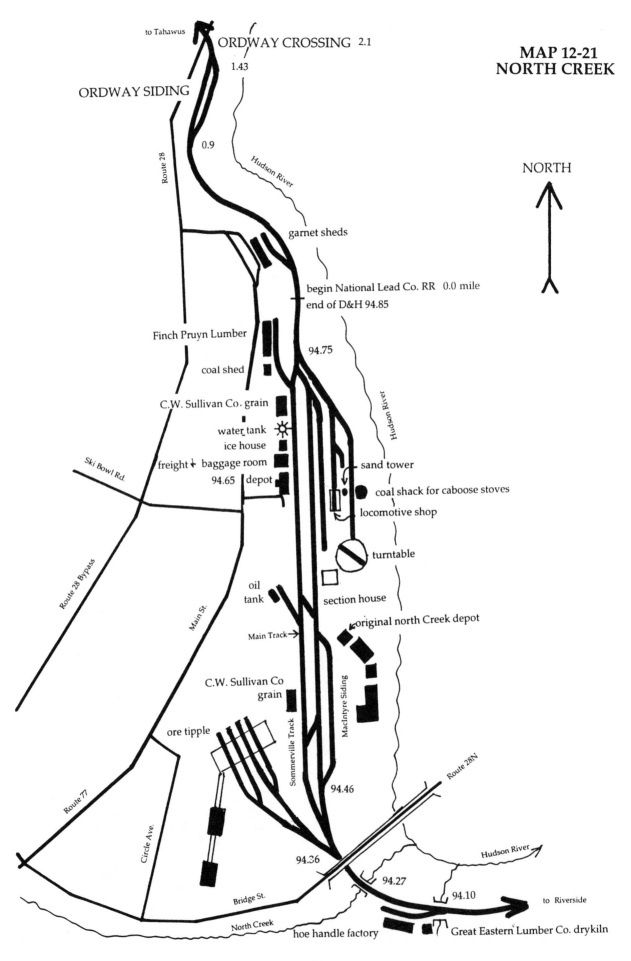

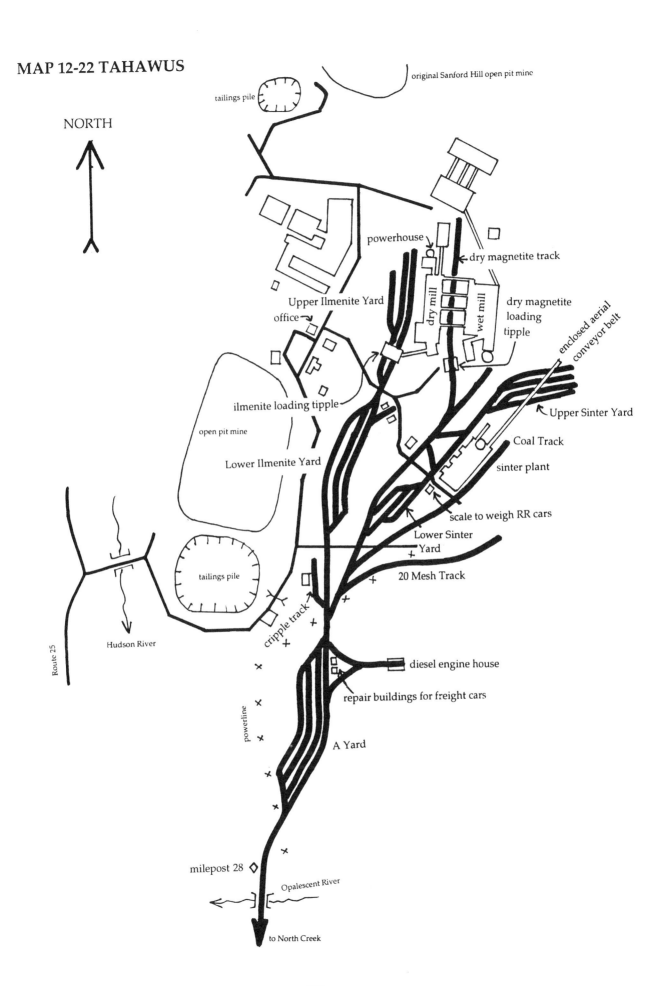

Chapter 13:
The Lake George Region

BECAUSE THIS REGION is at the periphery of the area covered in detail in this volume, and because there is so much historical information already available on the Lake George Region and its railroads, only a brief sketch is offered here.

D&H Caldwell Branch to Lake George

From the D&H Mainline at Fort Edward diverged a 14-mile-long branch which terminated at the south end of Lake George. Originally the station was called Caldwell, but between 1900 and 1906 it became known as Lake George. The branch was completed in 1882 and abandoned in 1958 between Lake George and the north end of Glens Falls. In 1995, the segment from the north end of the City of Glens Falls to downtown was abandoned. The segment between Fort Edward and downtown Glens Falls is still in service for freight only.

Photographs of the Lake George terminus occur in Shaughnessy (1967, pages 168. 179, 180, 203, 254, 256-257, 262-269, and 421) and in D&H (1925, page 361).

Gardner (1990, Volume 3, page 62) tells us in her photo captions that the first passenger station was built in 1882-1883 and torn down in 1911. The existing stone station, complete with tower, was built in 1912 on the site of the first station. A freight house, built in 1882, once stood at the water tank but was moved in 1909.

The facilities from 1915 through 1938 included four tracks with two platforms into the depot, a fifth to a coaling dock and pier, and the submerged track described in the next paragraph. In addition, the servicing and freight yard totaled 12 tracks and included a reversing loop, a water tank, a coaling platform, coal pockets, a turntable, two sheds, a sewage disposal plant, a one-track enginehouse, an ice house, a laundry, a barn, and a freight house. Trackage began to be removed gradually in 1929.

The *D&H Bulletin* (1937, Aug. 1) includes an article entitled "Sea-Going Railroad at Lake George." Box cars, lowered by a pulley and then partly submerged in the lake, were launching boats.

The Prospect Mountain Inclined Cable Railroad

The Prospect Mountain Cable Railroad, 1895 to 1903, west of Lake George Village, is well-described by Meyers (1973). The line, operated by The Horicon Improvement Company, was powered by a stationary Otis engine on the summit. Two passenger cars, serving as counterweights to one another, rode the 1.4-mile-long three-foot-gauge track. A passing siding, shown on the Glens Falls 15-minute Quadrangle surveyed in 1895 at elevation 1100 feet, was extant at mid-slope. Meyers writes that the rise was 40 feet per 100 or a 40% grade. The Quadrangle shows an ascent from 400 to 2000 feet in 1.3 horizontal miles, a 23.3% grade. Visitors soon lost interest in the hotel and view from the summit and the line was abandoned. Because the Cable Railroad was narrow gauge, no connection was ever made with the other railroads in Lake George.

**Hudson Valley Railway:
Electric Interurban Line into Warrensburg**

The Warren County Railroad was incorporated on June 29, 1899. An electric line, ten miles long, opened between Glens Falls and Caldwell (Lake George) on July 10, 1901. On August 14, 1901 it was consolidated into the Hudson Valley Railway and was extended and opened to Warrensburg, six more miles, on January 1, 1902.

Maps in Shaughnessy (1967, pp. 218 and 232) show the Hudson Valley Railway on its own private right-of-way parallel to and west of the D&H Caldwell Branch south of Lake George Village. The right-of-way can still easily be seen from U.S. Highway 9 between Lake George and Warrensburg: the old grade is now occupied by a power line paralleling the highway on the west. The 1927 Adirondack Land Map, published by the New York State Conservation Department, shows the private right-of-way ending just south of the Schroon River Bridge in Warrensburg. From here north, the track ran down the center of Main Street (U.S. Highway 9), crossed the Schroon River Bridge, and terminated at the intersection of Horicon Avenue (formerly River Road), County Route 10. The track apparently ended in the middle of the street, with only a boarding platform and no station building.

Abandonment took place between Warrensburg and Caldwell on January 1, 1928 and between Caldwell and Glens Falls on November 30, 1928. No connection was ever made between the electric railway and the Warrensburg Branch of the D&H (see Map 12-18) barely a third of a mile away.

Shaughnessy (1967) offers much detail on the Hudson Valley Railway which became a subsidiary of the D&H and continued southward to Saratoga Springs, Albany, and Troy.

Delaware & Hudson 810 with a three-car local headed for Lake George, summer 1946.
Arthur B. Martin photo from collection of Jeffrey G. Martin.

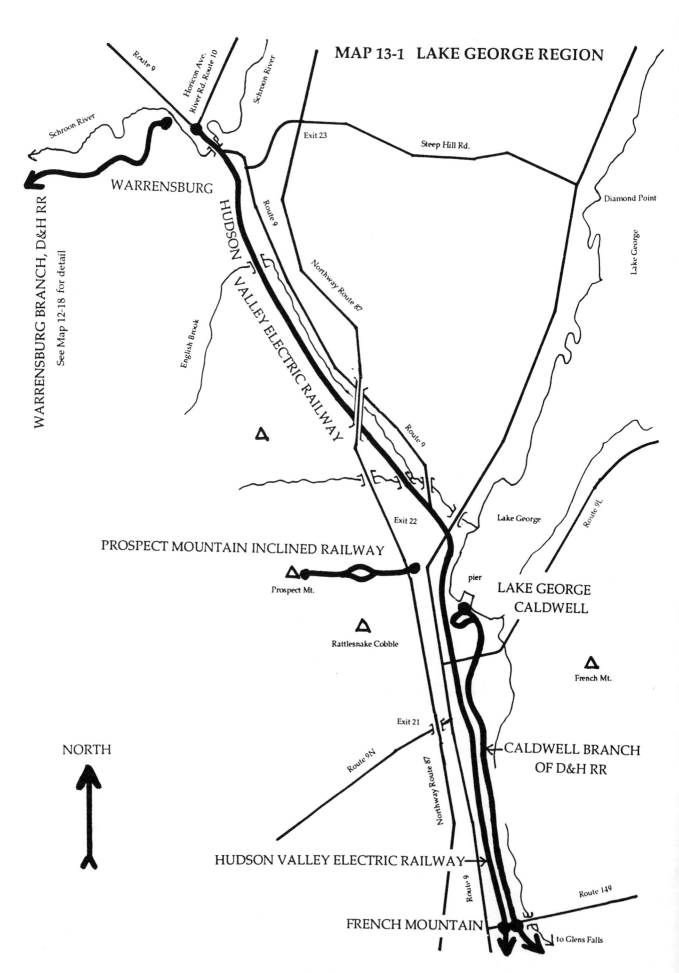

Chapter 14:
Baldwin Branch of the D&H and The Ticonderoga Terminal Railroad

THE 4.8-MILE-LONG BALDWIN BRANCH of the D&H diverged from the mainline at Delano, just north of Montcalm Landing, and followed the outlet to Lake George, Ticonderoga Creek, through the Village of Ticonderoga upstream to Baldwin (see Maps 11-4 and 14-1). Lake Champlain's elevation at Delano is between 95 and 101 feet, while Lake George's is 322, so that an ascent of about 225 feet was needed. Shaughnessy (1967, page 169) states that this Branch was built in 1874 and opened in May 1875 to connect steamboat service on Lake Champlain with that on Lake George. The original name was the Lake George Branch, but it was renamed the Baldwin Branch between 1900 and 1906, probably when the Caldwell Branch was renamed the Lake George Branch.

Photos on pages 180 and 181 in Shaughnessy show Baldwin and the nearby Rogers Rock Hotel. Gardner (1990, Volume 4) also has a photo of Baldwin on page 41.

Intermediate points from Montcalm Landing at 0.0 mile were Ticonderoga (Village) at 2.0 miles and Academy at 2.1 miles. Gardner (1990, Volume 4) includes photos taken in Ticonderoga Village. The captions indicate that the original station was a combination built in 1891, moved across the track to the south in 1913 and rebuilt into a freight house. Before 1891, Academy Station was used. A new passenger station was built in 1913-1914 on the site of the original depot, and stands today as an office building.

One passenger train each way daily served Baldwin, summers only, from 1875 through 1932. In addition, year-round shuttle trains connected Ticonderoga Village with Montcalm Landing. There were from three to seven shuttles each way daily depending on the year. This service stopped sometime between the timetables of June 26, 1932 and April 1, 1933.

Detail of the spurs serving the mills in Ticonderoga Village was obtained from a June 1926 International Paper Company map. Note that the Ticonderoga Terminal Railroad served the freight station and paper mills in the Village. The general area map is traced from the 1894 Ticonderoga Quadrangle.

Freight traffic into Ticonderoga Village ceased in 1980 or 1981, and the rails were pulled up.

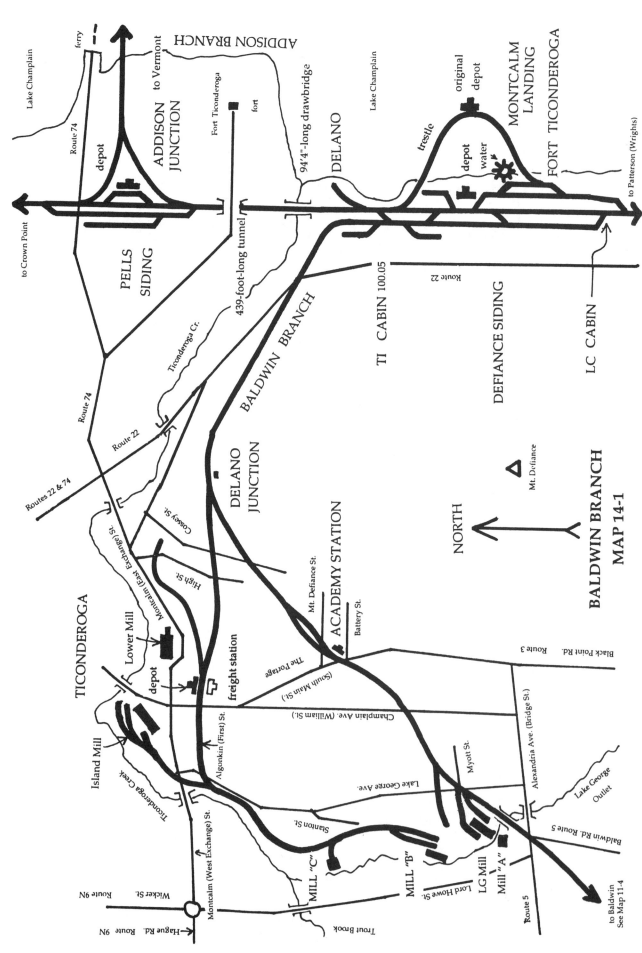

Chapter 15:
Crown Point Iron Company's Railroad

THE PURPOSE OF THIS RAILROAD was to connect the iron mines at Hammondville and the separator forges at Irondale, later Ironville, with the blast furnaces at Crown Point on Lake Champlain.

Surveying occurred in the winter of 1872-1873, with construction in 1873, and service beginning in January 1874. The whole line, with thirteen miles of main track and an additional seven of sidings and spurs, was three-foot narrow gauge. Hence, interchange with the D&H at Crown Point was impossible, although dual-gauge tracks served the blast furnaces and yards.

A nearly 1300-foot elevation change existed between Crown Point and Hammondville, a grade almost as steep as the Lake Champlain and Moriah's. Elevation ranged from 121 at the D&H Crown Point depot to about 930 feet at Ironville, 1330 at Hammondville and 1400 at #4 Shaft north of Hammondville.

Allen (1973) offers much detail on locomotives and equipment. A combine was used to carry employees and passengers. The line closed in July and August of 1893, partly due to the opening of the Mesabi Iron Range in Minnesota which eventually caused the decline of all Adirondack iron mines.

Publications on the Crown Point line abound. The Penfield Foundation, which currently operates the Penfield Homestead and Historical Museum Area in Ironville, has published a series of booklets and maps on the district. The three most valuable to this book are the superbly-detailed maps by E. E. Barker (1941) of Hammondville in 1876, and two by Steve Barker (1973) of Ironville. Other Penfield Foundation booklets are by Spaulding (1874), Allen (1968), E. E. Barker (1969), and a recent introductory pamphlet (post-1980). McMartin (1982) offers a history of Ironville, emphasizing the origin of the iron mines before the advent of the railroad, the villages and people; she includes some railroad history and description of the industrial process. Hyde (1974) and Mohr (1974) also have information on this railroad. Shaughnessy (1967) has photos on pp. 136, 138, 139, 178, and 430 and so does the Saranac Lake Free Library: #82.884 and #82.885. A recent description of the line will be found in the *Inventory of Abandoned Railroad Rights of Way*, published by the New York State Department of Transportation's Real Property Division in 1974.

Old maps are also very useful. Gray (1876) shows much detail at Crown Point and some at Ironville. The 1892 Port Henry and 1895 Paradox Lake U.S.G.S. quadrangles show the line in relation to roads, streams, and topography. Gray (1876) names the intermediate hamlet Irondale, but the 1892 Quadrangle already calls it Ironville.

Fortunately for us, Stoddard took a number of photographs of the Crown Point Railroad, including the famous one of a train crossing the Puts, or Putnam, Creek trestle. Railroad historian, Richard Wettereau of the *New York Times*, and the author relocated the approaches and footings for this trestle in 1991. Photographs of the Crown Point Blast Furnace were in 1985 at The Adirondack Museum's mining building, but not all photos on exhibit included railroads. At least fifteen different photographs, some of them Stoddard's, are readily available to us today in the abundant recent publications; some of the photos are used by more than one author.

Passenger service did exist for a time on the line. The summer 1883 Delaware & Hudson timetable lists a connection at Crown Point via the Crown Point Iron Company's Railroad to Hammondville.

From Hammondville by stagecoach, it was 6 miles to Paradox Lake and 15 miles to Schroon Lake.

Map 15-3 shows the blast furnace at Crown Point simplified as a single building. In actuality, Gray (1876) shows the blast furnace as a complex of at least nine buildings, eight of which are identified: two casting houses, two boiler houses, two ovens, an engine house, and possibly a steam saw mill labeled "s.s.m."

A Crown Point Iron Company locomotive and the blast furnace at Crown Point.
Collection of Feinberg Library, State University of New York at Plattsburgh.

MAP 15-1 CROWN POINT IRON COMPANY'S RAILROAD

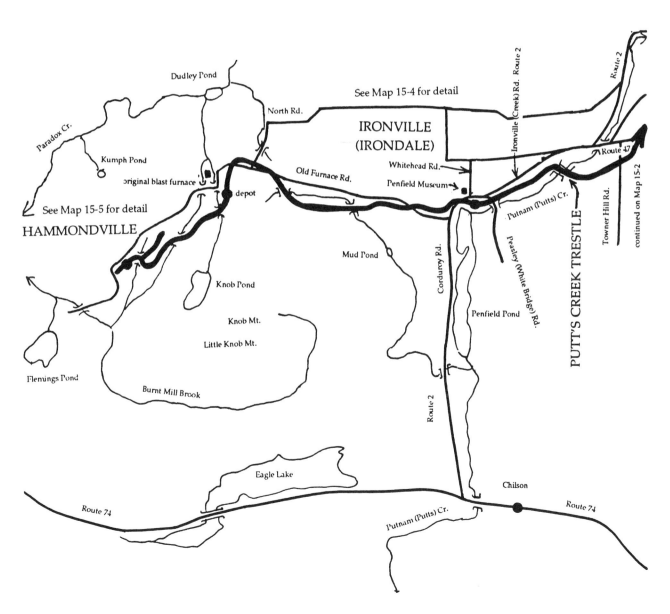

MAP 15-2   CROWN POINT IRON COMPANY'S RAILROAD

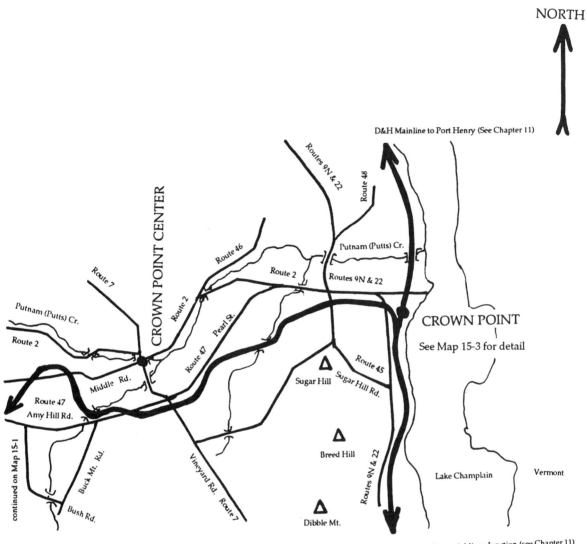

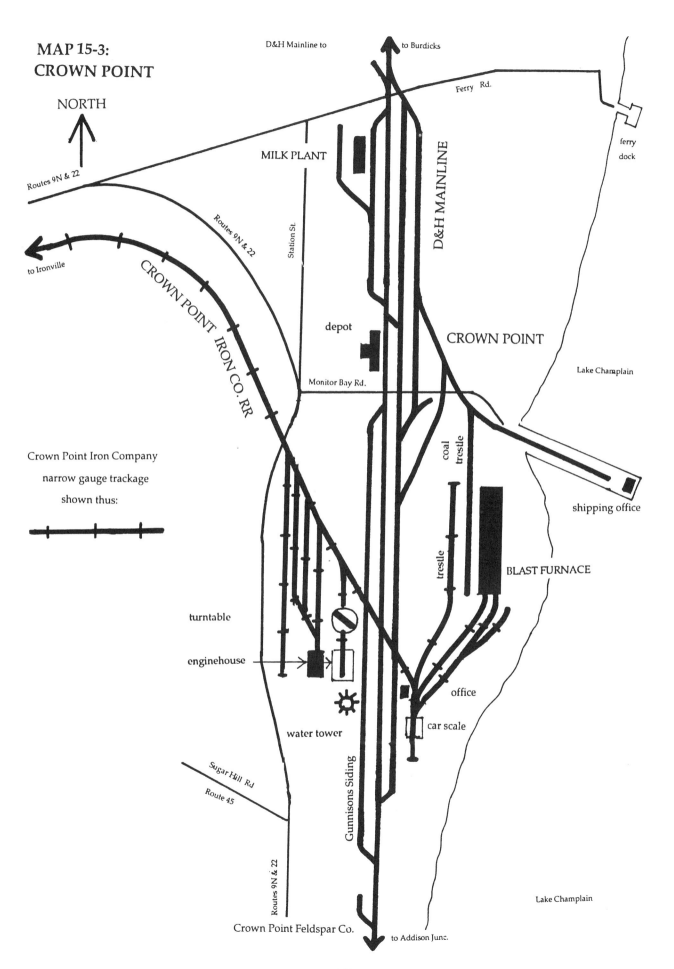

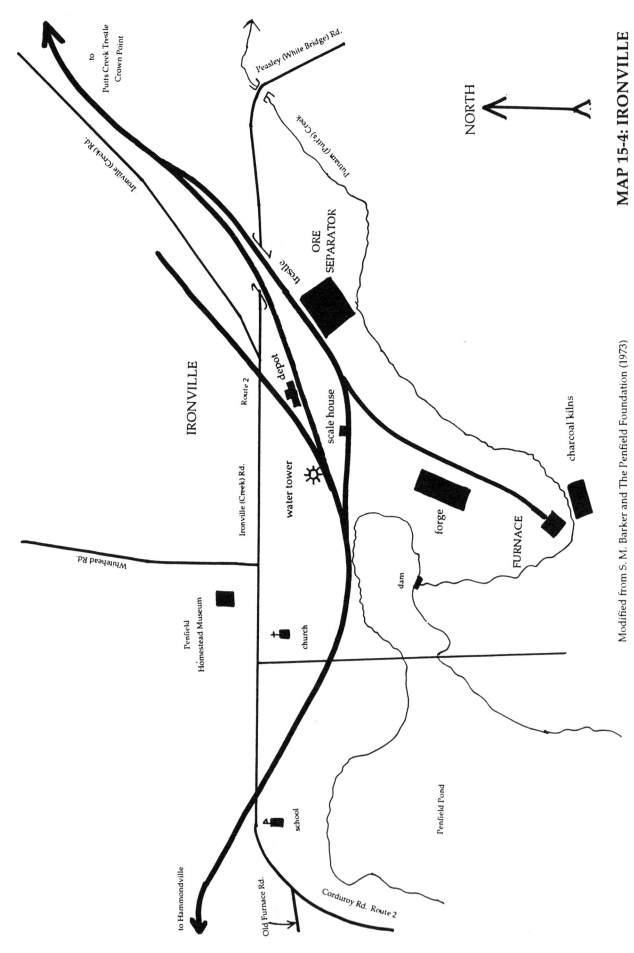

MAP 15-4: IRONVILLE

Modified from S. M. Barker and The Penfield Foundation (1973)

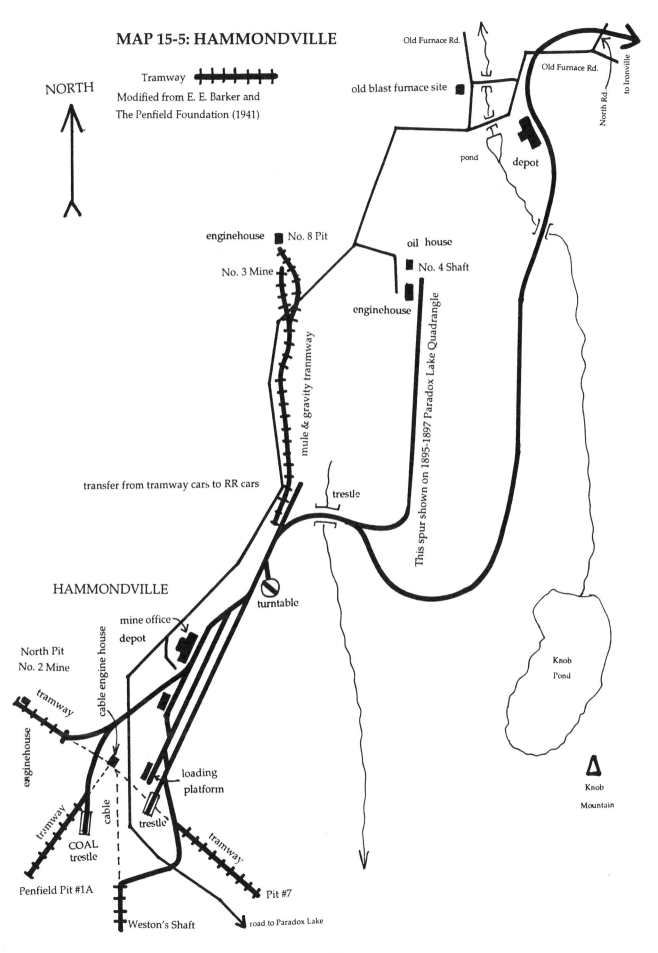

Chapter 16:
Lake Champlain and Moriah Railroad

THIS RAILROAD joined the Delaware & Hudson mainline at Port Henry and climbed to Mineville and Witherbee in the Town of Moriah to serve several iron mines. *The Annual Report of the New York State Board of Railroad Commissioners* (1893, p. 305) states that the line was chartered on December 4, 1867 and offers details on the equipment, income, and expenses. The Lake Champlain & Moriah was built jointly in 1868-1869 by the Witherbee Sherman Company and the Port Henry Iron Company. Initially wooden rails were used, but steel rails were already in service by 1873.

A railroad from Vermont via Addison Junction was completed to Port Henry in 1871, three years before the D&H Mainline was completed from Whitehall to Port Henry, and four years before the Mainline was completed from Port Henry to Plattsburgh. A section of the D&H Mainline between Port Henry and Addison Junction was under construction as early as 1869 and 1870 (D&H 1925, p. 242).

The LC&M climbed from elevation 103 feet at Port Henry along the D&H to an elevation of 1560 feet at the Fisher Hill Iron Mine in 8.7 miles. This is an average grade of 3.17%, although the steepest mile, when measured on a U.S.G.S. topographic quadrangle, ascended 250 feet at 4.7% between Mineville and Fisher Hill. Fortunately, the loaded ore cars came down and the empties went up; braking was a bigger problem than climbing. The LC&M had the steepest grade of any railroad in the Adirondack Region except for inclined cable railways.

Unraveling the history of this short line railroad has been the most difficult challenge during the preparation of this volume. Because the railroad operated for over a century and because the individual mines opened, became depleted of ore, and closed at different times, many track relocations were made. It is nearly impossible to record all of them, so that only the major changes are documented here. There were many separate iron companies operating in the area as early as the late 18th century, many of which did not survive for long and closed before the railroads arrived. When Gray (1876) was published, there were at least five companies operating: Witherbee Sherman & Company, Port Henry Iron Ore Company, Parrott and Thomas Iron Company, Cedar Point Iron Company, and Bay State Iron Company. Witherbee Sherman & Company controlled the Cedar Point and, later, in 1883, controlled the Bay State. A close partnership existed between Witherbee Sherman & Company and the Port Henry Iron Ore Company; these two major companies jointly built the Lake Champlain & Moriah Railroad.

References

Another difficulty in unraveling the history of this railroad that nil recent information has been published. There are occasional references to it in older, technical mining journals: Granbery (1906), Stephenson (1909), Birkinbine (1915), and *Mining and Metallurgy Journal* (1943). Early maps are helpful: Gray (1876), Burleigh (1889), and Lloyd (1892). The United States Geological Survey topographic quadrangles also provide insight: Port Henry 1892, 1945, and metric 1980; Elizabethtown 1892, 1955; and Witherbee metric 1978. By far the greatest accumulation of detail, regrettably unpublished, is by a researcher who requests to remain anonymous; fortunately, much of his historical material is available at the Sherman Library in Port Henry. This material includes some equipment rosters and some track schematics by Witherbee Sherman and Republic Steel. Babcock (1995) describes the mines.

Maps
A series of maps will assist the reader

Map 16-1 is a general orientation map showing the whole LC&M and its relation to hamlets, roads, brooks, the D&H, and Lake Champlain.

Map 16-2 shows detail of the south half of Port Henry including the depot, the D&H Mainline, and the Cedar Point Blast Furnace.

Map 16-3 shows detail of the north half of Port Henry including the Bay State Furnaces and Port Henry Tunnels on the D&H Mainline.

Map 16-4 shows detail of the LC&M servicing facilities in Port Henry, and the 1909 relocation at Terio Wye along McKenzie Brook.

Map 16-5 shows detail at Switchback, east of Moriah Center, including the #7 Mill.

Map 16-6 shows detail in the Mineville-Witherbee area in the 19th century.

Map 16-7 shows detail of the Mineville-Witherbee area in the 20th century.

Map 16-8 shows detail of the Fisher Hill and adjacent iron mines.

Blast Furnace and Ore Docks at Port Henry (Maps 16-2 and 16-3)

Blast furnaces produced cast iron in pigs whereas forges produced wrought iron. The Cedar Point Blast Furnace was under construction in 1872-1873 and was first operated in 1875, the same year that the D&H Mainline opened from Whitehall to Plattsburgh. Like the Lake Champlain & Moriah Railroad, the blast furnace was built jointly by the Witherbee Sherman Company and the Port Henry Iron Ore Company. It was located at milepost 116.5 on the D&H Mainline, about 0.2 mile south of the Port Henry Depot. In 1906, the furnace was operated under lease by the Northern Iron Company, although it was still owned by Witherbee Sherman.

On the west side of the furnace passed the D&H Mainline with extensive yard facilities (see photos in Shaughnessy, 1967, pp. 170 and 172). On the east (Lake Champlain) side of the furnace a southerly extension of the Witherbee Sherman ore docks, elevated trackage on trestles, served the blast furnace. The ore docks made it possible to ship the iron by barge as well as by rail.

A large overhead traveling crane was once at the edge of the lake, and used to transfer ore from rail to barge. The massive concrete foundation still stands, and is easily visible from the Port Henry Amtrak depot today. However, because of a later land fill, the foundation is now well inland from the lake shore.

The ore docks and travelling crane located south of the LC&M Railroad bridge over the D&H Mainline at milepost 116.91 were owned by Witherbee Sherman. Those ore docks north of the LC&M bridge were owned by the Port Henry Iron Ore Company and extended to a point adjacent to milepost 117.15 on the D&H. Photos of the ore docks appear in Stephenson (1909), pp. 418 and 419.

The blast furnace was closed in 1934 by Witherbee Sherman Company and was demolished by Republic Steel in 1939, about the same time that Republic Steel demolished the Standish Blast Furnace (see Chapter 20, and Map 20-15).

After demolition of the Cedar Point Blast Furnace, the adjacent powerhouse, southwest of the furnace and between it and Highway 9N-22, still stood. In 1940, Republic Steel moved equipment into this empty powerhouse, and Mill #6 was established. It ran until October 1946.

The Cheever Iron Ore Company, the Bay State Iron Company, and the Port Henry Tunnels (Maps 16-1 and 16-3)

The Cheever Iron Ore Company mine was about 2.2 miles north of the Port Henry depot, about 300 feet above the level of Lake Champlain, and just east of the present highway 9N-22. In 1870, an inclined tramway railroad, .75 mile long, was built to connect the mine with a barge pier on Lake Champlain. In 1870, the D&H Mainline here was still five years in the future. The tramway is shown on Gray's 1876 atlas of Essex County, but the owner is stated to be the Champlain & Essex Mining Company. Ore from the Cheever mine supplied the Bay State Iron Company furnace from 1867 to 1883. Today, the Cheever pier site is at about milepost 118.9 on the D&H.

The Cheever Iron Ore Company mine closed and reopened several times depending on the fluctuating iron market. The 1906 reopening was by the Witherbee Sherman Company; the tramway was rebuilt in 1907 and enlarged to three tracks. The permanent closing date of this mine was in late December 1918.

Two furnaces were built north of Mill Brook, one in 1854 and another in 1860. These were both bought by the Bay State Iron Company in 1867 which operated them until 1883. In 1883, the Port Henry Furnace Company, a subsidiary of Witherbee-Sherman, acquired these furnaces. One of the two was located on the shore of Lake Champlain, presently at D&H milepost 117.7. When the D&H Mainline was completed in 1875, it had to tunnel inland in order to avoid passing through the middle of this furnace (see also Chapter 11 and Map 11-5). The second furnace was located on the west side of the D&H. Each of these furnaces was shut down in 1892 and dismantled by Witherbee-Sherman in 1896. The D&H Mainline was then free to hug the Lake Champlain shoreline, the inland tunnel being no longer needed. The date of tunnel abandonment, however, was much later: between 1940 (D&H Employees' Timetables still listed low clearance) and 1945 (when the U.S.G.S. topographic Port Henry quadrangle was published and did not show it).

In 1907, a powerhouse on Lake Champlain at the north edge of the mouth of Mill Brook was built, adjacent to the steamboat landing and a short distance south of the Bay State Furnace site. A spur from the D&H Mainline diverged to the powerhouse at milepost 117.47, probably to bring in hopper cars with coal. The D&H bridge over Mill Brook is at milepost 117.46.

Lake Champlain & Moriah Railroad Shops and Servicing Facilities

These were located west of the bridge over South Main Street (Highways 9N-22) in Port Henry. See Map 16-4 for detail.

Terio Wye and the Relocation at McKenzie Brook (See Map 16-4).

The original route out of Port Henry in the vicinity of McKenzie Brook included a switchback called the Terio Wye. This was actually a switchback, not a wye. It is not to be confused with the locality named Switchback another two miles up the line. In 1909 the Terio Wye was replaced by a horseshoe curve which bridged Whitney Street, Lakeview Avenue, and McKenzie Brook—each with a massive concrete arch. These three arches still stand today and are inscribed with "LC&M RR 1909."

Relocations at Switchback (See Map 16-5)

This locality, east of the hamlet of Moriah Center, received its name from the original pair of switchbacks built by the LC&M in 1868-1869. On February 16, 1905 a runaway train, speeding down the grade from Mineville to the upper switchback, literally flew off the end of the track (Granbery, 1906, pp. 22 and 23). To avoid a repeat occurrence, a switch, named the Malone Switch, was installed above the upper switchback as an alternative route to stop any future runaway trains. Fortunately, there was none.

In either November of 1937 or in early 1938, Republic Steel leased the mining operations from Witherbee Sherman and in 1942-1943, built Mill #7, a concentrating facility and sintering plant. The original nineteenth century pair of switchbacks had been abandoned temporarily and a new switchback, along the north side of Mill Brook, was built. A wye was built at about the same time ca. one-third of a mile east of the new switchback. The United States Geological Survey Port Henry quadrangle in 1945 shows the track relocations. As Mill #7 spewed forth enormous quantities of waste materials, the gigantic tailings pile grew and grew to the point that it threatened to bury the new switchback and a portion of North Mill Road.

By the time aerial photographs were taken on July 1, 1957 for the New York State Office of Equalization and Assessment, both the railroad and the highway had, in fact, been buried and were relocated. The original 1868-1869 pair of switchbacks, though modified, was back in service!

In 1992 most of the buildings of Mill #7 still stand except for the sintering plant. The area is privately owned by Rhone-Poulenc, Inc., a French minerals company.

Relocations in the Mineville-Witherbee Area (Maps 16-6 and 16-7)

According to Gray (1876), the LC&M headed west from Mineville parallel to, and the north side of, what is now Essex County Highway #6. The railroad terminated at the intersection of Barton Hill Road, Hospital Road, and Route #6, serving the Old Bed mines and shafts.

By 1892, when the Elizabethtown quadrangle was surveyed, the railroad had been extended westward parallel to Highway #6, crossing what is now the Dalton Hill Road or Essex County Highway #7C or 70, and terminating at a New Bed shaft and sawmill at Roe Pond. Also by 1892, a branch had already been built, probably in 1883 when the Bonanza and Joker Mines were opened, crossing Highway #6 at Mineville and heading southwest in the direction of Witherbee. In 1901 this branch was extended to serve the just-completed Harmony A & B Shafts at Witherbee.

Sometime in the early twentieth century, the original line to New Bed Mine and Roe Pond was abandoned, leaving only the southwest branch extant. See the Legend to Map 16-7 for some detail on when various mines, shafts, and mills opened and closed. The remainder of the buildings were torn down in 1979-1980, except for the extant Harmony Change House and Central Power House.

Fisher Hill Iron Mine (Map 16-8)

By coincidence, the railroad into Fisher Hill was in existence both in 1892 and in 1955 when the Elizabethtown quadrangles were published, suggesting that this branch was in service the whole time. In actuality, the portion at Fisher Hill shut down in 1893 and did not reopen until 1941!

The 1891 *Poor's Directory of Railroad Officials* states that "surveys completed and contract let for private branch from Mineville to Fisher Hill, 2 miles." On the 1892 Elizabethtown quadrangle, the railroad is shown terminating about a tenth of a mile beyond the Moriah-Elizabethtown town line at the Fisher Hill Mine. *Mining and Metallurgy Journal* (1943) indicates that this mine was shut down in 1893 and not reopened until the summer of 1941. The LC&M built a new spur off the Fisher Hill line in 1903 to serve the Cook, O'Neil, Smith, and Thompson Shafts. A map in Granbery (1906, page 7) thus no longer shows the railroad serving the Fisher Hill Mine, but instead diverging off to the east below it and terminating at these shafts.

A comparison of the 1892 Elizabethtown quadrangle with the 1955 Elizabethtown quadrangle reveals not only that the Fisher Hill Mine railroad had been rebuilt but that the junction at Mineville was relocated. The original Fisher Hill extension joined the LC&M in 1891-1892 about a half-mile west of Mineville. The 1941 extension joined the LC&M directly in Mineville.

The Fisher Hill Iron mine shut down June 30, 1966 and the pumps were turned off on February 1, 1976. In May of 1988, the New York State Department of Corrections began rehabilitating the 1941 era Fisher Hill Mine buildings into the Moriah Shock Incarceration Camp which opened in February 1989.

Equipment

There were 20 locomotives in all, 15 steam and 5 diesel. Of course, not all operated simultaneously. The number of engines in service at any one time ranged from 5 to 9. Steam locomotives included a single 0-6-0T, one 0-4-4T, two 2-4-0s, seven 2-6-0s, two 4-6-0s, and two 2-8-2s. Diesels were industrial switchers.

There were three passenger cars used for carrying employees, but possibly not the general public, from Port Henry up to the mines. A waiting platform and shelter in Port Henry existed just east of the South Main Street (Highways 9N-22) overpass on the north side of the track. One passenger car is supposedly still in existence serving as a camp in the Crown Point area.

I have seen photographs of a single truck caboose. There were many ore cars, called jimmies, of various sizes and capacities; the derailed remains of seven of them still decorate the embankment just south of the Stone Street crossing between Port Henry and Switchback.

Starbird (1967) included a photo with detailed caption of a train underground in one of the Mineville mines. Because this underground railroad was not physically connected with the LC&M, a more complete description will be found in Chapter 8 on disconnecting railroads.

Closure

The mines and railroad ceased operations suddenly on July 23, 1971. Hyde (1974, p 154) says that the mining "operation is now shut down, but that the pumps which keep water from flooding the mines are kept running, with the thought that operations may possibly be resumed at some future date." They have not. Most of the buildings were demolished and the rails removed in 1979-1980. I had noted that the yard opposite the Port Henry depot plus the Sherman passing siding between Cabin SR and Cabin SN were still present in 1983, but gone by May 1990.

Legend to Map 16-7: Mineville in the Twentieth Century

1. Mill #1. Built in 1852 by American Mineral Company, long before the LC&M was opened. Burned

sometime between 1913 and 1917. Replaced later by Mill #5 (see entry on Mill #5 below).

2. Mill #2. Built 1902. Burned sometime between 1913 and 1917 when Mill #1 burned, but not replaced.
3. Mill #3. Built 1909-1910 to serve Harmony Mines. Burned May 18, 1923.
4. Mill #4. Built 1911 to serve Barton Hill Mine. Closed during the early 1930s.
5. Mill #5. Built 1918 on the site of the earlier Mill #1. Demolished 1979-1980.
6. Mill #6 is NOT shown on Map 16-7. (See Map 16-2 of Port Henry South. Mill #6 ran 1940 to October 1946 next to the site of the Cedar Point Blast Furnace).
7. Mill #7 is NOT shown on Map 16-7. (See Map 16-5 of Switchback).
8. Bonanza Shaft. Built summer 1883. Explosion on October 5, 1904 damaged the shaft and LC&M locomotive #7. Demolished before the 1940s.
9. Clonan Shaft. Built 1909-1910. In use through late 1950s. Demolished 1979-1980.
10. Clonan Hoist Building and 10A. Clonan coal trestle.
11. Joker Shaft. Built September 1908 although the mine had opened in 1883. 1892 Elizabethtown quadrangle shows track leading to it. Electric tramway already in operation underground by 1910. Burned April 1941 along with the Head House.
12. Joker Change House.
13. Joker Tailings Pile. Both still exist.
14. Don B Shaft built 1942 (to replace Joker Shaft?). Pumps shut down in the mine summer 1979. Shaft demolished 1979-1980.
15. Don B Electric Substation.
16. Don B Hoist Room.
17. Don B Crushing Plant.
18. Harmony A Shaft. Built January 1901 with railroad extension to it and to Harmony B Shaft. Burned May 19, 1922.
19. Harmony B Shaft. Built January 1901. Steep ramp track into it from the south.
20. Harmony Change House. Still stands.
21. Harmony Tailings Pile. Still exists.
22. Old Bed Power House. Built 1883 for Bonanza and Joker Shafts.
23. Coal track on trestle to serve Old Bed Power House.
24. Central Power House. Built 1902 with a coal track on trestle. Power House still stands, but trestle is long gone.
25. Barton Hill Mine loading facility for railroad cars.
26. Barton Hill Tailings Pile. Still exists.
27. Roe Shaft and Sawmill at Roe Pond. Railroad to them shown on 1892 Elizabethtown quadrangle.
28. Mineville School.
29. Memorial Hall. Built 1893 by Witherbee Sherman Company. Still stands as Veterans of Foreign Wars Hall.
30. Firehouse. Still stands.
31. Witherbee Sherman Company Office. Built 1907. Long stone staircase leading up to it from the south had three tracks crossing at different levels.
32. Shed for maintenance-of-way work car.
33. Harmony mine shops and warehouse.

Legend to Map 16-2: Port Henry South

A. Lake Champlain & Moriah Railroad Depot.
B. Lake Champlain & Moriah Railroad Office.
C. Witherbee-Sherman Office.
D. Chemistry laboratory for ore analysis.
E. Delaware & Hudson Railroad Depot. Milepost 116.81.
F. Delaware & Hudson Railroad Freight House.
G. Sherman's Warehouse.
H. Team tracks.
I. Roundhouse, 3 stalls, with turntable.
J. Foot bridge for pedestrians.
K. Water tower. Milepost 116.45.
L. Later turntable.
M. Signal bridges (two of them).
N. Stimpson Lumber.
O. Stimpson Coal.
P. Sawmill on pier.
Q. Witherbee-Sherman ore dock tracks on trestle.
R. Traveling crane on its own rails.
S. Witherbee-Sherman Ore dock.
T. Cedar Point Blast Furnace.
U. Sinter Plant.
V. Smoke stacks (two of them).
W. Power House. Converted into Mill #6 about 1940.
X. Building converted into Lake Champlain & Moriah Railroad Shop ca. 1940.
Y. Tailings pile.
AA. Powerhouse.
BB. Sand.
CC. Engine house for yard switcher.
DD. Scales.

MAP 16-1 LAKE CHAMPLAIN & MORIAH RAILROAD

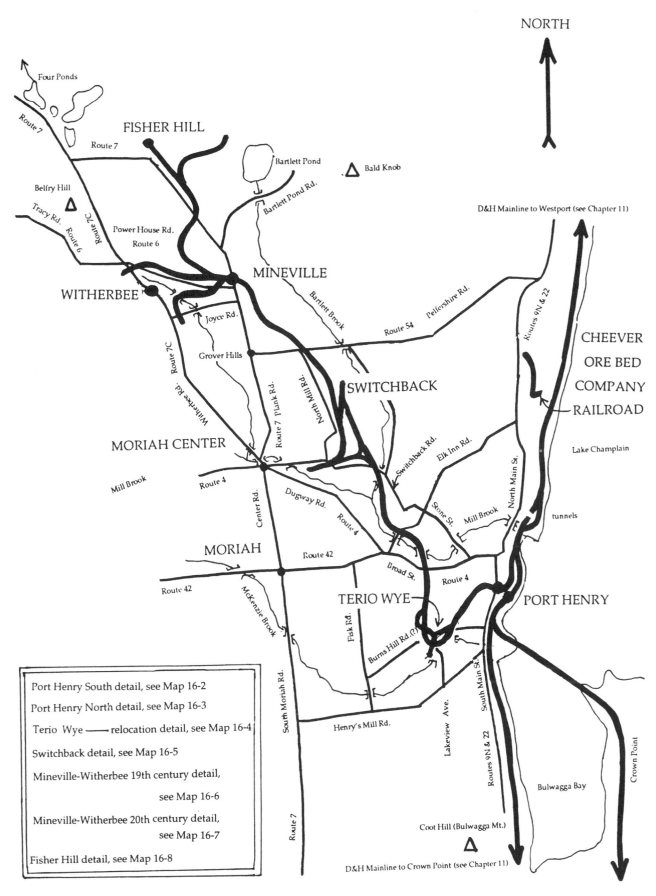

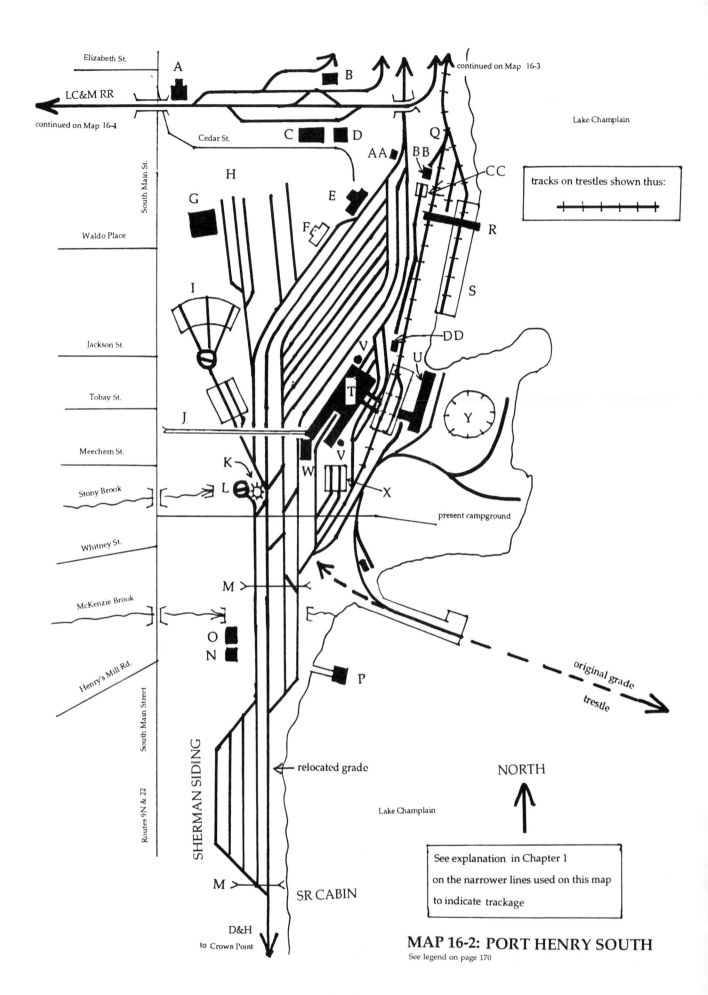

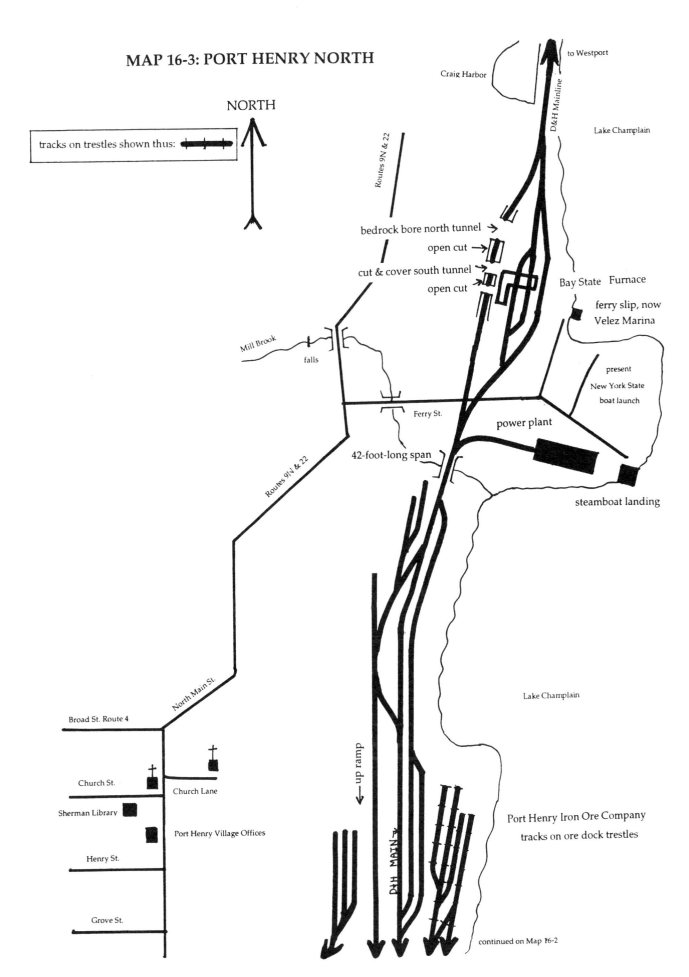

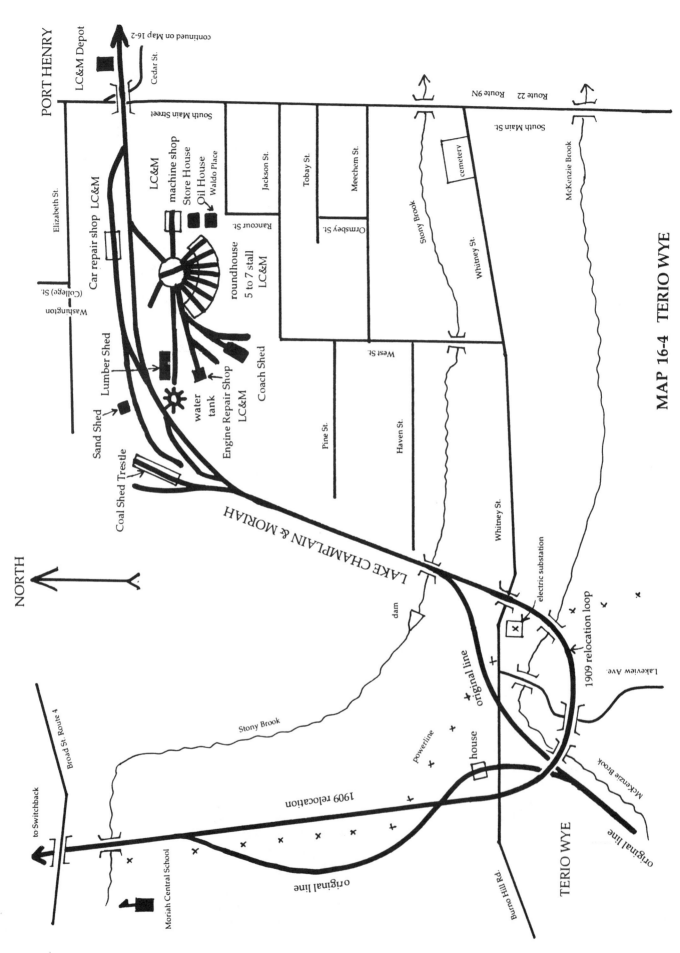

MAP 16-4 TERIO WYE

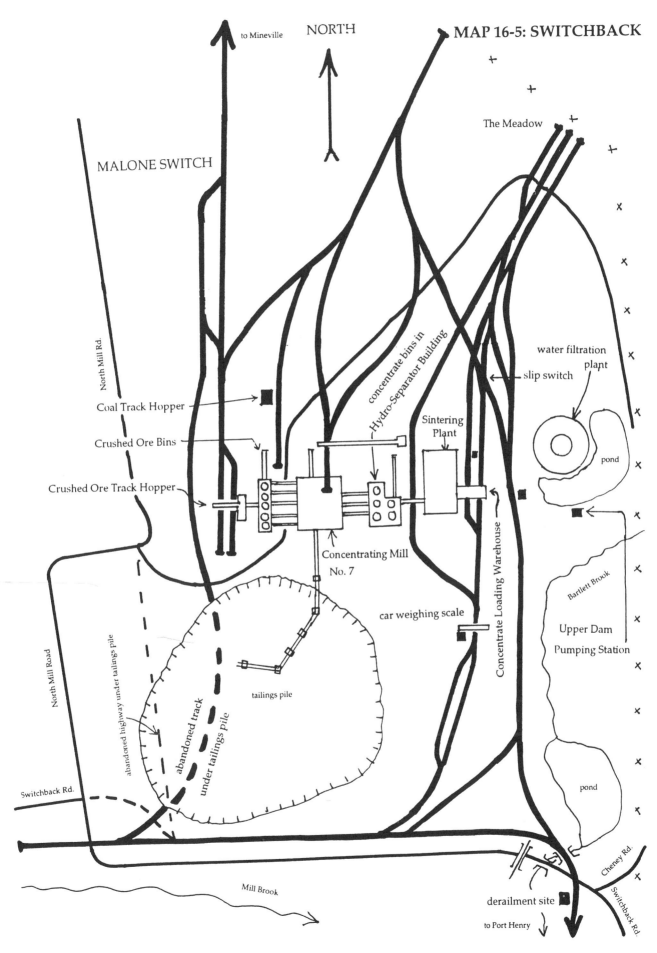

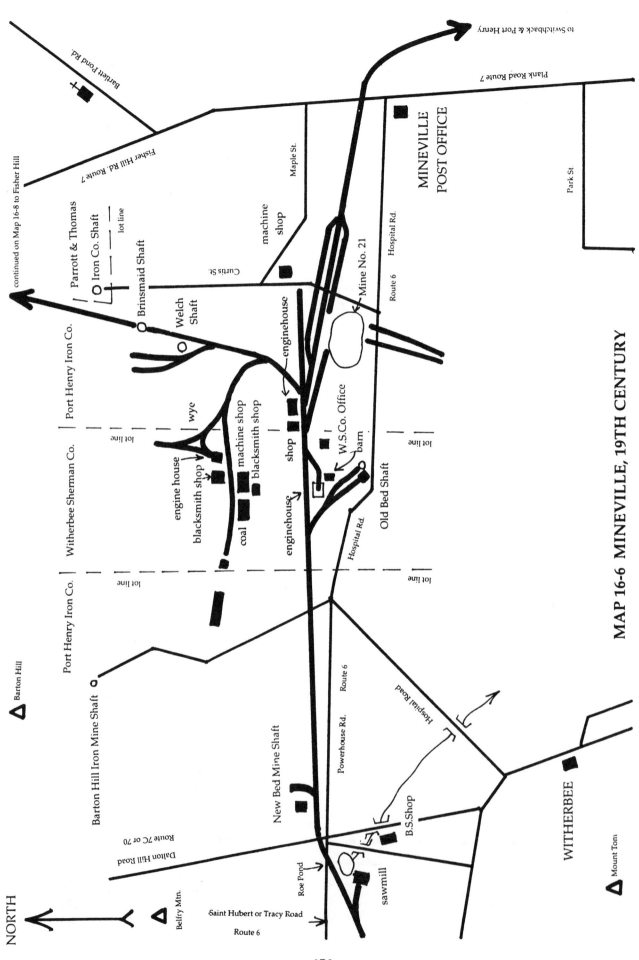

MAP 16-6 MINEVILLE, 19TH CENTURY

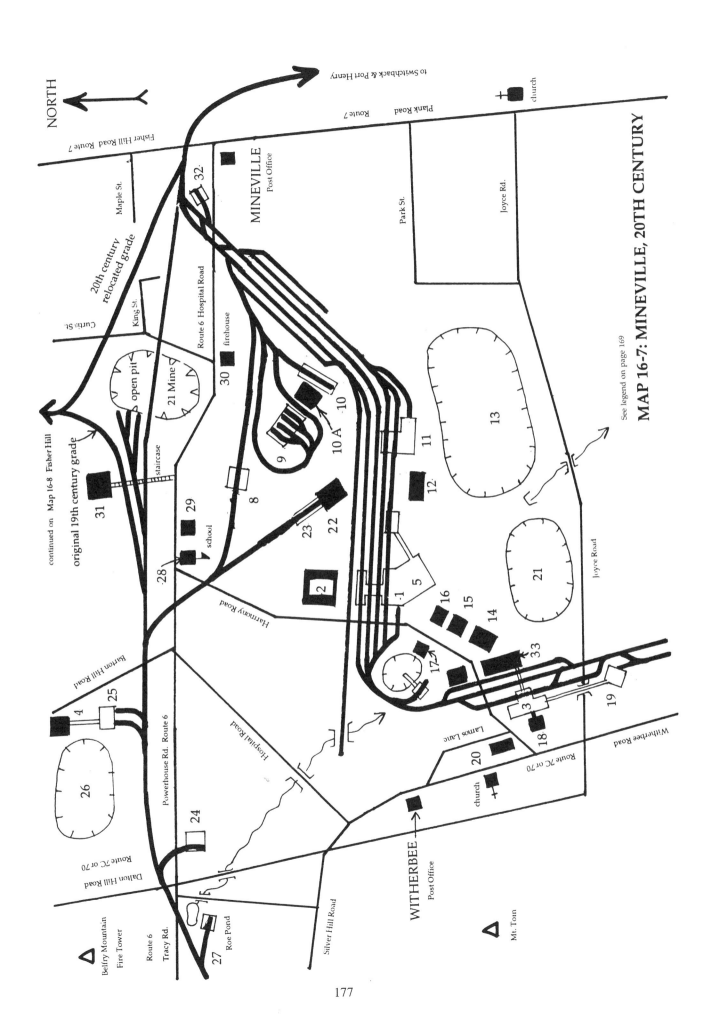

MAP 16-7: MINEVILLE, 20TH CENTURY

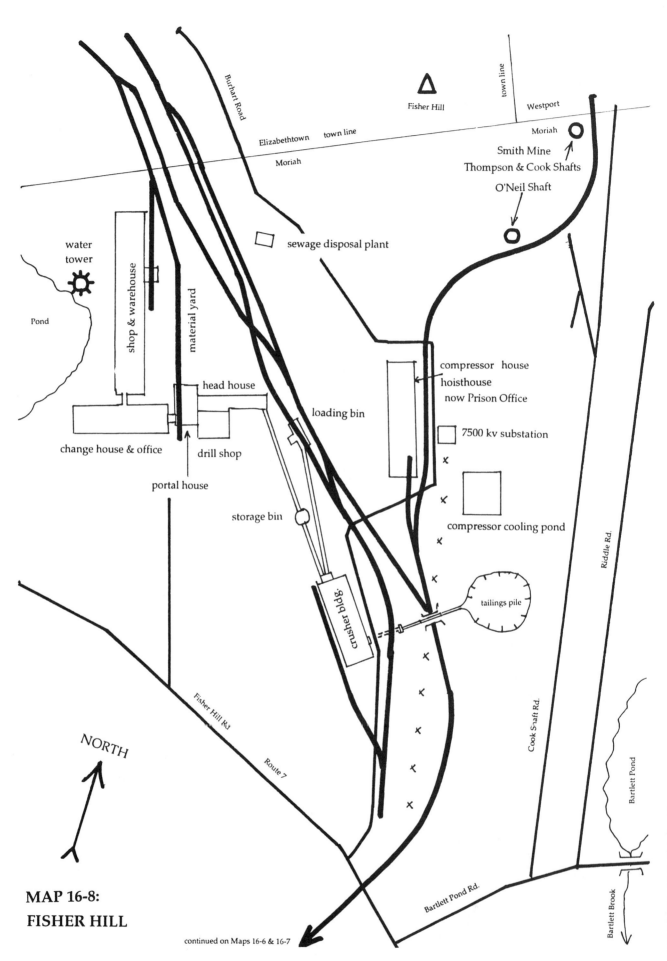

MAP 16-8:
FISHER HILL

Chapter 17:
Elizabethtown Terminal Railroad and the NY&P Railroad at Willsboro

A PROPOSED RAILROAD to connect the D&H Mainline at Westport with the Essex County seat at Elizabethtown was begun but never completed.

Most of the detail on Willsboro along the D&H Mainline will be found in Chapter 11 (Map 11-8). However, the New York and Pennsylvania Company had its own railroad, and this fact warrants inclusion in a short, separate chapter to further reduce the length of Chapter 11. See Map 17-3.

Elizabethtown Terminal Railroad

An article in the *Essex County Republican*, an Elizabethtown newspaper, reprinted in Kozma (1985) and dated March 31, 1910 describes the construction in progress. Another article dated June 2, 1910 shows a photo of the motor car purchased by the Elizabethtown Terminal Railroad Company. The car, built by the McKeen Motor Car Company of Omaha, Nebraska, apparently was never delivered as no rails were ever placed on the grade. The company had hoped to complete a 500-foot-long trestle over the Black River (not to be confused with the Black River separating the Adirondacks from the Tug Hill Plateau) by August 1, 1910. Stoddard's 1912 map of the Adirondacks shows the line as "to be built" and parallels what is currently State Highway 9N on the North. The eight-mile long line never opened, and Masters (1970) tells us that the finances and foreman both disappeared.

The grade is still visible in places. The best two localities to observe it today are (1) from the Mountain Shadows Restaurant, where the grade is between the restaurant and Highway 9N, eastward past the N.Y. State Department of Transportation yard to a high fill at Brainard's Forge Road west of the Black River and (2) between Route 9N and the cemetery east of Black River.

New York and Pennsylvania Company's Railroad at Willsboro

In the middle of the passing siding on the D&H Mainline, a spur once diverged eastward across Highway 22 and dropped steeply down to the Boquet River. See Wellman (1992) for details on the New York and Pennsylvania Company pulp mill, built in 1882 as the Champlain Pulp Mills, and its Shay and diesel locomotives. The Payne Library in Willsboro has a scrapbook of photos of the New York and Pennsylvania Company; Map 17-3 is based on these photos. West of the Highway 22 crossing was the mill's extensive pulpwood yard with at least nine tracks.

Wellman (1992) states that the mill was torn down in 1962. The tracks from the Route 22 grade crossing down to the mill and the pulpwood yard trackage were probably removed about the same time. One of the smaller mill buildings still stands and is now used by Ashline Produce. Sometime between 1962 and 1980 the Tambrands Company opened a plant on the site of the former pulpwood yard and operated it to ca. 1991. The spur from the D&H into the Tambrands plant still existed in 1992, but was no longer in service.

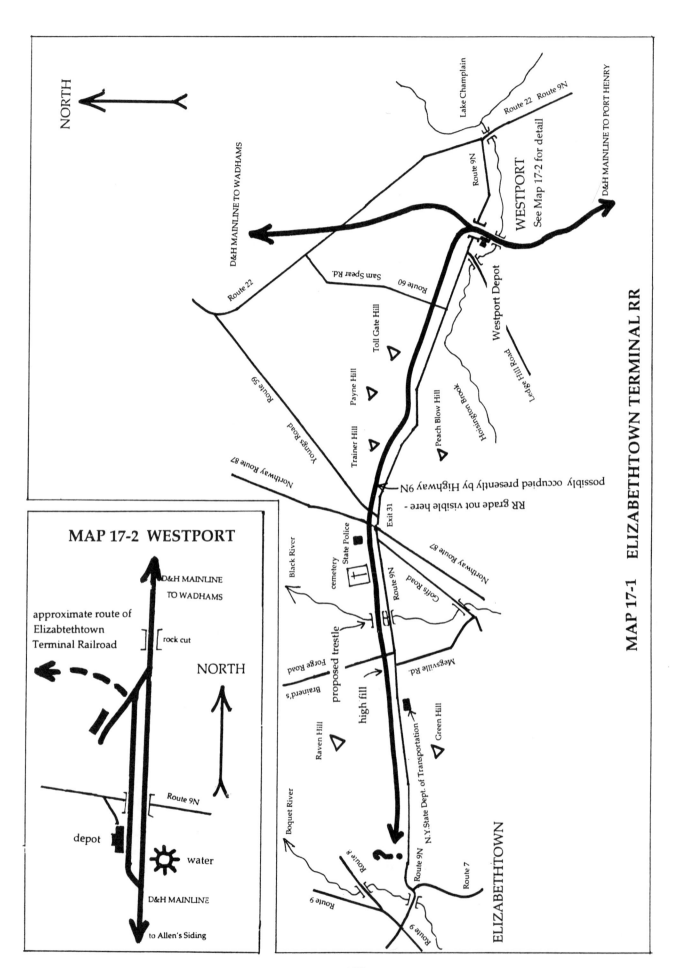

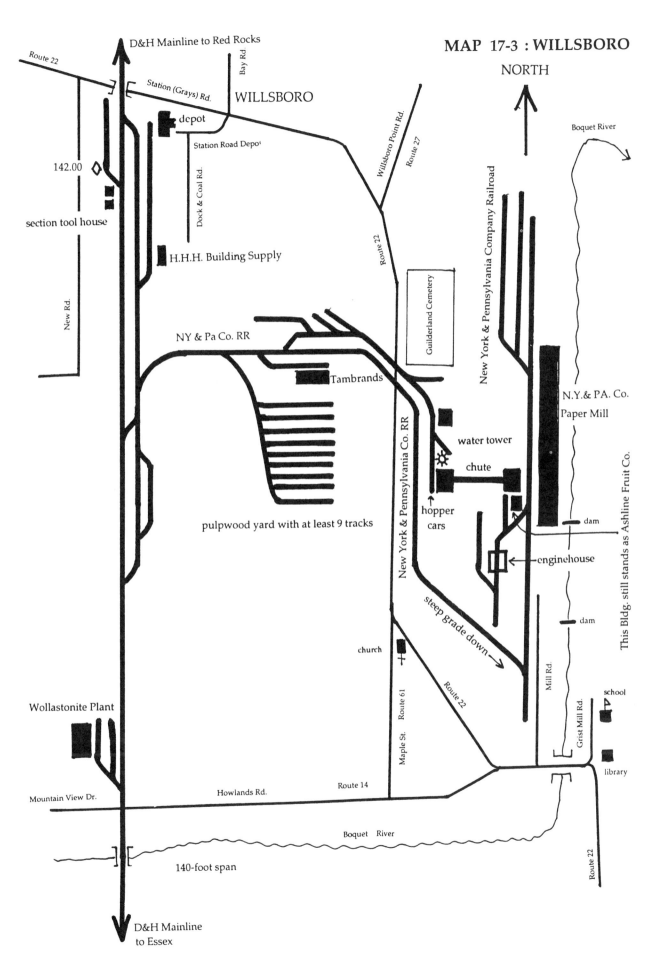

Chapter 18:
Keeseville, Ausable Chasm and Lake Champlain Railroad

THE KEESEVILLE, Ausable Chasm & Lake Champlain Railroad Company, a separately-owned line only 5.6 miles long, never became a branch of the D&H Railroad with which it connected at Port Kent (see Maps 11-9, 18-1 and 18-2). The *Annual Report of the New York State Board of Railroad Commissioners* (1893, p. 293) tells us that the line was chartered April 4, 1889 and began regular scheduled operations May 26, 1890. The first train to reach Keeseville, however, was on May 22. The Anderson Falls Heritage Society, a Keeseville area historical group, has a fine collection of photos, clippings and other materials on the line. Included in their collection is a photo of the trestle under construction over Ausable Chasm in (early?) May 1890. Clippings from the *Essex County Republican*, an Elizabethtown newspaper, dated March 21, 1889 and June 12, 1890 describe the proposed route and the opening of the railroad, respectively. The railroad was initially steam-powered.

The November 1, 1901 issue of the *Essex County Republican* describes a discussion between the KAC&LC personnel and that of the Paul Smith's Hotel Company, both at that time considering the construction of an electric railway. In 1903, articles in this newspaper still showed electrification in the planning stages, but by March 1, 1906 (according to Jim McFarlane, electric railroad historian, personal communication) the line was electrified. It ran with a third rail from Port Kent through the Route 9N highway crossing 0.4 mile east of Keeseville, but changed to catenary, i.e. overhead trolley wire, just outside the Keeseville terminal. A photo at the Anderson Falls Heritage Society shows the third rail on the river side of the track, in the vicinity of the match factory, supported by a short post rising from every fifth or sixth tie. Materials at the Anderson Falls Heritage Society suggest power failures as a major reason for de-electrification; legal problems with both stock holders and the Keeseville Power Company also made electrification ephemeral. Palmer (1979) lists February 1, 1911 as the last of the electric operation, but McFarlane informs me that it took place on December 31, 1911. The line continued to operate with steam.

A description of the line from Port Kent to Keeseville follows. Before electrification, the KAC&LC came in behind the Port Kent station on the D&H Mainline, according to a photo at the Society. McNamara (1914-1915) states that the KAC&LC depot was 85 yards north of the D&H depot, placing the former waiting shelter just north of the South Quay Street, Route 373, crossing. The present Amtrak open, but canopied, waiting shed was built in May 1995. Photos of Port Kent are available at The Adirondack Museum (catalog #P35716 and #35722), and in Shaughnessy (1967, pp. 378 and 381).

The KAC&LC gradually diverged northward from the D&H, climbing steeply, crossing Lake Street just north of North Street, and then swinging northwest, west, and southwest. Embankments of the old grade are still visible on and just outside the Port Kent Golf Course in three places. The railroad closely paralleled Route 373 for a short distance east of the Soper Road highway intersection. Apparently, there were neither industries nor spurs between Port Kent and Ausable Chasm.

The present U.S. Highway 9 bridge over Ausable Chasm, completed in 1932, is almost on the same site of the former railroad trestle. One can see today, by peering down into the bottom of the chasm from the Route 9 bridge, that the bases of both railroad trestle abutments are not exactly parallel to the highway bridge, but are rotated at an angle of about five to ten degrees. The track crossed the Ausable River in a slightly more north-south direction. The original highway bridge over the Chasm still stands about 0.2 mile upstream.

The Ausable Chasm station was 4.3 miles from Port Kent, or 1.3 miles from Keeseville. This would place the depot at the Old State Road highway crossing, and probably on the northwest corner according to the 1893 Plattsburgh U.S.G.S. 15-minute quadrangle. There were several hotels in the vicinity of the depot to serve the famous tourist attraction.

This quadrangle also shows a short spur diverging toward the river from the main track south of the Old State Road. The spur served the Alice Falls Pulp and/or Paper Mill, built in 1890 and purchased in 1905 by J. & J. Rogers (MacKinnon, 1995). In 1992, the old mill was being rebuilt as an electric power plant.

Upstream from the pulp mill was a rolling mill and, above that, a match factory. Photos of these industries at the Society show no sidings so that one wonders if and how freight cars were loaded and unloaded.

The old Keeseville station still stands but has been modified so that it no longer resembles a depot. It is currently the North Country Club Restaurant and is located on the northwest side of U.S. Highway 9 several hundred feet from the highway junction of Routes 9 and 9N. This writer has been told that a Chevrolet garage now stands on the site of the freight house, but this needs confirmation. Reproductions of a picture postcard, mailed August 27, 1908, are for sale at the Society offices in Keeseville; the card shows the Keeseville station with a high shed over two tracks, catenary, boxcab electric locomotive #3 with trolley poles and a pilot (cowcatcher), a coach, and two boxcars.

In addition to the electric locomotive #3 described above, the KAC&LC owned at least three steam locomotives, but not all necessarily simultaneously. Gardner (1975, p. 11) depicts two scenes of the 158-foot-high cantilever bridge over the Ausable Chasm. The first shows Mogul No. 1, a 2-6-0, with a sloping-rear tender pulling (backwards) a single open-vestibule combine. On page 203 of Shaughnessy (1967) is a close-up of No. 1 at the D&H Railroad's Colonie shops for repairs in 1913. Number 1 was sold to the Schoharie Valley Railway and was renumbered 6. The second Gardner photo shows another steam locomotive, a 2-4-4T tank engine with tender as a single unit, pulling a short mixed train. Photos at the Anderson Falls Heritage Society include a 4-4-0 on a trestle with flatcars and #1. Apparently, steam locomotives were not turned; trains were pulled westbound and pushed eastbound.

Gardner (1975, pp. 10 and 83) includes a KAC&LC timetable of June 26, 1916. There were seven round trips daily, three on Sunday, to meet the boats of the Champlain Transportation Company and the D&H Railroad trains. Trips originated at Keeseville and required a running time one-way of 20 minutes for the 5.6 miles. Thus a single train shuttling back and forth could provide all the passenger service. Two of the seven round trips daily were to meet boats only. D&H timetables show five round trips daily in other years.

The KAC&LC had proposed an extension up the Ausable River from Keeseville to Rogers Station (where it might have connected with the Ausable Branch) serving industries en route, but permission for this extension was denied and it was never built.

Closure of the KAC&LC was on February 5, 1924 (Shaughnessy, p. 203).

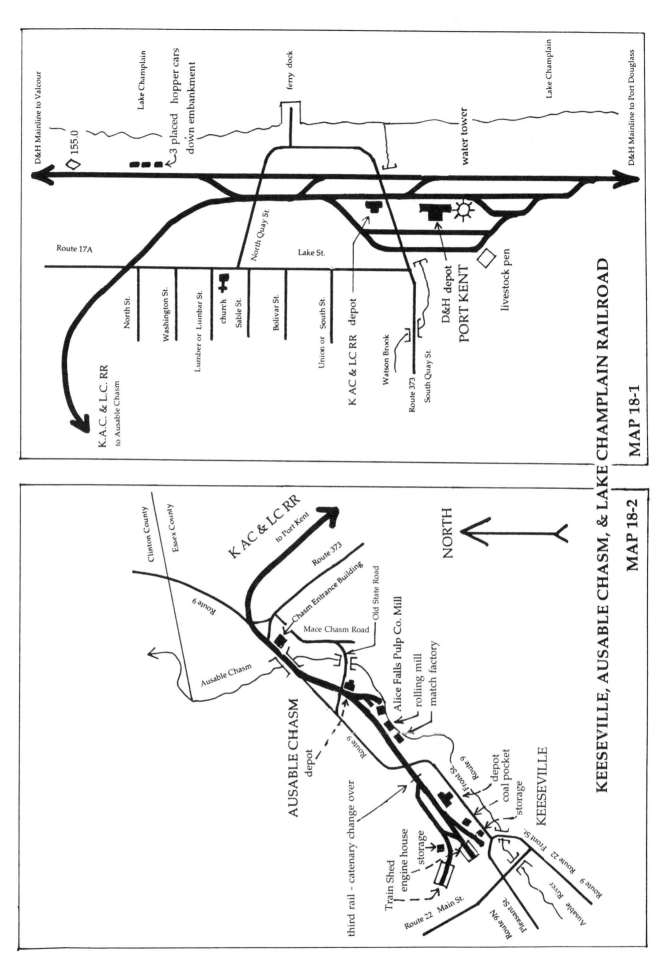

Chapter 19: Ausable Branch

THE CONSTRUCTION HISTORY of this branch is far more involved and fascinating than I ever imagined! It was built from Plattsburgh to Ausable River before the mainline through Port Kent. Shaughnessy (1967, p. 137) states that in 1866, the Whitehall & Plattsburgh was organized to build a railroad between these two points. Construction began at both ends, from Plattsburgh south toward Ausable River and from Ticonderoga north toward Port Henry (the Whitehall-Ticonderoga segment was built later). The idea was to avoid the rugged cliffs, known as the Red Rocks, along Lake Champlain north of Willsboro by constructing a line inland between Port Henry and Plattsburgh. The proposed Ausable River-Port Henry inland route never materialized, leaving the Plattsburgh-Ausable River segment "hanging" without a through-route mainline function. Thus Ausable River became a terminus and the Plattsburgh-Ausable River segment became only a branch.

Construction from Plattsburgh to Ausable River was completed in the latter part of 1868 (Shaughnessy, 1967, p. 137; D&H, 1925, p. 241; and Hardy, 1985, p. 137). The terminus was called Ausable River and later Rogers. Maps showing construction appear on pages 153 and 164 of Shaughnessy and Beers (1869).

When the D&H mainline was opened via Red Rocks in 1875, it joined the Ausable line at a point 0.86 mile south of the present Plattsburgh station. Saint Pierre (1990) emphasizes the attempts of Smith Weed to bring the railroad to Plattsburgh from Whitehall. She describes the competition, almost conflict, between New Yorkers and Vermonters about the route of the line.

Relocation of the junction with the mainline to South Junction occurred in 1894, and lengthened the line by 0.9 mile. Shaughnessy (1967, p. 202) states the reasons for the junction relocation: not enough room in downtown Plattsburgh for yard and storage tracks, and to get the line off the military reservation. The military reservation became the U.S. Air Force Base much later, with runway construction beginning in 1955-1956 forcing further railroad relocation: this time of the Chateaugay Branch (see Chapter 20 paragraphs on Bluff Point). The Air Force Base closed in 1995.

Also in 1894 the Ausable Branch was extended 2.7 miles upstream to Ausable Forks and another 1.2 miles to the J.& J. Rogers Pulp Mill.

For the first time, an article wholly devoted to the Ausable Branch has been published (Hardy, 1985) with the first photographs. The primary reason for construction of this branch, according to Hardy, was to serve the two iron mines, Peru's at Arnold and Rogers' at Palmer Hill further west. A secondary function was to serve passengers continuing further into the Adirondacks via connecting stagecoach, for example to Paul Smith's Hotel.

Because the segment of the current D&H mainline in the downtown portion of the City of Plattsburgh was originally part of the Ausable line, detail on the downtown Plattsburgh area is included in this chapter instead of in Chapter 11 on the D&H Mainline. (Enormous Chapter 11 on the D&H mainline is already overflowing with detail while this chapter has plenty of room for expansion.) Detail on the Furnace Branch, an originally narrow gauge spur of the Chateaugay Railroad in Plattsburgh, is found on Map 19-4. Detail on the Freydenburg Falls Branch, also off the Chateaugay, is also found in Chapter 20 and especially Map 20-9.

Mileages

The following list of stations and industries includes mileages after the 1894 relocation via South Junction. These mileages are from a 1919 D&H timetable. For mileages prior to 1894, estimate 0.9 mile less from Salmon River to Ausable River.

Station Descriptions

Plattsburgh. 0.0 mile. Elevation 118 feet. Maps 11-1, 11-10, 19-1, 19-3, 19-4, 19-5, 19-9, 20-1, and 20-2.

Passenger station: The original station was located out on the dock from 1852, when the railroad was completed from Mooers Junction, through at least 1877 according to the map in Shaughnessy (1967, p. 152). This must have been convenient for passengers transferring to and from steamboats, but what happened after 1868 when the line was extended south to Ausable River? Timetables of 1870 and 1872 (in Shaughnessy, 1964, pp. 31 and 43 respectively) show that there were no through trains at Plattsburgh; trains from Montreal and Ausable River did not always connect conveniently either. But what happened after 1875? Did through trains make a side trip down onto the dock to stop at the station and then back out?

Gardner (1990, Volume 4, page 66) includes several photos and drawings of passenger stations. She notes a station built in 1875 and torn down in 1886 when the present depot was built. She does not mention a depot which must have been in existence from 1852 to 1875. McLeod (1983) described a festival on October 5 of that year commencing the restoration of the depot as a historic site. Burdick (1985) describes contemporary Amtrak service through this station. McLeod (1993) wrote on restoration of the depot.

Plattsburgh Traction Company: Trolley cars served the station from 1895 or 1896 through 1929, stopping on Bridge street at the back of the building. See Borrup (1970-1971) for detail and Map 19-5 here based on his. Shaughnessy also has some information on the Plattsburgh Traction Company.

Photographs: Shaughnessy has photos of the Plattsburgh area on his pages 152, 155, 214, 215, 294, 374, 400, and 423. Zimmermann (1978) has photos on page 16 and 17, while Plant and Plant (1993) offer one on page 45.

Passing sidings: The D&H mainline was once double-tracked through Plattsburgh, and in some places even triple-tracked (see Maps 19-3 and 19-4).

Servicing facilities: In 1869 there was a woodshed. In 1889 there was a machine shop which stands to this day, although now abandoned. The turntable, also present in 1869, still stands but is also unused. The roundhouse was burned about 1992 and many historic records were apparently destroyed in the blaze. Steam lines once emerged from the machine shop to heat passenger cars on a nearby siding. The April 28, 1940 D&H Employees' Timetable, page 43, lists a machine shop track, an ice house at the shops, a turntable track, an engine house track, a ten-stall roundhouse, a coaling track, and a dump track with coal chute and sand spout.

The narrow gauge Chateaugay Railroad: This line from 1878 through 1903 had its own servicing facilities (see Chapter 20).

Freight station: There was one on the dock in 1869 along with a storehouse, according to Beers (1869). Gardner (1990, Volume 4, page 66) offers a photo of a freight house built in 1875 and burned in 1880. The second freight office was built in 1880, burned in 1911, and repaired in 1912.

Industrial sidings: In 1869 there were four: S. Carter's Tannery, G.W. Bodds Saw Factory, a bakery, and a G. Mill (possibly a grist mill?). In 1889, there was the Saranac Manufacturing Company; its buildings became the Lake Champlain Pulp & Paper Company's in 1916. The 1902 Sanborn Insurance Company maps indicate the Lozier Motor Company on the site of the present Georgia Pacific paper mill. Other industries in 1902 between the Saranac River and Lozier were W. Wilcox & Son coal, wood, and hay; and the Plattsburgh Creamery. Frank Pabst Headquarters Warehouse, out on the dock, burned during the winter of 1984-1985. In 1902 there was the Dock & Coal Company lumber yard. Armour Meats had been abandoned long before 1977. In the 1916 era, International Paper Company had a track at South Dock. In 1902, the Baker Brothers Planing Mill and lumber yard were about to be tied to their operation at Tekene (see Chapter 20). The April 28, 1940 D&H Employees' Timetable, page 43, lists but does not locate the following industries: Berst, Forster & Dixfield Company track; Plattsburgh Coal Company track, and Diamond Match Company track.

Steamboat: At the North Dock the steamboat *Oakes Ames* connected with the trains in 1869.

Saranac River and Cumberland Avenue Bridges: North of Plattsburgh depot is the 155-foot span over the Saranac River at milepost 167.80. Just north of bridge at 167.87, the D&H had to remove the old Cumberland Avenue overpass in 1974 to make clearance adequate for the then-new high-cube box cars and possibly the dome cars, leased from the Canadian Pacific by Amtrak. The City of Plattsburgh had to build the present Cumberland Avenue overpass.

Furnace Branch: 0.3 mile south of the present Plattsburgh depot, at Elevation 125, the Chateaugay Railroad's Furnace Branch diverged, initially narrow-gauged. See Maps 11-10, 19-1, 19-4, 19-5, 20-1 and 20-2 and Chapter 20 text.

Junction with Ausable Branch and D&H Mainline prior to 1894: This junction was 0.86 mile south of the present Plattsburgh depot at elevation 136. See Maps 11-10, 19-1, 19-4, 19-5, 20-1, 20-2, and 20-9. The original 1868 line to the Ausable River joined the subsequently built 1875 D&H Mainline here. During the period 1868 through 1894, the Ausable Branch proceeded to strike out in a southwesterly direction cutting across what is now the U.S. Air Force Base. After 1894, when the Ausable Branch's connecting point with the mainline was relocated to South Junction, this junction ceased to exist. All that remained was a short stub 0.4-mile long shown on the 1939-1956 15-minute Plattsburgh quadrangle. After 1894, Ausable Branch trains used the D&H mainline through Cliff Haven and Bluff Point to South Junction (See Chapter 11), then diverged from the mainline and headed west to:

Salmon River Junction. 6.1 miles from Plattsburgh via South Junction, but ca. 5.2 miles via the original 1868 route. Elevation 170. Maps 11-10, 19-1, 19-6, 20-1, and 20-2.

Passenger station: The station was in service from the 1868-1870 period through 1931.

Industrial siding: Quick Flame Gas Corporation was here in 1916, but in 1984 it was Par Gas. The Ausable Branch presently terminates just south of this siding after having been abandoned back from Ausable Forks in 1981.

Chateaugay Branch: At this point the Chateaugay Branch diverged from the Ausable Branch after the former's 1955 relocation off the Air Force Base runway. See Chapter 20. This point became Salmon River Junction in 1955.

Miscellany: The original Ausable Branch route, 1868 to 1894, joined the relocation via South Junction here.

Laphams Mills. 8.8 miles. Elevation 306. Maps 19-1 and 19-7.

Passenger station: The original name for this station was Bartonville Station. Between 1870 and 1875 the name was changed to Lapham's Mills, but by 1891 the name was shortened to Lapham's. Gardner (1990, Volume 4, page 49) offers a photo of the waiting room built in 1901. The station is still listed on a July 2, 1928 timetable, but did not reopen in 1931.

Passing siding: One is shown on the 1916 D&H map.

Industrial siding: I have neither information on the nature of the mills nor whether the railroad served them.

Peru. 10.9 miles. Elevation 348. Maps 19-1 and 19-7.

Passenger station: The station was in service from the 1868-1870 period through 1931. Gardner (1990, Volume 4, page 49) offers a photo of the combination passenger and freight station built in 1872. It still stood in 1991.

Passing sidings: There were two on a 1916 D&H map, the northerly with a crossover in the middle.

Industrial sidings: Several were shown on a 1916 D&H map. One served a creamery, the building occupied by Agway in 1991. A second served the Northern Orchard Company which shipped apples. A third siding served several industries including Peru Butter & Cheese Company; LaVarnway & Kennedy (nature of industry unknown); Clark & Holden, in 1914-1915 shippers of apples, fertilizers, hay and straw; and A. Mason & Son, in 1914-1915, a sawmill and lumber dealer). A refrigeration service is on the site in 1991 of Clark & Holden.

Harkness. 15.2 miles. Elevation 375. Maps 19-2 and 19-7.

Passenger station: One is shown on the 1911 Dannemora quadrangle as straddling both tracks south of the crossing, obviously an error. It was in service from the 1868-1870 period through 1931. Gardner (1990, volume 4, page 50) shows the shelter built in 1913. She notes that the original shelter was located about 200 feet to the south and burned.

Passing siding: The U.S.G.S. 1911 Dannemora quadrangle shows the passing siding on the west of the main, but a 1916 D&H map shows it on the east. Was the siding relocated?

Industrial siding: Sheffield Farms Company, Inc. Creamery is shown on the D&H 1916 map.

Arnold (Ferrona). 17.9 miles. Elevation 507. Maps 19-2 and 19-7.

Passenger station: Timetables from 1870 through 1900 list this stop as Ferrona, but by 1906 the name had become Arnold. The station was in service through 1931. I have never seen a photo of it.

Passing siding: The D&H 1916 map shows one.

Industrial sidings: The D&H 1916 map shows two. The Ausable quadrangle, surveyed in 1893-1903, indicates a railroad heading west up to the Arnold Hill iron mine, but with an ascent of some 500 feet in 1.2 miles, averaging 7.9%. Hardy (1985) informs us, "Arnold Hill and nearby Clintonville were thriving villages tied to the Peru Steel and Iron Company. A tramway, an ingenious miniature rail system operated by gravity and horses, connected the mines at Arnold Hill with Arnold Station, a distance of 1.5 miles." James Rogers III (owner of radio station WNBZ in Saranac Lake) tells me that the inclined railway was narrow gauge and had two tracks; in this case, then, there was no physical connection with the standard-gauged Ausable Branch. Loaded ore cars were let down on one track to Arnold Station while empties were drawn up as a counterweight on the other track. By the time the 1953 Ausable Forks quadrangle was surveyed, the Arnold hill iron mine railroad had long been abandoned.

Ausable River or Rogers. 20.8 miles. Elevation 578. Maps 19-2 and 19-8.

Passenger station: This was the terminus from 1868 through 1894. From here, the line from Plattsburgh was to cross the Ausable River and continue southward to be connected with the line being built northward from Port Henry and Westport. This southward connection was never built and the line into Ausable River was thus left "hanging" as a branch. We know, however, the approximate route of the proposed but never built inland mainline: James Bailey, Plattsburgh City Historian, has provided me with a map from the Asher and Adams atlas (See Chapter 11 in the section on Wadhams Mills). In this 1871 atlas, Ausable River is called New Sweden. The station name on the timetables was Ausable River in 1870, Ausable in 1872 and 1875, and Rogers in 1891 through at least July 2, 1928. It did not reopen in 1931. Another name for the station at one time was Point of Rocks. Industrial sidings: Hardy (1985, p. 8) includes a photo of this station taken in the late nineteenth century; it shows two tracks in front of the station and a third track around the rear of what looks like a freight station. The J.&J. Rogers Company was initially an iron company with mines at Palmer Hill, located north of Ausable Forks and nearly three miles west-southwest of the Peru Steel and Iron Company's mines at Arnold Hill. From 1868 through 1894, the nearest rail head to Palmer Hill was here at Ausable River 2.7 miles east-northeast. The photo in Hardy shows iron billets, presumably from Palmer Hill, lined up along a siding.

Stagecoach connections: Paul Smith's Hotel Company stagecoaches met the trains here from 1868 through 1886.

Ausable Forks. 23.5 miles. Elevation 551. Maps 19-2 and 19-8.

Passenger station: The station was in service from 1894 through 1931. Gardner (1990, Volume 4, page 50) has a photo of the combination passenger and freight station built in 1893. I have been told that the building had been built earlier at Rogers and moved to Ausable Forks in 1894. It was moved in 1967 diagonally across the street and is now the D&H Freight House Eatery. The original station site is now a picnic area.

Facilities: A 65-foot turntable and water tank were here.

Industrial sidings: Smith's Storehouse and Standard Oil Company were also served here. Observations were made by the author on July 11, 1975 of boxcars for Ward Lumber in Jay and Haselton Lumber in Haselton.

Miscellany: The three grade crossings within one-half mile of each other along Route 9N east of the hamlet, and the track running down the middle of the street were an unusual sight as late as 1981! The rails were still visible in the pavement as late as August 24, 1991, but by May 8, 1992 they had been paved over.

J.&J. Rogers Company (Rome). 24.7 miles. Elevation 600.

Maps 19-2 and 19-8.

Hardy (1985) and Mackinnon (1995) tell us that the J.&J. Rogers Company closed their iron industry in 1889 and began their paper industry in 1893. The Palmer Hill iron mines were abandoned and a pulp mill was constructed 1.2 miles west of Ausable Forks. The railroad was extended from Ausable River through Ausable Forks directly to the new pulp mill in November of 1894. The 1893 Ausable quadrangle, revised in 1903, labels the hamlet surrounding the mill as "Rome."

In 1902, the J.&J. Rogers Company built a paper mill roughly midway between the pulp mill and Ausable Forks. The Robeson Process Company mill treated some of the waste from the mills. The pulp mill closed first, sometime between 1923 and 1943. By 1953, the Ausable Forks quadrangle shows the track abandoned back from the pulp mill to the paper mill. The paper mill closed later, about 1970, but the unused track still reached it as late as 1981. Hardy (1985, page 9) offers two photos of the mills with the track in the foreground.

Timetable Operation

The timetables of May 6, 1870 through April 2, 1928, recorded two passenger train trips daily each way originating at Plattsburgh. The first was in the morning and the second, mixed with freight in 1870, was in the afternoon. An exceptional period is shown on the timetables from 1875 through 1893 when only a single round-trip daily operated. By 1898, there were two daily again. Running times varied over the years from a minimum of 45 minutes to a maximum of 120 minutes one-way, the latter for mixed trains.

After the 1894 relocation, Ausable Branch trains stopped at Cliff Haven from ca. 1902 through 1931, at Bluff Point from ca. 1894 through 1927, and at South Junction from ca. 1894 through 1931. See Chapter 11 on the D&H Mainline for detail on these three stations. Cliff Haven and Bluff Point were open during the summer months only.

The termination of passenger service on the Ausable Branch is a curious one. There were still two passenger trains daily shown on the timetable of April 2, 1928, but only one daily on July 2, 1928: odd because summer normally meant additional service, not a reduction. I have no timetables for 1929. The D&H system timetables of April 27 and June 29, 1930 no longer include passenger service on the Ausable Branch. However, the June 28, 1931 indicates a very temporary resurrection of service because by September 27, 1931 it disappeared for good. Trains in 1931 did not stop at Laphams Mills nor Rogers. Local historians in Ausable Forks have informed me that the temporary resurrection of passenger service in 1931 was accomplished by some prominent residents of that community successfully persuading the D&H.

Equipment and Abandonment

Equipment, because the Ausable Branch was standard-gauged and connected with the D&H mainline, could be shared with the mainline.

Hardy mentions that the last freight trains in Ausable Forks occurred in the late 1970s. This agrees with my sightings of boxcars there in 1975 and 1977. My sources indicate that the tracks were removed from just south of Salmon River Junction to Ausable Forks in August or September of 1981.

Legend to Map 19-4: Plattsburgh

1. Fouquet House, a hotel owned at one time by Paul Smith. Lowest two floors still exist in 1994.
2. Baker Brothers Planing and Saw Mill and Lumber Yard in 1902.
3. Platform in 1902, probably for Chateaugay Railroad narrow gauge passenger service and/or freight.
4. Chateaugay Railroad Company Car Repair Shop for narrow gauge in 1902 and freight house.
5. Armour & Company Meats before relocation to #13.
6. Plattsburgh Traction Company Trolley Barn from 1895 to 1929. See Map 19-5 for detail. Wilcox Ice House in 1889. Racine Auto Parts in 1984. Fasino's Auto Supply in 1985.
7. Kindling Wood Factory in 1889. Plattsburgh Light, Heat & Power Company in 1902 and 1916. Later the Plattsburgh Gas & Electric Company. New York State Gas & Electric until the 1970s.
8. The Williams Manufacturing Company, making sewing machines and bicycles in 1902. Police Station in 1984.

9-11. Plattsburgh Foundry, Chateaugay Ore & Iron Company in 1889 and in 1916. #9 is a machine shop. #10 is an engine house. #11 is a shed. The foundry was still operating in 1984, but had another owner, and a sign outside stated that the buildings were built in 1890.

12. Chateaugay Ore & Iron Company Furnace in 1889. Vacant in 1902.
13. Armour Meats, relocated from #5.
14. S. Carter's Tannery in 1869. Saranac Manufacturing Company in 1889. Lake Champlain Paper & Pulp Company in 1916.

15. G. Mill in 1869 (probably "G" stands for "grist" on the 1869 map).
16. G. W. Bodds Saw Factory in 1869.
17. Bakery in 1869.
18. Lake Champlain Paper & Pulp Company.
19. Grist mill in late 19th century.

The bridge over the Saranac River on the Furnace Branch was double-decker: Saranac Street below and the railroad above.

Compiled mainly from these major sources: James Bailey, Plattsburgh City Historian; 1869 and 1889 J. L. Beers' atlases of Clinton County; 1902 Sanborn Insurance Map; 1916 Delaware & Hudson valuation and track diagram; Chateaugay Railroad valuation and track diagram; 1984-1985 field checks.

The D&H freight house at Ausable Forks was moved a short distance and is now a restaurant.
Author photo, October 1993.

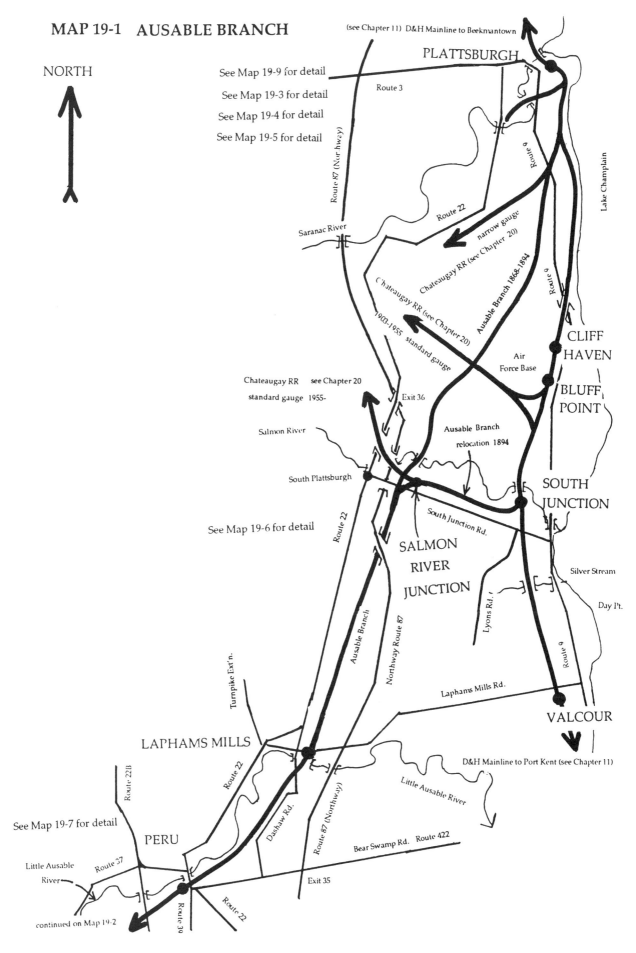

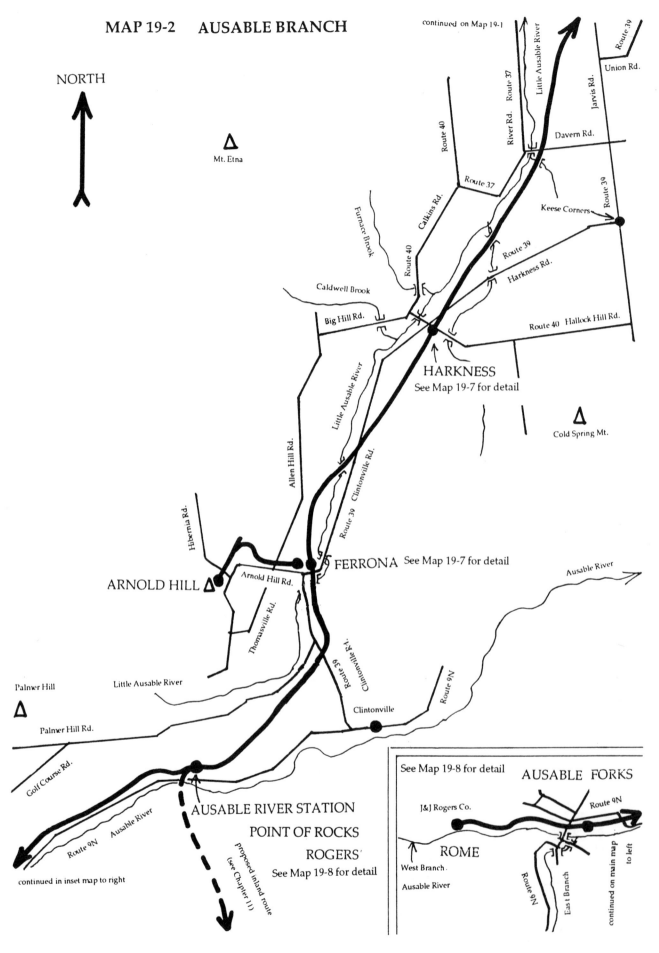

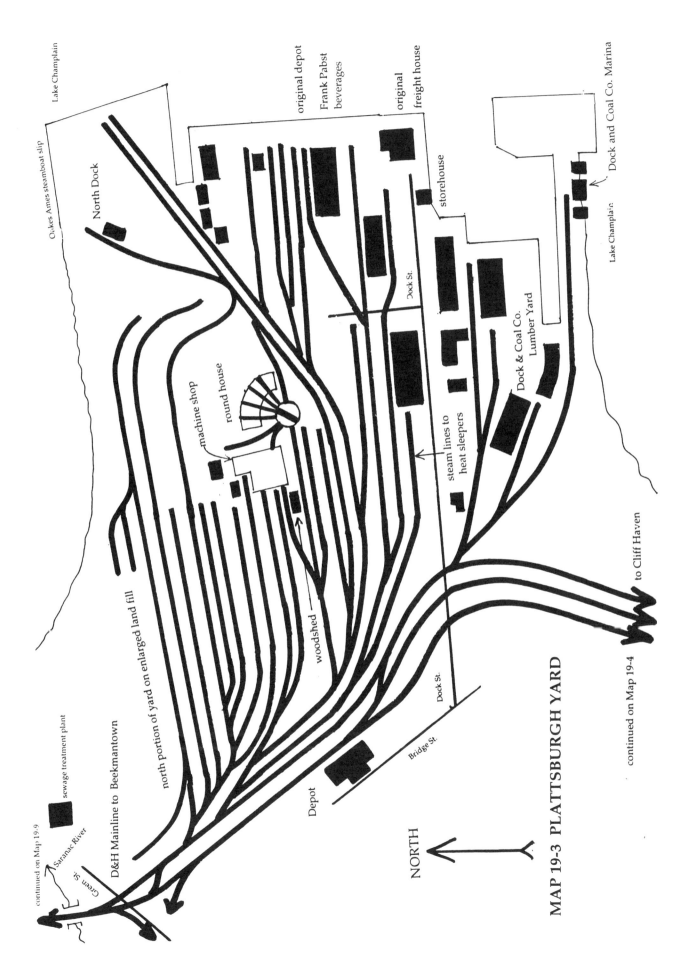

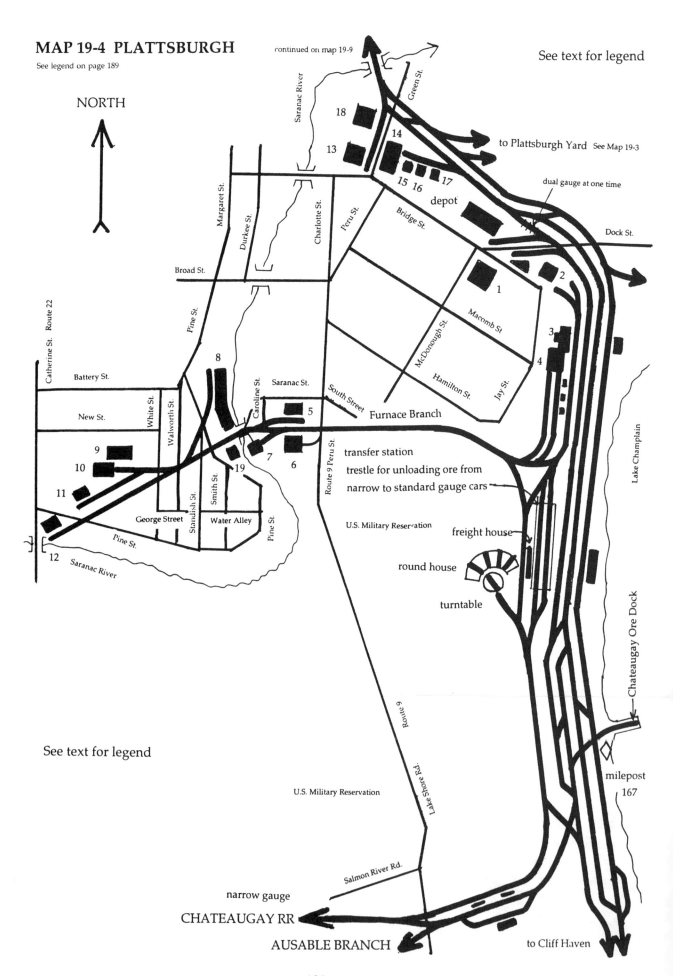

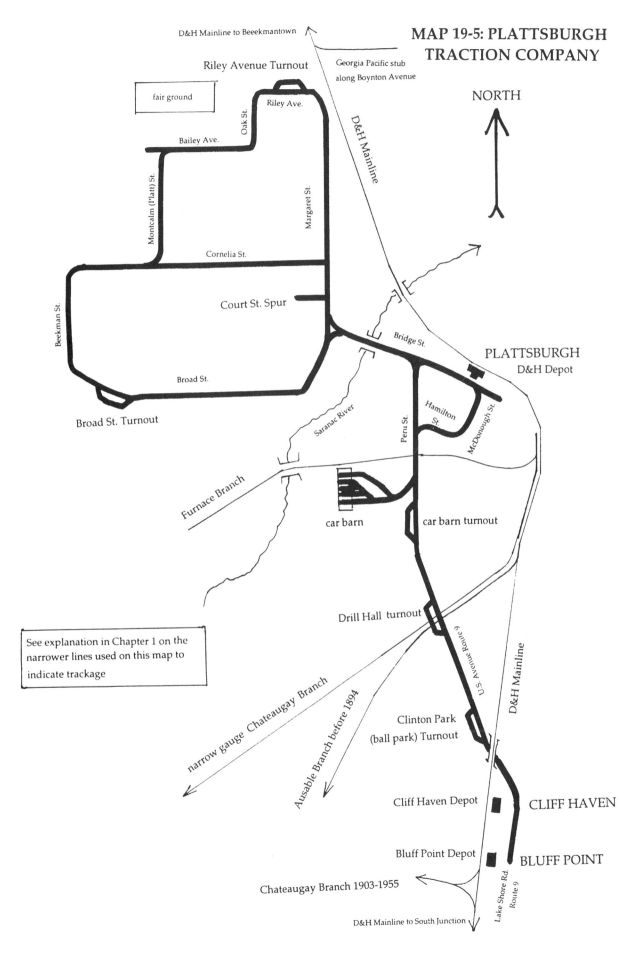

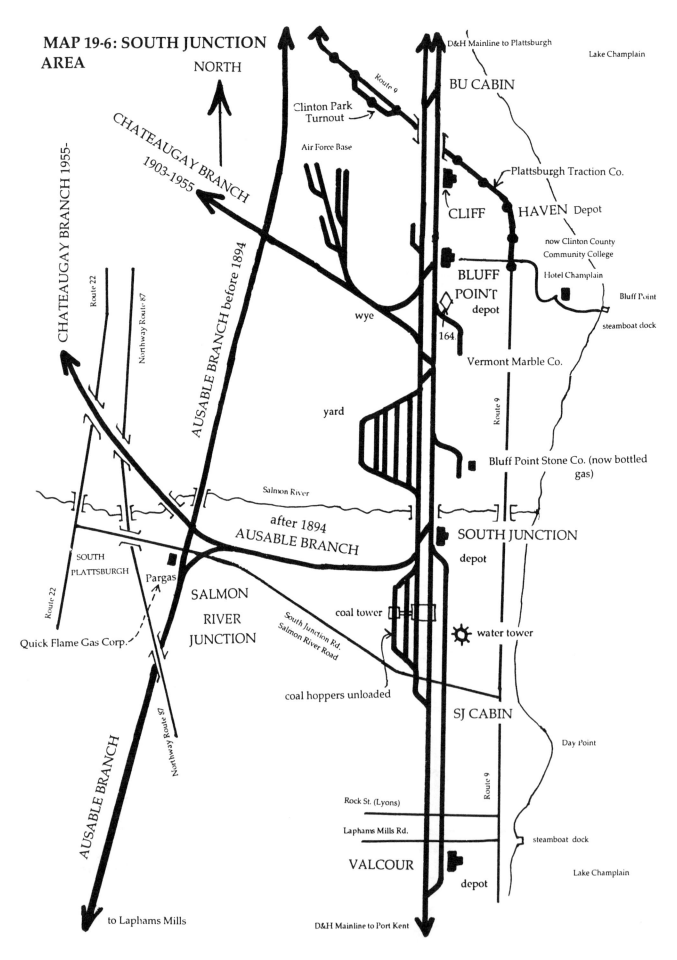

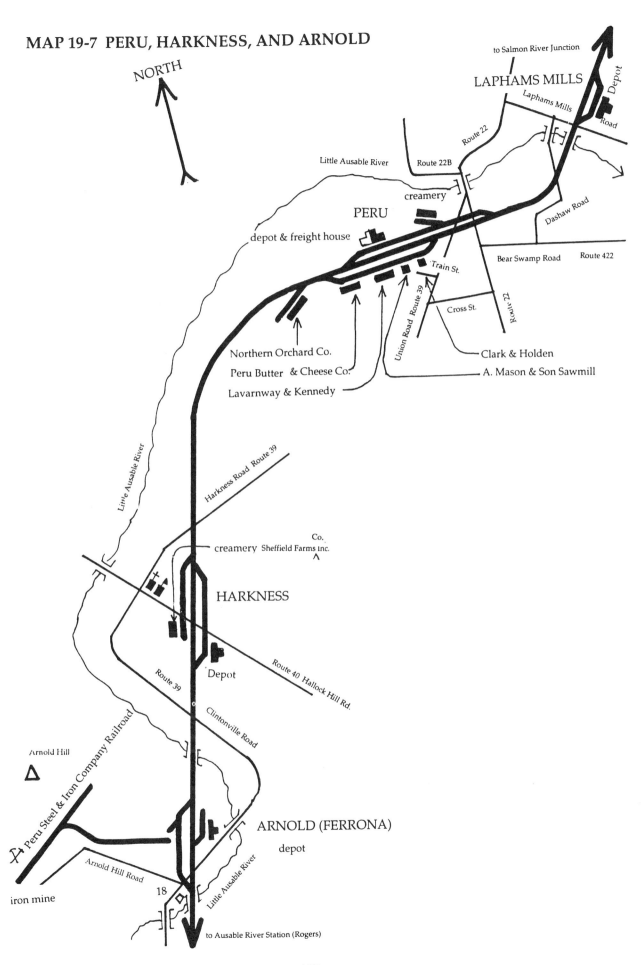

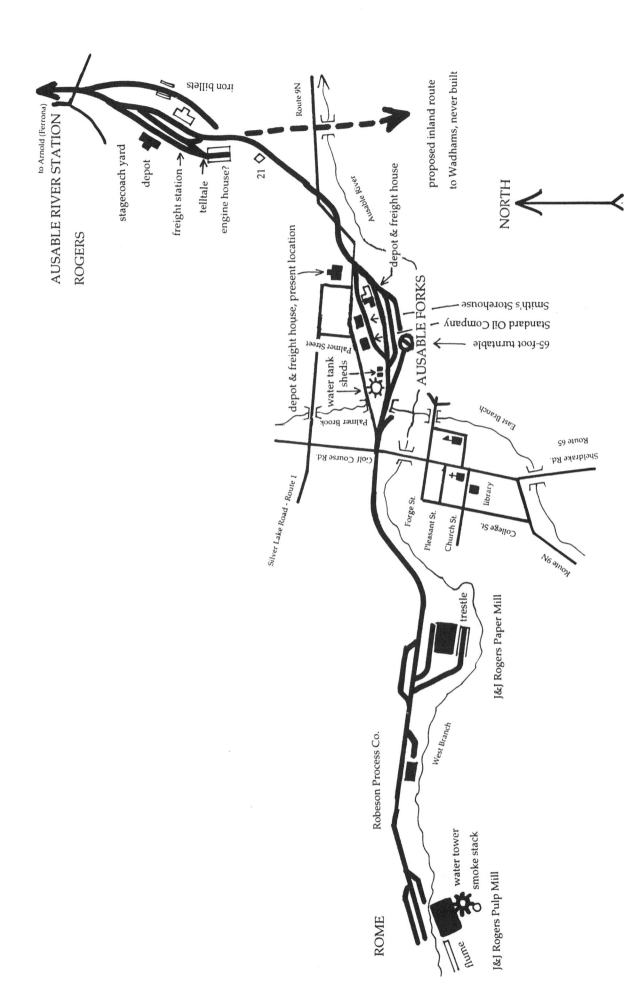

MAP 19-8: AUSABLE FORKS AREA

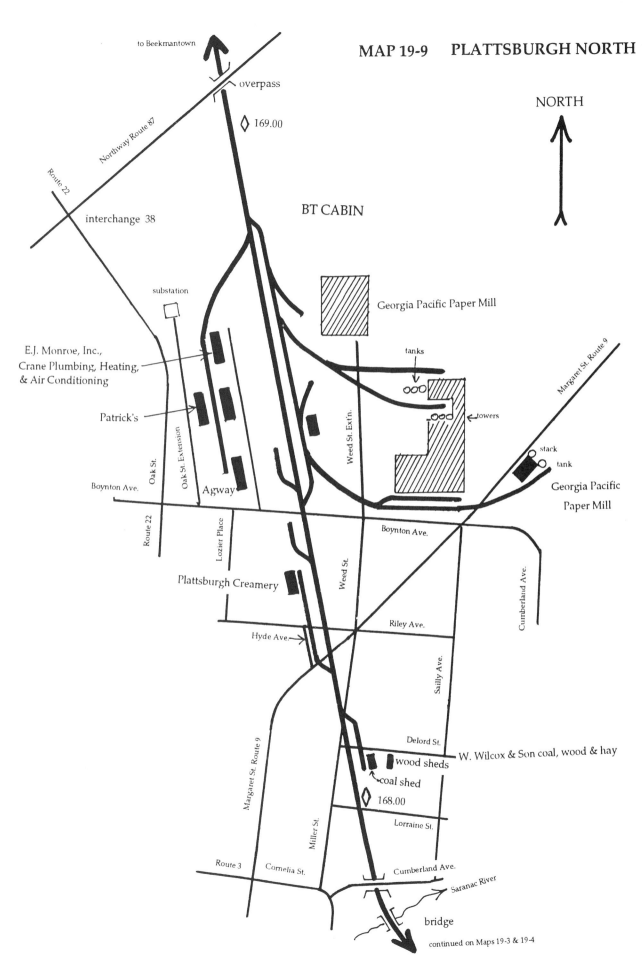

MAP 19-9 PLATTSBURGH NORTH

Chapter 20: Chateaugay Railroad

ON MAY 20, 1878 the Plattsburgh & Dannemora Railroad was organized by the State of New York to connect the State Prison at Dannemora with the then recently-completed D&H Mainline. Construction on the narrow three-foot gauge to Dannemora was completed by December 1878, but the locomotives and cars were not delivered until the next year. The narrow gauge diverged from the D&H mainline at Plattsburgh, not at Bluff Point and not at South Junction.

Great detail on the construction of this line is offered in Lewis (1880, pages 309-312) and in D&H (1925, pages 625-626). Between May 15 and 20, 1879 the Chateaugay Railroad was incorporated, took over the Plattsburgh & Dannemora, and began extending the line on June 8, 1879 from Dannemora to the Chateaugay Ore Bed at Lyon Mountain. The track reached the first mine shaft on December 6, 1879, and eleven days later the first regularly-scheduled freight train left Plattsburgh for the Ore Bed. It returned on December 18, 1879 to Plattsburgh with a load of ore. Transfer of the ore from the narrow gauge to the standard-gauged mainline D&H cars at Plattsburgh was necessary until 1903.

The line was completed and opened to Lyon Mountain by March 30, 1880 and extended to Standish in 1885 simultaneously with the construction of the blast furnace. Loon Lake was reached on November 15, 1886 and Saranac Lake on December 5, 1887. The reason for the extension toward Loon Lake was primarily for charcoal to fuel the blast furnace. The extension to Saranac Lake was made probably for tourists and local freight.

The Saranac & Lake Placid Railroad was organized June 13, 1890. When the line was completed between Saranac Lake and Lake Placid on August 1, 1893, it consisted of three rails to accommodate both the narrow gauge Chateaugay Railroad equipment and the standard-gauged Adirondack & Saint Lawrence equipment; the latter had arrived in Saranac Lake on July 15, 1892 and soon became a part of the New York Central. (The Saranac Lake & Lake Placid trackage is included in this chapter because the line between these two points was, between 1903 and 1946, under full D&H control; the New York Central had only trackage rights during this period.)

In 1901, the D&H began to assume greater and greater control of the Chateaugay and the Saranac & Lake Placid Railroads. In 1902 standard-gauging began, with the elimination of many curves and relocation of the track in many places. A junction was constructed at Bluff Point. By July 29, 1903, the entire line from Plattsburgh to Lake Placid was standard gauged and under full control of the D&H; it had become the Chateaugay Branch of the D&H.

Abandonment of the Chateaugay, as was its construction, was in stages. In 1940 the segment between Plumadore and Saranac Lake, which closely paralleled the New York Central Adirondack Division for the bulk of its length, was first to go. A connection was built at Plumadore so that D&H trains could use New York Central trackage from there to Lake Clear Junction and then to Saranac Lake (Shaughnessy, 1967, p. 355). On November 1, 1946 D&H trains ceased operating to Lake Placid, and the remaining trackage from Plumadore back to Lyon Mountain was abandoned. The line between Saranac Lake and Lake Placid was sold to the Central.

Construction of the Air Force Base at Plattsburgh in 1955 caused a relocation of the junction from Bluff Point southward to South Junction. Can you imagine what would have happened if this 1955 relocation were not made? There would have been a grade crossing on the runway!

The Chateaugay Branch was abandoned from Lyon Mountain to Dannemora in 1970 after Republic Steel shut down the mines.

Schuyler Falls Town Historian, Leo Perry, showed me a *Lease of the Plattsburgh & Dannemora Railroad by the State of New York to the Chateaugay Railroad, May 20, 1879*. The state was then completing the line to Dannemora. The 100-year lease specified one train daily each way except Sunday, and expired in 1979. Soon after, in August and September of 1981, the track was removed from Dannemora down to Otis Junction. This segment of trackage, first to be built, was the last to be abandoned!

Mileage

Mileage along the Chateaugay Branch has been especially difficult to calculate and compile not only because of the obvious disparity between the narrow gauge and the standard gauge lines. Disparities exist also within standard gauge mileage itself. For example, I have consulted two D&H Chateaugay Branch valuation diagrams. The diagram in the Clinton County Real Property Tax Office in Plattsburgh includes only the Clinton County segment, but offers much track schematic detail. The diagram in my files includes the complete branch in Clinton, Franklin and Essex Counties, but is limited in its track schematic detail. Milepost zero is not the same for the two diagrams. The Clinton County diagram's zero point is Plattsburgh depot on the D&H Mainline and mileage is measured via Bluff Point on the standard gauge route. The diagram in my files has its zero point at the north end of the wye where the Furnace Branch joins the Chateaugay Branch, some 0.23 mile south of Plattsburgh depot (this zero point, probably an earlier one, is a hold-over from the 19th century when it was also the zero point for the narrow gauge); standard gauge mileage is also measured via Bluff Point.

Also, there are discrepancies within the standard gauge mileage itself on the valuation diagram in my files! A short distance west of Twin Ponds, 42.619 miles without any explanation suddenly becomes 43.817 miles; some 1.198 miles of track are lost and unaccounted for! The D&H's civil engineers possibly made some relocations within the standard gauge over the years so that the mileposts would shift along the line. Another gap in mileage occurs northeast of Plumadore where 50.74 and 51.15 should be 0.39 mile apart but are only 0.09 mile; some 0.30 mile has been lost. A third but minor discrepancy occurs north of Tekene Junction at only 159 feet or about 0.03 mile.

For the sake of consistency, I have chosen to use in this book the standard gauge mileage shown on the valuation diagram in my files. The mileage of depots, sidings, spurs, bridges, highway crossings, and other facilities are listed in the text rather than creating clutter on the maps. Few mileposts are left today in the ground along the line. Milepost 50, still standing between Lake Kushaqua and Onchiota, and when measured along the valuation diagram, is at 60.37 miles.

The standard gauge line was built in 1903 partly to straighten many of the narrow gauge tight curves and thus shorten the distance from Plattsburgh to Lake Placid. However, because the standard gauge connection with the D&H Mainline was relocated to Bluff Point, the distance between Plattsburgh and Lake Placid remained about the same.

Station Descriptions

Plattsburgh. 0.00 mile at the north end of the wye where the Furnace Branch joins the Chateaugay Branch, some 0.23 mile south of the Plattsburgh depot (Amtrak station). Elevation 118 feet above sea level. Maps 11-10, 19-1, 19-3, 19-4, 19-5, and 20-2.

Passenger station: The Chateaugay narrow gauge line had a separate platform for loading passengers, probably built about 1879. No physical connection was made initially between the narrow and standard-gauged tracks between 1879 and about 1896 so that Plattsburgh could hardly be called a junction. But from about 1897 through 1903, the Chateaugay Railroad was dual-gauged so that both narrow and standard gauge trains could use it. Dual-gauge trackage is described by Rochette (1937), shown on 1902 Sanborn Insurance maps, and illustrated in a photograph in Lansing (1897, page 26). Lansing's photo reveals a dual gauge track approaching the D&H depot currently used by Amtrak. Hence the original narrow gauge platform had been abandoned by 1897.

Servicing facilities: Just south of the passenger platform was the Chateaugay Railroad Company repair shop. A roundhouse with turntable was nearby. Sanborn Insurance Company 1902 maps and J. L. Beers 1889 maps of Plattsburgh provide the best detail. (See Chapter 19 for standard-gauge facilities.

Freight house: The freight house either adjoined the repair shop or was part of the same building.

Industrial sidings: The narrow gauge track extended north of the passenger platform to serve the Baker Brothers Planing Mill (see also the paragraphs on Tekene Junction in this chapter). A track on a trestle south of the wye straddled a standard-gauged D&H track directly below it so that ore and other bulk commodities such as wood pulp could be easily transferred by gravity from one hopper car to another. A second trestle probably had the standard gauge track above and the narrow gauge below so that coal could be easily transferred by gravity from standard-gauged D&H hoppers to narrow gauge cars for the Dannemora prison and other consumers (Lewis, 1880, page 311).

Furnace Branch: A branch of the narrow-gauge diverged from its main, paralleling Hamilton Street on the south. This branch, which already appears on an 1889 Beers' map and on the first 1893 U.S.G.S. 15-minute Plattsburgh topographic quadrangle, headed west, crossed the Saranac River, and terminated at the Chateaugay Ore & Iron Company Foundry. It was standard-gauged in 1903. By 1956, the more recent Plattsburgh 15-minute quadrangle shows the shortened branch terminating before crossing the Saranac River. The 7.5-minute Plattsburgh quadrangle, based on 1964-1966 aerial photographs, no longer shows the branch at all. The Furnace Branch had a number of industries along it, but not all operating at one time; these included a kindling wood factory (later, in 1916, a power house of the Plattsburgh Light Heat & Power Company), the Williams Sewing Machine Factory, the Chateaugay Ore & Iron Company Foundry and Furnace, Plattsburgh Foundry and Machine Shop, and even an engine house. Adjacent to the Furnace Branch, but not connected with it, at Peru Street was the car barn for the Plattsburgh Traction Company trolley cars from 1895 through 1929 (see Borrup 1970-1971 and the paragraphs on Plattsburgh in Chapter 19).

Dual gauge trackage: Rochette (1937) stated that "For several years prior to that time (1903) they had operated cars of both gauges in trains over the three-rail line between Plattsburgh and Cadyville." In 1903, after completion of standard-gauging, the transfer trestles at Plattsburgh were no longer needed and were removed.

Divergence of the gauges: At 0.63 mile south of the narrow gauge Plattsburgh station, elevation 136, the narrow-gauge Chateaugay Railroad diverged from the standard-gauged mainline from 1879 through 1903. Also at this point, the standard-gauged Ausable Branch had a junction with the mainline from 1875 through 1894. See Maps 11-10, 19-1, 19-4, 19-6, 20-2 and 20-9.

Divergence of the narrow-gauged Chateaugay Railroad from the Ausable Branch: At 0.90 mile from the narrow guage Plattsburgh station, elevation 165, these two lines diverged from 1879 through 1894. This divergence was located almost directly on what is now Lake Shore Road, U.S. Highway 9. See Maps 19-1, 20-2, and 20-9. The Ausable Branch was abandoned through here in 1894, leaving the Chateaugay the only track crossing Lake Shore Road until 1903. See Maps 11-10, 19-1, 19-4, 19-5, 20-2 and 20-9.

Cliff Haven. 2.60 miles from the narrow guage Plattsburgh station. Elevation 135. Maps 11-10, 19-1, 19-5, 19-6, and 20-2.

Prior to the standard-gauging of the Chateaugay in 1903, only D&H mainline and Ausable Branch trains stopped at this summer-only station from 1902. But after 1903, standard-gauged Chateaugay trains also stopped here through 1944. See Chapter 11 for detail.

Bluff Point. 3.08 miles from the narrow guage Plattsburgh station. Elevation 143. Maps 11-10, 19-1, 19-5, 19-6, and 20-2.

Passenger station: Prior to the standard-gauging of the Chateaugay Railroad in 1903, only D&H mainline (from 1890) and Ausable Branch (from 1894) trains stopped at this summer-only station. But after 1903, standard-gauged Chateaugay trains also stopped here through 1928. At 3.10 miles, just south of the Bluff Point station, was the junction where the standard-gauged Chateaugay Branch headed westward from 1903 through 1955. This junction was at the north end of the wye. The west end of the wye was at 3.34 miles. See Chapter 11 for detail.

Junction relocation: From 1903 through 1955, Chateaugay Branch trains crossed what is now the Air Force Base. But after 1955 when the runway was built, these trains were rerouted around the south end of the base via South Junction and up the Ausable Forks Branch for 1.2 miles. Here, near South Plattsburgh, a new segment of track was built 2.4 miles long around the west side of the base and up the grade to connect with the original Chateaugay track at Otis Junction. The new junction near South

Plattsburgh with the Ausable Branch was called Salmon River Junction (see Chapter 19).

Industrial sidings: Remnants of the 1903 Chateaugay Branch still diverge from the D&H mainline today at Bluff Point but do not venture west very far. A present-day wye leads into the Air Force Base but the tracks no longer cross the runway!

Tree nursery: The D&H Woodlands Department nurseries were established at Bluff Point shortly before 1910 (D&H, 1925, page 456). See also the section on the Wolf Pond plantations in this chapter.

Mileage: The Chateaugay Branch crossed the original Ausable Branch right-of-way, already abandoned in 1903 for nine years, at 3.96 miles. Three highways once crossed the standard gauge Chateaugay Branch, but were eliminated when the Air Force Base opened in 1955: Summer School Road at 3.87, Salmon River Road at 4.77, and Irish Settlement Road at 5.14. The west switch into Carl B. Getman Concrete Building Supply Company was at 4.97 miles. The junction between the narrow and standard gauge Chateaugay branches was at 5.40 miles, and the junction between these and the 1946 relocation of the Freydenburg Falls Branch was at 5.72 miles. Today, between these two junctions, at 5.65 miles, is the Northway.

Otis Junction. 6.08 miles. Elevation 303. Maps 20-2 and 20-9.

The point where the 1903 standard gauge Chateaugay line and the 1955 Air Force Base rerouting met is called Otis Junction. Today, the Chateaugay Branch ends just east of the Old Military Turnpike crossing at about 6.64 miles; it is shown as a double-line barrier across the track on Map 20-9.

West End and the Freydenburg Falls Branch. 7.05 miles. Elevation 294. Maps 20-2 and 20-9.

Flagstop: The only timetable in my collection which shows Freydenburg Falls as a flagstop is dated October 7, 1901.

Freydenburg Falls Branch: From West End this Branch descended for about 3.6 miles along the south bank of the Saranac River to Plattsburgh. On December 26, 1893, the Treadwells Mills Pulp and Paper Company gave the Chateaugay Railroad the right to build a line across their lands to their sawmill. By 1902, the branch had been extended eastward, and, according to Sanborn Insurance Company maps, was already serving the Freydenburg Falls Pulp Mill. At the terminus of the branch, barely one mile from the terminus of the Furnace Branch but never connecting with it, was the Maine Pulp Mill built in 1880. It was later sold to the Progressive Pulp and Paper Company and again to the American Carbide Company who owned it in 1909. In 1984-1985, the Imperial Wallpaper Mill and Arpak Plastics were on the site. In 1995, the owners are C&A Wallcoverings and Mold-Rite Plastics, respectively, and the Bombardier Company is interested in locating in the adjacent Northgate Industrial Park to build railroad cars (Day, 1995).

In 1902-1903 all industries on this branch, as shown by Sanborn Insurance Company maps, were served by dual gauge trackage during a transition period between narrow and standard gauge operations.

On March 26, 1946 the junction between the Chateaugay Line and the Freydenburg Falls Branch was relocated from West End to milepost 5.72 where it is today, shortening the branch by about 1.3 miles. By 1946 the two mills at Treadwells Mills and Freydenburg Falls had closed.

Morrisonville. 10.42 miles. Elevation 450. Maps 20-2 and 20-10.

Passenger station: The earliest timetable in my collection showing this as a stop is dated March 10, 1879. The caption in Gardner (1990, Volume 4, page 51) states that the combination freight and passenger station was built in 1880. It closed sometime between the timetables of April 26, 1936 and April 25, 1937.

Passing sidings: Baker (1970, p. 33) notes that the Morrisonville side track was nearly completed on June 28, 1879. This was only several months after the line opened to Dannemora. The 1911 Dannemora quadrangle indicates a passing siding 0.3 mile long on the south side and a stub track 0.2 mile long on the north. If this quadrangle is correct, then the D&H made some fast changes, for their 1916 valuation diagram shows the passing siding on the north. The 1956 Dannemora quadrangle shows a passing siding, 0.4 mile long, also on the north.

Industrial sidings: The 1916 D&H valuation diagram shows a stub leading into the Hiland Beverage Company, Inc.. The building still stood in 1990.

Kent Falls Branch. 10.52 miles at the switch. Elevation 460. Maps 20-2 and 20-10.

Leo Perry, Town of Schuyler Falls historian, showed me *Miscellaneous Document #1995*, an agreement between the Chateaugay Railroad and the Glens Falls Paper Mill Company to construct and operate a mill on or about January 1, 1897. The 1.7-mile-long branch to Kents Falls was to be completed by December 1, 1896 for the reception of wood and the shipping of pulp. According to Baker (1970, p. 54), International Paper Company was running this mill, named Mill D, in 1901 and 1913.

Mr. Perry also had a blueprint entitled *Right-of-way Track Map, Plattsburgh & Dannemora Railroad, sheet V-16B/6A*. All tracks were removed by December 14, 1936 on the Kents Falls Branch. The site of Mill D is now occupied by a New York State Gas and Electric hydropower plant.

Woods Mills. 13.04 miles at Rock's Crossing of Sand Road (County Route 31). Elevation 718 at the railroad trestle over the Saranac River. Maps 20-2 and 20-10.

Woods Mills never had a passenger station.

Relocation: A few hundred feet west of the junction of the Kent Falls Branch began a relocation of the narrow gauge. The original line crossed Sand Road, now Clinton County Highway 31, twice within a distance of 1650 feet. The 1903 standard gauge was built on the south side of Sand Road so that both crossings were eliminated. A portion of the fill upon which the standard gauge was built was removed in 1989 by the farmer-owner who planted corn in its place (See Map 20-10). Industrial spurs: By 1902 two more pulp mills had been built along the Saranac River as shown in the Sanborn Insurance Company map of that year. The 1911 Dannemora quadrangle shows two spurs serving the mills diverging from the Chateaugay at Woods Mills. One spur at 13.29 miles headed 0.6 mile west, upstream, to International Paper Company's Pulp Mill B. The second spur at 13.41 miles, with a wye at 13.52, headed for 0.4 mile east, downstream, to International Paper Company's pulp Mill C. Baker (1970, p. 54) informs us that by 1913 Mill B had already been abandoned but was still standing. In 1922, the mills gradually began to be converted into hydroelectric generating plants. Baker (1970) facing page 46 has a photo of Mill C. The 1956 Dannemora quadrangle no longer shows the spurs into the mills.

Trestle and quarry: The Chateaugay crossed the Saranac River on a trestle at 13.38 miles over a gorge cut into the Potsdam Sandstone, a miniature Ausable or Chateaugay Chasm. Photographs of the 72-foot-high trestle appear in Shaughnessy (1967, page 159) and in Baker (1970, facing page 15). Baker (1970, page 29) mentions a state stone quarry near the railroad trestle, but does not reveal whether or not it was served by the railroad, or its precise location.

Cadyville. 13.90 miles standard. Elevation 729. Maps 20-3 and 20-10.

Passenger station: Cadyville was a station stop probably for the entire life of Chateaugay passenger service. The oldest timetable I have listing service is March 10, 1879 and the most recent September 25, 1949. By September 24, 1950 it had closed. Gardner (1990, Volume 4, page 51) includes a photo with the caption that the combination passenger and freight station was built in 1880.

Stagecoach connections: Timetables of January 16, 1893 through June 25, 1899 noted stagecoach connections for Moffitsville, Redford, Saranac (the hamlet of Saranac should not be confused with the Village of Saranac Lake), and Clayburg.

Passing siding: A passing siding and stub track are shown on the 1911 Dannemora quadrangle, but the 1916 D&H valuation diagram shows more trackage. The passing siding was also used probably for doubling the hill.

Facilities: A water tower existed here, the concrete base of which still stands in 1994. There was also a section speeder house. According to Rochette (1937), three-rail dual-gauge track ran from Plattsburgh to Cadyville for several years prior to standard-gauging.

Industrial sidings: There were several near the station as shown on Map 20-10. At 14.42 miles was a stub into Wilson Brothers, at 14.50 into the Chittenden Company, and at 16.11 into the Northern Concrete Pipe Corporation. For location purposes in the field currently, Church Street (also called Dannemora Plank Road and, today, Prison Road) crosses at 14.56, the Plattsburgh-Saranac Town Line is at 15.89, a cattle pass was at 16.71, and Separator Brook (now called Canfield Brook and not to be confused with Separator Brook at Lyon Mountain) is bridged at 16.82. A sand pit existed between 16.03 and 16.20 miles but I have no evidence of a track into it.

Steep grade: From Cadyville, the line steeply ascended to Dannemora. According to Rochette (1937) the most inclined mile climbed 169 feet, equivalent to 3.2%. Trains had to be doubled on this hill using the sidings at Cadyville and Dannemora.

The 5.58 miles between these two stations necessitated an ascent of 627 feet, averaging 2.1%.

Dannemora. 19.48 miles. Elevation 1356. Maps 20-3 and 20-11.

Passenger station: Like Cadyville, Dannemora was a station for the entire life of Chateaugay passenger service. The oldest timetable I have listing it is March 10, 1879 and the most recent September 25, 1949. It had closed by September 24, 1950. Gardner (1990, Volume 4, page 52) notes that a combination passenger and freight station was built in 1880. In 1912, the present building was constructed originally as a passenger station, but in 1991 serves as the Village of Dannemora offices.

Passing siding: Both the June 29, 1891 and the June 22, 1896 timetables indicated that trains in opposite directions met here, requiring a passing siding. The 1916 D&H valuation diagram shows the siding, from ca. 19.5 to 19.74 miles, also used when trains were doubled on the hill out of Cadyville.

Industrial sidings: The Clinton Prison site at Dannemora, according to Lewis (1880, pages 48 and 49), was chosen by the New York State Legislature in 1845 and the facility completed in 1846. Thus the prison had been in service for some 32 years before the Plattsburgh & Dannemora Railroad arrived in December 1878. The original purpose of this line was to serve the prison, bringing in coal and supplies. Dannemora was the terminus from December 1878 to December 1879 when the line was extended to the ore beds at Lyon Mountain. One stub serviced a powerhouse at 19.30 miles; perhaps here the coal hoppers were emptied to heat the prison.

Facilities: An earlier water tank was at 19.41 miles, but was apparently replaced later by one at 19.50 miles.

Prison iron mine railroad: See section 20D in Disconnecting Railroads of Chapter 8 for a description of a railroad entirely within the walls of the prison.

Abandonment: George Ryan, a railroad historian from Plattsburgh, informs me of his observations at Dannemora in recent years. The last D&H freight ran in 1974, and the tracks were removed in the summer of 1981.

Russia (Lobdell Post Office or Saranac Station). 24.12 miles. Elevation 1489. Maps 20-3 and 20-12.

Passenger station: Lewis (1880) informs us that when the line first opened, the station was called "Saranac Station" because it was only a few miles north of the hamlet of Saranac (Saranac should not be confused with the Village of Saranac Lake). The earliest timetable I have listing it is August 1, 1883 although it probably had opened in 1880. The timetable of October 6 (or December 5?), 1890 shows the name had already been changed to Russia. Gardner (1990, Volume 4, page 53) has a photo of the combination passenger and freight station built in 1879. Trains were still stopping here on June 28, 1931, but had ceased by September 10, 1931.

Passing siding: The timetable of June 25, 1899 indicates that two trains running in opposite directions passed at Russia, requiring a passing siding. This ca. 800-foot-long siding is shown on the 1911 Dannemora quadrangle. It was still here on November 1, 1942 when the D&H *Employees' Timetable* records the capacity as 18 cars.

Chazy Lake. 30.23 miles. Elevation 1665. Maps 20-4 and 20-13.

Passenger station: The station opened sometime between the timetables of August 1, 1883 and June 24, 1889. The timetable of January 1934 still shows a stop here, but service had been discontinued by September 30, 1934. Gardner (1990, Volume 4, page 53) notes that the passenger station in the photo was built in 1892. Railway Express Agency and post office signs hung under the huge eaves of this small building. A pavilion existed at 29.98 miles.

Steamboat connection: Timetables of January 16, 1893 and June 22, 1896 note that a steamer met trains near the station and crossed to the north end of the lake to the Chazy Lake House.

Passing siding: A siding is indicated on the September 24, 1916 timetable when two trains passed here. The siding began at 29.94 miles and ended at 30.26. Gardner (1975, page 64) shows the siding in his photo with trains passing.

Facilities: The D&H *Official List No. 57* of January 1, 1941 indicates a watering facility here at 30.25 miles.

Bradley Pond Switch. 34.36 miles. Elevation 1710. Maps 20-4, 20-14, and 20-14A.

From here a 1.35-mile-long spur descended to Bradley Pond, elevation 1630. An 1895 map by Bien labels the spur's terminus as Bradley Pond Kilns. A D&H Chateaugay Branch valuation diagram indicates two kilns here. This was one of several charcoal-producing areas for the Standish blast furnace. Others were at Twin Ponds, South Inlet, Middle Kilns, Upper Kilns, and Plumadore. The 1911 Lyon Mountain quadrangle still shows the spur. Bradley Pond Switch, the junction point with the Chateaugay, was not a passenger stop.

A siding existed on the south side of the main, east of the Switch, from 33.83 to 34.17 miles.

Old Line Junction. 34.53 miles. Elevation 1715. Maps 20-4, 20-14, and 20-14A.

From here, the narrow and standard gauged lines diverged, not to reunite until Twin Ponds at 42.04 miles. This was the longest segment of the Chateaugay, 7.51 miles, where the narrow and standard gauge lines did not follow the same grade. Old Line Junction was not a passenger stop.

Lyon Mountain. 36.25 miles at standard gauge depot. Elevation 1753. Maps 20-4, 20-14, and 20-14A.

Early history: Linney (1934) and Hyde (1974, pp. 156-165) offer detailed history of the mines. The Chateaugay Iron Company was founded about 1872 although large-scale mining operations did not begin until 1873. Between 1873 and the arrival of the Chateaugay Railroad in December of 1879, the ore was brought down from the mines by wagon to the south shore of Upper Chateaugay Lake. The ore was then loaded on a barge and floated down the lakes to the huge Belmont Forge (photo, Hyde, p. 159) at the north end. From here, the iron was once again loaded on wagons and transported to the Chateaugay Station on the Ogdensburg & Lake Champlain Railroad, the nearest railroad to Lyon Mountain between 1849 and 1879. What a difference in shipping the iron ore out was made in 1879 when the Chateaugay Railroad arrived at Lyon Mountain!

Construction of the narrow gauge: The narrow gauge arrived in Lyon Mountain in 1880, terminating at the Chateaugay Ore Bed. Soon the narrow gauge was extended west from the mines and looped around the north side of the first of four hills, called Parsons Knob, at about the 1850 foot level. It then headed southwest downgrade and arrived in Williamstown (shortly after renamed Standish) in 1885 and terminated at the just-completed blast furnace. In 1886 the narrow gauge was rapidly extended further west, continuing downgrade to Twin Ponds, then into Middle Kilns, and eventually to Loon Lake. An 1895 map of Clinton County by Julius Bien and Company of New York City shows this extension to Twin Ponds and beyond. The 1903 *Scarborough Map of New York* confirms this extension.

Narrow gauge passenger station: The station for the narrow gauge opened in 1880 and was in service as a passenger station through 1903 (See Map 20-14A). A photo of this station with a narrow-gauge train appears in several publications: D&H (1925, page 629), Linney (1934, page 39), and Shaughnessy (1967, page 165). D&H Board of Directors Inspection of Lines (1928, page 319) and Gardner (1990, Volume 4, page 54) include a more recent 20th century photo, showing the brick addition to the southwest end of the building used as the Chateaugay Ore and Iron Company's office. In 1993, the older wooden station portion of the building is gone, but the brick portion still stands although vacant.

Stagecoach connections: Timetables from 1889 through 1899 recorded stagecoach connections, some of which also necessitated a steamboat ride, made with the following hotels: Ralph's, The Chateaugay, Merrill's, Indian Point House, and Banner House. (DeSormo [1974, pages 79-83] includes a chapter on the Banner House on Lower Chateaugay Lake.) Narrow gauge servicing facilities: Because Lyon Mountain was the temporary terminus for the period 1880 through 1885, facilities for the servicing and turning of trains existed here near the depot. On Separator Brook, writes Lewis (1880, page 312) was an engine house with two pits for housing locomotives, a machine shop, and a carpentry shop to repair and build engines, and to do car work.

Narrow gauge industrial sidings: Lewis (1880, page 312) describes a trip made over the then brand-new Chateaugay Railroad from Plattsburgh to Lyon Mountain. He continues with a description of the mining and processing operation. Above the depot and shops was a side track upon which the mined rock with its impurities was brought up in railroad cars. The cars were then emptied by gravity into a separator and roasting kilns. The ore was finally washed and reloaded into empty cars below to be hauled to Plattsburgh. This procedure preceded the opening of the blast furnace at Standish in 1885. An immense high wooden trestle terminating a 2344-foot-long spur crossed over the narrow gauge tracks and entered the separator (see Map 20-14A). Photos of this trestle in the background appear in Linney (1934, pp. 26, 56, and 43). Linney's p. 43 photo also appears in Lansing (1897, page 90).

Standard-gauging: In 1902 standard-gauging began in Plattsburgh and was completed to Lyon

Mountain and Saranac Lake in 1903. There were many relocations of the old narrow gauge, requiring a rebuilding of major and minor portions of the line to avoid some sharp curves and steep grades. By far the longest relocation, 7.51 miles, was here at Lyon Mountain. The new standard gauged line followed a more northerly route. It was built roughly parallel to, but as much as 200 feet below, the narrow gauge and was called the Valley Line.

Lyon Mountain Branch: After standard-gauging, the route of the original narrow gauge line became a 2.5-mile-long spur, the Lyon Mountain Branch. Its junction with the new line was at Old Line Junction, and its terminus was at the Ore Bed. The segment from the Ore Bed southwest to Standish and Twin Ponds was abandoned.

Standard gauge passenger station: The station for the standard gauge should have opened in 1903, although the photo caption in D&H Board of Directors Inspection of Lines (1928, page 319) and Gardner (1990, Volume 4, page 54) reads 1913. If the 1913 date is correct, then a temporary depot was built and lasted only ten years. The standard gauge station was about 0.3 mile west of and 140 feet in elevation below the old narrow gauge station which it replaced. The caption reads that the new station was improved in 1914. It was in service through sometime between the timetables of September 25, 1949 and September 24, 1950 when passenger service ceased. In 1994, it still stands as a tavern. More photos appear in Parishoners from St. Bernard's Church et al. (1975).

Standard gauge servicing facilities: A standard-gauged turntable was constructed just east of the new station at 36.11 miles.

Passing siding: The siding began at 35.77 miles and ended at 36.22 miles, with a crossover midway at 35.89 miles. The Depot Street crossing was at 36.07 miles and Separator Brook bridge at 36.10. The First Street, Route 1 or highway to Standish, crossed at 36.27 miles.

Standard gauge industrial sidings: Information for Map 20-14 comes from several sources including the 1911 and 1968 Lyon Mountain topographic quadrangles, 1916 D&H valuation diagrams, an early Dwight Church aerial photo in Burdick (1992), a number of photos in Linney (1930, Jun. 1; 1934; and 1975), and observations in the field made by this writer from 1977 through 1994. Linney (1934) offers a number of photos of the Lyon Mountain area in pages 38, 39, 40, 49, 54, 70, 79, 86, and 95. A photo of the huge sintering plant and concentrator appears in numerous publications including Linney (1930, Jun. 1, page 167), Hyde (1974, page 168), *D&H RR Bulletin* (1935, Apr. 1, page 57), D&H Board of Directors Inspection of Lines (1931, page 90), an untitled 1933 D&H promotions brochure, and in Linney (1975).

Conkling Separator: From the narrow gauge depot, the 1895 Bien and 1903 Scarborough maps indicate a branch about 1.3 miles long diverging to the west-northwest to Rogersfield. Such a direct descent would have required at least a 5.5% grade. After 1903, the new standard-gauged line intersected the branch at 36.40 miles, about 0.8 mile from its original junction with the narrow gauge. Thus, the branch was shortened to only 0.50 mile, as shown on the 1911 U.S.G.S. Lyon Mountain quadrangle. A Chateaugay valuation diagram indicates the Conkling Separator at the end of this branch with two stubs into it.

More photographs: Hyde (1974) presents several photos of Lyon Mountain but with railroad facilities sometimes appearing only in the background; the photos appear on pages 163, 168, and 170. Aerial views appear in Hyde (1974, page 172) and Burdick (1992).

Underground railroad: See Chapter 8, #20 for details on this disconnecting railroad.

Abandonment: Republic Steel had taken over the Chateaugay Ore & Iron Company in 1939 one year after the former acquired the Witherbee Sherman operations at Mineville. An article in the (Watertown?) *Times* in 1970 states that the mines at Lyon Mountain shut down in June 1967 and that the Interstate Commerce Commission authorized the D&H to abandon the line by April 29, 1970. The article states that "in the last two years only four cars were shipped over the line that were not involved with the salvage operation."

The Gap. 38.81 miles. Elevation 1598. Map 20-4.

The 1911 Lyon Mountain quadrangle shows this stop. Sometime between September 24, 1916 and October 1, 1917, timetables began to contain a footnote that trains would stop at this flagstop. I have been informed, but have not confirmed, that a path led down from The Gap and provided access to Chateaugay Lake for pedestrians. The flagstop ceased to exist sometime between the timetables of June 26 and September 25, 1932.

Standish. 39.90 miles. Elevation 1575. Maps 20-4 and 20-15.

Passenger stations: The narrow gauge opened to Standish in 1885, but the first timetable I have listing it is October 5, 1890. Gardner (1990, Volume 4, page 55) and the D&H Board of Directors Inspection of Lines (1928, page 321) include one view, while Shaughnessy (1967, page 158) and Parishoners of St. Bernard's Church et al. (1975) present a second view of the narrow gauge station. This huge building also served as a freight station, offices for the Chateaugay Ore & Iron Company, a hotel, and a general store. The new station, also a combination station, was constructed in 1903 along the standard gauge at Standish about three-quarters of a mile northwest of the old narrow gauge station. Trains ceased stopping here on November 1, 1946 when the D&H abandoned the line from Plumadore back to Lyon Mountain.

Passing siding: The 1911 Lyon Mountain quadrangle shows a passing siding along the standard gauge. It began at 39.92 miles and ended at 40.13.

Facilities: A water tank was located across the highway from the narrow gauge depot. When the standard gauge line was built, the water tank was placed just east of its depot at 39.87 miles.

Catalan Forge: Before arrival of the railroad, a temporary Catalan forge was constructed at Standish. One photo of it appears in Linney (1934, page 44) and Lansing (1897, page 92). A second photo appears in Lansing (1897, page 90). Both photos reappear in Linney (1975).

Blast furnace: The narrow gauge railroad and the blast furnace were built in 1885. The approach was over a more southerly route from Lyon Mountain (see Map 20-4). When the standard gauge line was built in 1903 over a more northerly route, a new branch 0.9 mile long had to be constructed southward from the new depot into the blast furnace. This new branch was called the Standish Furnace Branch and its tracks climbed from 1575 to 1670 feet. The blast furnace produced pig iron which decreased transportation costs since pig iron is far less bulky than ore. The furnace was still operational in 1937. I suspect that when Republic Steel purchased the industry in 1939, the blast furnace was soon dismantled. It was certainly closed by 1946 when the D&H abandoned the Chateaugay line back to Lyon Mountain via Standish from Plumadore. The blast furnace office, a stone building, still stands as a private residence today where Depot Street ends.

Photos of the blast furnace are common. The frequently-published picture with ore hopper cars in the foreground appears in D&H (1925, page 164), Linney (1934, page 60), Linney (1930, Jun. 1, page 167), Hyde (1974, page 164), and the D&H Board of Directors Inspection of Lines (1931, page 89). A close-up picture of the top of the furnace appears in *D&H RR Bulletin* (1935, Apr. 1, page 55), on the front cover of *D&H RR* (1935b), and in Linney (1975). Other views of the furnace appear in Linney (1930, May 1, page 165), Linney (1934, page 50), and D&H (1925, page 500).

Reforestation: D&H (1925, p. 626) states that the initial Standish Blast Furnace fuel, charcoal, was replaced by coke in 1902. Coke could be brought in by rail from Pennsylvania by the D&H. This fuel change meant that heavy cutting of area hardwood timber for charcoal could cease and it did. In fact, tree plantations followed (see the paragraphs on Middle Kilns and Wolf Pond and on the tree nursery at Bluff Point).

Challenges of solving the narrow gauge relocation: After standard gauging, a highway relocation occurred which at first made it difficult to locate the old abandoned narrow gauge route. Standish Road, now Clinton County Highway #1, shown on the 1911 Lyon Mountain quadrangle passed through the col between hills #3 and #4 on its way southwest out of Lyon Mountain toward the hamlet of Standish. It was later rebuilt to its present location, shown on the 1968 7.5-minute Lyon Mountain quadrangle from aerial photos taken in 1965, directly upon portions of the old narrow gauge! A deviation from the narrow gauge route is at Parson's Knob (Hill #1); instead of detouring northward around the Knob, the Standish Highway took a short cut through the col between hills #1 and #2.

Standish Brook culvert: At 40.23 miles, this is a scenic spot today. The concrete culvert was built in 1903 with the brook making a decided bend midway through it.

Twin Ponds. Approximately 41.8 miles. Elevation 1443. Maps 20-4 and 20-16.

Standard gauge relocation: The new 1903 standard gauge line rejoined the original narrow gauge line at 42.04 miles just west of Twin Ponds. The two gauges had been on separate rights-of-way from Old Line Junction, some 7.51 miles to the northeast.

Passenger station: Twin Ponds station opened sometime between the timetables of June 29, 1891 and January 16, 1893. It closed sometime between the timetables of September 25, 1932 and September 24, 1933. A building is shown on the 1911 U.S. Geological Survey Lyon Mountain quadrangle between the

South Inlet Branch overpass at 41.77 miles and the connecting track to this Branch at 41.87 miles; if this building were the station, then it was at ca. 41.8 miles.

South Inlet Branch: The 1911 Lyon Mountain quadrangle indicates two branches diverging from the Chateaugay at Twin Ponds. One, the South Inlet Branch, headed 1.59 miles to the north from the standard gauge line terminating at 19 charcoal kilns. The kilns were just north of Middle Kilns (South Inlet) Brook, elevation 1315 and not far from the south end of Upper Chateaugay Lake. The other headed 0.41 mile to the South to ten charcoal kilns, according to the 1916 D&H valuation diagram. These kilns were providing fuel for the blast furnace at Standish.

Middle Kilns. 45.96 miles at the Wolf Pond Road crossing. Elevation 1488. Maps 20-5 and 20-17.

Passenger station: This station opened sometime between the timetables of June 25, 1906 and June 24, 1906. It closed sometime between the timetables of September 25, 1932 and September 24, 1933.

Passing siding: The June 25, 1899 timetable suggests that two trains passed here, roughly midway between Loon Lake and Lyon Mountain, although Middle Kilns is not listed. The siding began at 45.94 miles and ended at 46.27. A 1942 employees' timetable notes a capacity of 31 cars.

Reforestation: Linney (1934) gives us detail on the forestry aspects of the Chateaugay iron ore operation. His Chapter VI, pages 130-134, describes the acreage cut for charcoal according to timber types and discusses forest fires. A photo dated 1915 on page 134 shows a Scots pine plantation at Middle Kilns begun in 1910. See Chapter 4 in this book.

Stub: A stub of unknown function existed at 45.82 miles.

Upper Kilns Junction. 46.28 miles. Elevation 1490. Maps 20-5 and 20-17.

From here a spur 0.4 mile long diverged to the northwest to Upper Kilns, another site of charcoal production for the Standish Blast Furnace. This Junction was never a station stop.

Wolf Pond. Approximately 48.4 miles. Elevation 1514. Map 20-5.

Passenger station: This station opened sometime between the timetables of June 29, 1891 and January 16, 1893. It closed sometime between the timetables of September 25, 1932 and September 24, 1933. The 1912 and 1916 timetables list the stop as "Wolf Ponds" in the plural. The U.S. Geological Survey 1902 Loon Lake quadrangle shows two buildings along the track between the Wolf Pond Road crossing at 48.32 miles and the Salmon River Bridge at 48.56; if one of these buildings was the station, then it was at ca. 48.4 miles.

Reforestation: Apparently the whole area from Middle Kilns to Wolf Ponds was so heavily denuded of timber for the Standish Blast Furnace that the Chateaugay Ore & Iron Company began reforestation efforts. Photographs of the Wolf Pond Scots pine plantation begun in 1910 occur in D&H (1925, page 458) and in Linney (1934, page 133).

Bridges: At 48.56 miles was the bridge over the Salmon River and at 49.01 the one over Cold Brook. At 49.11 miles began the big bend from the west to the south.

Plumadore. 51.44 miles. Elevation 1705. Maps 20-5, 20-18 and 36-13.

Passenger station: This station opened sometime between the timetables of June 29, 1891 and January 16, 1893. It closed sometime between the timetables of September 25, 1932 and September 24, 1933.

Connection with the New York Central: If one examines maps from the period 1892 through 1940, the closely parallel trackage of the D&H and the New York Central Railroads becomes very obvious between Plumadore and Onchiota. In effect, the D&H trackage duplicated the Central's, and the D&H could eliminate maintenance costs if it abandoned this segment. So, on page 29 of the November 1, 1942 D&H employees' timetable there is an entry: "A connection to the New York Central has been made at a point 4600 feet south of milepost 49, north of Plumadore, to a point 236 feet south of milepost 50, to be known as Plumadore Junction, and for location purpose, a sign board will be located 2000 feet north of the New York Central Railroad clearance point at Plumadore Junction. . ." (note the discrepancy in the mileage between the 1942 Employees' timetable and the valuation diagram from which mileages were obtained for this book). According to Shaughnessy (1967, p. 355), the connection was built in 1940 so that the segment from Plumadore to Saranac Lake could be abandoned. D&H Chateaugay branch trains ran on the Central's tracks via Lake Clear Junction until November 1,

1946. The now-abandoned crossover connection was still plainly visible when one hiked the rights-of-way at Plumadore in 1978, but had become more obscure in 1994.

"The Beehives." 51.77 miles. Elevation 1705. Maps 20-5, 20-18, and 36-13.

While hiking the Chateaugay Branch right-of-way on November 5, 1978, our party found some puzzling artifacts. On the east side of the former track was a cut in the glacial outwash sands: a cut large enough to include a spur track. Why would anyone make such a large excavation unless a track were to be placed through it? We followed the cut and soon came out into a flat area with tie impressions still in the ground---definite evidence of a siding. Along this siding were five circular foundations, about 18 feet in diameter, made of bricks set in mortar. These ring-like foundations were largely overgrown, and we scratched our heads trying to figure out what they were. Then we remembered the photographs in Hyde (1974, pp. 109 and 168) of "beehive-type" charcoal kilns. Now, things were beginning to fit together! Why was the Chateaugay Railroad extended past Standish so hurriedly after 1885 towards Plumadore and Loon Lake? Charcoal! The blast furnace at Standish required vast quantities of charcoal for fuel, and charcoal required hardwood timber. That is why there were short branches along the Chateaugay: Bradley Pond, South Inlet Branch, Upper Kilns---logging spurs to get the hardwoods out of the woods. Even the very names of some of the places attest to charcoal: Middle Kilns, Upper Kilns.

What an opportunity for model railroaders who are seeking to recreate in miniature a fairly small area with tremendous diversity of railroading activities. Picture this and duplicate it in your living room, basement or attic:

(1) Ore trains from the Lyon Mountain mines to the Standish blast furnace.

(2) Trains carrying pig iron from Standish to Plattsburgh.

(3) Logging trains carrying hardwood timber to the charcoal kilns.

(4) Trains carrying charcoal from the kilns to the blast furnace.

(5) Local freights delivering supplies for Lyon Mountain Village.

(6) Passenger, mail and express trains: from Plattsburgh to Lake Placid.

Forest fires: The woods in the Plumadore area along the Chateaugay appear as if they had been severely burned. For details on forest fires closer to the Paul Smith's area, Onchiota to Saranac Lake along the Chateaugay, see Kudish (1976 and 1981) and Chapter 4 in this book.

Tekene Junction. 54.17 miles. Elevation 1700. Maps 20-5, 20-5A, 36-12, and 36-36.

Passenger station: This station opened sometime between the timetables of June 25, 1905 and June 24, 1906. Trains were still stopping here on June 27, 1909. It is still listed on the timetable of June 26, 1910, but trains no longer stopped here. By the timetable of February 11, 1912, Tekene Junction was no longer listed.

Tekene Branch: This little logging branch has a most obscure history. Its origins are uncertain even among earlier publications. According to Seaver (1918, page 363), the Kinsley Lumber Company built a line about 1898 west from the New York Central (not the D&H) 1.8 miles to Tekene. From here the track continued further west for another 2.8 miles, with a branch 2.5 miles long touching the south shore of Debar Pond. Seaver says that the Kinsley Lumber Company sold the line to a Plattsburgh firm, Baker Brothers, who were tied in with the D&H Railroad, not the New York Central. So, in order to get the timber and pulpwood out of the woods and on to the D&H, the Baker Brothers with the D&H Railroad had to build a connection from the Tekene line to the Chateaugay Branch. This necessitated a junction built on the Chateaugay, called Tekene Switch, and a bridge over the intervening New York Central Adirondack Division track. On November 6, 1976, our hiking party was amazed at the sheer size of the concrete bridge abutments which were still standing. The bridge was long gone, as were the tracks, but the massive structures loomed out of the marsh as a pair of gigantic parentheses around the Niagara-Mohawk power line (now occupying the old NYC right of way). A cornerstone revealed the year of construction: 1903, the same year that the D&H standard-gauged the Chateaugay!

A valuation diagram of the Chateaugay Railroad shows that when the D&H acquired the Tekene Branch, it was very curvy and had to be relocated and straightened in many places. One land parcel along the grade is identified as "The Chateaugay Ore & Iron Company to the Chateaugay & Lake Placid Railway Company and the D&H Company, October 1, 1903. Track as found October 1, 1903." Does this suggest that the C.O.& I. Co. bought the land from Kinsley and in turn immediately, on October 1, 1903, sold it to the D&H?

The *Delaware & Hudson RR Bulletin* (1938, Jan. 1) must contain three errors. First, it states that the Tekene Branch was built about 1888, ten years before Seaver's construction date. If this were true, when the New York Central was built in 1892 it would have bisected the Tekene Branch. Second, the *Bulletin* states that the Branch was built by the Chateaugay Railroad over a right of way obtained from the Chateaugay Ore & Iron Company; this contradicts Seaver's more likely builder, Kinsley Brothers. In actuality, the Chateaugay Railroad did not build in 1888 but instead rebuilt the line in 1903. Third, the *Bulletin* states that the Branch was abandoned and the rails taken up in February 1918, while Seaver says that it had been abandoned some time before 1918. The *Bulletin* article does, however, offer useful information on how beavers flood railroad grades.

The 1902-1906 Loon Lake quadrangle incorrectly labels the Kinsley-Baker line as Brooklyn Cooperage. Brooklyn Cooperage had all their operations near and along the New York & Ottawa from Tupper Lake to Saint Regis Falls (See Chapter 26), not here.

Passing siding: The timetable of June 21, 1908 shows that two trains met at Tekene Junction, requiring a passing siding. The valuation diagram shows two dead-end stubs ending at 54.33 miles.

Catamount. Approximately 54.8 miles. Elevation 1710. Maps 20-5 and 36-12.

The 1902-1906 Loon Lake quadrangle shows this station, but only the timetable of June 25, 1905 includes it. The October 7, 1901 and June 24, 1906 do not. The quadrangle also shows a cluster of three buildings along the track about 0.6 mile south of Tekene Junction and labels the area Catamount.

Loon Lake (Inman Post Office). 55.93 miles. Elevation 1730. Maps 20-6, 20-19, and 36-12.

Passenger station: Loon Lake was a station from 1886 through 1946. From 1940 through November 1, 1946, D&H trains were stopping at the New York Central station across the highway, not any longer at the D&H station. Gardner (1990, Volume 4, page 58) includes a photo of the combination station with a note that it was built in 1866 (!) and remodeled in 1904. How could it have been built 20 years before the narrow gauge reached Loon Lake in 1886? Shaughnessy (1967, pages 159, 162 and 165) includes photos of the Loon Lake station and area.

Stagecoach connections: Timetables from 1889 through 1899 indicate stagecoach connections to Loon Lake House (Chase's) three miles away. Much detail is available in DeSormo (1974, pp 43-54) on this major Adirondack hotel. Stagecoaches from Paul Smith's Hotel met the trains here for about one year, 1886-1887; afterwards the connecting point was Gabriels Station.

Passing siding: In 1896 and 1899, timetables inform us that trains met here, necessitating a passing siding. Gardner's (1990, Volume 4, page 58) photo shows the siding.

Freight house: One stood north of the station and west of the main along a stub track, along Highway 99. The switch was at 55.92, the freight house at 55.89, and the end of the stub at 55.86. This writer photographed the house in May 1993, but when he returned in June 1994 it was gone!

Servicing facilities: Loon Lake was the temporary terminus for the Chateaugay Railroad from November 15, 1886 when the line arrived to December 4, 1887 when it opened to Saranac Lake. A reversing loop is shown on Map 20-19 as a dashed line because the existence of such a loop has not been confirmed. A water tower appears in a photo on page 162 of Shaughnessy (1967); its foundation is still visible on the ground today at about 55.94 miles. The Highway 99 crossing is about 55.95.

Connection with the New York Central: When the Mohawk & Malone, soon to become the New York Central Adirondack Division, was under construction in 1891-1892, materials were brought in by the Chateaugay to Loon Lake (see Chapter 36). South of Loon Lake Station at about milepost 147.5 on the New York Central, the site marked today between Niagara Mohawk power poles #245 and #246, the narrow gauge Chateaugay and the Mohawk & Malone were very close together (see Map 20-19). What is not known is where the freight interchange track, listed in McNamara's *D&H Freight Shipper's Directory* of 1914-1915, was located---whether it was here at the Mohawk & Malone construction materials transfer point or built anew at the stations. In 1903, the standard gauged Chateaugay was rebuilt considerably east of the narrow gauge and as far as half a mile from the New York Central.

Mileages along the standard gauge are as follows: 56.37 divergence of the narrow gauge, 56.41 crossing of Kushaqua-Mud Pond Road, 59.06 narrow gauge rejoined the standard on Kate Island in Mud Pond, 59.50 bridge over North Branch Saranac River.

Passenger transfer to Paul Smith's Hotel: Travel recommendations in the first Paul Smith's Railway timetable of August 20, 1906 suggest that people from Plattsburgh board D&H trains for Loon Lake. Here, passengers walked across the highway to the New York Central station and waited for the southbound to take them to Lake Clear Junction. At the Junction, the Paul Smith's line could be boarded for the remaining 6.5 miles to the Hotel. In the afternoon or evening, the return trip could be made.

Lake Kushaqua (Round Pond). 59.63 miles. Elevation 1675. Maps 20-6, 20-19, and 36-12.

Passenger station: This station opened between the timetables of June 24, 1889 and October 6, 1890, but the initial name was Round Pond. The name was changed to Lake Kushaqua between the timetables of June 23, 1893 and June 22, 1896. The station closed sometime between the timetables of September 25, 1932 and September 24, 1933.

Relocation: Between the present highway bridge and the dam over the outlet to Lake Kushaqua can still be seen today the pilings for the narrow gauge line bridge which crossed the water above the dam. The standard gauge line crossed the outlet below the dam. Extensive relocations of the narrow gauge occurred between Lake Kushaqua and Onchiota stations.

Hartwell. Approximately 61 miles. Elevation ca. 1680.

This station appears on the January 16 and June 26, 1893 timetables only and must be where the Buck Pond State Campground is today.

Onchiota (Rainbow). 62.21 miles. Elevation 1690. Maps 20-6, 20-20, and 36-12.

Passenger station: This station opened sometime between 1887 and the timetable of June 21, 1889. It was initially named Rainbow on the earlier timetables through October 3, 1898. The June 25, 1899 timetable and October 7, 1901 timetables list Rainbow with Onchiota in parentheses, but by June 25, 1905 the name was totally Onchiota. Trains still stopped here on September 24, 1939, but no longer in 1940 when service was relocated over New York Central trackage.

Passing siding: An 1891 timetable records that two trains met here, requiring a passing siding.

Stagecoach connections: Stages from the Rainbow Lake House, four miles to the southwest, met trains here during the period 1893 through 1899 according to timetables. County Highway 30 crossed the track at 62.22 miles.

Industrial sidings: Tyler (1968, pages 14 through 17) states that Roak moved his sawmill from Roakdale to the south shore of Oregon Pond about 1895, and that Roak then sold the mill to Baker and Odell of Plattsburgh who ran it until 1913 or 1914. This conflicts with Seaver (1918, pp. 363-364) who mentions a series of other mill owners but not Roak (see Chapter 36). The Chateaugay Branch valuation diagram shows a spur into this mill from the narrow gauge at 62.10 miles, but oddly this spur continues past the mill and becomes the standard gauge spur from the New York Central! The narrow and standard gauge Chateaugay lines joined at 62.19 miles after several short relocations between Lake Kushaqua and Onchiota.

Roakdale Railroad: Tyler (1968) describes the nearly two-mile long narrow gauge railroad which connected the sawmill at Roakdale with Onchiota. She does not offer the date of construction, but it must have been 1887 or later, following the opening of the Chateaugay. A sawmill operator like Roak, wanting to get his lumber to market, would not build a railroad line to Onchiota without a connection to a larger railroad. Tyler writes that the Roakdale line shut down several months before November 4, 1895. The precise location of the Roakdale Railroad is difficult to determine. The present Franklin County Route 30 probably rests directly upon it. Exactly how it connected with the Chateaugay at Onchiota I do not know. According to Roakdale resident Lane Knight, reconstruction of the highway in the mid 1960s revealed old ties and rails just southeast of Boot Pond (Roakdale) Bog. He also recalls seeing the cement pilings for Roak's mill on the south side of the highway just east of the outlet to the bog; any evidence of the mill no longer exists. A complex of highway relocations in the Onchiota area does not help in the location of the railroad grades. For an area so close to Paul Smiths and home of this author, Onchiota still poses a challenging puzzle!

Vermontville Station. 65.735 miles at highway crossing. Elevation 1610. Map 20-6.

This station opened sometime between the timetables of June 24, 1889 and October 6, 1890. The last timetable listing the station was September 29, 1940, for by the end of that year the line had been abandoned from Plumadore to Saranac Lake. Chateaugay trains stopped not in the hamlet of Vermontville, but instead here some 2.5 miles to the west. The vicinity of Vermontville Station is called Oregon Plains, and extensive fire damage in 1903 occurred here (see Kudish, 1981).

Facility: At 64.835 miles was a water tank. For location purposes in the field today, the Oregon Plains Road crossing was at 64.07 miles and the second of four Negro Brook bridges at 64.97. Lyons, now Bigelow, Road flanked by the third (66.16 miles) and fourth (67.74 miles) bridges, crossed at 67.59 miles.

Bloomingdale Station. 68.136 miles. Elevation 1550. Maps 20-7 and 20-21.

Passenger station: This station was located one-and-three-quarters miles west of the center of Bloomingdale Village (now a hamlet). Trains stopped here from the time that the Chateaugay opened to Saranac Lake on December 5, 1887 through sometime between the timetables of September 30, 1934 and January 6, 1935. Gardner (1990, Volume 4, page 58) offers a photo of the station which she notes was built in 1888 and remodeled in 1904.

Stagecoach connections: Stages from the Paul Smith's Hotel, instead of traveling all the way to Loon Lake as they had since December of 1886, needed come only the seven miles to Bloomingdale Station. When Paul Smith opened his railway on August 20, 1906, regularly-scheduled stagecoach service to Bloomingdale Station ceased; however, an on-call conveyance service persisted at least through 1908: "Private conveyance for Paul Smith's can be secured promptly on telegraphing advice to Paul Smith's Hotel Company" stated the June 21, 1908 D&H Railroad timetable. Maps accompanying the 1896 and 1899 Chateaugay timetables announced connections by stage to the Crystal Springs House in Bloomingdale and Rice's House in Lake Clear.

Freight house: A photo of the freight house at 68.105 miles in Gardner (1990, Volume 4, page 58) has the caption that it was built in 1887. A stub continued north from the passing siding to serve the freight house and ended at 68.07 miles. Rickerson Brook crossed beneath the main at 67.96.

Passing siding: The siding began at 68.13 miles and ended at 68.44, with the County Highway 55 crossing at 68.16. The siding where trains met, according to a 1912 timetable, can be discerned on the 1902 Saranac quadrangle. Gardner's photos show two tracks in front of the depot and freight house. Tyler (1968, pp. 21-25) describes a family moving with all their belongings, including domesticated animals, from Bloomingdale, and loading a boxcar on the siding here.

Relocation south of Bloomingdale Bog. 71.21 to 72.20 miles. Elevation 1600 to 1640 feet. Maps 20-7 and 20-22.

South of Bloomingdale Station, the Chateaugay crossed the great Bloomingdale Bog for three miles on a fill. Then beyond, south of, the bog but before the rock cut where the Chateaugay approached very closely what is now State Highway 86, the narrow gauge had been built across a marsh on a long, high trestle at 71.73 miles. (This was not the only major wooden trestle in the area; another occurred over the Saranac River in the Village of Saranac Lake.) The standard gauge relocation in 1903 straightened the line and crossed the marsh on a fill, without a trestle, between 10 and 13 feet lower than the original 1887 line. Dick Finegan of Saranac Lake first pointed out this major relocation in 1992; it had escaped my notice for 21 years! Just as remarkable was the continuation of the relocation southeastward into the rock cut; the standard gauge was built again from about 6 to 13 feet lower, necessitating further blasting. In all, this relocation was 0.99 mile long, with the narrow gauge crossing the standard twice at 71.73 and at 72.08.

Saranac Lake. 74.51 miles. Elevation 1550. Maps 20-7, 20-23, 20-24, and 36-11.

Lake Colby Drive: Approaching Saranac Lake, the Chateaugay Railroad right-of-way from Peck's Corners (Trudeau Road) at 72.77 miles to Keene Street at 74.075 miles is now called Lake Colby Drive (State Highway 86). Upper Broadway, which parallels the Drive on the east, was the original turnpike. Note how level and straight Lake Colby Drive is today. At 74.30 miles, south of the Cedar Street crossings, the Chateaugay joined the Mohawk & Malone (later the New York Central Adirondack Division).

Chateaugay passenger and freight stations: Saranac Lake was the temporary terminus for the Chateaugay from December 5, 1887 through August 1, 1893. Rochette (1937) writes that a tent was set up for use as a station until a building could be constructed at 74.51 miles. Photos of this original 1887 wooden station appear in Hochschild (1962, p. 12), in Gardner (1990, Volume 4, page 60), and in the collection in the Saranac Lake Free Library as #82.620. Gardner also has a photo of the freight house built in 1888 across the tracks from (northeast of) the depot. In 1904, the original wooden D&H depot was moved across the tracks, coupled with the freight house, and made into an enlarged freight office at 74.485 miles. The present stone 1904 Union Depot was built on the same site as the original Chateaugay depot. The D&H freight house was still standing as late as 1953, seven years after the D&H pulled out.

New York Central passenger and freight stations: When the Mohawk & Malone arrived on July 16, 1892, its passenger station was located just west of Broadway. Later, the New York Central freight house resulted from the renovation of the original 1892 Mohawk & Malone depot. Still later Big D, a building supply retail store, owned the building. It burned during the winter of 1985-1986.

Union Station: Mary Hotaling, formerly of Historic Saranac Lake, found some detail in the Record of Minutes, Board of Trustees, Village of Saranac Lake for March 21, 1904: "The matter of moving the old Chateaugay Railroad Station and the erection of a new and larger station by the D&H Company was discussed at considerable length. . . ." We know that the extant stone station must have built shortly thereafter. Since two railroads shared the same station, this depot was a union station—that is, a station of a union of two or more railroads. The canopy over the station platform was removed on January 16, 1941. The porte-cochere was removed January 30, 1942. D&H trains continued to stop at the Union Depot through November 1, 1946 and New York Central trains through April 25, 1965. In 1980, the Adirondack Railway used the station which also doubled as the chief dispatcher's, Luke Wood's, office.

Stagecoach connections: A host of hotels sent stagecoaches and other conveyances to Union Depot. Before the Saranac Lake & Lake Placid Railroad was opened, only four points were listed in the 1889 timetable: Ray Brook House, Lake Placid, Saranac Inn, and Cascade Lake. However, between 1893 and 1899 the timetables and accompanying maps listed many more: Algonquin, Miller's, Ampersand Hotel, DelMonte, Berkley, Riverside Inn, Alexander's, Edgewater Inn, all Lake Placid hotels, and boats for Bartlett's and Corey's. In addition to the charcoal and iron industry which kept the Chateaugay Railroad operating further north, the passenger business at the south end of the line must have been of significance. Great detail on these hotels and others is available in *Summers on the Saranacs* by DeSormo (1980).

Passing siding: In 1896 Chateaugay trains were already meeting in Saranac Lake proving that the passing siding was already in existence. The siding was still in place during the summer of 1965, shortly after passenger service had ceased, and I suspect that it was removed shortly thereafter; it was gone by 1971. The siding began at approximately 74.31 miles and ended originally between the Margaret Street and Bloomingdale Avenue crossings. It was later shortened to end just short of the Margaret Street crossing.

Servicing facilities: Because the Chateaugay temporarily terminated in Saranac Lake, a complex of servicing facilities existed here. A map in the Franklin County Clerk's Office in Malone shows the track plan during this time, 1886-1893, complete with depot, engine house, freight house, and turning wye. A D&H valuation diagram indicates that the wye joined the main at 74.41 and 74.495 miles. The 1902 Saranac quadrangle also shows the wye, but the scale is so small that it is difficult to see. The *Essex County Republican* of October 19, 1899 describes a fire in the engine house: "There were two locomotives in the house at the time of the fire and they were both badly damaged. They were the *Loon Lake* and the *Lake Placid*." The New York Central had its own servicing facilities west of Broadway (see Map 20-23).

The Saranac Lake & Lake Placid Railroad: This line was organized in 1890 and began construction of an extension of the railroad from Saranac Lake to Lake Placid. This extension opened August 1, 1893 and accommodated both the narrow-gauged Chateaugay and the standard-gauged New York Central trains. The SL&LP was built as dual-gauge or three-rail track, but the track did not look like a Lionel model railroad O-gauge track because the middle rail on the S&LP was off-center. The first rail was shared by both railroads. The second rail was three feet from the first and used only by Chateaugay trains. The third rail was four feet, eight-and one-half inches from the first and used only by the Central. Can you imagine the complexity of the switches? (The only contemporary situation which I can think of that approximates this is the Mount Washington

Cog Railway in New Hampshire, where the middle cog creates extraordinary switches. The Newfoundland Railway as recently as 1988 had dual gauge switches at Port-Aux-Basques). Of course the Chateaugay and New York Central trains could not interchange cars until the Chateaugay was standard-gauged in 1903.

D.O.T. Map: A map given to the organization Historic Saranac Lake by the New York State Department of Transportation offers interesting but often unrelated tidbits of information about the Saranac Lake, Ray Brook and Lake Placid areas. This information is in the form of a commentary and the spurs in question are not identified on the map. The title of the map is *Description and Map of the Acquisition of Property Remsen-Lake Placid (abandoned Penn Central Transportation Company Right-of-Way)*, dated September 9, 1974 when the Penn central sold the line to the State of New York. A few examples of tidbits follow: On March 30, 1931 the LaTour Siding was added at the station. A spur track was removed at the station on March 8, 1938. On May 9, 1941 and again on January 30, 1942, 182 feet of main track was removed from the station---why on two dates seven months apart unless the removal was in stages?.

D&H industrial sidings: At ca. 73.4 miles, just south of the Saranac Lake General Hospital, was siding which served Latour's fuel storage tanks; these tanks were removed as recently as 1975. This segment of track, as has been mentioned before, was abandoned in 1940. However, I have heard that for several years after that, a dead-end spur persisted from the junction with the New York Central north to this siding. I have no documentation to confirm this, but the 1955 Saranac Lake quadrangle, based on 1953 aerial photos, shows Lake Colby Drive. Thus, if this spur persisted after 1940, it did not last until 1953. Numerous industries existed in the Village of Saranac Lake, appearing and disappearing over the years, some served only by the D&H, others only by the Central, and still others by both. The track plan during the peak years of operation, approximately the 1910 to 1920 era, as can best be reconstructed is shown on Maps 20-23 and 20-24. In 1979 the Adirondack Railway made a few modifications resulting in the trackage we still see today. A list of industries served at least by the D&H from north to south includes: D. Cohen & Sons Hardware; Adirondack Hardware Company and Stark's Hardware selling Lone Star Cement; Standard Oil Company siding built December 17, 1924, later Hyde Fuel Company; LaTour selling D&H Sterling Coal; a warehouse with owner unknown; Branch & Callanan Lumber & Hardware in use through 1972; a coal shed and lumber yard on either side of and almost connected to the D&H engine house which burned in February 1899; a coal and/or gravel spur trestle at about 74.7 miles behind the present Belvedere Restaurant (shown in an aerial photo taken in the 1930s and reproduced on page 92 of Dora and Keough, 1977) abandoned about 1935; and Adirondack Bottled Gas Company just south of the River Street crossing at 75.39 and in service through 1972. Just south of the Adirondack Bottled Gas siding, at about 75.5 miles, I recall in the early 1970s a pair of abandoned rails, no longer with a switch or connection, heading southeast into a gravel pit off Payeville Road. The pit is now the site of a North Country Community College playing field.

Siding at Will Rogers Hospital: A fellow railroad historian, Chris Brescia, noticed about 1978 evidence of a siding into the Will Rogers Hospital area at about milepost 76.7. We could find no documented evidence about this long-abandoned siding, the industry it served, or the dates of operation. When new ties were installed in preparation for Adirondack Railway operations in 1979, much of the evidence of the old siding was destroyed. The date on the cornerstone of the coal chute at Will Rogers is 1926, confirming the decade. The Route 86 crossing is at 76.83 miles.

New York Central industrial sidings: A series of industrial sidings was served by the New York Central only, not the D&H, west of Broadway. These include from west to east: Hulbert's Tri-Lakes Supply; Pyrofax Gas; Sterling Coal; Pabst Beverages; Boyce & Roberson Blue Coal; and Swift Meats to about 1970.

Trestle, bridge and relocation: The present long fill from Bloomingdale Avenue to the Saranac River was not always an embankment. A photo in the 1987 Saranac Lake Free Library calendar, on the back of the month March, shows an 1894 wooden trestle. I suspect that standard-gauging replaced the trestle in 1903. The East Pine Street bridge at 74.95 miles was being strengthened for highway traffic in 1976 when this writer noticed a plaque on it recording the D&H mileage from Albany: 233.79. This bridge was originally built in 1903-1904. A 1974 New York State Department of Transportation map indicates that a curve was relocated at Mc Kenzie Slough, at ca. 75.9 miles, with the original line further west than the existing line. No date is given for the relocation.

Photographs of Saranac Lake abound in publications:

Shaughnessy (1967), pp. 166, 190, 278. Page 166 shows dual gauge.

Dora and Keough (1977), pp. 89 and 90.

DeSormo (1974), page 113.

Gardner (1975), page 91.

Hochschild (1962), page 12 of *Adirondack Railroads Real and Phantom*.

Harter (1979), pages 67, 68 and 75; the page 67 photo is the same as in DeSormo.

Adirondack Daily Enterprise: April 22-25, 1965; April 9, 1972; April 28, 1976;

Adirondack Advertiser: September 14, 1977; September 21, 1977; May 31, 1978; and June 7, 1978 (this photo is the same as that in DeSormo and Harter).

Robbins (1975), page 26 (this is the same photo as in Staufer 1967, page 73).

Palmer and Roehl (1990), page 102.

A bibliography has been compiled on the New York Central Adirondack Division especially for Saranac Lake by Brescia and Hotaling (1990).

Ames Mill. 77.695 miles at highway crossing. Elevation 1570. Maps 20-8 and 20-25.

This was never a station, but is shown on some old turn-of-the-century maps and the 1902 Saranac quadrangle. Even a map in the 1908 D&H timetable shows Ames Mill. What kind of mill was here and whether or not a railroad siding served it are unknown.

A photo in Harter (1979, page 68) shows a wreck which occurred in September 1917 on the big 90-degree curve just northwest of Ames Mill. The original right-of-way is shown on Map 20-25 as a much tighter-radius, more easterly curve than the present broader, more westerly curve. The relocation took place in 1918, probably to avoid another wreck.

Ray Brook. 78.51 miles. Elevation 1575. Maps 20-8 and 20-25.

Passenger station: Ray Brook served D&H trains from August 1, 1893 when the Saranac Lake & Lake Placid Railroad opened through November 1, 1946. It served New York Central passenger trains through April 25, 1965. Gardner (1990, Volume 4, page 61) has a photo of an earlier Ray Brook combination passenger and freight station built in 1907. This wooden building burned December 9, 1928 and a new stone station opened by the time that the *D&H RR Bulletin* (1930, Nov. 15) was published. For a period in the 1970s the building served as the Ray Brook Post Office. The building still stands as of this writing.

Industrial sidings: On the north side of the track with switch at 78.44 miles was a stub track to spot occasional freight cars. South of the track, alongside the heating plant for the old sanatorium (now Camp Adirondack—a state prison), was a stub on which coal hoppers were set. The switch on the main was at 78.36 miles. A second stub was added between November 25, 1925 and May 12, 1932. These two coal stubs were in use through the spring of 1972 when the Penn Central Railroad abandoned freight service. In fact, when a washout down the line toward Utica prevented a locomotive from reaching Ray Brook and hauling away the last remaining hopper cars, the latter had to be hauled away by flatbed trailer over highways to Potsdam. I regret that I did not see this most unusual and entertaining movement through Saranac Lake streets! The trucks had to be removed from the hopper cars for powerline clearance purposes along the highways; they were reattached in Potsdam where the hoppers were removed from the flatbed trailers and re-railed on Penn Central tracks. The Adirondack Railway in 1979 removed the two coal sidings.

Olympic siding: A D&H valuation diagram informs us that a siding was added near Ray Brook station on October 26, 1927 and removed December 22, 1932. Oddly, a D&H employees' timetable of November 1, 1942 still lists Ray Brook Siding with a capacity of 24 cars. Were there two different sidings involved here or was there but one siding which had been removed at the end of 1932 and resurrected by 1942? An article in the *Lake Placid News*, June 30, 1977, featuring Ray Brook agent Tony Moreno stated: "That was the year [1932] the railroad put in a spur and siding at our station and dead trains laid in here overnight to accommodate the anticipated [Olympics] crowds that might be coming and going." A field check by the author located the west end of the Olympic siding at about 79.0 miles.

Photographs: The *Lake Placid News* of June 30, 1977 shows Ray Brook Station with agent Tony Moreno in the 1920s. Hastings (1950, page 25) shows the upgrade to the east. Harter (1979, page 29) and the *Adirondack Daily Enterprise* of April 9, 1972 include photos.

Accident: The *Essex County Republican* of October 19, 1899 described a derailment of a Wagner Palace Sleeping Car and a coach at Ray Brook. The wrecker came to the rescue from Plattsburgh making record time.

Lyons. 83.475 miles at Old Military Road crossing. Elevation 1742. Maps 20-8 and 20-25.

Industrial siding: Although never a passenger station stop, this locality is shown on a map included in the D&H June 21, 1908 timetable. Here, with switch at 83.41 miles, was a siding serving Standard Oil in 1932. More recently, Adirondack Bottled Gas and Raeoil Corporation, both local firms, had huge tank cars filled with bottled gas unloaded here as recently as 1972.

Olympic siding: Extra tracks were built at Lyons for the 1932 Winter Olympics. Mary MacKenzie, North Elba Town Historian, sent me copies of two clippings from the *Lake Placid News* dated September 25 and November 13, 1931. The September 25 article described New York Central officials studying the area prior to construction. Two tracks with a platform in between at Lyons Crossing (site of the present fire house) were to be built. About twenty-five Pullmans, housing approximately 500 guests, were to be spotted here. A locomotive would be coupled onto the Pullmans to provide heat and hot water; electrical power would also be provided. The November 13 article stated that the Lyons Crossing spurs were nearly completed. The Chubb River bridge is just east at 83.59 miles.

Lake Placid (Newman Post Office). 84.235 miles. Elevation 1736. Maps 20-8 and 20-26.

Passenger station: Last stop! As previously noted, both the Chateaugay-D&H and the New York Central trains began operating to and from here August 1, 1893. The D&H ceased service on November 1, 1946, the Central passenger service on April 25, 1965, and Penn Central freight in 1972. When the D&H pulled out in 1946 they sold the 10.01 miles of track between here and Saranac Lake to the Central on October 26. Gardner (1990, Volume 4, page 62) shows the original 1893 station, a converted house, located on the south side of the yard. She also includes a photo of the stone station built in 1904, when the Saranac Lake Union Depot was constructed, on the north side of the yard. The Lake Placid-North Elba Historical Association has used the extant stone station as a museum since 1967.

Freight house: Gardner (1990, Volume 4, page 62) includes a photo of the freight house built in 1893.

Servicing facilities: A runaround track adjacent to the main track provided engine escape from an arriving train and ended at 84.31 miles. There was a coal shed, an engine house, a hand car shed, a boiler house, a tool shed, an engine ash pit, a water tank, a warehouse, and a trestle for sand and gravel with a building housing a fuel oil tank. Before the turntable was built in 1916, engines were turned on a wye which headed south; the turntable was photographed by this writer in 1965, but it had been removed by 1971. The wye joined the main at 84.13 and 84.22 miles, and headed south for 0.11 mile. A New York Central employees' timetable dated September 30, 1951 stated that only steam locomotive watering facilities were in Lake Placid; the nearest diesel watering facilities were at Lake Clear Junction. A car body store house near the turntable was removed February 20, 1928.

Industrial sidings: There were two coal spurs, one owned by Hurley Brothers and the other by the Lake Placid Company; the latter's switch was at 84.07 miles. Hurley Brothers also had a wood shed.

Washburn's Crossing: The crossing at Averyville Road on a New York State 1974 Department of Transportation map is labelled "Washburn's Crossing." It is at 84.01 miles.

Olympic sidings: The *Lake Placid News* of September 25, 1931 stated that four additional tracks were to be built in the Lake Placid yard alongside the highway, Averyville Road, toward the station. Each track was to be 500 feet long and could hold about six Pullman cars serving as housing for visitors to the Olympics. The yard capacity would be doubled and about 500 people, in addition to the 500 at Lyons, could be housed. As at Lyons, a locomotive coupled to the Pullmans would provide heat, hot water, and electricity.

Gadsby's Tavern: A clipping from the *Adirondack Daily Enterprise* in the fall of 1968 (provided by railroad historian, Kenneth Campbell, but not precisely dated) states that a Penn Central freight brought the dining car, Gadsby's Tavern, into the Lake Placid Station. The diner had been built in 1922 by the Chesapeake & Ohio Railroad and had been sitting in the Baltimore yards. The car was removed in 1980 along with all other Adirondack Railway equipment.

Photographs: Hastings (1950) has photos on pages 22 and 26. The *Lake Placid News*, November 16, 1978 shows a picture of a steam-powered train entering Lake Placid; the track is standard gauged, hence post-1903. Harter (1979) has photos of it on pages 69, 71, 75, and 166. Page 69 shows dual-gauge. The photo of the turntable on page 71 is my own taken in July 1965. Shaughnessy (1967) has a photo on the top of page 166.

Chateaugay Equipment

There is a detailed roster in Shaughnessy (1967, page 470) of the narrow-gauge Chateaugay railroad locomotives with photographs of several of them with rolling stock (pp. 158, 159, 161, 162, 165, 167, 278). Additional information on Chateaugay equipment can be found in the Mohr (1974), Rochette (1937), and in Chateaugay Railroad timetables from the 1890s.

The Saranac & Lake Placid Railroad had its own engines for some time. Number 1, a ten-wheeler or 4-6-0, is shown on page 166 in Shaughnessy.

Once standard-gauging was completed in 1903, D&H mainline equipment could run over the Chateaugay Branch and did. In 1912 the timetable lists buffet-sleeping and parlor cars through to New York City.

Timetable Operation

Rochette (1937) records that during the period which the Chateaugay terminated at Lyon Mountain, 1880-1885, there were four passenger and three freight trains each way daily between Lyon Mountain and Plattsburgh.

Summer passenger service was more frequent than in other seasons. By 1889 there were two trains daily each way between Plattsburgh and Saranac Lake, three by 1896 between Plattsburgh and Lake Placid, four by 1905, three by 1912, two by 1920, and one by 1927. Fewer trains ran on Sundays. During the other seasons by 1890, there was one train daily each way between Plattsburgh and Lake Placid, two by 1893, and one by 1927. Some trains were sub-routed at Lyon Mountain or Standish.

Throughout the period 1893 through 1946, and continuing on into the era of New York Central ownership, additional trains were run all year, but more in summer, by the New York Central over D&H trackage between Saranac Lake, Ray Brook, and Lake Placid. These trains originated in Utica or shuttled from Lake Clear Junction (see Chapter 36).

Service to Lake Placid on the Chateaugay ceased on November 1, 1946. However, as recently as September 25, 1949, one passenger train was still running daily, except Sunday, each way between Lyon Mountain and Plattsburgh, stopping at Cadyville and Dannemora. This service ceased about a year later.

Minimum running time between Plattsburgh and Lake Placid was two hours and twenty-five minutes for an express in 1908. Maximum running time, slightly over four hours, occurred in the 1940s, when D&H trains were rerouted via Lake Clear Junction. There was another reason for this lethargic trip other than some additional miles: mixed trains!

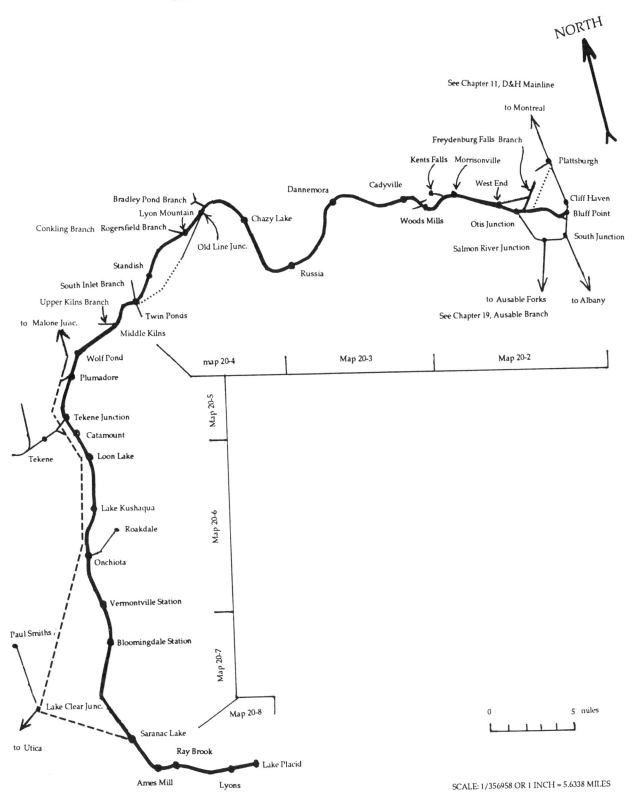

MAP 20-1 CHATEAUGAY RAILROAD

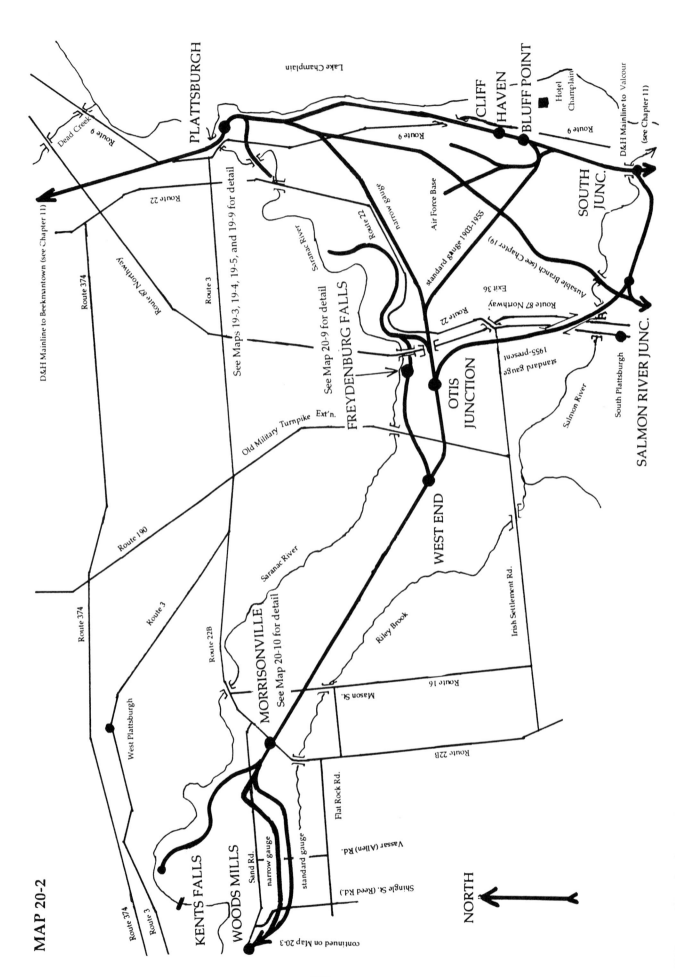

MAP 20-2

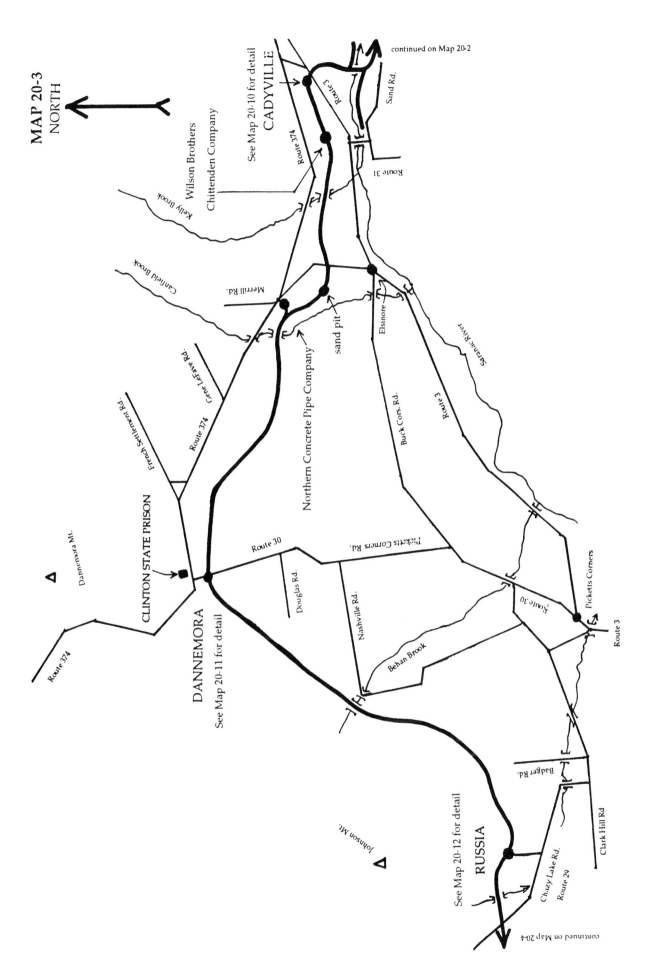

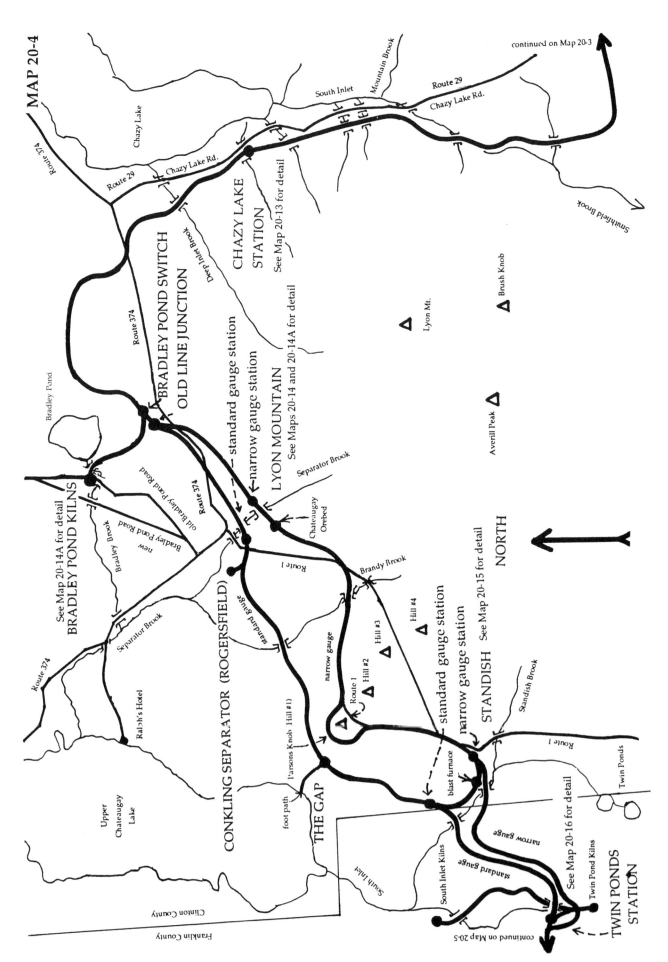

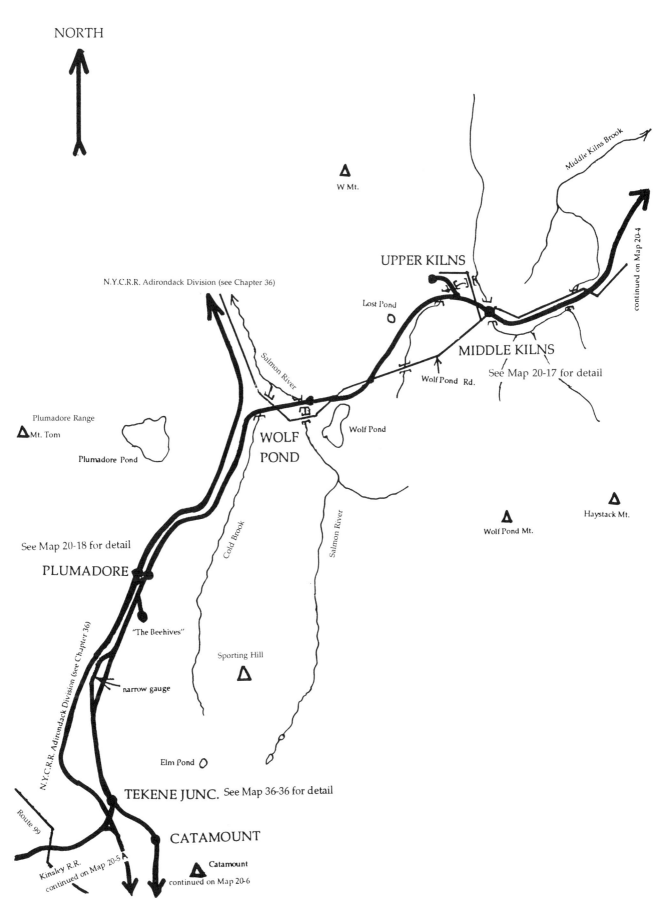

Map 20-5A: KINSLEY LUMBER COMPANY (BAKER BROTHERS)

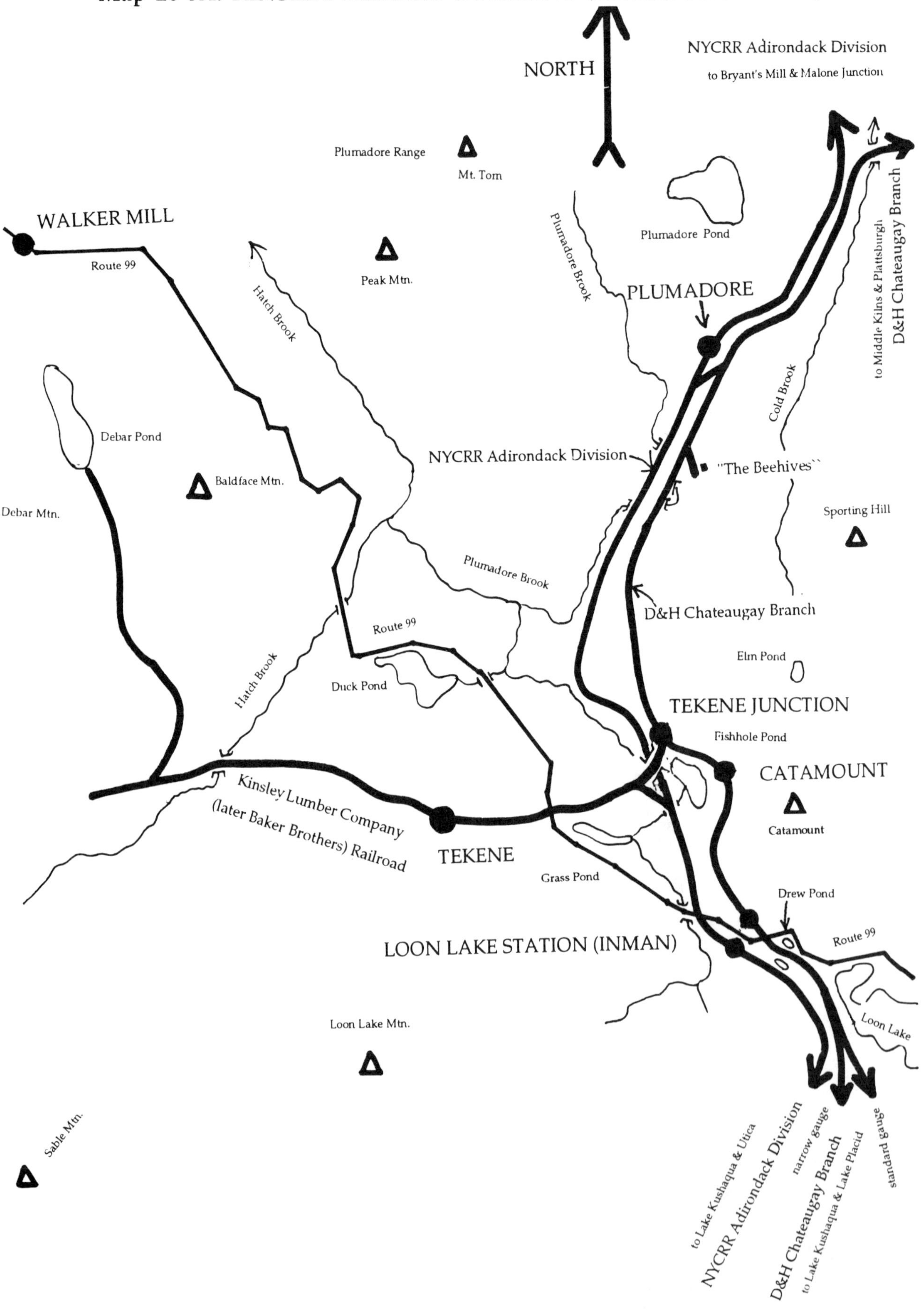

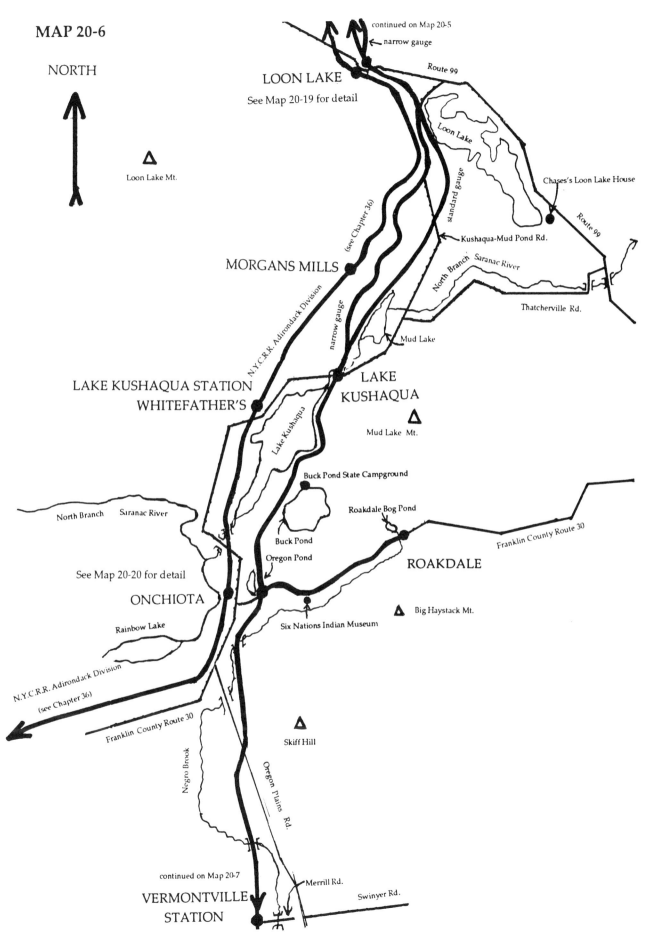

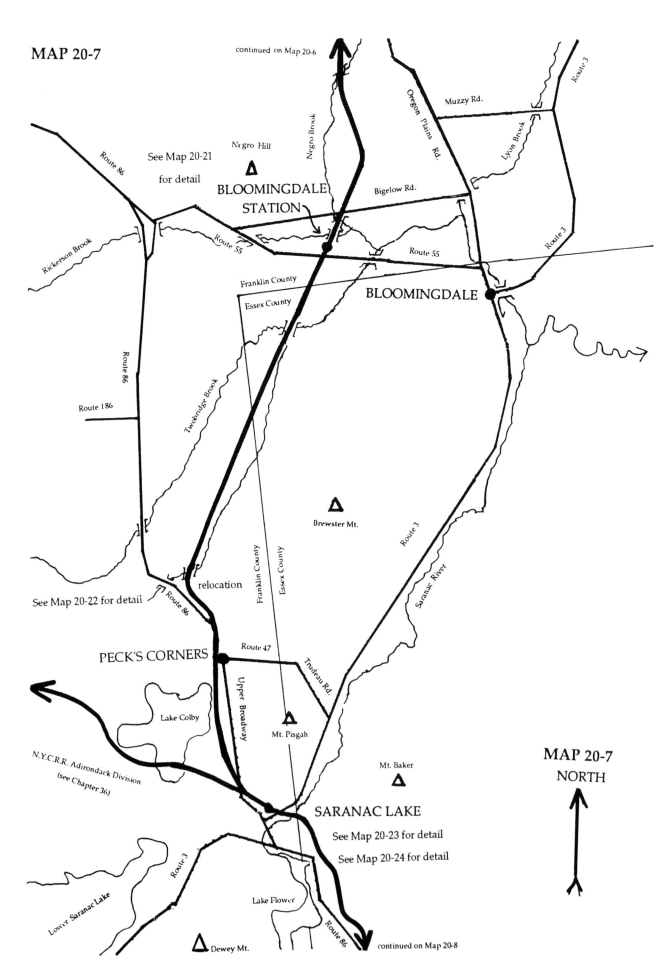

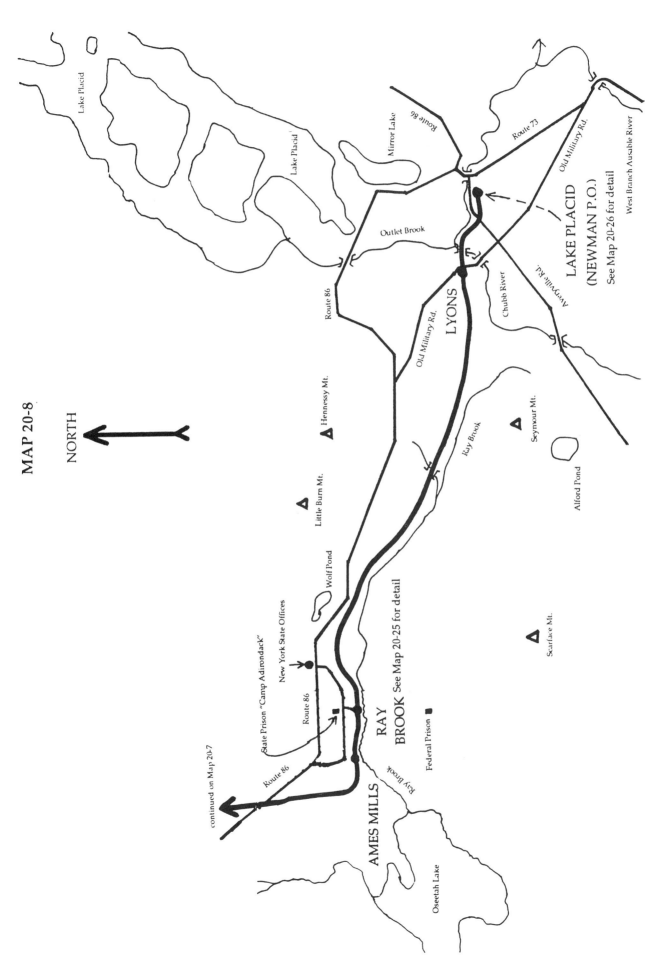

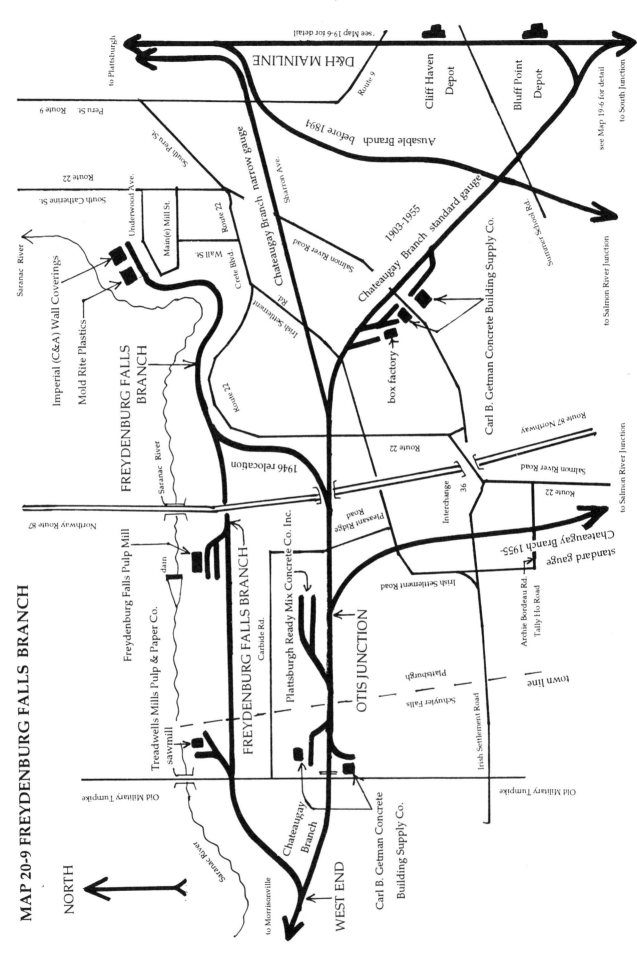

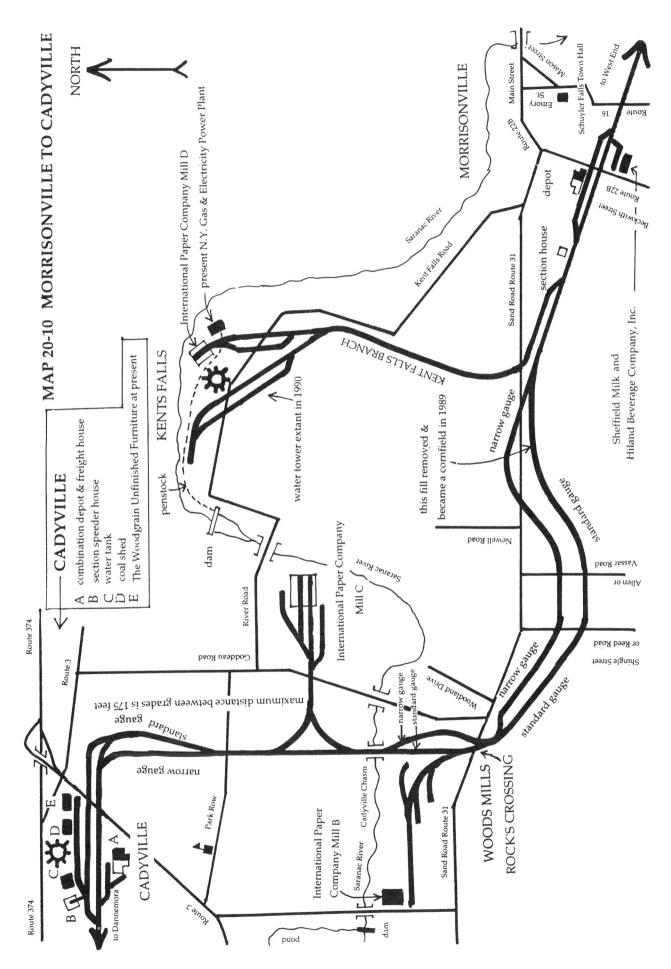

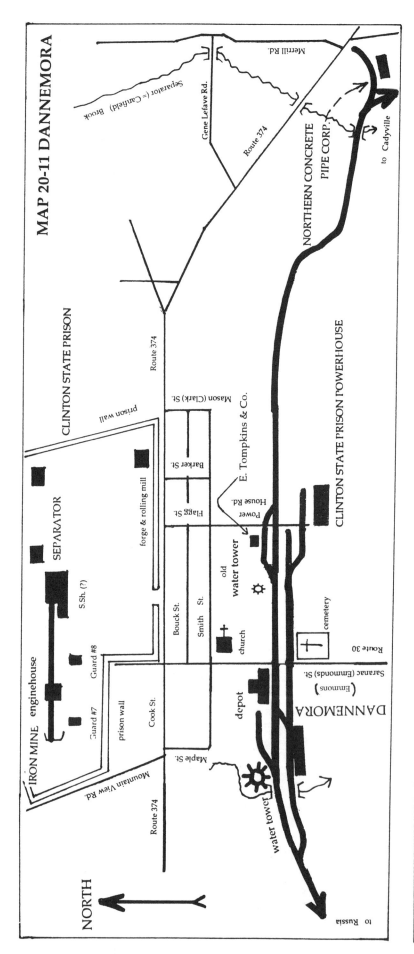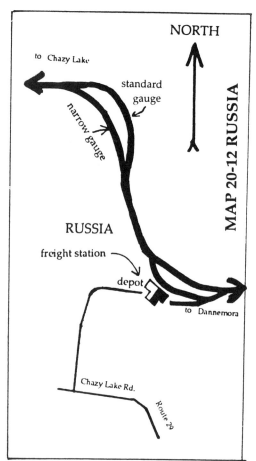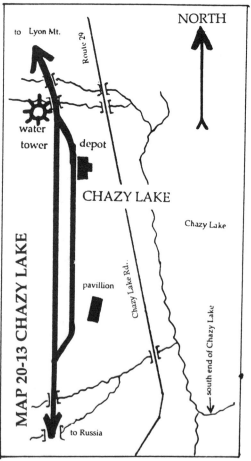

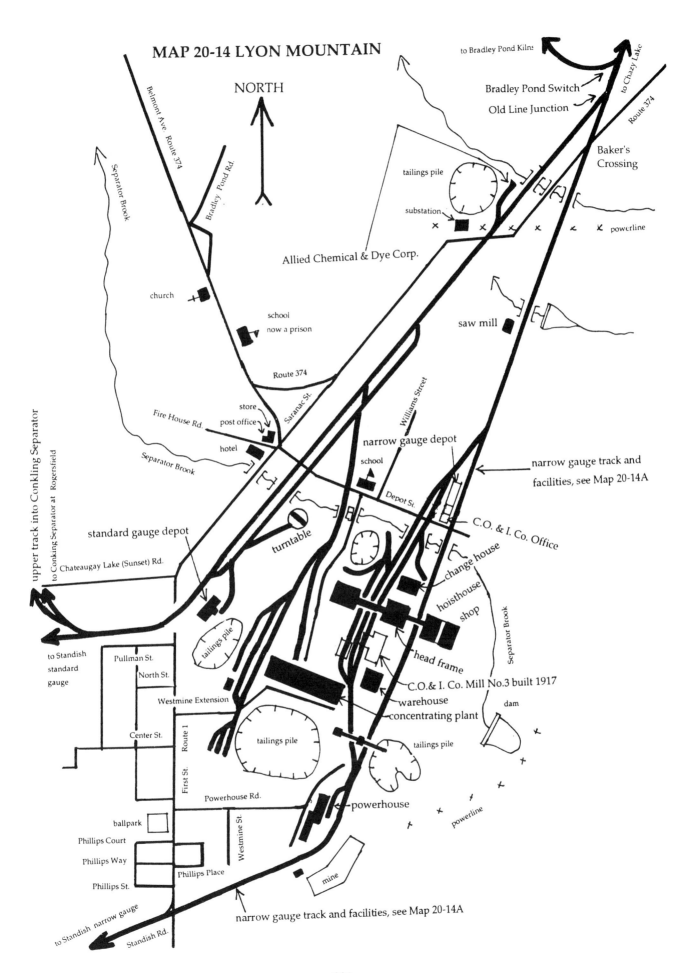

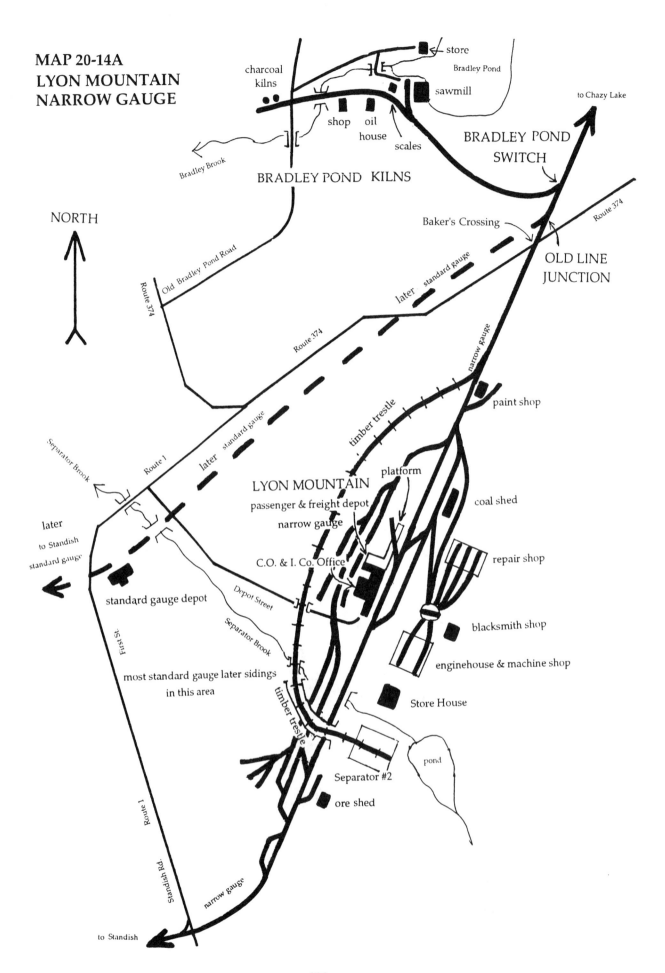

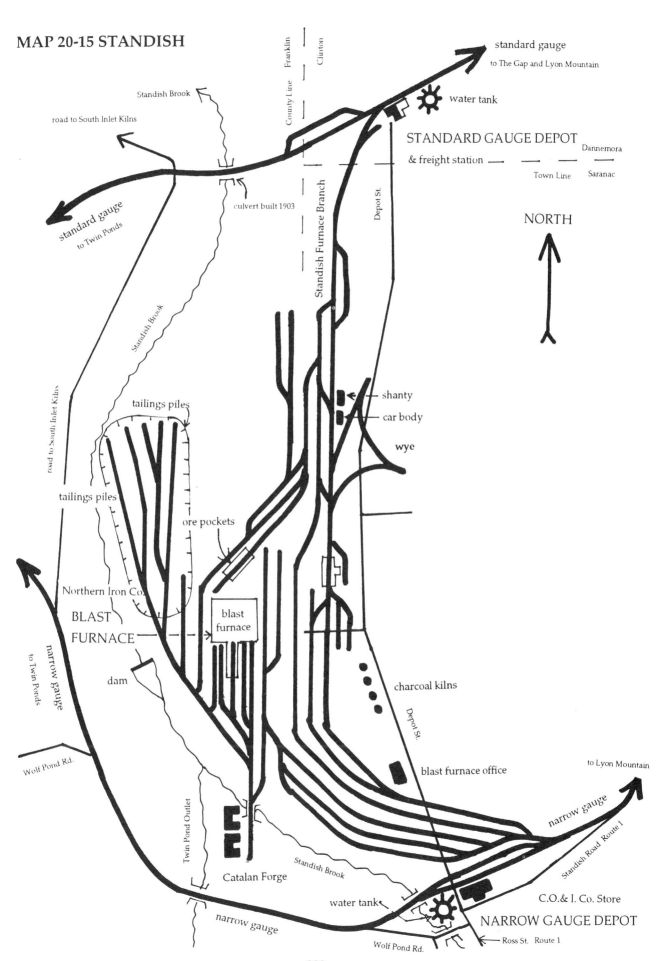

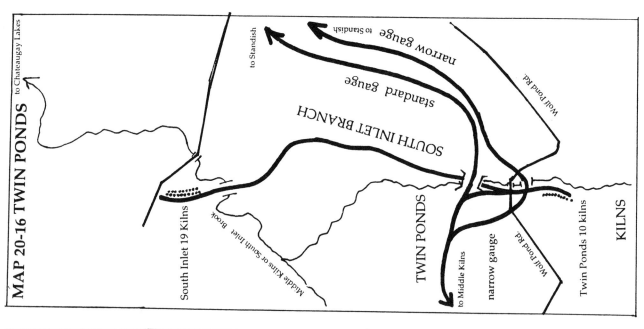
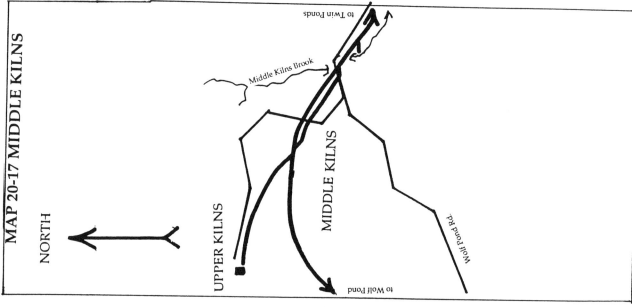
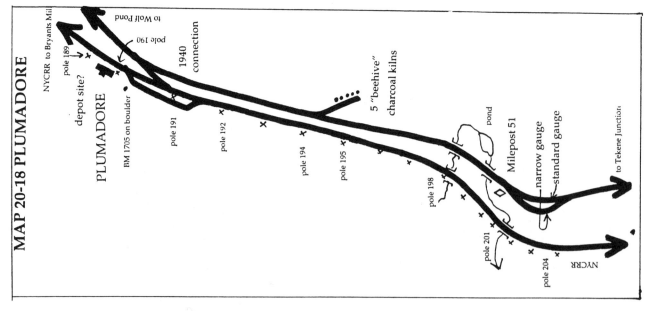

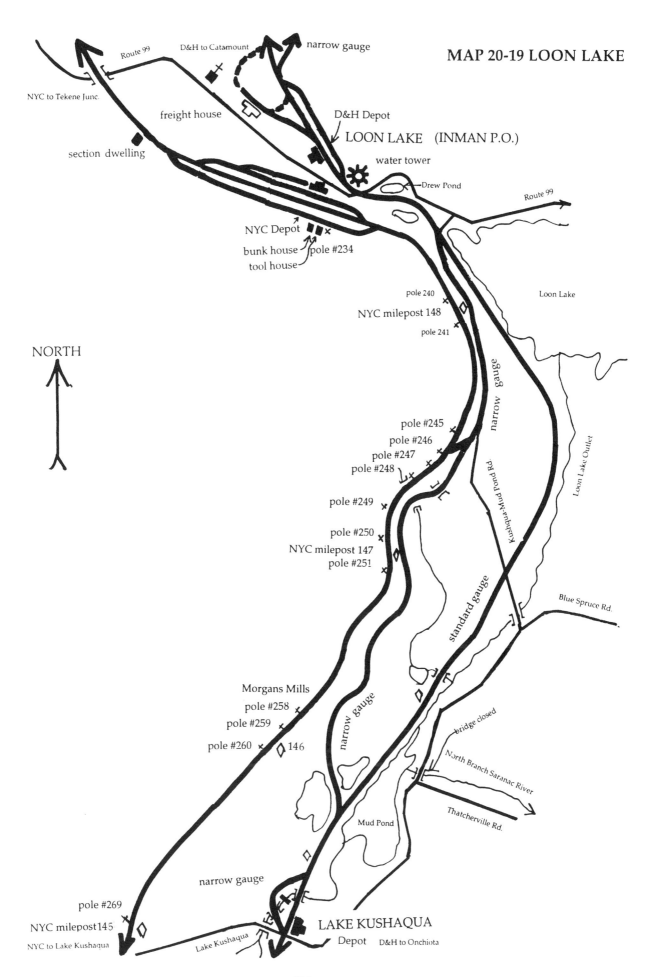

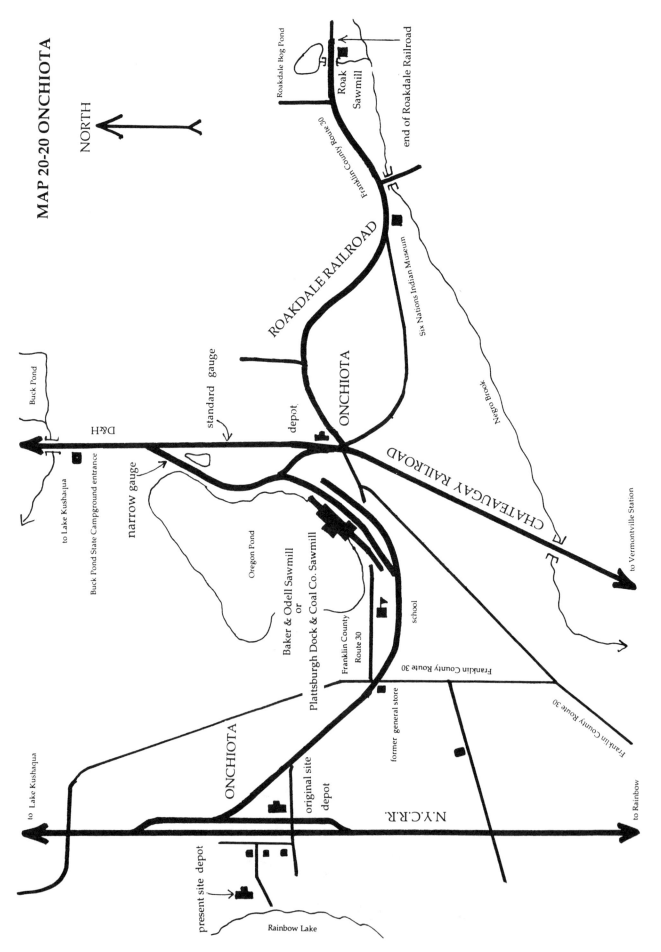

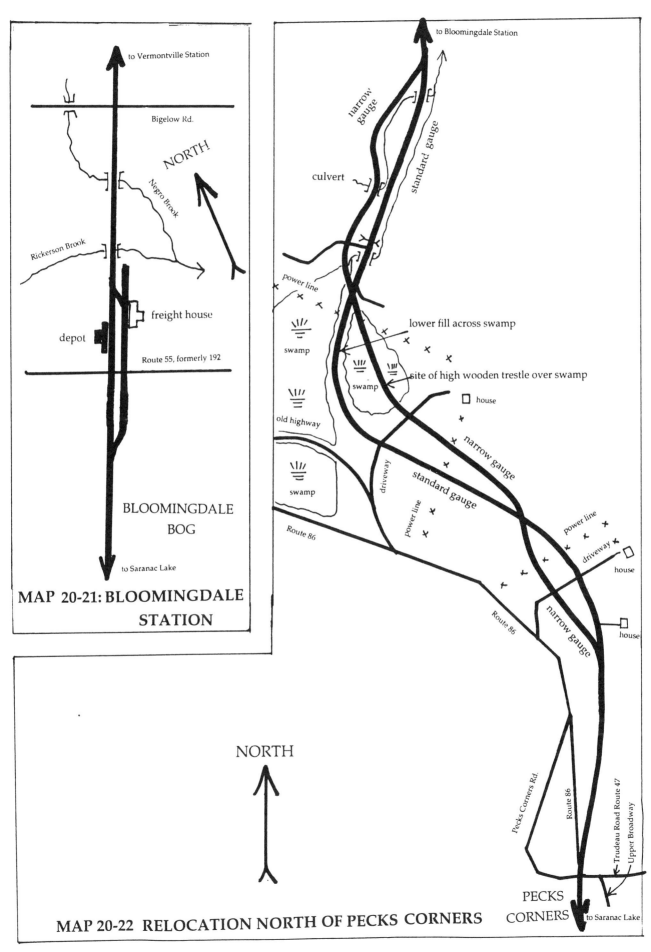

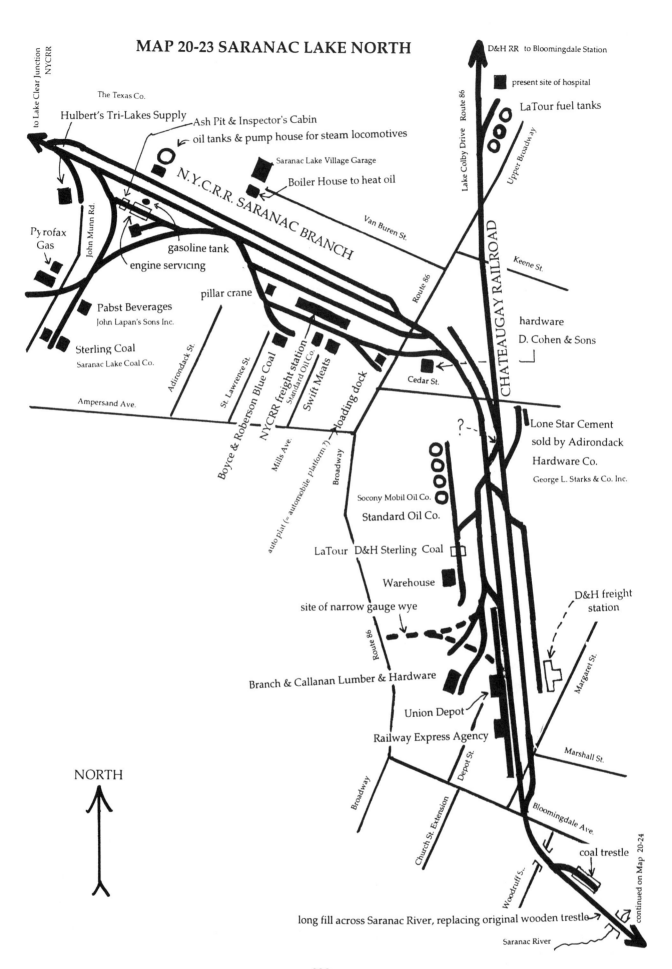

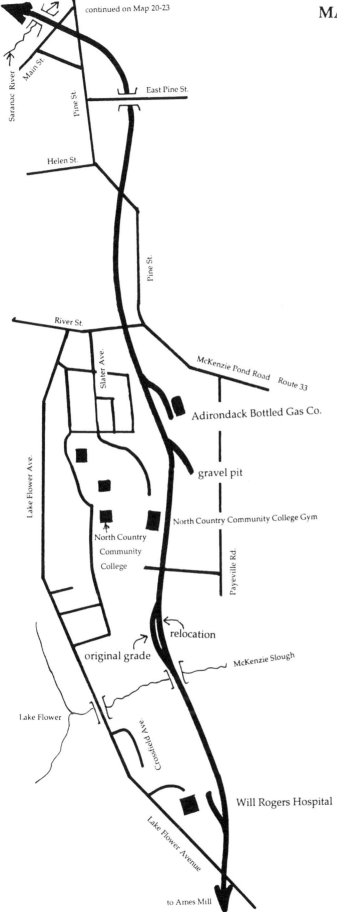

MAP 20-24 SARANAC LAKE SOUTH

MAP 20-25 RAYBROOK

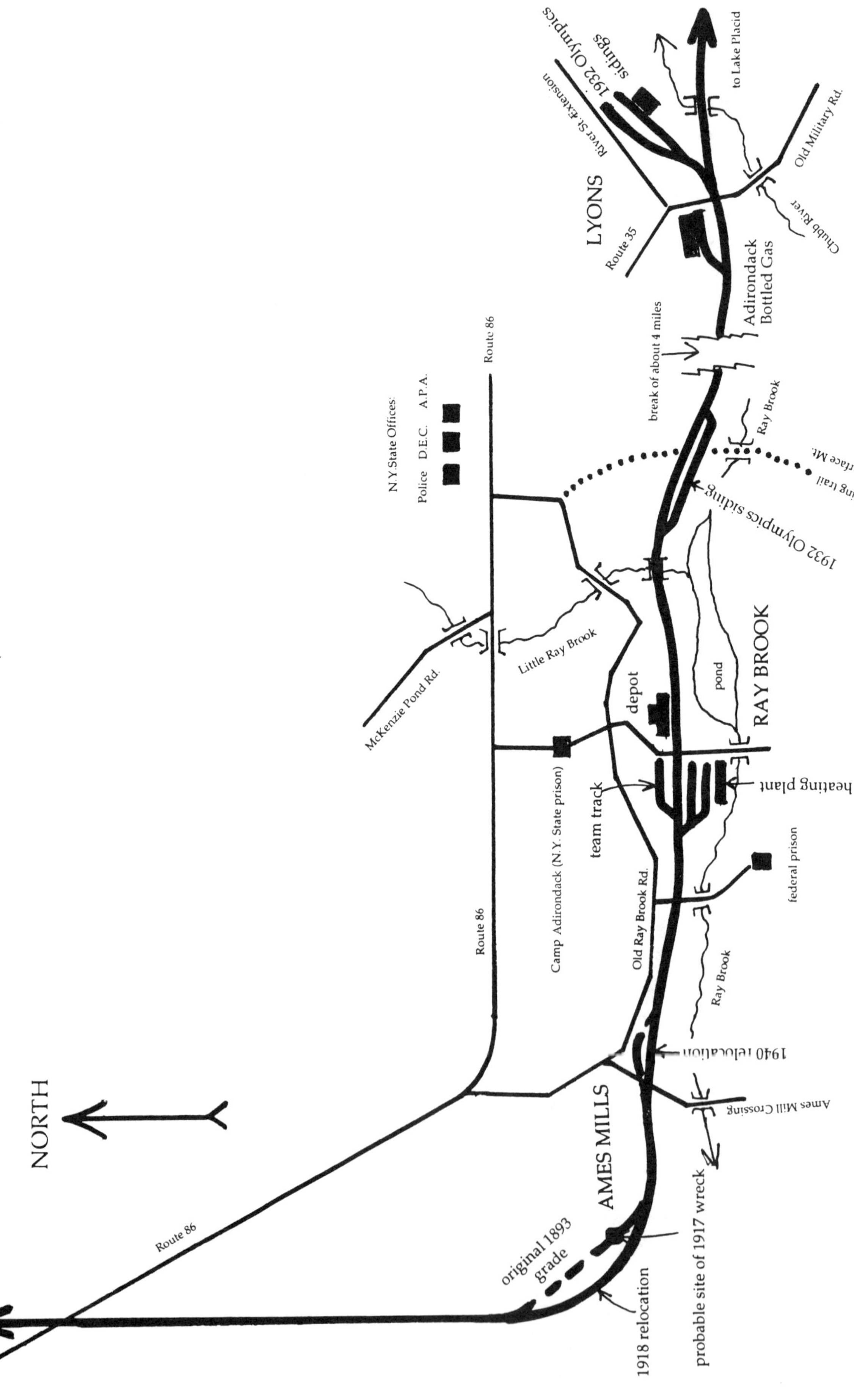

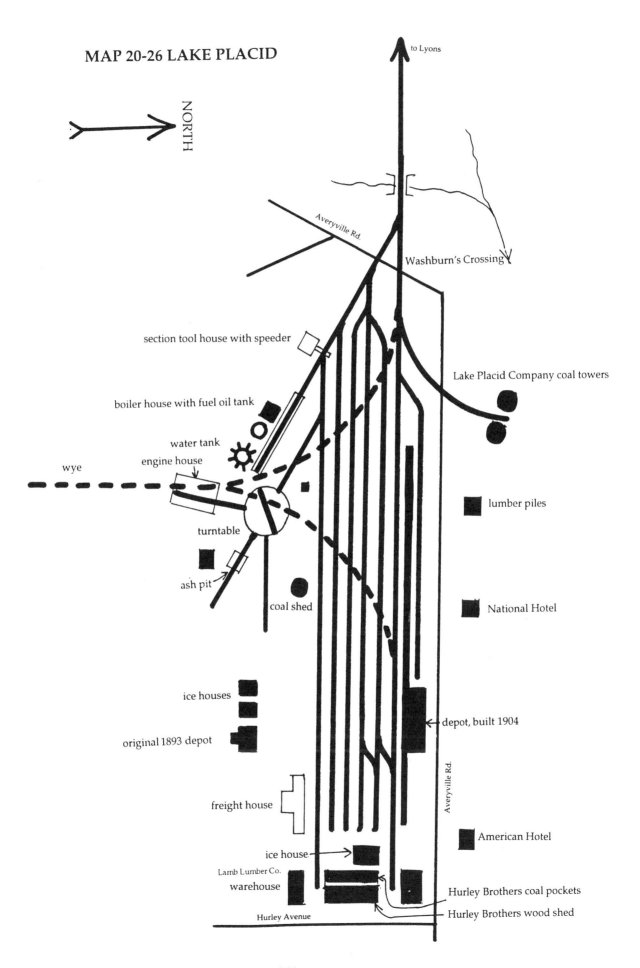

Chapter 21: Mooers Branch

ORIGINALLY THIS LINE was not a branch of the D&H Mainline at all, but in the early years rather a portion of it. A detailed history is available in McKnight (1989) with a brief summary of that history here. On July 22, 1852, the Montreal & Plattsburgh Railroad was completed northward from Plattsburgh to Mooers Junction, connecting with the Northern Railroad (later the Ogdensburg & Lake Champlain and finally the Rutland). The Canadian segment was being built southward from Caughnawaga via Hemmingford by the Lake Saint Louis and Province Line Railroad (soon to change its name to the Montreal & New York Railroad and then the Plattsburgh & Montreal Railroad), but did not reach Mooers Junction until several days before September 11, 1852. At this time a turntable was under construction at Caughnawaga. The first through passenger train from Plattsburgh to Caughnawaga ran on September 20, 1852. A ferry was needed to cross the Saint Lawrence River. The final link from Lachine into Montreal was provided by the Montreal and Lachine Railway.

In 1859, the Victoria Bridge over the Saint Lawrence River at Montreal was completed, and the Grand Trunk Railroad built south to Rouses Point.

The D&H wished to use the Rouses Point route rather than the Mooers Junction route to Montreal. On November 17, 1875, a special train with officials aboard ran from New York via Plattsburgh, Mooers Junction, east on the O. & L.C. to Rouses Point, and north to Montreal. During the summer of 1876, the D&H began construction of the present mainline cutoff via Chazy and Cooperville to Rouses Point and completed it by the end of the year. The old line through Sciota and Mooers Junction then became the Mooers Branch. The junction between the old and new lines became Canada Junction, just north of West Chazy at about milepost 178.

From 1876 through 1925 both lines were in service until the original via Mooers was abandoned. Mooers ceased to be a junction. Rutland trains continued to operate through here until September 25, 1961.

Sciota. 182.9 miles from Albany. Elevation 323.

The station here probably opened in 1852 or shortly thereafter and certainly was in existence in 1869 when F. W. Beers' Clinton County atlas was published (See Map 21-3 modified from this atlas). Note the several spurs serving the Sciota Mill Company; what products did it manufacture? The station closed in 1924 and was moved to Cooperville to replace a station which had burned there (Gardner, 1990, Volume 4, page 69).

Mooers Junction. 188.0 miles. Elevation 280.

Map 21-2 is based on McKnight (1989, page 115). One passenger train made one round trip daily on the Mooers Branch after 1876. It terminated not at Plattsburgh, but instead, went on through to Ausable Forks and served also the Ausable Branch.

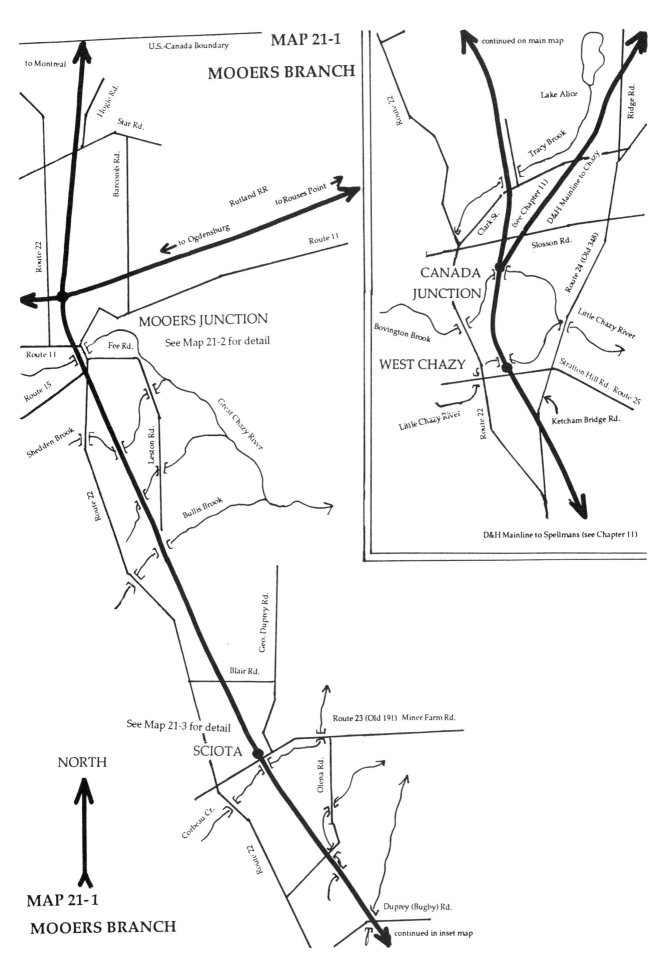

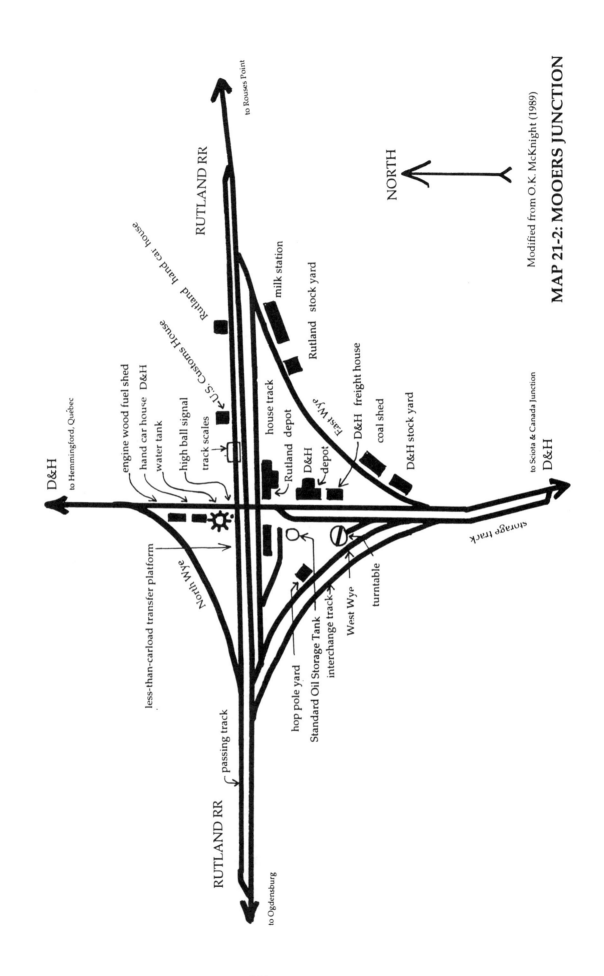

MAP 21-2: MOOERS JUNCTION

Modified from O.K. McKnight (1989)

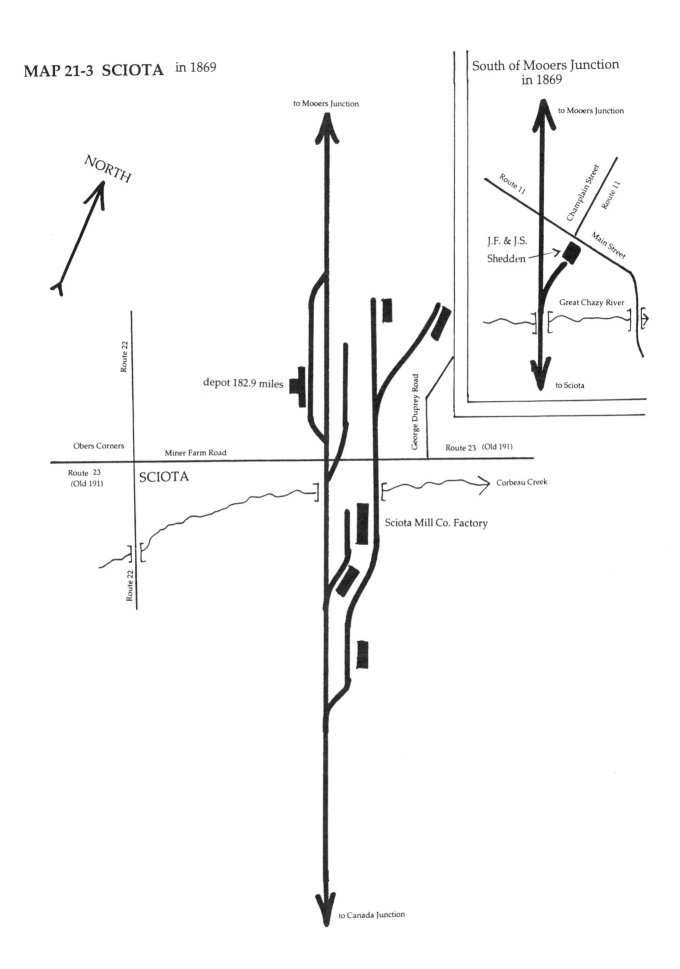

Chapter 22:
Amtrak's Adirondack

UNTIL APRIL 1971, the D&H had run the *Laurentian* from Albany to Montreal as a day train and the *Montreal Limited* by night with sleepers. With the inception of Amtrak on May 1, 1971, international passenger service, i.e. all trains crossing the border between the United States and Canada, was suspended. These two D&H trains in addition to those running from New York City to Montreal via Vermont stopped running.

Resurrection of Service along Lake Champlain

By September 1971 the New York State Legislature had passed a governor's bill which authorized the New York State Department of Transportation to contract with the National Railroad Passenger Corporation, Amtrak, for additional service. Although no funds were appropriated at that time to implement this action, the New York State Department of Transportation was working with Amtrak toward an agreement which would lead to restoration of the popular D&H route.

By April 1972, there was legislation pending in Congress which would allocate an additional $2 million to Amtrak to provide international service to Montreal. One of the options was through New England, not New York.

R. Thompson (1972) reported that Representative Carlton J. King of the New York State Assembly suggested that upstate New Yorkers write to Amtrak. Both houses of the U.S. Congress had passed legislation which required Amtrak to restore intercity rail passenger service to Montreal. The route to be used would be determined by Amtrak. A route via Albany, as well as one via Springfield, Massachusetts, was being considered.

The board of directors of Amtrak decided on August 24, 1972 to utilize the New England route in spite of the substantial efforts of the New York State Department of Transportation pleading for the restoration of the New York City—Albany—Montreal route. It took from August 24 to September 30 to restore the *Montrealer* in 1972—a fairly short time. Ironically, Amtrak has suspended the *Montrealer* in April of 1995, but the *Adirondack* still runs. To celebrate the 150th anniversary of the Delaware and Hudson Canal Company, the D&H Railway on April 28-29, 1973 ran a special excursion train from Albany to Montreal. Details were written up in the newspapers of that time and appeared simultaneously as announcements made by the D&H itself. The double-headed, steam-powered consist drew big crowds all along the line. In addition, the D&H had a second train touring its Albany-Binghamton Division; the Oneonta newspapers described the train stopped there with crowds passing through the historic exhibits.

Early in 1974 the New York State Legislature approved the $30 million Rail Services Preservation Fund. This fund was to be used as the first of a two-part program to rehabilitate New York railroads. Of this $30 million, one million dollars was used to upgrade the track from Albany to Rouses Point and to restore stations in preparation of the resurrection of passenger service along Lake Champlain. The second part came later in 1974, when on election day November 5, New York State voters approved a $250 million Rail Preservation Bond Act.

Amtrak alone hesitated to resurrect the *Adirondack* in fear of large financial losses, but Zimmermann (1978, page 43) states that "such a service could be initiated under the 403b provision of the Amtrak law, which allowed a state to sponsor additional Amtrak trains by paying two-thirds of their operating losses." In the first year of *Adirondack* operation, Amtrak expected to spend $1,200,000 on the run and earn only $700,000. Two-thirds of the $500,000 loss would be paid for by New York and the remaining one-third by Amtrak itself.

Detail on the funding and expenditure of that funding can be found in two 1974 publications by the New York State Department of Transportation: *Railroads Now and for the Future* and *New York State's Rail Program*. The D&H itself urged voters to pass the $250 million Rail Preservation Bond Act as did the Citizens Public Expenditure Survey of New York State.

State legislators and Department of Transportation officials made the *Adirondack* a reality with Amtrak on August 5, 1974. On that day a special train rolled north from Albany to Montreal carrying a host of dignitaries and stopping at principal stations along the way. Crowds turned out at each stop to see and hear the governor, New York State Department of Transportation commissioner, Commerce commissioner, mayors, state legislators, etc.. On August 6, 1974 regular daily service began with train #68 southbound and train #69 northbound between New York and Montreal via Albany and Plattsburgh. Lake Placid, Plattsburgh, and Watertown newspapers all carried descriptions of the August 5th festivities in their August 6th editions

The period from 1967 to 1977 was an exciting and historic one for the D&H (Zimmermann, 1978). Five of the ten years were financially in the black and five in the red. For a railroad in the northeastern United States to make a profit for at least one year in this era was indeed unusual. The purchase of secondhand diesel locomotives, especially Alco PAs and Baldwin Sharks, and passenger cars from other railroads attracted the attention of many rail buffs because this equipment was the last in service of its kind in the United States.

A *New York Times* article on September 9, 1974 is headed *D&H Railway Credits Black Ink to Workers*. A Syracuse *Herald American* article dated as recently as April 3, 1977 is entitled *Pride, Flexibility keep D&H on Right Track*. During this period, a deal with Conrail greatly extended geographically D&H operations over the lines of financially failing railroads. When Conrail began operating on April 1, 1976 the D&H was its only major competitor in the northeast (see *The Daily Star*, Oneonta, New York, March 10, 1976).

In contrast to earlier newspaper headlines from the 1974 to 1977 era, the *Adirondack Daily Enterprise* of Saranac Lake on August 4, 1978 headed an article with *D&H's Fight for Survival*. This article stated that the D&H was at that time a subsidiary of the Norfolk & Western Railway but that the N&W has "insulated itself from the liabilities of the Delaware line." An abrupt decline in D&H finances occurred between 1977 and 1978. Loans and grants from the United States Railway Association and the states of New York, Pennsylvania, and Vermont were keeping the D&H running in 1980. The May 29, 1981 *Enterprise* indicated that New York State was buying and rehabilitating 200 old run-down box cars from the D&H in a partial effort to bail the railroad out with 4.4 million dollars.

Burdick (1985) wrote that New York State covers 65%, or $725,000, of the operational loss. This suggests that the total loss is $1,115,385 and Amtrak covers the remaining 35% or $390,385. Although Burdick does not state so exactly, I suspect that these figures are for calendar or fiscal year 1983 or 1984.

From 1974 through 1978, the *Adirondack* headed north out of Albany via Watervliet and Mechanicville toward Saratoga Springs. This routing necessitated a reverse movement in downtown Albany in order to get from Amtrak-Conrail to D&H trackage. The last timetable indicating Watervliet and Mechanicville was January 8, 1978; the April 30, 1978 timetable no longer listed them. By this time the *Adirondack* was running via Schenectady toward Saratoga Springs. The route change, according to the Amtrak timetable, reduced the New York-Montreal total mileage from 382 to 375.

The second routing change came in 1986, when Windsor Station in Montreal was no longer used and arrivals and departures were shunted over to Central Station. The Amtrak timetable of October 27, 1985 still lists Windsor Station, while the April 27, 1986 timetable lists Central Station. The total mileage from New York to Montreal was extended some eight miles from 377 to 385, according to the timetables, counteracting the 1978 shortening! Along with the Montreal station change came a relocation of Canadian customs stops from LaColle to Cantic, Quebec.

A third routing change came on April 7, 1991 when the *Adirondack* began to operate out of Penn Station, not Grand Central, in New York City. By April 1995, when the *Montrealer* was discontinued, the *Adirondack's* run was extended to Washington D.C.

Port Henry and Willsboro were not station stops on the November 30, 1975 Amtrak timetable, but were in service by the October 31, 1976 timetable. Port Kent was added a little later: sometime between October 13, 1976 and May 1, 1977. Westmount, Quebec, a Montreal suburb, first appears on the May 1, 1977 timetable and is last listed on April 24, 1983. Montreal West, another Montreal suburban stop but in service from the very beginning in August 1974, also was last listed on April 24, 1983. Schenectady was added, first appearing in the October 28, 1979 timetable. It was not a stop on October 29, 1978 although *Adirondack* trains were passing through there since April of that year. The reason was that the Schenectady station had not been in service for all trains, including the Albany-to-Buffalo runs, for several years. All trains stopped at Colonie during that time before the Schenectady stop was resurrected.

Beginning in the fall of 1988, the *Adirondack* no longer stops at Port Kent during the winter timetable period, October through April. Port Kent has become a seasonal April through October summer stop primarily as a ferry connection only.

Beginning in the fall of 1983, the *Adirondack* no longer stopped at Willsboro during the winter timetable period, October through April. Willsboro had become a seasonal summer stop only from April through October. But by 1988, summer service had also ceased.

From 1974 through April 29, 1978 most *Adirondack* equipment was D&H. The famous last Alco PAs and occasional Alco RS-3s and 36s pulled the cars, including D&H baggage, coaches, and a full diner. Dome cars were first rented from the Canadian Pacific for service between Montreal and Albany (ironically, the D&H is now owned by the CP!). There was insufficient clearance in the tunnels south of Albany. An occasional old New York Central parlor car was coupled on the rear. Amtrak later supplied the dome cars.

The Amtrak timetable of April 30, 1978 announced that Turboliners had replaced the older D&H equipment. By August 3, 1980 Amtrak's timetable indicated that Amfleet had replaced the Turboliners. Turbos were running again in 1991 but Amfleet in 1992.

Great detail on the post-Shaughnessy decade of D&H locomotives and passenger cars will be found in Zimmermann (1978). Detail on post-Zimmermann era D&H equipment will be found in Sweetland (1992) and Plant and Plant (1993).

An analysis for specific times of station stops and running times can easily be made from examination of Amtrak timetables from 1974 through the present. Beginning on October 20, 1984, the southbound run began to leave Montreal daily in the afternoon instead of in the morning from October to April (cold season) to better accommodate skiers returning to New York City from Adirondack regional points late in the evening. From April to October (warm season) the traditional morning Montreal departure resumed. Beginning on October 26, 1986 the southbound left Montreal in the afternoon on Sundays, providing more convenient return service for New York City area people on weekend trips to northern New York or Montreal. Since then, the southbound has left Montreal at various times, but the northbound has always left New York City in the morning.

Running times have ranged from a minimum of 8 hours 30 minutes in October 1983 to 10 hours 20 minutes at the outset in August 1974.

Fares have increased markedly over the years. A one-way New York to Montreal coach fare was $22.25 on August 6, 1974, but $67.00 on May 27, 1988. However, the round trip excursion fare in 1988 was only $89.00.

The September 4, 1974 Saranac Lake *Adirondack Daily Enterprise* stated that during its first month of operation, the *Adirondack* averaged 330 people per day on northbound and southbound trains combined north of Albany. South of Albany, the ridership was and is much heavier and funding is all-Amtrak. Burdick (1985) states that the number of passengers on the *Adirondack* was 75,000 in 1983, equal to an average of 205 riders daily in both directions combined.

References

Abundant articles have been written on recent Amtrak *Adirondack* and D&H developments in addition to those listed above. The *Adirondack* is described in McLaughlin (1974), Hebard and Forrest (1974), Zimmermann (1975, 1978), Burdick (1985), Fenster (1994), and Crane in Crane, McClellan, and Folwell (1995). D&H finances are described in Mohr (1974), Faber (1974), Zimmermann (1978), and Chady (1977).

Consolidations #817 and #803 in the Fort Edward engine house, ca. 1947. Page 154.
Collection Chapman Historical Museum.

The Laurentian at Fort Edward in the mid-1940s. D&H passenger locomotives had many distinctive features.
Page 154.
Collection Chapman Historical Museum.

The tracks leading to the right form the north leg of the wye of the Lake George Branch at Fort Edward. The station, beyond the freight house, is scheduled for restoration. Page 154.

Kip Grant photo.

The remains of a typical ore car, Port Henry, May 1992. Page 166.
Author photo.

Lake Champlain & Moriah train, locomotive #15. Page 166.
Richard Wettereau colleciton.

LC&MRR #12 with an old D&H coach, Mineville yard. Page 166.
Richard Wettereau collection.

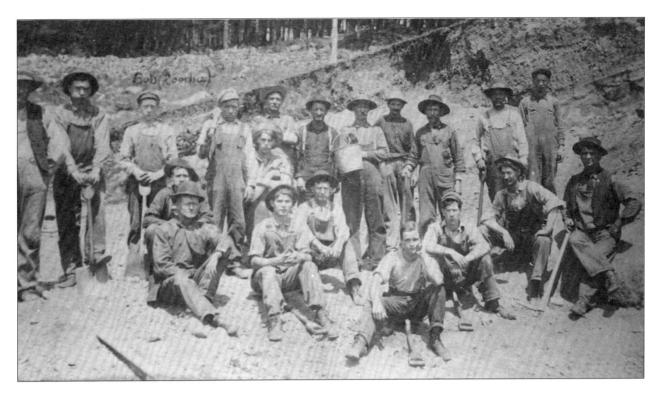

Work crew on the Lake Champlain & Moriah Railroad. Page 166.
Richard Wettereau colleciton.

The 1905 wreck at Switchback on the Lake Champlain & Moriah Railroad. Page 168.
Richard Wettereau collection.

Facilities between Mineville and Witherbee near Mill #5, looking southeast to Joker Tailings Pile. Page 168.
Warren Dobson photo, late 1971.

Facilities between Mineville and Witherbee. Mill #5 on right, hamlet of Witherbee in distance.
Looking southwest to Mt. Tom. Page 168.
Warren Dobson photo, late 1971.

Sintering plant at Switchback with Concentrating Mill #7 on the hillside. Looking southwest. Page 168.
Warren Dobson photo, late 1971.

The sintering plant at the extreme left has been demolished, but Concentrating Mill #7 still stands.
All built 1942-43 by Republic Steel. Photographed after the July 1971 closure. Page 168.
Warren Dobson photo.

The Lake Champlain & Moriah Railroad built this overpass over Whitney Street in Port Henry in 1909, photographed in 1994. The Terio wye was replaced by a horseshoe curve. Page 168.
Richard Wettereau collection.

Opposite page, top:
Lake Champlain & Moriah Railroad locomotive. Page 169.
Richard Wettereau collection.

Opposite page, bottom:
The D&H roundhouse at Plattsburgh, April 1973. It burned ca. 1992, but the turntable pit and shop (left) still exist. Apparently, many valuable D&H historic documents were lost in the blaze. Page 186.
Author photo.

Office of the Chateaugay Ore & Iron Company at Lyon Mountain. The narrow gauge depot, now demolished, was once attached to the rear of the office. August 1991. Page 206.

Author photos, above and below.

The few remaining industrial buildings at Lyon Mountain. The tallest is the Chateaugay Ore & Iron Company Mill #3, built in 1917. Looking southwest, August 1991. Page 206.

**Remains of the Standish blast furnace, abandoned shortly after 1939.
Page 208.**
Richard Wettereau photo, October 1994.

An early Ray Brook Station. The powerhouse in the background served the Ray Brook Sanitarium, now Camp Adirondack, a state prison. Page 216.
Photographer unknown.

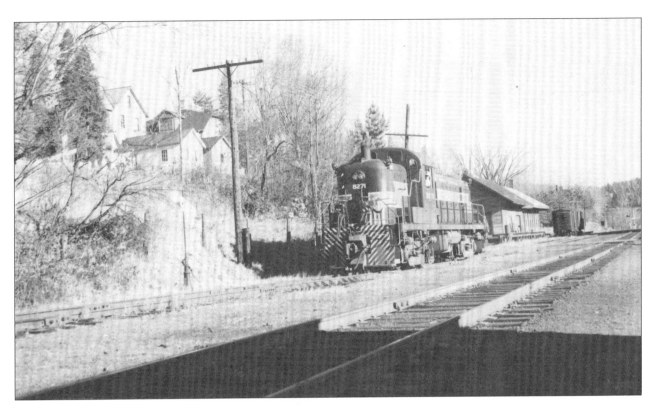
New York Central Alco locomotive switching in Saranac Lake, 1953. D&H freight house beyond. Page 214.
Alan Thomas photo.

Ray Brook station built in 1930 and still standing. Page 216.
Photographer unknown.

Former Reading class T-1 adapted to reproduce D&H Class K 4-8-4 #302 for the railroad's sesquicentennial trip to Montreal in April 1973. Page 246.
Kip Grant photo.

Train #69, Amtrak's northbound *Adirondack*, coming into Fort Edward in early 1975. The locomotives are former Boston & Maine units. Note the dome car. Page 248.

Kip Grant photo.

Section II:
Into the Adirondacks from the North

Chapter 23:
New York and Ottawa

"ADIRONDACK ENTERPRISES! A New Route to the Wilderness! Great Lumbering Industries! The Boom that has Come to Brandon, Brighton, and Waverly—Will it be Permanent?"

This newspaper quotation comes from the Plattsburgh *Sentinel* of April 10, 1885. John Hurd formed the Northern Adirondack Railroad Company on February 9, 1883 in order to timber the Adirondacks of Franklin County. Construction began on August 30, 1883 (Pope, 1972) at Moira, a station on the Ogdensburg & Lake Champlain (later the Rutland) Railroad. The new line was built to Saint Regis Falls in late September 1883, to Santa Clara in 1884, to Brandon in 1886, and terminated in Tupper Lake sometime between late 1889 and the summer of 1890.

On May 30, 1895, the Malone newspaper the *Palladium* stated that Hurd's bankruptcy forced him to sell the line (Pope, 1972). The railroad was reincorporated into the Northern New York Railroad; this was an unfortunate name because the Ogdensburg & Lake Champlain Railroad had used the same name from 1848 to 1858. In 1897, the second Northern New York Railroad became the New York & Ottawa, because the line was being extended northward from Moira toward the Canadian Capital. The bridge under construction over the Saint Lawrence River at Cornwall collapsed on September 6, 1898, delaying the commencement of service to Ottawa until 1900. On December 12, 1906 the New York Central and Hudson River Railroad took over the New York & Ottawa Railroad, and the line became the Ottawa Division.

A description of the New York & Ottawa Railroad follows on a station by station basis, beginning at Moira (milepost zero) and ending at Tupper Lake (milepost 54). In addition to the timber for sawmills and pulpwood for paper mills, Hurd's railroad also carried cordwood to Montreal for fuel, hemlock bark, and charcoal (Seaver, 1918, p. 535). Whereas

Webb's Adirondack & Saint Lawrence Railroad, built in 1892 (see Chapter 36), cut a swath only 100 feet wide through the forest and was more tourist-oriented, Hurd's Railroad removed the forest along the right-of-way for several hundred feet on each side at least (*Franklin Historical Review*, 1973, p. 57).

Detail on the major feeder logging railroads to the New York & Ottawa will be found in the following separate chapters: Watson Page Lumber Company Railroad (Chapter 25), Brooklyn Cooperage Company Railroad (Chapter 26), Bay Pond Inc. Railroad (Chapter 27), and Oval Wood Dish Company Railroad (Chapter 28). Detail on the Bombay & Moira Railroad, a connecting line but not primarily a logging line, is presented in Chapter 24.

Station Descriptions

Moira. 0.00 mile. Elevation 370 feet. Maps 23-2, 23-7, and 24-1.

It was from this point, on the Ogdensburg & Lake Champlain Railroad, where John Hurd began building his line southward in 1883.

Although the Ogdensburg & Lake Champlain Railroad lies outside the Adirondacks and thus is not included in this book, a brief chronology will be given here. Much information is available, the primary sources being Shaughnessy (1964, pp. 59 to 68), Doherty (1971), Shaw & Walsh (1982), Berry (1952, 1953) and Nimke (1986, 1989, 1990). The O.& L.C., one of the first railroads to be built in northern New York, connected the Saint Lawrence River with Boston via northern New England. A chronology:

1848----Northern New York Railroad construction began;
1850----first through train from Rouses Point on Lake Champlain to Ogdensburg on the Saint Lawrence River on Sept. 20;
1858----reorganization into the Ogdensburg Railroad;
1864----re-reorganization into the Ogdensburg & Lake Champlain Railroad;
1870----part of the Central Vermont System;
1898----Central Vermont System collapsed on February 14;
1901----The O.& L.C. Railroad became part of the Rutland Railroad on September 27;
1953----passenger service discontinued;
1961----freight service discontinued after September 25 strike;
1964 to 1966----rails removed.

The Ogdensburg & Lake Champlain Railroad is briefly mentioned in three other chapters in this book: in Chapter 11 on the Delaware & Hudson Mainline which it crossed at Rouses Point, in Chapter 21 on the Mooers Branch which it crossed at Mooers Junction, and in Chapter 36 on the New York Central Adirondack Division which it crossed at Malone Junction.

The track plan at Moira in 1902, presented here on Map 23-7, is modified from Nimke (1986, p. 21; 1989, Part 1, pp. 148-150; and 1989, Part 2, p. 146). By 1902, the Bombay & Moira had been abandoned and thus is not shown.

Passenger station: The original 1850 station location is shown in the Beers' 1876 atlas of Franklin County. Later, when Hurd's Northern Adirondack Railroad was built, the station was surrounded by the wye. Ottawa Division trains used the Moira depot until May 6, 1937, but the Rutland Railroad continued to use it until 1953. A second depot was built just east of the Fort Covington Street crossing (now State highway 95) where it still stands today as a tavern.

Passing sidings, interchange, and storage tracks: There were several on both the O.& L.C. and on the New York & Ottawa. The 1915 U.S.G.S. Moira 15-minute quadrangle shows the approximate track plan at that time.

Servicing facilities: Haworth (1954) lists a roundhouse. The June 26, 1932 Employees' Timetable lists an enginehouse, a coaling plant, and a water station.

Freight station: One is shown on Nimke's 1902 map.

Industrial sidings: In 1902, Nimke shows General Mills Inc.; GLF Feed Store (Agway in 1991); Ducey Lumber Company Mill; and a milk station owned first by Millett's, then Levy's, and finally by Dairymen's League. Haworth (1954) mentions two sawmills but offers no detail.

Alburgh. 3.2 miles. Elevation 490. Map 23-2.

This station is listed on a timetable of June 30, 1889 but no longer on August 10, 1896.

Mosher. 5.5 miles. Elevation 690. Map 23-2.

This station is listed on timetables of August 10, 1896 and March 7, 1898. It had not yet appeared by June 30, 1889 and was closed by June 25, 1905.

Dickinson Center. 8.39 miles. Elevation 958. Maps 23-2 and 23-8.

Passenger station: This station was in service probably throughout the whole life of the line; at least the timetables dated June 30, 1889 through June 28, 1936 list it.

The building still stood in 1992. A photo of the DickinsonCenter Station with a train appears on the front cover of the *Franklin Historical Review*, Volume 6, 1969.

Passing siding: The 1919 U.S.G.S. Nicholville quadrangle indicates one here 0.2 mile long and it still shows in a 1936 photo by the New York Central.

Bridge abutments: The concrete bridge abutments which still stand in 1992 on either side of Franklin County Highway 5 indicate a construction date of 1914.

Saint Regis Falls. 11.81 miles. Elevation 1256. Maps 23-3, 23-9, 25-1, 26-1, and 26-2.

Saint Regis Falls had one of the largest forest product mill concentrations along the New York & Ottawa Railroad. A description of the first train into Saint Regis Falls on September 25, 1883, rented from the Ogdensburg & Lake Champlain Railroad, will be found in Pope (1972). This train derailed!

Passenger station: This station was in service for the full life of the Ottawa, from 1883 to 1937. A photograph is found in Palmer (February 1970); I have in my files another taken in the summer of 1936 by the New York Central Railroad when it was still in service. The building was torn down to make way for the present Waverly Town Office and Fire House which were completed in 1964 on the same site.

Stagecoach connections: In 1898 and 1905 stagecoaches met the trains at Saint Regis Falls for Lake Ozonia and Fernwood Hall. By 1909, Hotel Oneita had been added to the stagecoach schedules.

Passing siding: The 1919 15-minute Nicholville quadrangle indicates one 0.35 mile long. This is confirmed by a 1900 Saint Regis Paper Company mill map modified here as Map 23-9. In 1932 it held 24 cars. The siding still existed in 1936.

Servicing facilities: Palmer (February 1970) mentions a wooden two-stall engine house and a small repair shop in service until the large shops were completed in 1885 in Santa Clara. In 1932 there was a water station.

Freight station: Palmer (February 1970) mentions one.

Industrial sidings: Because of a complex series of sales, moves, mergers and reorganizations of the industries at Saint Regis Falls, an accurately detailed history is difficult to trace. My primary source is Seaver (1918, pp. 547-550) combined with information provided by the Saint Regis Falls Historians Association. Industries served by the railroads were concentrated in two areas. The first area was located upstream along the Saint Regis River eastward above the Main Street Bridge. The second area was located downstream at the falls below the River Street Bridge.

In the first area, the Hammond sawmill was built ca. 1860 with the first dam, long before the arrival of the railroad. In 1882, Hurd, Hotchkiss & McFarlane greatly enlarged the old Hammond Mill, added a machine shop, and introduced steam power and machines to produce clapboards, lath, broomsticks, and boxes. Hurd's railroad arrived a year later to serve the mill. Dodge, Meigs & Company (the Santa Clara Lumber Company) then bought the mill and shortly after sold it to the Saint Regis Paper Company. Saint Regis Paper in 1896 leased (part of?) the mill to Watson Page and B. W. Babcock, but apparently still owned the plant in 1900 according to a map (modified here as Map 23-9) published that year by the paper company. Brooklyn Cooperage Company bought the mill in 1904 and ran it until about 1920 or 1921. Saint Regis Falls historians tell me that the mill was demolished about the time that the Ottawa Division was abandoned (1937).

In the second area, the Hammond Tannery was built in 1865, long before the railroad's arrival. Several other owners followed, the last being the Saint Regis Leather Company from 1884 to 1901. The 1893 *Map of Township No. 10 of Waverly* shows a siding into the tannery, but this siding could have been built and added to the map at a later date as was the Watson Page Lumber Company Railroad. In 1901, the Cascade Chair Company bought the old tannery and installed an electric lighting plant. See Chapter 25 for details on the Watson Page Lumber Company Railroad which served this chair factory from 1907 to about 1909 when the factory burned. Seaver notes us that the factory was rebuilt as the Cascade Wood Products Company with dam and pulpmill by Alex MacDonald and Dr. L. M. Wardner. Saint Regis Falls historians tell me that the rebuilt mill was located adjacent to the original but just downstream; the most recent owner, perhaps into the 1920s, was Saint Regis Paper, but this is unconfirmed. Both mill sites are now in the Town of Waverly Campground.

Saint Regis Falls historians also inform me of two sidings along the New York & Ottawa near but well above the tannery site. These were for the Mica Factory and Giffins Coal Company (Map 23-9) but have not been confirmed.

Nelda Y. Smith (1969) mentions several sawmills (at least some of which were bought by Hurd) and a box factory but does not locate them. A description in detail of a sawmill and a box factory appears in the Plattsburgh *Sentinel* of April 10, 1885 but without location.

Palmer (February 1970) lists the Hotchkiss Lumber Company Storehouse, and notes that one sawmill (probably the Hurd, Hotchkiss and McFarlane renvoation of the old Hammond sawmill) was altered for making clapboards, lath and broomsticks.

Furthest upstream where the N.Y. & Ottawa crossed the Saint Regis River the Saint Regis Paper Company built a steam-powered pulp rossing mill. It shows on the 1893 Town of Waverly Map but could have been built and added to the map at a later date. Former Town of Waverly Historian Ralph M. Farmer suggests that this mill ran only for a year or so, about 1908; this makes sense because after 1904, Brooklyn Cooperage was already operating on the site of the first Saint Regis Paper Company mill. Farmer also tells me that another, electrically-powered pulp rossing (debarking) mill was in operation in the 1930s just west of the Saint Regis rossing mill and was known as the Johnson Pulp Mill; it is shown in a summer 1936 photo taken by the New York Central (see Map 23-9).

Branches: See Chapter 25 on the Watson Page Lumber Company Railroad and Chapter 26 on the Brooklyn Cooperage Company Railroad. The latter Chapter also provides information on the Everton Railroad which originated from Saint Regis Falls.

Shanleys. 15.0 miles. Elevation 1256. Map 23-3.

Passenger station: Shanleys is shown as a station on the early timetables of June 30, 1889 and August 10, 1896, but no longer on March 7, 1898.

Industrial sidings: Nelda Y. Smith (1969) states that the Shanley and Alfred Lumber company had mills here.

Santa Clara. 18.09 miles. Elevation 1330. Maps 23-3, 23-10, 26-1, and 26-3.

According to Palmer's notes, the N.Y. & Ottawa Railroad reached Santa Clara in 1884. The shops and logging headquarters were moved here that year from Saint Regis Falls. Palmer writes that by 1885 the line had been extended to a point eight miles south of Saint Regis Falls (this would be equivalent to a point 1.8 miles south of Santa Clara), with another eight miles under construction. In other words, construction had reached beyond Meno by 1885.

A description of the construction and proposed construction as far as Brandon will be found in the Plattsburgh *Sentinel* of April 10, 1885. Much of the 75,000-acre Hurd and Hotchkiss Tract south of Saint Regis Falls (through Santa Clara) was still in first growth timber. The tract was about 13 miles wide around Santa Clara. Logs were to be skidded, i.e. dragged, by horses to railroad flat cars, rolled up onto the cars, transported by rail, and dumped into the river at Santa Clara, Saint Regis Falls, or Everton. The minimum diameter for harvested trees was to be nine inches, with more than one-third of it pine, part birch and maple, and the remainder spruce.

Passenger station: The station was in service for the whole life of the line, from 1884 through 1937. After abandonment, the building was moved a very short distance onto a site formerly occupied by the main track and was converted into a church which still stands today.

Stagecoach connections: In 1889, stagecoaches met the trains at Santa Clara for the Blue Mountain House Hotel, although Spring Cove became the stage connection site by 1896.

Servicing facilities: Here were car and machine shops established by Hurd (Seaver 1918, p. 535). Seaver notes that, along with former New York State Governor Alonzo B. Cornell, Hurd performed successful experiments in the Santa Clara shops in lighting passenger cars by electricity produced by the revolution of car wheels. The shops burned in October 1915 (Vanderwalker, 1972).

Industrial sidings: Santa Clara did not exist as a community until the railroad arrived. Here, Hurd established two sawmills and a chair factory (Seaver, 1918). Detailed descriptions of the two sawmills and the railway station will be found in the Plattsburgh *Sentinel* of April 10, 1885. Shingles, lath, boxes, broom handles and pickets were being produced. When Hurd became bankrupt in 1895, the Brooklyn Cooperage Company acquired the mills at Santa Clara until they burned in November 1903 (Seaver, 1918, p. 536).

Track plan: The track plan at Santa Clara is incompletely shown on the 1921 U.S.G.S. Santa Clara quadrangle; most conspicuous of what is shown is the wye to turn engines and cars. Photographs in Vanderwalker (1972) and in Gardner (1975, p. 10) show portions of the trackage. A series of five maps at the Champion International Corporation (formerly Saint Regis Paper Company) office in Santa Clara show much detail. None of the maps is dated, but the earliest offers "Northern New York Railroad;" this line, which took over Hurds's bankrupt Northern Adirondack Railroad on May 30, 1895, itself was reorganized in 1897 into the New York & Ottawa. Hence this map dates from late 1895 or 1896. It is redrafted here as Map 23-10.

Branch to Lake Ozonia: At 19.8 miles and elevation 1337, a Brooklyn Cooperage line diverged to Lake Ozonia (see Chapter 26). The junction is shown on the 1921 15-minute Santa Clara quadrangle.

Weidman. 21.3 miles. Elevation 1334. Maps 23-3 and 26-3.

Weidman is not listed on any timetable as a station, but it is a place-name on the 1920 and 1923 Adirondack Maps published by the New York State Conservation Commission. I think I have found in the field where Weidman was and what it was. On June 28, 1986, a party of five historians and I followed the N.Y. & Ottawa grade from Santa Clara to Meno. At milepost 21.5 is a bridge, with most recent concrete abutments rebuilt in 1927, over the Saint Regis River. Just north of it we found the right-of-way of a spur heading off to the southwest. We followed the spur, complete with cuts and fills and tie impressions, for about one-third of a mile but ran out of time.

Just how much further this "Weidman Branch" continues is unknown as I have never seen it on any map. The ownership of this branch is also a mystery. Saint Regis Falls historians inform me about the Weidman Lumber Company establishing their first sawmill about 1858 or 1859 in the region, but this is long before the railroad's arrival.

Spring Cove. 22.29 miles. Elevation 1343. Maps 23-4, 23-11, 26-3 and 26-4.

Passenger station: This was already a station on the June 30, 1889 timetable and existed as such through the June 28, 1936 timetable. A print in my files taken in August 1936 by a New York Central photographer shows the station as not more than a small shack. Trains stopped here probably through to abandonment in 1937.

Stagecoach connection: Between 1889 and 1909 Spring Cove was the stagecoach connection site to the Blue Mountain House at the base of Azure Mountain.

Industrial siding: Nelda Y. Smith (1969) described charcoal kilns here where coke was made from hardwood timber and then shipped out by rail as fuel. A stub track existed here for that purpose diverging from the mainline to the southeast. The *Watertown Daily Times* (1993) included a photo of a Brooklyn Cooperage Railroad log loader on a siding at Spring Cove about 1912. Our 1986 exploratory party located the stub as an embankment crossing an open meadow. See Map 23-11. A steep ascent then followed to Downey.

Downey. 24.59 miles. Elevation 1520. Maps 23-4 and 26-4.

The March 1, 1909 timetable lists this station. It is not yet listed on June 25, 1905 and no longer by June 23, 1912.

LeBoeufs. 25.39 miles. Elevation 1590. Maps 23-4 and 26-4.

Donaldson (1921, Volume II, pp. 137-140) states that this was the second point at which a railroad entered the Adirondack Park Blue Line. The first was the Adirondac Company's Railroad in 1871 (Hochschild, 1961). The Blue Line was located at LeBoeufs in 1886 when Hurd's Railroad arrived. Today the Blue Line is just north of Saint Regis Falls. A sawmill was established in 1886 along with the railroad at LeBoeufs. None of the timetables, however, lists LeBoeufs as a station. Our exploratory party in 1986 could not find any evidence of stubs at Downeys or at LeBoeufs.

Meno. 27.16 miles. Elevation 1605. Maps 23-4, 26-1, and 26-4.

Passenger station: Meno is not yet listed on the March 7, 1898 timetable, but it is listed as a station stop on the June 25, 1905 through June 28, 1936 timetables. The New York Central photographer captured it on film in August of 1936. It probably was in service to May 6, 1937.

Branches: For the Brooklyn Cooperage Company branches which diverged here, see Chapter 26.

Facilities: A water station and a section house existed in 1932.

Madawaska. 28.16 miles. Elevation 1600. Maps 23-4 and 26-4.

This is a station indicated on the timetables from August 10, 1896 through June 28, 1936. It was not yet in service on June 30, 1889 and probably operated until May 6, 1937. A New York Central photographer took a picture of it during August 1936.

Brandon. 32.25 miles. Elevation 1603. Maps 23-4, 23-12 and 27-1.

Brandon was the largest community between Santa Clara and Tupper Lake, and was the temporary terminus of the railroad from July 6, 1886 when the first train arrived (Pope, 1972) to late 1889.

Passenger station: The initial name of this 1886 station, as shown on the June 30, 1889 and July 17, 1892 timetables, was Paul Smith's Station, but by August 10, 1896 the name had already been changed to Brandon. For a short period, as stated in the July 2, 1902 *Adirondack Daily Enterprise* of Saranac Lake, trains did not stop here. It was still in service on June 28, 1936 and probably to May 6, 1937.

Stagecoach connections: Connections at Brandon were numerous. Concord coaches from Paul Smith's Hotel operated from 1886 to about 1906, when Paul Smith opened his own railway to Lake Clear Junction on the New York Central Adirondack Division. The 1889 timetable also indicates a stage connection for the Meacham Lake House, the Saranac Lakes, and at Paul Smith's a change of stage for Bloomingdale and Lake Placid. From 1896 through 1905 timetables appeared with advertisements for connections to Meacham Lake and McColloms. DeSormo (1974) offers detailed accounts of the hotels at Meacham Lake, McColloms and Paul Smith's as well as Gardner (1975, page 9).

Passing siding: The 1902-1903 U.S.G.S. Saint Regis quadrangle shows a passing siding east of the main track and north of the Paul Smith's-Azure Mountain highway crossing. The siding, about 0.2 mile long, is next to the station. Collins (1969) offers a village street map plus a photo of the station with a freight siding.

Servicing facilities: On October 3, 1987, I had the opportunity to explore the Brandon area in detail with Mr. Fred Joost, caretaker of Ross Park. A big surprise occurred when we discovered the turntable pit between the mill spur junction and the station. On page 78 of *Where did the Tracks Go* (1985) I inquired how engines were turned at Brandon during the three years, 1886 to 1889, when it was a terminus before the line was extended to Tupper Lake. Here was the answer! Detail on the Brandon area is shown on Map 23-12.

Industrial sidings: Patrick Ducey and John Torrent had purchased 28,000 acres in the Brandon area during the period from December 1881 to January 1882 (Pope, 1972) in a tract adjacent to and south of the Hurd, Hotchkiss, and McFarlane Tract acquired in August 1882. Ducey had begun building his sawmill on the Saint Regis River where Hurd's railroad crossed it, the mill being completed by March of 1887 (Pope, 1972). By 1895 after Hurd's bankruptcy, Ducey's mill activity began to decline; the machinery and tools from the mill were bought from Ducey in April 1897 by A.J. Norton and moved to Saint Regis Falls (Pope, 1972). On October 3, 1987 Fred Joost and I were looking for the precise site of Ducey's sawmill and the spur track which must have served it. The mill was east of the N.Y. & Ottawa and north of the Saint Regis River. This was not a water-powered mill as I had first assumed, but a steam-powered mill. The remains are high and dry and well above the river; no vestiges of penstocks or canals are present. Vestiges of the bandsaw are still present, however. The next step was to find where the spur track connected with the main; the surprise was that the spur track was not short, but paralleled the main track on the east for nearly half-a-mile before joining the latter just south of the Brandon Station site. A map entitled *Vilas Preserve and Vicinity* compiled by H. S. Meekham of Saint Regis Falls, dated 1892, shows the location of Ducey's mill exactly.

Land ownership: Following closing of Ducey's sawmill, a series of dramatic shifts in land ownership occurred; these are well-documented in a number of publications (Donaldson, 1921; Collins, 1969; Pope, 1972; Gove, 1981; and Surprenant, 1982). William Rockefeller began acquiring lands around Bay Pond and Brandon in 1898-1899. These were sold to Bay Pond Inc. in 1923 (see Chapter 27). In 1937, the year of the N.Y. & Ottawa abandonment, Bay Pond Inc. sold the northern half of its tract centering around Brandon to the Ross Family under whose ownership it is today. The southern half centering around Bay Pond was sold back to the Rockefeller Family also in 1937.

Forest fires: The area from Brandon southward past McDonald Station burned in 1903, the worst fire year in Adirondack history (Suter, 1903; Schmidt, 1916). On these sandy glacial outwash plains, the fires can be severe and the forest very slow to regenerate;

charred stumps of white pine logged during the Ducey era (1887-1895) are still apparent (Kudish, 1981, page 125).

Church trains: Tyler (1968, pp. 35-37) describes special Sunday church trains run by Hurd from Brandon to Santa Clara and Tupper Lake.

Reference: Surprenant (1982) offers the most complete history of Brandon.

McDonald. 33.47 miles. Elevation 1611. Maps 23-5, 23-12, and 27-1.

Passenger station: The station appears on timetables from May 18, 1924 through June 28, 1936. It had not yet opened by June 25, 1922. It might have been in service as late as May 6, 1937 and still was standing, though the building was modified, in 1987.

Branches: See Chapter 27 for detail on the logging railroad of Bay Pond Inc. which operated from here from about 1923 to 1937.

Facilities: In 1932 a section house was here.

Bay Pond. 35.29 miles. Elevation 1590. Maps 23-5, 23-13 and 27-1.

Passenger station: Bay Pond appeared as a station as early as on the August 10, 1896 timetable, and as late as on the June 28, 1936 timetable. It probably was in service until May 6, 1937. During the period 1899-1923 when the Rockefeller Family owned the tract, Bay Pond was a private station. In 1995, the (second?) station building still stands as a residence. I have been shown a much smaller building nearby which was supposed to have been the moved original station.

Passing sidings: The 1902-1903 U.S.G.S. Saint Regis quadrangle indicates a passing siding east of the main track and just north of the station, 0.1 mile long. I have seen photographs of this siding taken in 1936 and now in the collection of Philip Delarm of Paul Smiths. By 1936 there were still freight cars on the siding, but it was no longer double-ended; the switch at the southwest end had been removed.

Gove (1981) indicates a passing siding at the southwest end of Bay Pond (the pond itself) at about milepost 36.6 which he calls Collins Landing. This siding dates back to the Bay Pond Inc. era, 1923-1927, and not to the two Rockefeller eras, 1899-1923 and 1937-present.

Industries: Hyde (1974) presents photos of logging trains at Bay Pond on pages 46 and 47 of her text.

Refer to Chapter 27 and the section on McDonald above for detail on Bay Pond Inc..

Forest fire: It was during the Bay Pond Inc. era, 1923-1937, that the 1934 fire burned the region from Bay Pond southwestward downstream along the West Branch Saint Regis River and toward Derrick. See the annual report of the New York State Conservation Department for 1934 for details.

Black Rapids Junction. 38.9 miles. Elevation 1554. Maps 23-5 and 23-14

Passenger station: This Junction is listed on the August 10, 1896 and March 7, 1898 timetables only. It was no longer in service by June 25, 1905.

Black Rapids Spur: The 1892 *Map of the Vilas Preserve and Vicinity* compiled by H. S. Meekham indicates "Kickabuck Station" just south of the bridge over the West Branch Saint Regis River. Three-fourths of a mile south of this station is shown a wye, straddling the Waverly-Altamont Town Line. Leading away from the wye in a northwesterly direction is a branch which terminates in two spurs near a camp on the West Branch Saint Regis River. This terminal lies approximately midway between Black Rapids downstream and the New York & Ottawa bridge upstream. The junction is not named on this 1892 map. See Map 23-14 in this atlas.

The junction is shown and named on a 1896 New York Central Railroad publication entitled *Health and Pleasure on America's Greatest Railroad* along with the short spur terminating at Black Rapids.

Gove (1981) dates the Black Rapids branch to the Ducey era, 1887-1895, when the Brandon sawmill was in operation. Although Hurd's railroad did not reach Tupper Lake until the end of 1889 or early in 1890, it is likely that the railroad did reach the Black Rapids area by 1888 and that Ducey could make use of it by installing a jackworks.

This branch appears as an unpaved road on the 1953 15-minute Saint Regis U.S.G.S. quadrangle.

Derrick. 41.23 miles. Elevation 1551. Maps 23-5, 23-15, and 28-1.

Passenger station: The July 17, 1892 timetable lists this station as Saranac Inn Station while Wallace's *Guide to the Adirondacks* (1894) lists it as Blue Pond after a body of water just south of the station. The August 10, 1896 and March 7, 1898 timetables call this station Willis Pond after a body of water about a mile to the south. The June 25, 1905 timetable finally uses the name Derrick. Trains were still stopping here on November 15, 1932, but no longer stopping on April 26, 1936 despite the fact that the station was still listed in the timetable.

Stagecoach connections: Simmons (1976, p. 110) mentions that this was the station for the connecting stage for Saranac Inn from 1888 to 1892. In 1892 when Webb's Mohawk & Malone was completed, the new Saranac Inn Station was about seven miles closer to the Inn and replaced Derrick as the stagecoach connecting point.

Industrial sidings: Hyde (1974, p. 32) describes Charles H. Turners's sawmill running here from about 1896 to about 1910. For several more years following, C. H. Elliott shipped out three carloads a week of mangle rolls for laundries. Elliott's main mill was located at Tupper Lake Junction (see Chapter 36). Austin Bourn of Guilford, New York, has sent me a copy of a photograph of Derrick taken before 1906. The sawmill is on the west side of the N.Y.& Ottawa track along Blue Pond; a siding, with a box car, leads into the mill from the north. It is unknown whether the Derrick siding at one time reconnected with the main at the south end. A variety of houses and buildings forms the hamlet of Derrick on the east side of the track.

A New York Central photographer, active in the summer of 1936, took two pictures of Derrick which still show the siding and station. See Map 23-15.

Kildare. 45.18 miles. Elevation 1528. Maps 23-6, 28-1 and 28-3.

Passenger station: Kildare Station is currently on exhibit at The Adirondack Museum in Blue Mountain Lake. The exhibit notes that this station building was constructed before 1912 and closed in 1937. Kildare appears as a station on the timetables from August 10, 1896 through June 28, 1936, but probably continued to May 6, 1937.

Branches: From Kildare, the Oval Wood Dish Company had several diverging logging lines; detail is provided in Chapter 28.

Facilities: A water station and a section house existed in 1932.

Childwold. 48.69 miles. Elevation 1602. Maps 23-6, 23-17, and 28-1.

Passenger station: The station is listed in the timetables from August 10, 1896 through March 1, 1909, but no longer on June 23, 1912. It must not be confused with Childwold Station on the New York Central Adirondack Division, some six miles to the southwest (see Chapters 36 and 39).

Stagecoach connections: Stages from the Childwold Park House met trains here in 1896. An article in the *Tupper Lake Free Press and Herald* on a Wednesday of March 1973 described the hotel and the stage connection. The hotel had opened in 1878, some twelve years before the railroad.

Passing siding: The 1922 Childwold 15-minute quadrangle locates a passing siding 0.2 mile long just south of Pitchfork Pond at 48.7 miles. In summer 1936, the New York Central photographer informs us by his picture that the siding was on the east but no longer double-ended; the switch was only at the south end.

Tupper Lake Junction (Faust Post Office). 52.29 miles. Elevation 1550. Maps 23-6, 26-1, 26-6 and 36-30.

Passenger station: The Village of Tupper Lake was almost non existent until Hurd's Railroad reached the site with construction crews late in 1889. According to Simmons (1968, p. 32), the first train arrived on July 1, 1890. The junction, also called Faust Post Office, developed a little later as a result of the opening on July 15, 1892 of Webb's Adirondack & Saint Lawrence Railroad which crossed Hurd's at this point. In fact, construction of Webb's line in 1891-1892 was facilitated here both northward and southward by equipment and supplies brought in by Hurd's line.

The station was in service from 1892 through 1965, serving only the Adirondack Division after 1937. Photos of the station and the junction occur in several publications including Gardner (1975, p.29), Simmons (1976, pp. 146-149), and Harter (1979).

Passing sidings and servicing facilities: Abundant sidings and servicing facilities were located here but primarily for the Adirondack Division which had the bulk of the traffic. See Chapter 36 and Map 36-30 for details.

Industrial sidings: The number of wood products industries in the Tupper Lake Junction area had been numerous, and the complexity increased further by the fact that many mills changed owners several times. In many instances in reading different accounts published at different times, one realizes that not several industries were involved but only a single industry which had a different name each time! Those industries which were located directly along the N.Y.& Ottawa line are presented in this chapter. Those industries, such as the Santa Clara Lumber Company pulp rossing plant, Champlain Realty Company, Tupper Lake Chemical, etc., which were located directly along the New York Central Adirondack Division are presented in Chapter 36. The Brooklyn Cooperage Company is described in Chapter 26.

The primary reason for Hurd's Railroad reaching the shores of Tupper Lake (actually Raquette Pond) was the Big Mill, one of the largest of its time. Photos of this saw mill appear in Simmons (1976, pp. 135, 136, and 137) including descriptions of its size and operations. It was built in 1890 when the railroad arrived on the site of what is now the Municipal Park Grandstand (Simmons, 1976, p. 66). From Hurd's Big Mill an aerial tramway was built across what is now Demars Boulevard to a series of charcoal kilns which were situated along the north side of Railroad Street (now Pleasant Avenue). These kilns are mentioned in Simmons (1976, p. 67) and in Hyde (1974), and are shown on a May 24, 1899 map at the Franklin County Clerk's office in Malone. The tramway was nearly an eighth of a mile long and carried wood chips and other waste from the mill to the kilns. A railroad siding served the kilns presumably to haul away the charcoal. Simmons (1976, pp. 67 and 128) informs us that there was a succession of owners of the Big Mill following Hurd's bankruptcy in 1895. They were:

(1) Shepard and Morse, operating it for about a year;
(2) Patrick A. Ducey (the same of Brandon) and several otherowners for short period (Simmons, 1968, p.36);
(3) Norwood Manufacturing Company owned the Big Mill in 1900 (Simmons, 1976, p. 109) and in 1911 (photo, Simmons, p. 135).
(4) Santa Clara Lumber Company bought the Big Mill in 1913 (Simmons p. 128) and ran it until 1926. It was torn down in 1930.

See Map 23-18 for location of the Big Mill.

Howard H. Hobson's saw mill was the first built in Tupper Lake (Simmons, 1976, p. 67), a year or so earlier than Hurd's Big Mill, i.e. ca. 1889. The location (Simmons, p. 413) was on the shore of Raquette Pond where, later, Ohio Street and Michigan Avenue were built. A photo in Simmons (p. 135) shows this mill, roughly halfway between Hurd's Big Mill and Tupper Lake Junction. Hobson's Mill burned in 1894 (Simmons, p. 413) and was rebuilt by the A. Sherman Lumber Company (photo, Simmons, p. 137) in 1895. The Sherman Mill, known locally also as the Sisson Mill, operated until 1915 when it was sold to the Oval Wood Dish Company.

In 1915, The Oval Wood Dish Company bought the old Hobson Mill from Sherman (Sisson), but began to construct a new facility across Demars Boulevard closer to the Ottawa tracks. Simmons (1976, pp. 65 and 150-166) offers much detail on this facility which was completed in 1918. Oval Wood Dish owned it until 1964 when Adirondack Plywood took over. In 1969-1970 Tupper Lake Veneer and Major Rod Limited replaced Adirondack Plywood as the operators. The huge warehouse, with interior railroad track, just northwest of the Oval Wood Dish plant was also constructed in 1918, but burned in 1967. See Map 23-18 locating Hobson's and Oval Wood Dish industrial mills. Hyde (1974, pp. 43 to 45) offers aerial photos of the Oval Wood Dish Company. See Chapter 28. Palmer (1970) states that wood chips were converted into pulp and that hemlock bark was shipped by the ton to tanneries.

Tupper Lake. 53.99 miles. Elevation 1550. Maps 23-6, 23-18, and 26-6.

Passenger station: This station at Tupper Lake should not be confused with the the station at Tupper Lake Junction located 1.70 miles to the north. Simmons (1976, p. 65) notes that Hurd's first railroad station, post office, and store were located temporarily, in 1890, on the site of the future Oval Wood Dish Company. New York Central Railroad Valuation Map #V109/1 gives us an accurate picture of the station location, sidings, and industries during the period 1917 to ca. 1947. New York & Ottawa passenger trains stopped at both stations through the September 25, 1932 timetable, but by November 15, 1932 they were terminating at the Junction. The Valuation Map has a note that the station was retired in 1933.

Stagecoach connections: Between 1896 and 1909, timetables indicate stage connections from the Hotel Wawbeek and other resorts on Upper Saranac Lake. The steamer *Altamont* run by the Tupper Lake Navigation Company, connected with the trains to serve resorts on Big and Little Tupper Lakes, including the Tupper Lake House, Moodys, and the scenic attraction Bog River Falls. See DeSormo (1980).

Proposed extension: A map in Palmer (1970) indicates a proposed extension of the Northern Adirondack (Hurd's) Railroad southeastward from Tupper Lake up the Raquette River to Raquette Falls and Long Lake. Professor of surveying C. Creighton Fee of Paul Smith's College states that this proposed line had been surveyed to the Raquette Falls or the north end of Long Lake and graded a short distance out of Tupper Lake. A May 24, 1899 map at the Franklin County Clerk's Office shows the proposed extension. The tracks were never placed on the grade because State Forest Preserve Land ahead blocked the plans. It had been hoped that the extension would eventually connect with the Delaware & Hudson at North Creek.

Passing siding: A short passing siding, 578 feet long, existed across the main track from the station.

Servicing facilities: See Map 23-18.

Industrial sidings: There were several as shown on Valuation Map #V109/1, but these are not fully identified. One served a cattle pen and another a lumber shed (see Map 23-18).

Timetable Operation

The June 30, 1889 timetable indicated two round trips daily between Moira and Paul Smiths Station (later Brandon) and two additional sub-route trips daily between Moira and Santa Clara.

After the line was extended to Tupper Lake by 1890, the number of passenger trains each way daily between here and Moira varied between one and three. It was most commonly two through 1917, but by May 1920 the number had been reduced to one. The one train daily operated through the end of service in 1937. Sunday service was either non-existent or reduced.

Additional sub-route service was often provided at the north end of the line between Moira and Santa Clara or between Ottawa and Santa Clara.

After abandonment of the New York & Ottawa south of Moira in 1937, passenger service still continued through at least April 25, 1948 when one train operated between Helena and Ottawa.

Freight service must have been frequent in the early years when the forest product industries were most active. But by January 1936, according to a newspaper article in the Smallman Collection at the Paul Smith's College Library, the passenger train made one round trip out of Tupper Lake daily, with a freight crew attached for mixed runs on two days per week. Simmons (1976, p. 141) notes that one freight train worked the whole line three times weekly in 1936.

Running times varied one-way between Tupper Lake and Moira from two hours to two hours and fifty-five minutes. They varied between Tupper Lake and Ottawa, 128 miles, from four and one-half hours to seven hours and ten minutes.

Speed limits were 35 miles per hour on much of the Ottawa Division. The *Malone Palladium* of September 1, 1898 discussed track improvements, curves and grades and the fact that the line had been built from Moira to Tupper Lake with 80-pound rail. Five days after this article was written the bridge at Cornwall, Ontario, collapsed.

Equipment

Detail on the equipment of the Northern Adirondack is readily abundant in publications. Examples are the Plattsburgh *Sentinel* of April 10, 1885, Palmer's notes at The Adirondack Museum, a roster sent to me by railroad historian F. Ray McKnight, the cover of the *Franklin Historical Review* in 1969, an article in the *Tupper Lake Herald* of October 10 and 17, 1913, Haworth (1954), Palmer (February 1970), and timetables from the nineteenth century.

Abandonment

The last of the major forest products industries and feeder logging railroads had already closed by 1937, and freight business was nil.

Simmons (1976, pp. 141 and 142) and Doherty (1971) write that the last passenger train, #62, left Tupper Lake Junction on May 6, 1937, then describe the track removal. Detail is also available in the July 15, 1937 edition of the *Tupper Lake Free Press*. A work train promptly began removing the rails on May 7 of that year, and had them torn up to Kildare from Santa Clara by June 25. Tracks were also removed from Moira north to Helena.

Newspaper clippings from the *Watertown Times* dated February 13 and 15, 1957 describe the last northbound freight train operated on February 13; it ran from Massena over Canadian National tracks to Helena and thence over the Ottawa Division to Ottawa. The last southbound trains were a work train followed by a freight with engine #8304, an Alco RS-2, on February 14. The *Tupper Lake Free Press* of February 11, 1957 also describes the last run.

A remnant section of track is still in place from Helena northwestward for several miles ending short of the Saint Lawrence River at Rooseveltown, but Conrail no longer provides service on it.

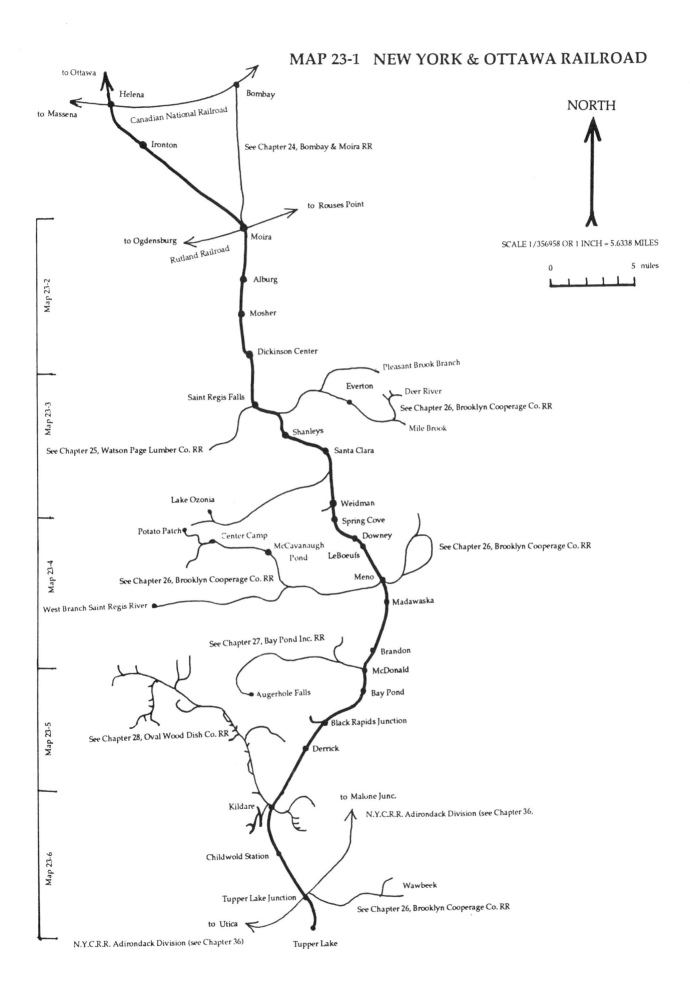

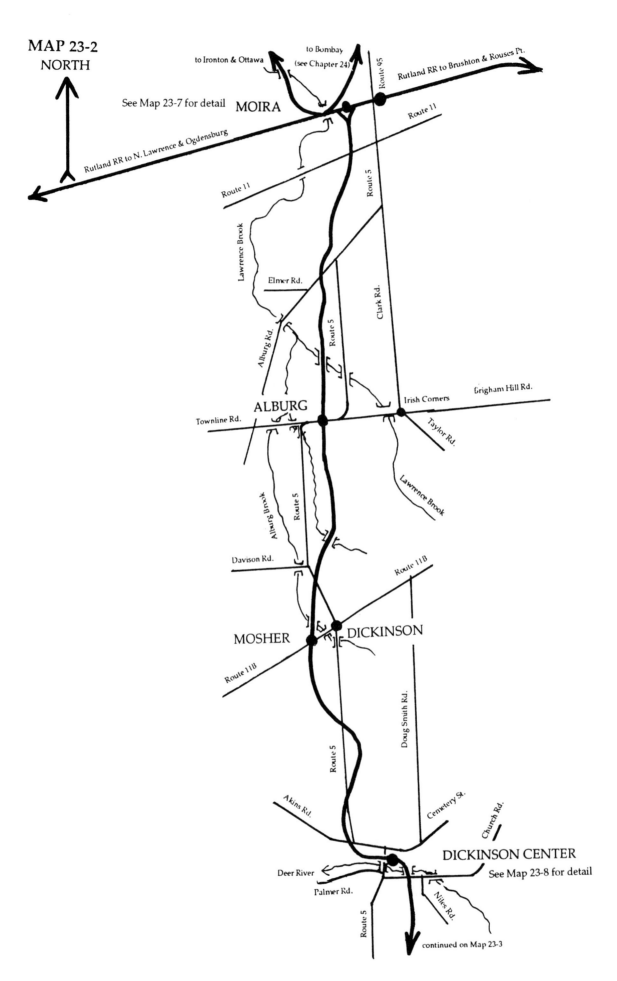

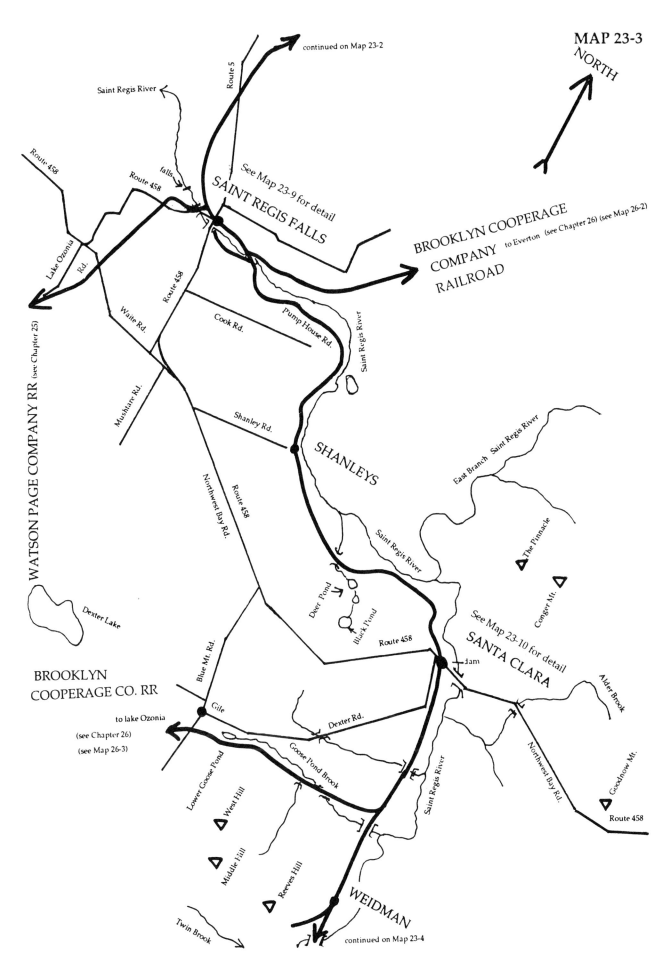

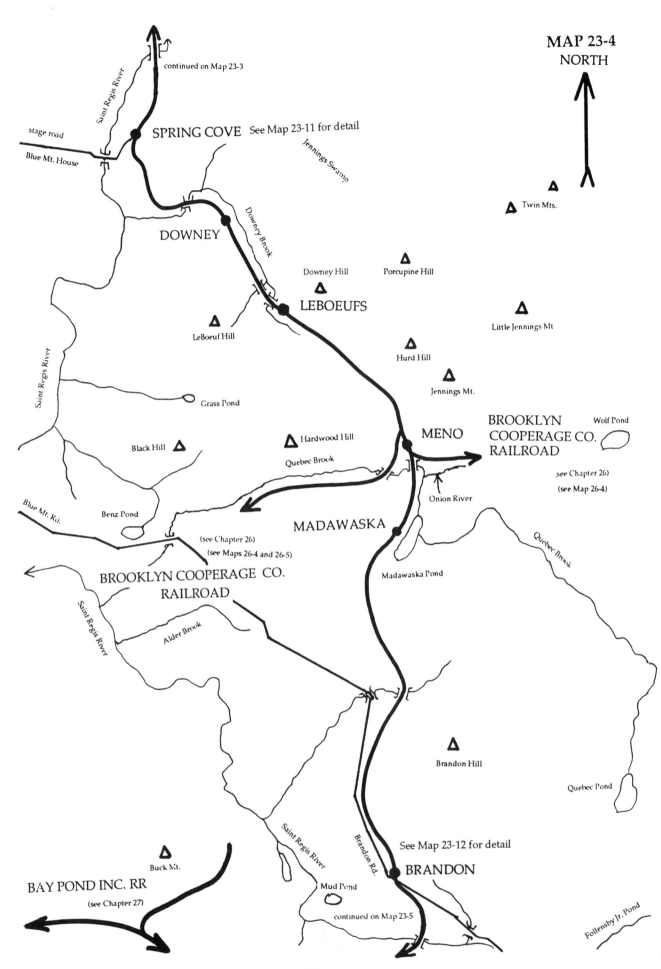

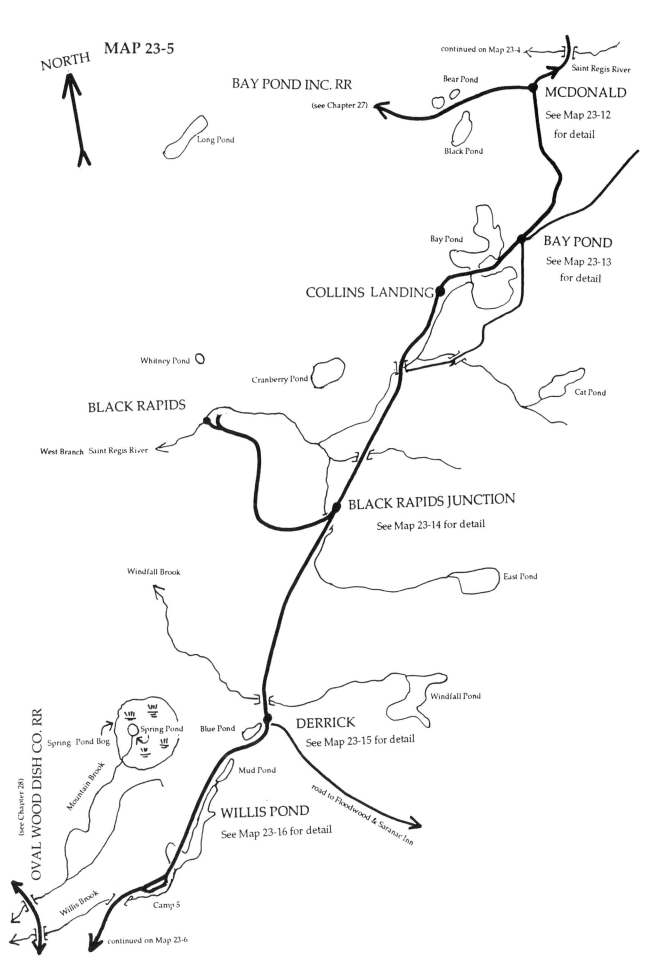

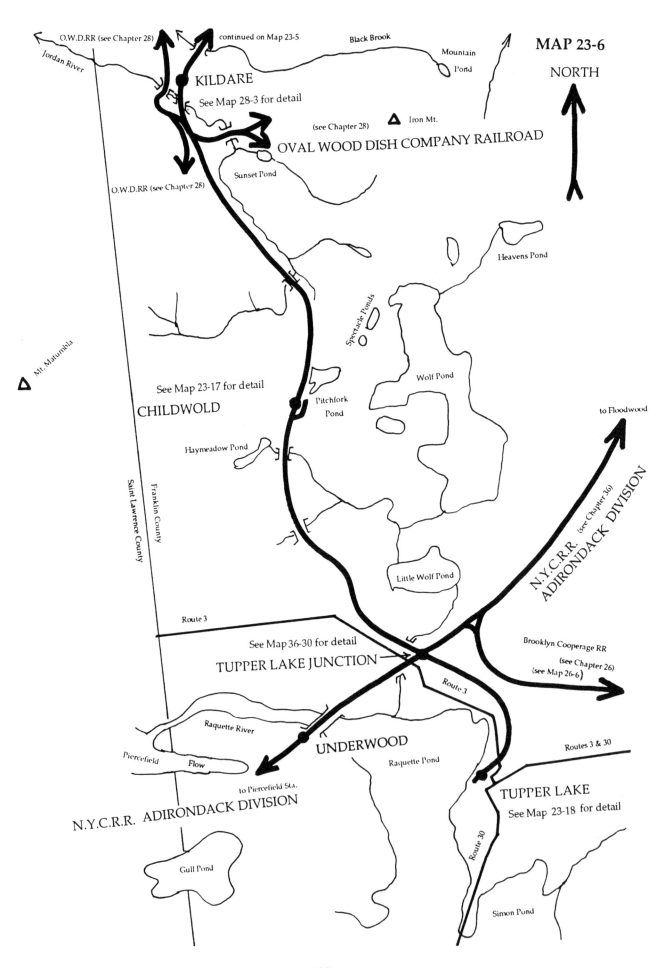

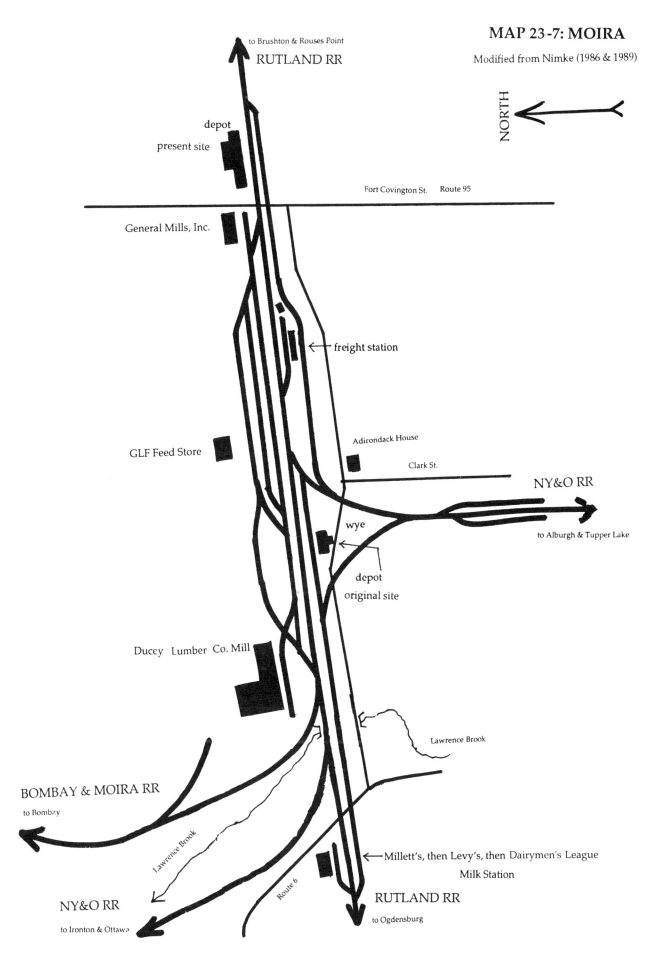

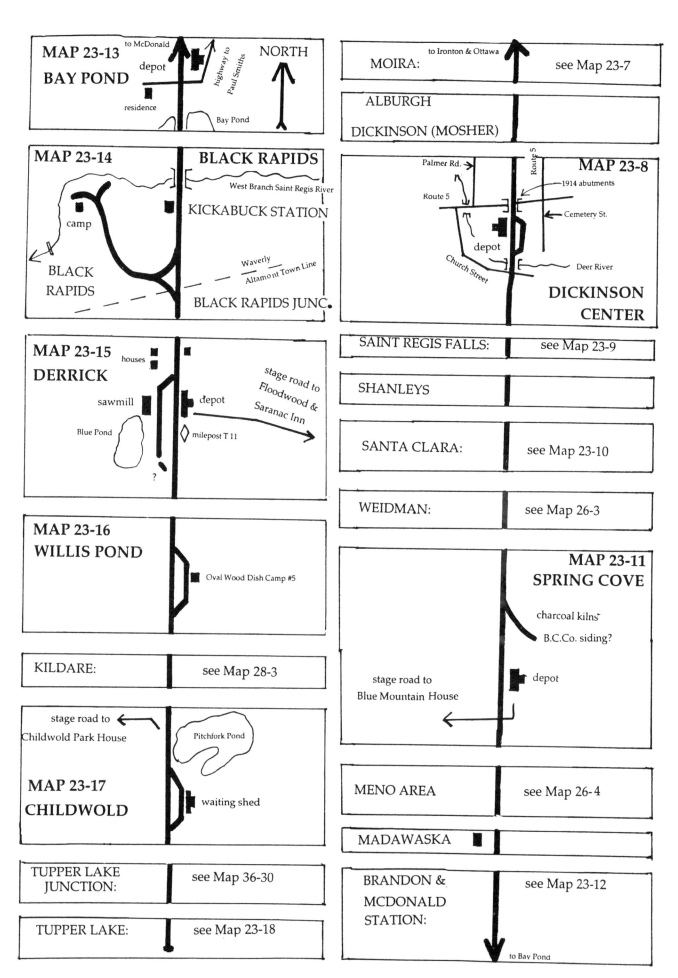

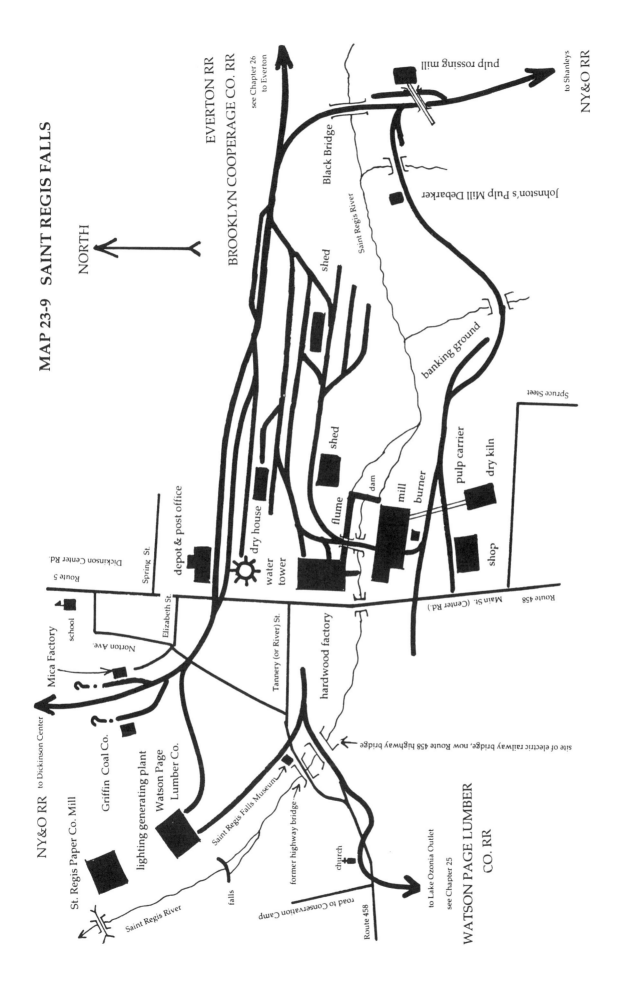
MAP 23-9 SAINT REGIS FALLS

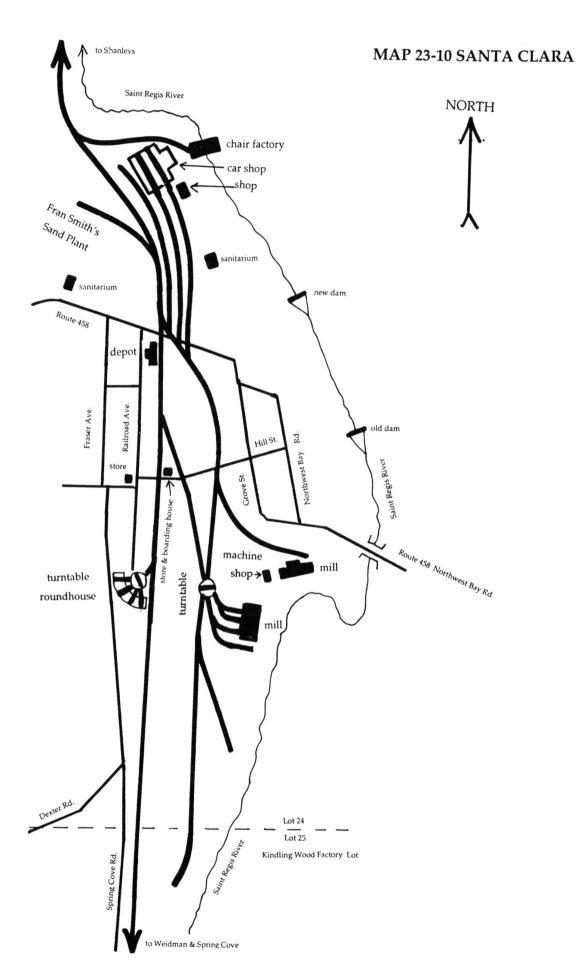

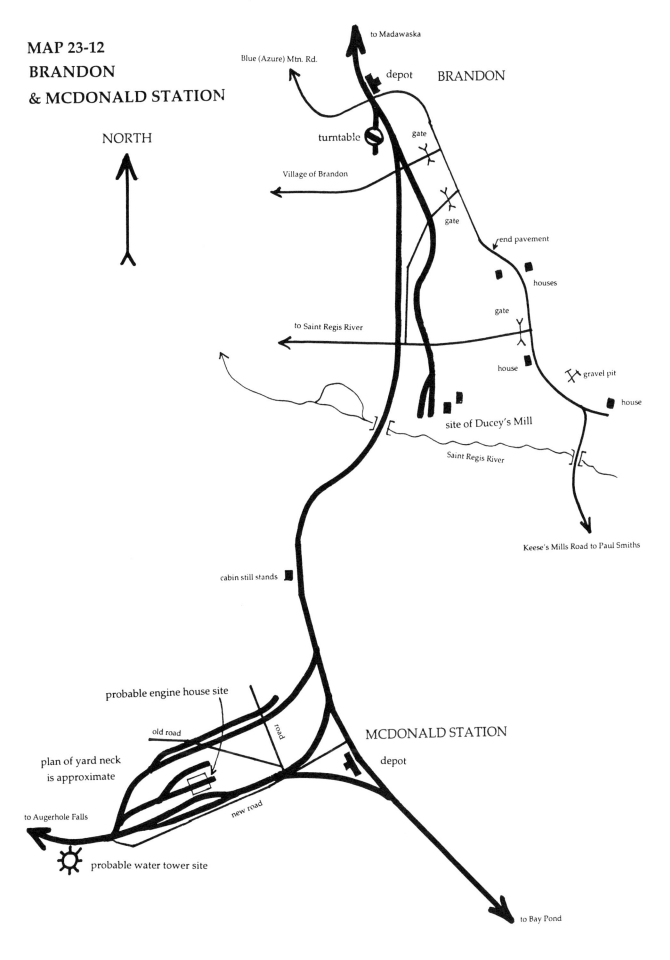

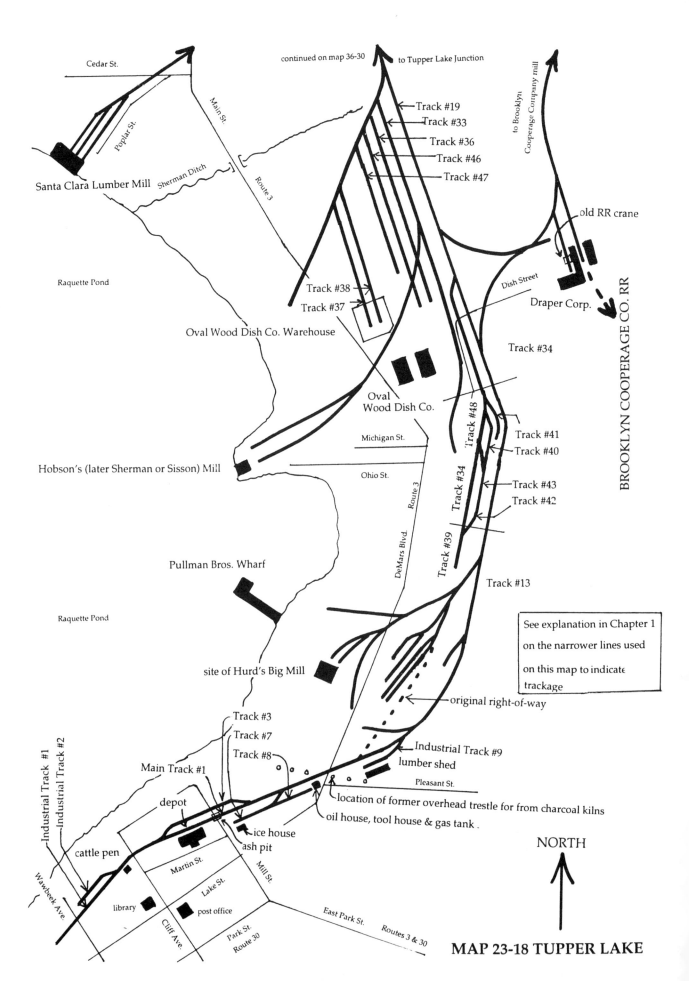

Chapter 24:
Bombay & Moira Railroad

A SHORT-LIVED RAILROAD once ran from Moira northward to Bombay, some eight miles in length via South Bombay. Some detail appears in a newspaper article housed in the Smallman Collection at the Paul Smith's College Cubley Library. The article is not dated nor the newspaper identified, but it is possibly the *Malone Evening Telegram*; the author is Neil Brush and the title is *Facts, Not Fallacies*. In 1889, Ernest G. Reynolds of Bombay, with the Central Vermont Railroad (a temporary owner following the Ogdensburg & Lake Champlain but preceding the Rutland) built this line. In 1891, a company was organized to extend the line to Hogansburg and the Saint Lawrence River, but the extension was never completed. The line from Moira to Bombay ran only until 1897 and the rails were torn up in 1900. A 1939 article in the *Malone Evening Telegram* also described the Bombay & Moira but added no detail useful for us here.

Maps 23-1, 23-2, 23-7, and 24-1

The only map which I have found showing the Bombay & Moira is an 1895 Franklin County map by Julius Bien and Company of New York City. This map, also in the Smallman Collection, labels the line "Central Vermont Railroad-Bombay and Moira Branch." There is a discrepancy between Bien's map, which shows the line further east and much closer to the paralleling highway (now State Highway 95), and the aerial photos of the United States Department of Agriculture's *Franklin County Soil Survey* (1958). The Bien map shows the railroad on the east side of the highway for one-and-one-half miles at South Bombay. Of course, a relocation was possible but the older grade would also appear on the aerial photo; it does not.

For detail on the Rutland Railroad through Moira, references are cited in Chapter 23 in the section on Moira.

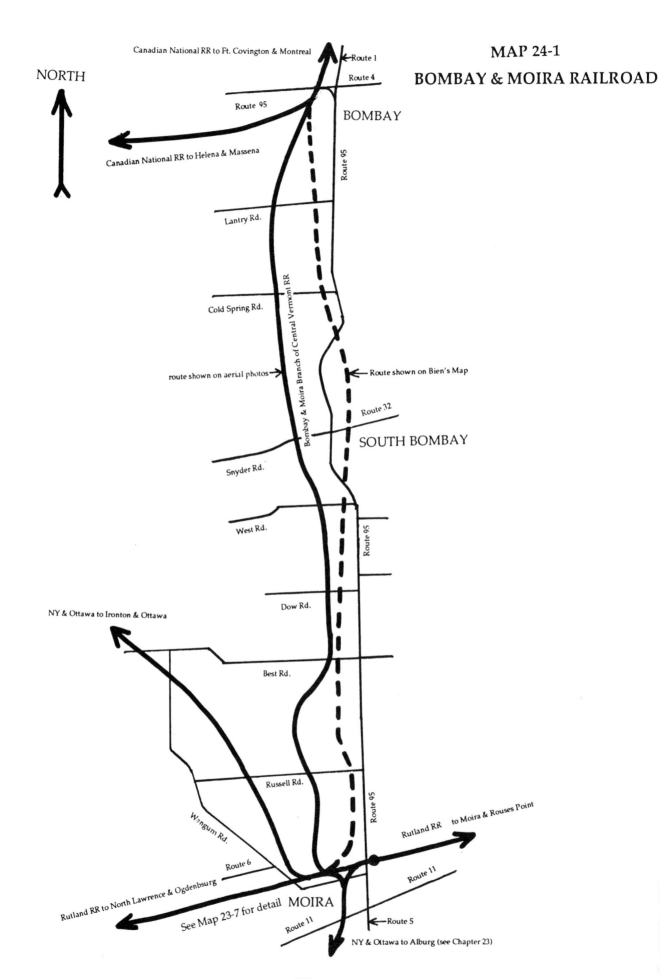

MAP 24-1
BOMBAY & MOIRA RAILROAD

Chapter 25:
Watson Page Lumber Company Railroad

Former town of Waverly historian, Ralph M. Farmer, has been carefully reading through issues of the *Adirondack News*, a Saint Regis Falls newspaper which was established in 1887 and published to ca. 1933. He compiled an unpublished report, *The Watson Page Lumber Company Cascade Chair Company Electric Railroad*, for the Saint Regis Falls Museum and Historical Association in 1992. From his report, I have extracted the following summary on construction:

April 21, 1906: Watson Page Lumber Company is constructing a railroad grade from River Street Bridge in Saint Regis Falls.

April 28, 1906: Rail-laying has begun.

September 29, 1906: Because the gasoline-powered locomotive has inadequate power, an electric locomotive is being considered.

March 2, 1907: Watson Page Lumber Company and Cascade Chair Company are merging.

April 6, 1907: The electric power-generating dynamo is being installed.

April 13, 1907: The electric locomotive is currently hauling sand and ballast (probably for completion of the distant end of the grade).

Maps 23-1, 23-2, 23-9, and 25-1

The only map which I have seen showing the railroad is the *Map of Township No. 10 of Waverly, Franklin County, New York* originally published in 1893. The railroad was added on to the map at a later date, probably 1907 or 1908, and the line incorrectly labeled "Saint Regis Electric Railroad." It traces the track about four miles to the Saint Lawrence County line. The last 0.8 mile is not shown and had to be located in the field by railroad historian Russell Nelson and the author in 1985 and 1986 (see Map 25-1). The line terminated at Lake Ozonia Outlet, two miles by air from the northern, or nearest, point on the lake and not at the lake itself. We found a short spur, long enough to accommodate several log cars, at the upper terminus. The old grade can still be seen today as it crosses Route 458, and the Waite, Lake Ozonia, and Howe Roads.

The 1893 map indicates a switchback in the hamlet of Saint Regis Falls in order to avoid a tight 180-degree turn into the Cascade Chair Factory. No connection is shown with the New York & Ottawa; I suspect the reason was that the electric line was narrow gauge so that a physical connection was impossible. By comparing very carefully the two photographs which I have seen of the electric locomotive and using the size of two gentlemen inside the cab, I have been able to determine that the rails were distinctly less than 4 feet, 8.5 inches apart; I am not sure exactly which narrow gauge they were. Trim (1984, p. 84) suggests that the rails were of a lighter-weight steel than those of the New York & Ottawa; this would be further supporting evidence for a narrow-gauge operation.

Before the merger, the Watson Page Lumber Company was to have provided and hauled the hardwood logs to the Cascade Chair Company factory. Because the merger occurred before the railroad was completed, operations were all under one company under the Cascade name.

Of the two photographs I have seen of the electric locomotive, the first was published in Trim (1984, p. 84) but the resolution is inadequate to discern much detail. Fortunately, railroad historian Richard Palmer sent me a better reproduction of the same photo and the locomotive clearly shows "Watson Page Lumber Co." lettered on it. It is a small, one-truck, four-wheel trolley, perhaps about eleven feet long and equally as high (except for the trolley pole on the roof). The appearance is of a box sitting upon a small platform. The photo has the caption "Earl J. LaPoint, Saint Regis Falls, N.Y."

The second photo was sent to me by electric railroad historian, Jim McFarlane. It appears to be an enlargement of an old picture post card because there is a caption printed on it: "Electric Railway between Saint Regis Falls and Lake Ozonia, Adirondack Mountains." The caption is in error in stating that the railway went all the way to the lake. The photo shows the railway and the old River Street highway bridge over the Saint Regis River, the steep railroad grade on the far (west) bank, the trolley locomotive, the catenary, and a switchback which leads to the Cascade Chair Factory.

A third photo available at the Saint Regis Falls Museum shows track and catenary only, not well-graded and following closely the undulating character of the land.

The precise date of abandonment is unknown. Seaver (1918, p. 550) states that "Both chair factory and the electric works were run successfully until 1909, when fire wiped them out." It would seem likely that the electric railroad ceased operations at this time. Seaver continues in 1918: "The railroad is no longer in existence, the rails having been taken up and sold for old iron."

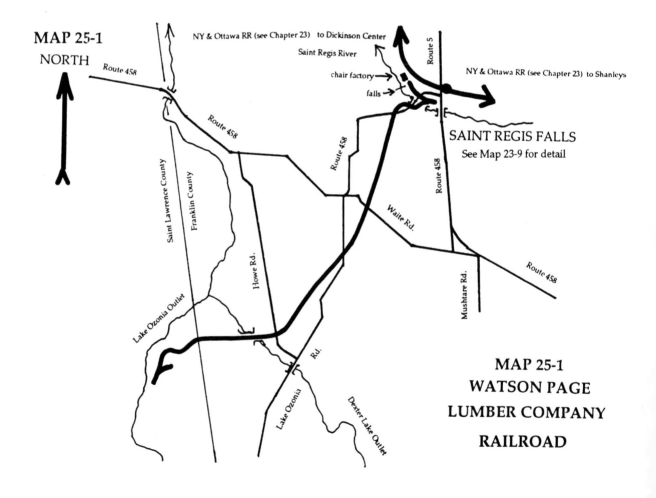

MAP 25-1 WATSON PAGE LUMBER COMPANY RAILROAD

Chapter 26:
Brooklyn Cooperage Company Railroad

THE BROOKLYN COOPERAGE COMPANY, with main offices in Brooklyn, New York, produced barrels for the shipment and storage of sugar. The company did not own the lands upon which they built their numerous hardwood-logging railroad spurs, but rather leased the lands from paper companies often after the softwood logs were harvested. Brooklyn Cooperage's major areas of activity were at Tupper Lake, at Saint Regis Falls (including Everton, Lake Ozonia, regions west of Meno, and regions east of Meno), and at Salisbury Center. This chapter is divided geographically following these areas of activity (See Map 26-1 for an overview). Operations were from 1900 into the early 1920s.

Tupper Lake:
Map 26-6

Northeast of McCarthy Street in Tupper Lake was the Brooklyn Cooperage Mill (Simmons, 1976, pp. 78 and 79, with photo p. 88), built in 1900. The mill made barrel staves and headings, and operated until 1921. A seven-mile-long logging railroad was built in May of 1900 east to near Wawbeek. Donaldson (1921, Volume II, pp. 202-207) describes the legal battle which soon developed between landowners along Upper Saranac Lake and the then recently-formed New York State College of Forestry at Cornell University (this College was soon moved to Syracuse). Smoke from the burning of some trees felled to make a clearing for the Fernow State Plantations resulted in numerous complaints from the landowners. The Brooklyn Cooperage Company, under contract to haul some of the hardwood from the State lands, became caught in the battle and shut down their railroad line in 1904.

The line split at its eastern end into two branches as shown on the Long Lake quadrangle surveyed in 1901-1902 and the Saint Regis quadrangle surveyed in 1902-1903. A portion of the south branch is presently occupied by State Highways 3 and 30 on a long, level stretch west of their junction. The Long Lake quadrangle also indicates a small rail yard which Brooklyn Cooperage built near its stave and heading mill. A stub track is shown north of what is now Sunmount State Developmental Center, but the function of this stub is unknown. Brooklyn Cooperage later built a second mill (Simmons, 1976, p. 79) about 1902 using the wood waste from the stave and heading mill to manufacture charcoal, wood alcohol, and acetate of lime; this second mill ran until ca. 1915.

With the cessation of logging operations along the Wawbeek line in 1904, Brooklyn Cooperage Company had to look elsewhere to obtain their hardwoods. They looked north and began building a series of spurs off the New York & Ottawa, beginning at Saint Regis Falls in 1904 and then later into Lake Ozonia and east and west of Meno.

Clippings from the *Tupper Lake Free Press* during the 1971-1974 era in the Smallman Collection at the Paul Smith's College Cubley Library include a photo of the Brooklyn Cooperage mill in Tupper Lake. A brick portion of the mill still stands in 1991.

In 1985, a brochure entitled *Fernow's Forest: Self-Guided Nature Trail* was published jointly by the N.Y. State Department of Environmental Conservation, the Adirondack Chapter of the Society of American Foresters, the Tupper Lake Rotary Club, and Paul Smith's College. This brochure provides detail into the historical forestry aspects of the controversial plantations. The trail is accessible to the public today and is located about a half-mile north on Route 30 from its junction with Route 3.

The Everton Railroad: Map 26-2

Palmer (February 1970) states that in 1886, McFarlane, Ross and Stearns built a railroad from Saint Regis Falls east six miles to Everton where they had previously built two sawmills. The Malone *Palladium* of July 29, 1886, page 2, confirms the railroad construction date as spring, 1886. The 1891 *Poor's Directory of Railroad Officials* mentions that McFarlane, Ross, and Stearns owned 16.50 miles of standard-gauged, 30-pound-rail line with one locomotive. Their address was Everton, New York. The Everton Railroad is shown on the 1895 and 1898 Adirondack Land Maps published by the New York State Forest Commission. The March 8, 1898 New York & Ottawa timetable still lists connections with the Everton Railroad indicating that perhaps some form of passenger service existed.

In 1904, the Brooklyn Cooperage Company took over the then-abandoned Everton Railroad, but it is not clear in Palmer (1971) whether the tracks were still present or had to be relaid. Former Waverly Town Historian, Ralph M. Farmer, says that the tracks indeed had to be relaid. A map drawn by J.M.B. (only initials given) of the Saint Regis Paper Company's lands in Franklin County Townships 10 through 15, dated April 1910, indicates the line ending just short of Bristol Brook between the highway and the East Branch Saint Regis River 0.1 mile below the falls at Everton. Perhaps this was as far as the Everton Railroad had been built in 1886.

Another map drawn by Saint Regis Paper Company surveyor A.A.Z. (again, only initials given) in May 1937 shows the Brooklyn Cooperage Company perhaps at its greatest extent east of Everton. This map was drawn, however, about 15 years after the Company had suspended operations. The map is entitled *Map of the Everton Tract, Townships 11 and 12, Franklin County, Sheet 3*. On this map, several additional spurs are shown which do not appear on the 1921 Santa Clara quadrangle. One is about a mile above Everton Falls and the other four at Deer River and Mile Brook. Several logging camps operating in 1919 and 1920 are shown on this map, one of them located along the track and labelled "Railroad Camp."

In *Where did the Tracks Go* (Kudish, 1985, p. 66), I indicated a 0.1-mile-long stub off the Brooklyn Cooperage line at the confluence of Pleasant Brook and the East Branch Saint Regis River. Little did I know then that this Pleasant Brook stub was a mere remnant of a 4.7-mile-long branch which followed Pleasant Brook to its source and continued east to cross the Deer River! A tour of the area by Clayton Winters of Bangor and the Mile Brook area in May of 1988 convinced me of the magnitude of Cooperage operations. The present Red Tavern Road (Franklin County Highway 14) occupies the Everton and Brooklyn Cooperage railroad grade between the west base of Trim Hill and Everton, a distance of about four miles. The original highway crosses the grade 0.3 mile west of Pleasant Brook.

Photos of the Brooklyn Cooperage Company Mill at Saint Regis Falls occur as #P2415 of The Adirondack Museum collection and several photos appear in Trim (1989).

Lake Ozonia: Map 26-3

From a point 1.8 miles south of Santa Clara station on the New York & Ottawa, Brooklyn Cooperage built an eight-mile-long line westward to and beyond the southern end of Lake Ozonia. Trim (1989, page 94) states that this line was built in 1917 to a jack works on the lake and continued on to the Frank A. Cutting Tract in the Town of Hopkinton, Saint Lawrence County. The hardwood logs from the Cutting Tract were going to the Brooklyn Cooperage Mill in Saint Regis Falls while the softwood logs assembled at the jack works were going to the Saint Regis Paper Company as pulp. The hemlock bark was intended for Cutting's own tanning business; he designed and built a number of special bark-hauling railroad cars (there is a photo of one in Trim (1989, page 94).

The 1919 Nicholville and 1921 Santa Clara quadrangles show the line with five short stubs mid-route and four short stubs at the Lake Ozonia terminus. On August 11, 1985 railroad historian Russell Nelson and I followed the old right-of-way from the Blue Mountain Road westward. Two of the five short stubs mid-route are still discernible, but we could not locate the four stubs at the Lake Ozonia terminal. Instead, Russell found a spur, not shown on any map I have seen, which continued westward about 0.75 mile and became obscure in an existing gravel Champion International Paper Corporation road. This spur must have entered the Cutting Tract in 1917.

Russell wondered whether this spur looped around southward then eastward to connect with the Brooklyn Cooperage line at Center Camp which originated from Meno. Modern log roads make such a determination almost impossible in the field, but the 1963-1964 Lake Ozonia 7.5-minute quadrangle and 1957 aerial photos at the New York Division of Equalization and Assessment office confirm it. Thus Palmer's (1971) statement that Brooklyn Cooperage built their line to Lake Ozonia from Meno is correct (see *Where did the Tracks Go*, 1985, page 67). Lake Ozonia was reached from two different directions!

West of Meno:
Maps 26-3, 26-4, and 26-5

Trim (1989, pages 94-95) states that after the 1908 forest fires on the Cutting Tract, Frank Cutting made a contract with the Brooklyn Cooperage Company to build railroad westward to salvage his hardwood logs. The line followed Quebec Brook and the Saint Regis River downstream, eventually crossing the River at a point 0.25 mile above the Blue Mountain Road bridge. Just west of the railroad bridge the line divided. The north branch headed past McCavanaugh Pond and followed Stony Brook downstream reaching Center Camp in 1911. The railroad was soon extended and a wye built just west of Center Camp. The south spur from the wye terminated a little over a mile further downstream along Stony Brook beyond what Trim calls the Babcock Camp. The north spur from the wye headed for a 15-acre cleared area called the Potato Patch; potatoes were grown here to feed the people at Center Camp and other nearby logging camps. From the Potato Patch, the spur looped around to the east and connected with the Lake Ozonia line described above.

The south branch followed Alder Brook and Long Pond Outlet downstream to the West Branch Saint Regis River, lands not owned by Cutting. Parts of both branches are shown on the Meno (1963-1964) and Lake Ozonia (1963-1964) 15-minute quadrangles as truck roads or trails.

None of the older 15-minute quadrangles, Santa Clara (1921) and Nicholville (1919), shows the Brooklyn Cooperage lines out of Meno except for, at Meno, a half-mile-long stub which is probably a remnant of the line heading west. However, a string of bench marks on these old quadrangles along both the Stony Brook (north) and Long Pond Outlet (south) locates the branches. The 1911 and 1920 Adirondack Land Maps, published by the New York State Conservation Commission, do indicate the two branches running west from Meno.

Another map showing the north branch line through Center Camp is one by the Saint Regis Paper Company, entitled *Cutting Tract, NE Quarter of Rivers Dale-Township 12, Sheet 15*. The surveyor was E.L. Hazen and the date March 10, 1938, although Brooklyn Cooperage had pulled out of this area 17 or 18 years before. Hazen's map does not show the loop connection with the Lake Ozonia line.

Trim (1989, page 95) says that "The sawmill was located on Stony Brook where the Bulger Camp now stands, next to the railroad." I inquired further for the precise location of the Bulger Camp and learned that the site is just inside Franklin County, probably within a tenth of a mile or so from the Saint Lawrence County Line. The mill produced ties for Brooklyn Cooperage Company and lumber for downstate dealers.

East of Meno:
Map 26-4

The 1911 and 1920 Adirondack Land maps show a Brooklyn Cooperage line also heading east from Meno and terminating almost on the Santa Clara-Brighton Town Line. In actuality, this Cooperage track extended considerably further than this, completely encircling Sugarloaf and Daniel Mountains and even looping back on itself. Jane Gardner, former forester for Champion International Corporation (formerly Saint Regis Paper Company), informed me of this additional trackage. In 1986 and 1987, she, along with colleagues Bud Delano and John Flynn, gave me a tour of the old grades. The only point which I could not reach was the vicinity of the confluence of Mountain Brook with the Onion River because of extensive beaver flooding. I suspected that the junction which created the loop was here and I finally confirmed the fact at the office of the New York Division of Equalization and Assessment; their 1956 aerial photos were taken before the flooding and clearly show the junction.

Along the line near Clear Brook (labeled Jenkins Brook on the Meacham Lake 7.5-minute quadrangle) we found evidence of a short stub, approximately 135 feet long and thus with a capacity of only several logging flatcars. This stub is shown on Map 26-4.

Map 26-4 is at a scale of 1/62500 as are all the scale-three maps in this book, based on the older 15-minute quadrangles. But there was difficulty in tracing this Brooklyn Cooperage line on the 1921 Santa Clara 15-minute quadrangle. Errors made by the United States Geological Survey cartographers resulted in omission of the Onion River and incorrect location of other streams. Fortunately, the more recent 7.5-minute Meno and Meacham Lake quadrangles show the streams and topography correctly so that I had to scale them down from 1/24000 to prepare the map here.

Salisbury Center: Map 34-1

Brooklyn Cooperage Company also had a mill at Salisbury Center at the southern edge of the Adirondacks, quite distant from the bulk of its operations along the New York & Ottawa in the northern region. See Chapter 34 on the Jerseyfield Railroad for details.

Equipment

The Brooklyn Cooperage Company, according to Palmer (March 1971) used a variety of geared locomotives, mostly Shays and Climaxes. Palmer includes a photo of a Climax at work with a Barnhardt steam log-loader crane on the flat cars. This photo is duplicated in Koch (1979, page 139, in Trim (1989), and in Wever et al. (1992, page 5). Wever et al. list engines # 1, #2, and #8.

Photos and descriptions of the Barnhardt log loader appear on pp. 18 and 22 of the Smallman Collection's black scrapbook at the Paul Smith's College Library.

Closure and a Surprise

Palmer (1970 and 1971) states that Brooklyn Cooperage pulled out of the Adirondacks about 1920. This is confirmed in Seaver (1918) who had predicted a closure of operations within a year or two of his writing because most hardwood timber had been removed by then. Simmons (1976) offers that the Tupper Lake mill closed in 1921, probably the last Cooperage operation in the Adirondacks.

To my utter amazement in 1986 a letter came from the Brooklyn Cooperage Company in Versailles, Connecticut! Mr. Andrew N. de Treville, plant manager, sent me a copy of his 1981 publication *A Brief Look at Brooklyn Cooperage, Past and Present*. Brooklyn Cooperage is now a subsidiary of Amstar Corporation, American Sugar Refining Company. The plant in Connecticut manufactures cartons for Domino Sugar, but on special occasions still receives an order to build barrels. Mr. de Treville gave me a tour of the plant in 1986. Brooklyn Cooperage is still alive and well despite seventy years of retirement from the Adirondacks!

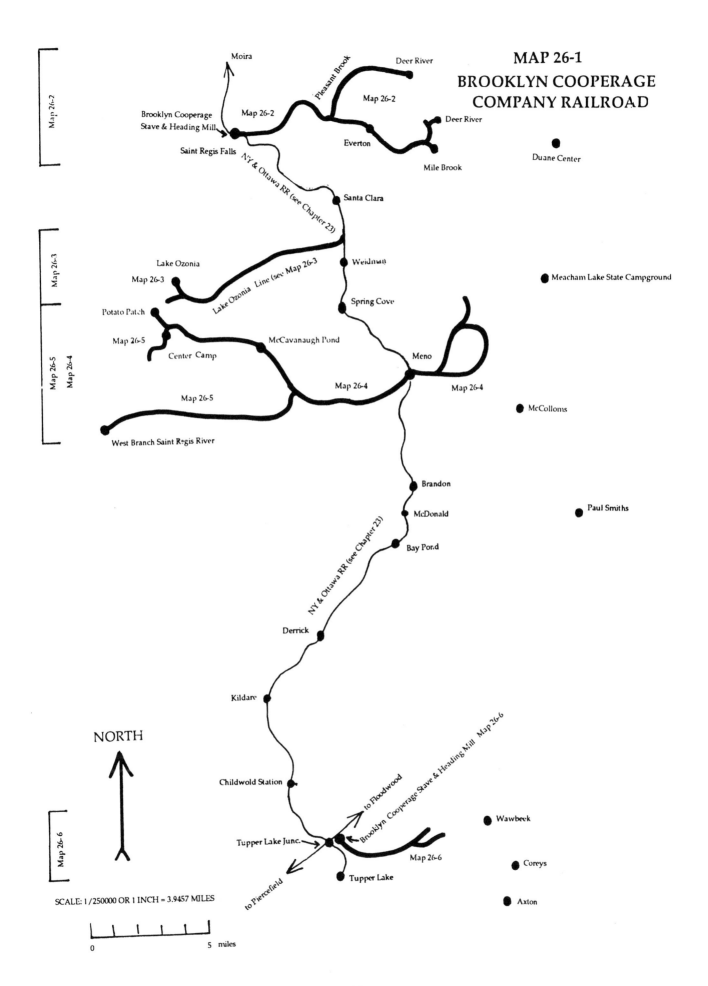

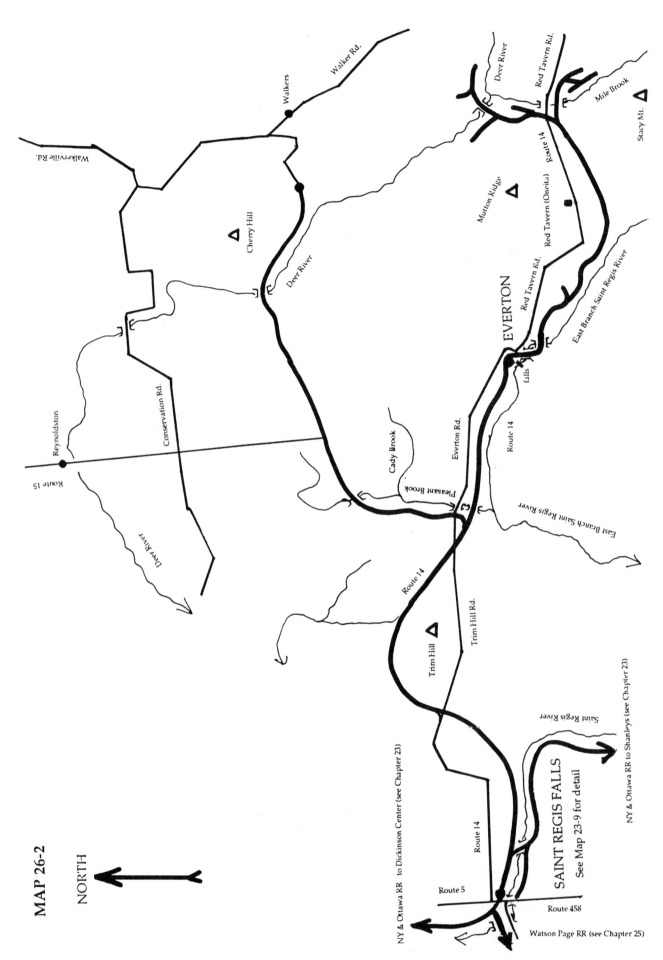

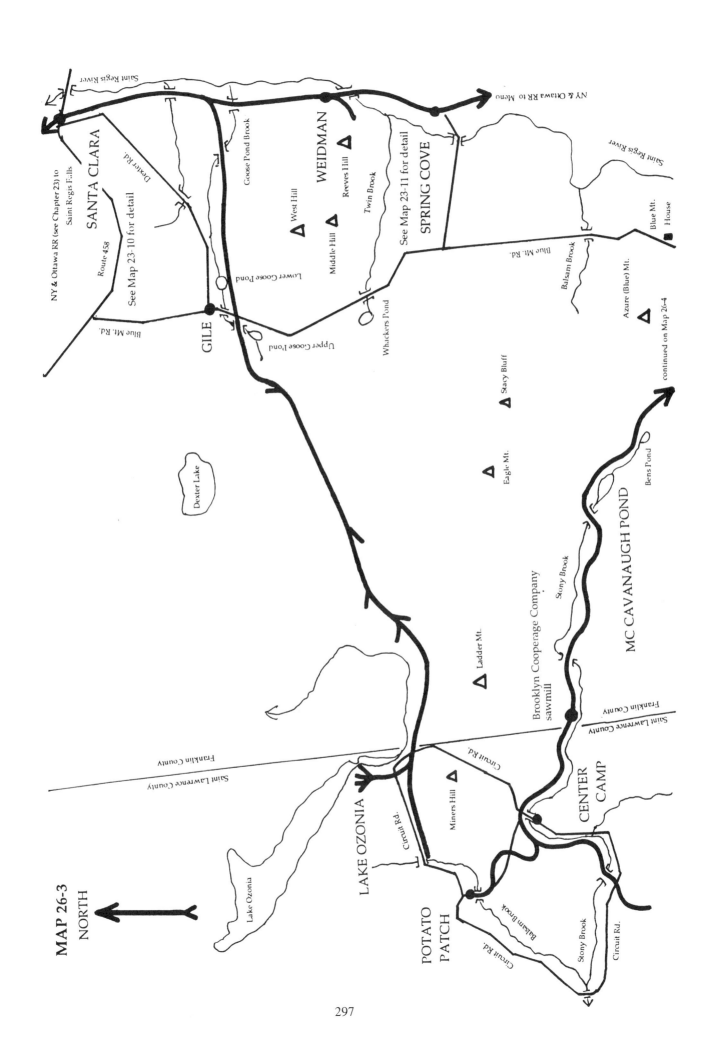

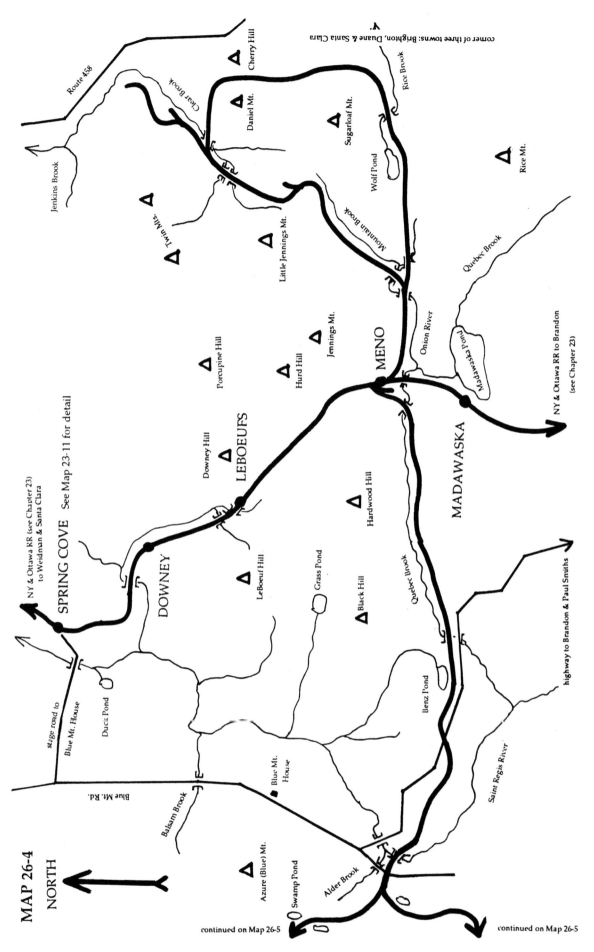

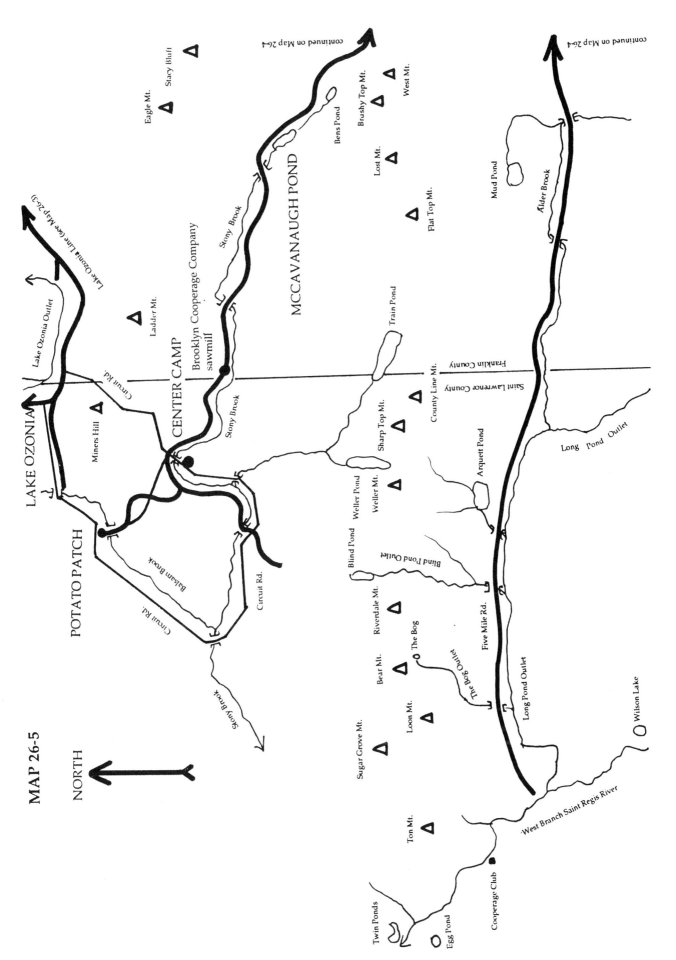

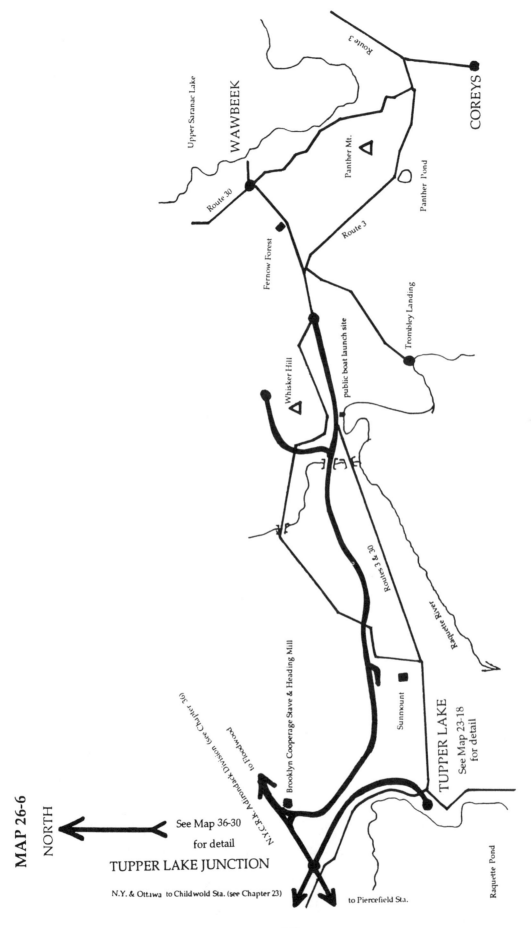

Chapter 27:
Bay Pond Inc.

GOVE (1981) offers a comprehensive history of Bay Pond Inc. John N. McDonald had been a partner in the Mac-a-Mac Corporation operations at Brandreth on the New York Central Adirondack Division (see Chapter 38). He, with four others, formed Bay Pond Inc. in 1923 and acquired the William Rockefeller tract surrounding Bay Pond. In 1924 logging operations began mostly for spruce pulpwood.

Maps 23-1, 23-5, 23-12, and 27-1

From a station on the Ottawa Division of the New York Central built and named McDonald, in 1924, a railroad was constructed 10.4 miles west to a point on the West Branch Saint Regis River just downstream from Augerhole Falls and almost to the Saint Lawrence County line (see Map 27-1. The Saint Regis Mountain metric topographic quadrangle (aerial photos 1976, published 1979) and 7.5-minute Augerhole Falls quadrangle (aerial photos 1967, published 1970) show the grade as a jeep trail.

On October 17, 1987 the author was given a tour of the junction by Fred Joost, caretaker of Ross Park, the current owner. We found much more than appears on the map of page 6 of Gove (1981). A wye surrounded the station which, although altered, still stood. To the west was a yard of six tracks (if one includes the two wye tracks), with the remains of an engine servicing facility under one of them; a large concrete slab exists today on the ground with a pit in it. I am not sure of the precise manner in which the six tracks merged at the neck at the west end of the yard so that Map 23-12 is an approximation. The water tower was west of this yard neck along the line to Augerhole Falls. Collins' (1969) photo of McDonald Station, incorrectly labeled Brandon Station, was taken with the photographer facing north and looking at the south end of the wye.

Gove's map shows a jackworks at both Wolf Pond and near Augerhole Falls. The author's field notes of July 11, 1978 indicate that the line terminated in two short stubs near Augerhole Falls.

Bay Pond Inc., according to Gove's 1981 article, ran two rod locomotives (as opposed to geared locomotives) because there were no steep grades. One was a 2-6-0 Mogul built by Alco-Schenectady in 1913. The other, used as a pusher at the rear of the train, is too distant in the photos to be identifiable. The two locomotives, one at each end of the train, brought a cut of about ten cars loaded with pulpwood to McDonald Station. The cars were later coupled on to an Ottawa Division train. Photos of the Bay Pond Inc. train appear in Gove (1981, p. 7) and Hyde (1974, pp. 46 and 47).

Gove (1981, p. 39) states that the Oval Wood Dish Company of Tupper Lake built a 1.5 mile-long spur off the Bay Pond Inc. railroad to harvest hardwood timber from the south and east slopes of Buck Mountain in 1925 (see Chapter 28 for more detail on the Oval Wood Dish Company whose railroad operated primarily out of Kildare). Gove's map indicates Haynes Camp at the junction of this spur with Bay Pond Inc.'s railroad, 2.8 miles west of McDonald Station.

Bill Gove has recently (1991) given me a copy of a map drawn by F.E.L. (only initials known) on May 25, 1927 entitled *Plan of Proposed Railroad, on Bay Pond Inc. Tract, at McDonald, N.Y. for the Oval Wood Dish Corp., Tupper Lake, New York*. This proposed spur is fully within the Town of Santa Clara, runs much closer to the Saint Regis River, and terminates further north around the base of Buck Mountain than the 1925 spur. Whether the spur proposed in 1927 was ever built I do not know; my tour guides on our July 11, 1978 field trip made no mention of it. I have included a sketch of the spur in Map 27-1.

The last year of operation for Bay Pond Inc. was, according to Gove, 1932. McDonald Station was still listed, however, in the 1936 Ottawa Division timetables. The New York Central abandoned this Division in 1937, and it was about this time that Bay Pond Inc. sold the tract back to the William Rockefeller family.

The author in the engine service pit at McDonald Station, October 1987. Bay Pond Inc. operated from 1924 to 1932.

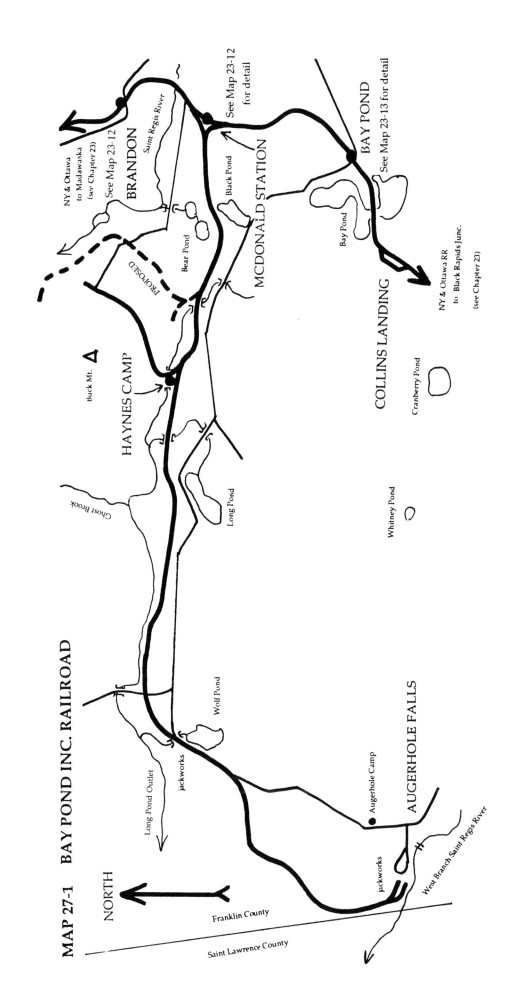

Chapter 28: Oval Wood Dish Corporation's Railroad at Kildare

PALMER (March 1970) described in detail how the Oval Wood Dish Corporation, with main offices and plant at Tupper Lake, set up logging headquarters at Kildare in 1916. Construction of railroads began in 1917.

Maps 23-1, 23-5, 23-6, 28-1, 28-2, and 28-3

Map 28-1 in this book shows Oval Wood Dish lines in Franklin County, while Map 28-2 shows lines continuing westward into Saint Lawrence County. Map 28-3 shows detail at Kildare.

The 15-minute Childwold quadrangle, surveyed in 1919-1920, shows a 7.7-mile-long line terminating at Buckley and Sullivan Camps with an 0.8-mile-long spur, the #10 spur, heading west downstream along the south side of Potter Brook. The quadrangle also shows two branches heading east and southeast from Kildare wrapping around the west end of Iron Mountain. The *Inventory of Abandoned Rights-of-Way* (1974) published by the New York State Department of Transportation is in error, assigning ownership of the Iron Mountain branches to Brooklyn Cooperage. The easterly branch continues onto the 1955 Saint Regis quadrangle, aerial photos taken 1953, where the grade is designated as abandoned. These quadrangles show only a mere fraction of the total trackage which Oval Wood Dish had built in this region.

Forest historian and author, Bill Gove, of Vermont has given me photocopies of two maps drawn by Floyd A. Hutchins of the Oval Wood Dish Corporation lands. These maps show not only the railroad spurs, but also when certain tracts of land were logged, which were burned, which were waste lands, and which were State Land and therefore could not be logged. There is a wealth of detail on forest history on these maps.

The Timber Lands map by Hutchins of Township 19 in Franklin County shows blocks of timber already cut by April 1, 1919 as well as those proposed for cutting later in 1919, in 1920, and in 1921. No clues are given on this map of precisely when the logging spurs were in service. Because the logging spurs and camps operated for as short a period as several months to several years, keeping track of which was in service at what time is complex. The Township 19 map also indicates the Blue Mountain Line ascending the northeast slopes of Mount Matumbla with a series of three switchbacks. I estimate this line attaining elevations of between 2000 and 2060 feet, a climb of 500 feet above Kildare. Switchbacks to climb steep grades were rare in the Adirondacks; I know of no others used in logging railroads, although the Lake Champlain & Moriah used them on their iron mining railroad.

The Timber Map by Hutchins in Townships 8 and 9 in Saint Lawrence County was dated January 10, 1920 and was compiled from field notes of J. D. Lacey. It shows tracts cut in 1918 and 1919, and proposed cuts for the years 1920 through 1923. It also indicates railroad grades completed with steel laid, those abandoned with steel taken up, and those with only grade completed and steel not yet laid as of January 10, 1920. Those spurs already abandoned by January 10, 1920 ran north and northwest from Kettle Pond in Saint Lawrence County toward Whitney Pond and the West Branch Saint Regis River, respectively. The spur in one of the Buckley Camps, #17, also had been abandoned. A spur which had been graded by January 10, 1920 but with rails not yet laid crossed Cold Brook, the outlet to Amber

Lake, just below its confluence with Cedar Brook. One wonders whether all spurs graded actually had steel rail laid, and whether additional trackage was built after 1923. See Map 28-2 modified from Hutchins.

Professor C. Creighton Fee of Paul Smith's College has given me a copy of another map drafted by Hutchins, dated April 14, 1922 and entitled *Plan of the Proposed Extension of the Oval Wood Dish Corporation railroad Yard at Kildare, New York*. This map is sketched as Map 28-3, but how much of this proposed extension was actually constructed is not known. No indication of the Blue Mountain Line switchbacking up the slopes of Mt. Matumbla is shown on the 1922 map, suggesting that this line had already been abandoned.

Palmer (March 1970) tells us that Oval Wood Dish owned two locomotives, both Heisler 63-ton geared engines. These had to cross the New York Central's Ottawa Division to work both their east and west lines at Kildare. Simmons (1976, p. 134) includes a photo of one of these Heislers. Oval Wood Dish also had 65 standard flat cars for transporting logs to Tupper Lake (Simmons, 1976, p. 135 photo).

A series of *Tupper Lake Free Press* clippings at the Paul Smith's College Library Smallman Collection includes photos of Oval Wood Dish operations. Several clippings which were dated supply the following detail:

February 27, 1974 on page 77.1 in the black scrapbook: photo of the Patent Slide at O.W.D. Camp #5.

January 16, 1974 and several other dates in a series of articles on pp. 92, 92A, 93, 93A, and 96: O.W.D. had only two camps along the Ottawa Division mainline, #5 at Willis Pond and #1 at Kildare. Logs were lowered by cable down the steep slopes of Mt. Matumbla by a device known as a Lidgerwood Skidder.

Several additional articles were undated. One includes a photo showing the switchback junction of tracks "A" and "B" on the slopes of Mt. Matumbla. In another, on page 65 of the black scrapbook, there is a statement that the Santa Clara Lumber Company used only conifers, and that they sold their lands and hardwood timber afterward to Oval Wood Dish in December of 1914. Some of the undated articles listed above are probably from the 1967-1968 era.

Palmer (March 1970) reveals that in 1926, the Sisson White Company took over the logging railroad and removed the tracks about a year later.

See Chapter 27 and Map 27-1 for the O.W.D. branch off the Bay Pond Inc. Railroad around Buck Mountain west of Brandon.

The Kildare depot, August 1936, near the Oval Wood Dish operations, is now at The Adirondack Museum in Blue Mountain Lake.
Collection of New York Central System Historical Society, Inc.

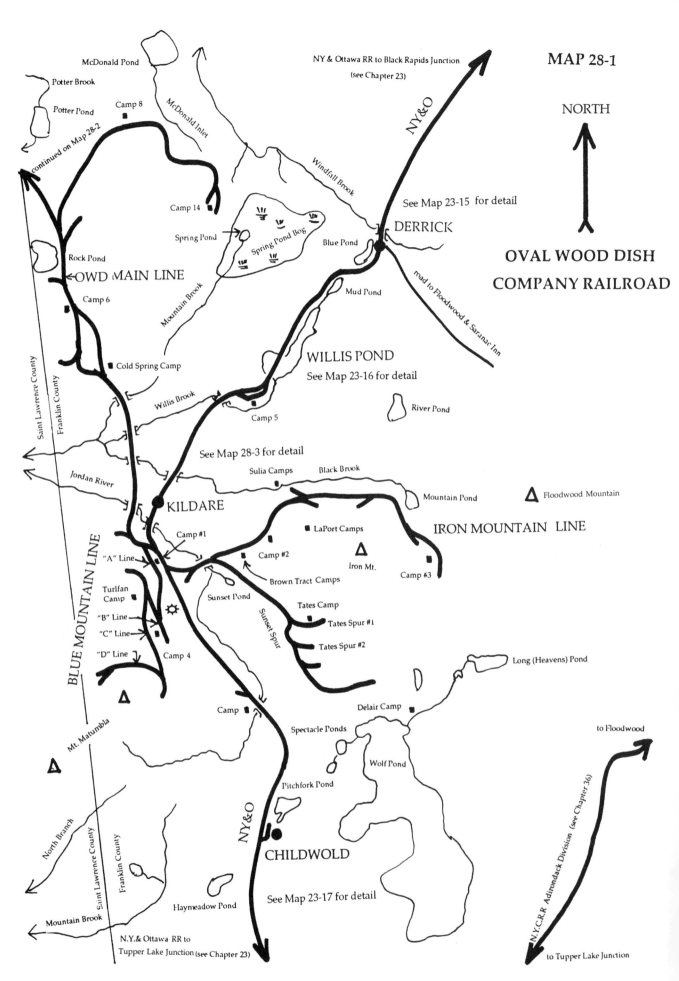

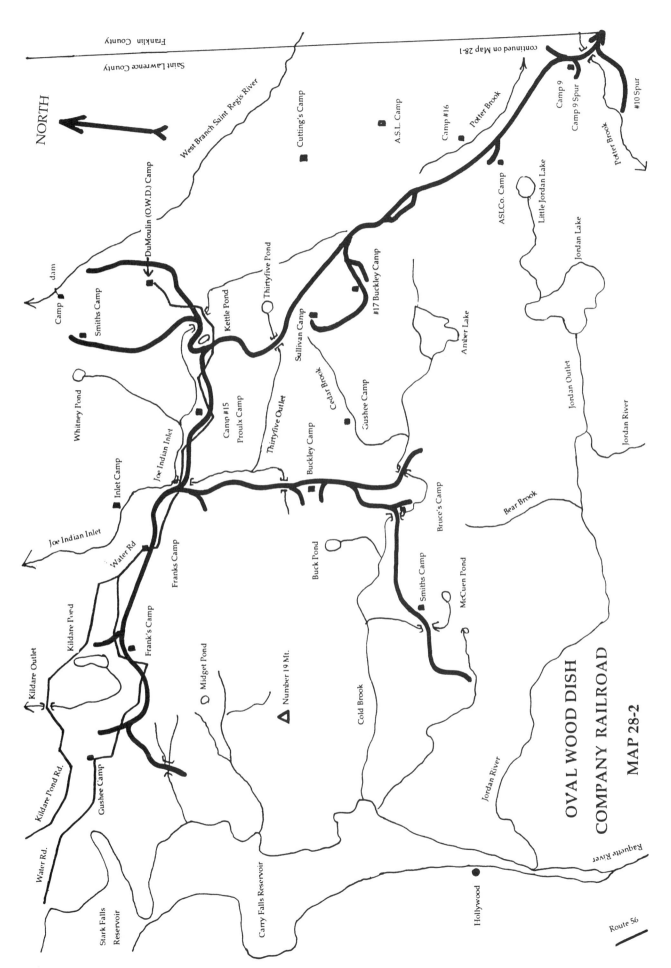

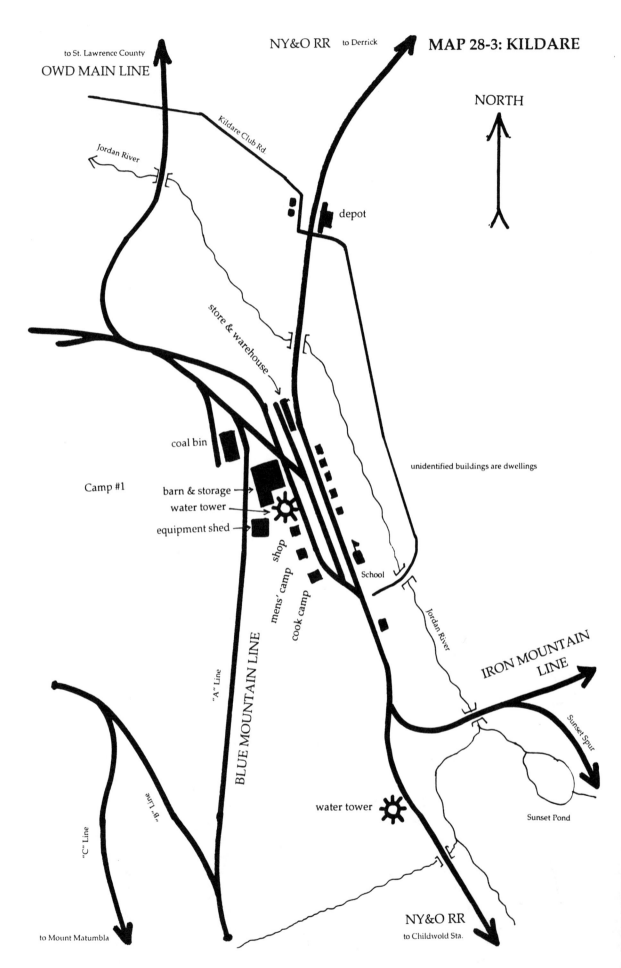

Northbound Amtrak *Adirondack* arriving at Fort Edward in February 1976. The Alco PA locomotive served the Santa Fe and was rebuilt to serve the D&H from 1967 to 1977. Page 248.

Thomas C. Curran photo.

Dickinson Center, August 4, 1936. Much of the building still stands. Page 266.
Collection of the New York Central System Historical Society, Inc.

Santa Clara, looking south. It is August 1936 and the Ottawa Division will be abandoned in a year. Page 268.
Collection of the New York Central System Historical Society, Inc.

Derrick on August 4, 1936. Left of center, note the remains of Turner's sawmill, later Elliott's mangle roll mill. Page 271.

Collection of the New York Central System Historical Society, Inc.

New York & Ottawa train at Tupper Lake (not Tupper Lake Junction)
sometime between 1897 and 1906. Page 272.

Richard Wettereau collection.

The Bay Pond Station still stands as a private residence. View looking northeast, August 1987. Page 271.
Author photo.

Opposite page, top:
Watson Page Lumber Co. electric locomotive, Saint Regis Falls, ca. 1908. Page 289.
Earl J. LaPoint collection.

Opposite page, bottom:
Watson Page Lumber Co. electric locomotive. Track at left ascends to Lake Ozonia Outlet.
The track at right goes to the mill. The old highway bridge beyond has been abandonded. Page 289.
Bill Gove collection.

Above:
Brooklyn Cooperage Company is still alive and well in Versailles, Connecticut, seventy-five years after departing from the Adirondacks. The company is now part of Amstar Corporation, the American Sugar Refining Company. Page 291.
Author photo, January 1987.

Left:
Mohawk, Adirondack & Northern freight at Benson Mines, August 26, 1993, headed for Newton Falls. The new railroad replaced Conrail on May 1, 1991. Pages 331 & 336.
Author photo.

Newton Falls Paper Company was established about 1896.
Recently it has changed hands several times. Page 336.

Author photo, November 1990.

Northbound train at Big Moose, 1964. Page 394.
Alan Thomas photo.

Northbound train at Sabattis, 1964. The station burned about 1990. Page 397.
Alan Thomas photo.

Above:
New York Central Pacific Class K-3, #4667, at Thendara in the mid-1930s. Page 393.
Arthur G. Martin photo, Jeffrey G. Martin collection.

Right:
Adirondack Centennial Railroad, August 9, 1992, the first year of operation, at Thendara. Pages 393 & 475.
Author photo.

Above:
Southbound train in the summer 1939 at Blue Rock curve near milepost 125 and Saranac Inn. Hoel pond in view. Page 400.
Alan Thomas photo.

Right:
Saranac Inn, 1953. Page 400.

Freight bound for Montreal at Lake Clear Junction in 1953. Page 400.
Alan Thomas photo.

Lake Clear Junction. The building still stands. Page 400.
Photographer unknown.

Lake Clear Junction.
Above: Southbound General Motors Convention train, 1953.
The freight station persisted until the early 1970s.
Below: Train at right to Montreal, at left to Lake Placid, 1954.
Page 400.
Alan Thomas photos.

Gabriels Station, the second on the site, was built in 1927. Page 400.
Lynda Edris collection.

Lake Kushaqua Station, New York Central Railroad Adirondack Division. Page 401.
Richard Wettereau collection.

Section III:
Into the Adirondacks from the Saint Lawrence on the Northwest and West

Chapter 29:
Hannawa Railroad

THE HANNAWA RAILROAD is shown on the 1905-1906 Potsdam 15-minute quadrangle. Calvert (1975), however, is my prime source. According to her, the Hannawa Falls Water power Company was incorporated on March 30, 1899. Shortly thereafter it built a hydroelectric plant at the Falls. A pulp mill was also built just downstream from the hydroelectric plant, as well as a 3.8-mile-long railroad to connect the mill with the New York Central's Saint Lawrence Division in Potsdam. In a series of articles for the *Watertown Daily Times*, Berry (1955) described how he had difficulty in purchasing pulpwood for the Hannawa Falls Water Power Company mill and had to travel much in Canada in his search; his company did not own lands from which to obtain pulpwood.

Maps 29-1, 29-2 and 33-1

According to Calvert, the Potsdam Red Sandstone Company had the same board of directors as the hydroelectric plant and pulp mill. The railroad, in addition to hauling pulpwood into the mill, also hauled sandstone out of the quarry on the west side of the Raquette River to Potsdam.

Calvert mentions that although the line had no formal passenger service, pulp mill crews, Hannawa Falls residents, and children searching for an amusement park-like ride rode the train. Dr. Arthur Johnson, Professor of History at the State University of New York at Potsdam, lecturing on February 11, 1979 stated that the railroad provided special berry-picker service trains on Sundays.

Note how the Hannawa Railroad diverged from the present Conrail line at what is now the busy intersection of Routes 11, 345, and 138 (Map 29-2). The line headed southeastward through a cut which is still visible and then island-hopped up the Raquette River to the quarry and pulpmill (Map 29-1).

Calvert includes two photographs: a train about 1915 on the rails and another off the rails in 1910.

I cannot determine the precise date of closure. Calvert offers no help. The best estimate may be from information provided by Palmer and Timmerman (1973, pp. 171 and 172) discussing the Adirondack & Saint Lawrence Railroad from DeKalb Junction to Hermon (see Chapter 33). The rails were removed from the Hannawa Railroad and used in construction of a spur into the then new Hires Condensed Milk Company plant in DeKalb Junction. The spur and milk plant were built after World War I began on July 28, 1914, but before the United States became involved on April 6, 1917; hence, the Hannawa Railroad must have been abandoned between late 1914 and early 1917.

A northbound freight, DM-11, on the New York Central's Saint Lawrence Division passes through Potsdam with a mix of Alco power in May 1967. The lead engine is FA-2 #1169. The junction with Hannawa Railroad was just to the south.
Jeffrey G. Martin photo.

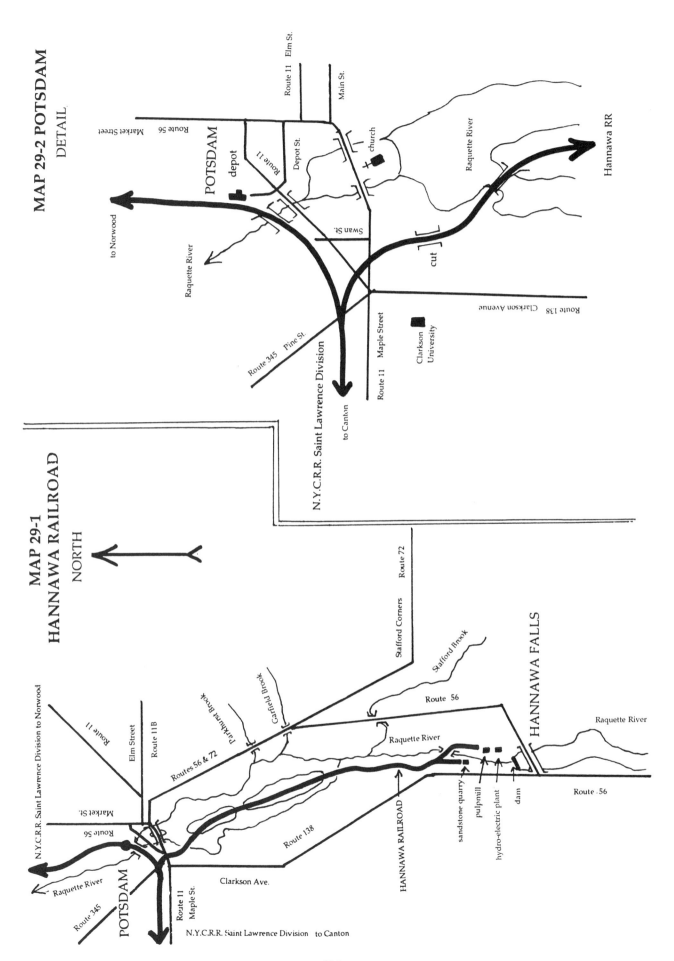

Chapter 30:
Clifton Iron Company's Railroad

An almost disproportionately large volume of literature has been written on this small railroad---probably because it was so unusual: one of the earliest short lines in northern New York, one of the shortest-lived, and one of only four which used wooden rails. In this book, only a brief summary is presented, but the reader is referred to other sources for further detail.

Maps 30-1, 30-2, and 33-1

The Clifton Iron Company's Railroad was surveyed in 1866 and opened January 1, 1868. Beginning at East DeKalb and connecting there with the New York Central's Saint Lawrence Division, the line was built 23.5 miles to the southeast, passing through Marshville, Stalbird, Grant's Crossing, Silverhill, Degrasse P.O. (Monterey), and Clarksboro. Clarksboro was the residential village located about 1.5 miles north of the mines and blast furnaces. A fire on September 4, 1869 destroyed much of the equipment; as a result, operations were suspended. A chimney, 160 feet tall and built about 1867, was not torn down until 1942 when the Hanna Ore Company operated the mine.

Maps showing the Clifton Iron Company's Railroad are Ely's (1878), Asher & Adams (1871), and an 1882 map on page 178 in Reynolds et al. (1976) with no original publisher given.

I was able to obtain the precise route of the Clifton Iron Company's Railroad from historian Russell Nelson of Potsdam, who had, in turn, obtained it from John Thomas, co-author of the 1969 article with Richard Palmer. I drew the route first on the 1904 Gouverneur and 1919 Russell quadrangles, and then traced it as shown here on Maps 30-1 and 30-2.

Additional references on the Clifton Iron Company's Railroad are as follows: An article in the *Ogdensburg Advance* reprinted in the *New York Times* August 6, 1868 offers some detail on the track, train speeds, and the mines. On August 23, 1920 an article in the *Saint Lawrence Plaindealer* describes Clifton in the early 20th century. An article in the *Canton Commerical Advertiser*, (1950) has detail on the wooden track, trestles, locomotives, cars, furnaces and mines. Barnes (1962) offers a description of the reopening of the mines from 1941 to 1952 when the Hanna Ore Company operated their railroad from a very different direction: via Newton Falls and Newbridge (see Chapter 31). Palmer (1967) and Palmer and Thomas (1969) present the most thorough account of the 19th and 20th century aspects of the railroads and mines; they note a siding at Grant's Crossing. Dodge (1950) describes the cars, locomotives, track, trestles, furnaces, and mines of the Clifton Iron Company. Kirkbride (1977) summarizes the earlier references. Angus (1991) includes photos of the chimney and furnace ruins at Clifton.

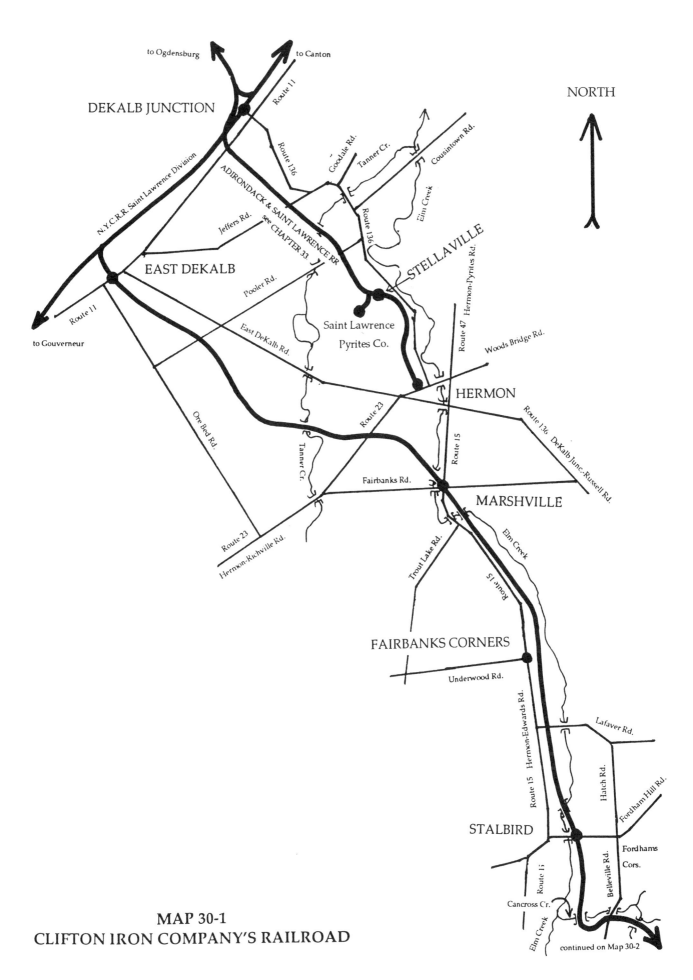

MAP 30-1
CLIFTON IRON COMPANY'S RAILROAD

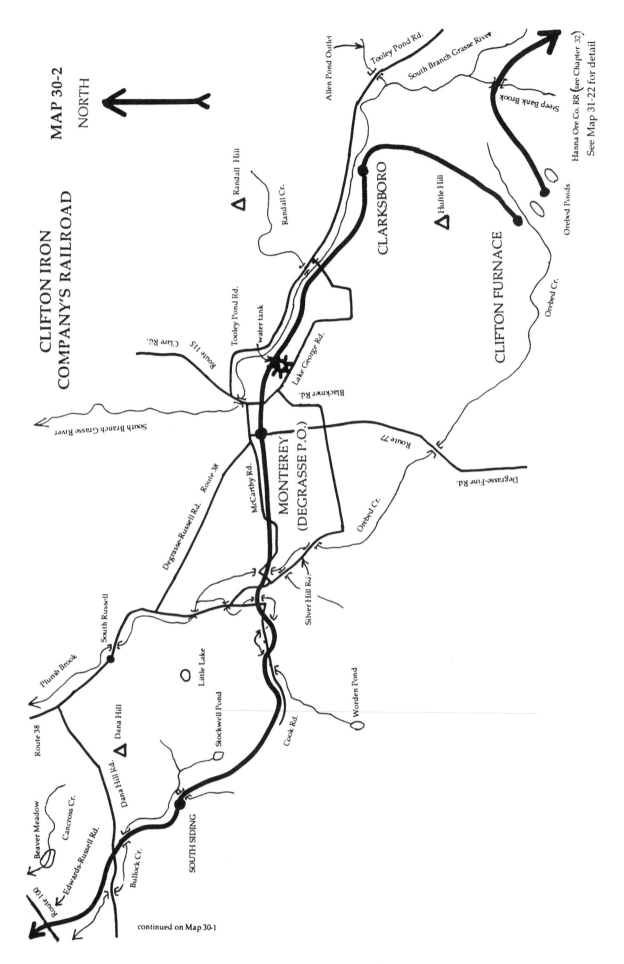

Chapter 31:
Carthage and Adirondack Railroad

THIS RAILROAD was built from the Rome, Watertown & Ogdensburg Railroad eastward into the Adirondacks, and was soon to become the Carthage & Adirondack Branch of the New York Central Railroad. The tenth *Annual Report of the New York State Board of Railroad Commissioners* (1893, page 152) states that the line was chartered March 28, 1883 and opened to Jayville on January 1, 1887. It was extended to Oswegatchie on February 1889 and to the Little River iron ore beds, later called Benson Mines, on August 22, 1889. In 1896, the line was continued to Newton Falls, then to Newbridge in 1902, and ultimately to Clifton Mines in 1941. The purpose was to transport wood products, pulp and paper, marble, talc, and iron ore out of the Adirondacks.

The mileposts for this line begin at Sackets Harbor on Lake Ontario, not Carthage; all mileages will be offered likewise in this chapter. Watertown is at milepost 12.01, and Carthage at 29.68. Mileages have been compiled from several employees' timetables over the years from 1906 through 1937. Mileage discrepancies which exist are probably due to several factors: Curves can be straightened and the mainline relocated, as at Benson Mines. Station buildings can be demolished and new ones erected at a different site. Sidings can be lengthened, shortened, and/or relocated.

Years of service for the stations, flagstops, and sidings are approximate because the author does not possess a complete set of timetables. The earliest available is 1901 and the latest 1957, with some 26 in between.

Passenger service was reduced from two trains to one each way daily between January 27, 1932 and January 2, 1933. By 1937, trains were mixed. Passenger service ceased between June 19, 1942 and April 19, 1944, although freight service continues twice weekly through the present. Conrail operated the line through April of 1991. On May 1, 1991 the new Mohawk & Adirondack Northern Railroad began operating the line. Only three industries are still served by the line: Slack Chemical Company just west of Wilna at about milepost 30.8; Clark Minerals talc mine at Rock, milepost about 41.1; and Newton Falls Paper Company at milepost 75.4.

An excursion on this line, sponsored by the Central New York Chapter of the National Railway Historical Society and the Mohawk, Adirondack & Northern Railroad on October 19, 1991, revealed to the writer that few sidings and switches remain. In addition to the industrial spurs mentioned above and the Carthage yard, there still exist the following: two stubs at Harrisville Station, milepost 50.3; a stub at Collins, milepost ca. 62.7 used occasionally for doubling a hill; the old spur into Benson Mines at milepost 72.2, now abandoned; and a passing siding-runaround at milepost 73.5 between Benson Mines and Newton Falls.

Sizeable villages were once at Kalurah, Jayville, and Aldrich, although in 1991 no obvious evidence remains of these industrial centers. Hunting and fishing camps are common between Bacon (Backus) and Oswegatchie today, but few year-round residences remain.

The trackage from Sackets Harbor to Watertown was abandoned in 1949. The trackage from Watertown directly to Carthage via Black River, Felts Mills, and Great Bend was abandoned between 1966 and 1970. Today, to reach Carthage Conrail trains must diverge from the Saint Lawrence Division main track at Philadelphia. They interchange with the Mohawk, Adirondack & Northern at

Carthage. The latter new railroad also serves Lowville, Beaver River, and Croghan.

An overview of the whole Carthage & Adirondack will be found on Map 31-1.

Station Descriptions

Carthage. 29.68 miles from Sackets Harbor. Elevation 742 feet. Maps 31-2 and 31-8.

The Carthage & Adirondack Railroad begins at this point on the former Rome, Watertown & Ogdensburg. The latter railroad was built through here in 1851. As of May 1, 1991 the interchange with Conrail, as mentioned above, is here with the Mohawk, Adirondack & Northern.

Passenger station: The building still exists, but it is used currently as freight offices. The last C&A passenger trains, as stated above, were between 1942 and 1944. In January 1961, the Lowville Village Board protested the discontinuation of the last passenger trains through their village (and, of course, Carthage); the protest was ignored because by 1962, New York Central timetables were no longer showing trains between Utica, Watertown and Ogdensburg over the old R.W.& O. Palmer and Roehl (1990, page 98) include a photo of the Carthage depot.

Passing sidings: Through trains to and from Sackets Harbor and Newton Falls met here in 1906, 1913, and 1923, necessitating at least one passing siding. Track #8 opposite the station held between 19 and 23 freight cars over the years 1911 through 1925. Track #14 held 19 cars in 1940.

Servicing facilities: A water tower was here from or before 1911 through 1948, but no longer in 1957. A 1920 employees' timetable mentions an ice house switch in Carthage.

Freight station: This building still stands in 1991.

Industrial sidings: One track still diverges westward into the James River Paper Mill, formerly Crown Zellerbach Corporation.

Branches: The former direct line from Sackets Harbor and Watertown, abandoned between 1966 and 1970, joined here.

Wilna. 30.85 miles. Elevation 742. Maps 31-2 and 31-8.

Passing siding: Wilna was never a passenger stop. It is already present on a 1906 employees' timetable, still present in 1925, but gone by 1930. The passing siding here accommodated between 24 and 28 freight cars over the years. Trains met here in 1913. Despite the fact that the passing siding has been gone for over half a century, a sign "Wilna" marking the spot still stands in 1991.

Industrial siding: In 1991, the Slack Chemical Company occasionally was serviced by freight cars on a spur located just west of Wilna.

Yard: The 1902 Carthage 15-minute quadrangle shows a small yard of 2 tracks midway between Carthage Station and Wilna with a spur to an industry along the Black River.

Rogers. 34.58 miles. Elevation 844. Map 31-2.

Passenger station: This flagstop first appears on a June 17, 1906 timetable; the January 26, 1903 timetable does not yet indicate it. Trains stopped here on January 28, 1940, but no longer on June 23, 1940. (This station should not be confused with another of the same name on the D&H Ausable Branch; see Chapter 19.)

Carter (Karter). 36.42 miles. Elevation 884. Map 31-2.

Passing siding: A passing siding existed here with a capacity of between 12 and 15 freight cars over the years. Trains met here in 1906. A 1925 employees' timetable still lists it, but a 1930 does no longer. This was never a passenger stop. On the June 17, 1906 timetable the name was Carter, but by August 6, 1911 it had become Karter or Karter Crossing. (This station should not be confused with Carter Station on the New York Central Adirondack Division, Chapter 36, Maps 36-5, 37-1, and 37-4.)

North Croghan. 37.23 miles. Elevation 880. Map 31-2.

Passenger station: This first appears as a flagstop on the June 17, 1906 timetable. Trains stopped here on January 28, 1940, but no longer on June 23, 1940.

Natural Bridge. 39.51 miles. Elevation 839. Maps 31-3 and 31-9.

Passenger station: A passenger station was located here from 1901 or earlier through at least June 23, 1940. It had closed by April 19, 1944. Palmer and Roehl (1990, page 98) include a photo of the Natural Bridge depot.

Passing siding: A passing siding was located here and is shown on the 1912 Lake Bonaparte 15-minute quadrangle on the south side of the main track. Its capacity varied from 8 to 21 cars depending on the year, from 1906 through 1940. The Natural Bridge 7.5-minute quadrangle, based on 1950 aerial photos, shows the siding as 0.3 mile long, but on the north side of the main.

Industry: An old milk depot still stands in 1994 south of the track and east of the Slye Road crossing. Worthington (1943) describes switching movements here.

Burnett. 40.05 miles. Elevation 825. Maps 31-3 and 31-10.

Industrial sidings: Burnett was never a passenger stop, nor was it listed as a passing siding. It was a junction with a spur, 3.5 miles long, which headed north to a quarry about 1.5 miles east-southeast of the hamlet of Lewisburg. The 1912 Lake Bonaparte 15-minute quadrangle shows the spur. The *Map of New York State Showing Mineral Occurrences* (1956), published also by the United States Geological Survey, reveals that the mineral quarried here was a dolomitic marble. Burnett is listed in the 1906 and 1913 employees' timetables but no longer in 1919.

The 1912 Bonaparte quadrangle also shows a half-mile-long spur paralleling the main track from Burnett eastward with a small stub. The industry served on this is unknown, but it could have been used for switching cars loaded with marble.

Rock. 41.14 miles. Elevation 857. Maps 31-3 and 31-10.

Passenger station: Rock first appears on the June 24, 1919 timetable as a flagstop; the November 30, 1913 timetable does not yet indicate it. Rock continued to be a flagstop through January 28, 1940, but trains no longer stopped here by June 23, 1940.

Industrial siding: The 1912 Lake Bonaparte quadrangle indicates a spur about 0.4-mile long diverging to the northwest into a quarry. The Map of New York State Showing Mineral Occurrences (1956) records that the mineral is talc. In 1992, the spur is still in use to serve the mills and office of the Diana Plant of Clark Minerals, Inc. Worthington (1943) describes switching movements here.

Diana. 42.80 or 42.81 miles. Elevation 829. Maps 31-3 and 31-11.

Passenger station: This was a flagstop during the early years, from June 25, 1901 through November 30, 1913, but no longer by September 28, 1919.

Passing siding: One existed here from 1906 through 1925, but is no longer shown in an employees' timetable of 1937. However, the 1950 Natural Bridge 7.5-minute quadrangle still shows it on the north side of the main track. The siding began at milepost ca. 42.68 and ended at ca. 43.00. It had a capacity of from 18 to 33 freight cars over the years.

Servicing facilities: A water tower was located here as early as 1911 and as late as 1948. It is still shown on the 1950 Natural Bridge 7.5 minute quadrangle at milepost 42.80 or 42.81.

Fitzgerald. 43.91, 43.92, or 44.03 miles. Elevation 820. Map 31-3.

Passenger station: This first appears on the June 17, 1906 timetable as a flagstop; the January 26, 1903 timetable does not yet show it. Fitzgerald continued to be a flagstop through January 28, 1940, but trains no longer stopped here by June 23, 1940.

Miscellany: The 1912 Lake Bonaparte quadrangle shows a short stub of unknown function from a switch at milepost ca. 43.91 to its end at ca. 44.01. At 44.03 was a road which led to Highway 3.

South Bonaparte. 46.64 miles. Elevation 770. Map 31-3.

This is listed from June 28, 1931 through January 24, 1937 on employees' timetables as a flagstop. It was not yet in existence on November 1, 1925 and was no longer listed on June 27, 1937.

Lake Bonaparte. 47.41 or 47.43 miles. Elevation 770. Map 31-3.

Passenger station: This was a flagstop by June 25, 1901, and continued to be so through 1903. It was a station from 1906 through 1925. By 1930 it had become a flagstop again, continuing as such through June 23, 1940 and possibly a little later. Lake Bonaparte was named after Napoleon Bonaparte's brother, Joseph, who had an estate here.

Harrisville. 50.30 miles. Elevation 809. Maps 31-4 and 31-12.

Passenger station: This was a station by June 25, 1901 through June 23, 1940 and probably a little later. The building still stands in 1994.

Passing sidings: In 1906 and in 1913, the eastbound and westbound freights met here in late morning. The passing siding held from 17 to 53 cars depending on the year between 1911 and 1948. The 1912 and 1950 topographic quadrangles suggest the track plan reproduced here as Map 31-12. In 1948, only one passing siding outside Carthage was listed on the employees' timetables, and that was at Harrisville. By 1957, the Harrisville passing siding was no longer listed. In 1991, only two dead-end stubs remain. A 1920 employee's timetable mentions the first and sixth switches in the Harrisville yard, suggesting a more complex track plan. Worthington (1943) describes switching at Harrisville.

Industrial sidings: Two longer industrial spurs headed down to the West Branch Oswegatchie River. According to a mural painted on the outside of the Harrisville Library, the Diana Paper Company Mill was established in 1907 and later sold to the Saint Regis Paper Company. The mill, located just downstream from the railroad trestle, operated through the 1950s. The 0.45-mile-long spur diverged from the C&A immediately west of the State Highway 3 overpass. The 1912 Lake Bonaparte quadrangle shows the second spur diverging from the west end of the Harrisville yard and heading south for about 1.2 miles to the river; here, International Paper Company had a mill.

Photograph: One appears in Gardner (1975, page 29) showing a mail train near Harrisville on April 6, 1907. The train consists of one 4-4-0 locomotive with tender, two mail cars and three coaches.

Bacon (Backus). 52.84 or 52.85 miles. Elevation 894. Maps 31-4 and 31-13.

Passenger station: This was a flagstop by June 25, 1901. It continued to be so through January 28, 1940, but trains were no longer stopping here on June 23, 1940. The name was changed from Bacon to Backus between 1916 and 1919: a New York Central 1916 map of the Adirondacks still shows Bacon while the June 24, 1919 timetable lists Backus. The Bacon station, a small enclosed waiting shelter, sits in 1993 in the back yard of a private residence in Harrisville.

Siding: A stub shows on the 1912 Lake Bonaparte quadrangle east of the highway crossing and north of the main track. New York Central Valuation Section blueprint #V97, updated to 1955, shows a very wide, 150-foot, right-of-way west of the crossing, where the waiting shelter stood. Typically the right-of-way was 80 feet wide.

Kalurah. 56.71 or 56.85 miles. Elevation 1080. Maps 31-4 and 31-13.

Passenger station: Initially Kalurah was called Little Mill. The January 26, 1903 timetable does not yet list Kalurah, while the June 17, 1906 one lists it as a flagstop. It continued to be one through 1940 and perhaps a little later.

Passing siding: An article (not dated but published shortly prior to 1964) in the Syracuse *Post Standard* mentions a passing siding here with a capacity of 20 cars. This siding was used to cut off cars if there were difficulty ascending the hill ahead up to Jayville and Briggs. I have not yet found an employee's timetable which lists this siding. The average speed of ore trains on the C&A at this time, early 1960s, was 20 miles per hour.

Servicing facilities: From 1923 through 1948, a water station was located at about milepost 55.75 or 55.8. It replaced the water station at Jayville which operated during the period 1911-1920. The dam on Gulf Stream with a pipe leading out of it near milepost 56.50 still existed in 1993; it had supplied the water station about a three-quarters of a mile to the west.

Grade crossings: The public highway now known as Jayville Road crosses the C&A at four localities in the Kalurah area. The New York Central valuation diagrams updated to 1955 list four different older highway names as follows: Millers Road at milepost 52.85, Hayes Falls Road at 55.54, Shingle (or Single) Shanty Road at 56.86, and Little Long Lake Road at 57.16.

Mecca Lumber Company Railroad: See Chapter 32.

Jayville. 58.48 miles. Elevation 1121. Maps 31-4 and 31-13.

Passenger station: Jayville was the temporary terminus for the railroad from 1887 to 1889 when it was extended to Oswegatchie. It was a station stop probably from this period through 1920. From 1923 through January 28, 1940 it was reduced to a flagstop. Trains were no longer stopping here by June 23, 1940.

Passing siding: The passing siding held between 11 and 13 cars during the period 1911 to 1925. Trains passed here in 1913.

Servicing facilities: From 1911 through 1920 a water station was located here, but was moved to milepost 55.75 or 55.8 west of Kalurah by 1923.

Industrial sidings: A spur 0.3 mile long is shown on the 1915 Oswegatchie quadrangle headed north. A New York Central valuation diagram, updated through 1955, still shows the then-abandoned spur, about 2500 feet long and owned by the Magnetic Iron Ore Company. Cecil Graham, a railroad historian from Gouverneur, had lectured at the Saint Lawrence County Historical Association in Canton in October 1988 that it was this iron mine which brought the railroad to Jayville initially. He said that the mine closed about 1919 or 1920; this coincides with the time that the water station was moved and the passenger station became a flagstop.

Palmer (March 1970) states that Post & Henderson opened a sawmill here in the early 1890s.

Bear Lake. 61.00 miles. Elevation 1320. Map 31-4.

This was a flagstop on the November 5, 1905 timetable. The January 26, 1903 and June 17, 1906 timetables do not list it.

Briggs. 62.31 or 62.32 miles. Elevation 1411. Maps 31-5 and 31-14.

Passenger station: Trains were not yet stopping here by January 26, 1903, but the June 17, 1906 timetable lists it as a flagstop. It remained in service through at least June 23, 1940. Reynolds et al. (1976, p.68) have some detail on this station.

Passing siding: The 1915 Oswegatchie quadrangle indicates a passing siding 0.1 mile long here, although the employees' timetables list the siding at Collins, 0.3 mile further east.

Steep grade: Note the ascent from Jayville.

Collins. 62.62 miles. Elevation ca. 1423. Maps 31-5 and 31-15.

Passing siding: Collins was never a passenger stop. It is first listed on a 1911 employees' timetable as a passing siding. The capacity ranged from 11 to 16 freight cars during the period through 1930. In 1991, a dead-end stub was used to lay up cars if doubling the hill were necessary.

Vaughns. 63.66 miles. Elevation 1407. Map 31-5.

This was never a flagstop or a passing siding. It appears only on a 1906 employees' timetable without further detail.

Aldrich. 64.72 or 64.76 miles. Elevation 1333. Maps 31-5 and 31-16.

Passenger station: Aldrich does not yet appear on the January 26, 1903 timetable, but is present by June 17, 1906 timetable as a flagstop. During the period 1911 to 1925, it was a station stop. From 1930 through 1940, it was used again only a flagstop. Trains were still stopping here on June 23, 1940 and probably for a short while longer.

Newton Falls Paper Company Railroad: See Chapter 32.

Reference: Reynolds et al. (1976, p. 68) have some detail on Aldrich.

Coffins Mills. 66.98 miles. Elevation 1366. Maps 31-5 and 31-16.

Passenger station: This was already a flagstop on June 25, 1901 and continued to be through at least June 23, 1940.

Industrial siding: Reynolds et al. (1976, p. 94) list W.S. Coffin's sawmill and butter tub factory, but I have no evidence indicating if or where a siding existed.

Oswegatchie. 68.19 miles. Elevation 1372. Maps 31-5 and 31-16.

Passenger station: Oswegatchie was already a station stop on June 25, 1901, and continued to be through at least June 23, 1940.

Passing siding: One on the north side held between 10 and 15 cars between 1913 and 1940. The siding is shown on the 1915 Oswegatchie quadrangle as 0.25 mile long. It is still present on New York Central Valuation Section blueprint #V97 updated to 1955. By 1991 it had been long abandoned, but evidence of its location was still strong on the ground.

Anderson. 69.57 or 69.58 miles. Elevation 1368 at the east end. Maps 31-5 and 31-17.

Passing siding: The 1915 Oswegatchie quadrangle shows a passing siding 0.25 mile long on the north. It is listed on 1906 through 1913 employees' timetables, but no clue to a passing siding is given. By 1919 it is no longer listed. No passenger station or flagstop existed here.

Benson Mines. 72.15 or 72.16 miles. Elevation 1416. Maps 31-6, 31-18, 31-19, and 31-20.

The history of Benson Mines has been a most difficult one to unravel. A major relocation of the mainline in 1942-1944 because of the expansion of the quarry had repercussions on the whole area: the station, the Little River, the hamlet, and the highways. The only way to understand well the changes is to compare very carefully the old and the new maps. Map 31-18 summarizes the trackage in the last decade of the 19th century. Map 31-19, continued on Map 31-20, shows the trackage after the 1940s relocation. Maps 31-19 and 31-20 show the location of the railroad, station, and highways in the 19th century as dashed lines for the clearest comparison. The old concentrating plant and associated buildings with trackage shown on Map 31-19 as fine dashed lines are now all under water in a flooded mine pit.

Passenger station: The station was present for the whole life of passenger service from 1889 through about 1942. The relocation came at about the same time of the cessation of passenger service. After the station was moved, it served freight crews only. New York Central Valuation Section blueprint #V97, updated to 1955, still shows the new station. The original location of the station was at 72.15 or 72.16 miles from Sackets Harbor, and the new location at 71.53 miles. Photos of the old depot are in Reynolds et al. (1976, pp. 41 and 79). Palmer (March 1970) also includes one.

Passing siding: Timetables show that trains met at Benson Mines in 1906.

Servicing facilities: A water facility was here from before or in 1911 through 1957.

Industrial sidings: The operation of Benson Mines is described in Hyde (1974 with a photo on page 177) and by Reynolds et al. (1976, pp. 79-84 and 107 with several photos). Kenneth Campbell, a former railroad historian of the Town of Fine, had given me several clippings from the Watertown *Daily Times* and the Syracuse *Post Standard* on the ore trains operating out of the Jones & Laughlin Steel Corporation's quarries here. Unfortunately, most of the clippings are not dated, but probably are from the late 1950s and early 1960s. In one clipping, four Alco locomotives, FA and FB diesel units, are pictured; one FA is numbered 1038. The train left Watertown at 4 A.M. and arrived at Benson Mines later that morning with a string of empty hopper cars. The locomotives quickly uncoupled from the empties and coupled on to a waiting train of hoppers containing sintered iron ore; the waiting loaded cars had been assembled by a mine switch engine. Within a half hour the train (one photo showing 65 hoppers) was on its way back to Watertown where it arrived shortly after noon. Another clipping describes some of these cars derailing at Dunkirk, New York, on February 22, 1954 on route to Pittsburgh, Cleveland, and Alquippa, PA. Moravek (1981) notes that the mine was shut down in 1977 by Jones & Laughlin.

This writer noted an industrial switcher at the mines on May 17, 1968, but no detail on the locomotive was recorded except that its number was 7.

Post & Henderson Company Railroad: See Chapter 32.

Cranberry Lake Railroad: At Benson Mines was the connection with the Cranberry Lake Railroad (see Chapter 32).

Reference: A "Perspective drawing showing arrangement of plant at Benson Mines" was published in *Mining and Metallurgy* magazine, November 1943, page 524. The drawing shows trackage and identifies all the buildings.

Miscellany: Benson Mines was originally named Little River Iron Ore Beds.

Newton Falls. 75.43 or 75.44 miles. Elevation 1383. Maps 31-7 and 31-21.

A Saint Lawrence County map, dated 1896-1897 and formerly owned by Kenneth Campbell, shows the railroad already extended to Newton Falls. An 1895 New York Central map, appearing on page 55 of Harter (1979) does not yet show it; hence the line must have opened to Newton Falls in 1896 or early 1897.

Passenger station: Newton Falls was a station already by June 25, 1901, and continued to be through at least June 19, 1942. By April 19, 1944, passenger trains were no longer running. Reynolds et al. (1976, p. 41) include a photo of the depot.

Passing siding and wye: There was a passing siding, named Ball Park Siding, between mileposts 74.16 and 74.43, although trains were turned on the wye adjacent to the depot.

Industrial sidings: Here was and is the Newton Falls Paper Mill. On September 15, 1985, the caretaker at the mill informed me that Conrail trains at that time were running on Tuesdays, Thursdays, and Saturdays——a schedule which was continued until Conrail turned service over to the new Mohawk, Adirondack & Northern Railroad on May 1, 1991. Initially, M. A. & N. trains ran on Mondays, Wednesdays, and Fridays, although in 1994 it was twice weekly. Map 31-21, showing detail on Newton Falls, is a combination of information taken from New York Central Valuation Section blueprint #V97 updated to 1955, and the author's field notes made in 1985 and in 1990. Reynolds et al. (1976) has information on the paper mill on pages 98-102 and 105, with photos of the mill on pages 66 and 101. A 1948 employees' timetable lists McGraw-Hill Publication Company and Chilton Company sidings at Newton Falls.

Newton Falls & Northern Railroad: See Chapter 32.

Hanna Ore Company Railroad: See Chapter 32.

References

No single major publication has been found to date on the Carthage & Adirondack. Several short articles do exist, however, some of which have been cited in the text above: Worthington (1943), Berry (1958), Barnes (1962), Graham (1966), Palmer (March 1970), Hyde (1974), and Reynolds et al. (1976).

This old coach served as crew quarters at Benson Mines.
Author photo, May 1991.

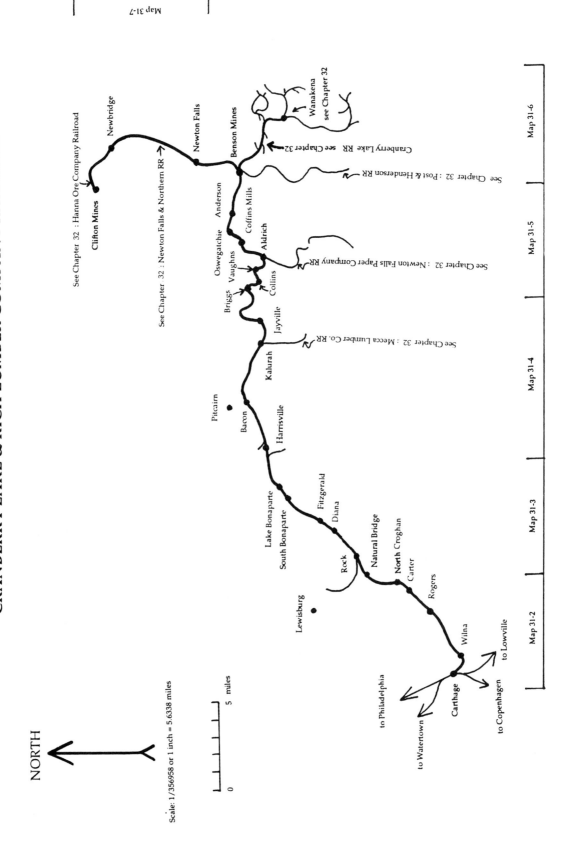

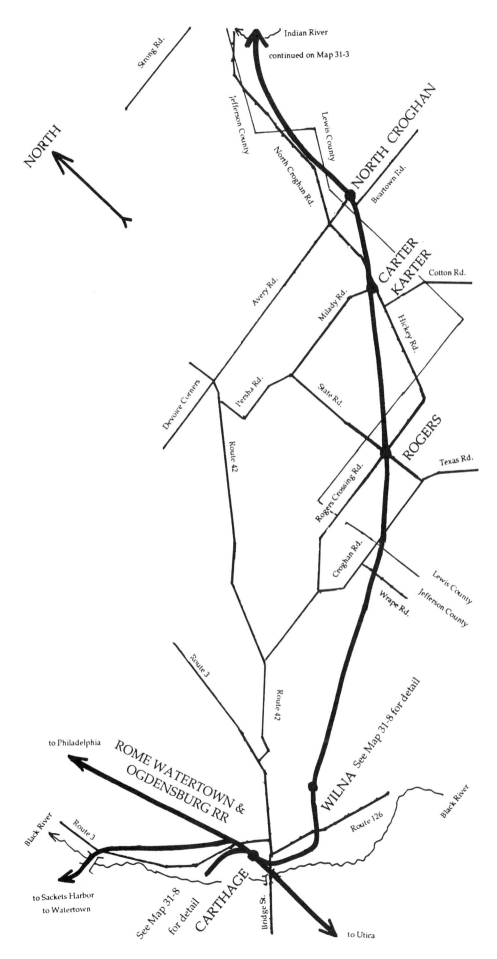

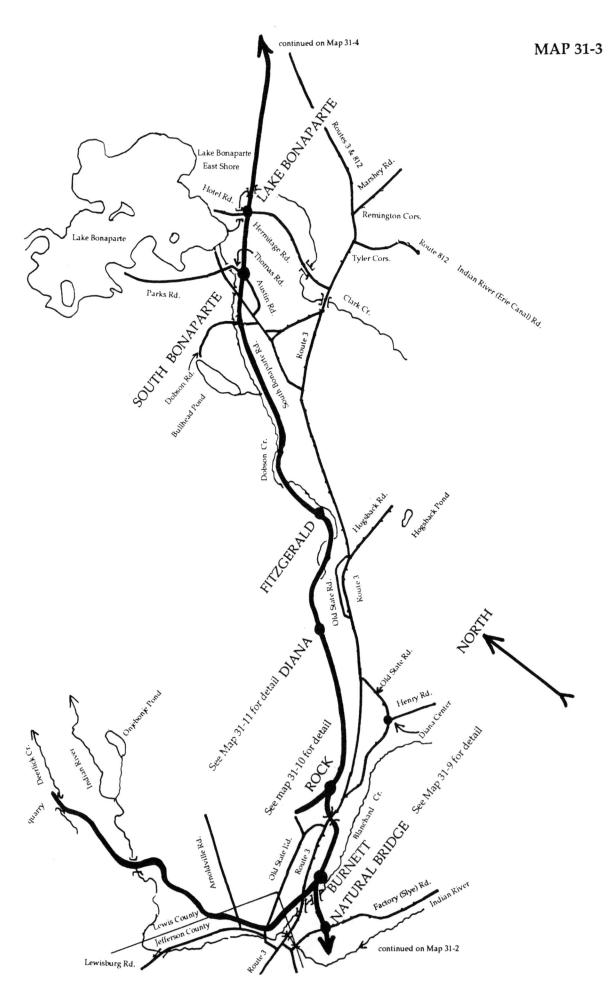

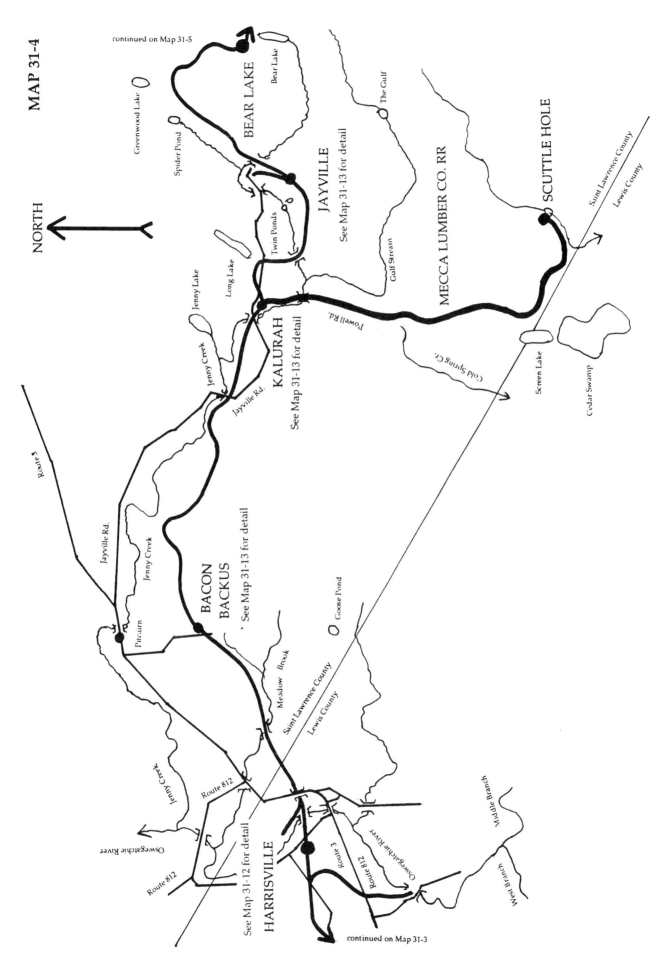

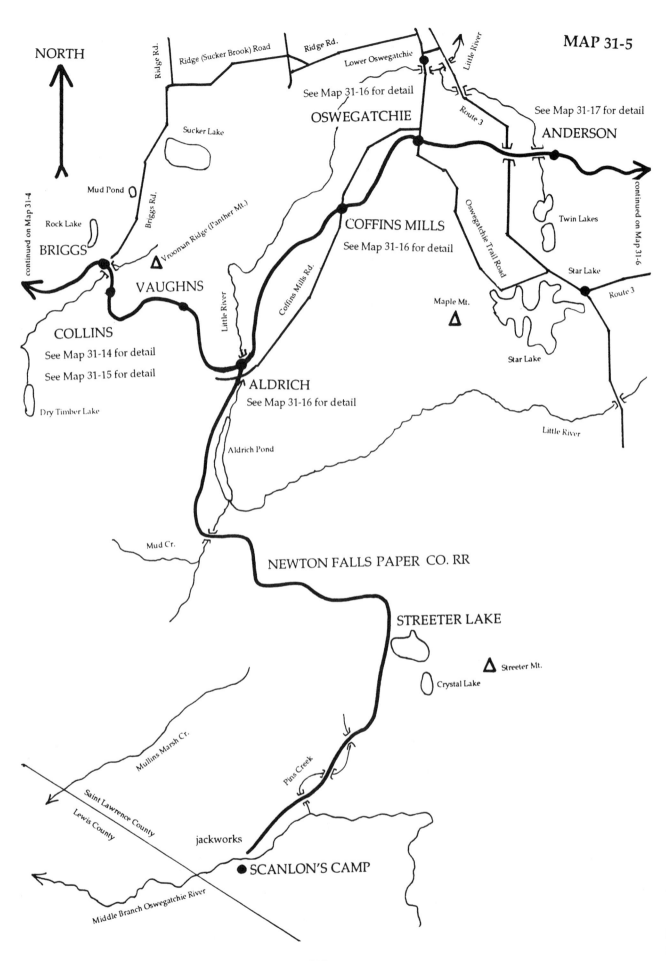

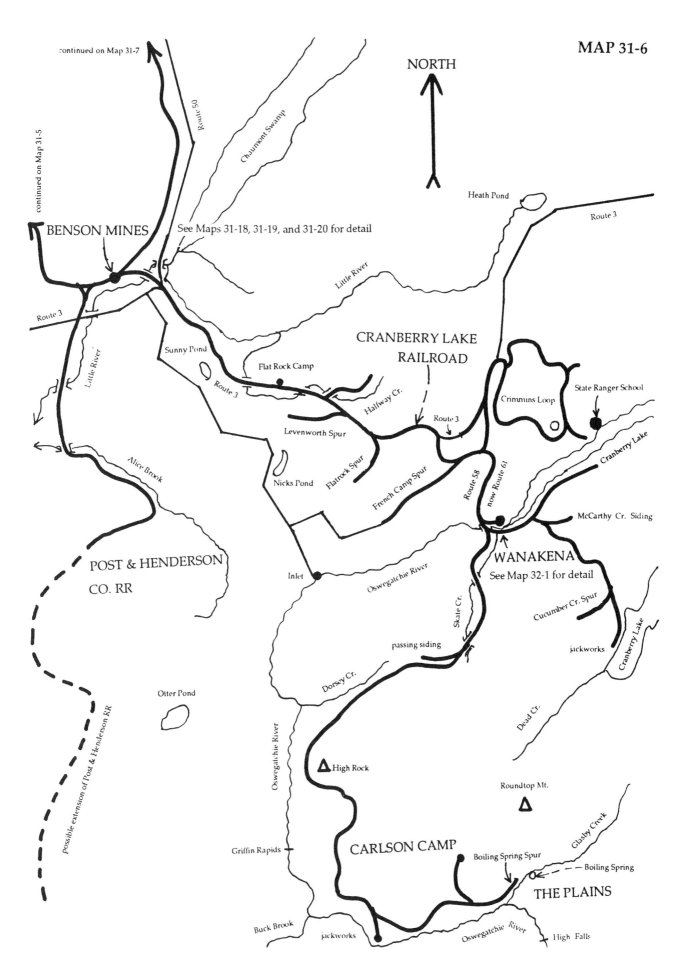
MAP 31-6

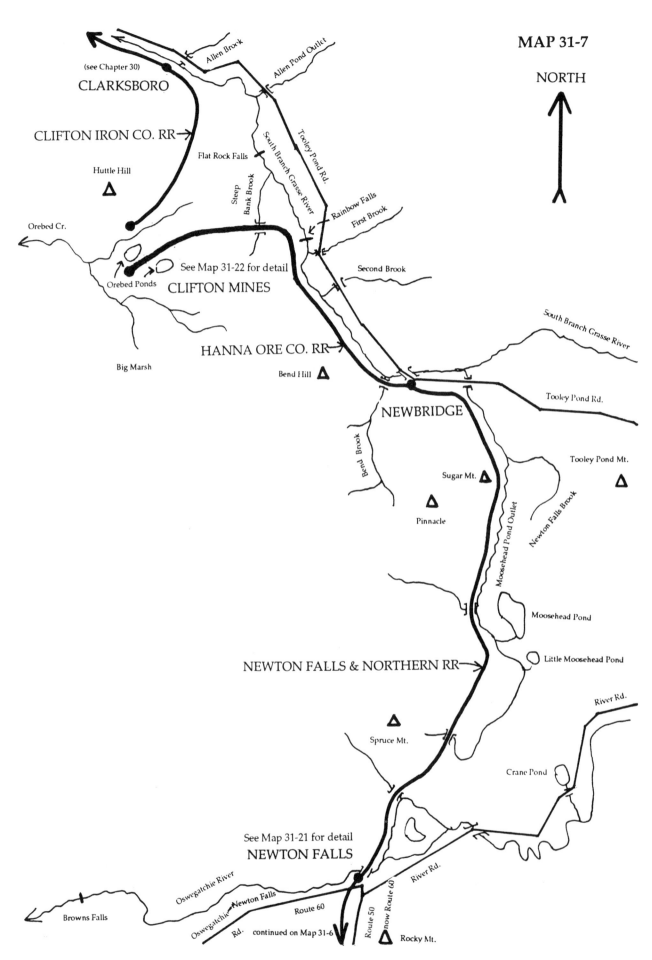

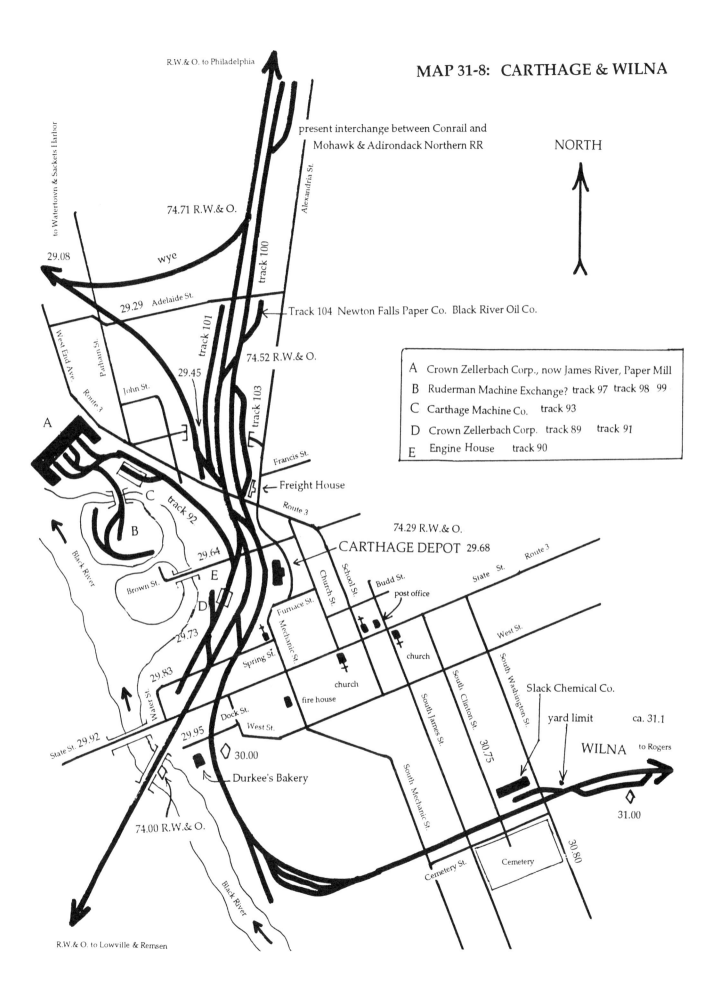

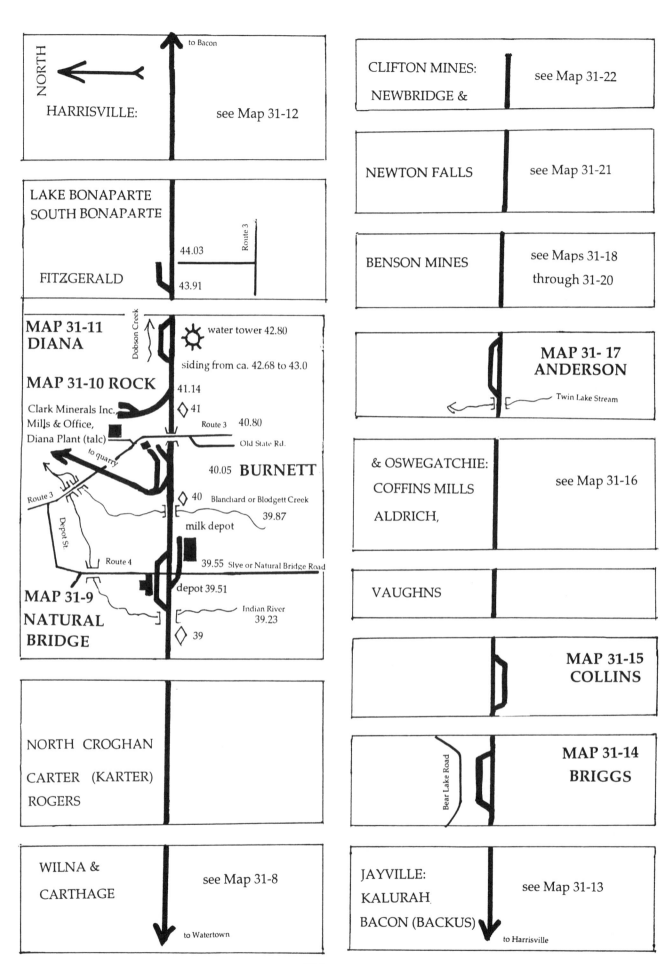

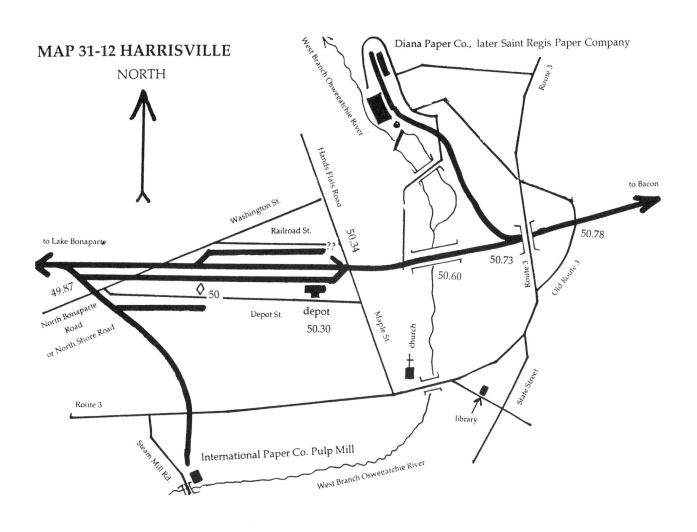

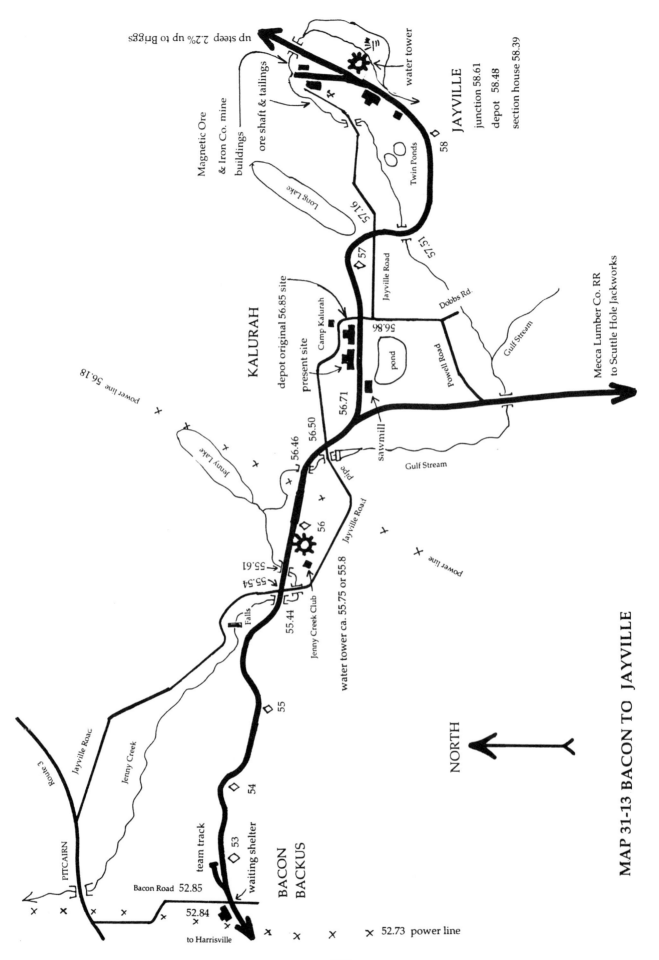

MAP 31-13 BACON TO JAYVILLE

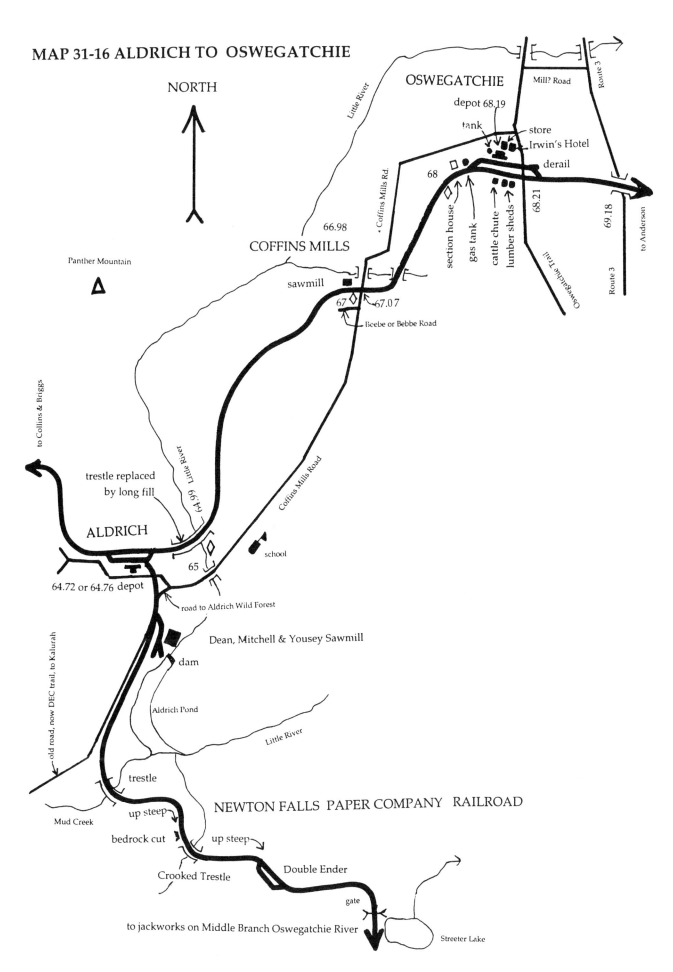

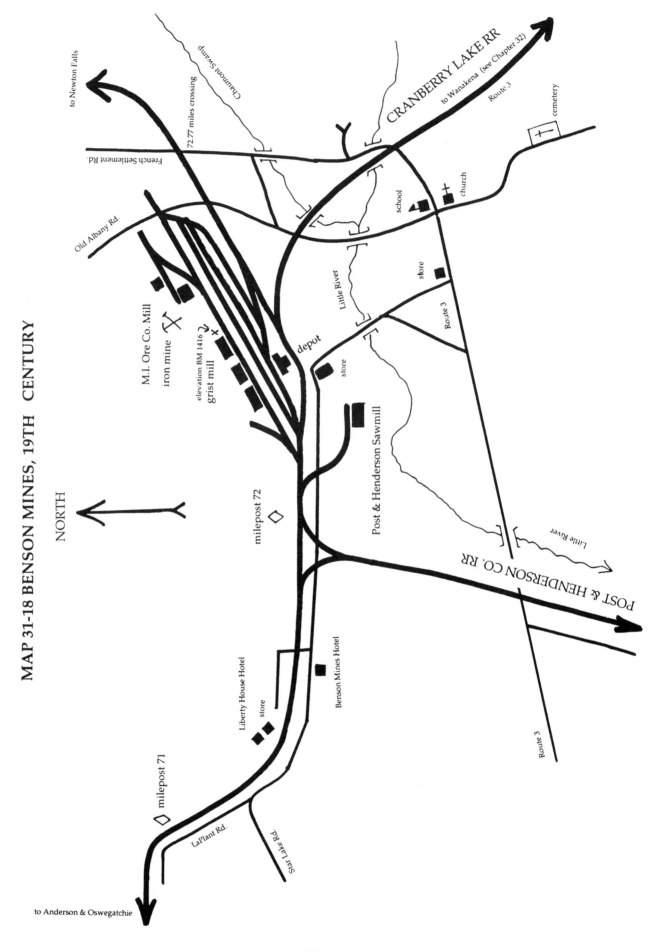

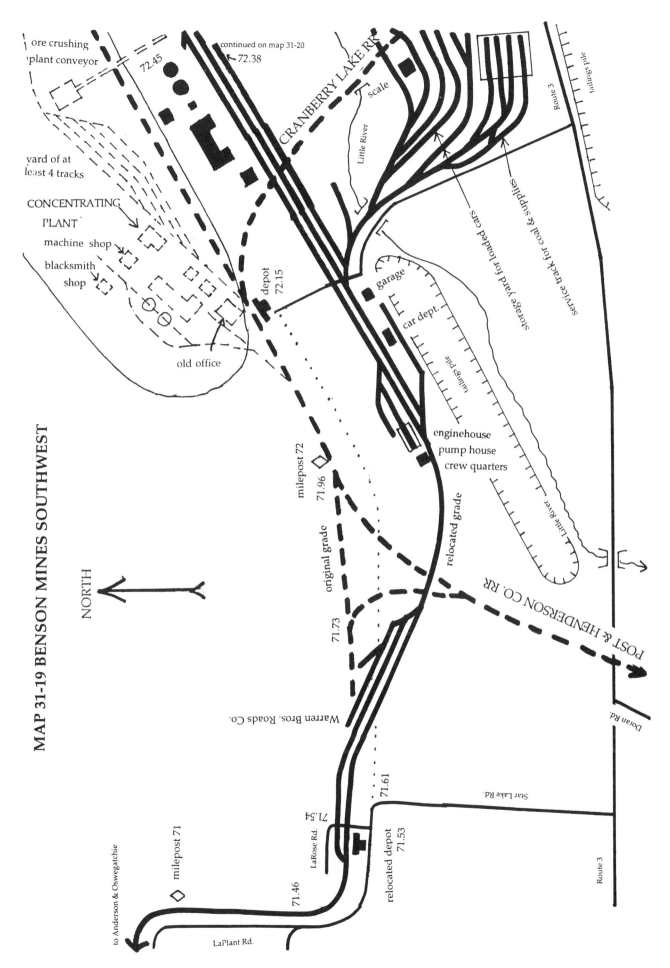

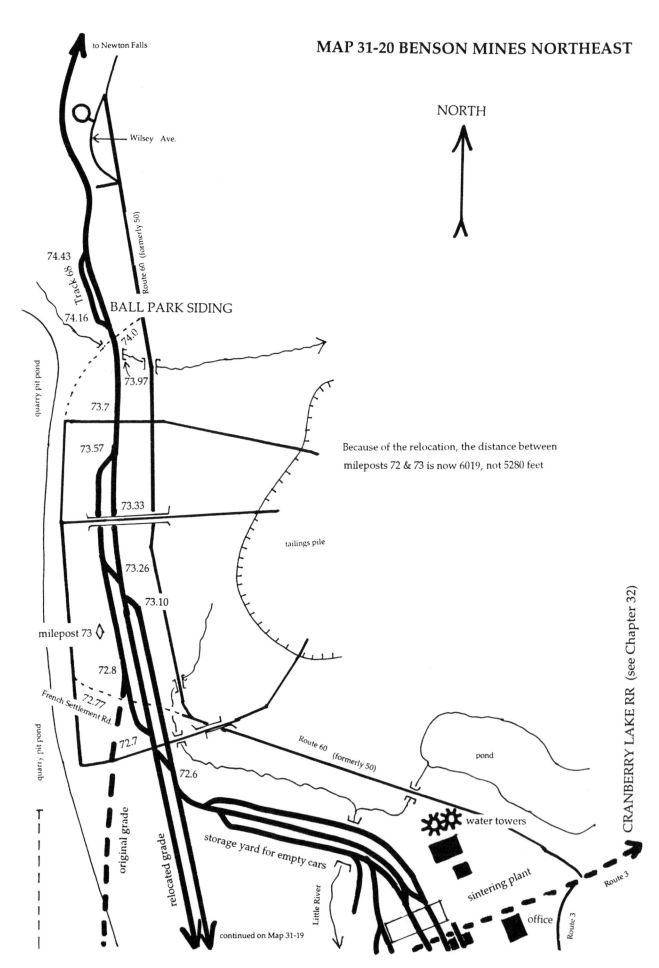

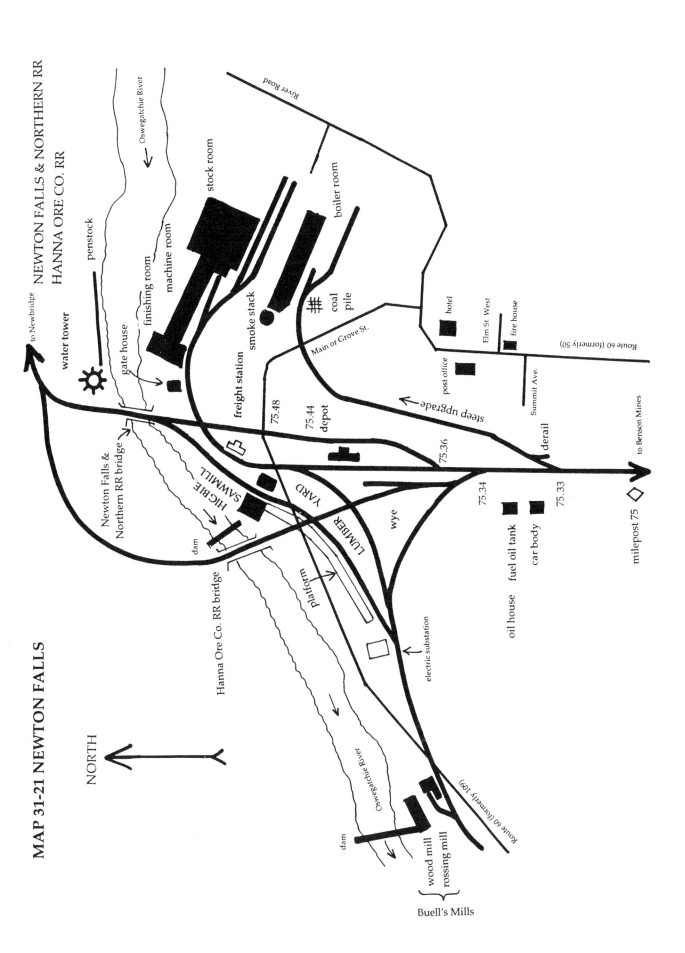

MAP 31-21 NEWTON FALLS

NEWTON FALLS & NORTHERN RR
HANNA ORE CO. RR

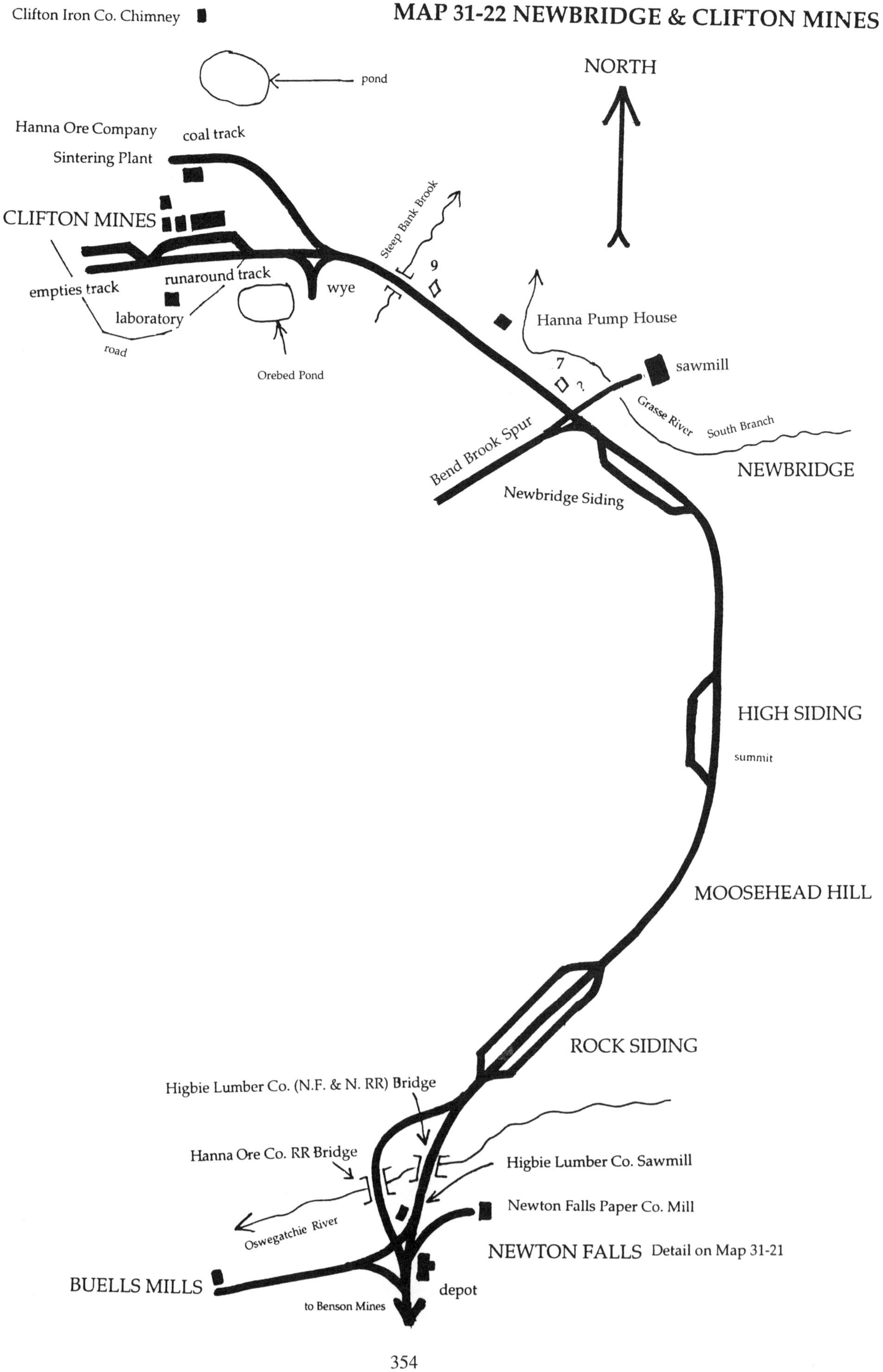

MAP 31-22 NEWBRIDGE & CLIFTON MINES

- Clifton Iron Co. Chimney
- pond
- Hanna Ore Company Sintering Plant
- coal track
- NORTH
- CLIFTON MINES
- Steep Bank Brook
- empties track
- runaround track
- wye
- 9
- laboratory
- road
- Orebed Pond
- Hanna Pump House
- 7 ?
- sawmill
- Bend Brook Spur
- Grasse River South Branch
- Newbridge Siding
- NEWBRIDGE
- HIGH SIDING
- summit
- MOOSEHEAD HILL
- ROCK SIDING
- Higbie Lumber Co. (N.F. & N. RR) Bridge
- Hanna Ore Co. RR Bridge
- Higbie Lumber Co. Sawmill
- Newton Falls Paper Co. Mill
- Oswegatchie River
- NEWTON FALLS Detail on Map 31-21
- BUELLS MILLS
- depot
- to Benson Mines

354

Chapter 32:
Six Short Railroads Connecting with the Carthage and Adirondack

THE PRIMARY PUBLISHED SOURCE on these short lines is Gove (1973) who offers great detail, photos, and a superb map showing locations of most of the logging spurs. Palmer also has notes at The Adirondack Museum on these railroads. Reynolds et al. (1976) include some information and photos on pages 67 and 103. To further reduce the length of Chapter 31, six of the shorter branch lines diverging from the Carthage & Adirondack Railroad have been combined in to this single chapter. (The reader will find less interruption in the trend of thought following the Carthage & Adirondack because of the elimination of these six shorter side trips.)

Cranberry Lake and Rich Lumber Company Railroads: Maps 31-6 and 32-1

The Cranberry Lake Railroad was chartered on February 24, 1902 and opened officially on May 18, 1903. Six miles of common carrier railroad (including passenger and freight service) between Benson Mines and Wanakena, plus about fifteen miles of Rich Lumber Company logging trackage were built. Benson Mines station became a union station, shared jointly by the Cranberry Lake and the Carthage & Adirondack Railroads (photo, Gove 1973, p. 25) where connections were made.

Passenger service was provided by a 2-8-0 locomotive, a combine, and a coach, making two round trips daily on June 23, 1912 according to a New York Central System timetable, pages 11 and 12. Photos of the passenger train appear in Gove on pp. 25 and 29, the latter at Wanakena. Gove (p. 17) also provides a photo of the locomotive shops. Palmer and Roehl (1990, page 95) also offer a photograph.

Several mills were built at Wanakena as soon as the railroad arrived in 1903, but all were short-lived. The last to cease functioning was the Shoe Last Factory which burned on February 12, 1912 (Gove, 1973, p. 20). By carefully examining the photos in Gove (pp. 20 through 22), in Keith (1972, pp. 11 and 80), and in Reynolds et al. (1976, p. 103), I was able to reconstruct the mill detail presented in this book on Map 32-1. Because the photos do not show all track stubs into the mills, the track plan here is probably incomplete.

Gove's (p. 23) map is the most informative in locating the logging spur grades of the Rich Lumber Company, but some spurs are omitted probably because not all spurs were in service simultaneously. Spurs not shown by Gove are presented in three other sources: (1) On exhibit at the Logging Building at The Adirondack Museum is a *Map of 1800 Original Acres New York State Ranger School* by F. R. Wilcox, dated November 22, 1922 showing a spur following up Halfway Creek for a distance of perhaps 0.67 mile. (2) The 1909 Adirondack Land Map published by the New York State Forest Fish and Game Commission indicates a spur following along the southeast bank of the Oswegatchie River downstream to about the Clifton-Fine Town Line. This spur, about one mile long, terminated almost directly across the River from the State Ranger School. It is also shown in the 1912 *New York State Atlas* published by the New Century Company. (3) Keith (1972, p. 5) includes a map which shows several additional spurs absent on Gove's map: Levenworth Spur, Flatrock Spur, French Camp Spur, a complete loop from Crimmins Switch, McCarthy Creek Siding, Cucumber Creek Spur, a passing siding at the head of Skate Creek, and a spur part way to High Falls.

Much of the present State Highway 3 follows the old Cranberry Lake Railroad grade in the Town of Fine. I had surmised this for years, and finally set out to prove it. I compared two *Adirondack Land Maps*, the 1909 and the 1938 (the latter published by the New York State Conservation Department). On this, State Highway 3 is in precisely the same location as the railroad was in 1909.

As one travels east along State Route 3 today, one sees that the old Cranberry Lake Railroad grade diverges from the highway almost exactly one mile by air northwest of the Wanakena depot site. The railroad grade strikes south to cross the Hayes Creek trestle, but the highway continues east for a distance of 0.2 mile, not following any railroad grade. Then, shortly, the highway is again built upon an old grade, but this time a spur of the Rich Lumber Company. In another 0.2 mile, the present highway intersection with County Route 61 into Wanakena is reached.

The Rich Lumber Company was served by Shay locomotives, #2 and #4, a Barnhardt log loader, twenty flat cars, 27 log cars, speeders, and fire-fighting cars stationed at the engine house in Wanakena (Gove, 1973, p. 24). Photos of the Shays appear in Gove (pp. 14, 16, and 17), in Reynolds et al. (pp. 68 and 103), and in Koch (1979, page 130). The Barnhardt log loader is shown in Gove on p. 17 and in Reynolds et al. on p. 68. The "speeder" is not the typical small hand-pumped car, but a converted highway bus with an open canopy over the seats.

Because of the depletion of much merchantable timber, and the forest fires of 1908, the Cranberry Lake and Rich Lumber Company Railroads ran only until 1914. The rails were removed in 1917. The New York Central timetable of November 16, 1913 still shows passenger service from Benson Mines to Wanakena. The Cranberry Lake 15-minute quadrangle, surveyed from 1916 to 1919, does not show the line.

Mecca Lumber Company Railroad at Kalurah: Maps 31-4 and 31-13.

Palmer (March 1970) describes the Mecca Lumber Company, organized by Nellis, Amos, and Swift in 1903. A logging railroad six to eight miles long was built from Kalurah south to a jackworks at the Scuttle Hole where operations continued to about 1910. I have traced the right-of-way on the aerial photos at the New York State Office of Equalization and Assessment because no map shows the Mecca spur. The present Powell Road apparently follows much of this spur (see Map 31-4).

The junction with the C&A was at about milepost 56.71 with the Mecca sawmill at the edge of a pond just to the East (see Map 31-13).

Newton Falls Paper Company Railroad at Aldrich: Maps 31-5 and 31-16.

A photo of a mill at Aldrich appears in Palmer (March 1970) with the caption "Aldrich, a few miles west of Star Lake, was a busy place on the C&A branch of the New York Central Railroad. Prior to World War I, the Newton Falls Paper Company operated a logging railroad from there to Streeter Lake."

A pulp mill existed at Aldrich adjacent to the sawmill of Dean, Mitchell, and Yousey. I am not certain of the owner of this pulp mill. The Newton Falls Paper Company mill is still at Newton Falls (see Chapter 31).

The Newton Falls Paper Company Railroad appears on the 1915 Oswegatchie Quadrangle. The ca. 7.6-mile-long spur passes Streeter Lake and terminates across the Middle Branch Oswegatchie River from Scanlon's Camp about a half-mile short of the Saint Lawrence-Herkimer County line.

Charles Kellogg of Adams Center, New York, writes me that his father, William N. Kellogg, surveyed the route for the Newton Falls Paper Company, completing the project about 1915. Berry (1958) describes the donation by Charles Kellogg to The Adirondack Museum of photographs taken by his father. Four of these photos show the construction out of Aldrich in 1915.

The New York State Department of Transportation's *Inventory* (1974) in error attributes this spur to the International Hydro Electric Corporation. However, the year of abandonment and track removal, recorded as 1922, seems correct.

Presently, mileage along this old railroad, now an unpaved road, is as follows: 0.0 junction with C&A at Aldrich, 1.5 hiking trail to Kalurah, 4.4 gate on road near Streeter Lake, 7.6 jackworks site at end of line.

Post & Henderson Company Railroad at Benson Mines: Maps 31-6, 31-18, and 31-19.

In addition to the iron mines, Palmer (March 1970) notes that there was significant lumbering activity at Benson Mines, supporting this fact with a photo. Post & Henderson, who earlier operated a sawmill at Jayville, established operations in the Benson mines area with headquarters and a second sawmill. About 1905 they built a logging railroad south out of Benson Mines. Examination of the 1915 Oswegatchie Quadrangle reveals a wye here which looks as if it were originally used to turn steam locomotives, but is far too long, about 0.4 mile, to have done so. I believe that this wye is the remaining stub of the Post & Henderson Railroad. Russell McKittrick of the New York State Office of Equalization and Assessment found a part of the old grade with ties still in place along Alice Brook. I have traced the line as best as possible on Map 31-6.

Newton Falls & Northern Railroad at Newton Falls. Maps 31-7, 31-21, and 31-22.

Palmer (March 1970) informs us that the Robert W. Higbie Lumber Company formed the Newton Falls & Northern Railroad on June 24, 1908 and built a line about seven miles long to Newbridge, located about 82.4 miles from Sackets Harbor. It ran until November 14, 1919 when the company dissolved and the rails were removed. The right-of-way of this line, but oddly not the track, is shown on the 1915 Oswegatchie Quadrangle and on the 1920 Stark Quadrangle as a trail with railroad survey benchmarks: 1443, 1458, 1354, and at Newbridge, 1237 feet elevation, respectively.

A photo on the cover of *Northern Logger* magazine March 1970, shows Higbie Lumber Company Climax locomotive #1 pulling a lumber train out of the sawmill at Newton Falls. This photo is reproduced again in Angus (1991, page 11) and in Koch (1979, page 140). The original photo in the archives of the Saint Lawrence County Historical Association in Canton shows two tracks crossing left of the train, a feature cropped in the two published pictures; the crossing is shown on Map 31-21.

Angus (1991) briefly describes the large mill which made broom handles and other buildings at Newbridge.

There are unconfirmed reports that the Newton Falls & Northern had a number of spurs in the Newbridge area. One report which seems reliable is that a spur headed up Bend Brook for several miles in a southwesterly direction. Another is a spur which followed the South Branch Grasse River downstream for a distance part way to Clifton Mines; if the latter spur did exist, then the Hanna Ore Company in 1941 did not need to build a full three-plus miles of new grade by using the old logging spur.

Hanna Ore Company Railroad: Maps 31-7, 31-21, and 31-22.

Palmer (March 1970) comes to the rescue here in unraveling a complicated sequence of events. The Hanna Ore Company relaid track on the old Newton Falls & Northern grade between Newton Falls and Newbridge. Then they built nearly three miles of new trackage, possibly less than that (see paragraph above), into Clifton Mines. Clifton Mines was 85.48 miles from Sackets Harbor and at elevation 1200 feet. The first train arrived on December 22, 1941 (Barnes, 1962).

The Hanna Ore Company was the parent company with operations in other states as well. Locally, Hanna's subsidiary was the Clifton Ore Company, Inc. of DeGrasse, New York. The latter was issuing paychecks to employees in October of 1942 and should not be confused with the 19th century Clifton Iron Company described in Chapter 30.

Palmer (1979) indicates that the date of abandonment of this 10.04-mile-long mining extension (total from Newton Falls) as 1955. This is three years after the date of closing of operations, 1952, offered by Barnes (1962). The only map which I have showing this line is a 1956 publication entitled "Bulletin 1072, Plate 9, Map of New York State showing Mineral Occurrences," published by the United States Geological Survey.

Worthington (1943) describes the construction of the Hanna Ore Company Railroad with Newton Falls yard as "choked with traffic." The 200-foot-long steel bridge across the Oswegatchie River at Newton Falls was brand new then when Worthington wrote. This bridge still stands in 1995 and is at a site downstream from the earlier Newton Falls & Northern Railroad bridge (see Map 31-21).

A description of the Hanna Ore Company Railroad is as follows:

Milepost zero: bridge over Oswegatchie River at Newton Falls, elevation 1380 feet.

0.75 mile: Rock Cut Siding. A siding existed on either side of the main, for storage of empty cars. The material removed from the rock cut was used for making the adjacent two causeways over bays of the Oswegatchie River. The Newton Falls & Northern Railroad had used wooden trestles.

2.5 miles. Highest point on the line. Elevation 1458 feet.

4.3 miles. Cross line from Town of Clifton into Town of Clare.

4.7 miles. High Siding. Elevation 1390 feet. Siding west of main was used for reassembling southbound trains which had doubled the hill.

6.8 miles. Newbridge Siding. Elevation 1230 feet. Siding south of main was used for breaking up southbound trains for doubling the hill.

6.9 miles. Former Newton Falls & Northern Railroad spur up Bend Brook diverged from this point. Higbie sawmill is reported to have been across the South Branch Grasse River from here.

7.0 miles. Wooden milepost still stands in 1995, but the number 7 has faded.

8.7 miles. Pumphouse still stands along bank of Grasse River. Water was pumped from here via a subterranean aqueduct parallel to the track to the mines.

9.0 miles. Wooden milepost still stands in 1995 but the number 9 has faded. Elevation 1240 feet.

9.4 miles. Cross Steep Bank Brook.

10.0 miles. Wye and entrance to yard at Clifton Mines. Chemical laboratory still stands in 1995 at elevation 1228 feet.

A railroad had been built into Clifton Mines at a much earlier date and from a very different direction. Detail on the Clifton Iron Company's Railroad will be found in Chapter 30.

Hanna Ore Company facilities at Clifton Mines. The ball mill crusher building is on the right with Pennsylvania Railroad coal hoppers.
William LaBounty photo, summer 1948.

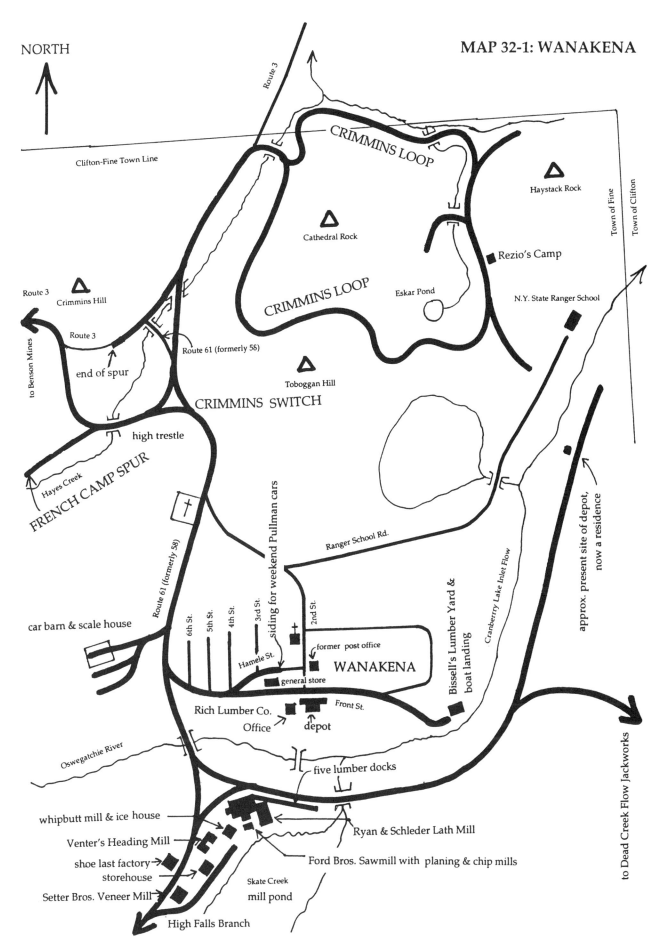

Chapter 33:
Three Peripheral Railroads

THERE are three railroads peripheral to the Adirondacks which should be considered: The Adirondack & Saint Lawrence, The Gouverneur & Oswegatchie, and the Lowville & Beaver River (Map 33-1).

The Adirondack & Saint Lawrence Railroad: Map 30-1

The Saint Lawrence Pyrites Company built a railroad in the 1890s from DeKalb Junction on the Saint Lawrence Division of the New York Central 2.2 miles to their mine in Stellaville. In 1906, the Adirondack & Saint Lawrence Railroad was incorporated as a common carrier and the line was extended 1.3 miles to Hermon where the primary industry was dairy and the secondary lumber. In 1912, there were four passenger trains each way daily, three on Sunday, with a running time one way of fifteen minutes. The pyrite mines closed in 1921 and the milk condensing plant shortly thereafter. The rails were torn up in 1924 and 1925. See Chapter 29 on the Hannawa Railroad for a relation between these two short lines. Palmer (1973) is the prime source for the Adirondack & Saint Lawrence.

The Gouverneur & Oswegatchie Railroad: Maps 33-4 and 33-5

Winters (1978) is the main source for detail on this line, chartered in April 1892 and opened to Edwards with the first passenger train on August 1, 1893. The line almost immediately became a branch of the New York Central's Saint Lawrence Division with which it connected at Gouverneur Junction, 0.92 mile from Gouverneur Station. Along the route, measured from the Station and not from the Junction, were Hailesboro (3.26 miles), York (5.94 miles), Emeryville (7.72 miles), Hyatt (10.37 miles), Talcville (11.32 miles), and Edwards (13.82) miles.

Winters (1978) lists the 24 larger industries served by the Gouverneur & Oswegatchie. This list includes nine talc companies, six pulp and paper companies, two ore companies, two companies whose names suggest minerals, a milk plant at Edwards, a lumber company, a limestone company, a zinc company, and Saint Joseph Minerals at Balmat.

In 1929, a branch 4.25 miles long was built from a junction at milepost 7 west of Emeryville, to the then newly-opened Saint Joseph Lead Company zinc mines at Balmat.

An article, from the Watertown *Daily Times*, undated but probably from the 1960s, describes a disconnecting railroad underground at the Wight Talc Mine, between Emeryville and Balmat. Three battery-powered locomotives were in service (see Chapter 8).

Passenger service terminated in January 1933, while Conrail abandoned freight service along the track through Emeryville, Talcville, and Edwards on December 22, 1977. Conrail still serves the Balmat Branch today.

The Lowville & Beaver River Railroad: Maps 33-2 and 33-3

Consult Maloney (1973) for abundant information on this line. The railroad was incorporated in 1903 and opened in January 1906 from Lowville to Croghan, 10.5 miles, with intermediate stations at New Bremen (5 miles) and Beaver Falls (8 miles). The primary industries served were agriculture (dairy and potatoes mainly), the J. P. Lewis Paper Mill at Beaver Falls, lumber, a block factory, and a rubber plant.

Passenger service operated from 1906 through January 1947.

Palmer and Roehl (1989, pages 103 and 104) include an early photo of the Lowville depot and a mixed train crossing the Black River trestle, respectively.

Hendrickson (1989) described the purchase by Livingston Lansing of a 1918 Shay locomotive from the Eureka Springs and North Arkansas Railroad. The locomotive arrived on April 18, 1989 at The Rome Locomotive Works for overhauling. Then, the October 16, 1991 *Journal and Republican*, a Lowville newspaper, announced the arrival of the Shay in Lowville from Rome. Both the 1989 and 1991 moves were over the highway on a flatbed trailer, not by rail. The intentions were to run the Shay as a summer tourist attraction on the Lowville & Beaver River.

On May 1, 1991 The Lowville and Beaver River became part of the new Mohawk, Adirondack & Northern Railroad. Conrail now terminates and interchanges at Carthage. The Mohawk, Adirondack & Northern now also owns two former Conrail lines out of Carthage: Newton Falls Branch and the line to Lowville. Freight service continues at present to serve the paper mill at Beaver Falls, and tourist passenger excursions to Croghan are run in the summer. Detail of the trackage at Lowville (Map 33-3) is provided by Walt Cooga of the Central New York Chapter of the National Railway Historical Society, and 1968 New York Central Railroad valuation diagrams.

Class K-11d Pacifics were the usual power on the New York Central's northern divisions, the Saint Lawrence and the Adirondack, for several decades, ending about 1950. This is #4521 built by Alco in 1912 and still in service on March 3, 1940 when F. Ray McKnight photographed it. The Saint Lawrence Division lines connected with the three railroads described in Chapter 33: at DeKalb Junction, Gouverneur Junction, and Lowville.

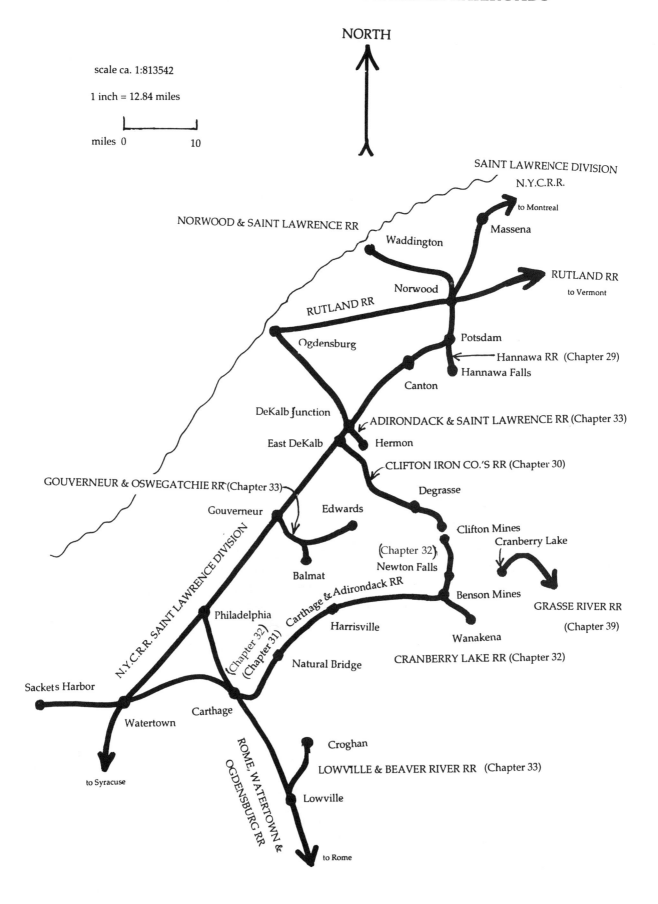

MAP 33-1 THREE PERIPHERAL RAILROADS

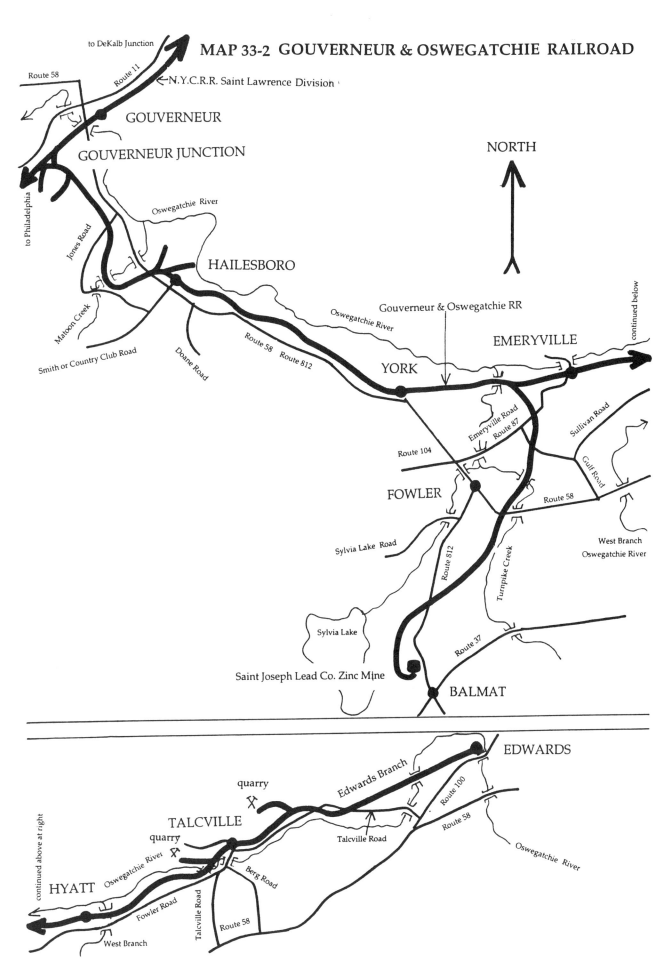

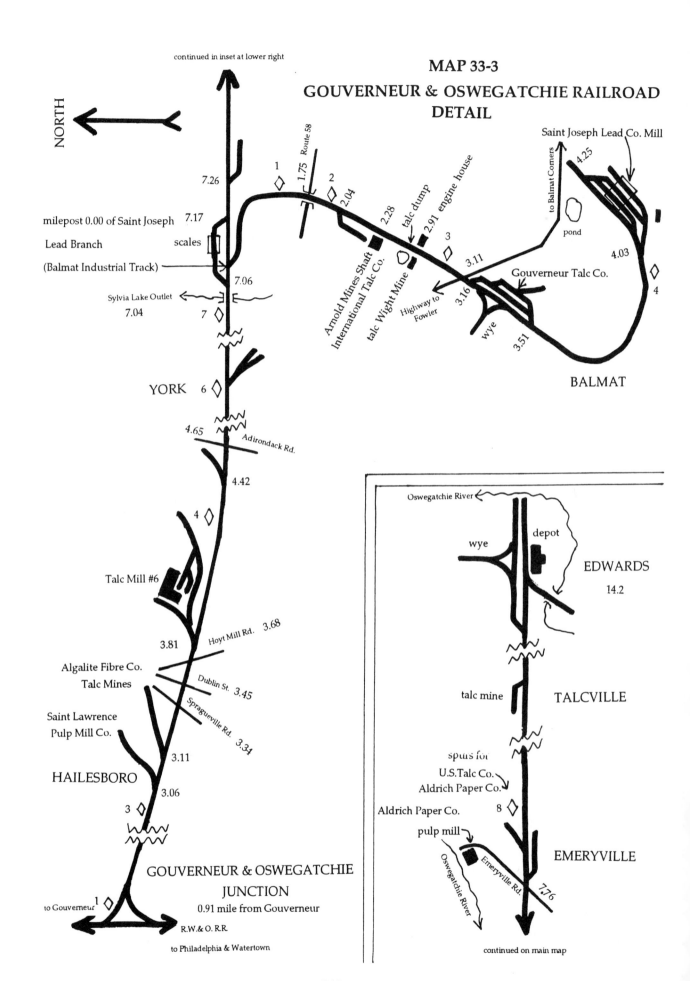

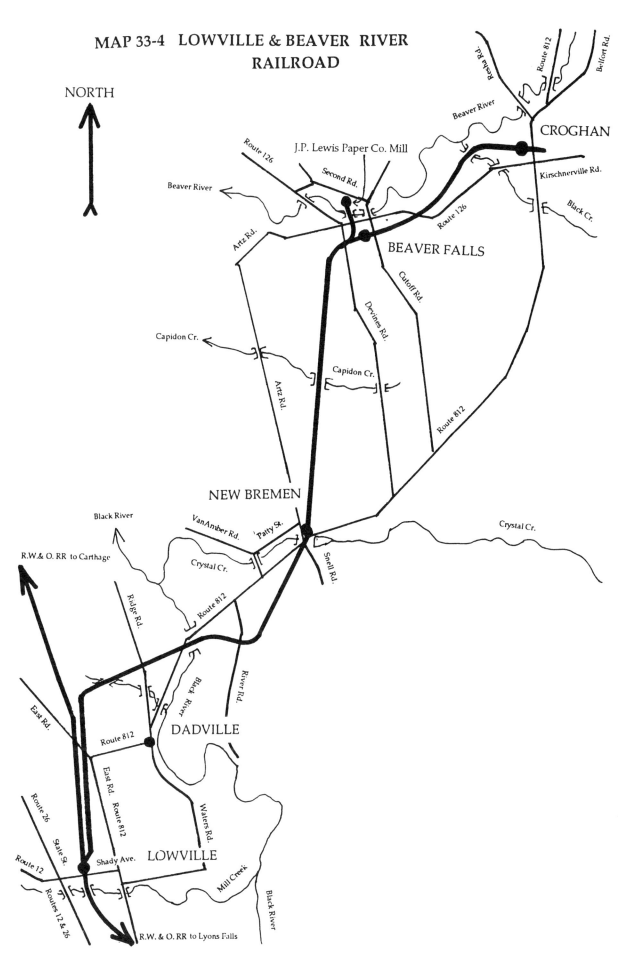

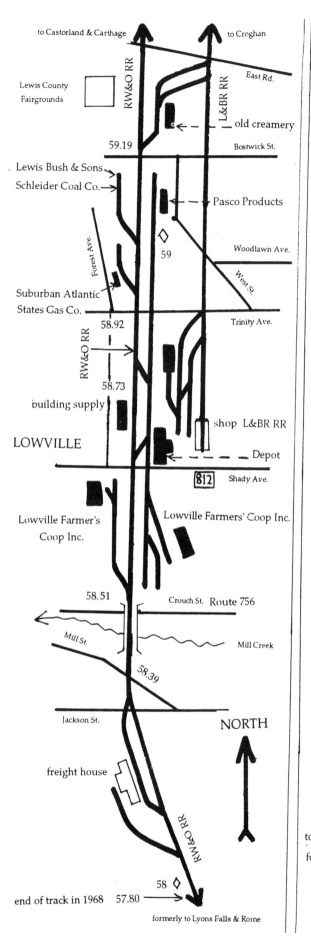
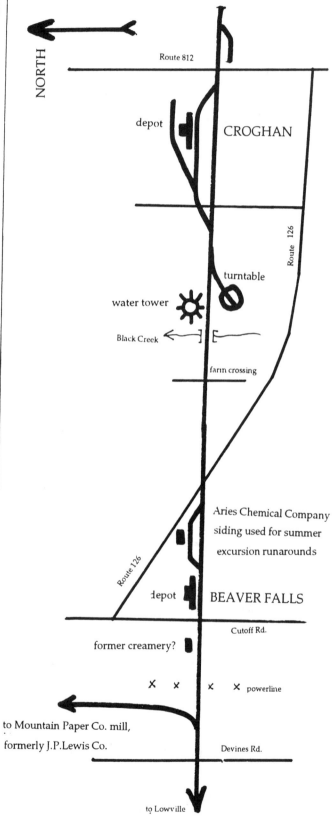

MAP 33-5
LOWVILLE & BEAVER RIVER RAILROAD DETAIL

Marion River Carry Railroad train approaching the Upper Carry Station. Page 430.
Richard Palmer collection.

New York Central Railroad engine #4503 (Class K-11, a 4-6-2)
on the turntable at Lake Placid, February 4, 1940. Page 400.

Gus Portelance photo.

Big Moose in 1991. Page 394.

Author photo.

Above:
Saranac Inn Station in March 1940. Note cattle chute at the left. Page 400.
F. Ray McKnight photo.

Right:
From 1961 through 1965, the New York Central Adirondack Division terminated at Gabriels, about five miles north of Lake Clear Junction, to bring in materials to build Paul Smith's College dormitories. Page 401.
Charles Ballard photo, April 1965.

Grasse River Railroad rail-bus, a rebuilt White bus, in 1942 at Cranberry Lake. Page 444.
Gould Hoyt photo.

Childwold Station, ca. 1954. Grasse River Railroad, on the lower level, persisted for only three more years.
Pages 397 and 443.

Alan Thomas photo.

Lake Clear Junction. Paul Smith's Electric Railway car at left. Page 453.
Photographer unknown.

Before Paul Smith electrictrified his railroad, he used this locomotive purchased from the New York Central in 1906. **Page 453.**

Photographer unknown.

Left:
**Motor-generator inside the Paul Smith's Electric Railway car's baggage compartment.
Page 454.**
Alan Thomas photo.

Below:
**Paul Smith's Electric Railway car with private car in tow.
Ca. 1913.
Page 456.**
Post card, author's collection.

Right:
Paul Smith's Electric Railway car midway between the hotel and Lake Clear Junction. The car was used to haul flatcars with logs in winter for several years. Page 456.
Alan Thomas collection.

Below:
Paul Smith's Electric Railway car. Builder's photo by J. G. Brill Company, Philadelphia, 1907. Page 454.
Charles L. Ballard collection.

Paul Smith (left) and his sons Paul Jr. and Phelps in front of their electric railway car.
A gasoline-powered car is at the right. Between 1907 and 1912. Page 453.
Collection of Currier Press, Saranac Lake.

Lower Dam on the Bog River. A. A. Low used a spur of his Horse Shoe Forestry Company Railroad to build it in 1903. Here it is being reconstructed by the New York State Department of Environmental Conservation, but without a railroad, July 1992. Page 463.
Author photo.

Two Adirondack Railway trains meet at Tupper Lake Junction on July 10, 1980.
Note the canoe strapped to the locomotive in the foreground. Page 472.

Author photo from the locomotive cab.

Section IV:
Into the Adirondacks from the Mohawk Valley on the South

Chapter 34:
The Jerseyfield Railroad

PARKER (1987) writes that the Little Falls and Dolgeville Railroad, connecting with the New York Central mainline along the Mohawk River at Little Falls, was opened in 1892. It was eight miles long and was taken over as the Dolgeville Branch of the New York Central in 1906. Palmer and Roehl (1989, pages 8 and 9) offer some construction detail and two photos at Gulf Curve, Little Falls.

Maps 34-1 and 34-2

Passenger service was abandoned in 1933, and freight in 1964. At Dolgeville was the West Virginia Pulp and Paper Company mill.

The Dolgeville & Salisbury Railway Company opened in 1908 and, in actuality, was a three-mile-long extension of the L.F.& D. Passenger service ceased in 1925, and freight in 1945 or 1946. The Salisbury Steel & Iron Company opened mines at Irondale (not to be confused with Irondale on the Crown Point Iron Company's Railroad of Chapter 15) in 1902 and a railroad into them from Salisbury Center, about 1.5 miles, in 1909. The concentrating plant, where the iron was separated from the ore, was in Salisbury Center until the whole industry closed in 1913.

Brooklyn Cooperage Company, which had extensive operations along the New York Central Ottawa Division between Tupper Lake and Saint Regis Falls (see Chapter 26), also had a barrel mill at Salisbury Center from sometime between 1910 and 1915 until 1925. Brooklyn Cooperage bought the hardwood lumber from the Jerseyfield Lumber Company. The location of the cooperage mill, according to Parker, was at the wye, but this wye is not precisely located for us.

Parker states that the Jerseyfield Lumber Company was established sometime between 1910 and 1915 and ran until 1925 or 1926. It had two Shays and a Marion Log Loader, and was about twenty miles long.

Locating the route of the Jerseyfield Railroad has been troublesome. Parker's (1987, page 41) map shows it paralleling the Jerseyfield Road at a close distance and continuing all the way to Jerseyfield Lake. The New York State Conservation Commission *Adirondack Land Map* of 1923 shows it a distance further east and terminating in several branches at Black Creek, some 2.5 miles short of Jerseyfield Lake. I have denoted the Parker route as a dotted line north of Curtis on my maps and the *Adirondack Land Map* route as a solid line. The City Street Directory (1974) *Adirondack Region Atlas* shows the abandoned grade more accurately between Salisbury Center and Trammel Creek, and it is this book from which I have tried to trace the line on the 1898 Little Falls and the 1902 Wilmurt 15-minute topographic quadrangles. The quadrangles were surveyed, of course, before the Jerseyfield Railroad was built.

The discrepancy between the maps of Parker and the State Conservation Commission might be attributed to the following: When the 1923 *Adirondack Land Map* was published, the logging line could have reached only as far as Black Creek. In contrast, Parker's map might show the line reaching the shore of Jerseyfield Lake either at a later date (with the line already abandoned back to Black Creek) or at an earlier date (not yet built to Jerseyfield Lake).

Like the Jerseyfield Railroad, the New York & Ottawa was primarily a wood-products line. Mills like this one at Saint Regis Falls (on the New York & Ottawa) were common, 1936.
Photo collection of the New York Central System Historical Society, Inc..

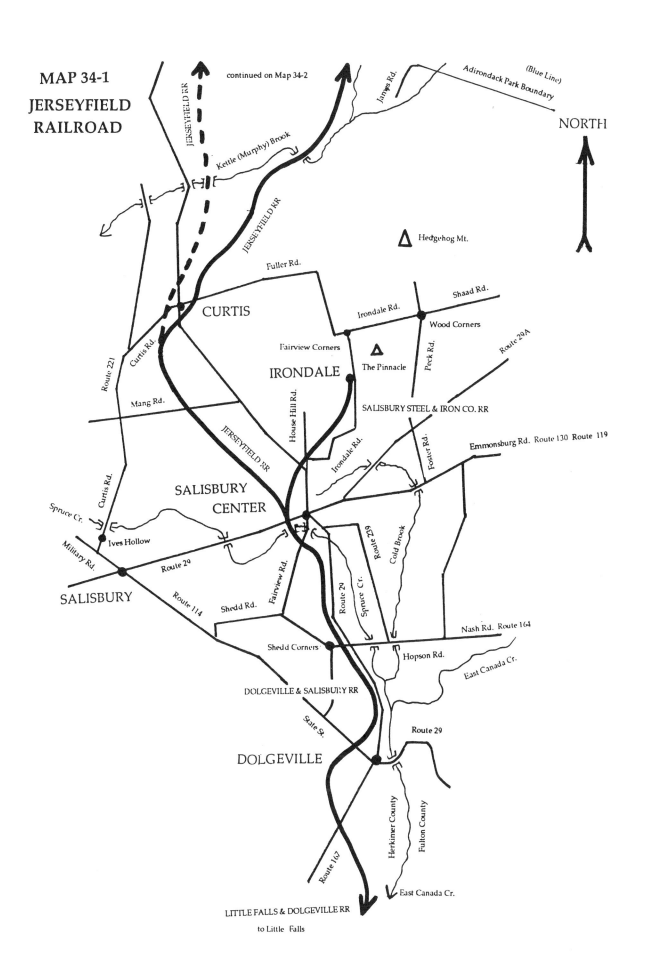

MAP 34-2 JERSEYFIELD RAILROAD

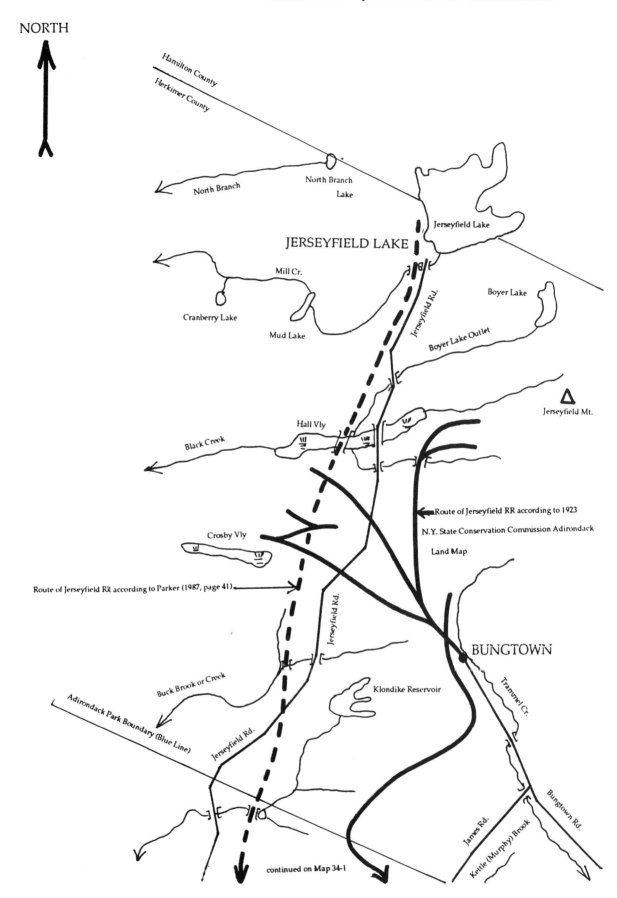

Chapter 35:
Fonda, Johnstown & Gloversville Railroad

THIS RAILROAD must be mentioned, but little more will be done in this book for two reasons. First, the line barely touches on the extreme southern edge of the Adirondacks at Northville; it is largely a Mohawk Valley railroad. Second, the railroad has been described in great detail by Gordon and Mowers (publication date not stated, but about 1971), Gordon (1980), and others listed below.

Map 35-1

The railroad was opened from Fonda, where it connected with the New York Central mainline, to Gloversville on November 29, 1870. In 1872, a company was organized to extend the line to Northville which it did, also on November 29, but in 1875. The distance from Fonda to Gloversville is about ten miles, and the extension another sixteen. The Gloversville and Northville railroad was soon combined with the F.J.& G.

In August 1895, a six-mile long branch was constructed from Broadalbin Junction eastward to Broadalbin.

Electrification occurred between 1891 and 1894 when several small trolley lines merged between Fonda and Gloversville. From Gloversville to Northville and Broadalbin the line was always steam-powered.

In 1930, the Sacandaga River was dammed, creating the Sacandaga Reservoir, and flooding and closing the extension to Northville. By 1936 electrification was being phased out, although a 1938 photo in Maguire and Reifschneider (1950, unnumbered but 13th page), still shows an electric car in service. Passenger service continued as a mixed train through to Broadalbin until August 15, 1956; Palmer and Roehl (1990, page 5) include a photo of Broadalbin. Freight service continued until 1990. I found the grade crossing still in place on State Highway 30A northeast of Gloversville on October 18, 1990, but a colleague reported the track being removed there and in Fonda on May 25, 1991.

Additional references on the Fonda, Johnstown & Gloversville are as follows:

Goldsmith (1936) describes a joint field trip on September 6, 1936 by the National Railway Historical Society and the Electric Railroaders' Association. At that time only electric baggage, mail, and express, but no longer electric passenger, cars were running between Fonda and Johnstown. Electric passenger cars were still running, however, between Johnstown and Schenectady.

Maguire and Reifschneider (1950) include four photos on their thirteenth and fourteenth (but unnumbered) pages.

The book of Nestle and Gordon (1958) is reviewed in *The Bulletin* of the National Railway Historical Society, 3rd quarter 1958 issue.

Wessels (1961, pp. 146-153) included a description with photos of Sacandaga Park, a famous amusement park, and a F.J.& G. timetable of September 4, 1919.

Adele Thompson (1976) described Sacandaga Park and its relation to the F.J.& G. in much greater detail. The Sacandaga Park depot still stands in 1995 as a private residence north of McKinley Avenue about 0.1 mile east of State Highway 30.

An unsigned article appears in the March 1991, issue of the Bridge Line Historical Society *Bulletin*, page 20. It describes a wastewater pipeline on the former railroad right-of-way.

Rominger (1994, pp. 20 and 23) offers a reprint of the descriptive 1911 *Trolley Trips through the Hudson Valley* with portions on the F.J. & G.

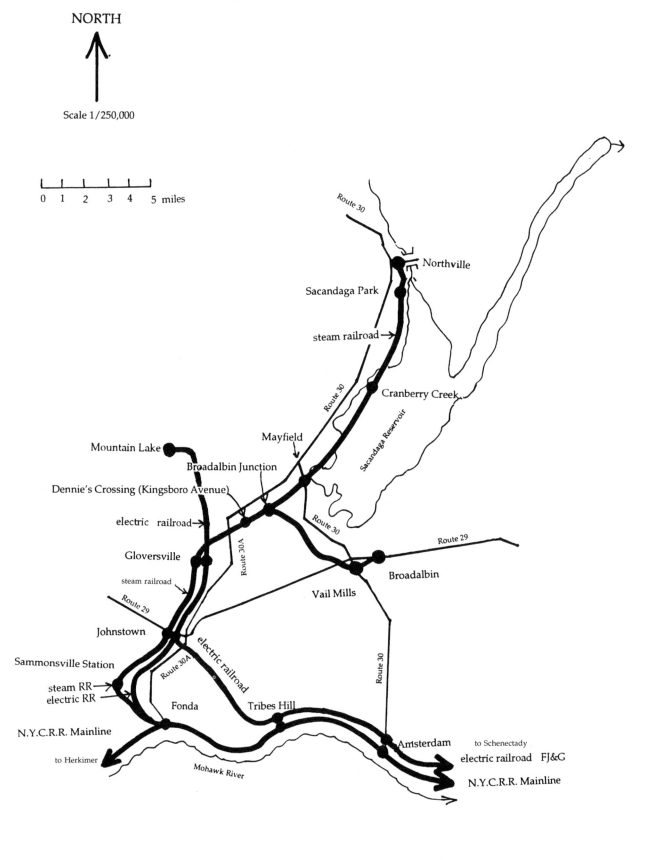

Chapter 36
New York Central Adirondack Division

CONSTRUCTION of this line was begun in 1891 by William Seward Webb of the Adirondack & Saint Lawrence or Mohawk & Malone Railway. Construction crews had simultaneously built the railroad from several points: First, the Herkimer, Newport & Poland had been built as a narrow gauge, reaching Poland in 1882. Webb standard-gauged it in June 1891 and began extending it to Remsen. A February 15, 1892 timetable shows passenger service between Herkimer and Poland. Second, crews were building track northward out of Remsen. Third, other crews were building track northward (and perhaps also southward) out of Minnehaha, the first Fulton Chain or "Peg Leg" Railroad bringing in materials and supplies. As a result, by July 16, 1892, trains were running from Herkimer to Fulton Chain Station (Thendara).

Fourth, crews were building the railroad south out of Malone Junction, the Ogdensburg & Lake Champlain hauling in the materials. Fifth, crews were building the railroad north and south from Loon Lake, with materials delivered by the Chateaugay Railroad (see Chapter 20). Sixth, crews were laying rail from Tupper Lake Junction north and south, with materials delivered by Hurd's Northern Adirondack Railroad. As a result, by July 16, 1892, trains were running from Malone Junction to Childwold Station; this included branch service from Saranac Junction (renamed Lake Clear Junction the following year) into Saranac Lake.

After the last spike was driven north of Twitchell Creek trestle on October 12, 1892, trains commenced operating between Fulton Chain and Childwold Stations twelve days later. Thus, it was possible on October 24, 1892 to travel directly from Herkimer through to Montreal by rail.

Connecting trains ran from Saranac Junction only to Saranac Lake from July 16, 1892 through July 31, 1893. On August 1, 1893, the Saranac and Lake Placid Railroad opened, and connecting trains operated through from Lake Clear Junction to Lake Placid.

On May 1, 1893, when the New York Central took over the Mohawk & Malone, the southern terminus became Utica, no longer Herkimer.

Mileposts along the grade, however, always tied into Herkimer, hence the "H" preceding each numbered mile.

Branch railroads

To reduce the length of this chapter, detail on a number of its longer branches has been separated into distinct chapters as follows:

Branch	Junction Point	Chapt.
Black River & Woodhull RR	Forestport	42
Moose River Lumber Co. RR	McKeever	42
1st Fulton Chain or "Peg Leg"	Minnehaha	42
2nd Fulton Chain RR or Old Forge Branch	Fulton Chain Sta.	42
Raquette Lake Railway and Marion River Carry RR	Clearwater	37
Champlain Realty Co. Spur	Woods Lake	42
Mac-a-Mac and Whitney RRs	Brandreth	38
Partlow Lake Railway	Partlow	42
Horse Shoe Forestry Co. RR	Horse Shoe	41
Grasse River Railroad	Childwold Sta.	39
Piercefield Spur	Piercefield Sta.	42
Brooklyn Cooperage Co. RR	Tupper Lake Junc.	26
Paul Smith's Electric RY	Lake Clear Junc.	40
Saranac Branch into L. Placid	Lake Clear Junc.	20
Tekene Branch	Tekene Junc.	20

Much detail on the Tupper Lake area will also be found in Chapter 23.

(Detail between Herkimer and Remsen and between Utica and Remsen is not presented in this book because of space limitations and distance from the Adirondacks.)

Station Descriptions

The dates of opening and closing given for stations refer only to passenger service. Mileages are from Herkimer, not Utica, in order to agree with contemporary mileposts. Elevations are in feet taken from U.S.G.S. topographic quadrangles.

Remsen. 27.67 miles from Herkimer. Elevation 1172 feet. Maps 36-2 and 36-15.

Passenger station: Remsen was a busy junction point at one time with railroads coming in from four directions: Herkimer, Utica, Boonville-Ogdensburg, and Malone Junction-Montreal. Harter (1979, pp.1-33 and 287-289) offers the details of construction. First to arrive in Remsen was the Utica & Black River Railroad which was built from Utica to Boonville; it was later to become part of the Rome, Watertown & Ogdensburg Railroad and was extended north to Carthage. Harter does not date the construction of the Utica & Black River, but Hochschild in his *Real and Phantom* (1962, p. 9) offers an 1866 map with the line already in place. On July 16, 1892, Webb's Adirondack & Saint Lawrence (the first railroad with this name; the second is described in Chapter 33) or Mohawk & Malone opened through Remsen.

Eventually, the Herkimer-Remsen line was abandoned between Remsen and Poland in 1943. A Watertown *Daily Times* article dated August 27, 1959 stated that the New York Central was first given approval by the Public Service Commission to end agency service at Remsen, retire the building, and terminate passenger service. By October 25, 1959 service had been suspended.

Passing sidings: Several were present, often simultaneously, at Remsen over the years with capacities of between 12 and 72 cars, as described in employee timetables from 1906 through 1957.

Servicing facilities: A water tower located in Remsen already by 1906 was still present in 1940, but gone by 1948. A turntable was still present in the 1950s era, the pit remaining in 1992 but much overgrown. A freight station appears in many of the photos because it was near the depot.

Industrial sidings: The Dairylea Creamery building, abandoned but still standing in 1992, dominates a photo in Harter (1979), page 172. See Map 36-15 for others.

Photographs: Photos of Remsen are common. Harter (1979) has several on pages 170-172. Gardner's (1975) photo on page 49 is the same as Harter's on page 170. Gardner offers two additional photos on pages 55 and 60.

Track-plan: The track plans shown in this book are compiled from the photographs, from 35 mm slides taken about 1950 by New York Central fireman, Bob Morgan, from the 15 and 7.5-minute Remsen topographic quadrangles, from the author's field notes of 1980 and 1992, and from an undated New York Central valuation diagram in the Harter Collection.

Snow Junction. About 29.5 miles from Herkimer. Elevation 1210. Map 36-2.

The Adirondack Division and Lyons Falls Branch of the New York Central ran parallel for nearly two miles north out of Remsen. To eliminate the duplicate trackage, the Central removed a portion of the Lyons Falls Branch sometime between 1965 and 1972. Lyons Falls trains, therefore, ran on the Adirondack Division track. A new junction called Snow was built at the north end of the removal.

A telephone existed at Snow, when the Adirondack Railway operated in 1980, so that the crew could call the Conrail dispatcher in Utica for clearance to enter or leave the Lyons Falls Branch.

On May 1, 1991 the Mohawk Adirondack & Northern Railroad took over Conrail's Lyons Falls Branch, and currently operates freight trains on it through Remsen, Snow, Boonville, and Lyons Falls.

Honnedaga (Delavan or Desmond). 31.66 miles. Elevation 1237. Maps 36-2 and 36-16.

Passenger station: This station opened in September 1892 and had three different names at different times. It was first called Honnedaga. Between September 22, 1914 and October 3, 1915 the name was changed to Delavan (although Harter spells it Delevan). Then, between September 27, 1925 and June 27, 1926 the name was changed to Desmond. It closed between June 24, 1928 and September 29, 1929.

Industrial siding: A stub siding, east of the main track and heading north, existed here at one time. A New York Central valuation diagram shows a cheese factory on the west side of the main. Whether the siding served the factory or not is unknown.

Kayuta. 33.45 miles. Elevation ca. 1190. Map 36-3.

Passenger station: Kayuta opened as a station between March 31 and June 14, 1912 although a photo in Harter (1979, page 174) shows that it was no more than flagstop shelter. It closed between September 29, 1940 and September 24, 1944. Just north of the shelter, at milepost 33.75, was the trestle (Harter photo, page 175) over the Kayuta Reservoir----actually the Black River dammed up at Forestport.

Tracy's Spur. Ca. 34.5 miles. Elevation 1190. Map 36-3.

The remains of a former siding north of Kayuta at about milepost 34.5, east of the main and heading north, was still in evidence in 1980. A New York Central 1914 publication, *Station Numbers*, lists Tracy's Spur here. The October 1905 New York Central *Official Freight Shippers' Directory* tells us that Frank Tracy had a pulpwood business at Forestport.

Forestport. 35.57 miles. Elevation 1199. Maps 36-3 and 36-17.

Passenger station: This station opened in September 1892 and closed sometime between April 29, 1956 and April 28, 1957. Harter includes photos of it on page 174. The building still stands in 1992.
Buffalo Head Hotel: Across the highway and track from the depot is the Buffalo Head Hotel, still open.
Stagecoach connection: A stage connected Forestport Station with Woodhull, 0.5 mile to the west, and Forestport, 1.5 miles to the west.
Passing siding: One on the west existed and held between 37 and 47 cars. It was already extant in 1906, still present in 1948, but gone by April 28, 1957.
Black River & Woodhull Railroad: See Chapter 42.

Meekerville. Ca. 36.0 miles. Elevation 1199. Map 36-3.

This was never a station but only a small community along the track. Meekerville Road crosses the main track at 35.95 miles.
The function of Taffarn's Siding is unknown.

Anos (Anos Siding). 38.03 miles. Elevation 1296. Maps 36-3 and 36-18.

The only employees' timetable which I have in my collection listing Anos Siding is June 19, 1910. It was never a passenger station. The 1897 Remsen 15-minute quadrangle indicates a stub 0.15-mile long on the east and heading north. My observations in 1980 reveal that this siding was double-ended. Harter (1979, p. 279) lists Boonville Sand here.

Pit Four. 39.70 miles. Elevation 1347. Map 36-3.

This stub siding was on the east side of the main heading north, was 960 feet long, and served a sand pit. Harter (1979, p. 279) includes it as well as a New York Central station list from the 1926-1928 era.

Johnson Siding (Johnston Siding or Johnson Track). 39.81 miles. Elevation 1347. Map 36-3.

The function of this siding is unknown. It might have been on the east side of the main, but I am not certain. Harter (1979, p. 279), as well as a 1926-1928 era New York Central station listing, includes it.

Nichols Mills. 39.94 miles. Elevation 1347. Map 36-3.

Nichols Mills was never a station stop but an industrial siding just south of the 96-foot-long Big Woodhull Creek trestle. Harter (1979, p. 279) includes it as well as a 1926-1928 era New York Central station listing. Between the Big Woodhull and Bear Creek trestles (the former at 39.98 miles and the latter at ca. 40.3 miles), the 1897 Remsen quadrangle shows another siding on the east, stub-ended and heading north at about 40.1 miles. I cannot find the function of either. Nichols Mills appears on maps in employees' timetables from 1906 through 1918, but not in 1940.

White Lake (Woodgate). 42.50 miles. Elevation 1417. Maps 36-3 and 36-19.

Passenger station: This station opened July 16, 1892. From its opening through May 18, 1924 it was called White Lake, but by September 27, 1925 the name had been changed to Woodgate. Service was suspended here for passengers between December 6, 1953 and April 29, 1956. Harter (1979, page 178) presents a photo of the depot; Palmer and Roehl

(1990, page 102) do likewise. In 1980 the building was owned by the Adirondack Railway; the building still stands as a private home in 1992.

Passing siding: At the station were two stubs headed north, one of them probably the remains of a former passing siding. This siding held from 37 to 58 cars and was already present in 1906, still extant in 1948, but gone by 1957.

Servicing facilities: A water tower was present at White Lake in 1906, still present in 1918, but gone by 1940.

George C. Wood Ice Company Spur. Ca. 43.5 miles. Elevation 1430. Map 36-4.

A New York Central valuation diagram describes the George C. Wood Ice Company House 0.3 mile west of the main track. It is listed in a 1914 New York Central publication, *Station Numbers*. A spur shows on the 1910 McKeever quadrangle heading west to the shore of White Lake. Harter calls this spur Utica City Ice.

White Lake Sand Pit. Ca. 44.2 miles. Elevation ca. 1450. Map 36-4.

The White Lake Sand Pit spur diverged to the east of the main heading north to about milepost 44.5. It also shows on the 1910 McKeever quadrangle and on a N.Y.C.R.R. valuation diagram.

Purgatory Hill. Ca. 44 to 46 miles. Elevation ca. 1450 to 1550. Map 36-4.

This was one of the steepest on the Division. Harter (1979, page 180) states that the grade is 1.87%. The track crosses Purgatory Creek at about 46.4 miles.

Otter Lake (Otter). 47.57, 47.58, or 47.59 miles. Elevation 1551. Maps 36-4 and 36-20.

Passenger station: Otter Lake appears on a Mohawk & Malone map dated September 1892, but does not appear on the timetables until April 23, 1893. On some timetables and maps the name is Otter Lake and on others, Otter. Harter (p. 178) and Gardner (1975, p. 39) present the same photo of the station which resembled more a house than a depot. The station closed between April 27, 1958 and October 25, 1959, and still stands in 1994.

Passing siding: One was already present by 1906 and still present in 1957. It held between 25 and 35 cars, and appears on the 1958 McKeever quadrangle as 0.3 mile long on the east.

McKeever. 49.15 miles. Elevation 1538. Maps 36-4 and 42-1.

Passenger station: This station appears on a Mohawk & Malone timetable of September 1892. Harter (page 179) shows the station with two trains passing, plus a 1978 photo of the bridge over the Moose River at 49.50 miles. The station closed between May 13, 1957 and April 27, 1958, but the building still stands in 1995.

Passing siding: There was one on the east already extant in 1906, still present in 1948, but gone by 1957. It held between 30 and 50 cars.

Moose River Lumber Company Railroad: See Chapter 42.

Nelson (Nelson Lake). 52.12 or 52.19 miles. Elevation 1620. Maps 36-4 and 36-21.

Passenger station: This station opened between June 18, 1905 and June 17, 1906. It closed between September 29, 1940 and September 24, 1944.

Passing siding: A passing siding existed at 51.8 miles on the west side and had a capacity of between 43 and 46 cars. It was already present in 1906, extant in 1918, but gone by 1939.

Section buildings: A valuation diagram shows a tool house and a bunk house along the Nelson Lake siding on the west and a section dwelling along the main track on the east. Behind the dwelling, also at 51.8 miles, was a dam on the Moose River and two camps.

Minnehaha. 53.75 miles. Elevation 1683. Maps 36-4 and 42-2.

Passenger station: This station had not yet opened when the May 29, 1893 timetable was printed, but does appear on an April 1895 timetable. It closed between June 13, 1948 and September 25, 1949.

First Fulton Chain or "Peg Leg" Railroad: See Chapter 42. A New York Central valuation diagram indicates a former junction at about 53.79 miles or some 200 feet north of the station. This could have been the "Peg Leg."

Bridges over the Moose River: There are two in the Minnehaha area: one at 52.8 miles, and the other at 53.69 miles and about 300 feet south of the station.

Onekio. 55.01 miles. Elevation 1740. Map 36-4.

This station is not yet shown on an 1896 New York Central map, but was open when the August 29, 1902 timetable was printed. It closed between June 22 and October 12, 1913. Not a trace of it remains in 1992.

Fulton Chain Station (Thendara). 57.93 miles. Elevation 1712. Maps 36-5 and 42-3.

Passenger station: Fulton Chain Station was the terminus of the Adirondack & Saint Lawrence railroad temporarily from July 16 through October 24, 1892. On the latter date, the first through train ran from Herkimer to Malone Junction. On June 27, 1920 the name was changed to Thendara (Harter, p. 183) which remained the station name through April 25, 1965 when the New York Central suspended passenger service. When the Adirondack Railway operated in 1979 and 1980, Thendara was the site of offices and shops. Beginning in 1992, The Adirondack Railway Preservation Society has been running their Adirondack Centennial Railroad from here to Minnehaha as a highly successful passenger excursion.

Passing sidings: Employees' timetables list a passing siding here accommodating between 73 and 76 cars during the 1906 to 1948 era, but only 35 cars in 1957. This siding was west of the main track and had been long removed by the time the Adirondack Railway began operations in the late 1970s. Between October 9, 1979 and January 12, 1980 the Adirondack Railway added a stub-ended track on the site of this former siding, connecting at the north end with the main track. A second siding was east of the main track and ran directly in front of the station; this siding was left still intact when the Penn Central ceased freight service in 1972, and still exists. A third siding was in existence on the far west side during the early decades of the twentieth century.

Servicing facilities: A water tower located here already in 1906, was still present in 1957, but probably removed shortly thereafter. Also at Thendara were a freight house, a tool house, a coal bin, a section house, a gas tank, a pump house, and a turntable. The turntable had been removed by 1953. The Adirondack Railway and Adirondack Centennial Railroad's car shop is on the site of the former freight house.

Photographs: Photos of Thendara abound: Harter (1979, pp. 188 and 262); Gardner (1975, pp. 23, 39, 40, and 75); Hochschild (1962, *Life and Leisure*--p. 35); and DeSormo (1974, p. 108).

Industrial sidings: On exhibit in 1992 in the Thendara Station was a relief map by Daryl Carman of the Town of Webb Historical Society showing Thendara during the 1900 to early 1930s era. Carman locates, at the south end of the Thendara yard, the Pullman Brothers' mill, abandoned in the 1920s. This mill produced sounding board lumber for pianos, and is listed in both the October 1905 New York Central *Official Freight Shippers' Directory* and the employees' timetable of June 30, 1918. The latter mentions the Pullman Brothers' piano track, suggesting a siding.

Carman locates the first Brown's Tract Lumber Company Mill which burned about 1918 further north. This mill had two tracks on trestles over a bay of the pond serving a log boom. The October 1905 *Shippers Directory* states that this was a sawmill for lumber and lath. Carman also locates the Deis Mill, part of which is now the Foley Lumber Company. Foley still existed in 1992, but was of course not served by a railroad.

Old Forge Branch: See Chapter 42.

Moulin. 60.66 miles. Elevation 1748. Map 36-5.

This flagstop first appears on a map in a June 17, 1906 employees' timetable and then intermittently on passenger timetables beginning in 1912. It closed between June 13, 1948 and September 25, 1949. A 1914 New York Central publication, *Station Numbers*, notes that there was no freight siding at Moulin.

Lotus Siding. Ca. 63 miles. Elevation 1750. Map 36-5.

Lotus Siding appears on maps in employees' timetables from 1906 through 1918, but not in 1940. A New York Central 1914 publication, *Station Numbers*, lists the nearest milepost as 63. The function escapes me.

Clear Water, Clearwater, or Carter. 64.12 miles. Elevation 1752. Maps 36-5, 37-1 and 37-4.

Passenger station: Clear Water had not appeared yet in the May 29, 1893 timetable, but it is listed in one of April 1895. The Raquette Lake Railway (See Chapter 37) opened for private and logging use in 1899; on July 11, 1900, this branch line opened to the public (Harter, 1979, p.291) and Hochschild (1962, *Life and Leisure--*, pp. 38 and 97), connecting with the Adirondack Division at this point. Until 1905 the name on the timetables consisted of two words, Clear Water, but by 1906 the name had become one word: Clearwater. Harter (p. 186, photo p. 94) notes that the name was changed again to Carter on June 23, 1912. The New York State Museum has also a photo, #P14273. Service for passengers continued to sometime between April 29, 1956 and May 13, 1957, although the Raquette Lake Railway had closed in 1933.

Passing siding: One on the Adirondack Division west of the main track held between 28 and 51 cars. It was already present in 1906, still extant in 1918, but was gone by 1939. A valuation diagram indicates "Industrial track #2," stub-ended and heading north on the west side of the main.

Raquette Lake Railway: See Chapter 37 in this book for details on this branch line. The Raquette Lake Railway had two double-ended sidings at Clear Water during the period 1906 to 1913. One was west of the Adirondack Division passing siding and held between 14 and 22 cars; the other was east of the station and held 8 to 10 cars. A wye was present to turn Raquette Lake Railway engines. A water tower and oil tank were present at one time.

Remaining buildings in 1988: Only the station foundation remains. Two old buildings and the old store remain and are currently residences.

Upgrade: From Clear Water, the Adirondack Division began the long, steep climb, with several spectacular rock cuts, to Big Moose. Harter (p. 180) describes the 1.1% grade which often caused problems.

Big Moose. 69.31 then 69.29 miles. Elevation 2034 or 2035. Maps 36-6 and 36-22.

Passenger station: Big Moose appears on a Mohawk & Malone map dated September 1892, but is named Buck Pond. When the station first appeared on the April 23, 1893 timetable, the name had been changed to Big Moose. Marleau's (1986) photos on pages 256 and 257 show that a second station building replaced the first sometime between 1920 and 1928. What happened to the first? Because the first building is listed on employees' timetables at milepost 69.31 and the second at milepost 69.29, the second building must have been constructed just to the south of the first. The second station was in service through April 25, 1965 and still stands.

Passing siding: One was on the east and held between 27 and 35 cars; it was in existence from or before 1906 through 1980 when the Adirondack Railway used it to store coaches waiting to be refurbished. At one time a second siding existed on the east and in the later years was reduced to a stub-ended track at the north end only; it had been removed by the time New York Central fireman Bob Morgan took photographs ca. 1950.

Wye: At Big Moose was a wye to turn back pusher, or helper, engines toward Thendara or Utica to meet the next northbound train. Marleau (1986, page XV) offers a map showing that there were two wyes. One of the wyes was laid out in 1901 and built in 1906 (pp. 239 and 240 in Marleau); why did construction require five years? Although Marleau does not state so, his map suggests that the two wyes did not exist simultaneously. I suggest that the second wye was an enlargement of the first to accommodate larger engines in later years, e.g. Pacifics. A field check by this author on August 9, 1992 revealed that only the north end of the wye had been relocated. Apparently both the old and new wyes shared the same south leg, the one nearest the station, because there was but one fill across the swamp. The larger, relocated north leg of the wye, required quite a cut through a bedrock ledge, and joined the main track immediately south of the highest point on the Division.

Servicing facilities: In addition to the wyes was a section tool house.

Photographs: Photos of the Big Moose area abound. In addition to those mentioned above in Marleau, Harter has one on page 189, Gardner (1975) on page 94, and Hochschild in his *Real and Phantom* on page 11. (Railroad historian Frank E. Carey has supplied me with several others.)

Highest point on the Division: Just north of the wye there is a rock cut on the main track at 69.7 miles marking the highest point on the Adirondack Division at 2040 feet. Other surveys offer 2044 as the value.

Industrial siding: Just north of the highest point a siding diverged to the east, gradually descending but paralleling the main track, and terminating along the shore of Buck Pond just short of milepost 70. Gove (1978) notes that this siding was owned by Champlain Realty Company, a division of International Paper, and used for loading pulpwood onto railroad cars as part of the Woods Lake operation from about 1916 to about 1926 (see Chapter 42). The map on page 17 in Gove (1978) shows the siding connection at the north end at Buck Pond, but there is no evidence for this in the field. Marleau says that the siding at Buck Pond was built about 1921 for George Vincent's logging operation and sawmill, but does not tell us what the relation between Vincent and Champlain Realty was. Possibly Vincent was a contractor for Champlain Realty? Near Buck Pond on August 9, 1992, our exploratory party found two remnant pieces of a jackworks conveyor belt chain, one piece partly buried in the ground and the other suspended in a beech tree which had partly grown around it! The remnant pieces are now safely stored at Paul Smith's College.

Twitchell Creek Bridge: At 71.5 miles is the Twitchell Creek Bridge (Harter, photo page 199). Marleau (1986, page 47) writes that the track, on the highest trestle along the division, is 42 feet above the creek here.

Last Spike: At 72.0 miles was the spot where the last spike was driven on October 12, 1892 completing the Adirondack & Saint Lawrence Railway between Herkimer and Malone Junction. The first regularly-scheduled through train ran twelve days later.

Woods Lake (Woods). 73.47 miles. Elevation 1875 or 1882. Maps 36-6 and 42-5.

Passenger station: This station was not yet present when the May 29, 1893 timetable was printed, but was in service by April 1895. The name varied from Woods to Woods Lake over the years. The station closed between December 6, 1953 and April 29, 1956. It had been on the east side of the track. West of the track still stands in 1992 what might have been a hotel or boarding house (photo in Gove, 1978, page 17), but it was not the station.

Passing siding: One on the west held between 37 and 65 cars, and was in existence by 1906. It was still present on September 24, 1939 but gone by June 23, 1940.

Servicing facilities: A valuation diagram shows a bunk house, tool house, and gas tank.

Champlain Realty Company Railroad: see Chapter 42.

Beaver River. 77.69 miles. Elevation 1692. Maps 36-6 and 36-23.

Passenger station: Beaver River appears on a Mohawk & Malone map dated September 1892, but does not appear on timetables until April 23, 1893. It might have opened soon after trains started running through here on October 24, 1892. The depot burned in 1940 (Harter, p.190), but trains continued to stop here until April 25, 1965. In 1979 and 1980, the Adirondack Railway stopped here often to bring supplies to the present (second) hotel.

Passing siding: One on the east held between 29 and 37 cars. It was already functional in 1906 and still exists in 1992. A photo, undated but prior to 1914, supplied by Frank E. Carey shows a second siding west of the main and north of the station.

Servicing facilities: A water tower was here already in 1906, still present in 1948, but gone by 1957. Its foundation can still be seen in 1992.

Norridgewock Hotel: This building stood southwest of the station and burned in 1914 (Harter, page 140). Its foundation can still be seen in 1992 between the foundation of the water tower and the site of the station. The present hotel is directly across the main track from the station site, on the east.

Industrial siding: A photo in Harter (page 190) shows a track diverging to the northeast from south of the station downgrade into a gravel pit. Photos supplied to me by Frank Carey include those of the pit itself and what appears to be a view taken looking north from the top of the water tower. In the latter photo, a track diverges to the southeast from the north end of the station; if this track also heads to the gravel pit then the pit was accessible by means of a wye. Today, the pit site is apparently under water.

Little Rapids. 80.23 or 80.24 miles. Elevation 1689. Map 36-6.

This station was in service as a private station according to the timetables of April 23, 1893, May 29, 1893 and April 1895. It then disappeared from the timetables by September 1, 1902, but was resurrected some time between June 28, 1936 and September 24, 1939. It then operated as a public station, and closed between October 25, 1959 and April 29, 1962. Elevations range from 1685 through 1721; 1689 is the most common. In 1980, the site was marked by a sign board reading "Little Rapids." South of Little Rapids at 78.5 miles, the Division crossed Alder Creek.

Brandreth (Brandreth Lake). 81.37 miles. Elevation 1690. Maps 36-7, 38-1, and 38-2.

For detail on Brandreth, the Mac-a-Mac and Whitney Industries Railroads, see Chapter 38.

Passenger station: An 1896 New York Central map does not yet indicate this station, but a 1900 map does. Gove (April 1981) notes, however, that the Brandreth Lake Station had opened in 1895 for people with nearby summer homes. The name was changed from Brandreth Lake to Brandreth some time between the timetables of June 23, 1912 and March 20, 1913. It closed on April 25, 1965.

Industrial sidings: At Brandreth, a remnant stub of the Mac-a-Mac line persisted until 1953 or later. A New York Central valuation diagram indicates an office building, an engine house, a coal shed, a barn, a cement house, a sand house, a Mac-a-Mac freight house, and several homes. At 81.9 miles is the bridge over the Beaver River. An aerial photo from 1956 shows a spur track heading southeast at about 82.0 miles, crossing the Beaver River on a separate bridge and ending shortly; the function of this spur is unknown.

Photographs: Harter has photos on his page 198.

Keepawa. 82.77 miles. Elevation 1721. Maps 36-7 and 36-24.

Passenger station: Harter (p. 200) states that there were three stations within Webb's private Nehasane Park. Keepawa was for his staff of caretakers. Keepawa is shown on a 1900 New York Central Railroad map. It is then listed on employees' timetables from June 19, 1910 to June 23, 1940, but no trains stopped here.

Passing sidings: Here were two, one on each side of the main track. One of them which held 27 or 28 cars was already in place in 1906, still extant in 1913, but gone by 1917.

Partlow (Pulpwood Post Office). 84.27 or 84.32 miles. Elevation 1730. Maps 36-7 and 42-6.

Passenger station: Partlow, the second station within Webb's private Nehasane Park, was used primarily for logging operations. An 1896 New York Central Railroad map does not yet show Partlow, although a 1900 New York Central Railroad map does. Timetables list it from August 29, 1902 through June 18, 1905.

Siding: According to Marleau, page 242, a siding was built at Partlow in 1919. Because this siding was not listed in employees' timetables, it was probably not a passing siding but only a junction.

Partlow Lake Railroad: See Chapter 42.

Nehasane. 87.82 miles. Elevation 1787. Maps 36-7 and 36-25.

Passenger station: Nehasane first appears on a Mohawk & Malone map dated September 1892, but is called Lake Lila. It does not appear on timetables until April 23, 1893 when the name was changed to Nehasane. This was Webb's private station for his nearby Nehasane Lodge on Lake Lila. The name was hyphenated Ne-ha-sa-ne until 1914, but the hyphenation dropped by 1917. The waiting shed and station still stood in 1980, although the New York Central ceased stopping here on April 25, 1965. The land had been acquired by the State of New York, and is now open to the public. Nehasane Lodge had become so dilapidated that the New York State Department of Environmental Conservation had to demolish it, simultaneously with seven other nearby buildings, on April 3, 1984.

Passing siding: One on the west was already present in 1906 and still extant in 1957. It held between 21 and 34, cars and was gone when the Penn Central abandoned service in 1972.

Photographs: Harter has several on his pages 202 through 205, and on 210. The State Museum Library in Albany has a photo, catalog #P22379, which shows the Nehasane Park Fire Service train (see Chapter 4).

Washout: At about 87.5 miles, a washout present in 1992 will have to be filled in and the track rebuilt in order for any kind of service to resume. The rails are suspended in space over the creek. The other major washout in 1992 is near Rollins Pond at about milepost 120.

Bog Lake (Robinwood). 90.7, 90.89 or 90.95 miles. Elevation 1756. Maps 36-7 and 36-26.

Passenger station: There is some confusion here. The timetable of April 23, 1893 lists Bog Lake at 90.7 miles. The name was still Bog Lake on the June 19, 1904 timetable. By June 27, 1906, however, the timetable no longer lists Bog Lake, but offers Robinwood instead. Then the employees' timetable of June 17, 1906 records the mileage of Robinwood as 90.89 miles and the employees' timetable of June 26, 1932 as 90.95 miles. The timetables lead one to believe that this was one flagstop with a name-change, but why the 0.25-mile relocation? Clark (1974) states that the name "Robinwood" was Marian Low's (wife of Abbot Augustus Low) suggestion for the point of access to their Bog Lake Camp. The station closed between October 25, 1959 and April 29, 1962.

Passing siding: A passing siding was located here on the east, holding 16 or 17 cars, already in existence in 1906, still present in 1913, but gone by 1917.

Industrial siding: An examination of the 1903-1904 Tupper Lake 15-minute quadrangle at about milepost 91.8 reveals a small stub siding on the east, heading north 0.15 mile to a building. The function of this siding is a mystery.

Long Lake West (Sabattis). 94.78 miles. Elevation 1788 or 1789. Maps 36-8 and 36-27.

Passenger station: An 1895 New York Central Railroad map does not yet show Long Lake West, but an 1896 map does. Harter (p.209) notes that the name was changed from Long Lake West to Sabattis on June 26, 1923. This had been the station for Long Lake, hence the original name, with stagecoaches running between here, Little Tupper Lake, and Long Lake. The last passenger train to stop here was on April 25, 1965. The station burned about 1990.

Passing siding: Employees' timetables list a passing siding accommodating between 41 and 62 cars. It was present in 1906 and still so in 1957. The dead-end stub remaining in 1980 was in such poor condition that dispatchers of the Adirondack Railway used it for meets only in emergencies; it was a long haul between passing sidings, Beaver River to Tupper Lake Junction, in 1980. The 1903-1904 and 1953 Tupper Lake quadrangles show a change of track plan during the half-century; the two plans are combined into Map 36-27.

Photographs: Photos occur in Harter (pp. 205, 210, and 211). Robbins (1975, p. 27 and 29) includes photos of Sabattis, but he calls this station Brandreth! Why?

Forest fire: *The Conservationist*, magazine of the New York State Department of Environmental Conservation, October-November 1963, page 16, includes a photo of the September 1908 forest fire here. See Chapter 4, Railroads and Forest Fires, in this book for some detail on this burn.

Horse Shoe (American Legion). 99.91 miles. Elevation 1738. Maps 36-8 and 41-1.

Passenger station: Horse Shoe Pond appears on a Mohawk & Malone map dated September 1892, but the name does not appear on timetables until April 23, 1893. The "Pond" was soon dropped from the name by August 29, 1902. Harter (p. 282) uses one word, and sometimes two, for Horse Shoe. Abbot Augustus Low built the station in 1896 with the same design as the Garden City Station on the Long Island Railroad. The name was changed to American Legion between January 19 and December 7, 1947. Timetables list American Legion to the end of passenger service on April 25, 1965, but the building had been removed before that. Aerial photographs #EA-A-80-19 and 20 at the New York State Office of Equalization and Assessment taken on October 1, 1958 no longer show the station. Its foundation still exists in 1992.

Passing siding: Passing siding data are for between 52 and 65 cars. The siding was already present in 1906, still present in 1940, but gone by 1948.

Servicing facilities: A water tower was already here in 1906, present in 1918, but gone by 1940.

Horse Shoe Forestry Company and Wake Robin Railroads: See Chapter 41.

A. A. Low's Siding. Ca. 102 miles. Elevation 1754. Map 36-8.

The April 1, 1914 New York Central publication *Station Numbers* lists this siding with the nearest milepost as 102. How, and whether or not, it tied in with the Horseshoe Forestry Railroad I do not know.

G. A. McCoy Siding. 103.14 miles. Elevation 1700. Map 36-8.

An April 1, 1914 New York Central Publication *Station Numbers* lists this siding, and Harter (1979, page 282) informs us of its precise mileage: 103.14. (I cannot find what this siding was used for).

Pleasant Lake (Mount Arab). 104.01 miles. Elevation 1676. Maps 36-9 and 36-28.

Passenger station: This is yet another name-change station! Pleasant Lake first appeared in timetables between June 19, 1910 and June 18, 1911. The name was changed to Mount Arab between October 2, 1921 and June 25, 1922. The station closed between April 27, 1958 and October 25, 1959. Gardner (1975, page 75) has a photo of it.

Childwold Station. 106.75 or 106.76 miles. Elevation 1713. Maps 36-9, 39-2 and 39-6.

Passenger station and stagecoach connection: From July 16 through October 24, 1892, this station was the temporary terminus of the Mohawk & Malone Railroad being built southward from Malone Junction. It served the nearby Childwold Park House Hotel, but should not be confused with the New York & Ottawa station some six miles to the northeast which also, via another stage route, served the same hotel (See Chapter 23). The Adirondack Division station closed between October 25, 1959 and April 29, 1962.

Passing siding: One here on the east held between 26 and 56 cars. It was already present in 1906, still so in 1957, but gone by the time the Penn Central abandoned freight service in 1972.

Grasse River Railroad: See Chapter 39 for detail on this line which diverged at Childwold Station.

Piercefield Station. 109.22 or 109.23 miles. Elevation 1673 or 1674. Maps 36-9 and 42-7.

Passenger station: This station is not yet indicated on the May 29, 1893 timetable but is indicated by that of April 1895. It closed between September 29, 1940 and September 24, 1944. Harter includes a photo of the station on his page 211.

Passing siding: A passing siding was built here between 1906 and 1910, was still present in 1918, but gone by 1939. It had a capacity of between 23 and 25 cars.

Piercefield spur: See Chapter 42.

Underwood. 112.3 miles. Elevation 1550. Maps 36-9 and 36-29.

Simmons (1976, pp. 79 and 80 with photo on p. 88) provides details of activities at Underwood. In 1898 and 1899, George Underwood built a pulp rossing plant (to remove the bark from pulpwood) at the west bank of the Raquette River near the railroad bridge. The plant ran until 1909, shipping debarked pulp to the International Paper Company mill at Piercefield. Simmons notes that Underwood worked for the Champlain Realty Company, a subsidiary of International Paper. At a later time, the Underwood site was used as a jackworks, but Simmons offers no date for this.

At milepost 113 was a spur leading to a jackworks on Raquette Pond across from Underwood. It is present on both the 1901-1902 and 1955 Long Lake quadrangles, but had been abandoned before the Penn Central ceased operations in 1972. I have seen a film made in the 1930s by Whitney Industries of a jackworks in operation on Raquette Pond (see Chapter 38); this is probably the one which they used.

Tupper Lake Junction. (Faust Post Office). 113.64 miles. Elevation 1556. Maps 23-6, 26-6, 36-9 and 36-30.

Passenger station: This busy station was in service from July 16, 1892 through April 25, 1965 and then, again, in 1980 by the Adirondack Railway. The Northern Adirondack Railroad, built by John Hurd in 1889-1890, predated the Mohawk & Malone built by William Webb by about 2.5 years. The two railroads crossed here at Tupper Lake Junction. Webb's Railroad was taken over by the New York Central in 1893 and Hurd's in 1906 (the latter becoming the Ottawa Division) so that one railroad then operated both lines. For details on the New York & Ottawa, which operated until 1937, see Chapter 23. Although passenger service terminated on the Adirondack Division on April 25, 1965, Tupper Lake Junction station was not demolished until 1975. A photo of the station, #P38332, is at the State Museum Library in Albany.

Stagecoach connections: In the earlier years, the station was served by stagecoaches from Tupper Lake Village (almost two miles away), the Wawbeek Lodge, Rustic Lodge, and the Waukesha.

Delivery of railroad car to The Adirondack Museum: The Louisville & Nashville private car on exhibit at The Adirondack Museum came to Tupper Lake Junction by rail in 1958 and, then, was hauled over the highway to Blue Mountain Lake by a truck with flatbed trailer. The *Tupper Lake Free Press* of March 13-20, 1958 describes the procedure. The *Syracuse Herald*, March 12, 1978 does also, but with more detail.

Servicing facilities: Northeast of the junction were the elaborate yards and servicing facilities stretched out along the Adirondack Division for 0.4 mile to McCarthy Street and beyond. Seaver (1918) describes the railroad machine shops, probably connected with the engine house already in existence in 1910. The engine house was served originally by four tracks and later two. It burned on May 20, 1951 (Simmons, 1976, pp. 143-144); also destroyed were offices and a locomotive. In 1953 the remains of the house were razed. About the same time, along with dieselization, the fuel oil tanks and coal tower were removed. The twin water towers were a landmark adjacent to Main Street crossing, already in place in

1906 and still present in 1957. A freight house, a sand house, and an ash pit also existed. In the yard, freight trains, heading for Utica, Lake Placid, and Malone Junction, were made up.

Photographs: Numerous photos of Tupper Lake are available: Harter (1979, pp. 218, 219, 256, 302); R. B. Miller (1956, page 19); Staufer (1967, pages 71 and 215); Gardner (1975, page 29); Simmons (1976, pages 86, 134, 135, 146-149, 164-166, and 336); and Palmer and Roehl (1990, page 97).

Industries: Those industries along the Ottawa Division are described in Chapter 23. The major ones include Hurd's Big Mill, the Hobson Mill, and the Oval Wood Dish Company. Only those industries served directly by the Adirondack Division are described in this chapter.

The spur leading to the Santa Clara Lumber Company pulp rossing plant on Raquette Pond crossed Main Street (Route 3) twice, once at the station and, again, at a diagonal near Water Street. It followed Poplar Street to the plant which was built in 1899 and ran until 1913 (Simmons, p.36). The Santa Clara plant, like the Underwood Mill, removed the bark from the pulpwood logs. The Santa Clara Lumber Company then bought John Hurd's old Big Mill and ran it as a saw mill from 1913 to 1926.

Two short stubs off the Santa Clara Mill spur but near the station served several industries to possibly as recently as 1972: Armour Meat Company (photo in Simmons, 1976, p. 86); Socony Vacuum Oil Company in 1954 which became Standard Oil in 1956 and finally Mobil; and the Texas Company in 1954, later Texaco Oil-o-Matic and coal.

The Santa Clara Mill spur was cut back later to just beyond Cedar Street until the Penn Central abandoned service in 1972. Between Cedar and Main Street crossings was the Tupper Lake Supply Company which also could have been served by the railroad as late as 1972.

A spur to the Parish Oil Company in 1954 was located on the then-abandoned right-of-way of the Ottawa Division. It was the only industry on the northwest side of the Adirondack Division in the Tupper Lake Junction vicinity.

Southwest of McCarthy Street and on the southeast side of the yard was the U.S. Bobbin and Shuttle Company (Simmons, p. 311 and photo on p. 312) built in 1948-1949 and running to 1953. Bobbin spools and shuttles were made for the textile industry, and were shipped to other plants for finishing. In 1960, Jamestown Adirondack Corporation took over the mill and made furniture parts until 1967 (Simmons, p. 312).

Northeast of McCarthy Street was the Brooklyn Cooperage Mill. A single remnant brick building still stands in 1991. Detail is available in this book in Chapter 26 on the railroad of the Brooklyn Cooperage Company, including the line which headed east out of Tupper Lake to near Wawbeek.

After 1915, the Tupper Lake Chemical Company took over the Brooklyn Cooperage Company Mill and ran it until 1919. Palmer's unpublished notes at the Library of The Adirondack Museum state that the Tupper Lake Chemical Company had an industrial 0-4-0 steam switcher. In 1948-1949 the Draper Corporation, now part of Rockwell International, built a mill on the site of the former Tupper Lake Chemical Company, using the original smokestack. The Draper Mill has produced a variety of hardwood products since, including bobbin blanks for textile mills, lumber, bowling pin blanks, and furniture components (Simmons, 1976, pp. 310 and 311). Observations made by this writer on October 30, 1977 include an old railroad crane sitting on a piece of track, disconnected from what the Penn Central had left in 1972, in the Draper Corporation yard; in addition was some track of a 6.5-foot gauge also not connected to any other track.

In 1915, Clayton Elliott built a mangle roller plant adjacent to the Brooklyn Cooperage's stave and heading mill which consumed waste materials that came from the Cooperage Mill. Simmons (1976, p. 80) describes a narrow gauge railroad which connected the Cooperage Mill with the Elliott Plant (See Chapter 8 section on disconnecting railroads). The latter shut down after 1921 and relocated to the site of Hurd's Big Mill on Demars Boulevard from 1924 through 1931.

Between Tupper Lake Junction and Floodwood were two sidings which raise questions. The New York Central booklet *Station Numbers* of April 1, 1914 lists a Champlain Realty Company siding with nearest milepost 116 and Turner's Jackworks at nearest milepost 118. The October 1905 New York Central *Official Freight Shippers' Directory* indicates that C. H. Turner had a lumber and pulpwood business in Malone. On a field check on October 29, 1978, our exploratory party found the remains of an old siding on the east side of the main heading southward at about milepost 117.1. Was this Champlain Realty's, Turner's, or neither?

399

Floodwood. 121.57 and 121.84 miles. Elevation 1585. Maps 36-10 and 36-31.

Passenger station: The timetable of May 29, 1893 does not yet show Floodwood, but the April 1895 timetable does. There is some confusion in the location of the station because the 1910 through 1915 employees' timetables list the mileage from Herkimer as 121.57, while the 1939 employees' timetable lists the mileage as 121.84. Sometime during the 1920s and 1930s, the station might have been moved north 0.27 mile.

Passing siding: One did exist here on the west side of the main track, south of the station. It was already in existence by 1906, still extant in 1918, but gone by 1939. Its capacity ranged from 52 to 60 cars.

Industrial sidings: The old 1902-1903 Saint Regis quadrangle indicated a short stub on the west side, heading south at the highway to Derrick. This stub was about 0.1 mile long and its function is unknown.

Saranac Inn. 128.56 miles. Elevation 1626. Maps 36-10 and 36-32.

Passenger station: This station opened on July 16, 1892 and closed sometime between April 29, 1956 and April 28, 1957.

Stagecoach connection: This station replaced the Derrick station on the New York & Ottawa as the nearest point on a railroad to the Saranac Inn hotel. Derrick station was considerably further away, about nine miles, when it opened in 1890. Saranac Inn station opened two years later, and was only a two-mile stage ride from the hotel.

Passing siding: One was located west of the main track, a double-ended team track, and a stub. The main siding held between 16 and 25 cars. It was already in existence by 1906, extant in 1940, but gone by 1948.

Photographs: Harter includes them on pages 165, 166, 220, 221, 262, and 263. Staufer has a photo on page 73, but calls the station Saranac Lake!

Lake Clear Junction (Saranac Junction). 131.68 miles. Elev. 1629. Maps 36-11 and 40-1.

Passenger station: When this station opened on July 16, 1892, it was called Saranac Junction because here the Saranac Lake Branch diverged from the Mohawk & Malone main line. The name was changed to Lake Clear Junction by April 23, 1893. Passenger service from here north to Malone Junction was discontinued on December 13, 1957, although service continued to Saranac Lake and Lake Placid out on the branch until April 25, 1965 when the station closed.

Passing sidings: There were several. The longest was already in existence in 1906 and still extant in 1957. Its capacity, ranging from 63 to 84 cars, was the greatest on the Division between 1910 and 1918 when the latter number of cars was accommodated. Two additional sidings were on the east within the wye. A dead-end stub was on the west side at the south end of the station. In 1972, the Penn Central left a short stub which the Adirondack Railway removed in 1980; the stub could hold only one or two freight cars.

Servicing facilities: A water tower was already present in 1906, still extant in 1948, but gone by 1957. It was, in the earlier years, located south of the wye on the west side near where Highway 30 now crosses. Sometime between 1913 and 1927 the water tower was moved inside the wye. The wye was provided for turning engines which worked the Saranac Branch with connecting trains.

Saranac Branch: For detail on this 5.82-mile-long branch to Saranac Lake and continuing on to Lake Placid, see Chapter 20 on the D&H Chateaugay Branch.

Paul Smith's Electric Railway: See chapter 40.

Highway 30 overpass: A November 2, 1927 blueprint of the then-proposed highway crossing elimination is on file in the Lands Department office at Paul Smith's College. This blueprint also provides much detail used in the preparation of Map 40-1. The overpass was built in 1929, a short distance south of the station, and removed during the summer of 1989.

Photographs: There are many: Harter (1979, pp. 221, 225, 226, 259); Hastings (1950, p. 24); Kudish (1976, pp. 24 and 25).

Paul Smith's Station (Gabriels). 136.69 miles. Elevation 1705. Maps 36-11 and 36-33.

Passenger station and stagecoach connection: When this station opened on July 16, 1892 stagecoaches to and from Paul Smith's Hotel met the trains so that the station was named Paul Smith's Station. On August 20, 1906 when the Paul Smith's Railway opened to Lake Clear Junction, stagecoaches no longer met trains at Paul Smith's Station; the name was changed to Gabriels. The station building burned on August 22, 1927 according to Collins (1977, p. 19), and was replaced by a smaller building until passenger trains ceased stopping here between December 6, 1953 and April 29, 1956.

Passing siding: One already existed in 1906 on the west side of the main and north of the State Highway 86 crossing. It held between 33 and 44 cars. It was still extant in 1918 but gone by 1939.

Industrial sidings: A stub curved north and west from the passing siding to bring in coal cars to heat the Sisters of Mercy Sanatorium. Ben Muncil's sawmill on the east side of the main track had a stub serving it heading north. An article in the Plattsburgh *Press Republican* in May 1982 by Bill McLaughlin entitled *Changes Loom for Gabriel Prison Nears* mentions that Muncil's sawmill was established about 1920, burned in 1948, and closed in the late 1950s. It has been said that potatoes and Christmas trees were shipped out in railroad cars from Gabriels, but no documentation of this has been found to date.

Temporary terminus: When freight service was abandoned between Lake Clear Junction and Malone Junction on April 1, 1961, the almost 42-mile-long segment of track was removed except for five miles between Lake Clear Junction and Gabriels. The stub continued to be in use for the delivery of materials for construction of Livermore and Currier Dormitories at Paul Smith's College. Charles L. Ballard has given me several photographs which he took on April 24, 1965 showing the track terminating a few hundred feet short of the Route 86 grade crossing. By October 14, 1966 Niagara Mohawk had not yet connected the high voltage transmission line to the poles which had just been installed. The transmission line follows the Adirondack Division right-of-way from milepost 135 almost to Malone Junction.

Overpass: The overpass at milepost 137.7 over the Gabriels-Rainbow Road, County Highway #30, was built in 1932, and removed by October 1987.

Photographs and references: The proximity of Gabriels to the Paul Smith's Electric Railway has prompted this writer to catalogue all photos of Gabriels Station, published and unpublished, along with those of Lake Clear Junction. For more detail on the Gabriels area, see Collins (1977) and Kudish (1976, 1981).

Rainbow Lake (Rainbow). 139.19 miles. Elevation 1702. Maps 36-11 and 36-34.

Passenger station: This station first appears on a Mohawk & Malone timetable of September 1892. It closed between June 18, 1950 and December 6, 1953. Photos in Collins (1977) show the station and the nearby Rainbow Lake House hotel. See especially the photo which appears on the ninth (unnumbered) page in the picture section following page 118. Before 1893 the nearest station to the Rainbow Lake House was Onchiota on the Chateaugay Railroad which opened in 1887. The Rainbow Lake Sanatorium was also located near the station.

Onchiota. 142.51 miles. Elevation 1710. Maps 20-6, 20-20, and 36-12.

Passenger station: The May 29, 1893 timetable does not indicate Onchiota, but the April 1895 timetable does. It was in service until December 13, 1957 when passenger service ceased. The station itself was a small, one room waiting shed, later moved several hundred feet to the west of the right-of-way (to private land).

Passing siding: One east of the main track held 20 cars. It was already in existence in 1906, present in 1913, but gone by 1917.

Industrial siding: From the passing siding, a spur headed south and east to a steam saw mill on Oregon Pond. Tyler (1968) informs us that the first mill at Oregon Pond was moved by Roak about 1895 from its original site at Roakdale. According to Seaver (1918, pages 363-364), Warren B. Walker built the mill about 1910 and later sold it to Baker Brothers of Plattsburgh. By 1918, Baker Brothers had sold it to the Plattsburgh Dock and Coal Company. Seaver does not mention Roak so that there is a disparity between his and Tyler's early history of this mill. Whether another spur served this mill from the D&H Chateaugay Branch on the east is still unknown.

Kushaqua Viaduct: At about 143.2 miles, the Adirondack Division crossed the Kushaqua Narrows on a large concrete viaduct about 25 feet high built in 1904. A photo of this viaduct with double-headed steam locomotives appears on page 230 of Harter. (One can canoe through the culvert today.)

Lake Kushaqua (Stonywold). 144.50 miles. Elevation 1726. Maps 20-6, 36-12 and 36-35.

Passenger station: The timetable of July 16, 1892 does not yet list Lake Kushaqua, but the September 1892 timetable does. From 1892 through June 18, 1950 the name was Lake Kushaqua, but it was changed to Stonywold by December 6, 1953. Passenger trains served this stop through December 13, 1957. Gardner (1975, page 94), has a photo of this station. The building itself was moved during the summer of 1975 to a point southwest of the intersection of New York State Routes 3 and 99, adjacent to the Pine Grove Restaurant. The top of the roof had been removed in order to clear powerlines while the station moved on a flatbed trailer along the highway. Because of this, rain and rot set in, and the old station had been demolished into a pile of boards and rubble when the author last checked it in September 1990.

Passing siding: In 1906 one held 12 cars, but it was gone by 1910. When New York Central fireman, Bob Morgan, photographed it about 1950, it was a stub heading south with an adjacent section house. This stub was used to unload coal into a chute for the heating of the Stonywold Sanatorium, later Whitefathers.

Servicing facilities: A water tower was located here already in 1906, still present in 1918, but gone by 1940.

Whitefathers Chapel: Part of the Whitefathers property was sold to the State of New York which proceeded to tear down the old sanatorium buildings in the late 1970s. The chapel alone still stands in 1991, privately owned, and diagonally across the highway from the site of the depot.

Derailment: Harter (page 230) includes photos of a freight train wreck about three miles north of Lake Kushaqua Station. He describes the wreck on page 228.

Morgan's (Morgan's Mills or Morgan's Siding). 146.21 miles. Elevation 1761. Maps 20-6, 20-19 and 36-12.

Hyde (1970, page 25) states that the mill at Bryant's, milepost 158.6, was dismantled and moved to this site in 1915. Seaver (1918, page 364) writes us that the mill at Morgan's was erected by International Paper Company, but was used for cutting hard wood instead of pulp. This might have been a Champlain Realty Company operation, a subsidiary of International Paper, but who was Morgan? A 1926 map in a New York Central employees' timetable shows Morgan's Siding, and a station listing from about that period lists it as Morgan's. Harter (1979, page 284) calls it Morgan's Mills. This was never a passenger station. On May 30, 1977, our exploratory party found an old clearing on the east side of the right-of-way at this point, between Niagara Mohawk power poles #257 and #258.

Loon Lake (Inman Post Office). 148.76 miles. Elevation 1749. Maps 20-6, 36-10 and 20-19.

Passenger station: Passenger trains stopped here from July 16, 1892 through December 13, 1957. It was the highest elevation station on the Adirondack Division north of Sabattis. Across the highway from the New York Central station was the Chateaugay Railroad's station of the same name, built six years earlier (see Chapter 20). Hence Loon Lake was a transfer point for passengers between the two lines.

Stagecoach connection: Loon Lake was the also the connecting point for stagecoaches for the three-mile ride to Chases's Loon Lake House (see Chapter 20 for details).

Passing siding: The passing siding, west of the main track, was already extant in 1906, present still in 1940, but gone by 1948. It held between 20 and 35 cars. On the east of the main track directly in front of the station, was a double-ended team track.

Connection with the D&H: At milepost ca. 147.5 (between the present Niagara Mohawk power poles # 245 and #246) the Mohawk & Malone grade was adjacent to the narrow gauge Chateaugay Railroad. The Chateaugay, built six years earlier, brought in construction materials in 1891-1892 for the Mohawk & Malone. McNamara (1914-1915) in his D&H *Official Freight Shipper's Directory*, page 31, lists a freight connection between the two railroads at Loon Lake; I am not certain whether the connection was built at the original 147.5 site or at the depots.

Tekene. 150.13 miles. Elevation 1680. Maps 20-5, 20-18A, 36-12 and 36-36.

The complex history of Tekene is presented in Chapter 20. It was never a passenger station, but rather a junction point with the Kinsley Lumber Company timber and pulpwood railroad built, according to Seaver (1918, page 363), about 1898. The logging line was later sold, about 1903, to Baker Brothers of Plattsburgh, and the connection moved to the D&H Chateaugay Branch. The Loon Lake 15-minute quadrangle, published in 1902-1906, incorrectly names this logging line as Brooklyn Cooperage!

Passing siding: One was located here west of the main track with a capacity of between 20 and 30 cars. A map in the June 17, 1906 New York Central employees' timetable shows Tekene, but no siding is listed here yet. By June 19, 1910, the siding is listed, was still present in 1913, but gone by 1917. By 1910, however, the Tekene Branch had been tied in with the D&H for seven years, so why did the New York Central install the siding then?

Plumadore. 153.48 miles. Elevation 1705. Maps 20-5, 20-18 and 36-13.

Passing siding: Plumadore was not a passenger station. A passing siding did exist here on the west with a capacity of 34 or 35 cars, according to employees' timetables. Plumadore is first shown on an 1896 New York Central map. It was still extant in 1918, but gone by 1939.

Connection with the D&H Chateaugay Branch: In 1940 a connection was made so that D&H trains could be routed over New York Central tracks from here south to Saranac Lake via Lake Clear Junction. Details are available in Shaughnessy (1967, page 335) and in this book, Chapter 20. This connection lasted until November 1, 1946 when the D&H abandoned service beyond Lyon Mountain.

Little Bryant's. 157.6 miles. Elevation 1508. Maps 36-13 and 36-37.

On the 1902-1906 Loon Lake 15-minute quadrangle appears a short stub, barely 0.1 mile long on the west, crossing Wolf Pond Road, and heading northwest. Hyde (1970, page 65, writes us that this was Little Bryant's, but offers no detail. Was there a saw mill here?

Bryant's Mill. 158.6 miles. Elevation 1506. Maps 36-13 and 36-38.

Seaver (1918, page 179) informs us that Edwin R. Bryant of Syracuse built a sawmill here "a number of years ago" but offers no specific year. The mill was beset with legal problems, burned, was rebuilt by Felix Cardinal, and then run by a series of additional owners. In 1915, it was dismantled and moved south. Hyde (1970, page 25) writes, specifically, that the mill was moved to Morgan's at milepost 146.21.

A loading siding, and a spur heading almost to the south end of the lake were located here, according to Hyde (pages 64 and 65). She states that after the mill here was moved to Morgan's in 1915, only firewood and pulpwood were shipped out for a time.

Employees' timetables do not list the loading siding because it was not used for passing. On July 30, 1994, our exploratory party found that the loading siding was located on the west side of the main, north of the Bryant's Siding Road grade crossing. We also found that the spur switch was just south of the grade crossing; the spur headed northeast down toward Mountain View Lake with West Road currently occupying the right-of-way (see Map 36-38).

Mountain View. 160.19 miles. Elevation 1498 or 1501. Maps 36-13 and 36-39.

Passenger station: This station opened with the July 16, 1892 timetable, and was in service through December 13, 1957. Much detail is available thanks to Hyde (1970, with photos on pp. 63, 64, 65 and 186); Harter (1979 with photos on pp. 231, 232, 233, 261); Dumas (1962, with photo on p. 11); and DeSormo (1974, with photo on p. 108). The DeSormo photo, and the one on the back of Harter's dust jacket, duplicates Harter's on page 231. The first station at Mountain View was apparently no more than a small waiting shack; a more substantial building had been built by 1916. However, a photo in Dumas (1962, page 11) shows that the third and last station at Mountain View was also a small waiting shack!

Passing siding: Hyde (1970, p. 64) states that, initially, there was a siding to serve a lumber yard. When the lumber yard closed or reduced its operation, this siding was extended and converted into a passing siding. It was west of the main track, held 14 or 15 cars, was present already in 1906, extant in 1918 and about 1923, but gone by 1939.

Industrial siding: An additional stub was built to accommodate local freight on the east (Hyde, 1970, p. 64).

Berry pickers: Hyde and Dumas both mention the fact that berry pickers would come up from Malone Junction on the Sunday morning train and return in the evening. This sometimes necessitated extra coaches being cut off at Mountain View during the day.

Servicing facilities: A photo in Harter (p. 232) shows a station agent's cottage and what appears to be a small section house.

Owls Head (Ringville). 162.83 miles. Elevation 1526. Maps 36-13 and 36-40.

Passenger station: Owls Head was not yet a stop on July 16, 1892. The September 1892 timetable lists Ringville. The name was changed to Owls Head by April 23, 1893. Service for passengers continued here through December 13, 1957. Harter includes a photo of the station on page 232, taken while trains were still running. Dumas' photo (1962, p. 11) shows the station after the tracks were removed in 1961. Osborn (1992) includes two photos of the station, one of which is an aerial view.

Passing siding: One holding from 26 to 46 cars was already built by 1906, and still in service in 1957. The Loon Lake 15-minute quadrangle of 1902-1906 indicates a passing siding on both sides of the main track.

Servicing facilities: A water tower was here already in 1906, still present in 1948, but gone by 1957. Owls Head was the summit of the long upgrade out of Malone Junction. Some engines had to be watered here to continue on their way southbound. Pusher engines returned to Malone Junction to assist with the next southbound train. On July 30, 1994, our exploratory party found that the water supply for the tower probably came from Owls Head Pond via a ditch (see Map 36-40).

Industries: Seaver (1918, page 178) describes Scott G. Boyce's saw and planing mill operating until 1916 or 1917. The 1902-1906 Loon Lake quadrangle shows an industry, most likely Boyce's, with two stubs heading to Owls Head Pond.

Relocation: An article in the Malone *Evening Telegram*, dated January 1956, states that the present highway, south out of Owls Head for 0.25 mile toward Mountain View, is straight, and lies atop the original railroad grade. This original grade was abandoned at a time unknown to this writer, and rebuilt further to the east.

Chasm Falls. 165.61 miles. Elevation 1300. Maps 36-14 and 36-41.

Passenger station: This station had not yet appeared in the May 29, 1893 timetable, but does appear on the April 1895 timetable. It served passengers until sometime between June 28, 1936 and September 24, 1939.

Siding: Employees' timetables do not list a passing siding, but a dead-end stub 0.2 mile long on the east, heading north is shown on the 1912-1913 Chateaugay 15-minute quadrangle.

Todd's Pit. 166.52 miles. Elevation 1269. Maps 36-14 and 36-42.

This was not a passenger station, but employees' timetables between 1906 and 1913 do list it. The 1906 timetable mentions a 17-car passing siding. The 1912-1913 Chateaugay 15-minute quadrangle shows a short stub on the east heading south. When this author hiked the right-of-way on August 13, 1985 the sand and gravel pit was still in use, but of course no longer by the railroad. The east side of the Salmon River from Owls Head to Malone Junction is one great glacial outwash deposit—a vast supply of sand and gravel.

Whippleville. 169.28 miles. Elevation 970. Maps 46-14 and 36-43.

Passenger station: This station appears on the September 1892 timetable and operated through sometime between June 28, 1936 and September 24, 1939.

Stub track: The 1912-1913 Chateaugay 15-minute quadrangle denotes a short stub on the east, heading south.

Duquette's Pit. Ca. 171.3 miles. Elevation 920. Maps 36-14 and 36-44.

There was never a station here. When this writer hiked the line on August 13, 1985 the sand and gravel pit was still active, but it was operated by the Malone Concrete Products Company. The Niagara Mohawk powerline diverges from the railroad right-of-way at pole #31, just south of Duquette's Pit, and heads northeast. The grade of the old spur into the pit left the main and headed southeast (see Map 36-44).

Malone Junction. 173.31 miles. Elevation 730. Maps 36-14 and 36-45.

Passenger station: This is as far a we will go on the Adirondack Division, although the line continued north through Constable, crossed the border into Canada, and headed for Montreal. The station opened on July 16, 1892. In earlier years, some Utica trains terminated here, but most headed through the junction to Montreal. From sometime between September 30, 1951 and December 6, 1953 through December 13, 1957, all trains from Utica terminated here. However, commuter trains still continued to run north between Malone Junction and Montreal until October 25, 1958. The depot, at the southwest corner of the crossing between the Rutland and the New York Central, still stands in 1990. In 1984, it had been converted into a restaurant and catering service with a small addition put on across the former Rutland right-of-way.

Rutland Railroad interchange: Here was the connection with the Rutland (earlier the Ogdensburg & Lake Champlain, built in 1850). See Chapter 23 at Moira for a brief history of this railroad. The last Rutland passenger train ran in 1953, and the last freight on September 25, 1961. The Rutland's station in downtown Malone was a mile west of Malone Junction. Track plans, photographs, and railroad building blueprints are available in three of Nimke's books (1986, p. 19; 1989 Part I, pp. 117-125 and the folded map; 1989, Part II, pp. 104-106, 140, and 180). These, though highly detailed, include only the Rutland facilities and interchange tracks at Malone Junction. New York Central facilities distant from the Rutland tracks are not shown.

Servicing facilities: Facilities and yards were extensive here. A roundhouse was located northeast of the crossing between the two railroads. There was also a water tower already present in 1906, and still present in 1957. The coaling station stood at the north end of the New York Central yard. There were also fuel oil tanks, car shops, a freight house, and snowplow storage.

Sources of track plans: The maps in this book were compiled from several sources in addition to the Nimke references listed above. Historian Richard Palmer sent me blueprints drawn in 1906 and in 1917 by the New York Central Maintenance of Way Department.

Photographs: Photos, published in the following references, also assisted in the compilation of the track plans: Harter (1979, pages 164, 234-239, 255-261); *Franklin Historical Review* (1973, pages 53 and 55); and DeSormo (1974, pp. 14 and 107, the latter showing construction in 1891 south out of Malone Junction). Ray Russell in the Malone *Evening Telegram*, October 15, 1983, page 5, shows the New York Central roundhouse in 1920 or 1921. On February 12, 1983, page 5, the same newspaper offered an old photo of the Junction. The Smallman Collection at the Paul Smith's College Library includes many newspaper clippings, some with photos, taken over the years on Malone Junction from the Malone *Evening Telegram*.

Abandonment

Passenger service was suspended on December 13, 1957 between Malone and Lake Clear Junctions. On October 25, 1958, the last train commuted from Malone Junction to Montreal. The last northbound passenger train from Utica to Lake Placid operated on April 24, 1965; the last southbound return-trip passenger train from Lake Placid to Utica was on the 25th. A Watertown *Daily Times* article of April 26, 1965 describes these trains. Fourteen years later, Adirondack Railway trains re-entered Lake Placid for barely another year (See Chapter 42).

Dumas, writing in the Watertown *Daily Times* of October 27 and 28, 1961, states that the last through freight service operated between Lake Clear and Malone Junctions in the fall of 1960. However, the line was not officially abandoned until April 1, 1961. She includes photos of the track, already removed, at Mountain View, with ties piled up, as well as some of the abandoned Owls Head station. Freight service from Lake Clear Junction to Gabriels continued through at least April 25, 1965.

A Syracuse newspaper article by Richard Palmer, probably dated April 24, 1965, states that the weekly freight continued on, going north on Sunday and south on Monday, after passenger service ceased to Lake Placid. When this writer arrived in Saranac Lake in the fall of 1971, the freight came every two weeks, northbound on Saturdays and southbound on Sundays, until the Penn Central abandoned it the following spring. Another unidentifiable newspaper article in the Smallman Collection, dated August 16, 1972 stated that the last Penn Central freight into Lake Placid was on April 10, 1972.

On March 30, 1980, the last Conrail freight arrived in Malone Junction from Huntingdon, Quebec. Ray Russell's article and photo in the Malone *Evening Telegram* on October 15, 1983, is the source.

Equipment

Because the Adirondack Division connected with the New York Central mainline at Utica, it was easy for nearly every conceivable type of locomotive (except the very heaviest) and car to run on the Utica-Montreal line. Great detail of the Mohawk & Malone's roster of locomotives is presented in Harter (1979, pp. 303-305) and in Palmer's notes at The Adirondack Museum library. The Mohawk & Malone ran only a year from 1892 to 1893 when the New York Central took it over.

Hastings (1950) and Staufer (1967) also described equipment. Seely (1928) described the equipment used by the Adirondack and Ottawa Divisions for fighting forest fires: five flat cars bearing each a 7000-gallon water tank and pump with hose (see Chapter 4).

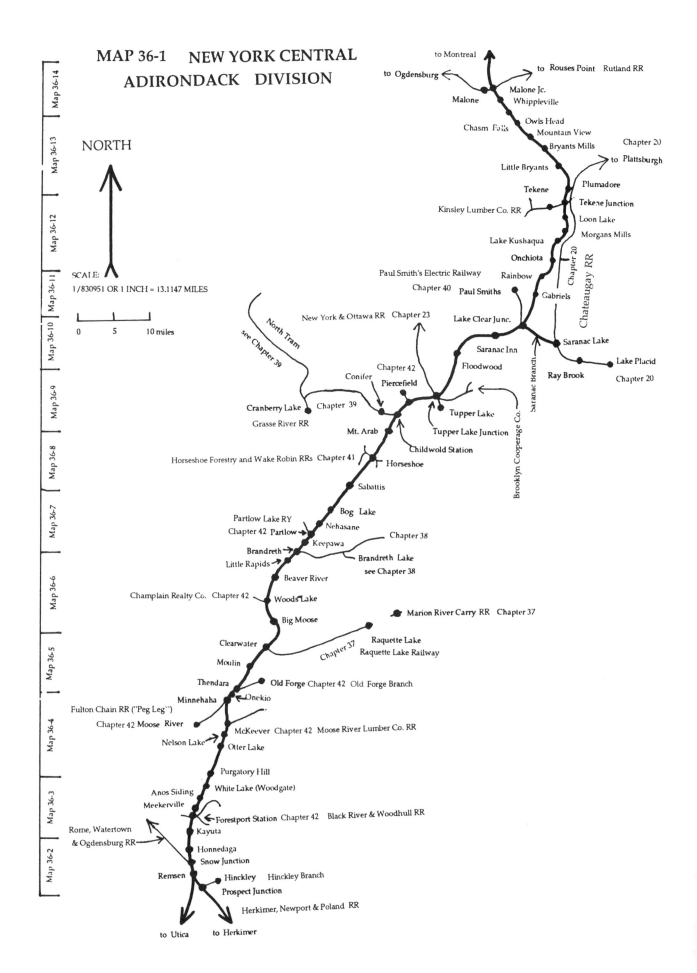

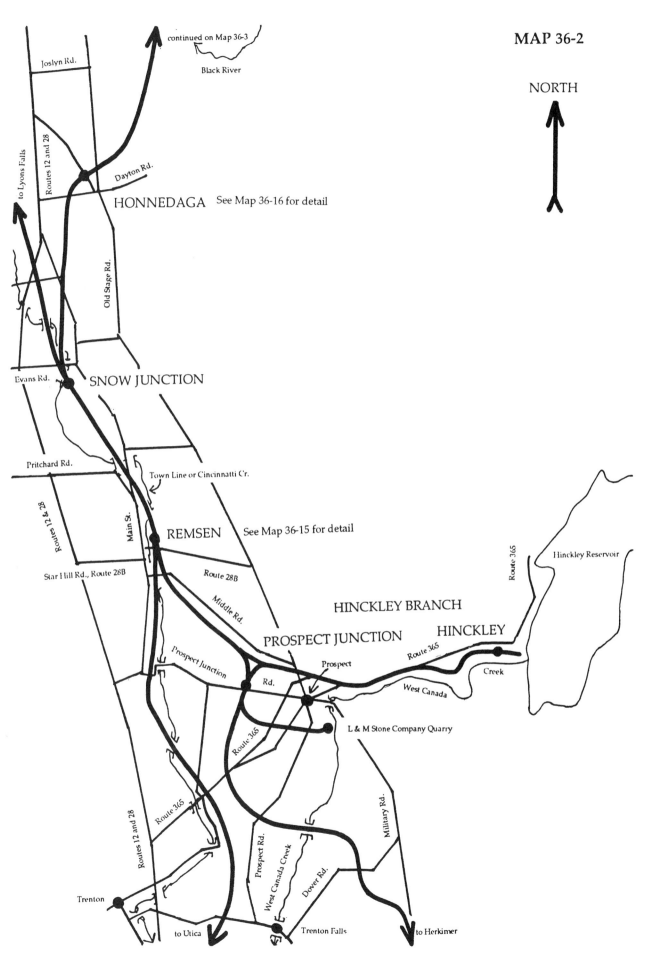

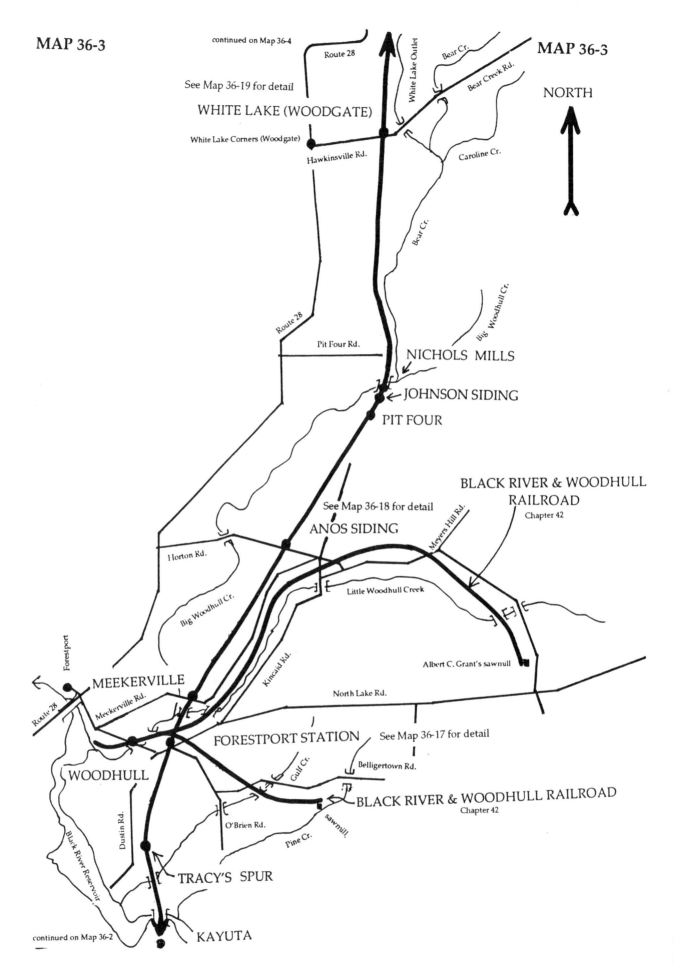

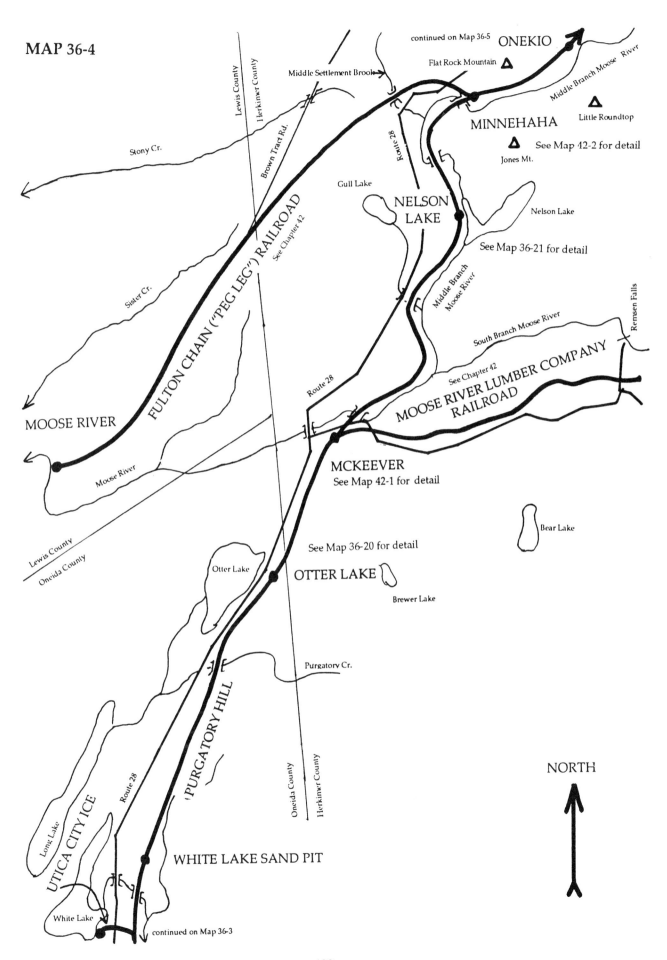

MAP 36-5

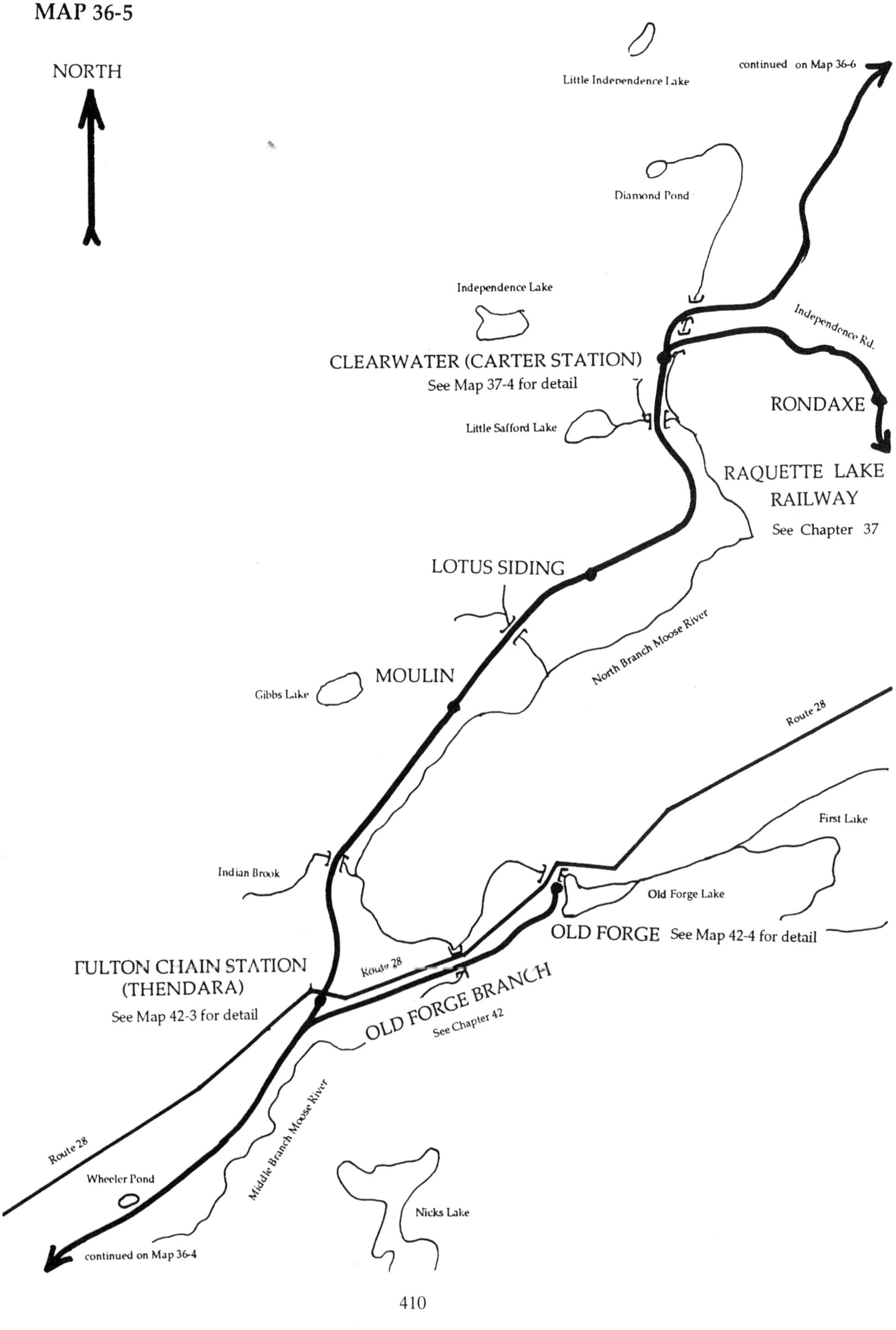

NORTH

continued on Map 36-6

Little Independence Lake

Diamond Pond

Independence Rd.

Independence Lake

CLEARWATER (CARTER STATION)
See Map 37-4 for detail

Little Safford Lake

RONDAXE

RAQUETTE LAKE RAILWAY
See Chapter 37

LOTUS SIDING

North Branch Moose River

MOULIN

Gibbs Lake

Route 28

First Lake

Indian Brook

Old Forge Lake

OLD FORGE See Map 42-4 for detail

FULTON CHAIN STATION (THENDARA)
See Map 42-3 for detail

Route 28

OLD FORGE BRANCH See Chapter 42

Route 28

Wheeler Pond

Middle Branch Moose River

Nicks Lake

continued on Map 36-4

410

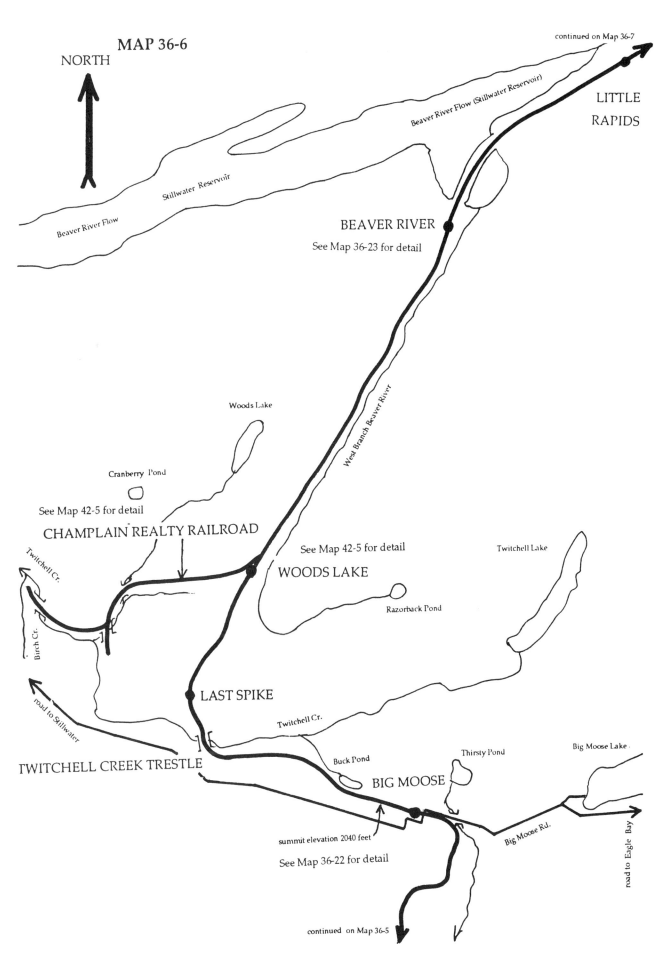

MAP 36-7

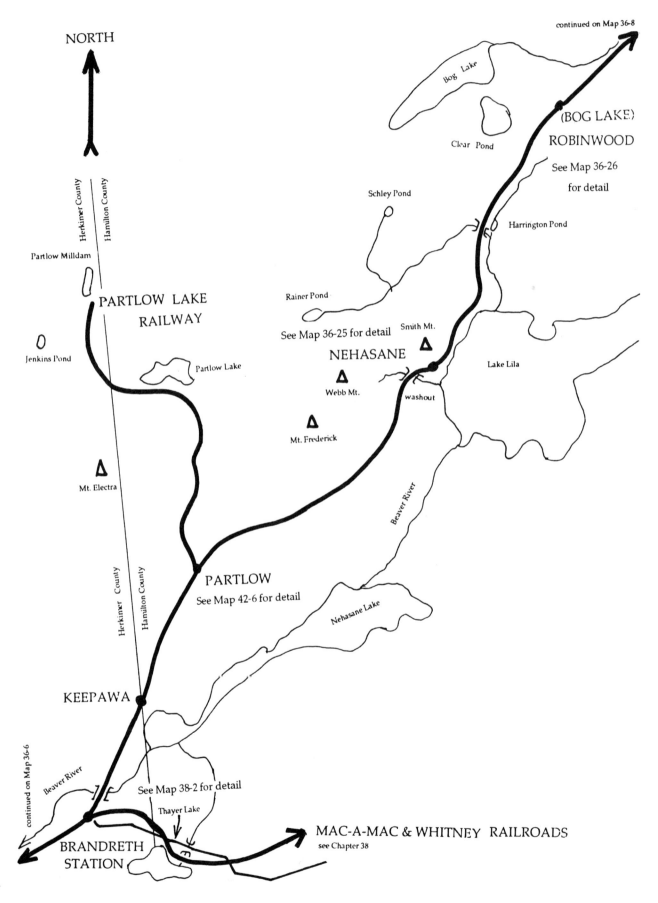

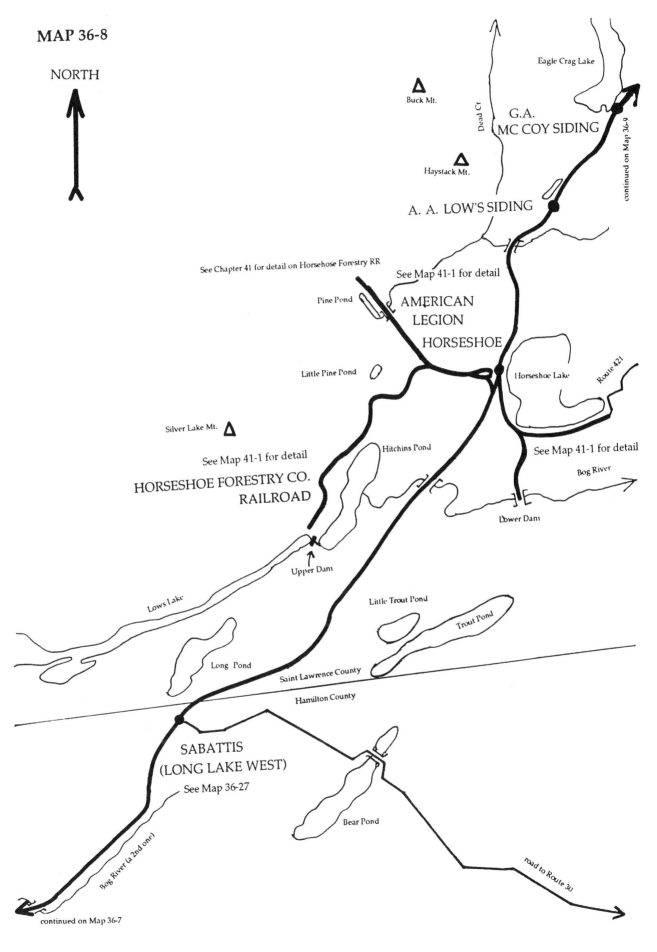

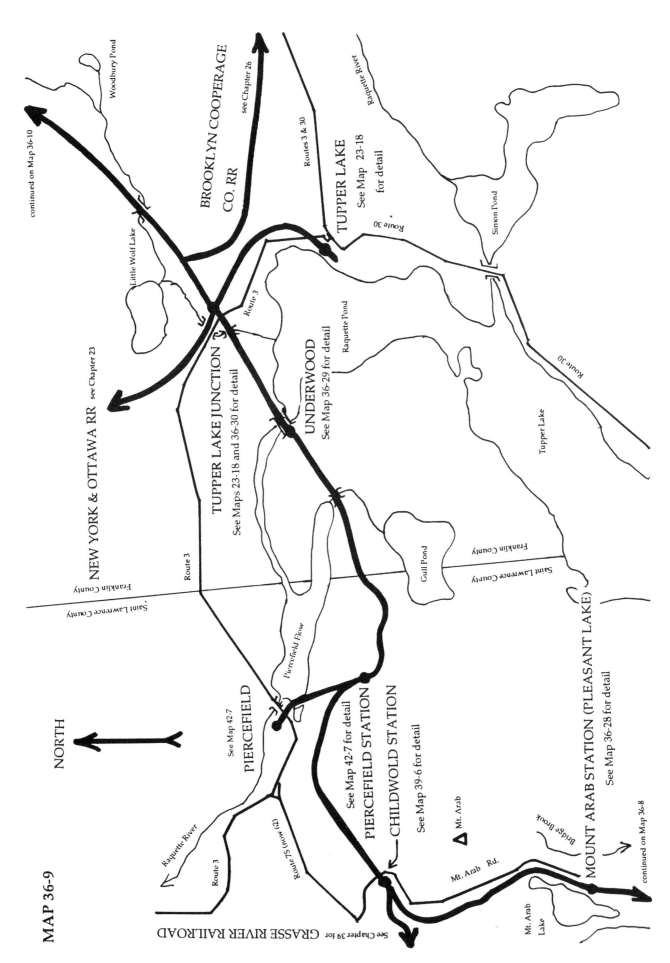

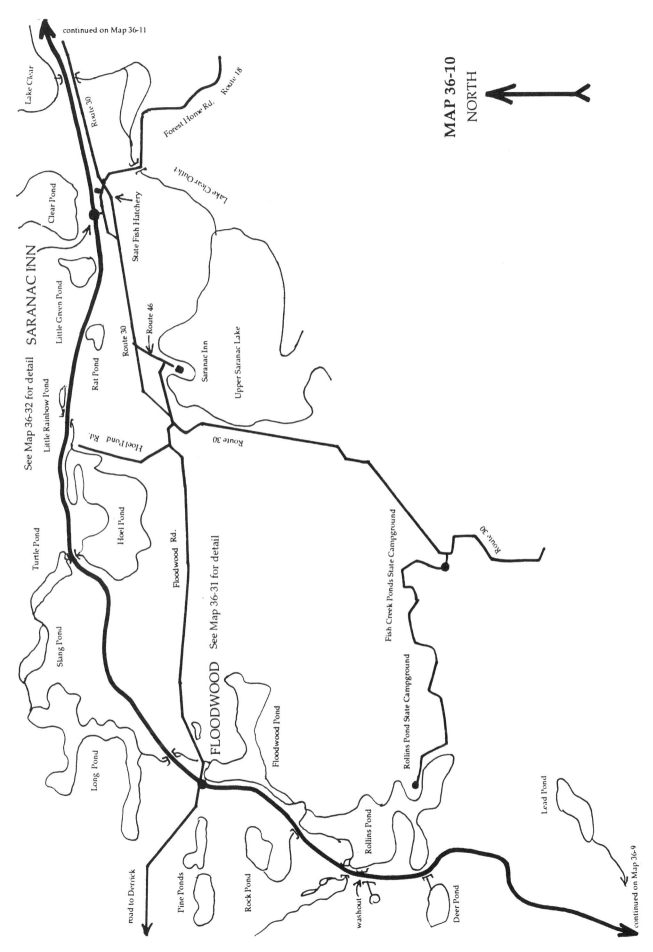

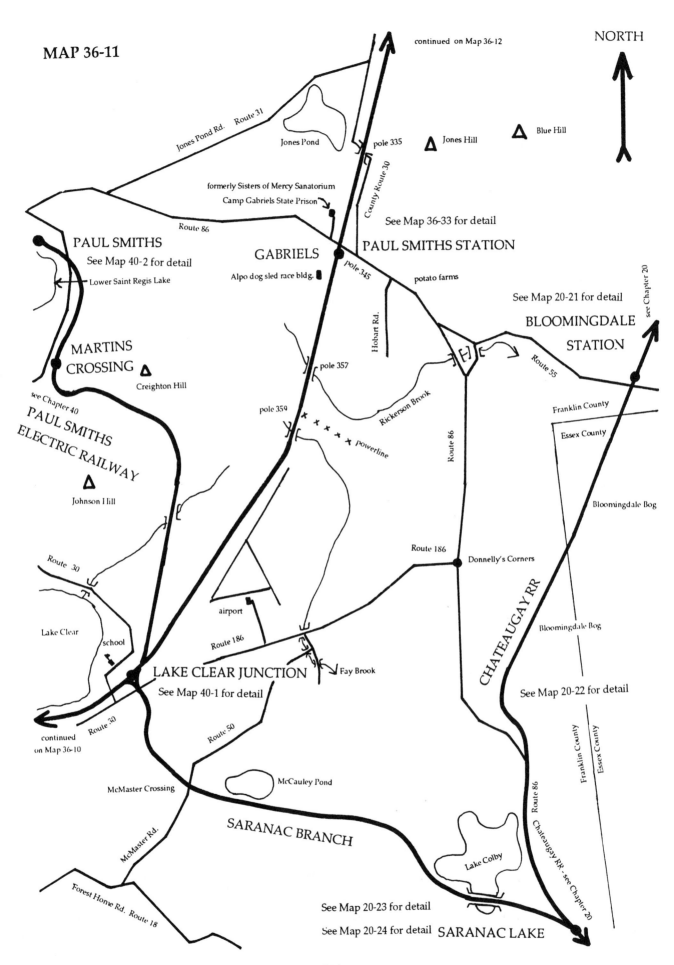

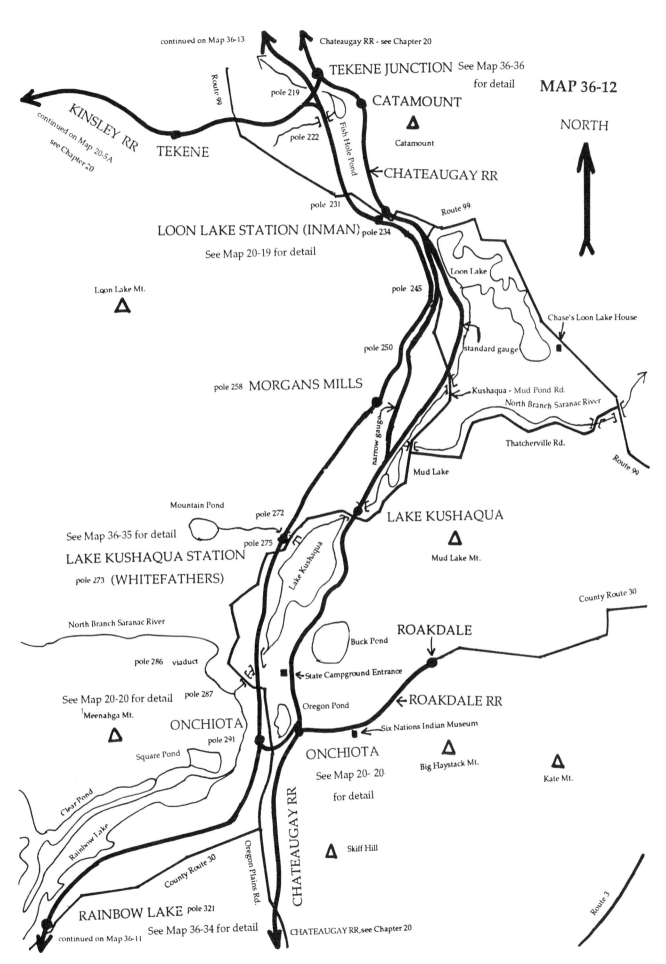

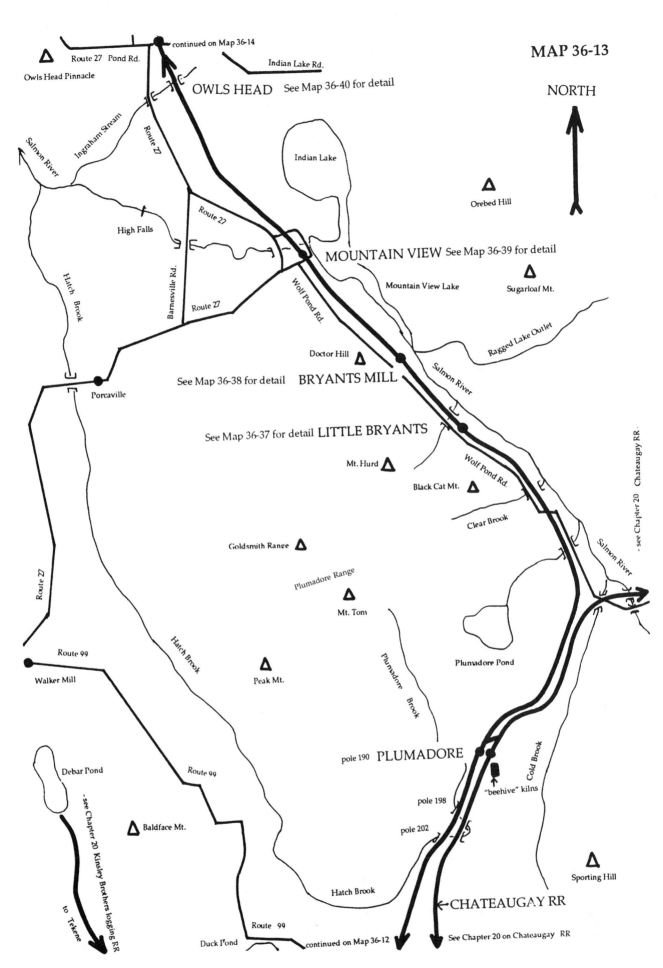

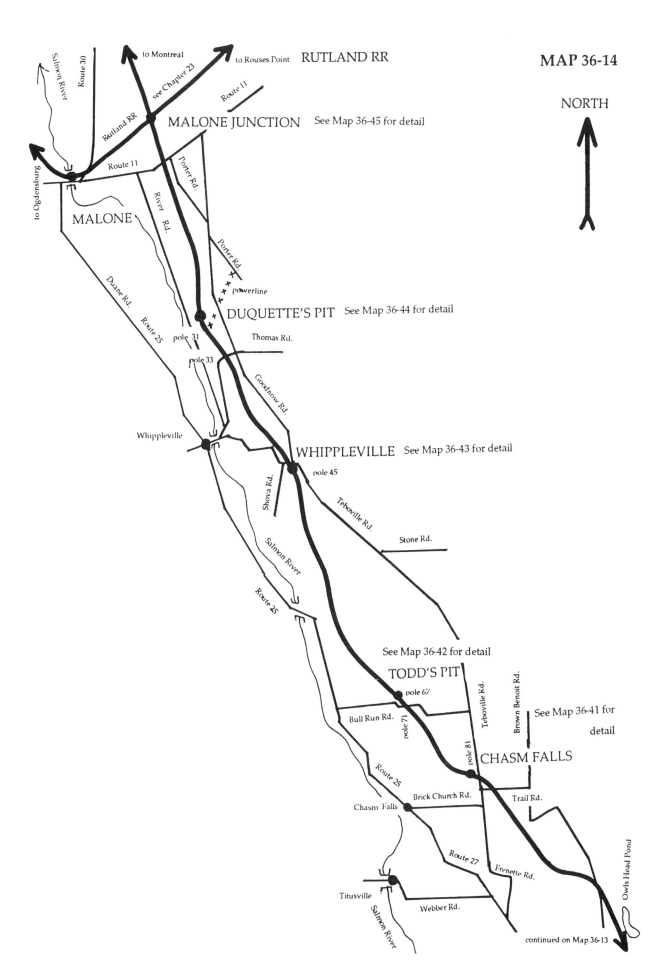

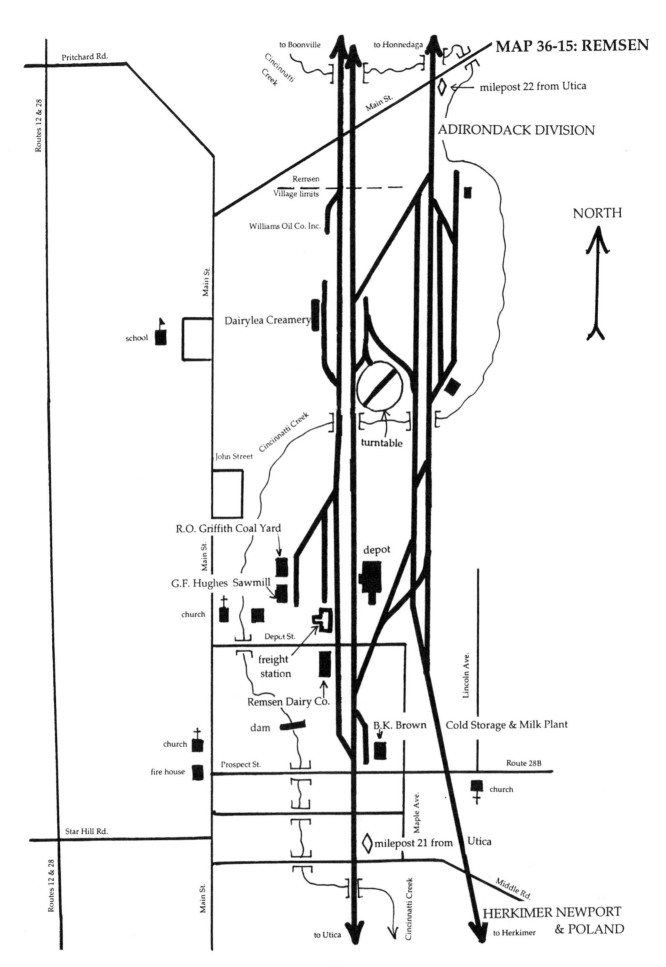

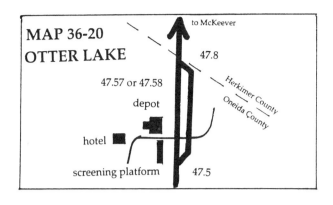
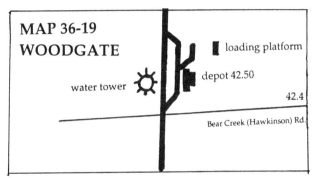
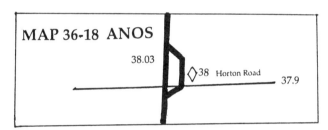
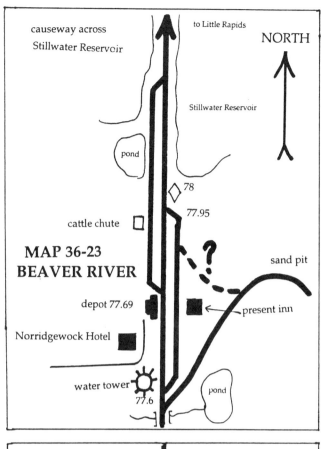
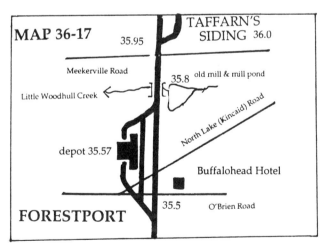
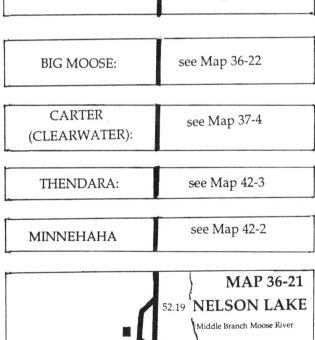
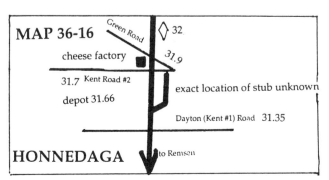
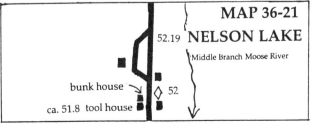

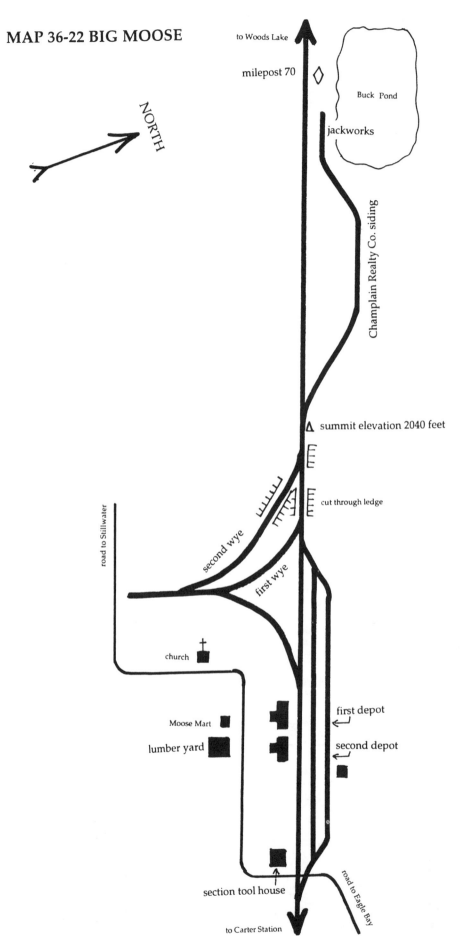

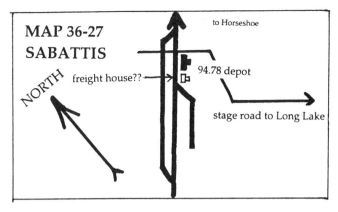
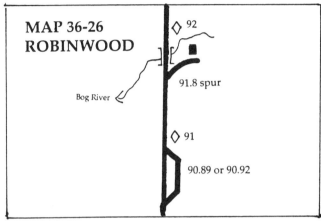
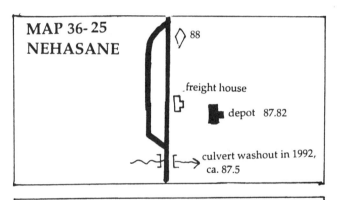
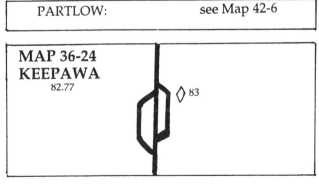
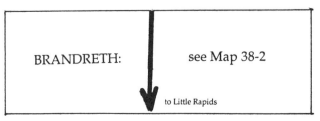
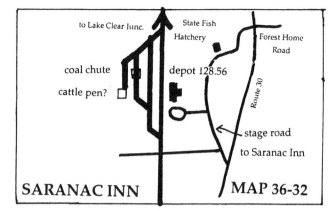
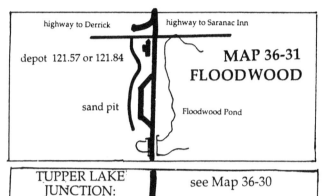
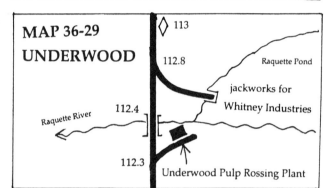
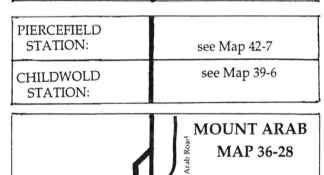
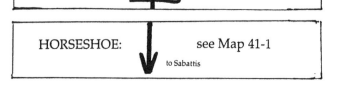

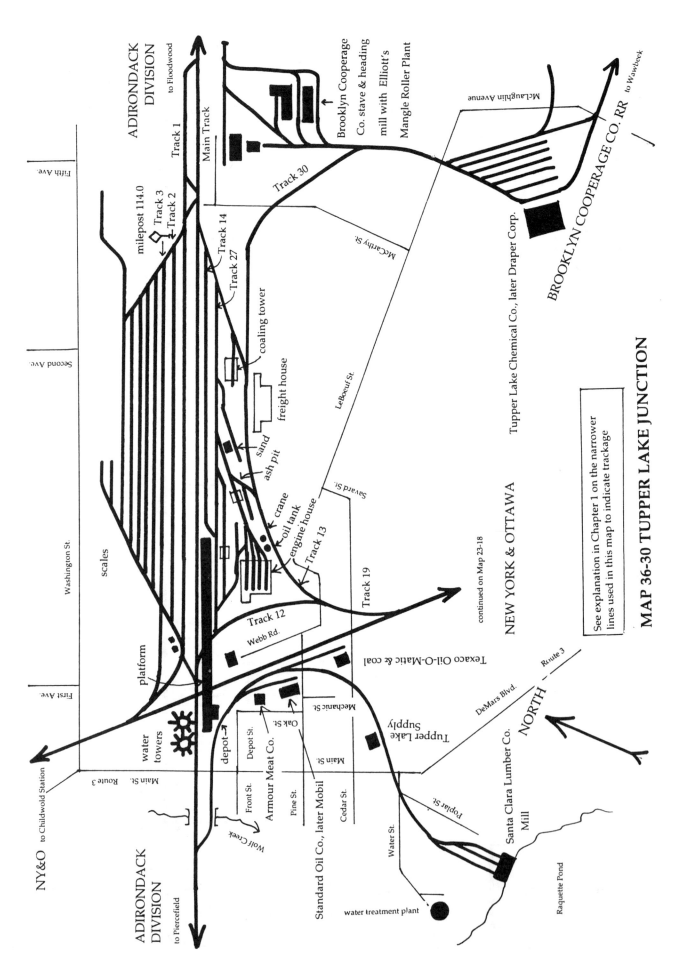

MAP 36-30 TUPPER LAKE JUNCTION

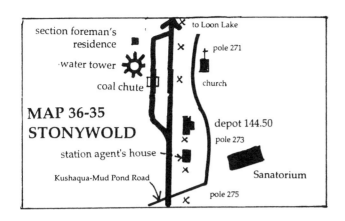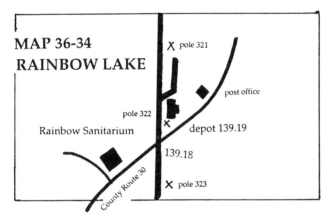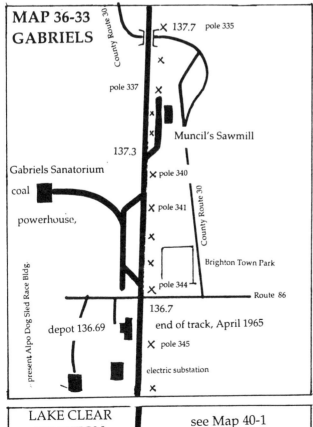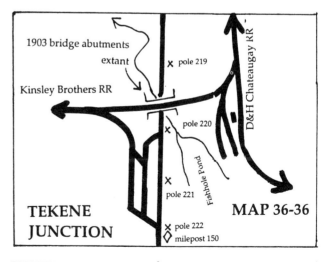

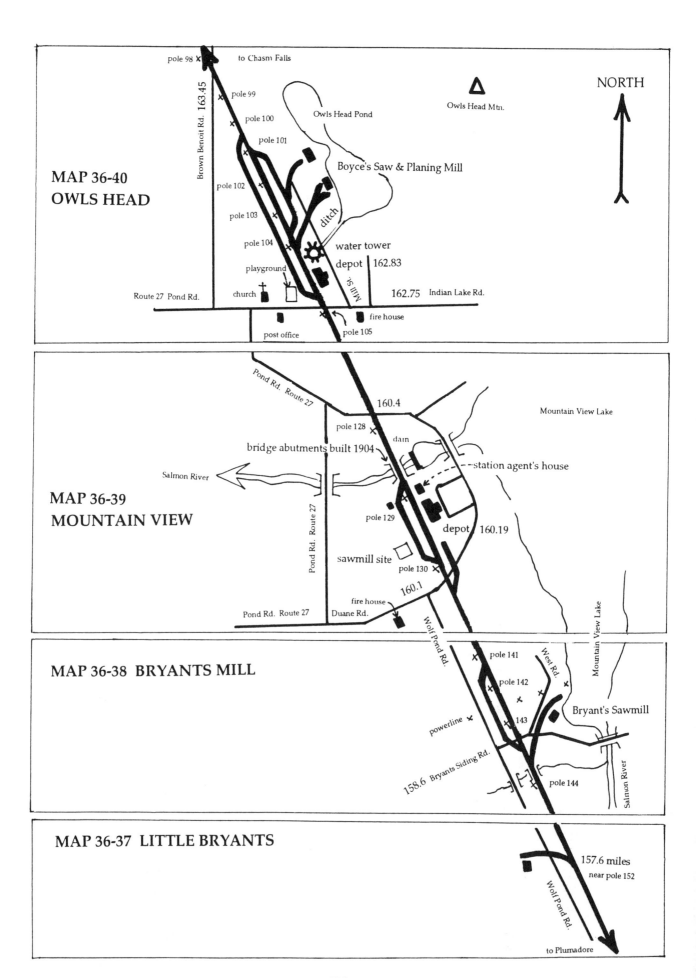

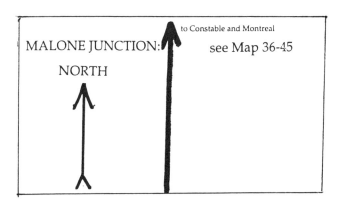

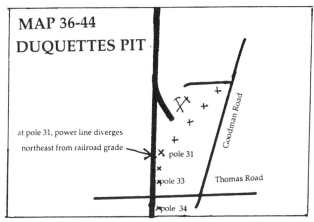

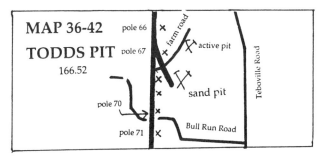

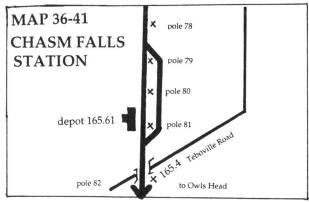

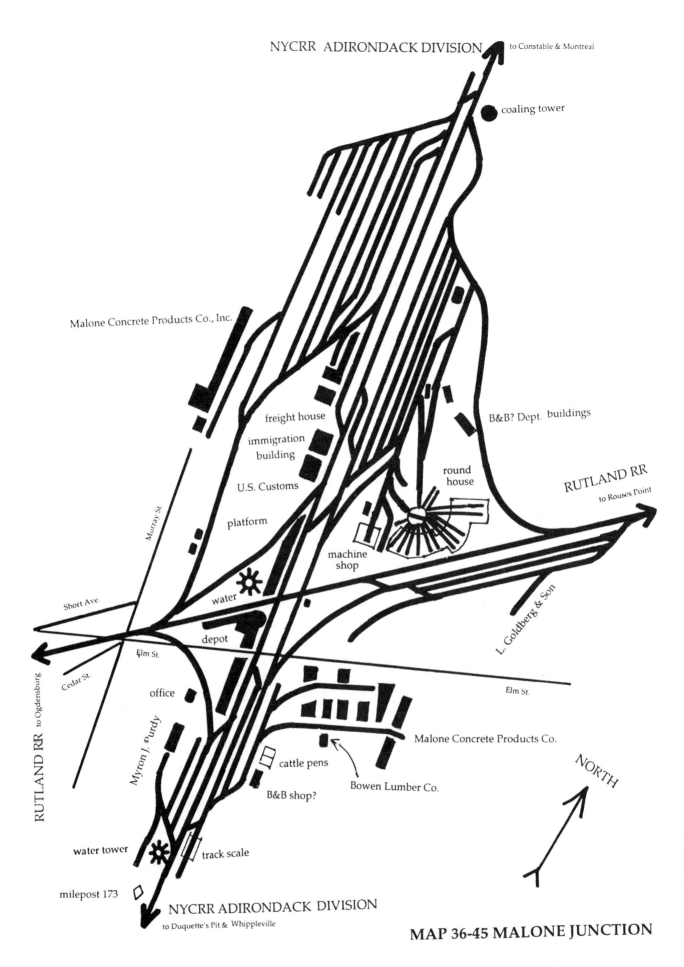

Chapter 37:
Raquette Lake and
Marion River Carry Railroads

I HAVE HEARD that the Raquette Lake Railway began as the Dix Lumber Company's railroad out of Clearwater, later renamed Carter Station, on the New York Central Adirondack Division. The line was later extended to Raquette Lake, but I cannot confirm these facts from publications of that period. Timm (1989, p. 261) writes that the line opened privately on September 12, 1899 to enable people such as the Durants, Huntingtons, and Vanderbilts to reach their camps. The railroad opened to the public on July 1, 1900, although Harter (1979, p. 291) claims that the line opened on July 11. The New York Central acquired the Raquette Lake Railway in 1917 (Hochschild, 1962, *Life and Leisure* --, page 97).

New York Central Railroad employees' timetables and Harter (1979, pp. 280 and 281) list the following intermediate stations with mileages. Several of these stations, Minnowbrook, Fairview, and Skensowane, do not appear on the 1900 Big Moose 15-minute topographic quadrangle.

Raquette Lake Railway
Station Descriptions

Clearwater (Carter Station). 0.00 mile. Elevation 1752. Maps 37-1 and 37-4.

Warren Lipa, director of railroad history field trips for the Sagamore Institute at Raquette Lake, has a photograph which shows that the station at Carter was extended from both ends with open canopies in later years. In 1988, we found that only the foundation still exists. See Chapter 36 for more detail about Clearwater on the New York Central Adirondack Division.

Rondaxe. 2.50 miles. Elevation also 1752. Map 37-1.

Photographs of this station in Warren Lipa's collection show a small shed-like building with an attached open canopy. No siding is visible. The station is located on the 1900 Big Moose quadrangle. Between Rondaxe and Carter Station, the abandoned railroad grade is occupied now by unpaved Independence Road.

Summit. 3.99 miles. Elevation 1880. Map 37-1.

I doubt that there was ever a station here, for observations made during a hike to this point in 1989 indicated to our group that there were neither buildings nor connecting highways. At about milepost five, an historic marker describing the railway stands today along the present grade just west of a marsh crossing.

Minnowbrook. 5.55 miles. Elevation 1820. Maps 37-1 and 37-7.

At about this point, the railroad grade approached and began to parallel the highway which we now call State Route 28.

Bald Mountain. 5.7 miles. Elevation 1800. Maps 37-1 and 37-7.

This station is shown on the 1900 Big Moose quadrangle. Two miles away to the southwest was the Bald Mountain House hotel on Third Lake.

Fairview. 7.01 miles. Elevation 1750. Maps 37-1 and 37-7.

About 0.4 mile west of this station stands a historic marker which reads "Train Wreck on November 9, 1913. Train struck log here, derailed, and went over cliff killing 3 of crew." The sign is attached to power pole #230 on the railroad grade, and is visible from Highway 28 today if one knows precisely where to look. See Map 37-7.

Skensowane. 8.08 miles. Elevation 1750. Maps 37-1 and 37-7.

A 1902 New York Central blueprint shows no siding here.

Eagle Bay. 9.14 miles. Elevation 1760. Maps 37-1 and 37-7.

One photo in Warren Lipa's collection does show a passing siding here. A 1906 New York Central employees' timetable indicates that it held fourteen cars. This siding must have been short-lived, for a 1910 employees' timetable no longer lists it. The depot still stands in 1994 on the north side of the highway, and just west of the Hamilton-Herkimer County line. The railroad grade is behind the station.

Uncas (or Uncas Road). 12.14 miles. Elevation 1850. Map 37-2.

The 1900 Big Moose quadrangle indicates a station, while the New York Central 1902 blueprint shows no siding. From Eagle Bay to here, the track paralleled Uncas Road on the north. Today, the road still exists, and it continues east from here to Browns Tract Ponds State Campground and Raquette Lake. When the railroad was in operation, Uncas Road turned southeast from Uncas Station, and provided access by private conveyance to summer camps such as the Vanderbilts' at Sagamore Lake and the Durants' at Uncas on Mohegan Lake. The first part of this old Uncas Road, today diverging from the Uncas Station site, is a hiking trail leading to Black Bear Mountain.

Raquette Lake. 17.89 miles. Elevation 1762. Maps 37-2 and 37-5.

Map #153 of the Adirondack Museum Library shows the track plan of this terminus when it was under construction in October of 1899. Map 37-5 of this book depicts the track plan after it was completed. The source is a New York Central plan entitled *Map of Station Grounds at Raquette Lake*, March 27, 1902, and updated several times through December 21, 1915. A copy of this map was given to me by Jimmy Dillon of Raquette Lake.

Map 37-5 shows the relation of trackage with both former and existing buildings. Note the following: (1) the reversing loop for locomotives; (2) the depot which more recently served as a restaurant and then burned on December 8, 1972 (Timm 1989, p. 293); (3) the freight transfer dock where boxcars were pushed onto barges; (4) the extension of track past depot for loading coal into steamboats from railroad hopper cars, and loading ice in winter from the lake into boxcars (photo of the latter in Timm, 1989, p. 237); (5) the siding into the Huntington Train Shed to store private cars—the Chapel marks the site today; (6) the engine house and fuel oil tank spurs; and (7) three additional spurs constructed to serve the Raquette Lake House Hotel and hamlet, much of which burned on February 20, 1927.

The New York Central employees' timetables indicate a water tower here during the period 1906 through 1918, and probably before and after. The passing siding in 1906 held 30 freight cars.

Abandonment

The October 1, 1932 New York Central Adirondack Division timetable announced that service had been discontinued from that day through the fall, winter, and spring until June 15, 1933. Trains operated for the last time during the Summer of 1933. Harter (1979, p. 292) states that service terminated permanently on September 30, 1933.

Marion River Carry Railroad. Maps 37-3 and 37-6.

Much publicity and publication have been given to the Marion River Carry Railroad for several reasons. First, it was reported to be the shortest standard-gauged railroad in the United States at 0.87 mile. Second, it connected with steamboat routes, not other railroads, at both ends. Third, the locomotive and a rebuilt passenger car are on exhibit today at The Adirondack Museum in Blue Mountain Lake. Publications on this line follow chronologically. Page numbers are cited for photos where the publication is a full book; no page numbers are cited for short articles. See Beals (1928), Dales (1940), R. B. Miller (1955-1956 and 1956-1957), Fynmore (1957),

Hochschild (1962, *Life and Leisure--*, pp. 38, 39, 49, 51, 55, 80, 86, 89, 92, and 93), DeSormo (1974, p. 180), Timm (1979), Harter (1979, pp. 92-95), Egan (1981), Timm (1989, pp. 10, 237-240, 269-270, and 275), Dedrick (1989), O'Hern (1990), and Shields (1994).

It was possible to travel from the Raquette Lake railway station to Blue Mountain Lake by boat except on the rapids on the Marion River which the Carry was built to bypass. The railroad, along with the Raquette Lake Railway, opened in 1900 for the summer season.

Before the railroad was built, a sawmill existed at Bassett's Carry (or Bassett's Camp), the original name for most likely the lower terminus of the line. Hochschild (1962, in *Life and Leisure in the Adirondack Backwoods*, p. 42) notes a sawmill at the Carry run by W. W. Durant, and shows a photo of it on page 49. Timm (1989, p. 240) also shows a photo of the mill with tracks built on elevated platforms, not unlike the high docks used by the Emporium Forestry Company some years later. These tracks were probably not connected with the Marion River Carry railroad as the mill operated earlier in the 1890s. The upper terminus might have been called Bissell's Landing before the Carry Railroad was built.

Photos in DeSormo (1974, p. 180) and Timm (1979, p. 264) show the original railroad with horses and three horse-drawn street cars obtained from Brooklyn Rapid Transit. Egan (1981, p. 42) tells us that the first two years of operation were marked by two unsuccessful locomotives. The third engine, a Porter Tank Engine from the New York City elevated, went into service on June 13, 1902. This engine's front end always faced east towards Utowana Lake. Thus, it pulled the train from the Lower to the Upper Carry, and pushed it back down to the Lower Carry. Because the locomotive was never turned, the directions east and west are obvious, therefore, when one finds a captionless photograph of the engine. The locomotive was stored in the engine house from the time of abandonment in 1929, because of the construction of State Highway 28, to the time of transfer to The Adirondack Museum in 1955 (R. B. Miller, 1955-1956).

Warren Lipa has, in his collection, a photograph of Durant's Inspection Car (a locomotive with a large cab to seat several passengers) which came on a barge from Raquette Lake to the Marion River Carry. What a weight for the barge! The Inspection Car was lettered F P & L Co which Warren believes stands for "Forest Products and Land Company."

The Marion River Carry Railroad must have modified one of the three open-sided Brooklyn Rapid Transit cars by removing seats in order to convert it into a baggage car. The single passenger coach on exhibit at The Museum was rebuilt from parts of the three original cars. On a 1989 field trip sponsored by Sagamore Institute and conducted by Mr. Lipa, our group found remains of the other cars cast down the embankment from the grade.

Freight cars were ferried by barges from Raquette Lake to Blue Mountain Lake using the Carry Railroad. There were only three switches on the line. One, at the lower terminus, was used to separate freight cars entering or leaving the Raquette Lake barge from the passenger cars leaving or arriving at the depot. The second switch served the engine house. Boxcars carried coal and kerosene mainly for the Prospect House and Callahan's Store on Blue Mountain Lake. These freight cars never left the barge and were unloaded while still upon it. One boxcar was apparently accidentally dumped into and still lies in the lake near the Prospect House point! Each boxcar was pulled off the barge at the lower terminus, tugged up to the engine house switch, and uncoupled; then, according to a procedure which I do not fully understand, the boxcar was manually jacked past the switch so that the locomotive, now on the engine house spur, could get behind the car and push it the rest of the way up to the upper carry dock and onto the barge. I would assume that coal destined for the steamboats on Blue Mountain, Eagle, and Utowana Lakes also came via boxcar on barge across Raquette Lake. A third switch with unknown function existed at the upper terminus.

The decomposing wooden barge still exists at the upper carry at Utowana Lake, but three authors, Egan (1981), Dedrick (1989), and Shields (1994), identify it as the dock.

Harter (1979, p. 292) states that the Marion River Carry Railroad closed on September 15, 1929.

In 1989 and 1990, the lower half of the Marion River Carry Railroad grade below the trestle site was privately-owned, probably still is, and appears as a grassy road. The Marion River Carry Inn is now a private residence. The upper half, above the trestle site, is on state land, and serves as a public canoe carry trail for boaters traveling to and from Utowana Lake and the Marion River. The trestle itself is long gone, and one must ford the river on foot to walk the whole length of the grade.

MAP 37-1 RAQUETTE LAKE RAILWAY

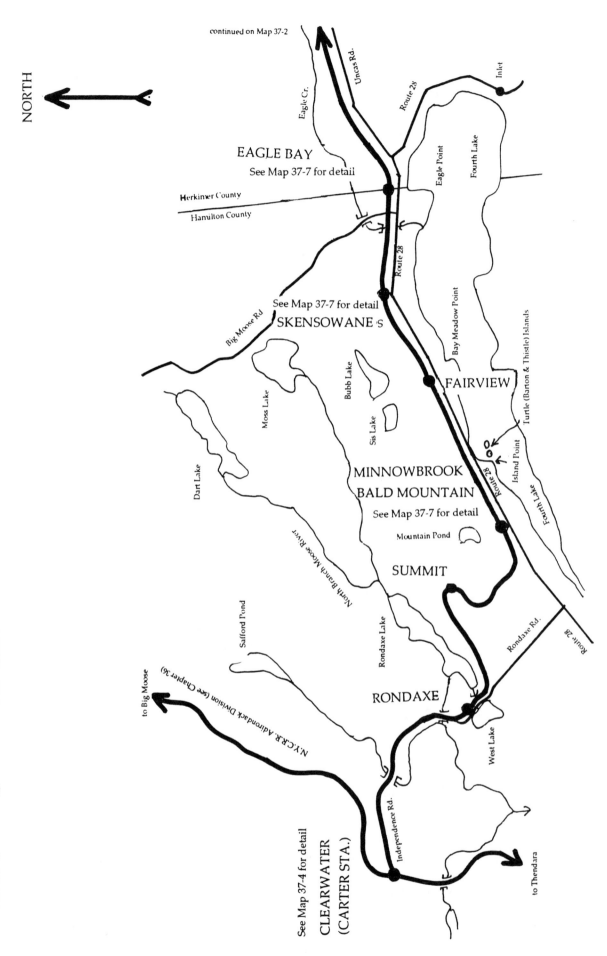

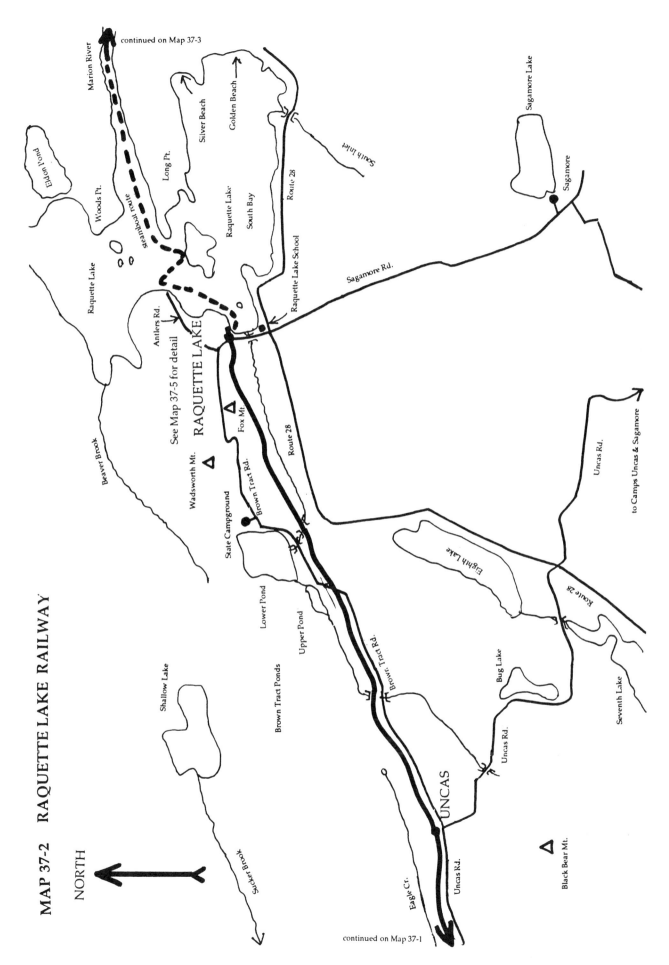

MAP 37-3 MARION RIVER CARRY RAILROAD

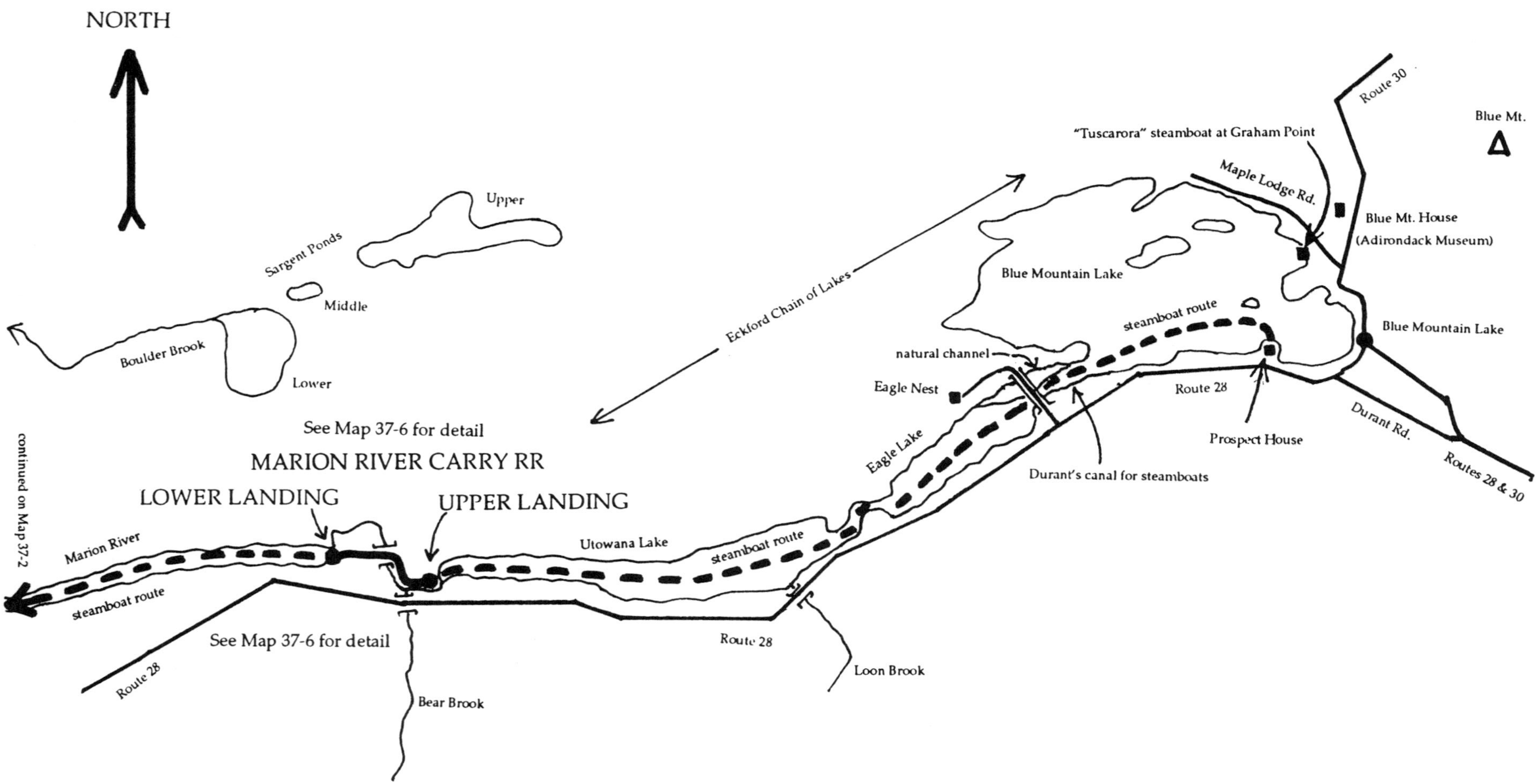

continued on Map 37-2

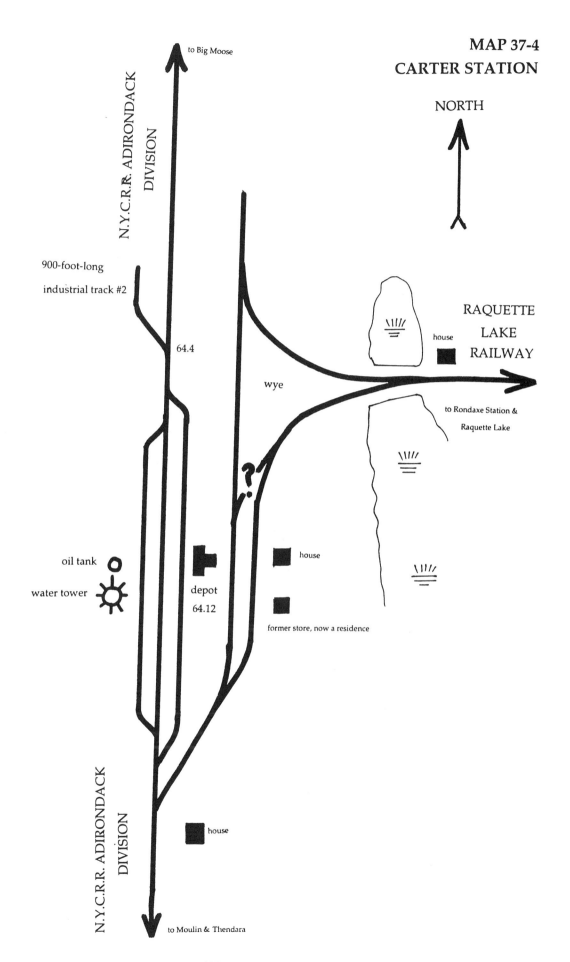

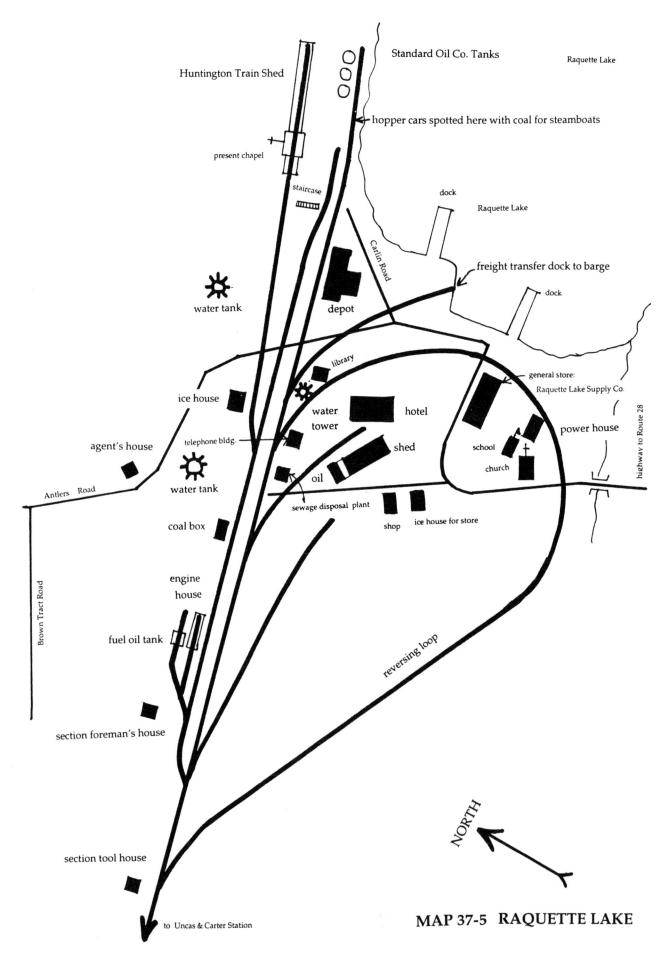

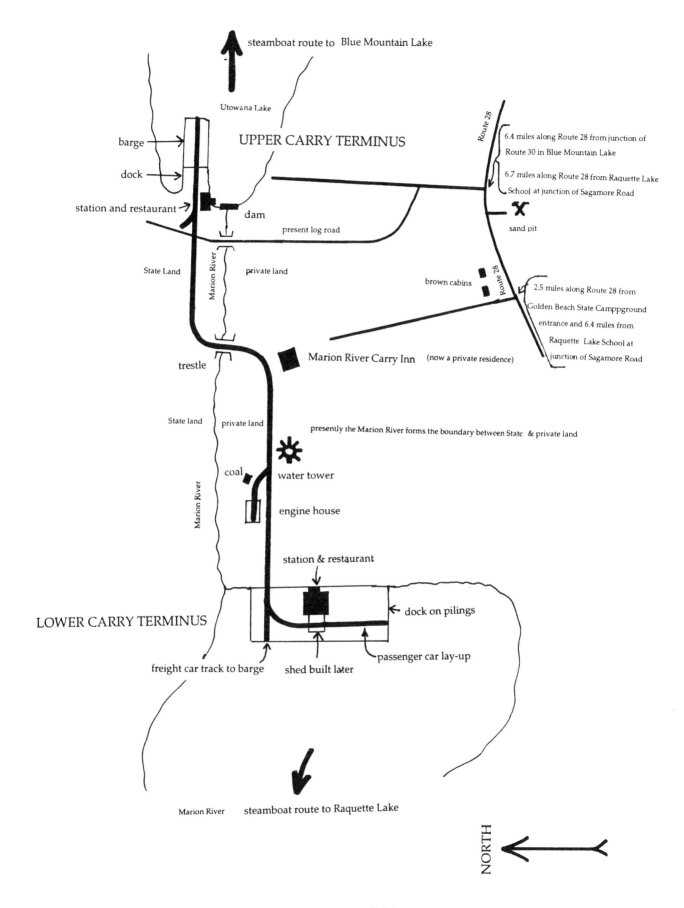

MAP 37-6 MARION RIVER CARRY

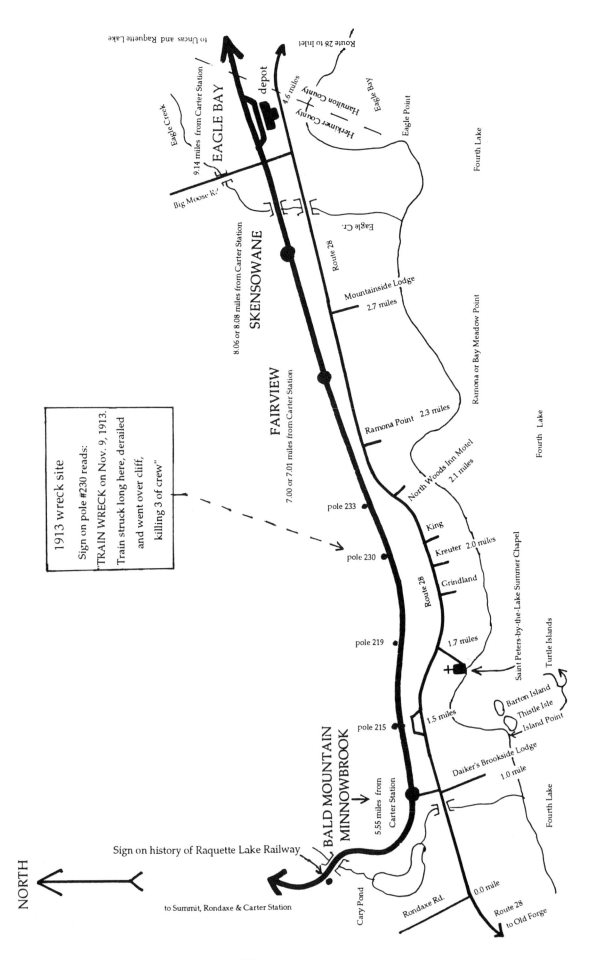

MAP 37-7 1913 WRECK SITE

Chapter 38:
Mac-A-Mac and Whitney Industries Railroads at Brandreth.

GOVE (April 1981) and a tour which the author received of Brandreth Park from the Potter and Wardner Families on August 1, 1991 are the sources for most detail on these two logging railroads. There are only three instances in the Adirondacks where a railroad had been built and abandoned, and another railroad some years later rebuilt on the earlier right-of-way. Brandreth is one. The other two are at Everton (Chapter 26) and at Newbridge (Chapter 32).

Maps 38-1 and 38-2

Gove records the fact that in order to make travel easier to their lodge on Brandreth Lake, the Brandreth Family constructed a small depot on the New York Central Adirondack Division at a point which they named Brandreth in 1895. From here, they travelled by wagon over the Old Mountain Road to the Lodge. The earliest New York Central timetable in my collection which shows Brandreth is in 1900.

In 1912, John N. McDonald, Vasco P. Abbott, and Benjamin B. McAlpin formed the Mac-a-Mac Corporation. Under agreement with the Brandreth Family, they were to remove conifer pulp logs from Brandreth Park, the tract of land owned by the family. Mac-a-Mac built a railroad line nine miles long to Brandreth Lake as well as three more miles of spurs (see Map 38-1). Logging of old growth forest began after April 15, 1912. There were four jackworks: one was at Thayer Lake, the second at North Pond Flowground, the third at West Pond, and the fourth on the Arm of Brandreth Lake. The junction between the Mac-a-Mac mainline to Brandreth Lake and the branch to North Pond Flowground was named Saint Agnes. Offices, a small village, and an engine house to shelter their Heisler and Mogul locomotives were built at Brandreth Depot. The connection with the New York Central was south of the depot (see Map 38-2). Pulpwood was shipped out on flatcars via the New York Central to the Saint Regis Paper Company mill at Deferiet.

Mac-a-Mac suspended operations at Brandreth Park in 1920 and, within a few years, McDonald had moved his equipment north to near Bay Pond. He then established Bay Pond Inc., and logged a tract from McDonald Station west to near Augerhole Falls on the West Branch Saint Regis River (see Chapter 27).

A photograph of the jackworks at North Pond Flowground was shown to me by Dr. LeRoy Wardner and is probably the jackworks shown on the front cover of *The Northern Logger and Timber Processor*, April 1981. It was steam-powered. The remains of the original dam and coal pile still exist in 1991 next to the railroad grade which is currently used as a logging road for trucks.

Gove writes that a sawmill was constructed in 1925 near Brandreth Depot by the Little Rapids Lumber Company. Here, hardwoods left over from the softwood logging by Mac-a-Mac on Brandreth Park were consumed. The mill yard, with hot pond to rid the logs of soil and bark, was located about one-fourth of a mile east of the depot along the former Mac-a-Mac line (see Map 38-2). No railroad was used in this logging operation (only Linn Tractors) which ended in 1931.

Whitney Industries Inc. was formed to log hardwoods from Whitney Park, the tract of land adjacent to Brandreth Park on the northeast, to sell to Oval Wood Dish Company of Tupper Lake (see Chapter 28). In 1935 and 1936, Whitney Industries relaid track on the former right-of-way of the Mac-a-Mac Railroad from the Little Rapids Lumber Company saw mill site some 6.5 miles to a point about one-half mile beyond Saint Agnes on the North Pond Flowground spur. From this point, Whitney Industries constructed a new grade northeastward across the last two miles of Brandreth Park and then into Whitney Park. Within Whitney Park, the line continued about four more miles to Rock Pond, a total distance of almost 13 miles from Brandreth Depot (see Map 38-1). No jackworks were involved at Rock Pond because this was a hardwood logging operation, and hardwood logs were not floated on bodies of water. Whitney Industries operated their railroad for only several years, ceasing in 1939. The 1954 Raquette Lake 15-minute quadrangle, based on 1953 aerial photos, shows the abandoned grade to Rock Pond. The junction which Mac-a-Mac had used with the New York Central was not utilized by Whitney Industries; instead, a new junction was built northward almost as far as the bridge over the Beaver River. The new north junction probably better facilitated moving logging trains northward toward Tupper Lake.

Arthur Potter, a descendant of the Brandreth Family, has given Paul Smith's College a most fascinating film of Whitney Industries' logging and railroad construction in 1935 and 1936. Most labor was done by human muscle and horse beside the steam-powered machines. There were no chain saws. The locomotive shown in the film is #33, an 0-6-0 saddle tank switcher.

A photo taken by railroad historian, Luke Wood, in the early 1950s from the cab of a diesel locomotive shows the depot and the store; the latter building had a sign which read "Brandreth Lake Corp. Forest Products." The 1954 Big Moose 15-minute quadrangle, based on aerial photos from 1953, shows the siding and other buildings. An aerial photo from the New York State Office of Equalization and Assessment, dated September 28, 1956, reveals the depot, the store, other buildings and, in addition, several boxcars on the siding behind the store. The siding was a short remnant stub of the former Mac-a-Mac Railroad line. The depot burned during the winter of 1968, and the two last remaining houses burned in 1975 (MacDonald, 1975, page 13).

Published photos are readily available. Gove (1981) includes several of Mac-a-Mac operations. Harter (1979, pp. 198 and 199) has three: of Brandreth Depot, of a Heisler locomotive, and of the jackworks at Brandreth Lake. Berry (1956) includes a photo of a Mac-a-Mac log train in 1914, ready for the New York Central. Koch (1979, page 140) has a photo of Mac-a-Mac Heisler #1, an oil burner.

Further examination of the 1956 aerial photo from Equalization and Assessment reveals a previously undetected, unreported spur joining the Adirondack Division north of the Beaver River bridge. The spur headed south also crossing the Beaver River, but on separate bridge and terminated within a few tenths of a mile. The function of this spur is unknown (see Map 38-2).

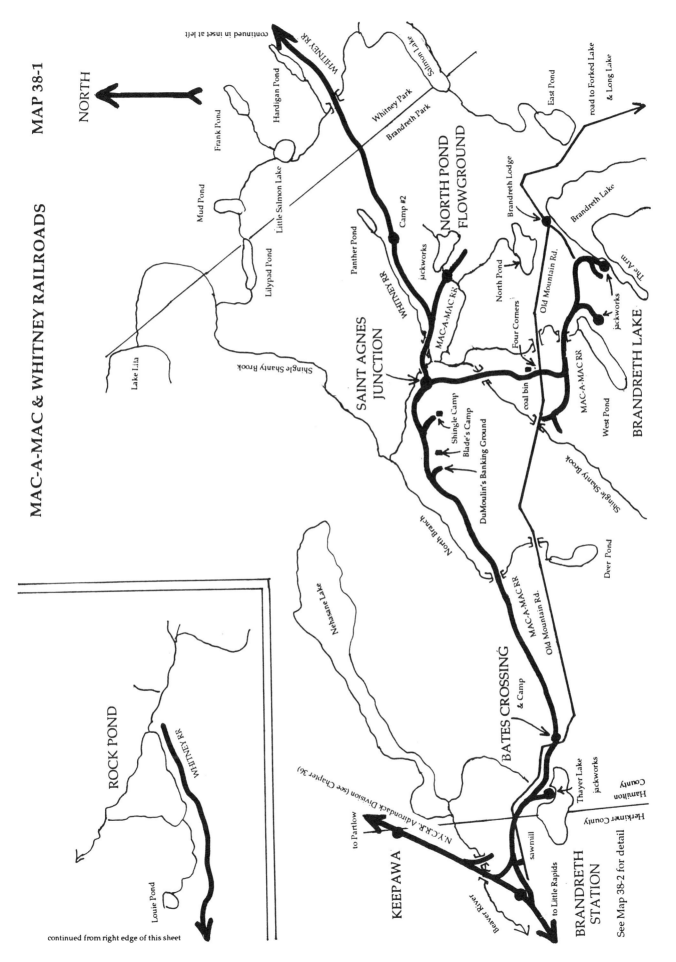

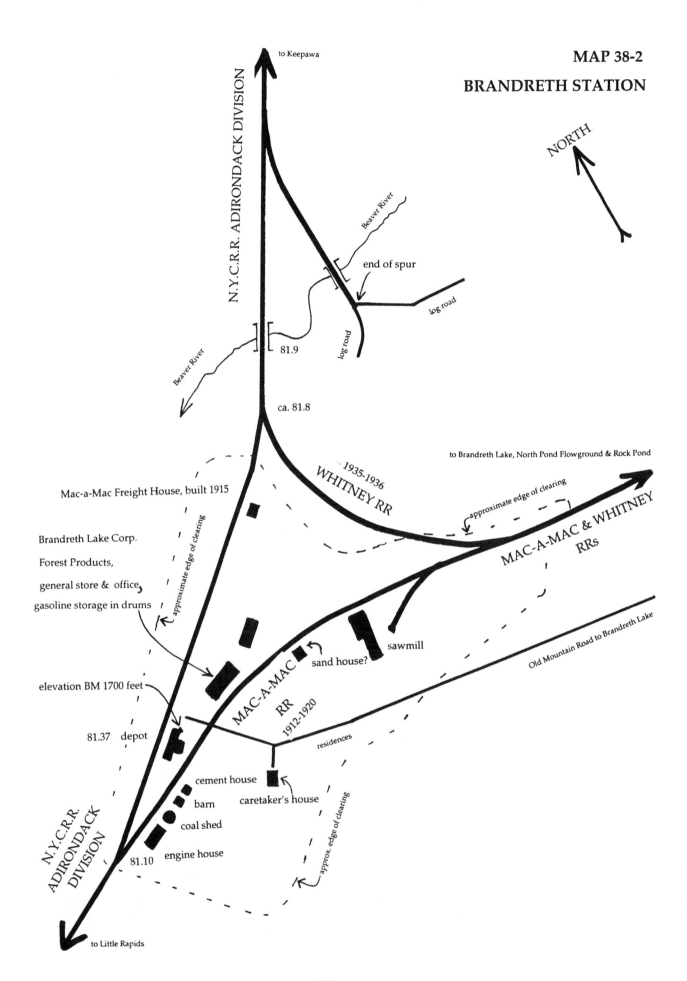

Chapter 39:
Grasse River Railroad.

AT CHILDWOLD STATION, the Grasse River Railroad connected with the New York Central Adirondack Division from 1913 to 1957. The primary source for detail on the Grasse River Railroad is Gove (September 1970, December 1970, and 1973) who also offers much detail on the various locomotive power and passenger service car roster. William L. Sykes and his Emporium Forestry Company built a sawmill at Conifer in 1911, and in 1913 built a railroad 1.2 miles long to it from Childwold Station. The railroad offices and shops were also located in Conifer. A rapid extension of the railroad then ensued, with over fourteen miles of track laid to Cranberry Lake during the same year, 1913. A sawmill at Cranberry Lake was constructed in 1917, and many logging spurs were built. Fowler (1968, p. 149) offers a photo of the Grasse River Railroad under construction.

Map 39-1

It is not always easy to plot all the spurs on the 15-minute topographic quadrangles and trace them here because: (1) Gove's map shows no contours and (2) the 15-minute quadrangles are incorrect in places. For an example of the latter, between Bear Creek and Alder Brook, the Stark quadrangle shows a climb over a 60-foot-plus-high ridge and down the other side. On the 7.5-minute Albert Marsh quadrangle (1970), the grade barely had to ascend over a ridge at all. Thus, most of the spurs are shown only approximately. Several should be accurately plotted, however, because I have found them on other maps, e.g. at Silver Brook and at Brandy Brook.

Passenger service probably began in 1915 or shortly after the Grasse River Railroad was incorporated. Passenger trains ran to Cranberry Lake until at least 1942 and, perhaps, as late as 1945 or 1948. To Conifer, Kutta (1981) includes a timetable of September 25, 1949.

Childwold Station. 0.0 mile. Elevation 1713 feet. Maps 39-2 and 39-6.

This was the junction point with the Adirondack Division. It is described in Gove (1973 with photos on pp. 82, 85, 96, and 99) and in Bragdon (1940). See also Chapter 36 paragraphs on Childwold Station.

Conifer. 1.2 miles. Elevation 1560. Maps 39-2 and 39-6.

Here were the railroad offices and the shops plus the main Emporium Forestry Company mill. Photos are plentiful: Palmer (1965, p. 12); Gove (1970, September, p. 12), Smallman Collection at Paul Smith's College Library (1971, pp. 72, 83); Gove (1973, pp. 74, 76, 83, 91, 93, 100, 101, 104); Harter (1979, p. 111); and Kiernan (1984).

An exhibit at the Saint Lawrence University Library at Canton in April 1985 concentrated on Conifer. One aerial photo not only revealed the track plan but also identified and labeled all the buildings of the mill. This aerial photo has been converted into Map 39-6. Kiernan (1984) described the exhibit. Hyde (1974, p. 40) and Simmons (1976, p. 366) show the same or a very similar photo as the one on exhibit at Saint Lawrence University but fail to identify the buildings. Hydes's photo has clearer resolution and records ca. 1955.

Gove (1973, p. 77) states that the first logging spurs were built up the valley of Dead Creek before the mainline was extended westward to the Silver Brook area and Cranberry Lake. All this construction was done in 1913.

Grasse River Club. 4.0 miles. Elevation 1530. Map 39-2.

This was a private fishing club. Trains stopped here according to timetables from 1918 through 1939, and probably before and after this period.

Silver Brook Junction. 6.1 miles. Elevation 1515. Map 39-2.

Trains stopped here in 1922 and 1923 when, I assume, the Silver Brook spurs were active. Trains did not stop here in 1918, 1930, nor in 1932 and 1939.

Jeanne Reynolds, Clifton-Fine Towns Historian, has shown me an Emporium Forestry Company blueprint which presents several areas including the Silver Brook spurs. Note the passing or storage siding on the spur. Gove (1973, p.77) states that these were built during the first year of operation: 1913.

Shurtleff's. 8.7 miles. Elevation 1520. Map 39-2.

This was a stop from 1918 through 1939 or later, serving Shurtleff's Hotel. The 1932 timetable lists the mileage as 9.0 as opposed to the 1918 timetable's 8.7; could the station or stop have been moved?

Brandy Brook Junction. 10.4 miles. Elevation 1470. Map 39-3.

The name included "Junction" in a 1918 timetable, but did not in 1930 and 1939. This suggests that the Brandy Brook spurs were in service in 1918 but abandoned by the 1930s. Neither name was listed in the 1922 nor 1923 timetables.

The 1916 Schmitt Adirondack forest fire map published by the New York State Conservation Commission already shows the Brandy Brook Spurs so that they had been built within three years of the opening of the Grasse River Railroad.

Clark's. 12.0 miles. Elevation 1470. Map 39-3.

This was not yet a stop in 1918, but became one on a 1922 timetable. The 1923 through 1939 timetables also list it.

Lines. 13.8 miles. Elevation 1441. Map 39-3.

This does not appear on any timetable, but is shown on the 15-minute Cranberry Lake quadrangle, surveyed between 1916 and 1919.

Dodge Brook Wye. 15.1 miles. Elevation 1503. Maps 39-3 and 39-7.

This is the junction point where the North Tram joined the mainline. It is also the point where passenger trains and railcars from Childwold Station turned around and backed down to the Cranberry Lake depot. Dodge Brook Wye is not listed on timetables, but it is named by Gove on his map.

Cranberry Lake. 16.0 miles. Elevation 1490. Maps 39-3 and 39-7.

This was the western terminus for passenger service, and the site of the second Emporium sawmill from 1917 (Gove, Sept. 1970, p. 33) to 1927 (Gove, Dec. 1970, p. 35). The track plan at Cranberry Lake illustrated here as Map 39-7 is compiled from four sources: (1) *Emporium Forestry Company Layout of Mill, Cranberry Lake*, dated July 14, 1919, a blueprint shown to me by Jeanne Reynolds, Clifton-Fine Towns Historian. This layout reveals only the immediate area around the sawmill, and excludes the lumber docks and wharves into Cranberry Lake. (2) I was able to gather the detail on the lumber docks and wharves plus the sawmill area from an aerial view picture postcard. The card, undated, is an aerial photo entitled *Cranberry Lake Village----Skyview*, copyright by D.P. Church. The publisher is the $5 Photo Company, Photo Park, Canton, New York. (3) A field trip taken by the author on September 20, 1986 with Dr. Ed Dreby, present owner of much of the lands. The foundations for the sawmill and locomotive shop are still visible. The horsebarn, company office, warehouse, and depot building doubling as the company store still stood. (4) The photo in Fowler (1968, p. 130) shows the high docks.

Photos of the mill at Cranberry Lake appear in Gove (1973, p. 88), Reynolds et al. (1976, pp. 59 and 65), and on the Church postcard mentioned above.

Bragdon (1940) records that the passenger train backed down to the edge of Cranberry Lake from the Dodge Brook Wye, and that the combine was left unattended next to the depot while the locomotive performed other duties elsewhere. A photo caption in Reynolds, page 45, informs us that railbus #11 also backed down toward the lake and stood at the depot in later years; this is confirmed by a photo taken in

1942 by Professor Gould Hoyt of Paul Smith's College.

The North Tram: Maps 39-3, 39-4, and 39-5

Shortly after arrival at Cranberry Lake in 1913, the Emporium Forestry Company began building the North Tram, connecting with the mainline at Dodge Brook Wye. By 1920-1921, when the Stark 15-minute quadrangle was surveyed, the North Tram had been built almost to the foot of Pleasant Lake, about 25 miles from Childwold Station, and ten miles from Dodge Brook Wye.

Jeanne Reynolds has several maps of the North Tram. One, dated September 5, 1925, shows that the survey for the railroad was completed to a point roughly midway between Bear Creek and Alder Brook, about 37 miles from Childwold Station. The survey at this time had begun to Alder Brook, but was not yet completed.

Gove (December, 1970, p. 35) tells us that construction of the North Tram and its spurs continued to about 1937. I measured the mileage along the Stark 15-minute quadrangle and found that the northeastern-most point of the Tram was about 40.5 miles from Childwold station and 25.4 miles from Dodge Brook Wye. Gove (Sept. 1970, pp. 32 and 35) states that there were about thirty miles of main Tram track; this figure may be more accurate because I could not measure all the small curves from the sometimes inaccurate Stark quadrangle. The mileage, including all the spurs, totaled almost 100 miles. The North Tram ceased operating, and the rails began to be removed about 1941 (Gove, Dec. 1970, p. 35). Then Gove says "The rail on the remainder of the north tram road was taken up soon after Draper Corporation bought the property in 1945, and in 1948 the rail on the Grasse River Line was taken up from Cranberry Lake village east to a point one mile west of Conifer village."

Photos of the North Tram appear in Gove (Dec. 1970, p. 13 and 1973, pp. 77 and 85).

Mystery Spurs

A map at the library of The Adirondack Museum in Blue Mountain Lake shows two spurs which I cannot locate on any other map. One is named the "Black Brook Line" on the south of the main, and the other "McClinton Tram Road" on the north of the main and further west. The only clue is that these spurs were near the South Branch Grasse River possibly in the area between Conifer and Lines.

Railroad Logging Operations

In all his articles, Gove offers much detail on logging operations. A Shay required, for example, six hours to run the whole North Tram. In the later 1920s until 1931, pulpwood was brought out to Childwold Station, and then run the 2.5 miles on the Adirondack Division to Piercefield Station. From here it was brought down the Piercefield Spur to the International Paper Company Pulp Mill.

Equipment and Additional Reading

Gove (September 1970, December 1970, 1973, pp. 108-110) provides a complete roster of locomotive power and motor rail cars used in passenger service.

Additional material will be found on the Grasse River Railroad in Bragdon (1940), Palmer (1965), Fowler (1968), Hyde (1974, p. 40), Reynolds et al. (1976), Simmons (1976, p. 366), Harter (1979), Koch (1979), Kutta (1981), Kiernan (1984), and in the *Tupper Lake Free Press and Herald* of January 28, 1971. A series of articles on this railroad appeared in this period (January 1971) and in the 1967-1968 era in this Tupper Lake newspaper; it is available currently in the Smallman Collection at the Paul Smith's College Library.

Abandonment

After the North Tram was gradually abandoned, from Cranberry Lake to a point a mile west of Conifer, the track was removed in 1948. The mill at Conifer burned on November 29, 1957, and the last two or so miles of track into Childwold Station were abandoned almost immediately.

In early July 1992, nearly twenty miles of Grasse River railroad right-of-way was donated to The Adirondack Nature Conservancy. See *The Flicker*, Fall 1992, cover page.

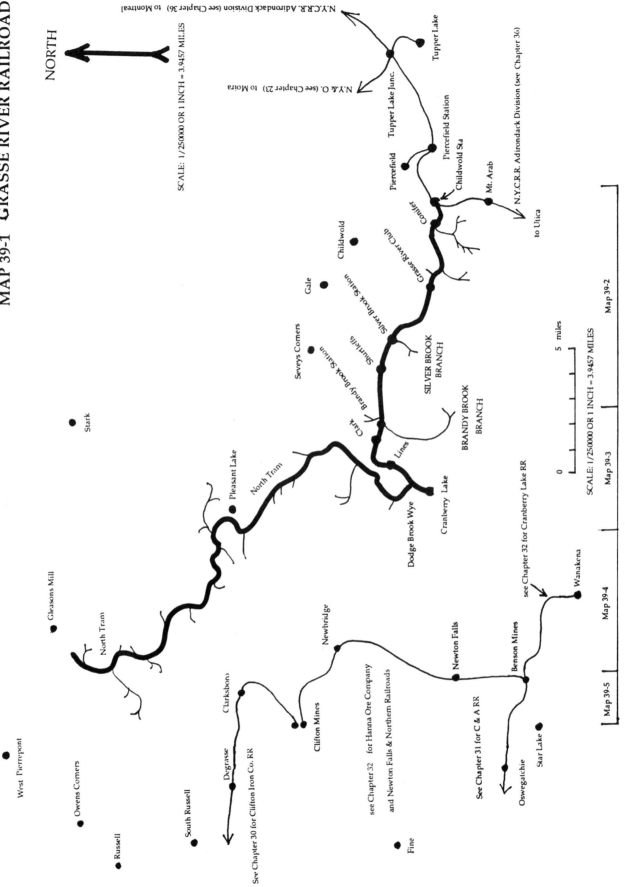

MAP 39-1 GRASSE RIVER RAILROAD

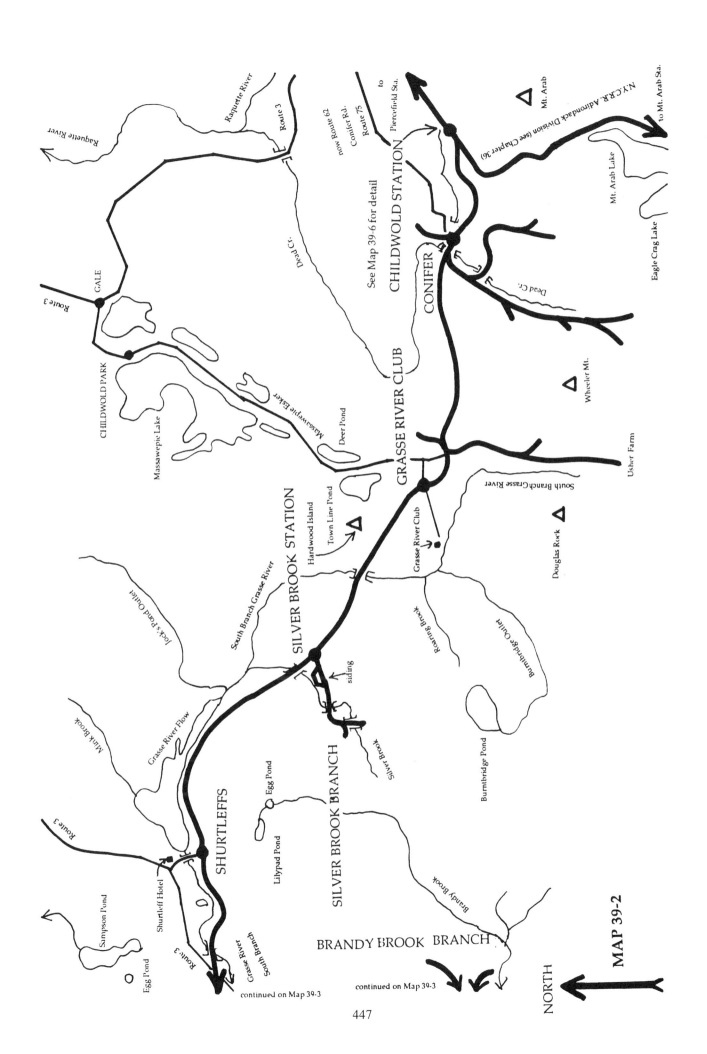

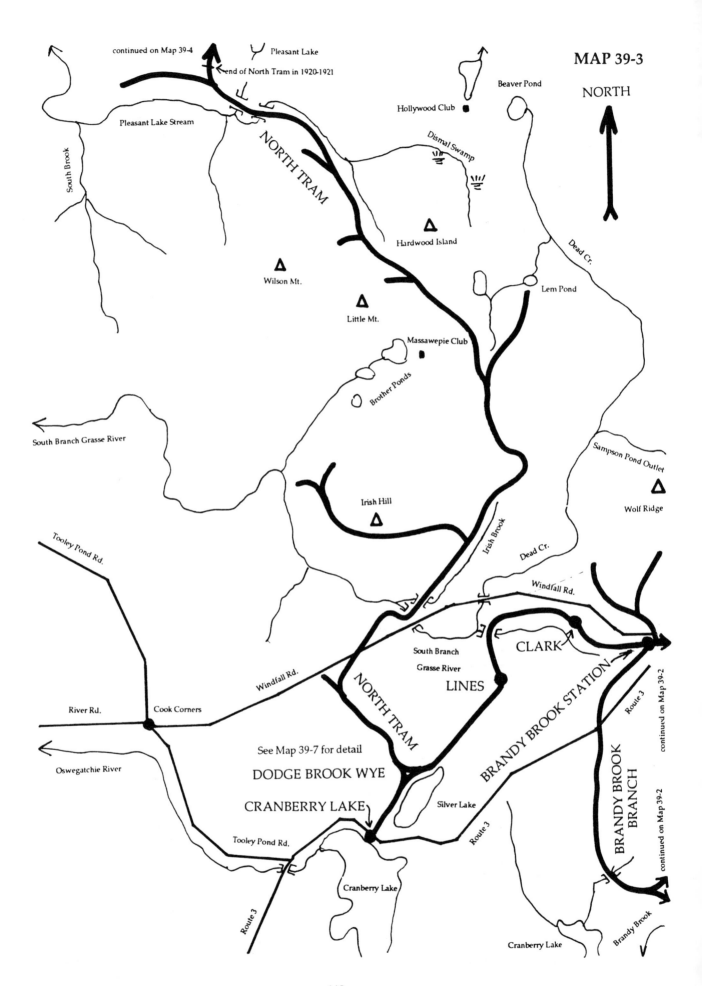

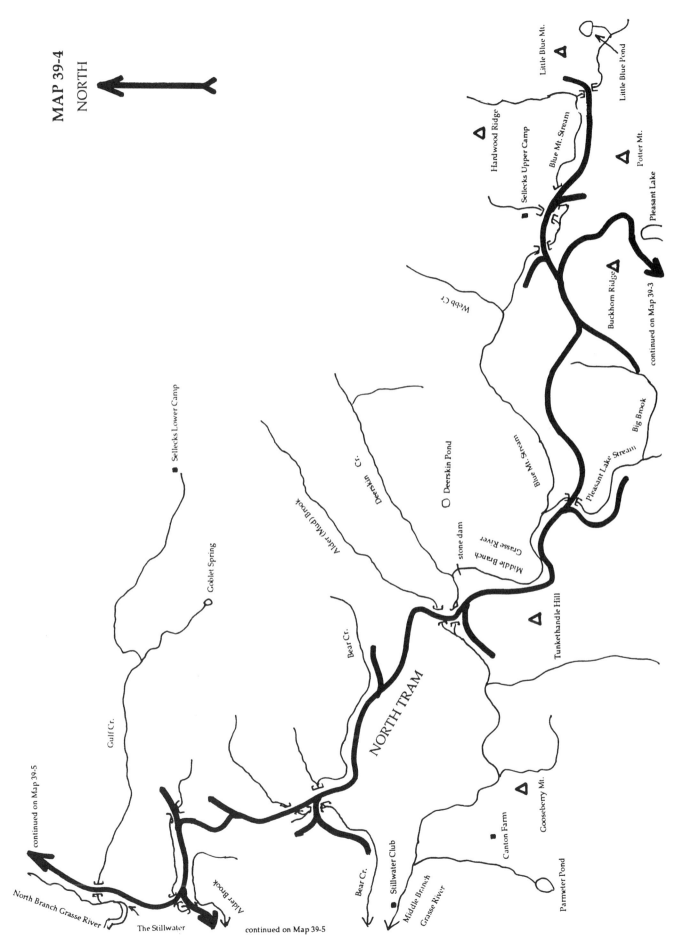

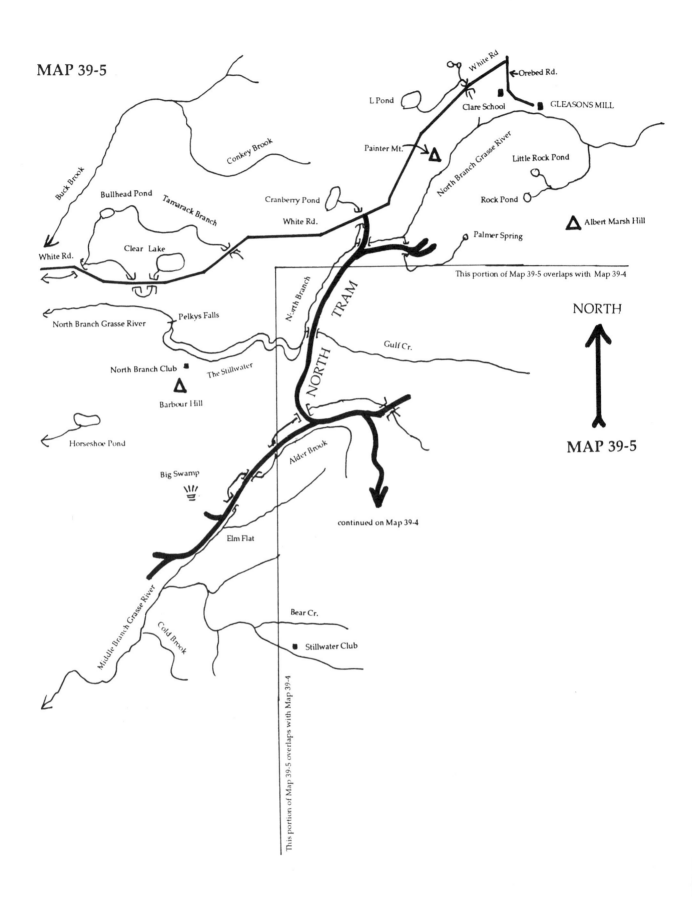

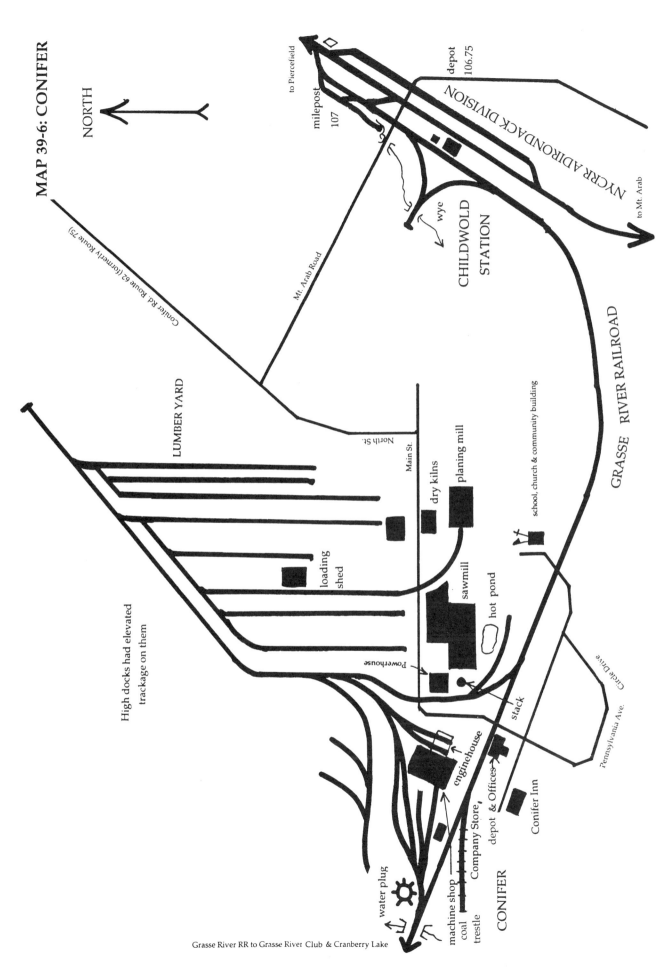

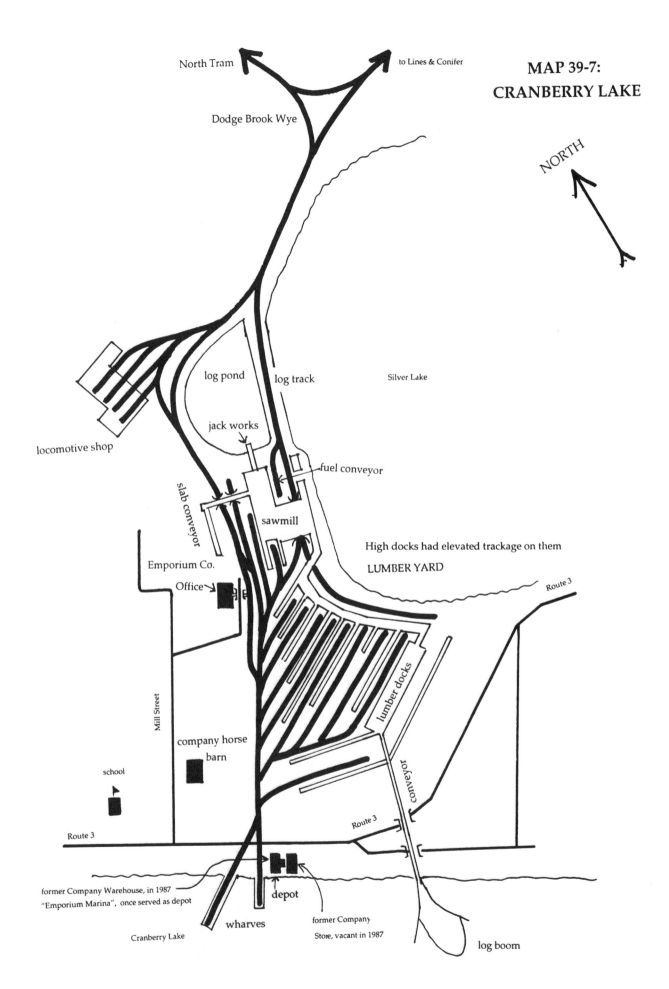

Chapter 40:
Paul Smith's Electric Railway

PRIOR TO THE OPENING of the Paul Smith's Railway on August 20, 1906, travel to the Paul Smith's Hotel was solely by stagecoach or by other horse-drawn vehicles. In 1886 two different railroads were built into the northern Adirondacks at the same time as the establishment of regularly-scheduled connecting service via the Paul Smith's stage (see Figure 1 in Kudish, 1976, p. 20). The Chateaugay Railroad, later to become part of the Delaware & Hudson in 1903 and described in Chapter 20, reached Loon Lake on November 15, 1886 after seven years of construction from Plattsburgh; the Paul Smith's stage met the trains here, about 14 miles northeast of the Hotel. On December 15, 1887 the railroad was extended to Bloomingdale and Saranac Lake; the stage then needed to travel only half the distance, seven miles, to Bloomingdale Station.

The second railroad, the Northern Adirondack or Hurd's and described in Chapter 23, was begun at Moira. It was built southward arriving in Brandon, about eight miles west-northwest of Paul Smiths, in 1886. A timetable dated June 30, 1889 lists the connecting stage for Paul Smiths. Brandon was then the temporary terminus of the railroad. In late 1889 or early 1890 the tracks reached Tupper Lake. This railroad was to become the New York & Ottawa Division of the New York Central in 1906.

On July 16, 1892 a third railroad, Webb's Mohawk & Malone or the Adirondack & Saint Lawrence described in Chapter 36, was built southward from Malone and opened with trains to Childwold. The Paul Smith's stage then had the shortest run yet to reach a railroad station—four miles to Paul Smith's Station. When Paul Smith opened his own railway in 1906, the name of this New York Central Railroad station was changed to Gabriels. On October 12th of that year, 1892, the Mohawk & Malone was completed through to Herkimer, although regularly-scheduled through trains did not begin operating until October 24th.

With at least two stages and a tally-ho connecting with as many as fourteen trains daily of three different railroads after 1892, Paul Smith decided to simplify the transportation arrangements of his guests to travel, without change of pullman or private car, directly from New York, Boston, Chicago, Albany, Buffalo, Montreal or other major city of origin.

The closest connecting point to an existing railroad (Gabriels, four miles away), necessitated an ascent of Easy Street Hill, prohibitively steep for a railroad. The next closest connecting point was at Lake Clear Junction, 6.5 miles to the south and nearly on the level. M. J. Corbett in 1904 surveyed two possible routes, one passing west of Johnson Hill through Upper Saint Regis Post Office and the second passing east of Johnson Hill; this second route was selected.

Duquette (1987) writes: "Paul purchased a steam locomotive from the New York Central to serve as a the workhorse during the laying of the rails" (in 1906). He continues: "By this time Paul had purchased another steam locomotive. . . ." According to Richard Palmer's notes at The Adirondack Museum in Blue Mountain Lake, the first locomotive was #3723, an ex-New York Central Alco-Cooke 0-6-0 built in March 1902 lettered "Adirondack Light and Power Company." The second locomotive was a 4-4-0 built, according to Palmer, in 1886 in the west Albany Shops of the New York Central. Photographs of this second locomotive exist, but none of the first.

A hike by the writer on May 1, 1976 from Paul Smiths to Lake Clear Junction revealed that much of the 6.5-mile length of the line necessitated long fills across swamps as well as several sand cuts. The cuts were made very wide to provide tons of material for the fills. Such railroad equipment as steam locomotives, steam shovels, and gondola cars would have begun work at the Lake Clear Junction area and worked northward.

The Lake Clear-Paul Smiths highway had to be relocated further to the west when the railroad was built. The railroad crossed the abandoned turnpike twice (the southerly crossing was known as Martin's), and the track was at a superior elevation of several feet (see Map 40-2).

DeSormo (1974) offers an account of the initial trip: Mr. Brown, an official of the New York Central, brought one of his regular mainline locomotives and heavy car over the new Paul Smith's line with an apprehensive Paul riding with him. Fortunately the roadbed was substantial enough to prevent an incident. The Paul Smith's line was laid with 60-pound rail (i.e. a yard-long segment of rail weighing 60 pounds), in contrast to the 80-pound rail with which the Adirondack & Saint Lawrence was built in 1892, and the 105-pound rail later used until 1972.

The first schedule published by the Paul Smith's Railway was dated August 20, 1906 when regular passenger service began. The timetable, printed by the *Adirondack Enterprise* of Saranac Lake, indicates five round trips daily, requiring a half-hour for the one way, 6.5-mile, trip.

When service began on August 20, 1906, stagecoach connections at Gabriels with the New York Central, at Bloomingdale with the Delaware & Hudson, and at Brandon with the New York & Ottawa were no longer needed and probably suspended.

An Electrical Experiment with Malfunctions

Paul Smith had been generating electric power for his hotel and the surrounding area since about 1898 from his Keese's Mills Plant, about 2.5 miles west of the hotel. It thus was a relatively easy matter to electrify the railroad so that Paul Smith ordered an electric interurban combine car. J.G. Brill of Philadelphia built the body while General Electric of Schenectady provided the motors and electrical equipment. According to Mr. James Brown of Bloomingdale, the car cost $25,000 and supposedly the whole railroad cost $75,000.

The Paul Smith's Electric Railway car, because it was an experimental first of its kind, had malfunctions during its initial years of operation. It had to be hauled back to General Electric at Schenectady at least once, and possibly several times, by New York Central Adirondack Division trains for rebuilding, and hauled again to Lake Clear Junction and Paul Smiths for retesting. Joseph Cunningham, an electric railroad historian, brought my attention to this imperfect beginning (see Cunningham, 1991, pp. 7, 9, and 10). Because the car arrived at Paul Smiths at least twice, the exact dates of its being pressed into service are uncertain.

We know that on August 31, 1906, eleven days after the steam operation began, Paul Smith Junior wrote to a Mr. Davis at General Electric in Schenectady inviting him to come to Paul Smiths to look over the line and recommend trolley equipment. He asked Mr. Davis to either change coach trains at Lake Clear Junction or to take the through Pullman to the hotel.

Brill's Magazine, a publication by the Philadelphia builder of trolley and interurban bodies, included an article on the Paul Smiths car in their November 15, 1907 issue. The article begins: "A type of interurban car recently furnished by The J.G. Brill Company to Paul Smith's Electric Light Power & Railroad Company of Paul Smiths, New York, has an electrical equipment of unusual interest." Hence, the electric car had already been first delivered to Paul Smiths by the fall of 1907.

Middleton (1974 and 1976) writes that the initial electrical equipment in the car was a mercury air rectifier (also called a mercury arc rectifier) designed to change alternating current from the overhead trolley wire to direct current in order to run the car's motors. This apparatus did not operate to expectations.

The mercury air rectifiers were replaced in Schenectady by a General Electric motor-generator. A General Electric blueprint, # T 205352, entitled "Car Layout Showing Motor Generator Support," is dated March 10 and 17, 1908. It took a week for the engineer to draw these plans specifically for the Paul Smith's car. Hence, the motor-generator was constructed and installed probably in the Spring or Summer of 1908.

Another blueprint entitled "Connections of a Sprague-General Electric Multiple Unit Control System, Type M, for 4 Motors, AC & DC Operation with Motor Generator Set, Paul Smith's Electric Light Power and Railway Company" was also specific to the car. It was begun on February 4, 1906 and completed January 21, 1909, three years later. Hence, the final touches on the car's electrical apparatus did not occur until 1909.

These blueprints, plus about ten others not specific to the Paul Smith's car but to interurban cars in general, are on file at the Paul Smith's College Lands Department. The blueprints, including some of the trolley wire catenary system, date from 1902 through 1909. Apparently, the motor-generator set was successful and served the car until its retirement about 1930.

There were several unusual features: first, the car drew 5200 volts AC from the overhead wire and converted them internally by means of the large motor-generator (described above) in the baggage-mail section, to 600 volts DC. The 600 volt DC current then powered the motors which were mounted on the trucks adjacent to the axles. Second, the car was originally equipped with four trolley poles on the roof, two at each end of the car on both the right and left sides. Because the wire was strung off-center of the car, only the two poles on the northeast side of the car could come in contact with the wire; the two other poles were later removed (see Figure 3, page 27, of Kudish, 1976).

Additional electrification information was made available by John Duquette, former Town of Harrietstown-Saranac Lake Historian. In 1911 The Union Falls generators, and in 1912 the Franklin Falls generators, were pressed into service with an output of 22,000 volts AC. The transmission line which originated at Union Falls was routed to Paul Smiths via Franklin Falls, Bloomingdale, and Gabriels. At the hotel, the voltage was dropped by transformers to 5200 volts AC to feed the trolley wire. The railroad right-of-way also served as a 22,000-volt transmission line to Lake Clear Junction. Thus by 1912 it was possible to switch the electric power source supplying the railway, the hotel, and the surrounding area from the Keese's Mills Dam to the Union Falls-Franklin Falls complex or vice-versa, as needed. Mr. Duquette has a booklet, *The Power Development on the Saranac River below Saranac Chain of Lakes*, which yields further detail: the purpose of the newly-organized Paul Smith's Electric Light Power and Railroad Company was "to construct and operate an electric railroad." The date of the booklet was 1906.

Overnight Pullman and private cars were switched by New York Central locomotives onto the electrified Paul Smith's track at Lake Clear Junction (see Map 40-1) where the electric car could push them to the hotel. Day passengers riding coaches were required to change trains at the junction. Timetables from 1906 through about 1928 or 1929 indicate connections with trains to and from Malone, Saranac Lake, Lake Placid, and Utica. For passengers originating at Plattsburgh on the Delaware & Hudson, it was necessary to change trains twice: to New York Central trains at Loon Lake and to the Paul Smith's car at Lake Clear Junction.

Figure 4 of Kudish (1976, pp. 24 and 25) shows the electric car at Lake Clear Junction. Every photo observed indicates that the baggage-mail end was always pointed to the junction, and the passenger end toward Paul Smiths. Obviously, the car was never turned around because no electrified wye, loop, or turntable ever existed (a wye had been proposed for near the warehouse but never was built). The electric car had to push passenger and freight cars to the hotel, but pull them to Lake Clear Junction.

Conductor's Trip Reports

John Duquette has donated nearly a thousand of Paul Smith's Electric Railway conductors' trip reports to the Paul Smith's Museum. An analysis of these reports reveals much about the daily routine of the railroad. Some conductors may not have been as thorough in writing down unusual events as others. Some conductors could not spell, and others had illegible script, making analysis difficult at times. The span of time ranges from November 29, 1909 through September 23, 1928. For one year, 1915, all reports are present. For other years, e.g. 1917 and 1923 through 1926, none is present. For the remaining years, several months' worth of reports are present, the duration varying from year to year. There were seven motormen and twenty-two conductors over the twenty years represented in the reports.

Fares were always fifty cents one way except to Martin's Crossing and other part-way destinations; then they were twenty-five cents. A listing of half-fare destinations other than Martin's Crossing is as follows: Duset Camp in 1917, Creighton's Crossing in 1917, Creighton's Camp in 1917, Coal Spring Camp in 1917, Lumber Camp in 1915, Delcores' Landing in 1921, and Martin's Landing in 1921. Some conductors may not have recorded Martin's Crossing for the half-fare, leaving one wondering whether the half-fare was for a shorter trip or for a child. There was no fare increase from 1909 through 1928 except for a war tax in 1917 and 1919; the tax was approximately 8% but inconsistent, varying from 5 to 15%.

Fares were recorded on a Duplex fare register machine.

Running times for regularly-scheduled, or timetable, runs were usually 30 minutes each way with an average speed of 13 miles per hour. The shortest scheduled runs were 25 minutes. The running time was as short as 20 minutes on a few extra runs without passengers. The record is 18 minutes on November 2, 1915 for the 6.5 miles, an average speed of 21.7 miles per hour. Slow speeds were because of the rough roadbed, not inadequate power.

Layovers at Lake Clear Junction usually occupied from 20 to 40 minutes. The car was always stationed at the hotel between runs.

The number of runs scheduled in winter, spring and fall was two round trips daily. On some Sundays there was one or none. In the summer, there were five round trips daily. The maximum number of runs on a single day, due to unscheduled extras was six, seven, with a maximum of eight.

The car seated 24 people, but it was rarely full, and many runs were empty. The following table will give an idea of the number of passengers carried at different times of the year and over different years. The numbers in the table are the passengers per day, not per trip:

Year 1912 Jan. & Feb.	Year 1912 Summer	Year 1928 Summer
minimum zero	minimum 5	none on 12 days
median 5	median 40*	median 3.5
maximum 29	maximum 92	maximum 28

*40 people spread out over the five round trips indicates only 4 people per trip on the average—hardly a congested car! A busy period was July 28-31, 1910 when 33 to 105 fares were collected daily. Except for summers in the early years, the electric railway must have run almost constantly as a financial loss.

The electric railway car brought in private railroad cars of the wealthy who either stayed at the Paul Smith's Hotel or had their own camps on the Saint Regis Chain of Lakes. For examples: On July 30, 1910 an extra run at dawn was made for an unspecified private car. On September 26, 1915 several families left Paul Smiths in their private railway cars: The Bakers, Reids, and Brewsters. Mr. A. S. White of the White's Pine Camp had his private car hauled on June 26, 1915. On July 3, 1915 baggage car #552 and the sleeper, Louisiana, left Paul Smiths at 10:58 A.M.; these might have been New York Central cars and not cars owned by private individuals.

On occasion the Smith Family would "deadhead" out or in to meet trains at Lake Clear Junction. The term "deadhead" identifies in this case the owners, but also railroad workers or officials who pay no fare. Phelps did it on March 14, 1913. Paul Smith Jr. did it three times in November and December of 1915 to catch a New York Central train about 11 P.M. During one of these extra unscheduled trips, the record time of 18 minutes was made. Paul Smith Jr. also created an extra trip on March 9, 1913.

On occasion, there were specially reduced group rates and charters. On June 9, 1912 a group of 63 people chartered the car at half fare and attended a ball game. On February 2 through 4, 1915 special rates, 75 cents round trip instead of one dollar, were in effect during the Saranac Lake Winter Carnival. On January 29 and 30, 1913 there were special half-fare excursion rates for 34 and 47 people, respectively, with no reason given by the conductor for the trip.

Extra trips were made in winter to plow snow when needed. These were done ahead of the noon and early evening scheduled passenger runs in 1910, 1912, and 1913. Snow plowing was a slow process, some round trips requiring from 90 to 135 minutes. The electric car itself did the plowing, probably, with a plow attachment on the pilot; there is no evidence that a whole separate plow car was pushed ahead of it.

In 1910, on April 26, 27, and 29, extra runs were made for "drawing sand for the road." No detail is offered by the conductor why sand was hauled. Could it have been for storage of sand for dusting the icy rails during the following winter? Sand to widen a fill or repair a beaver washout? Sand to sell to the public?

Between passenger and mail runs, it was not uncommon to see the railway car used as a freight locomotive. Several photographs in the Paul Smith's College Library show the electric car hauling several flat cars with logs. At one time, a spur was built in winter out onto the ice of Lower Saint Regis Lake to unload logs. The logs were then floated down the lake in spring after the ice melted in a boom to the sawmill.

A short distance south of the more northerly of the two grade crossings with the abandoned turnpike existed a short siding for loading flat cars with logs. Today, this site is about a quarter-mile southeast of the intersection of State Highway 30 and the Hoffman Road (see Map 40-2). According to James Brown of Bloomingdale who personally remembered the electric railway, the maximum number of railway flatcars loaded with 16-foot logs pulled out of this siding at one time by the electric car to Lake Clear Junction was seven. In 1975, at the end of the siding, railroad historian Christopher Brescia and this writer found a trolley wire support pole with guy wires still standing, and a brake wheel from one of the old flat cars.

On November 29, 1909 pulpwood was being loaded. On August 28 and November 16, 1915 a car of pulp was going out to Lake Clear Junction. On October 24, 1912 lumber was being hauled in. On January 16 and 23, 1915 half-fares were collected for the Lumber Camp. On September 24, 1915 a trip was made for the logs. A trip was made on August 14, 1915 for wood for the boiler house. In late August and September 1915 wood was being hauled several days per week.

Occasionally freight cars, other than those used for hauling pulpwood, lumber or logs, were seen on the Paul Smith's line. On October 12, 1913 a special trip was made for "Paino Bar of S. White" (did the conductor intend to write a "piano for White's Pine Camp"?. On November 9 and 10, 1916 a run was made for the *Democratic Times* (name unclear in conductor's script, but possibly a newspaper). On September 1, 1916 a special run was made for unspecified freight. On July 3, 1915 two LS&MS freight cars were brought to the hotel (which railroad then had the initials, L.S.& M.S.?). On November 16, 1915 two freight cars were brought to the hotel. Freight running times one way to or from the Junction were often only twenty minutes in contrast to thirty minutes for passenger runs.

Power failures and mechanical breakdowns were quite common. On October 29, 1912 the car had a broken air brake pump and did not operate. 1915 was the worst year for repairs and malfunctions. Between March 27 and June 16 there were eleven days, and two more days in September, when the electric car could not operate. In November of 1915 there were power failures on three days. On those days when the electric car could not operate, mail and passengers were carried to and from the junction by either hand car, livery (horse & wagon), automobile, or gas car. In no instance over all the years have I found a record of the steam locomotive being used to replace the electric car. Specific reasons for annulments were "air pump broke," "car laid up for repairs," "transformer in car burned out," "overhauling car," "car undergoing repairs," "car being painted," "trolley trouble," "motor burned out," "power failure," "truck broke in Lake Clear Yards," and "reverser on car broken." On June 5 and 6, 1915 the car was being painted, and no trips were made. Before the paint job, the lettering on the sides of the car read: "The St. Regis Chain of Lakes." After the paint job, the lettering on the sides of the car read: "St. Regis and Osgood Chain of Lakes" and "U.S. Mail." Therefore, when one sees for the first time an undated photo of the electric car, it is possible to date the photo by the lettering on the car as either before or after June 1915.

In 1927 and 1928, both electric and gas cars were used, the proportion of trips made by each varying day by day. A gradual phasing out of the electric car was occurring here in favor of the smaller, less-expensive-to-operate gas car.

Track Plan

The track plan at the hotel is shown on Map 40-2. There were two tracks upon which to lay-up private cars and Pullmans, both tracks terminating at the store. By 1914 the more northerly of the two was abandoned back to the warehouse so that a photo taken about 1928 (Figure 3 of Kudish, 1976, page 27) shows but a single track at the end of the line. A third track serviced the north side of the warehouse; this track, originally for freight cars, was later used to store the abandoned 4-4-0 steam locomotive. A temporary fourth track in 1914 turned north of the warehouse to assist in construction of the automobile garage. A fifth track, described above, was built out onto the lake ice to unload logs. All these tracks were apparently electrified so that freight and passenger cars could be readily switched.

Another proposed but never built track was to continue northwestward from the warehouse to the sawmill on the bay between Kellogg Point and the mouth of Barnum Pond Outlet. A cut, presently occupied by a road at the Paul Smiths Post Office, was made for this track, according to Professor Charles Kirche, former chairman of the Paul Smith's College Department of Mathematics, who recalls as a young man the line in service. The proposals which never came to be, the wye and the sawmill spur, were made in the 1915-1917 era.

At least one more, perhaps two more, sidings existed further south along the line in addition to the logging siding already described. Evidence is thin due to thick brush which has grown. Christopher Brescia found a frog and other portions of a switch, suggesting a siding which is indicated on Map 40-2 as the more southerly of the two. James Brown described a construction camp without a siding; the most likely site for such a camp is shown on the map as "Woodpecker Inn."

Abandonment

The precise date of the closing of the Paul Smith's Railway is uncertain. Figure 3 on page 27 of Kudish (1976) shows the car in front of the store shortly prior to abandonment. The lettering on the side of the car had faded. The main hotel building in the background burned on September 5, 1930 so that the caption date of about 1928 under the original photo in the Paul Smith's College Library is reasonably accurate. The automobiles in the photo have been dated also to the 1928 era as a confirmation.

A New York Central timetable of September 29, 1929 no longer indicates a connection at Lake Clear Junction. Collins (1971) states that the line closed in 1932. Assuming that this is the case, then the line ran for the last three or four years according to Professor Kirche by the small gasoline-powered car. Such operation was for mail and freight only. The present State Highway 30 was built in 1929 between Lake Clear Junction and Paul Smiths; by then, automobile and truck traffic had increased to such a point that rail service was no longer needed. Photos at the College Library show the electric car aiding in the construction of the State Highway and thus contributing to its own demise!

Figures 1 through 5 in Kudish (1976) are from the collection at the Cubley Library at Paul Smith's College; figures 6 and 7 are by Kudish. Relics, such as a car builder's plate, railway grade crossing sign, brake wheel, trolley wire support pole parts, switch frog, and rail are on file at Paul Smith's College.

Over a Half-Century of Being in the News

Following the abandonment of the Paul Smiths Electric Railway in the 1930s, articles and news items continue to be written about the line for over half a century. Many of these publications include photos of the car.

An unpublished photograph taken on September 26, 1938 by John Duquette shows the grade crossing of the railroad and Route 30 where the present Niagara-Mohawk substation exists, about a half-mile southeast of the College. The rails were still in place at that time, although service of any kind had ceased years before. Mr. Duquette says that the rails were removed shortly thereafter.

The writings of Cunningham (1991) and Middleton (1974 and 1976) on electrification have already been mentioned. Reifschneider (1947) writes that "a variety of rolling stock seems to have been used, all large double truck cars, even including some sort of gas-electric car at one time." There is no evidence of ownership beyond the one electric car, the one, possibly two, steam locomotives, the small gasoline-powered car, and perhaps several freight cars used for hauling logs and sand. Reifschneider places the last trip on November 26, 1936, but does not claim his source. He also writes "perhaps a few more freight trips may have been made at a later date." Since no New York Central timetables show passenger connections after September 1929, any sporadic runs from 1930 through 1936 might have been for freight only. This writer suspects that the 1936 Reifschneider closure date may have been the official abandonment year with the Interstate Commerce Commission, years after the last train actually operated.

Maguire and Reifschneider (1950) offered a photo of the electric car taken in 1935. The trucks, trolley poles, and trolley wires were still intact at that time. I have been told that the trucks and other electrical apparatus were removed during World War II for salvaging. Figure 7 of Kudish (1976, page 28) shows the car in early 1975. It had stood all these years directly on the main track, but was later moved about one hundred feet to the east on November 17, 1975 to permit access to the nearly-completed fire house. The car was located from the time of its move in 1975 to its demolition in 1984 where the wood shed stood.

In February 1968 an article appeared in *Trains* magazine, unsigned, but probably by Steve Maguire. The article was prompted by a visit, possibly in 1967, to the car by J. B. Puchalski of Ferris State College in Big Rapids Michigan. This article claims that the Paul Smiths line had two cars when all other evidence points toward one (perhaps the author was referring to one electric car and one small gasoline-powered car?). Reference has already been made to Middleton's article in *Trains* of September 1976.

In 1976 this author wrote an article on the Paul Smiths Electric Railway for the Franklin County Historical and Museum Society's *Franklin Historical Review*. It was this article which forms the basis for this chapter. Maguire (1977) responded to the 1976 Kudish article.

Published Photographs of the Paul Smith's Electric Railway

Subject	Publication	Kudish Catalog Number
Steam locomotive	Kudish (1976, pp. 22 & 23 as Figure 2), also Harter (1979, p. 117)	1502
Lake Clear Junction, ca. 1910	Kudish (1976, pp. 24 & 25 as Figure 4), also Duquette (1987, p. 3), Maguire?? (1968), and *St. Regian** (1974, p.13)	1201
Stagecoach	Kudish (1976, p. 20 as Figure 1), also Harter (1979, p. 117) and *St. Regian* (1974, p. 15)	----
Electric car at woodshed	Kudish (1976, p.26 as Figure 5), also Harter (1979, p. 119) and *St. Regian* (1974, p.14)	1405
Electric car at end-of-line	Kudish (1976, p. 27 as Figure 3), also Harter (1979, p. 119) and *St. Regian* (1974, p. 12)	1503
Paul, Phelps & Paul Jr. and car	Duquette (1987, p. 1)	1501
Motor-generator	Duquette (1987, p. 3)	1601
Elec. car in 1974	Kudish (1976, p. 28 as Figure 7)	1416
Elec. car in 1975	Harter (1979, p. 119)	1414
Interior of car	*Brill's Magazine* (1907, p. 221)	1607
Right-of-way	*Brill's Magazine* (1907, p. 220)	1306
Builder's photo of brand new car	*Brill's Magazine* (1907, p. 220)	1606
Electric car in 1935	Maguire & Reifschneider (1950, p. 29) Also Maguire (1968, p. 52)	1412
Electric car ca. 1967	Maguire (1968, p. 37)	1413
Electric car with coach/passengers	Collins (1977, p. "118L")	1506
Tickets	Duquette (1987, p. 3)	2301
Electric car in 1950s	McLaughlin (1972)	1410
Electric car with two pullmans	"Paul Smith's Adirondack Park"** (ca. 1908, p. 32)	1507
Paul Smiths Station at Gabriels	"Paul Smith's Adirondack Park"** (1893, p. 13)	1102

*The *St. Regian* is the Paul Smith's College yearbook.
**"Paul Smith's Adirondack Park" was an advertising pamphlet published by the Paul Smith's Hotel.

McLaughlin (1972), Collins (1977), Harter (1979), Duquette (1987), and Tyler (1988) most recently have written on the line. Shields has an article in press for the *Gazette* in 1996.

The author's attempts and those made by others to save the old electric car failed. On May 10, 1984 the old car body was dragged by two front-end loaders a few hundred feet to the east and demolished. By May 17, it was buried in a landfill between the College's new sawmill and the sewage treatment plant.

The interior of the Paul Smith's Electric Railway car in 1976, eight years before its demolition.
Author photo.

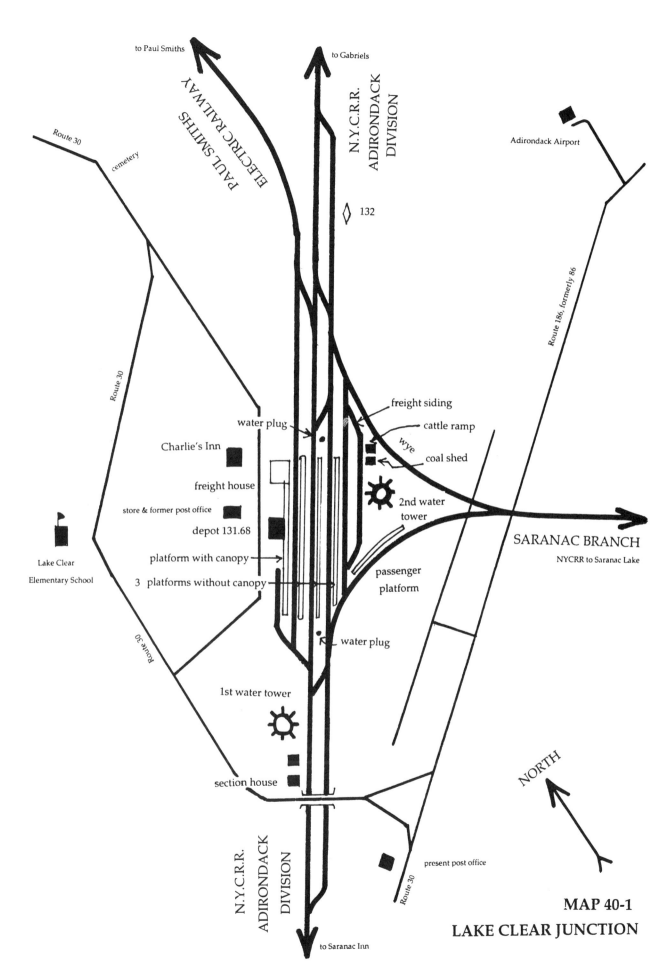

MAP 40-1
LAKE CLEAR JUNCTION

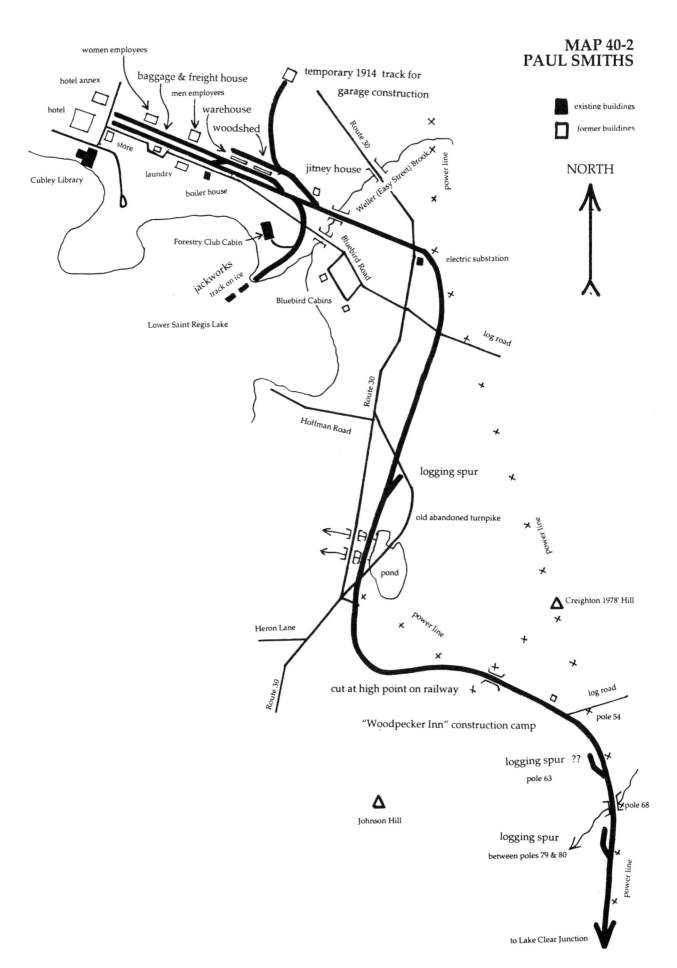

Chapter 41:
Horse Shoe Forestry Company and Wake Robin Railroads

IN 1892, Abbot Augustus Low began acquiring lands in the Adirondacks, beginning with his Bog Lake Camp accessible via the Bog Lake station, later renamed Robinwood, on the Adirondack Division. In fact, Clark (1974) states that Low's wife, Marian, named the locality "'Robinwood."

Map 41-1

By 1896, most of the Low Tract had been acquired. Low had a replica of the Garden City station of the Long Island Railroad built that year. This station at Horse Shoe was operated, under an agreement with the owner, Low, by the New York Central Railroad as a full service depot.

In 1897, a railroad was built by Low to haul logs to the Bog River for spring drives beginning in 1898. Clark (p. 9) lists a roster of equipment: two locomotives, a crane, a shovel, a log loader, and several flat cars. He states that there were 15 miles of track. If this were so, then I cannot account for 12.6 miles of those 15. The main Horse Shoe Forestry Company railroad line headed east from Horse Shoe Station around the south side of Horse Shoe Pond, some 1.7 miles, with the branch to the Bog River, another 0.7 mile. The total is 2.4 miles.

In 1897 or 1898, a sawmill with edger was constructed at Hitchins Pond. Machinery was also present for making shipping boxes for products such as bottled spring water, a variety of jellies and preserves (e.g. cranberry, crabapple, elderberry), maple sugar, and maple vinegar (Hughes, 1990). A stave and heading mill for wine barrels, and a drying yard were also built at Hitchins Pond. The Wake Robin Railroad was built west and south from Horse Shoe station to serve these mills. It was about 3.1 miles long with a 1.1 mile-long branch northwest to Pine Pond.

In 1898 a sap evaporator was built at Maple Valley, and was served by the Wake Robin Railroad. A photo of their locomotive, a 4-4-0 named *Washington*, plus tender and a flatcar with two sap-collecting vats, is published in Koch (1979, p. 138). In 1899, the Virgin Forest Springs bottled water plant opened and was also served by Wake Robin (Clark, p. 10). Each of these operations was located roughly midway between Horse Shoe Station and Hitchins Pond; Maple Valley was the more northerly of the two according to Clark (1974, map on page 13).

There is some uncertainty in the gauge of the Horseshoe Forestry and Wake Robin Railroads. Cushing (1900, pages r54 and r55), doing highly-detailed field work for the New York State Geologist's Office, mentions on three occasions that Low's railroads were narrow gauge. He hiked the lines, examining the then-fresh rock cuts and describes them 0.25 mile east of and 0.25 mile southwest of Horseshoe Station. The former rock cut would have been on the Horseshoe Forestry line, and the latter on the Wake Robin. The locomotive *Washington* in Koch's photo, mentioned above, does appear to be narrow-gauged.

In 1903 the first of two Bog River Dams, southeast of Horse Shoe Station, was built for both electric power generation and control of water levels for the spring log drives down to Tupper Lake. *Engineering News* of April 9, 1908 included an article about the dam as well as a photograph with a locomotive on top of it. F. Ray McKnight states that the locomotive is an ex 0-4-4 New York City Elevated engine. The article reveals that the track over the dam was on a branch line of the Horse Shoe Forestry Company and that there were about twelve miles of standard gauge logging trackage at that time. This conflicts with Cushing's (1900) observations that both Low's lines were narrow gauge. Could Low have standard-gauged one or both of his lines between 1900 and 1908? The 1903-1904 Tupper Lake quadrangle and Map 41-1 in this book show both Low's lines connecting with the Adirondack Division at Horseshoe, suggesting standard gauge. Narrow gauge lines would have meant that there was no physical track connection with the New York Central.

The 1903-1904 Tupper Lake quadrangle shows the main Horse Shoe Forestry Company track to the southeast end of Horse Shoe Pond, but not the branch to the first Bog River Dam. This quadrangle also shows the Wake Robin Railroad to Hitchins Pond and the branch to Pine Pond.

Clark (page 12) includes a photograph of the first dam under construction with a steam shovel in the foreground excavating footings; in the background was a locomotive pushing a dump-gondola car.

Hiking the gravel highway on July 21, 1992, this writer observed that the former Horseshoe Forestry Railroad branch line climbed a steep grade from the main, passed over a divide and down the other side, and terminated at the south end of the Bog River dam. This 250-foot long dam was in the process of being rebuilt by the New York State Department of Environmental Conservation in the summer of 1992.

In 1907 a second, but much smaller, dam creating Low's Lake was built across the Bog River above Hitchins Pond for generating more electric power. Apparently, no railroad track crossed this second dam.

In September 1908, forest fires contributed to the eventual demise of the Horse Shoe Forestry Company operations. Hughes (1990, page 40) presents several telegrams sent by Low to the New York Central complaining that the railroad's fire-fighting forces and prevention techniques were inadequate. The hamlet of Long Lake West, in addition to much of Low's forests, was lost in these fires. By August 1911, the Horse Shoe Forestry Company Railroad was no longer operating.

New York Central timetables continued to list Horse Shoe. Between January 19 and December 7, 1947, the station name was changed to American Legion. By August 1, 1958, according to New York State Equalization and Assessment photographs #EA-A-80-19 and #EA-A-80-20, the station had already been demolished. The last passenger train stopped here up to the end of service in April 1965.

A. A. Low's old Maple Valley evaporator building, now a hunting club, July 1995.
Author photo.

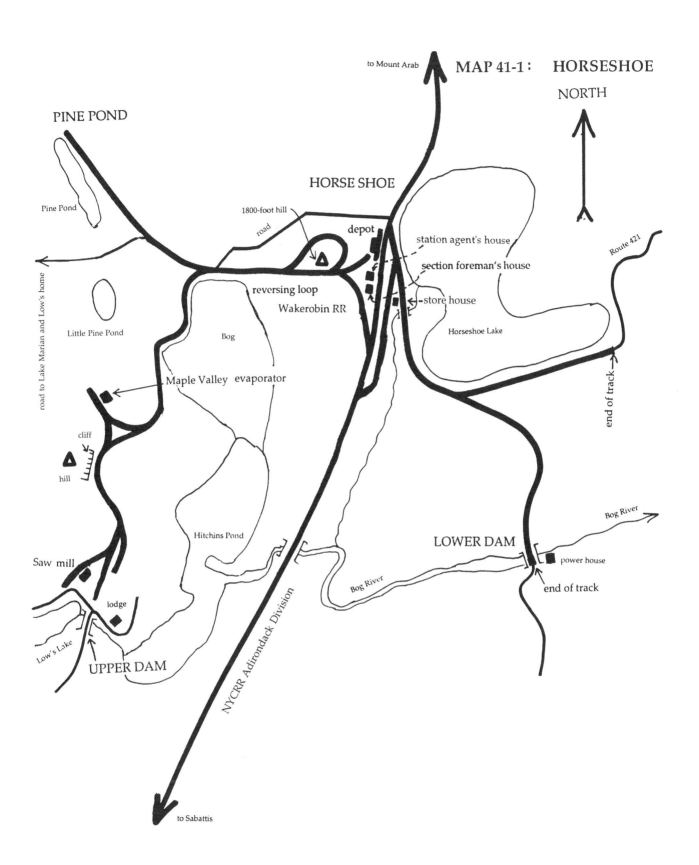

Chapter 42:
Seven Short Line Railroads along the New York Central Adirondack Division

To further reduce the length of Chapter 36, seven of the shorter branch lines diverging from the New York Central Adirondack Division have been combined into this single chapter, #42. (The reader will find less interruption in the trend-of-thought following the main Adirondack Division route because of the elimination of these seven shorter side trips.)

Black River and Woodhull Railroad: Map 36-3

The Black River and Woodhull Railroad crossed the right-of-way of the future New York Central Adirondack Division at about milepost 35.5, near Forestport Station. Of the seven short lines described in this chapter, this is the only one which did not physically connect with the Adirondack Division because it preceded the latter by over two decades. It operated until 1868 and 1869, and possibly into the early 1870s. Abandonment occurred long before Webb's Adirondack & Saint Lawrence railroad opened at Forestport Station in 1892.

Palmer's article (April 1970) entitled *Wooden Rails in the Wilderness* describes the Black River & Woodhull Railroad. The rails of this early line, 13 miles long, were made of wood. Only horses, never locomotives, pulled the cars loaded primarily with logs for sawmills. Palmer offers a map of the Black River & Woodhull which I have imposed upon the Remsen 1897 15-minute topographic quadrangle as best as possible.

Moose River Lumber Company Railroad: Maps 36-4 and 42-1

The Moose River Lumber Company Railroad diverged from the Adirondack Division at McKeever, milepost 49.15. Marleau (1986, page 239) states that this lumber company built a logging railroad in 1894. The 1910 McKeever 15-minute topographic quadrangle shows the line as 3.5 miles long heading east toward Woodhull Mountain on the south side of, but well above, the South Branch Moose River. Palmer has notes on the Moose River Lumber Company at the Adirondack Museum Library. Harter (p. 177) states that the Moose River Lumber Company sold their operation to the Gould Paper Company, and that the logging railroad was abandoned in 1914 or 1915. The June 13, 1948 Adirondack Division employees' timetable still lists a Gould Paper Company siding at McKeever. An undated New York Central valuation diagram supplies us with the detail of this branch with all it spurs.

The 1910 McKeever quadrangle shows also a spur, 0.4 mile long, following the Moose River downstream from the Adirondack Division bridge to the mill. Moose River Lumber Company logging trains must have crossed the Adirondack Division main track at McKeever to proceed from their logging line to their mill.

The only photograph of the Moose River Railroad which I have found occurs in Koch (1979), page 139.

Fulton Chain Railroad, the first or "Peg Leg": Maps 36-4 and 42-2

The Fulton Chain Railroad, the first of two with this name, was also known as the "Peg Leg Railroad." This short line diverged from the Adirondack Division at about milepost 53.79, just north of Minnehaha.

Palmer's 1971 article, reprinted in 1973, is the major reference on this short line. Photos appear on page 42 and 56 of the 1971 article and on pages 151 and 155 of the 1973 reprint. The line was built in 1888 and ceased running on July 1, 1892 when Webb's Adirondack & Saint Lawrence was completed to Fulton Chain Station, later called Thendara. The "Peg Leg" was eight miles long, and like the Black River & Woodhull, had wooden rails, hence the nickname "Peg Leg." Palmer offers great detail on the 36-inch narrow-gauge locomotive and operations. The "Peg Leg" ran only during the summer months to bring passengers from the Boonville-Port Leyden area at Moose River to the Fulton Chain of Lakes. From Minnehaha, they boarded a steamboat which followed the Middle Branch Moose River upstream to Old Forge. The "Peg Leg" also carried some freight, especially during construction of Webb's Railroad. Mihalyi (1991) also wrote about the "Peg Leg." A New York Central valuation diagram indicates a former junction at about 53.79 miles or some 200 feet north of Minnehaha station; this junction might have been the "Peg Leg." Poor's *Directory of Railroad Officials* for 1891 lists the owners, one locomotive, one passenger car and six work cars.

Fulton Chain Railroad, the second or Old Forge Branch: Maps 36-5, 42-3, and 42-4

The Fulton Chain Railroad, the second of two with this name, became the Old Forge Branch when the New York Central acquired it in 1917 (Hochschild, 1962, *Life and Leisure* --, page 97). It diverged from the Adirondack Division just south of Fulton Chain Station, later renamed Thendara, at about milepost 57.8. The 2.21-mile-long branch was constructed in 1896 (Harter, p. 290) to Old Forge. The branch was confusedly also called the Fulton Chain Railroad, and became the second railroad in the region with this name; the first was the "Peg Leg" at Minnehaha. The Old Forge Branch ran until July 11, 1932.

See also Hochschild's 1962 *Life and Leisure* -- p. 33 for details. The *New Century Atlas of Herkimer County*, 1906, published by the Century Map Company of Philadelphia, Pennsylvania, shows a track plan at Old Forge. This and other plans available of Old Forge show no facility for turning locomotives, only a few stub-end tracks, so that trains must have backed down to Thendara on the return trip. Carman's Relief Map in the Thendara Station in 1992 showed several industries along the Branch between Thendara Station and the bridge over the Middle Branch Moose River: oil storage tanks, coal yards, the second Brown Tract Mill (which burned again during reconstruction in the 1930s) with log boom, and a siding to jackworks one-quarter mile upstream in the Middle Branch Moose River.

Palmer and Roehl (1989, page 96) offer a photo of the Old Forge depot. New York State Museum photo #P1746 shows a train at the Old Forge depot.

Champlain Realty Company Railroad at Woods Lake: Maps 36-6 and 42-5

The Champlain Realty Company, a subsidiary of International Paper Company, built a railroad from Woods Lake. The logging railroad began at the north end of the passing siding at milepost 73.6 and followed Twitchell Creek westward downstream for about three miles. Construction was about 1916. Gove (1978) offers full detail, including photographs, on the operation. He says that the logging railroad ceased running about 1926, and that the rails were pulled up about 1932. The Buck Pond siding near Big Moose was also linked with this operation (see Map 36-22). Marleau (1986, page 240) states that Gove's approximate 1916 to 1926 dates are definite. He also tells us that George Bushey was the contractor here for the Champlain Realty Company and offers on his page 314 a 1927 map of the Woods Lake area. Marleau's map, along with Gove's, an International Paper Company Forest Map of Township Number 6 - John Brown's Tract, and New York Central valuation diagrams are combined here into Map 42-5.

Partlow Lake Railway: Maps 36-7 and 42-6

The Partlow Lake Railway diverged at Partlow, at milepost ca. 84.3. A 1900 New York Central map shows that the Partlow Lake Railway had already been built five miles northwest to Sylvan Lake, later called Partlow Mill Dam. This short line was used for logging operations on Webb's private Nehasane Park estate.

Piercefield Spur: Maps 36-9 and 42-7

The Piercefield Spur diverged from the Adirondack Division at Piercefield Station, milepost ca.

109.25. This 1.4 mile-long spur ran northwest down to the Raquette River at Piercefield. International Paper Company had a mill which was already running when the 1903-1904 Tupper Lake 15-minute quadrangle was printed. It was still running in 1931, but the 1936 *Adirondack Land Map* published by the Conservation Department no longer shows the spur. Where this spur crossed old State Highway 3, just south of the present State Highway 3, the rails were still in place in the concrete in 1991!

**The Adirondack Railway at Thendara, July 1980.
The Old Forge Branch diverged from Thendara until 1932.**
Author photo.

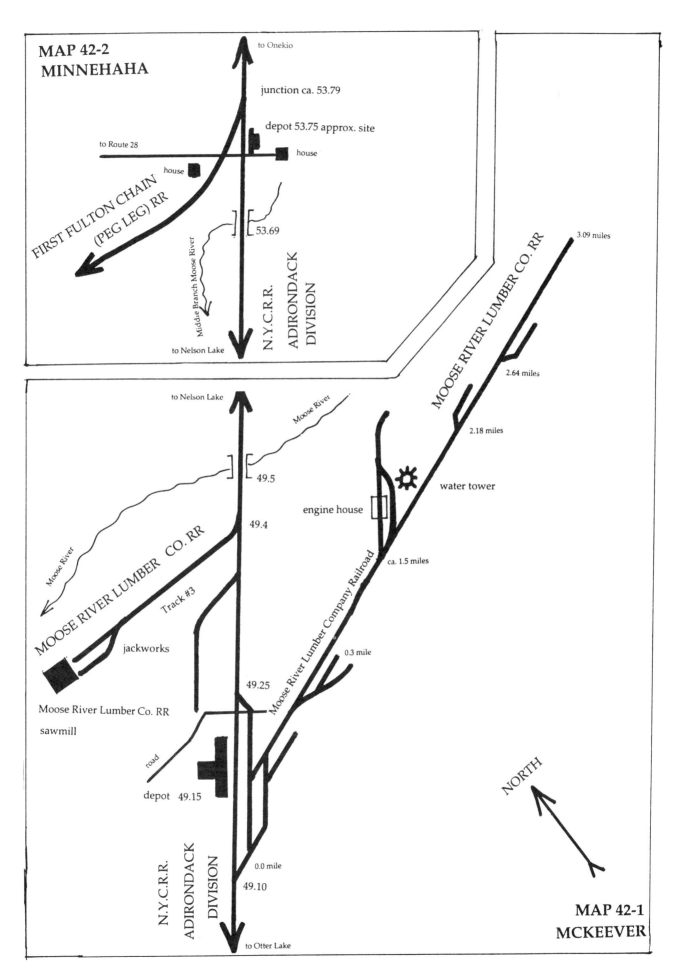

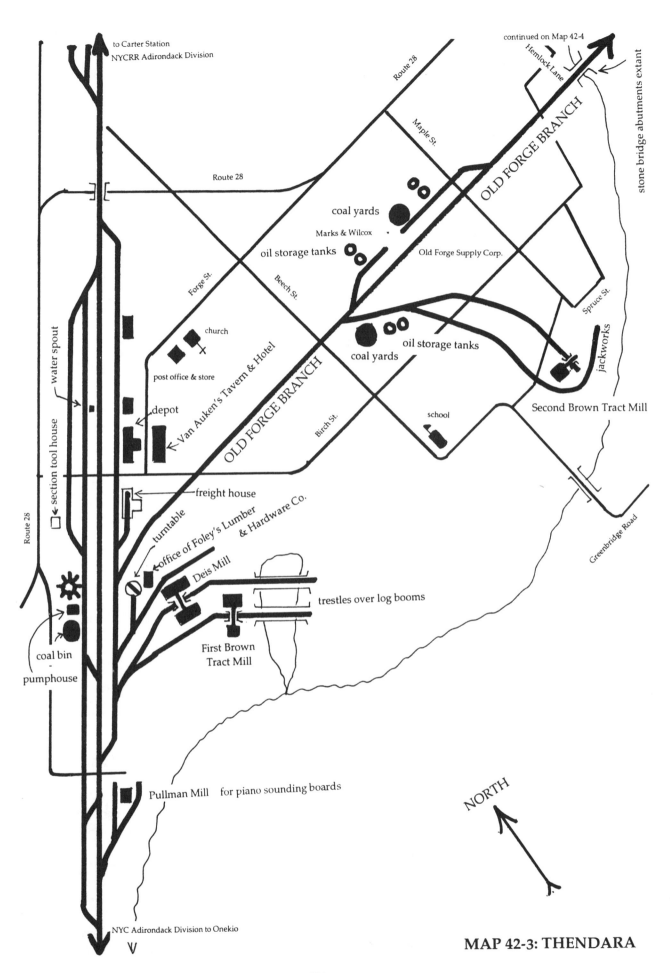

MAP 42-3: THENDARA

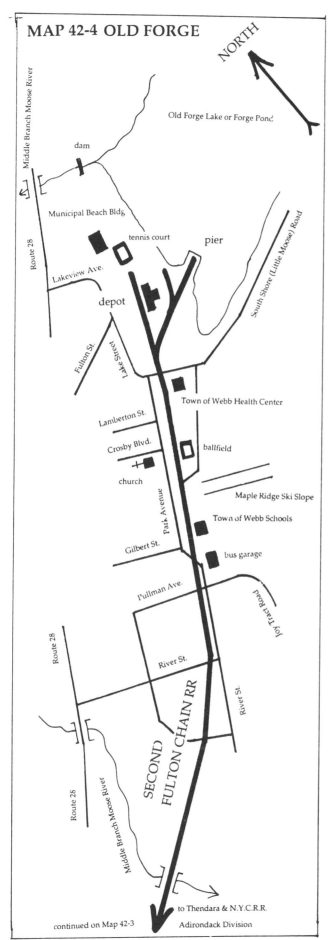
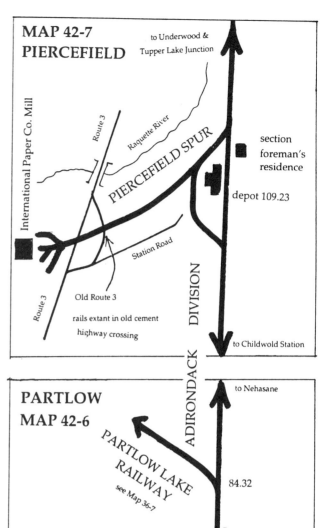
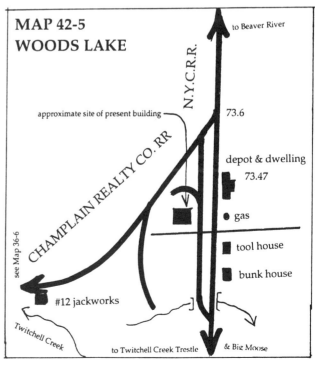

Chapter 43:
The Rise and Fall of The Adirondack Railway

BECAUSE THE HISTORY of the Adirondack Railway is so recent and because hundreds of still readily-accessible articles have been published about it, only a brief selection of articles and a summary are offered here. Consult the selected references, most of which are from newspapers, for details. The selection has been made by including only those articles signed by the authors and those sent to this writer by rail buffs with precise dates included. Mele (1990, Aug. 26) offers a good chronological historical summary.

The last Penn Central freight train to serve the Remsen-Lake Placid Branch was on April 10, 1972 (Lodge, 1972). Because of declining revenues, the Penn Central had applied in March 1971 to the Interstate Commerce Commission for permission to abandon the line. The Commission decided to grant the request on July 6, 1972, and released an official report on July 14.

In the meantime, the New York State Department of Transportation (D.O.T.) held a hearing in Saranac Lake on July 13, 1972 to gather information relative to the potential future use of rail freight service. The record of the hearing had been examined by the Technical Assistance Center of the State University of New York at Plattsburgh. When their study was completed by Lodge (1972) on September 14, including supplemental contacts with potential customers, the D.O.T. was in a position to determine what role, if any, the State should play in supporting or assisting the resumption of rail service in this area. The report presented the results of the survey to 140 potential shippers. Note that the Center was asked to study freight service, a study which, by 1980, had become nearly useless to the almost all-passenger operations!

Legislation was introduced to enable New York State to purchase the abandoned Penn Central line at the beginning of February 1974. See Doolittle (1974, Feb. 19) and (1974, Jul. 16) for details. At that time, a salvage company was already pulling spikes and removing rail on some sections of track; such a state purchase eliminated continued salvaging.

On April 17 (1974), Governor Wilson directed the D.O.T. to proceed with acquisition of the Lake Placid Branch line, including rails and structures. The purchase was to accomplish this with funds from the $30 million essential rail preservation appropriation recently approved by the legislature. An April 23, 1974 order by Federal District Court handling the Penn Central bankruptcy proceedings halted all further dismantling of the Adirondack Line. Department of Transportation Commissioner Schuler has begun negotiations to buy the line for the State.

An inspection tour was made of the line in July 1974 by State assemblymen, local politicians, and D.O.T. officials. At about the same time Albi Fetzer and Frank Menair, organizers of the Adirondack Railway Corporation, were at Lake Clear driving spikes which had been pulled by salvage crews the year before. A washout had developed between Lake Clear Junction and Tupper Lake (possibly south of Floodwood?).

Robbins (1975) and Roberts (1976) summarized events up to that time, the latter discussing financing in some detail. McLaughlin (1976) included a picture of the last train (two Alco road switchers and snow plow) which passed through Saranac Lake some four years before.

The construction era occurred from February 1977 to just prior to the Inaugural Run on October 9, 1979. In February 1977, the New York State

Department of Transportation (D.O.T.) approved the plans for the resurrection of railroad service. The D.O.T. at that time was applying to the Economic Development Administration (E.D.A.) for funding to cover the estimated $1.7 million rehabilitation cost. The federal agency was ready in time for the 1980 Winter Olympics at Lake Placid. Any costs not covered by the federal grant would have been shared between the State and the Adirondack Railway Corporation, a company formed to operate the railroad. The company leased the track from the State and would have been responsible for all maintenance and operation. Greenhouse (1977) and Nordwind (1977) summarized the then-recent, February 1977 events.

Rehabilitation of the track began finally on June 19, 1978 south of Beaver River, and on July 19 between Beaver River and Tupper Lake. Crews were hired, worked northward, and were past Tupper Lake by mid-October, concentrating on washouts (the one at Floodwood was a bad one). Viscome (1978) described the section crews and work trains, and included a photo of the bunk cars.

A group of people was organized by the Friends of the Union Depot to restore the Saranac Lake station. Their first meeting was on April 3, 1979 followed by a work party clean-up on April 28th and 29th. Their *FUD News* newsletters offer detail.

The Heart Association ran a benefit train from Utica on July 21, 1979 which went only as far as Tupper Lake. The Adirondack Conservancy's Great Adirondack Railway Excursion to Ne-ha-sa-ne Park, Saturday, August 25, 1979, never took place because a locomotive wheel broke en route from Thendara and the train never arrived in Tupper Lake for the crowd to board!

Pilcher (1979) described the route and some of the equipment, and offered a little history.

The Inaugural Run occurred on October 9, 1979. Detail on the this can be found in Peel (1979), Odato (1979), Bishop (1979), Reinman (1979), Palmer (1979), and Kizzia (1979).

Bishop (1979) wrote that the first freight arrived at Tupper Lake on the recently restored Adirondack Railway on Friday, October 19. A coal car containing 50 to 60 tons of fine coal was unloaded on a downtown siding off Washington Street by the W. D. Wilson Company. A small portion of the coal went to heat a local Tupper Lake home and the bulk to heat the "castle" at Litchfield Park. The coal originated in the anthracite fields of northeastern Pennsylvania and was about the only freight delivered during the operation of the Railway.

Another hopper car, not carrying freight for income, had a load of gravel for track maintenance at Ray Brook and derailed in mid-November 1979. A crane was used to rerail the car.

S. Thompson (1979), public relations and passenger service director of the Adirondack Railway, wrote about the line in the fall of that year.

Regular passenger operation occurred intermittently from January through October 1980. In January 1980, prior to the February Olympics, the Adirondack Railway ran weekend trains including a northbound run from Utica to Lake Placid on Friday evenings, a southbound return trip on Sunday midday, and a Lake Placid to Thendara run with a return trip on Saturdays. The first train out of Utica was on Friday January 4. McConnell (1980) described and praised the weekend service.

During the Olympics in February 1980, the trains ran daily. In March and April, trains did not run regularly.

An excursion for the weekend of May 3 and 4 from Utica to Lake Placid and return was operated. Newcombe (1980) described the summer service which had just begun to run and offered superb publicity.

Regular service resumed on weekends from May 16 through June 22, and on a daily basis beginning on June 28, according to the Spring-Summer 1980 Adirondack Railway timetable. This timetable also provides fares and running times. When no baggage car was available, canoes rode outside the locomotive on the catwalk within the handrails! One unique feature of the Adirondack Railway was its willingness to make extra unscheduled stops at remote locations to pick up or discharge passengers on fishing, hunting, camping or canoeing trips.

Because of many minor derailments (fortunately no injuries), in August 1980, the Adirondack Railway was shut down temporarily by the D.O.T. while track renovations could be made. The cause of the problem, according to some sources (but this has not been confirmed), was locomotive #25 whose wheels were out-of-gauge and spread the rails. A notice of the shut-down was made by the Railway itself in August 1980 in an open letter to the public urging letters be written to John Ladd of the Mohawk Valley Economic Development District, Inc. and State Senator James Donovan in support of restoration of service. In this notice, the statement was made that a total of 22,000 people rode the train: some 10,000 during the Olympics and some 12,000 more between May 18 and August 5.

Service was restored between Lake Placid and Tupper Lake in the fall of 1980 for a short time on weekends and holidays. The autumn Adirondack Railway timetable cited fares and running times. Faber (1980) rode the train on September 27 and then described and praised the service. Shortly after this, further derailments shut the operation down for good.

J. Moore (1980) described the railroad in general; then he discussed the use of DuPont herbicides to control unwanted vegetation along the right-of-way, and the use of DuPont paints in both the inside and outside of the railway cars.

Track changes were made during the operation of the Adirondack Railway at Thendara, Lake Clear Junction, and Lake Placid. See the sections on these stations in Chapters 36 and 20 for detail. (Those changes made at Utica are out of the geographic range of this book.)

In November 1980, the Adirondack Railway ceased operation. The causes of cancellation of service were financial problems, roadbed condition, and inadequate equipment for heating passenger cars in winter. Details on the closure and the Adirondack Railways's finances are found in Viscome (1980), and T. Rice (1980).

In April 1981 the Adirondack Railway filed for bankruptcy and New York State cancelled its lease. Carman (1981) wrote on the closure of the line. By June, Viscome (1981: Apr. 16, Jun. 11, Jun. 25) reported that New York State was looking for another operator; she described some of the potential investing operators and then wrote on a special post-closure run on June 20, 1981 from Utica to Lake Placid designed to entice additional investors. By the end of July 1981, six different groups were interested. Landfried (1981, Oct. 1) explained that by October, none of the six groups had submitted satisfactory proposals to the D.O.T. Another "scare" that the tracks would be removed by this state department came in early November (Viscome, 1981, Jul. 16), but supporters of the railroads were soon pacified because two agencies, one State and one federal, came to the rescue. By the end of November, the Adirondack Park Agency voted to ask the D.O.T. to delay track removal. Also, the Economic Development Administration (E.D.A.) which had earlier partially funded the railroad, stated that track removal by the D.O.T. would go against E.D.A. stipulations. Landfried (1981, Dec, 17) revealed that the state offered a ninety day reprieve so that potential operators could submit new proposals; Viscome (1981: Jul. 30, Nov. 12, Nov. 26) mentioned that the meeting of operators took place on December 15.

Events of 1982 began with two potential operators, one from the Utica area, the "Goldstone Group," and the other from the Rochester area, the "Minetree Group." See Viscome (1982: Mar. 18, Apr. 8) for a description. Adirondack Railway locomotives and cars were auctioned off at Webster, outside Rochester, on March 27, 1982 (Resnick, 1982).

By July 1982, yet another "scare" took place—the D.O.T. was threatening to remove the tracks once again (Gleaves, 1982: Jul. 22, Jul. 29, Sep. 2). Railroad supporters were pacified when the D.O.T. granted another time extension to potential operators to October 1. The Economic Development and Technical Assistance Center, State University of New York at Plattsburgh, published another survey in October 1982 to determine if re-resurrection for passenger and/or freight service was warranted. Burlage (1982) wrote on the causes of the Adirondack Railway's closure.

During July of the following year, Bruce (1983) reported on how Tupper Lake Village applied for an Urban Development Action Grant from the federal Housing and Urban Development agency (HUD) to assist the railroad resurrection. They failed. The report also describes the President of the Adirondack Transportation Corporation, Dr. Ronald Goldstone's, attempts at resurrection.

In January Frenette (1984) wrote that the Federal bankruptcy court denied the D.O.T. permission to remove the tracks until the 30-year lease with the Adirondack Railway expired in the year 2007. Tooley (1984) provided an update on the activities of the Adirondack Transportation Corporation and its President, Dr. Ronald Goldstone.

Tooley (1985) and Gymburch (1985) in November wrote about a firewood shipping proposal by William Kuntz III and Westrail Transportation System. Tooley (1986) wrote again, but this time on the finances.

A most extraordinary complex and lengthy series of legal proceedings followed a June 1987 decision by a federal district judge in Syracuse. These involved the federal district judge, a federal bankruptcy court judge, the New York State Department of Transportation, the Adirondack Railway and its bankruptcy trustee, the Adirondack Transportation Corporation which was hoping to be the new operator of the line, attorneys on all sides, the lease, and the ownership. Buck (1987), Mele and Olchvary (1987), Olchvary (1987), Mele (1988: Sep. 16, Sep. 23), and Gymburch (1988) attempted to explain this nearly incomprehensible tangle to the public.

Olchvary (1988) wrote about the telephone-linked, simultaneous Lake Placid and Utica meetings of January 18, 1988. Creditors had been invited but few appeared. Instead, most people who attended were discussing various ideas about how to re-resurrect the line.

Rappaport (1988) in November reported that the New York State D.O.T. outbid a group of Saranac Lake area businessmen for ownership of the line.

B. Rice (1989) wrote on the Adirondack North Country Association meeting in July 1989 for strategies on keeping the line open. This meeting resulted in a report dated May 3, 1990, and summarized by Russell (1990) and Mele (1990, Jul. 15). In July 1990 the North Country Railroad Association, as a project of the Mohawk Valley Chapter of the National Railway Historical Society, published a pamphlet entitled *Why should we save the Railroad through the Adirondacks*.

Mele (1990) in August supplied a brief but very well done chronological history of the Adirondack Railway.

In October 1991 a New York State inter-departmental (D.E.C. and D.O.T.) task force held three public hearings: in Ray Brook on the 8th, in Old Forge on the 9th, and in Utica on the 10th. Most people in attendance supported the re-resurrection of the railway. Russell (1991, Sep. 27-29) and Mele (1991) then reported on the hearings.

Adirondack Architectural Heritage sponsored summer walking tours of the railroad (Matteson, 1992; Bounds, 1993) led by Christopher Brescia, chief engineer for WNBZ, the Saranac Lake radio station. In September (Lamothe, 1993) interviewed Mark Kavouksorian, project director for the Utica-Mohawk Chapter of the National Railway Historical Society. Thill (1994) and Russell (1994) have brought us more recently up to date.

The Adirondack Railway Preservation Society was formed shortly after these activities and was soliciting membership in March 1992. Their first newsletter was mailed from Utica on July 3, 1992. Subsequent newsletters offer a running commentary on developments through to the present.

During the summer of 1992 trains began operating from Thendara to Minnehaha, celebrating the 100th anniversary of the opening of Webb's Mohawk and Malone (see Chapter 36). Appropriately, the line was called the Adirondack Centennial Railroad, but the name was changed in 1994 to the Adirondack Scenic Railroad. The operation has become very popular and successful. At the time of this writing it has opened for the 1995 season with an extension to Carter Station (Clearwater). See Folwell's article in Crane, McClellan and Folwell (1995).

Meanwhile at the other end of the line, volunteer crews were clearing brush off the track from Saranac Lake to Lake Placid in 1994. Much activity is beginning in 1995 to once again restore the Saranac Lake station, in essence a resurrection of the activities the Friends of Union Depot.

Annotated Bibliography

Adey, W. H. 1928. "College Boys at Student Camp." *Delaware & Hudson Railroad Bulletin* 8 (16): 247-249, 252, 253 (August 15). [On Thurman.]

Adirondack Company's Railroad (North Creek Line). Pamphlets in Saranac Lake Free Library: A235, 2 through 6.

Adirondack Nature Conservancy. 1992. "Gift of 20 Miles of Railroad Bed Helps Protect Massawepie Mire." In *The Flicker*: 1 (Fall).

Adirondack North Country Association. 1990. *Railroad Feasibility Study and Business Plan for the Utica to Lake Placid Rail Line*. Phase One Report. May 3, 1990. Prepared by Northwest Engineering, Inc., Tidioute, PA.

Adirondack Railway. 1980. *Time Table Number 1*. [January-February.]

-----. *Schedule of Trains*. May 16-October 13.

-----. 1980. *Fall Schedule of Trains*.

Allen, Richard S. 1973. "The Crown Point Iron Company's Railroad." In *Rails of the North Woods*: 175-194. Lakemont, NY: North Country Books. [Originally published by the Penfield Foundation in 1968.]

Angus, Chris. 1991. "Reclaiming an Historic Waterway." *Adirondac* 55, 4: 10-13 (July-August). [On Grasse River with photos of Higbie Lumber Co. locomotive at Newton Falls and the Clifton Furnace ruins.]

Asher and Adams. 1869 and 1871. *New Topographical Atlas and Gazetteer of New York*. New York City: Asher and Adams.

Babcock, Erland R. 1995. "The Iron Mines of Mineville, New York." *Bridge Line Historical Society Bulletin* 5, no. 6 (June): 13 and 14. [Published by Bridge Line Historical Society, Albany, NY.]

Baker, Sarah. 1970. *The Saranac Valley*. Saranac (Clinton County), NY: published by the author. Three volumes. [Volume II contains industries and railroads.]

Barker, Elmer Eugene. 1969. *The Story of Crown Point Iron*. Ironville, Crown Point, NY: The Penfield Foundation. Historical publication no. 3. Reprinted from *New York History*, October 1942.

Barker, Steve. 1973. "A Bird's Eye View of the Village of Ironville N.Y. and the Ironville Works of the Crown Point Iron Company." Map in *Your Own History: A Self-Guided Tour Through Ironville and The Historic Ironworks Area*. Ironville, NY: The Penfield Foundation.

Barnes, Jeanette D. 1962. "Clifton Mines." *The Quarterly* 7 (1):13 and 14 (January). [Publication of the Saint Lawrence County Historical Association, Canton, NY.]

Baumgartner, Edward P. 1996. "A Brief Chronology of the Lake Champlain & Moriah Railroad." *Bridge Line Historical Society Bulletin* 6, 4: 7-9,21,22

Beals, Clyde. 1928. "Tiniest Railroad is Now Menaced." *New York Times* (August 19).

Beers, D. G. & Co. 1876. *Atlas of Franklin County, New York*. Philadelphia: D. G. Beers & Co.

Beers, F. W. 1869. *Atlas of Clinton County, New York*. New York City: F. W. Beers, A. D. Ellis and G. G. Soule. [In 1889, J. L. Beers published a map of Plattsburgh; whether this was a portion of a Clinton County atlas is unknown.]

-----. 1876. *County Atlas of Warren, New York*. New York City: F. W. Beers.

Bernard, Robert. 1991. "Years of Fire." *Adirondack Life* 12 (2): 42- 46 (March-April).

Berry, Watson B. 1948-1956. "A North Country Chronicle." *Watertown Daily Times*. Many articles over many years. Specific ones of interest are:

1952: August 9,16,23,30; Sept. 6,13,20; October 11,25; November 22; December 6,13,27. [Rutland RR construction in the 1850s.]

1953: January 17; February 7,28; March 7,14,21,28: more on Rutland RR.

1953: May 23,29. [Sackets Harbor RR.]

1955: October 15. [Hannawa Falls Water Power Company.]

1956: January 21 and March 31. [Brandreth.]

1958: May 24. "Old Photographs Tell Story of Lumbering, Mill Operation." Page 6. [On Newton Falls Paper Company Railroad.]

Bien, Julius. 1895. *Map of Clinton County*. New York City: Julius Bien & Co. [Also, *Map of Franklin County*, 1895.]

Bird, David. 1971. "Forest Preserve in Adirondacks is Concern of Environmentalists." *New York Times*, November 28, 1971: 68. [Concerns railroad to Tahawus.]

Birkinbine, John. 1915. *The ABCs of Iron and Steel*. Cleveland, OH: The Penton Publishing Co. [Pp. 266 and 267 include photos of Mineville.]

Bishop, Harold. 1979. "Railroad Delivers First Freight Load." Saranac Lake: *Adirondack Daily Enterprise* (October 22).

Blankman, E. G. 1902. *New Popular Map of the Adirondacks*. Canton, NY: The Adirondack Map Company, Limited.

Board of Railroad Commissioners, State of New York. 1893. *Tenth Annual Report for the Fiscal Year Ending June 30, 1892*. Albany: James B. Lyon, State Printer.

Borrup, Roger. 1970-1971. "Plattsburgh Traction Company, Plattsburgh, New York." Reprint from *Transportation Bulletin* no. 78, September 1970-December 1971: 1-48. [Published by Connecticut Valley Chapter of the National Railway Historical Society, Warehouse Point.]

Bounds, Jeff. 1993. "Centennial: First Train to Lake Placid was 100 Years Ago Today." Plattsburgh *Press Republican* August 1: A-1.

Bourcier, Paul G. 1985. *History in the Mapping: Four Centuries of Adirondack Cartography*. Blue Mountain Lake, NY: The Adirondack Museum.

Bragdon, Henry. 1940. "The Passing of the Grasse River Railroad." *High Spots Yearbook*: 71-74. [Published by the Adirondack Mountain Club.]

Brescia, Christopher and Mary B. Hotaling. 1990. *Bibliography: Adirondack Division, New York Central Railroad*. Saranac Lake, NY: Historic Saranac Lake (unpublished).

Bridge Line Historical Society. 1991. "F.J.&G. Still in the News." *Bridge Line Historical Society Bulletin* 1 (3): 20 (March).

Brill, J. G. 1907. "Interesting Car for Paul Smith's Adirondacks." *Brill's Magazine*, 1, no.11 (November 15, 1907): 219-221.

Brown, William. 1963. *History of Warren County*. Glens Falls, NY: Board of Supervisors of Warren County.

Bruce, Carol. 1983. "Major Setback: HUD Grant Denied For Railroad Fund." Saranac Lake: *Adirondack Daily Enterprise* July 13.

Buck, Timothy. 1987. "State Loses Case Over Cause of Adirondack Railroad Bankruptcy." Saranac Lake *Adirondack Daily Enterprise* June 16.

Burdick, Neal S. 1985. "Amtrak in the Adirondacks." *Adirondack Life* 16 (2): 27-33 (March-April).

-----. 1992. "A Wing And A Prayer: Dwight Church Was the North Country's First Flying Photographer." *Adirondack Life* 23 (4): 52-57 (July-August).

Burlage, John W., Jr. 1982. "Taps for the Adirondack Railway: The 'Eager Beaver Line' Runs No More." *Block Line*, Bulletin of the Tri-State Chapter, National Railway Historical Society: 18-21 (January).

Burleigh, L. H. 1889. "Port Henry, New York." Lithograph drawn and published by the author, Troy, New York.

Burnett, Charles H. 1932. *Conquering the Wilderness: The Building of the Adirondack and Saint Lawrence Railway*. Published privately by the author.

Calkins, Alison. 1995. "Train Derails in Moriah." Plattsburgh *Press Republican* March 2, 1995: A-1.

-----. 1995. "Train Wreck Worst Ever in Area." Plattsburgh *Press Republican* March 3, 1995: 1,13, and 20.

Calvert, Trudie. 1975. "Gone But Not Forgotten—The Way We Were." *The Quarterly* 20 (2): 3,4 (April). [On the Hannawa Falls Railroad. Publication of the Saint Lawrence County Historical Association, Canton, NY.]

Canton Commercial Advertiser. March 6, 1950. [Article on the Clifton Iron Company's Railroad.]

Carman, Bernard R. 1981. "Derailed." *Adirondack Life* 12 (4): 4,5 (July-August). [On Adirondack Railway.]

Century Map Company. 1906. *New Century Atlas of Herkimer County*. Philadelphia: New Century Co.

-----. 1912. *New Century Atlas of Counties of the State of New York*. New York City and Philadelphia: Everts Publishing Company.

City Street Directory. 1974. *Adirondack Region Atlas*. Poughkeepsie NY: City Street Directory, Inc.

Clark, Mark. 1974. "The Low Dynasty." *The Quarterly* 19 (4): 9-15 and front cover (January). [Publication of the Saint Lawrence County Historical Association, Canton, NY.]

Collins, Geraldine. 1969. "Brandon—Ghost Town of Franklin County." *Franklin Historical Review* 6: 22-28.

-----. 1977. *The Brighton Story*. Lakemont, NY: North Country Books.

-----. 1971. "Railroad History of Franklin County." *Franklin Historical Review* 8: 6-16. [Article is unsigned, but Collins supplies an editor's note on page 13.]

Crane, Galen, Sandra McClellan, and Elizabeth Folwell. 1995. "Railroad Treks in the Adirondacks: Autumn Splendor from a Trio of Trains." *Adirondack Life* 26,6: 32-36 (September-October).

Cunningham, Joseph. 1991. *New Haven EP-5 Jets: Classic Power No.9*. Hicksville, NY: N.J. International, Inc. [Paul Smith's Electric Railway on pp. 7, 9, and 10.]

Cupp, Fred. 1994. "Up North." *Bridge Line Historical Society Bulletin* 4 (9): 23 (September). [On Riverside and North Creek.]

Cushing, H.P. 1900. "Recent Geologic Work in Franklin and Saint Lawrence Counties." New York State Museum, Albany: *Report to the Director and State Geologist, 1900*: r54 and r55. [On Horseshoe Lake Railway.]

Dales, Douglas S. 1940. "Seven-eighths of a Mile." *Railroad Magazine* 27, 6: 74-76 (May). [On the Marion River Carry RR.]

Day, Wally. 1995. "North Country News." *Bridge Line Historical Society Bulletin* 5, no.4 (April): 14. [On Bombardier's proposed railroad car building plant at Plattsburgh.]

Dedrick, Marion R. 1989. "The Marion River Carry, Then and Now." *Adirondac* 53 (7): 24, 25 (August). [Publication of the Adirondack Mountain Club.]

Delaware & Hudson Railroad Corporation. 1925. *A Century of Progress, 1823-1923*. Albany: J. B. Lyon Co.

-----. 1928. *Board of Directors----Inspection of Lines*, June 7 to 10. Pages 9-360: "Passenger and Freight Stations on the Delaware & Hudson."

-----. 1931. *Board of Directors - Inspection of Lines*, June 11 to 14. Pages 88 to 90: "Iron and Steel." [Port Henry and Lyon Mountain.]

-----. 1934. *Board of Directors - Inspection of Lines*, June 7 to 10. Pages 1 to 176: "A History of the Chateaugay Ore and Iron Company" by Joseph R. Linney.

-----. 1933. [Untitled promotion brochure.]

-----. 1941. *Official List No. 57*. January 1, 1941.

-----. 1973. *The D&H, the Bridge Line to New England and Canada*, 1823-1973. Map.

-----. *Delaware and Hudson Railroad Bulletin*:
  1926. 6 (19): 3 and 4 (October 1). "Forest Fires Once a Handicap."
  1927. 7 (1): front cover (January 1). [Photo of South Junction coaling tower.]
  1928. 8 (1): front cover (January 1). [Photo of Willsboro Tunnel south entrance.]
  1928. (8) 2: front cover and page 30 (January 15). [Willsboro Tunnel.]
  1928. 8 (14): front cover (July 15). [Photo of new station at Merriam.]
  1928. 8 (18): 278 (September 15). "The New Station at Merriam, NY."
  1928. (see Adey).
  1929. 9 (13): 195, 196 (July 1)."Pulled Roosevelt's Special."
  1930. (see Linney).
  1930. 10 (24): 376, 377, 381 (December 15). [New station at Lacolle, PQ.]
  1930. 10 (23): 356-359, 364, 365 (December 1). "Harnessing the Hudson." [Construction railroad at Sacandaga Reservoir]
  1930. 10 (22): 348 (November 15). "New Stone Station Opened at Ray Brook."
  1931. (see Gibbs).
  1931. 11 (9): 141 (May 1). [Photo of interior of new station, LaColle, PQ.]
  1931. 11 (20): 6 (October 15). "Currier's Crossing is No More."
  1932. (see MacMartin).
  1932. 12 (11): 282-283 (November 1). [Photo skirting Lake Champlain near Willsboro, NY.]
  1932. 12 (12): front cover (December 1). [Photo in the Red Rocks near Willsboro.]
  1933. 13 (8): 119-121, 123 (August 1). "The Milk We Drink."
  1934. 14 (3): 44, 45 (March 1). "Whitehall Crossings Eliminated."
  1934. 14 (3): 37, 43. (March 1). "Harvesting the Ice for D&H Use."
  1935. 15 (4): 55-57 (April 1). "Chateaugay Iron, Part One." [Photo of Lyon Mountain sintering and concentrating plant.]
  1935. 15 (5): front cover, 71-77 (May 1). "Chateaugay Iron, Part Two." [Photo of top of Standish blast furnace.]
  1935. 15 (4): 53, 54, 60 (April 1). "Snow Trains." [North Creek.]
  1936. 16 (8): 117-119,125 (August 1). "Crossing the Border."
  1936. 16 (12): 181-183 (December 1). "Canada's Customs and Immigration Regulations."
  1936. (see Schwarz).
  1936. 16 (4): 56, 59 (April 1). "How the D&H Delivers the Milk by Rail."
  1937. (see Rochette).
  1937. 17 (8): 117, 118 (August 1). " 'Sea-Going' Railroad at Lake George."
  1938. 18 (1): front cover, 5-7, 12, 13 (January 1). "Beaver Dams Flood Abandoned Tekene Branch."
  1938. 18 (3): 39-41, 46 (March 1). "Snow Trains." [North Creek.]

DeMarco, Mary. 1992. "Delaware & Hudson Day in Greenfield." *Bridge Line Historical Society Bulletin* 2, no. 9 (September): 3. Continued in 2, no. 11 (November): 8. [On restoration of Kings Station.]

DeSormo, Maitland. 1968. "The Three Macs of McColloms." *Franklin Historical Review* 5: 19-26.

-----. 1974. *The Heydays of the Adirondacks*. Saranac Lake: Adirondack Yesteryears.

-----. 1980. *Summers on the Saranacs*. Saranac Lake: Adirondack Yesteryears.

de Treville, Andrew N. 1981. *A Brief Look at Brooklyn Cooperage, Past and Present*. Versailles, CT: Amstar Corporation, Brooklyn Cooperage Company Carton Plant.

Dodge, William E. 1950. "Clifton Mining Operations and Old Railroad Recalled." *Watertown Daily Times* (March 16).

Doherty, Lawrence. 1971. "Railroad History of Franklin County." *Franklin Historical Review* 8: 6-22. [Mostly on the Rutland RR.]

Doolittle, William. 1974. "Introduce Legislation to Save Rail Service on Tri-lake Line." Saranac Lake: *Adirondack Daily Enterprise* (February 19): 1.

-----. 1974. "Will the Plan for the Railroad Work?" Saranac Lake: *Adirondack Daily Enterprise* (July 16).

Duquette, John. 1987. "Paul Smith's Trolley." Saranac Lake: *Adirondack Daily Enterprise* (December 12): 1,2,3,4,6.

Donaldson, Alfred. 1921. *A History of the Adirondacks*. New York: The Century Company. [Volume 2, pp. 131-141, on railroads with discussion on Brooklyn Cooperage line to near Wawbeek.]

Dora, Donna and Mildred Keough, ed. 1977. *A Past to Remember, A Future to Mold*. Saranac Lake: Women's Civic Chamber.

Dumas, Eleanor L. 1962. "End of an Era." *The Quarterly* 7 (3): 6. [Publication of the Saint Lawrence County Historical Association, Canton NY. Abandonment of the New York Central Adirondack Division at Mountain View and Owls Head.]

Egan, Patrick. 1981. "The Marion River Railroad." *Adirondack Life* 12 (1): 40-43 (January-February).

Elizabethtown Press. 1910. "Working on the Railroad." March 31.

-----. 1910. "200 Horse Power Motor Car Purchased By The Elizabethtown Terminal Railroad Company." June 2.

Ely, W. W., M. D. (1878). *Map of the New York Wilderness and the Adirondacks*. New York City: G. W. and C. B. Colton Company.

Empire State Railway Museum. *Steam Passenger Service Directory*. Richmond, Vermont: Great Eastern Publishing. Annual publication, 1966-present.

Faber, Harold. 1974. "D&H Railway Credits Black Ink to Workers." *New York Times* (September 9): page B19.

-----. 1980. "An Adirondack Train Ride Revives Memories for Buff." *New York Times*: 53-55 (September 29).

Farmer, Ralph. 1992. *The Watson Page Lumber Company----Cascade Chair Factory Electric Railroad*. Saint Regis Falls Historians Association, unpublished manuscript.

Fennessy, Lana. 1988. *The History of Newcomb*. Garretson, SD: published by the author. Pages 70- 88 are on Tahawus Mines.]

Fenster, J. M. 1994. "Train to Another Country: Vive La Difference of Montreal and the Charm of Approaching It on Amtrak's *Adirondack*." *Amtrak Express* (September-October): 30-33.

Fowler, Albert Vann. 1968. "Cranberry Lake from Wilderness to Adirondack Park." Blue Mountain Lake, NY: The Adirondack Museum and Syracuse University.

Franklin Historical Review. 1973. "Dr. Webb's Adirondack Railroad." 10: 49-61. [Excerpts from *New York Herald* June 1, 1897.]

Frenette, Liza. 1984. "State Denied Permission to Tear Our RR Tracks." Saranac Lake: *Adirondack Daily Enterprise* January 20: 1.

Friends of the Union Depot. 1919. *FUD News* (May 18). [Saranac Lake Union Depot.]

Fynmore, Jim. 1957. "Relics of 1890 Travel in the Central Adirondacks." *North Country Life* 11 (4): 36-41 (Fall).

Gardner, Ed. 1975. *Adirondack Vistas*. Harrison, NY: Harbor Hill Books.

Gardner, Ruth. 1990. *D&H Railroad, Champlain Division----Lake George Steamboat Co.----Pictures and Timetables*. Vol. 4. Mountaintop, PA: published by the author.

-----. 1990. *The D&H Railroad Corp.: Station Pictures, Timetables, Saratoga Division*. Vol. 3. Mountaintop PA: published by the author.

Gates, Albert. 1973. "Eulogy to the Rails." *Adirondack Life* 4 (2): 40-43 (Spring). [On Westport Station.]

Gibbs, Frederick J. 1931a. "Whitehall Tunnel Closed in Winter." *D&H RR Bulletin* 11 (9): 131-132 (May 1).

Gleaves, Melanie. 1982. "DOT Set To Tear Up Adirondack Rails." *Lake Placid News* July 22.

-----. 1982. "DOT Rejects Low Bid on Rail Salvage." *Lake Placid News* July 29.

-----. 1982. "Deadline for Rail Proposals Extended." *Lake Placid News* September 2.

Goldsmith, Frank. 1936. "The Fonda Johnstown & Gloversville Railroad Field Trip." *National Railway Historical Society Bulletin* 1, no. 8 (October-November): 4-6.

Gordon, William Reed. 1980. "Fonda, Johnstown & Gloversville." *National Railway Historical Society Bulletin* 45, no. 6: 20-35. [See also the *N.R.H.S. Bulletin* 23, no. 3 (3rd Quarter 1958): 13 for a book review on the F.J.& G. The book is by David F. Nestle and William Reed Gordon.]

Gordon, William Reed and Robert D. Mowers. 1970? *Trolleys Down the Mohawk Valley*. Rochester NY: published by the author. [Chapter on the Fonda, Johnstown & Gloversville Railroad.]

Gove, William. Articles in the *Northern Logger and Timber Processor*:

"William L. Sykes and The Emporium."
   [Part I is in Pennsylvania.]
   "Part II, The Emporium Forestry Company of New York and the Grasse River Railroad": 19 (3): 10-13,32,33 (September 1970).
   "Part III, Latter Days": 19 (6): 12,13,32,35,38 (December 1970). [The Grasse River Railroad article, in addition to being published in three installments in the *Northern Logger and Timber Processor*, was reprinted in 1973 as a chapter in *Rails of the North Woods*, pp. 69-110. Lakemont NY: North Country Books.]

"The Adirondack's Shortest Logging Railroad": 26 (12): 16,17,30,31,33 (June 1978).

"The Mac-a-Mac Railroad of Brandreth." 29 (10): 10-12,40-42,44 (April 1981).

"John McDonald's Railroad at Bay Pond." 30 (3): 6-8, and 38 (September 1981).

----. 1973. "Rich Lumber Company." In *Rails of the North Woods*. Lakemont, NY: North Country Books: 11-33.

Graham, Cecil H. 1966. "The C & A Railroad." *The Quarterly* 11, no. 1 (January): 16-17. [Publication of the Saint Lawrence County Historical Association, Canton, NY.]

Granbery, J. H. 1906. "The Port Henry Iron Mines." *The Engineering and Mining Journal*. Pages 1-31 in nine parts reprinted with author's revisions: May 12 (pp.1-4), May 26 (pp. 5-8), June 2 (pp. 9-13), June 9 (pp.14-16), June 16 (pp. 17-19), June 23 (pp. 20-23), June 30 (pp.24-28), July 21 (pp.29-31) and Sept. 22.

Gray, O. W. 1876. *New Topographical Atlas of Essex County, New York*. Philadelphia: O. W. Gray & Son.

Greenhouse, Linda. 1977. "Adirondack Railway Plans Approved by State Officials." *New York Times* (February 23).

Gymburch, Dave. 1985. "Proposal Made to Revive Rail Line: Broker's Bid to Haul Firewood on Adirondack Railroad Termed 'Speculative.' " Utica *Observer Dispatch* November 17.

-----. 1988. "Adirondack Rail, DOT Return to Court, Seek New Solution." Utica *Observer-Dispatch* March 31.

Hardy, Philip. 1985. "The Ausable Branch." *Adirondac* 49 (2): 8-12 (February-March). [Publication of the Adirondack Mountain Club.]

Harter, Henry A. 1979. *Fairy Tale Railroad: The Mohawk and Malone from the Mohawk, through the Adirondacks, to the Saint Lawrence----The Golden Chariot Route*. Sylvan Beach, NY: North Country Books.

Hastings, Philip R. 1950. "Pacifics to Placid." *Trains* 10 (11): 22-26 (September).

Haworth, James A. 1954. "Wilderness Railroad." *North Country Life* 8 (2): 20-22 (Spring). [On the New York & Ottawa.]

Hebard, Cliff and Lisa Forrest. 1974. "Cheers Greet Passenger Train and *Adirondack* Preview Greeted With Festivities, Respectively." Plattsburgh *Press-Republican*: 1-3 (August 6).

Heller, Murray. 1989. *Call Me Adirondack*. Saranac, NY: The Chauncy Press. [On Adirondack place-name origins.]

Hendrickson, Patti. 1989. "Veteran Publisher and Weatherman Engineers Boy's Dream to Reality." Rome *Daily Sentinel* (March 2): 2. [On Livingston Lansing's purchase of a Shay locomotive for the Lowville & Beaver River RR.]

Hochschild, Harold. *Township 34*. A series of Adirondack Museum Publications:
Dr. Durant and His Iron Horse. 1961.
Adirondack Railroads Real and Phantom. 1962.
Life And Leisure in the Adirondack Backwoods. 1962.
The Macintyre Mine----From Failure to Fortune. 1962.
Lumberjacks and Rivermen in the Central Adirondacks, 1850 to 1950. 1962.
An Adirondack Resort in the 19th Century: Blue Mountain Lake, 1870-1890: Stages And Luxury Hotels. 1962.

Horace and Thayer Company. 1852. Map of New York State.

Hotaling, Mary B. 1993. "North Creek Railroad Station on Track." *Adirondack Architectural Heritage Newsletter* 2 (2): 1, 3 (November).

Hough, Franklin B. 1853. *A History of Saint Lawrence and Franklin Counties, New York*. 1970 reprint. Baltimore: Regional Publishing Company. [Originally published in Albany.]

Hughes, Tom. 1990. "A Patent Genius." *Adirondack Life* 21 (3): 36- 41 (May-June). [On A. A. Low.]

Hyde, Floy Salls. 1974. *Adirondack Forests, Fields, and Mines*. Lakemont, NY: North Country Books.

-----. 1970. *Water Over the Dam at Mountain View*. Binghamton, NY: Vail-Baillou Press. [Chapter IV, pp. 55-66, is on the NYCentral Adirondack Division.]

Johnson, Arthur L. 1995. "Interviews of Retired and Active Railroad Workers Done at Malone, New York, on March 27, 1979." *Franklin Historical Review* 30: 12-17. Malone: Franklin County Historical and Museum Society. [On the Rutland RR and the NYCRR Adirondack Division.]

Johnson, Ernie. 1994. "The Lake Champlain & Moriah RR." *Bridge Line Historical Society Bulletin* 4 (6): 18 (June).

Journal and Republican. 1991. "Steamer on Track." October 16: 1. [Published by Lowville Newspapers Corp. On arrival of the Shay locomotive at Lowville.]

Kaplan, Alan. 1992. "Bridge Line Memories." *Bridge Line Historical Society Bulletin*. 2 (9): 35 (September). [On Port Henry.]

Kaplan, Mitchell. 1991. "The North Creek Ski Train." *Adirondack Life* 22 (1): 66, 67 (January-February).

Keith, Herbert F. 1972. *Man of the Woods*. Blue Mountain Lake, NY: The Adirondack Museum and Syracuse University Press. [On the Wanakena area.]

Kiernan, Betsy. 1984. "Conifer Remembered." *Ogdensburg Advance News* (November 18): 3.

Kirkbride, James. 1977. "The Old Clifton Railroad." [Lecture delivered at the Edwards Historical Association April 27, 1977.]

Kizzia, Tom. 1979. "In New York, A Railroad is Reborn." *Railway Age* (December 10): 40, 42, 43.

Koch, Michael. 1979. *Steam and Thunder in the Timber*. Denver, CO: World Press.

Kozma, Ethel. 1985. *Remember When: Lakeshore Rails Come to the North Country*. Wadhams, NY: unpublished report.

Krieger, Medora Hooper. 1937. "Geology of the Thirteenth Lake Quadrangle." *New York State Museum Bulletin* 308. [On page 105 is a photo of a narrow gauge disconnecting railway in the Barton Garnet Quarry, Gore Mountain.]

Kudish, Michael. 1975. *Where Did The Tracks Go*. Saranac Lake, NY: The Chauncy Press.

Kutta, Paul. 1981. "A Brief Glimpse of the Grasse River Railroad." *National Railway Bulletin* 46, no.1: 40-43.

Lamothe, Katherine. 1993. "RR Backers Sure of Success." *Lake Placid News* July 22.

Lamy, Margaret, 1965. "You Can't Get There From Here By Rail Any More." *New York Times* July 18 (Section 10): xx1, xx7. [On the abandonment of passenger service on the New York Central Adirondack Division.]

LaMoureux, John. 1995. "Huge Train Derailment Tears Up Tracks At Port Henry." Plattsburgh *Press Republican* March 5: A-4.

Landfried, Ron. 1981. "State Gets No Bids to Run Adirondack Railway." *Lake Placid News* October 1.

-----. 1981b. "Adirondack Railroad Gets 90-day Reprieve." *Lake Placid News* December 17.

Landon, Harry F. 1932. *The North Country: A History Embracing Jefferson, Saint Lawrence, Oswego, Lewis and Franklin Counties, New York*. Indianapolis, IN: Historical Publishing Co. [Volume 1 of the 3 volume set includes Chapter XV: "The Iron Horse Reaches the North Country."]

Landon, Richard. 1992. "A Day Away—Camps, Views Highlight Cruise on Lake Placid." Plattsburgh *Press Republican* June 7: B-10. [Includes description of Cone Family Camp inclined and disconnecting railroad.]

Lansing, W. 1897. *The Souvenir Industrial Edition of Plattsburgh, 1897*. Plattsburgh, NY: W. Lansing & Son.

Lewis, J. W. & Co. 1880. *History of Clinton and Franklin Counties, New York*. Philadelphia, PA: J. W. Lewis & Co. [Reprinted in 1978 by Clinton County American Revolution Bicentennial Commission.]

Lezette, Doug. 1994. "The D&H's Glens Falls Branch Today." *Bridge Line Historical Society Bulletin* 4, no. 4 (April): 4,5,24.

Lindsey, James. 1958-1959. "The Fish Car," *New York State Conservationist* 13 (3): 31 (December-January). [On the State fish hatchery railroad car.]

Linney, Joseph R. 1930. "Adirondack Iron Ores." *Delaware & Hudson Railroad Bulletin* 10 (11): 165-167, 172-173 (June 1). [On Lyon Mountain and Standish.]

-----. 1934. *A History of the Chateaugay Ore and Iron Company*. New York: Chateaugay Ore and Iron Company. [Published for the D&H Board of Directors' Inspection of lines June 7-10, 1934.]

-----. 1975. A chapter in *Ecumenical Edition*. See Parishoners from Saint Bernard's Church et al.

Lloyd, J. K. 1892. Map of the Village of Port Henry. December 1892, reprinted 1943. [Hanging on wall of Port Henry Vilage Offices.]

Lodge, Donald E. 1972. *The Freight Carloadings Market on the Lake Placid Branch of the Penn Central Transportation Company*. Technical Assistance Center at State University of New York, Plattsburgh.

MacDonald, Norman T. 1975. "Misplaced Station." *Adirondack Life* 6 (3): 13 (Summer). [Corrects the Robbins (1975) photo caption identifying Sabattis station as Brandreth.]

MacKinnon, Anne. 1995. "Rise and Fall of a Company Town: The Tangled Fortunes of J. & J. Rogers and Ausable Forks." *Adirondack Life* 26 (2): 50-56, 63 (March-April).

MacMartin, James. 1932. "Taking The Roof Off Whitehall's Tunnel: How Changes Are Being Carried Out in Connection With Grade Crossing Elimination." *Delaware & Hudson Railroad Bulletin* 12 (6): front cover, 168-170 (June 1).

Maguire, Stephen. 1968. Photographs of the Paul Smith's Electric Railway in *Railroad Magazine* vol. and no. unknown (February): 37,52.

-----. 1977. New electric publications. *Railroad Magazine* vol. and no. unknown (February): page no. unknown. [On Paul Smith's Electric Railway.]

Maguire, Stephen and Felix E. Reifschneider. 1950. *Trolley Pictures of the Empire State*. Orlando, FL: published by Reifschneider. [Includes photos of the Paul Smith's Electric Railway and the Fonda, Johnstown & Gloversville Railroad.]

Maloney, Keith F. 1973. "Lowville & Beaver River Railroad". In *Rails in the North Woods*, pp. 111-148. Lakemont, NY: North Country Books.

Manor, Steve. 1991. "Village, County Both Get Refusal Rights on D&H Site." Plattsburgh *Press Republican* (January 26): 15. [About Rouses Point yard.]

-----. 1992. "CP Upgrades Tracks, Service." Plattsburgh *Press Republican* (May 11): 13.

Marleau, William R. 1986. *Big Moose Station: A Story from 1893 to 1983*. Eagle Bay, NY: Marleau Family Press.

Martin, Ben. 1995. "Whitehall." *Bridge Line Historical Society Bulletin* 5 (1): 7, 8, 19 (January).

Martin, Ben. 1996. "Examining Saratoga to Willsboro." *Bridge Line Historical Society Bulletin* 6, 2: 27-30 (February).

Martin, Jeffrey G. 1994. "A Brief History of Railroads in The Greater Glens Falls Area." *Bridge Line Historical Society Bulletin* 4 (4): 9-13, 24 (April).

-----. 1995. "Whitehall: A Junction Through the Ages." *Bridge Line Historial Society Bulletin* 5, no.4 (April): 5.

Masters, Bob. 1970. "A Railroad To The Rescue: They Planned a Railroad to Save the County Seat and Lost Their Shirt. *Adirondack Life* 1 (3): 30-31 (Summer). [On Elizabethtown Terminal Railroad.]

Matteson, Michele. 1992. "Walking on the Railroad: Tour to Take Participants on a Walk Through Track History." Glens Falls *Post Star* August 5.

McConnell, Helen. 1980. "Fun, Food on Adirondack." Syracuse *Herald-American* (January 13).

McDonald, G. M., ed. 1977. "Adirondack Railway." *The Short Line* 5 (3): 11 (May). [This magazine is published in Greensboro, NC.]

McDonald and Foy. 1910-1911. *Adirondack Directory*. Saranac Lake: McDonald & Foy. [Includes track plan of Saranac Lake.]

McKinstry, Rohr. 1995. "Back On Track: Rail Service Resumes in Wake of Wreck. Plattsburgh *Press Republican* (March 7): 13.

-----. 1995." Derailment Investigation: Tracks Were in Good Shape." Plattsburgh *Press Republican*. (March 14): 13.

McKnight, Orville K. 1989. "Mooers Junction." *Canadian Rail* 411 (July-August): 111-131.

McLaughlin, Bill. 1972. "Effort to Preserve Adirondack Artifacts." Saranac Lake: *Adirondack Daily Enterprise*: page 1 (February 23). [Photo of abandoned Paul Smith's lectric railway car with caption.]

-----. 1974. "The 'Adirondack' Pulls In." Saranac Lake: *Adirondack Daily Enterprise* 81 (151): page 1 (August 6).

-----. 1976. "RR's Optimistic Light Dimmed By $$ Sign." Saranac Lake: *Adirondack Daily Enterprise* (April 28).

McLeod, Helen. 1983. "Railroad Festival Fetes Depot Restoration". Plattsburgh *Press Republican*: 8 (October 6).

McMartin, Barbara. 1982. "Ironville." *Adirondack Life* 13 (4): 24, 25, 48, 49 (July-August).

-----. 1994. *The Great Forest of the Adirondacks*. Utica, NY: North Country Books.

McNamara, T. J. 1914-1915. *Official Freight Shippers' Directory* Vol. II. Albany: Delaware & Hudson Railroad.

Mele, Chris and Paul Olchvary. 1987. "Development Group Backs Adirondack Railroad." Saranac Lake: *Adirondack Daily Enterprise* October 8: 1.

Mele, Chris. 1988. "Trustee Backs Auction of Railroad Track Lease." Saranac Lake: *Adirondack Daily Enterprise* September 16.

-----. 1988. "Judge OK's Auction of RR Lease." Saranac Lake: *Adironack Daily Enterprise* September 23.

-----. 1990. "Officials Hope to Put Railroad Back on Track." Saranac Lake: *Adirondack Daily Enterprise* July 21: 15.

-----. 1990. "Can the Adirondack Railroad Run Again: Local Rail Line Has Traveled a Rough Road." Plattsburgh *Press Republican* August 26 [This is the article with the good historical summary.]

-----. 1991." We Need Adirondack Railroad, Public Tells State." Plattsburgh *Press Republican* October 9.

Meyers, Roy Dean. 1973. "When the Bullwheel Turned—and the Mightiest Cable Railroad of Them All Climbed Prospect Mountain." *Adironack Life* 4 (2): 20-23 (Spring).

Middleton, William D. 1974. *When the Steam Railroads Electrified*. Milwaukee, WI: Kalmbach Publications. [Page 424 on Paul Smith's.]

-----. 1976. "Henry Ford and His Electric Locomotives." *Trains: The Magazine of Railroading* 36 (11): 22-26 (September). [Paul Smith's line is mentioned.]

Mihalyi, Louis. 1991. "The Peg-Leg Railroad." *Adirondack Life* 22 (3): 68-69 (May-June).

Miller, Clinton H. 1983. "Three Mines Left in the North Country." *Adirondac* 47 (1): 3-5, 22-24, 27 (February). [Publication of the Adirondack Mountain Club.]

-----. 1985. "The Tahawus Railroad: A Disappearing Controversy." *Adirondac* 49 (2): 13-14 (February-March). [Publication of the Adirondack Mountain Club.]

Miller, Erwin H. 1976. "In Search of the Adirondack Ruby." *Adirondack Life* 7 (2): 4-8 (Spring). [Photo of disconnecting railroad at Thirteenth Lake Mine.]

Miller, Roland B. 1956 and 1957. "Iron Horses in the Adirondacks, Part I." *New York State Conservationist* 11 (2): 18-19 (October- November). Part II is in 11 (5): 9 (April-May). [A photo of the Marion River Carry locomotive occurs also on page 37 of the December-January 1955-1956 issue, volume 10, no. 3.]

Mining and Metallurgy: Journal of the American Institute of Mining and Metallurgic Engineers. 1943. "Fisher Hill Mine, Mill, and Sintering Plant." (November): 497-524. [Page 524 includes a plan of Benson Mines.]

Mohr, William A. 1974. "Delaware & Hudson." *Adirondack Life* 5 (2): 15-20 (Spring).

Moore, James. 1980. "Working on the Railroad: On Track to the Olympics." *Dupont Magazine* (January/February): 8-11.

Moore, Robert W. 1995. "Derailment at Port Henry." *Bridge Line Historical Society Bulletin* 5 (5): 25 (May).

Moravek, J. R. 1981. "Iron and Smelting: Ghost Towns and Forgotten People." Plattsburgh: Department of Geography, State University of New York, unpublished manuscript.

Morton, Doris Begor. 1977. *Day Before Yesterday*. Whitehall, NY: Whitehall Town Board.

Murray, Neil. 1995. "Group Working to Restore Historic Railroad Station in North Creek. *Bridge Line Historical Society Bulletin* 5 (10): 7 (October).

Myers, Jim. 1992. "Pieces of a Failed Dream, The Adirondack Railroad, Auctioned at Webster." Rochester *Democrat and Chronicle*: March 28.

National Lead Company. 1967. *Tahawus Cloud Splitter: 25th Anniversary Issue, 1942-1967*. Houston, Texas: National Lead Company. [National Lead Co. is now Kronos, Inc., of National Lead Industries, Inc.]

National Railway Publication Company. *Official Guide to the Railways*. New York: published monthly.

Nestle, David F. and William Reed Gordon. 1958. *Steam and Trolley Days on the Fonda, Johnstown, & Gloversville RR*. Milford and Rochester, NY: Published by the authors. Book review in the National Railway Historical Society *Bulletin* 23, (3): 14 (3rd Quarter).

Newcombe, Jack. 1980. "Taking a Ride Into the Past on the Adirondack Railway." *New York Times* (June 29): xx3.

New York State Board of Railroad Commissioners. 1893. *Tenth Annual Report of the Board of Railroad Commissioners of the State of New York for the Fiscal Year Ending June 30, 1892*, Volume II. Albany: James B. Lyon, State Printer.

New York Central Railroad. 1893. *Health and Pleasure on America's Greatest Railroad*. New York City: New York Central Railroad. Published annually as part of the *Four-Track Series*. Other years include 1896, 1903. [These show fares, hotel accommodations, stage connections, excursions and running times, but no timetables. Maps are very general and of small scale.]

-----. 1905. *Official Freight Shippers' Directory*. Issued by Freight Department, October 1905.

-----. 1914. *Station Numbers*. Issued by New York Central & Hudson River Railroad and leased lines, April 1.

New York State—Annual Reports, Adirondack maps, *New York State Conservationist*, etc. appear chronologically with the following sequence of organizations:
New York State Forest Commission, 1885-1894;
New York State Fisheries, Game and Forest Commission, 1895-1910;
New York State Conservation Commission, 1911-1926.
New York State Conservation Department, 1927-1969.

New York State Department of Environmental Conservation, 1970-present.

New York State Forest Commission. 1891. *Annual Report of the Forest Commission, State of New York, for the Year 1891*. [Contains map entitled "Great Forest of Northern New York" and shows areas burned through 1891 plus old growth.]

-----. 1893. *Annual Report of the Forest Commission, State of New York, for the year 1893.*[This report included granting of charters to railroads in the Adirondacks, pp. 245-293 up to 1887. This and other annual reports also contain forest fire data.]

New York State Fisheries, Game and Forest Commission. 1896. *Second Annual Report for 1896*. [Page 505 has photo of pulp wood at the International Paper Company mill at Palmer.]

New York State Conservation Commission. *Adirondack Map*. Published over the years including 1909, 1911, 1920, 1923, 1927. [Many show logging railroads.]

New York State Department of Environmental Conservation. 1972. "Commissioner Protests Sale of Railroad. *New York State Conservationist* 26 (4): 36 (February-March). [Tahawus.]

-----. 1972. "Tahawus Railroad Sale Postponed." *New York State Conservationist* 26 (6): 36 (June-July).

New York State Department of Transportation. 1974. *Inventory of Abandoned Rights-of-Way*. Albany: Real Property Division of D.O.T.

Nielsen, Wally "Caboose." 1970. "Walking the Railroad or Trompin' the Tracks." *The ETM Log* (Autumn). Annapolis, MD: The Explorers Trademart. [Abandoned railroads in New York State as of 1969.]

Nimke, R. W. 1986. "Rutland Railroad Side Track Diagram, December 1, 1934." Walpole, NH: published by the author. [Includes the Ogdensburg & Lake Champlain in New York.]

-----. 1989. *The Rutland: 60 years of Trying*. Walpole, NH: published by the author. [Volume VI, Parts 1 and 2 are on the Ogdensburg & Lake Champlain Division.]

-----. 1990. *The Rutland: Arrivals and Departures----Train schedules 1901-1961*. Walpole, NH: published by the author.

Nordwind, Richard. 1977. "A Little Railroad That Could." *Lake Placid News* (March 16).

Norman, Robert, Jr. 1987. "Old As Dirt: Train Station Now Just A Memory." *The Whitehall Times* (April 30): 1, 5.

North Country Railroad Association. 1990. *Why Should We Save the Railroad Through the Adirondacks?* [A project of the Mohawk Valley Chapter of the National Railway Historical Society, July.]

Odato, James M. 1979. "Train is Late But Welcomed." Saranac Lake: *Adirondack Daily Enterprise* (October 10): 1, 5.

O'Hern, William J. 1990. "Mountain Tramps to Sargent Ponds: An Historical Bushwhack." *Adirondac* 54 (2): 11-16. [Publication of the Adirondack Mountain Club. Page 14 has Marion River Carry Railroad photo.]

Olchvary, Paul. 1987. "Court Rejects Adironack RR Settlement." Saranac Lake *Adirondack Daily Enterprise* November 30: 1.

-----. 1988. "Telephone Links Railroad Creditors in Lake Placid and Utica." Saranac Lake: *Adirondack Daily Enterprise* January 18: 10.

Osborn, Darlene A. 1992. *Owls Head New York Post Office Centennial Celebration*. Owls Head, NY: Owls Head Post Office.

Palmer, Richard F. 1970, 1971. "Logging Railroads in the Adirondacks." A four-part series in the *Northern Logger and Timber Processor*:

Part I. "John Hurd---A Man With a Dream." 18 (8): 28, 29, 47 (February 1970). [New York & Ottawa.]

Part II. 18 (9): 14, 15 (March 1970). [Includes Oval Wood Dish Company and Benson Mines area.]

Part III. "Wooden Rails in the Wilderness." 18 (10): 26, 27, 47 (April 1970). [Black River & Woodhull RR.]

Part IV. "Brooklyn Cooperage Operations." 19 (9): 16, 17, 25 (March 1971).

-----. 1971. "Peg-Leg Railroad." *Northern Logger* 19 (10): 14, 15, 37 (April). [This article was reprinted as a chapter in *Rails in the North Woods*. Lakemont, NY: North Country Books. 1973.

-----. 1965. "Iron Horse Is Dead." Syracuse, NY: *Herald American Stars Magazine* (April 18): 3, 12. [Last New York Central passenger train to Lake Placid.]

-----. 1965. "Adirondack Train Has Last Toot." Syracuse, NY: *Herald American Empire Magazine* (November 7): 9-11. [Excursion by Central NY Chapter of National Railway Historical Society from Syracuse to Tupper Lake.]

Palmer, Richard F. and John Thomas. 1969. "Wooden Rails in the Wilderness." A three-part series in *The Quarterly*. [Publication of the Saint Lawrence County Historical Association. Clifton Iron Co. Railroad.]

Part I. 14 (2): 3, 11-14, 22 (April).

Part II. 14 (3): 3, 11, 14, 22 (July).

Part III. 14 (4): 11, 14 (October).

Palmer, Richard F. and H. F. Timmerman. 1973. "The Adirondack & Saint Lawrence Railroad." In *Rails in the North Woods*. Lakemont, NY: North Country Books: 165-174. [Railroad from DeKalb Junction to Hermon.]

-----. 1979. Railway Traverses Memories. Syracuse *Herald-American* (October 14): 12.

-----. 1967. Part I, "Once Prosperous Mines Sparked Clarksboro." *Watertown Daily Times* (September 12): 2. Part II, "Remains of Clifton Mines Belong to 'Mother Nature.'" *Watertown Daily Times* (September 13): page no. unknown.

Palmer, Richard F. and Harvey Roehl. 1990. *Railroads in Early Postcards*, Volume 1. Vestal, NY: Vestal Press Ltd. [Includes some Adirondack regional views.]

Parishoners from Saint Bernard's Church of Lyon Mountain, Saint Michael's Church of Standish, and Memorial Methodist Church of Lyon Mountain. 1975. *A Century: Mining for Souls, 1895-1975. Ecumenical Edition.*

Parker, Lucinda. 1986. *Little Falls and Dolgeville Railroad: 72 Years of Shortline*. Brookfield NY: Worden Press, published by the author.

-----. 1987. *Into Salisbury Country*. Brookfield NY: Worden Press, published by the author.

Peel, Bob. 1979. "Reborn Train Provides Restful, Colorful Ride." Syracuse *Post Standard* (October 10).

Penfield Foundation publications on the Crown Point Iron Company's Railroad: See Barker, Steve (1973); Allen (1968 and 1973); Barker, Elmer Eugene (1969); and Spaulding (1874 and 1988).

Phelan, Kevin. 1994. "Tracks to Tahawus---Route of the Iron Ore." *Bridge Line Historical Society Bulletin* 4 (5): 7-9 (May) is part one. Part two is 4 (6): 13-15 (June).

Pierce, Harry H. 1953. *Railroads of New York: A Study of Government Aid, 1826-1875*. Cambridge, MA: Harvard University Press.

Pilcher, Edith. 1979. "The Adirondack Railway: Long Abandoned But Now Rebuilt, A Historic Adirondack Railroad Runs Again." *Adirondack Life* 10 (6): 16-19, 49 (November-December).

Plant, Jeremy F. and Jeffrey G. Plant. 1993. *Delaware & Hudson in Color*, Volume 2. Edison, NJ: Morning Sun Books.

Plum, Dorothy and Lynette L. Scribner. 1958. *Adirondack Bibliography*. Gabriels, NY: Adirondack Mountain Club. [Railroads on pp. 183-187 and in update to the original edition, pp. 66 and 67.]

Poor, Henry V., ed. 1849. "Sisco Furnace and Cheever Ore Bed." *American Railroad Journal: Steam Navigation, Commerce, Mining, Manufactures*. Second Quarto Series 5 (36): 559-562 (September 8). New York City: J. H. Schultz Co.

Poor's Railroad Manual Company in New York City. Several periodicals published annually from about 1868 into the first decade of the twentieth century. These include the *Directory of Railroad Officials, Private Railroads of the United States*, and *Poor's Manual of Railroads of the United States*.

Pope, Connie. 1972. "Brandon---A Legendary Ghost Town." *York State Tradition* 26 (3): 37-47 (Summer).

Porter, Marjorie Lansing. 1964. *Plattsburgh, 1785-1815-1902*. Burlington, VT: George Little Press, published by the author.

Rappaport, Laura. 1988. "RR Lease is Bought by State." Saranac Lake: *Adirondack Daily Enterprise* November 11.

-----. 1988. "Tracks Eyed For Recreation: Bidders Question 'Secret' EnCon Role in RR Auction." Saranac Lake: *Adirondack Daily Enterprise* November 14.

-----. 1988. "Altamont Urged to Buy Bridge, Old Rail Yard." Saranac Lake: *Adirondack Daily Enterprise* November 15.

Reifschneider, Felix E. 1947. *Toonervilles of the Empire State*. Orlando, FL, and Fairton, NJ: published by the author.

Reinman, Mary. 1979. "Train Whistle Marks Return of Rail Travel to Placid." *Lake Placid News* (October 11): 1, 4.

Resnick, Seth, photographer. 1982. "Railroad For Sale." Syracuse *Post-Standard* (March 27): T-1.

Reynolds, Jeanne, Bessie Decosse, and Kenneth Campbell. 1976. *Two Towns----Two Centuries, 1776-1976*. Gouverneur, NY: MRS Press and the Clifton-Fine Bicentennial Committee.

Rice, Barbara. 1989. "Railroad Backers See Hope for Service: State Hasn't Formally 'Abandoned' Line." Saranac Lake: *Adirondack Daily Enterprise* July 27.

Rice, Tim. 1980. "Opened 20 Months Ahead of Schedule: Rush to Olympics Hurt Adirondack Railway." Utica *Observer-Dispatch* (December 23): 9.

Robbins, Stephen A. 1975. "A Second Chance for the Adironack Division?" *Adirondack Life* 6 (2): 24-29 (Spring). [The photo of Sabattis, called Brandreth by Robbins, is corrected in the summer issue, p. 13, by MacDonald.]

Roberts, Steve. 1976. "Big Switch on Rail Line." *Lake Placid News* (October 13): 1, 2.

Rochette, Frank. 1937. "Frogs Croaked Sole Greeting As First Passenger Train Reached Saranac Lake's Tent Station." *Delaware and Hudson Railroad Bulletin* 17 (2): 19, 20 (February 1).

Rominger, Wray, ed. 1994. *Trolley Trips Through the Hudson Valley, 1911*. Fleischmanns, NY: Purple Mountain Press. [Reprint from The Trolley Press (1911). Includes Fonda, Johnstown & Gloversville RR; Lake George Branch of D&H; and Saratoga Springs.]

Rosenquist, Mitch. 1995. "Little Damage Now Seen From Wrecked Train." *Plattsburgh Press Republican* (March 4): 1,3.

Russell, Matthew. 1990. "ANCA Working To Put Adirondack Railroad Back On Line." Saranac Lake: *Adirondack Daily Enterprise* July 23.

-----. 1991. "Adirondack Intercounty Group Tackles Railroad, Etc." Saranac Lake: *Adirondack Daily Enterprise* September 27-29.

-----. 1991. "Locals Tell State to Keep Adirondack Railroad Line Intact." Saranac Lake: *Adirondack Daily Enterprise* October 9.

-----. 1994. "Group Seeks Other Funds For Depot Project." Saranac Lake: *Adirondack Daily Enterprise* December 13: 1.

-----. 1996. "Train Plan Derailed? Federal Funding Application for Ad'k Rail Line in Jeopardy." Saranac Lake: *Adirondack Daily Enterprise*: 1 (January 12).

Saint Pierre, Elise Miller. 1990. "Smith Weed and the Political Economy of Northern New York." Lecture delivered at the Kent Delord House Museum, Plattsburgh.

Sanborn Insurance Company. 1902. *Map of Plattsburgh*.

Saranac Lake Free Library. 1986. "Times Gone By." Calendar. [Photo accompanying April 1987 shows a long wooden trestle from Bloomingdale Avenue to the

Saranac River before the fill embankment was built on the Saranac & Lake Placid RR.]

Scarborough Company. 1903. *Scarborough's New Railroad, Post Office, Township and County Map of New York With Distances Between Stations*. Boston, MA: The Scarborough Company.

Schmitt, Karl. 1916. *Fire Protection Map of the Adirondack Forest*. Albany: New York State Conservation Commission.

Schwarz, G. V. 1936. Forestry on the Delaware & Hudson. *Delaware & Hudson Railroad Bulletin* 16 (1): 8, 9, 13 (January 1). Continued in 16 (2): 26, 27, 29, 30 (February 1).

Seaver, Frederick J. 1918. *Historical Sketches of Franklin County*. Albany, NY: J. B. Lyon Company.

Seely, S. A. 1928. "A Mountain Railroad Arms Against Fire." *American Forests* 34 (7): 427, 428 (July).

Shaughnessy, James. 1964. *The Rutland Road*. Berkeley, CA: Howell North.

-----. 1967. *Delaware and Hudson*. Berkeley, CA: Howell North.

Shaw, Robert B. and Stephen G. Walsh. 1982. "Along the 'Lower Route': A History of the Northern Railroad." *The Quarterly*. [Publication of the Saint Lawrence County Historical Association, Canton, NY.]
Part I: 27 (1): 7-13 (January).
Part II: 27 (2): 15-20 (April). [On the Ogdensburg & Lake Champlain RR.]

Shepherd, Chris. 1994. "Grant Enables Moriah Rail, Mine Museum." *Bridge Line Historical Society Bulletin* 4 (7): 18 (July).

Shields, Robert A. 1994. "The Marion River Carry Railroad." *Gazette: Narrow Gauge and Shortline Magazine* 19 (6): 42-47 (January). Los Altos, CA: Benchmark Publications, Ltd.

Simmons, Louis J. 1968. "Tupper Lake." *Franklin Historical Review* 5: 27-41.

-----. 1976. *Mostly Spruce and Hemlock: Historical Highlights of Tupper Lake and the Town of Altamont*. Binghamton, NY: Vail-Ballou Press.

Smith, Henry Perry. 1880. *History of Essex County*. Syracuse, NY: D. Mason & Company.

Smith, Nelda Young. 1969. "John Hurd's Railroad." *Franklin Historical Review* 6: 29-32.

Smithers, Nina. 1962. The Railroad Made Dekalb Junction. *The Quarterly* 7 (4): 7. [Publication of the Saint Lawrence County Historical Association, Canton, NY.]

Spaulding, Samuel S. 1873. *History of Crown Point New York from 1800 to 1874*. Ironville, Crown Point, NY: The Penfield Foundation, reprinted 1988.

Starbird, Ethel A. 1967. "From Sword to Scythe in Champlain Country." *National Geographic* 132 (2): 153-202 (August). [Pages 182 and 183 show interior of a mine at Mineville with an underground ore train.]

Staufer, Alvin F. 1967. *Steam Power of the New York Central, Volume 1, 1915-1955*. Medina, OH: published by the author.

Stephenson, B. S. 1909. "Magnetite Ore Deposits at Mineville." *The Iron Trade Review* August 26: 371-377 and September 2: 416-424.

Stoddard, Seneca Ray. 1912. Stoddard's Map of the Adirondacks. Glens Falls: S. R. Stoddard.

Surprenant, Neil. 1982. *Brandon: Boom Town to Nature Preserve*. Paul Smiths, NY: Ross Park.

Suter, H. M. 1903. *Forest Fires in the Adirondacks in 1903*. Bureau of Forestry, U.S. Department of Agriculture, Washington, D.C. Circular #26.

Sweetland, David R. 1992. *Delaware and Hudson in Color*. Volume 1. Edison NJ: Morning Sun Books, Inc.

Thill, Mary. 1994. "Revived Rail Service May Be Profitable." Plattsburgh *Press Republican* March 31: 15.

Thomas, Lester Saint John. 1979. *Timber, Tannery, and Tourists: Lake Luzerne, NY*. Lake Luzerne: Committee on Publication of Local History.

Thompson, Adele S. 1976. "Sacandaga: Coney Island of the North." *Adirondack Life* 7 (2): 14-17 (Spring). [Sacandaga Park and the F.J.&G.R.R.]

Thompson, Ralph. 1972. "King Urges Citizens: 'Write For Amtrak.'" Albany *Times-Union* May 5: page unknown. [Carleton J. King was a state assemblyman at that time.]

Thompson, Scott. 1979. "The Adirondack Railway: A Great 'Old' Idea." *Day and Night in Central New York* (Fall 1979): 1, 6, 7. [Published by *Day and Night Magazine*, Utica, NY.]

Timm, Ruth. 1979. "Profile of Raquette Lake: The Era of the Railroad and Steamboat." *Boonville Herald* April 18: 10.

-----. 1989. *Raquette Lake: A Time to Remember*. Utica: North Country Books.

Tooley, Shawn. 1984. "If Train Runs Again, Its First Stops Won't Be Local." Saranac Lake: *Adironack Daily Enterprise* April 3: 6.

-----. 1985. "Obstacles Derail Plan to Ship Firewood Over Adironack Railroad." Saranac Lake: *Adirondack Daily Enterprise* November 8: 1.

Trim, Paula LaVoy. 1984. *Water Over the Falls: Saint Regis Falls History*. Saranac Lake, NY: published by the author.

-----. 1989. *Looking Back Upstream: Saint Regis Falls and Its Past*. Saranac Lake, NY (?): published by the author.

Tyler, Helen Escha. 1968. *In Them Thar Hills: Folk Tales of the Adirondacks*. Saranac Lake: Currier Press. Chapters: "A Train's Last Run," 14-17. [On Roakdale.] "The Gospel Train," 35-37. [On church trains run by John Hurd to Tupper Lake and Santa Clara from Brandon.] "Moving Day, 1917," 21-25. [A family uses the siding at Bloomingdale Station chartering a boxcar.]

-----. 1988. *Born Smart: The Story of Paul Smith*. Utica NY: North Country Books. [Pages 165-169 on railroads.]

United States Department of Agriculture, Soil Conservation Service, in cooperation with the Cornell University Agricultural Experiment Station. 1958. *Soil Survey Franklin County New York* May 1958. Washington,

DC: Superintendent of Documents. Series 1952, number 1, May 1958.

United States Geological Survey 15-minute topographic quadrangles. When two years are connected by a hyphen, the first year is the year of survey or aerial photo, and the second is the year of publication.

Ausable 1893-1903 and Ausable Forks 1953; Big Moose 1900-1903 and 1953-1954; Chateaugay 1912-1913; Childwold 1919-1920; Cranberry Lake 1916-1919; Dannemora 1911 and 1954; Elizabethtown 1892 and 1955; Glens Falls 1895; Lake Placid 1893-1894 and 1942-1953; Long Lake 1901-1902 and 1955; Loon Lake 1902-1906; Luzerne 1900-1903 and 1947-1955; Lyon Mountain 1911; Malone 1914-1915; McKeever 1910 and 1958; Moira 1915; Newcomb 1953-1954; Nicholville 1919; North Creek 1895-1897 and 1942-1958; Old Forge 1892-1898 and 1954; Oswegatchie 1915-1916; Paradox Lake 1895 and 1942-1947; Plattsburgh 1893 and 1939-1956; Port Henry 1892-1898 and 1945; Raquette Lake 1899 and 1953-1954; Remsen 1897; Russell 1919; Saint Regis 1902-1903 and 1953-1955; Santa Clara 1921; Santanoni 1952-1953; Saranac 1902 and Saranac Lake 1953-1955; Saratoga 1899; Stark 1920-1921; Thirteenth Lake 1953-1954; Ticonderoga 1894; Tupper Lake 1903-1904 and 1953-1954; Willsboro 1938-1939.

-----. 1956. *Map of New York State Showing Mineral Occurrences*. Bulletin 1072, plate 9.

-----. 1961. *Ogdensburg*. Topographic map at 1/250000 scale and 100-foot contour.

Vanderwalker, Mrs. David B. 1972. *Town of Santa Clara: A Pictorial History, Book One*. Santa Clara, NY: Town Historian.

Viscome, Laura. 1978. "You Can Hear That Whistle Down the Line," *Lake Placid News* (October 25).

-----. 1980. "Train Cancels Winter Service." *Lake Placid News* (December 11): 2.

-----. 1981. "Railway Broke With $1.5 Million Debt." *Lake Placid News* April 16.

-----. 1981. "Proposed Rail Sale Starts on Right Track." *Lake Placid News* June 11: 1.

-----. 1981. "Adirondack Train Takes Special Run to Entice Investors." *Lake Placid News* June 25: 2.

-----. 1981. "Meetings of Minds on Railroad" *Lake Placid News* July 16.

-----. 1981. "Six Groups Interested in Railroad." *Lake Placid News* July 30: 2.

-----. 1981. "State Set to Tear Up Tracks." *Lake Placid News* November 12.

-----. 1981. "APA Votes to Delay Railroad Salvage." *Lake Placid News* November 26.

-----. 1981." Meeting to Save Railroad Planned December 15." *Lake Placid News* December 10.

-----. 1982. "Two Groups Eyeing Adirondack Railroad." *Lake Placid News*. March 18.

-----. 1982. "Rail Investors Present Proposal." *Lake Placid News*. April 8.

Waddington, David L. 1970. "A.C. Traction Brings Reaction." *National Model Railroad Association Bulletin* December: 27-28. [Paul Smith's Electric Railway.]

Wallace, Edward R. 1875. *Wallace's Guide to the Adirondacks*. New York City: The American News Company. [Updated at least through 1898.]

Watertown *Daily Times* (1993). "North Country Remembered" 4802. March 21, 1993, page E-4. [Photo of Brooklyn Cooperage log loader at Spring Cove.]

Weatherwax, David S. 1948. "Locomotives of the Adirondack Railway Company, 1864-1902." The Railway and Locomotive Historical Society Inc. Bulletin 74: 36-38 (October). [Published at the Baker Library, Harvard Business School. On the North Creek Line.]

Weed, Smith M. 1915. "Story of the Chateaugay Road." Plattsburgh *Evening Star-Republican*: page no. unknown (June 26).

Weitzman, David. 1980. *Traces of the Past: A Field Guide to Industrial Archaeology*. New York City: Charles Scribner's Sons. [Chapter 1, 3-40, is on railroads.]

Wellman, Bill. 1992. The New York and Pennsylvania Company. *Bridge Line Historical Society Bulletin* 2 (12): 10-11. (December).

Wessels, William L. 1961. *Adirondack Profiles*. Lake George, NY: Adirondack Resorts Press, Inc. [Fonda, Johnstown & Gloversville RR on pp. 148-149.]

Wever, Judy et al. 1992. *Historical Facts and Photos of Saint Regis Falls*, Volume 1, Number 1. Saint Regis Falls, NY: Saint Regis Falls Historians Association.

Wilcox, F. R. 1922. College Forest of the New York State College of Forestry Near Wanakena. Topographic map dated November 22 on exhibit at the Forestry Building at The Adirondack Museum, Blue Mountain Lake, NY, shows Rich Lumber Company railroad spurs.

Winters, Nelson B. 1978. "The G&O or the E&B or the B&B or . . . ? RR." *The Quarterly* 23 (3): 15-19 (July). [Publication of the Saint Lawrence County Historical Association, Canton NY.]

Worthington, Samuel P. 1943. "Riding the C&A." *National Railway Historical Society Bulletin* 8 (1): 4, 5, 16 (April).

Wright, Jack. 1991. "Along the Line: Adirondack Ore." *Bridge Line Historical Society Bulletin* 1 (5): 5, 6 (May) is part one. Part two is 1 (6): 5, 6 (June). [Tahawus.]

Zimmermann, Karl R. 1975. "The 'Adirondack': Remembrance of Trains Past." *New York Times* (July 13): page xx19 of Travel Section.

-----. 1978. *A Decade of D&H*. Oradell, NJ: Delford Press.

Index

Boldface type indicates the page number of a map.

Individudal industries which did not own a railroad will be found in this index under their products. Turn to the appropriate page in Chapters 2, 3, 5, 6, or 7 to locate the industry.

abandonment - 79-81, **82**.
Academy - 117, **157**, **158**.
acetate of lime - 34.
AD Cabin - **132**, **139**.
Addison Branch, Rutland RR - 103, **117**, **158**, 166.
Addison Junction - 103, **117**, **158**.
Adirondack, Amtrak's - 79, 100, 246-248.
Adirondack & Saint Lawrence RR -
    N.Y. Central Adirondack Division - 389-428, **406**.
    DeKalb Junction to Hermon - **329**, 360.
Adirondack Centennial RR - 475.
Adirondac Company's RR - 79, 131-153, **138**.
Adirondack Division, N.Y. Central RR - 79, 389-428, **406**, 472-475.
Adirondack Railway (1979-1980) - 79, 472-475.
Adironack Railway Preservation Society - 475.
Adirondack Scenic RR - 475.
aesthetics - 84.
agriculture - 48-51.
Air Force Base, U.S., at Plattsburgh - 185, 200, 202.
Alburgh - 266, **276**.
Aldrich - 335, **342**, **349**, 356.
Allen's Siding - 105, **119**, **128**.
Ames Mill - 216, **227**, **240**.
American Legion - see Horse Shoe.
Amtrak's *Adirondack* - 79, 100, 246-248.
Anderson - 335, **342**, 346.
Anos (Anos Siding) - 391, **408**, **421**.
apples - 49.
Arnold - 188, **192**, 197.
Ausable - 188.
Ausable Branch of D&H - 79, **123**, 185-190, **191** to **199**.
Ausable Chasm - **122**, 182, 184.

Ausable Forks - 188, **192**, **198**.
Ausable River - 188, **192**, **198**.

Bacon (Backus) - 334, **341**, **348**.
Baker Brothers RR - see Kinsley Lumber RR.
Bald Mountain - 429, **432**, **438**.
Baldwin and D&H Baldwin Branch - 79, **117**, 157, **158**.
Balmat - 360, **363**, **364**.
barges -
    on Chateaugay Lake - 206.
    on Raquette Lake - 431.
barrels - 34, **42**.
Bartonville Station - 187.
Bassett's Sawmill RR - 72, 431.
Bay Pond - 271, **279**, **282**, 303.
Bay Pond, Inc. RR - 301, **278**, 303.
Bay State Iron Company - 167.
Bear Lake - 335, **341**.
Beaver Falls - 360, **365**, **366**.
Beaver River - 395, **411**, **421**.
"Beehives" - 210, **224**, **234**, **417**.
Beekmantown - 110, **124**, **129**.
Belmont Forge - 206.
Benson Mines - 335, **343**, 350 to **352**, 355, 357.
berry-picker special trains - 27, 49, 403.
beverages - 60.
Big Moose- 394, **411**, **422**.
Black Rapids Junction - 271, **279**, **282**.
Black River & Woodhull RR - 466, **408**.
blast furnaces -
    at Clarksboro - 328.
    at Crown Point - 159.
    at Port Henry - 167.
    at Standish - 208.
Bloomingdale Bog - 213.
Bloomingdale Station - 213, **226**, **237**, **416**.
blueberries - 27, 49, 403.
Blue Mountain Lake - 431, **434**.
Blue Mountain Line - 304, 305, 306.
Blue Pond (Derrick) - 271.
Bluff Point - 109, **123**, **191**, **196**, **202**, **220**.

489

bobbin spools - 34.
Bog Lake - 396, **412**.
Bombay & Moira RR - 287, **288**.
Boreas River Gorge and Stillwater - 136, **144, 145**.
bottled gas - 60, **65**.
bowling pin blanks - 34.
boxes - 34, 35.
Bradley Pond Switch - 205, **222, 232**.
Brandon - 270, **278, 285, 303**.
Brandreth - 395, **412, 439, 441, 442**.
bridges - see trestles.
Brandy Brook Junction and Station - 444, **447, 448**.
Briggs - 335, **342, 346**.
Broadalbin - 387, **388**.
Brooklyn Cooperage Company - 72, **277, 278**, 291-294, **295** to **300, 383, 414**.
broomsticks - 34.
Bryant's Mill - 403, **418, 426**.
BT Cabin - 110, **123, 199**.
BU Cabin - 108, **109, 123, 196**.
Buck Pond (Big Moose) - 394, **422, 467**.
Buell's Mills - **353**.
Bulwagga Bay Trestle - 104, **118**.
Burdicks' Crossing and Siding - 104, **118, 127**.
Burnham's - 108, **121, 128**.
Burnett - 333, **340, 346**.
burns - see forest fires.
buttertubs - 34.

cabins, D&H (see also individual cabin names) - 100.
cable railways - see inclined railways and Prospect Mt. Cable RY.
Cadyville - 204, **221, 429**.
calcite - 53.
Caldwell Branch of D&H - 154, **156**.
Canada Junction - 110, **124, 129, 242, 243**.
Canadian National RR - 111, **125**.
Canadian Pacific RR - 112.
Carter-Adirondack Division of NY Central RR - 393, **410, 429, 432, 435**.
Carthage & Adirondack RR - 332, **339**.
Carthage - 332, **339, 345**.
Carthage & Adirondack RR (C&A Branch of NYCRR) - 331-337, **338** to **354**.
Cascade Wood Products (Chair) Co. RR - 289, **290**.
Catamount - 211, **223, 224, 417**.
cattle chutes and pens - 49.
Caughnawaga, Quebec - 242.
Cedar Point Blast Furnace - 72, **167**.
Center Camp - 293, **297, 299**.
centralized traffic control - 100.
Central Vermont RR - 266.
chairs - 34.
Champlain - **125**.
Champlain Division, D&H RR - 99-130, **114**, 246-248.
Champlain Realty Company (International Paper Company) -
    at Buck Pond (Big Moose) - 394, **422, 467**.
    at Morgan's Mills - 402.
    at Underwood - 398.
    at Woods Lake (railroad) - 395, **411, 471**.
Champlain Transportation Company (steamboats) - 100.
charcoal - 33, **41**.
Chasm Falls - 404, **419, 427**.
Chateaugay Lake - 206.
Chateaugay Ore & Iron Company - 206.
Chateaugay Railroad (Chateaugay Branch, D&H RR) - 79, **123**, 191, 200-218, **219** to **241**.
Chazy - 111, **125, 129**.
Chazy Lake - 205, **222, 230**.
Cheever Ore Bed Company RR - 105, **119, 167, 171**.
chemicals - 60.
Childwold (N.Y. & Ottawa) - 272, **280, 282**.
Childwold Station (N.Y.C. Adirondack Div'n.) - 397, **414, 443, 447, 451**.
Christmas trees - 34, 401.
Chubb's Dock - see Clemons.
church trains, Hurd's Sunday - 27.
clapboards - 34.
Clark - 444, **448**.
Clarksboro - 328, **330, 344**.
Clearwater - see Carter on NYCRR Adirondack Division.
Clemons - 101, **115, 127**.
Cliff Haven - 109, **123, 191, 196, 202, 220**.
Clifton Iron Company's RR - 328, **329, 330, 344**.
Clifton Furnace - 328, **330**.
Clifton Mines - 328, **330, 344, 354, 357, 358**.
Clifton Ore Company - 357.
Clinton State Prison RR at Dannemora - 72, 205, **221, 230**.
coal dealers - 60, **64**.
coal for locomotives - 59, **63**.
coal towers and trestles - 59.
Coffins Mills - 335, **342, 349**.
Collins - 335, **342, 346**.
Collins Landing - 279, **303**.
commuter train, Malone Junction - 404, 405.
concrete and concrete pipes - 60.
Cone Family Camp RR - 71.
Conifer - 443, **447, 451**.
Conkling Separator - 207, **222, 231**.
Conrail - 331, **332, 336, 390**.
cooperage - see barrels and Brooklyn Cooperage Company.
Cooperville - 111, **125, 129**.
Corinth - 132, **140, 148**.
Cornell, Alonzo B. - 268.
Cornwall, Ontario, bridge collapse - 265.
Cranberry Lake - 444, **448, 452**.
Cranberry Lake RR - 343, **355, 359**.
cranberries - 463.
creameries - 48, **50**.
Creighton's Camp and Crossing - 455.
Croghan - 360, **365, 366**.
Crown Point - 103, **118, 159, 162, 163**.
Crown Point Iron Company's RR - **118, 159, 160, 161** to **165**.
Cumming's Siding - 102, **116, 127**.
Currier's Crossing - 104, **118**.

Curtis - 384, **385**.
CV Cabin - 111, **125**, **129**.
CY Cabin and Siding - 110, **124**, **129**.

Dadville - **365**.
Dannemora- 72, 205, **221**, **230**.
Defense Plant Corporation - 136.
Defiance Siding - 103, **117**, **158**.
DeGrasse Post Office - see Monterey.
DeKalb Junction - 79, **329**, 360.
Delano and Delano Junction - **117**, **158**.
Delevan - see Honnedaga.
Delaware & Hudson RR -
    Mainline - 99-130, **114**, 246-248.
    Branches - 131-245.
dependability of railroads - 83.
depots - see individual station names.
derailments -
    at Lake Kushaqua - 402.
    at Port Henry - 105.
    on Raquette Lake Railway - **438**.
    at Ray Brook - 216, **240**.
    at Switchback - 169.
Derrick - 271, **279**, **282**, 306.
Desmond - see Honnedaga.
DH Cabin - 106, **128**.
Diana - 333, **340**, **346**.
Dickinson Center - 266, **276**, **282**.
disconnecting railroads - 71, **77**, **78**.
dishes, wooden - 34.
disposition of abandoned railroads - 79.
division points -
    Rouses Point - 111.
    Whitehall - 100, 101.
Dodge Brook Wye - 444, **448**.
Dolgeville - 383, **385**.
Dolgeville & Salisbury RR - 383, **385**.
dolostone - 53.
doubling the hill -
    at Big Moose - 394.
    at Dannemora - 204.
    at Stillwater (Boreas River Gorge) - 136.
Douglass - 108, **122**, **128**.
Downey - 269, **278**, **298**.
drawbridge at Addison Junction - 103.
drawbridge at South Bay - 101.
Dresden - 102, **116**, **127**.
dual gauge trackage -
  at Crown Point - 159.
  between Plattsburgh and Cadyville - 202.
  between Saranac Lake and Lake Placid- 214.
Ducey, Patrick - 270, 273.
Durant, Dr. Thomas Clark - 131.
Duquette's Pit - 404, **419**, **427**.

Eagle Bay - 430, **432**, **438**.
East DeKalb - 328, **329**.
economics of railroads - 83.
education - 83.

Edwards - 360, **363**, **364**.
electric lighting of passenger cars - 268.
electric railroads - 70, **75**.
Elizabethtown Terminal RR - 119, 179, **180**.
Elliott's Mangle Roller Plant RR - 72, 399.
Emeryville - 360, **363**, **364**.
Emporium Forestry Company - 443-452.
energy efficiency or railroads - 83.
enginehouses - 61, **68**.
Essex - 107, **120**, **128**.
Everton RR - 292, **296**.

Fairview - 429, **432**, **438**.
farm products - 48-51.
Faust Post Office - 272.
feed for livestock - 48.
feldspar- 53.
Ferrona - 118, **192**, **197**.
fires, forest -
  general - 45-47.
    at Bay Pond - 271.
    at Brandon - 270.
    at Horse Shoe - 464.
    at Middle Kilns - 209.
    at Oregon Plains - 213.
    at Sabattis - 397.
    at Wanakena - 356.
fire prevention and control - 45-47.
firewood - 34.
first growth forest - 35.
Fisher Hill Iron Mine - 169, **171**, **178**.
Fitzgerald - 333, **340**.
Floodwood - 400, **415**, **423**.
Fonda, Johnstown & Gloversville RR - 79, 387, **388**.
Forestport - 391, 408, **421**, 466.
forest fires - see fires, forest.
Forest Preserve, New York State - 80.
forest products - 30-44.
forges -
  at Belmont - 206.
  at Standish - 208.
Fort Ticonderoga - 102, **117**, 157, **158**.
French Mountain - **156**.
Freydenburg Falls Branch - 203, **220**, **228**.
Friends Lake - 134.
fuel oil - 60, **65**.
Fulton Chain RR -
  "Peg Leg" - 409, **466**, **469**.
  Old Forge Branch - 467, **471**.
Fulton Chain Station - see Thendara
Furnace Branch - **194**, 202.
furniture - 34.

Gabriels - 400, **425**, 453.
Gadsby's Tavern car - 217.
Gap, The - 207, **222**.
garnet - 53.
gauge, dual - 159, 202, 214.
gauge, narrow - 70.

gas, bottled - 60, **65**.
Gloversville - 387, **388**.
Gore Mountain Ski Center - 135.
Gouverneur & Oswegatchie RR - 360, **363**, **364**.
grades, abandoned - 79-82.
grades, steep -
    Cadyville to Dannemora - 204.
    Carter to Big Moose - 394.
    Crown Point Iron Company's RR - 159.
    Lake Champlain & Moriah RR - 166.
    Malone Junction to Owl's Head - 404.
    Purgatory Hill - 392.
    Spring Cove to LeBoeufs - 269.
Grand Trunk RR - 242.
Grant's Crossing - 328.
graphite - 73.
Grasse River Club - 444, **447**.
Grasse River RR - 443-452, **446**.
gravel pits - 53, **58**.
Greenfield - 132, **139**, **147**.
Gunnison's Siding - 104, **118**, **163**.

Hadley - 133, **140**, **147**.
Hague, graphite mine RR at - 73.
Hailesboro - 360, **363**, **364**.
Hammonds Corners - see Crown Point.
Hammondville - 71, 159, **161**, **165**.
Hanna Ore Company RR - 344, 357, **358**, **354**.
Hannawa RR - 325, 326, **327**.
hardware dealers - 60.
Harkness - 187, **192**, **197**.
Harrisville - 333, **341**, **347**.
Hartwell - 212.
heading mills - 34, **42**.
Helena - **275**.
Hemmingford, Quebec - 242.
Herkimer, Newport & Poland RR - 389.
Hermon - 360, **329**.
Higbie Lumber Company - 357.
High Siding - **354**, **358**.
Highby Creek Trestle - 107, **121**, **128**.
Hinckley branch - **407**.
hoe handles - 34.
Honnedaga - 390, **407**, **421**.
Horse Shoe and Horse Shoe Forestry Company RR - 397, 413, **463**, **464**, **465**.
hotels - 26.
hotel-stagecoach connections - 27.
Howard's Siding - 105, **119**, **128**.
HS Cabin - 105, **119**, **127**.
Hudson Valley (electric) Railway - 142, 151, 154, **156**.
Huntingdon, Quebec - 79.
Hurd, John - 265.
Hyatt - 360, **363**.
hydroelectric plants - see powerhouses.

ice - 54
inclined railroads - 71, **77**.
ilmenite - 53.

Inman - see Loon Lake.
International Paper Company (see also Champlain Realty Company) - **117**, **127**, 149, 158, 229, 471.
iron - 52, 56.
Iron Mountain Line - 304, **306**.
Irondale -
    Crown Point Iron Co. - 159, **161**, **164**.
    Salisbury Iron Co. - 383, **385**.
Ironville - 159, **161**, **164**.

J. & J. Rogers Company RR - 72, 188.
jackworks - 35, **44**.
Jayville - 334, **341**, **348**.
Jerseyfield RR - 383, 384, **385**, **386**.
Jessup's Landing - see Corinth.
Johnson's Siding or Johnson Track - **391**, **408**.
Johnstown - 387, **388**.

Kalurah - 334, **341**, **348**, **356**.
Karter - 332, **339**.
Kayuta - 391, **408**.
Keepawa - 396, **412**, **423**, **441**.
Keeseville, Ausable Chasm & Lake Champlain RR - 122, 182, 183, **184**.
Kent's Falls Branch - 203, **220**, **229**.
KG Cabin - 112, **126**.
Kickabuck Station - 271, **282**.
Kildare - 272, **280**, 304, **306**, **308**.
Kings - 132, **139**, **147**.
Kinney Junction (Kinney & Palmer RR) - 108.
Kinsley Lumber Company RR - 210, **224**, **402**.

Lake Bonaparte - 333, **340**.
Lake Champlain & Moriah RR - **118**, 166-170, **171** to **178**.
Lake Champlain Granite Company RR - 72.
Lake George - 154, **156**.
Lake Clear Junction - 400, **416**, **453**, **461**.
Lake Kushaqua -
    D&H - 212, **225**, **235**, **417**.
    NYC - **225**, 401, **417**, **425**.
Lake Luzerne - 133, **140**.
Lake Ozonia - 289, **292**, **297**, **299**.
Lake Placid - 217, **227**, **241**.
Lake Saint Louis & Province Line RR - 242.
Lake Station - 101, **115**, **126**.
Lapham's Mills - 187, **191**, **197**.
lath - 34.
LC Cabin - 103, **117**, **158**.
LeBoeufs - 269, **278**, **298**.
Leicester Junction, Vermont - 103.
legend to scale-four map symbols - 24.
lighting of passenger cars - 268.
limestone - 53.
Lines - 444, **448**.
Little Bryant's - 403, **418**, **426**.
Little Falls & Dolgeville RR - 383, **385**.
Little Mill - see Kalurah.
Little Rapids - 395, **411**.
Little River - see Benson Mines.

livestock - 48, **51**.
Lobdell Post Office - see Russia.
local Adirondack residents - 27.
locomotive shops - see enginehouses.
Long Lake West - see Sabattis.
Loon Lake -
    D&H - 211, **224, 225, 235, 417**.
    NYC - **224, 225, 402, 417**.
loop tracks for reversing - 62.
Lotus Siding - 393, **410**.
Low, Abbot Augustus - 463.
Low's Siding - 397, **413**.
Lowville & Beaver River RR - 360, **365, 366**.
lumber yards and dealers - 32, **39**.
Lyon Mountain - 206, **222, 231, 232**
Lyon Mountain Branch - 207.
Lyons - 217, **227, 240**.
Lyons Falls Branch - 390.

Mac-a-Mac Corporation RR - 439, **440, 441, 442**.
Madawaska - 270, **278, 298**.
Mainline, D&H - see Delaware & Hudson RR Mainline.
Malone - **419**.
Malone Junction - 404, **419, 428**.
Malone Switch - 168, **175**.
mangle rolls for laundries - 34.
Maple Valley and maple syrup - 34, **463**.
maps - 13-25.
marble - 53.
Marion River Carry RR - 70, 430, **434, 437**.
Marshville - 328, **329**.
Martin's Crossing - **416, 455**.
MB Cabin - 110, **124, 129**.
McCoy's Siding - 397, **413**.
McDonald, John - 301.
McDonald Station - 271, **279, 285**, 301, 303.
McKeever - 392, **409, 466, 469**.
McKinley, President William - 135.
MD Siding - 103.
meat packing plants - 48, 49.
Mecca Lumber Company RR - **341, 356**.
Meekerville - 391, **408**.
Meno - 269, 293, **278, 298**.
Merriam - 106, **120, 128**.
Mesabi Iron Range, Minnesota - 159.
mica - 53.
Middle Kilns - 209, **223, 234**.
"Milepost 60" - 136, **144**.
Mineville - 72, 168, map legend 169-170, **171, 176, 177**.
mining - 52-58.
Minnehaha - 392, **409, 466, 469**.
Minnowbrook - 429, **432, 438**.
Mohawk River - 383.
Mohawk, Adirondack & Northern RR - 331, 360, 390.
Mohawk & Malone RR - 389.
Moira - 266, **276, 281, 287, 288**.
Montcalm Landing - 102, **117, 157, 158**.
Monterey - 328, **330**.
Montreal, Quebec - 242, 246-248.

Montreal & Lachine Railway - 242.
Montreal & New York RR - 242.
Montreal & Plattsburgh RR - 242.
Mooers Branch and Junction - 242, **243, 244**.
Morgan's Mills and Siding - **225, 235**, 402, 417.
Moriah Center - **171**.
Morrisonville - 203, **220, 229**.
Moose River - 409.
Moose River Lumber Company RR - **409, 466, 469**.
Mosher - 266, **276**.
Moulin - 393, **410**.
Mount Arab - 397, **414, 423**.
Mountain View - 403, **418, 426**.

Napierville Junction Railway - 111, **125**.
narrow gauge railroads - 70, **74**.
National Lead Company RR - 136, 137, **144 to 146**.
Natural Bridge - 332, **346**.
Nehasane - 396, **412, 423**.
New Bremen - 360, **365**.
Newbridge - **344, 354, 358**.
Newman Post Office - see Lake Placid.
New Sweden - see Ausable River.
Newton Falls - 335, **344, 353, 357**.
Newton Falls & Northern RR - **344, 354, 357**.
Newton Falls Paper Company RR - 336, **342, 349, 356**.
New York & Ottawa RR - 265-286, **275**.
New York & Pennsylvania Company RR - **121**, 179, **181**.
New York Central RR -
    Adirondack Division - 79, 389-428, **406, 472-475**.
    Carthage & Adirondack Branch - 331-354, **338**.
    Ottawa Division - 265-286, **275**.
    Saint Lawrence Division - **327, 329**, 360, **363**.
Niagara Mohawk Power Corporation powerline - see powerlines.
Nichols Mills - 391, **408**.
North Creek - 135, **143, 152**.
North Croghan - 332, **339**.
North River - 136, **144**.
North River Garnet Company RR - 72.
North Tram - 445, **448 to 450**.
Northern RR - see Rutland RR.
Northern Adirondack RR - 265.
Northern New York RR -
  (first) Rutland - 265, 266.
  (second) New York & Ottawa - 265.
Northville - 387, **388**.
NR Cabin - 111, **125, 129**.

Ogdensburg - 79.
Ogdensburg & Lake Champlain RR - see Rutland RR.
oil-burning steam locomotives - 46, 47.
oil dealers and storage tanks - 60.
Old Forge - **471**.
Old Forge Branch - **410, 467**.
old growth forests - 35.
Old Line Junction - 206, **220, 232**.
Olympics, 1932 and 1980 - 216, 217.
Onchiota -

    D&H - 212, **225**, **236**, **417**.
    NYC - **225**, **401**, **417**.
Onekio - 393, **409**.
orchards, apple - 49.
Ordway Crossing and Siding - 136, **144**, **152**.
ore docks - 167.
Oregon Plains - 213.
Oswegatchie - 335, **342**, **349**.
Ottawa, Ontario - 265.
Otter Lake - 392, **409**, **421**.
Otis Junction - 203, **220**, **228**.
Oval Wood Dish Company RR - **279**, **280**, **304**, **306** to **308**.
Owls Head - **403**, **418**, **426**.

Palmer - 133, map legend **137**, **140**, **149**.
paper mills - see pulp.
Partlow and the Partlow Lake RR - **396**, **412**, **467**, **471**.
passengers - 26-28, **29**, 83-84, 246-248, 472-475.
Patterson - see Wrights.
Paul Smith's Electric Railway - **416**, 453-460, **461**, **462**.
Paul Smith's Station -
    at Brandon - 270, **278**, **285**, **303**.
    at Gabriels - **400**, **416**, **425**.
Peck's Corners relocation - **226**, **237**.
"Peg Leg" RR - **409**, **466**, **469**.
Pell's Siding - 103, **117**, **158**.
Penn Central RR - 217, **405**.
Peru - 187, **191**, **197**.
Peru Steel and Iron Company RR - 188, **192**.
piano sounding boards - 35.
pickets for fences - 35.
Piercefield Spur and Station - **397**, **414**, **467**, **471**.
Pit Four - 391, **408**.
plantations, forest - 203, 208, 209.
plastics - 60.
Plattsburgh - 109, **123**, 186, **191**, **193** to **195**, **199**, **201**, **220**.
Plattsburgh & Dannemora RR - 200.
Plattsburgh & Montreal RR - 242.
Plattsburgh Traction Company RR - 186, **195**.
Pleasant Lake - see Mount Arab.
Plumadore - 209, **223**, **224**, **234**, **403**, **418**.
Poland - 389, **390**.
Port Douglass - see Douglass.
Port Henry - 104, **118**, 166, 167, map legend **170**, **171** to **174**.
Port Henry Iron Company - 166-178.
Port Kent - 108, **122**, 182, **184**.
Porter's Spur - 104, **118**.
Post, Marjorie's RR at Camp Topridge - 71.
Post & Henderson RR - **343**, **356**.
Potato Patch - 293, **297**, **299**.
potatoes - 48, 401.
Potsdam - 325, **327**.
powerhouses and hydro-electric plants -
    at Conifer - **451**.
    at Hannawa Falls - 325, **327**.
    at Kents Falls - 204, **229**.
    at Lyon Mountain - **231**.
    at Mineville and Witherbee - 170, **177**.
    at Port Henry - 168, 170, **173**.
power lines, electric, Gabriels to Malone Junction - 19, 80, **401**.
preservation of railroads - 83-84.
propane gas - 60.
Prospect Junction - **407**.
Prospect Mountain Cable RR - 154, **156**.
pulp mills, pulp rossing plants, and pulp wood loading sidings - 33, 40.
Pulpwood Post Office - see Partlow.
Purgatory Hill - 392, **409**.
Putnam - 102, **116**, **127**.
Putt's (Putnam's) Creek Trestle - 159, **161**.
pyrite - 53.

Quarry Switch - see Wolf Creek.

Rainbow - 212, **401**.
Rainbow Lake - **401**, **417**, **425**.
Raquette Lake - 430, **436**.
Raquette Lake Railway - **410**, 429-438, **432**, **433**.
Ray Brook - 216, **227**, **240**.
reforestation - 35, 203, 208, 209.
Red Rocks - 107, **121**.
Rensselaer & Saratoga RR - 131.
Republic Steel underground RRs -
    at Lyon Mountain - 72.
    at Mineville - 72.
Rich Lumber Company - 355.
Remsen - **390**, **407**, **420**.
reversing loops - 62, **69**.
Ringville - see Owls Head.
Riparius Station - see Riverside.
Riverside - 134, **143**, **150**.
RK Cabin - 108, **122**, **128**.
Roakdale - 212, **225**, **417**.
Robinwood - **396**, **412**, **423**.
Rock - 333, **340**, **346**.
Rock Cut Siding - **354**, 357.
Rock Pond - 440, **441**.
Rockland Siding - 108, **121**, **128**.
Rogers -
    Ausable Branch - 183, **188**, **192**, **198**.
    Carthage & Adirondack RR - **332**, **339**.
Rogers, J. & J. Company RR - 33, 72, 188.
Rogersfield - 207, **222**.
Rome (Ausable Forks) - 188, **192**, **198**.
Rome, Watertown & Ogdensburg RR - 331, **339**, **390**.
Rondaxe - **410**, **429**, **432**.
Roosevelt, President Theodore - 135.
Roth's Forge RR - 72.
roundhouses - 62.
Round Pond - see Lake Kushaqua.
Rouses Point - 111, map legend **113**, **125**, **130**, 242.
Russia - 205, **221**, **230**.
Rutland Branch of the D&H RR - **115**, **126**.
Rutland RR -
    at Rouses Point - 111, map legend **113**, **125**, **130**.

at Mooers Junction - 242, **243, 244**.
at Malone Junction - 404, **419, 428**.
at Moira - 266, **276, 281**, 288.
RW Cabin - 108, **121, 128**.

Sabattis - 397, **413, 423**.
Sacandaga Park - 387.
Sacandaga Reservoir - **388**.
Sacandaga Reservoir construction RR - 73, 133.
Sackets Harbor - 331.
safety, railroad - 83.
Saint Agnes Junction - 439-440, **441**.
Saint Lawrence Division, NY Central RR - **327**, 329, 360, 363.
Saint Regis Falls - 267, **277, 283**, 289, 290, 292, **296**.
Salisbury Center - 294, 383, **385**.
Salmon River Junction - **123**, 187, **191, 196**, 203, **220**.
sanatoria, tuberculosis - 27.
sand and gravel pits - 53, **58**.
sandstone - 53.
Sanford Lake - 136, **146**.
Santa Clara - 268, **277, 284, 297**.
Saranac Branch - 389, **416**.
Saranac Inn - 400, **415, 423**.
Saranac Junction - see Lake Clear Junction.
Saranac Lake - 213, **226, 238, 239**, 389, **416**.
Saranac Lake & Lake Placid RR - 200, 214.
Saranac Station - see Russia.
Saratoga Springs - 132, **139**.
sawmills - 32, **38**.
SC Cabin - 101, **115, 126**.
Sciota - 242, **243, 245**.
separators -
   at Ironville - **164**.
   at Lyon Mountain - 206.
Shanley's 268, **277**.
Sherman Siding - 105, **118, 172**.
shingles - 35.
shoe lasts - 35.
shops, railroad repair - 61.
shortest standard gauge RR - see Marion River Carry RR.
Shurtleff's - 444, **447**.
shuttles for textiles - 35.
Silver Brook Branch, Junction, and Station - 444, **447**.
Silver Hill - 328.
sintering plants -
   at Clifton Mines - **354**.
   at Lyon Mountain - 207.
   at Switchback - 168, **175**.
Sisco Furnace RR - 72.
SJ Cabin - **196**.
Skensowane - 430, **432, 438**.
ski trains to north Creek - 135.
SN Cabin - 105, **118**.
Snow Junction - 390, **407**.
snow plows at Malone Junction - **405**.
social aspects of railroads - 83.
soils and forest fires - 46.
South Bay Siding - 101, **115, 127**.

South Bombay - 287, **288**.
South Bonaparte - 333, **340**.
South Corinth - 132, **139, 147**.
South Inlet Branch - 209, **234**.
South Junction - 109, **123**, 185, **191, 196**, 200, **220**.
specials, railroad - 27.
Spellmans - 110, **124, 129**.
speeders - 47.
Spring Cove - 269, **278, 282, 297, 298**.
spring water, bottled - 463.
SR Cabin - 105, **172**.
stagecoaches - 27.
Stalbird - 328, **329**.
standard gauge - 70.
Standish and Standish Furnace Branch - 207, 208, **222, 233**.
stave and heading mills - 34, **42**.
steamboat connections - 26.
Stellaville - 360, **329**.
Stillwater -
   Reservoir - **411**.
   Siding - 136, **145**.
stock pens - 48, 49.
Stoddard, Seneca Ray - 107, 133, 159.
Stony Creek - 134, **141, 150**.
Stonywold - see Lake Kushaqua on the NYCRR.
Summit - 429, **432**.
Switchback - 168, **171, 175**.
switchbacks -
   at Mount Matumbla, Kildare - 304, 305, **306**.
   at Switchback, Moriah - 168, **171, 175**.
   at Terio Wye, Port Henry - 168, **171, 174**.
Sykes, William L. - 443.

Taffarn's Siding - 391, **421**.
Tahawus - 136, **146, 153**.
talc - 53.
Talcville - 360, **363, 364**.
Tekene and Tekene Junction - 210, **223, 224**, 402, **417, 425**.
Terio Wye - 168, **171, 174**.
The Gap - 207, **222**.
The Glen - 134, **142, 150**.
Thendara - 393, **410**, 467, 470.
Thurman - 134, **142, 151**.
TI Cabin - 103, **117, 158**.
Ticonderoga - 79, **117, 157, 158**.
Ticonderoga Terminal RR - 157.
timetables - 8.
titanium - see ilmenite.
Todd's Pit - 404, **419, 427**.
tourist railroads - 83-84, 472-475.
towers, coal - 59
towers, sand -
   at North Creek - 135, **152**.
   at Rouses Point - 113, **130**.
towers, water - 61.
track (see also dual gauge, narrow gauge, standard gauge, wooden-railed) - 70.
Tracy's Siding or Spur - 391, **408**.
Treadwell's Mills - 203, **228**.

tree nursery- 203.
trestles and bridges (see also coal trestles) -
    at Addison Junction - 103, **117**.
    at Bear Creek - 391, **408**.
    at Bulwagga Bay - 104, **118**.
    at Cornwall, Ontario - 265.
    at Hadley - 133, **147**.
    at Highby Creek - 107, **121**, **128**.
    at Kayuta Reservoir - 391, **408**.
    at Kushaqua Narrows - 401, **417**.
    at Lyon Mountain - 206, **232**.
    at Moose River - 393, **469**.
    at Plattsburgh - 202, **194**.
    at Port Henry - 167, **172**, **173**.
    at Putt's (Putnam) Creek - 159, **161**.
    at Saranac Lake - 213, 215, **237**, **238**.
    at Stillwater Reservoir, **411**.
    at Stony Creek - 134, **150**.
    at Twitchell Creek - 395, **411**.
trolley cars - see electric RRs.
Trudeau, Dr. Edward Livingston - 27.
tuberculosis sanatoria - 27.
tunnels -
    at Port Henry - 168, **118**, **173**.
    at Red Rocks, Willsboro - 107, **121**.
    at Fort Ticonderoga - 103, **158**.
    at Whitehall - 101, **126**.
Tupper Lake - 273, **280**, **286**, 291, 300, 414.
Tupper Lake Junction - 272, **280**, 291, 300, 397, 414, 424.
turntables - 62, **69**.
Twin Ponds - 208, **222**, **234**.
Twitchell Creek Trestle - 395, **411**.

Uncas - 430, **433**.
Underwood - **280**, 397, 414, 423.
union stations -
    at Childwold - 397, **443**.
    at Lake Placid - 217.
    at Lowville - 360.
    at Malone Junction - 404.
    at Moira - 266.
    at Saranac Lake - 213.
United States Air Force Base at Plattsburgh - 185, 200, 202.
Upper Kilns - 209, **223**, **234**.
Utica - 389.
Utica & Black River RR - 390.
Utica City Ice - **409**.

Valley line - 207.
Valcour - 108, **122**, 191, **196**.
Vaughns - 335, **342**.
veneer mills - 35.
Vermontville Station - 212, **225**.

Wadhams Mills - 106, **120**, **128**.
Wake Robin RR - 413, **463**, **464**, **465**.

wall coverings - 60.
Wanakena- 343, 355, **359**.
Washburn's Eddy - 134.
Warrensburg, Warrensburg Branch and Junction - 79, 134, 142, 151, 155, **156**.
water tanks and water towers - 61, **67**.
Watertown - 331.
Watson Page Lumber Company RR - **277**, 289, **290**.
WD Cabin - 106, **128**.
Webb, Dr. William Seward - 389.
Weidman - 269, **277**, **297**.
West Chazy - 110, **124**, **129**, 242, 243.
West End - 203, **220**, **228**.
West Kilns, RR at - 72.
Westport - 105, **119**, 179, **180**.
Whallonsburg - 107, **120**, **128**.
whipbutt mills - 35.
Whippleville Station - 404, **419**, **427**.
White Lake - 391, **408**, **421**.
White Lake Sand Pit - 392, **409**.
Whiteface Mountain, construction RR at - 72.
Whitefather's - see Lake Kushaqua on the NYCRR.
Whitehall - 100, 101, legend on 112, **115**, **126**.
Whitehall & Plattsburgh RR - 185.
White's Sand - 132, **140**, **147**.
Whitney Industries RR - 439, **440**, **441**.
Wight Talc Mine RR - 73.
Williamstown - see Standish.
Willis Pond - 271, **279**, **282**, 306.
Willsboro - 107, **121**, 179, **181**.
Willsboro Bay - Red Rocks area - 107, **121**.
Wilna - 332, **339**, 345.
Windsor - see Cooperville.
Witherbee - 168, **176**, 177.
Witherbee-Sherman Company - 166-178.
Wolf Creek - 133, **141**, **147**.
Wolf Pond - 209, **223**.
wollastonite - 53.
wood alcohol - 35.
Wood, George C., Utica City Ice Company Spur - 392, **409**.
wood waste and chips - 35.
wooden-railed railroads - 71, **76**.
Woodgate - 391, **408**, **421**.
Woodhull - **408**.
Woods Lake - 395, **411**, **467**, **471**.
Woods Mills - 204, **220**, **229**.
wrecks - see derailments.
Wrights - 102, **116**, **127**.
wyes - 62, **69**.

yards - see under individual major station names.
York - 360, **364**.

zinc - 53.